games and information [4E]
information

games and ^{4E}
information

An Introduction to Game Theory

eric rasmusen

Blackwell
Publishing

BLACKWELL PUBLISHING
350 Main Street, Malden, MA 02148-5020, USA
9600 Garsington Road, Oxford OX4 2DQ, UK
550 Swanston Street, Carlton, Victoria 3053, Australia

The right of Eric Rasmusen to be identified as the Author of this Work has been asserted in accordance with
the Copyright, Designs and Patents Act 1988.

First published 1989
Second edition published 1994
Third edition published 2001
Fourth edition published 2007 by Blackwell Publishing Ltd

9   2013

Library of Congress Cataloging-in-Publication Data

Rasmusen, Eric.
   Games and information : an introduction to game theory / Eric Rasmusen. – 4th ed.
      p. cm.
   Includes bibliographical references and index.
   ISBN 978-1-4051-3666-2 (hardback)
   1. Game theory. I. Title

   QA269.R37 2007
   519.3—dc22

                                                                                 2006029009

A catalogue record for this title is available from the British Library.

Set in 10/12 pt Times
by Newgen Imaging Systems (P) Ltd., Chennai, India

The publisher's policy is to use permanent paper from mills that operate a sustainable forestry policy, and which
has been manufactured from pulp processed using acid-free and elementary chlorine-free practices. Furthermore,
the publisher ensures that the text paper and cover board used have met acceptable environmental accreditation
standards.

For further information on
Blackwell Publishing, visit our website:
www.blackwellpublishing.com

contents

*Sections that are starred are less important

figures

tables

games

preface

Contents and Purpose

This book is about noncooperative game theory and asymmetric information. In the introduction, I will say why I think these subjects are important, but here in the preface I will try to help you decide whether this is the appropriate book to read if they do interest you.

I write as an applied theoretical economist, not as a game theorist, and readers in anthropology, law, physics, accounting, and management science have helped me to be aware of the provincialisms of economics and game theory. My aim is to present the game theory and information economics that currently exist in journal articles and oral tradition in a way that shows how to build simple models using a standard format. Journal articles are more complicated and less clear than seems necessary in retrospect; precisely because it is original, even the discoverer rarely understands a truly novel idea. After a few dozen successor articles have appeared, we all understand it and marvel at its simplicity. But journal editors are unreceptive to new articles that admit to containing exactly the same idea as old articles, just presented more clearly. At best, the clarification is hidden in some new article's introduction or condensed to a paragraph in a survey. Students, who find every idea as complex as the originators of the ideas did when they were new, must learn either from the confused original articles or the oral tradition of a top economics department. This book tries to help.

Changes in the Second Edition, 1994

By now, just a few years later after the First Edition, those trying to learn game theory have more to help them than just this book, and I will list a number of excellent books below. I have also thoroughly revised *Games and Information*. George Stigler used to say that it was a great pity Alfred Marshall spent so much time on the eight editions of *Principles of Economics* that appeared between 1890 and 1920, given the opportunity cost of the other books he might have written. I am no Marshall, so I have been willing to sacrifice a Rasmusen article or two for this new edition, though I doubt I will keep it up till 2019.

What I have done for the Second Edition is to add a number of new topics, increase the number of exercises (and provide detailed answers), update the references, change the terminology here and there, and rework the entire book for clarity. A book, like a poem, is never finished, only abandoned (which is itself a good example of a fundamental economic principle). The one section I have dropped is the somewhat obtrusive discussion of existence theorems; I recommend Fudenberg & Tirole (1991a) on that subject. The new topics include auditing games, nuisance suits, recoordination in equilibria, renegotiation in contracts, supermodularity, signal jamming, market microstructure, and government procurement. The discussion of moral hazard has been reorganized. The total number of chapters has increased by two, the topics of repeated games and entry having been given their own chapters.

Changes in the Third Edition, 2001

Besides numerous minor changes in wording, I have added new material and reorganized some sections of the book.

The new topics are 10.3 "Price Discrimination"; 12.6 "Setting up a Way to Bargain: The Myerson–Satterthwaite Mechanism"; 13.3 "Risk and Uncertainty over Values" (for private-value auctions); A.7 "Fixed-Point Theorems"; and A.8 "Genericity."

To accommodate the additions, I have dropped 9.5 "Other Equilibrium Concepts: Wilson Equilibrium and Reactive Equilibrium" (which is still available on the book's website), and Appendix A, "Answers to Odd-Numbered Problems." These answers are very important, but I have moved them to the website because most readers who care to look at them will have web access and problem answers are peculiarly in need of updating. Ideally, I would like to discuss all likely wrong answers as well as the right answers, but I learn the wrong answers only slowly, with the help of new generations of students.

Chapter 10, "Mechanism Design in Adverse Selection and in Moral Hazard with Hidden Information," is new. It includes two sections from chapter 8 (8.1 "Pooling versus Separating Equilibrium and the Revelation Principle" is now section 10.1; 8.2 "An Example of Moral Hazard with Hidden Knowledge: the Salesman Game" is now section 10.2) and one from chapter 9 (9.6 "The Groves Mechanism" is now section 10.5).

Chapter 15 "The New Industrial Organization," has been eliminated and its sections real-located. Section 15.1 "Why Established Firms Pay Less for Capital: The Diamond Model" is now section 6.6; section 15.2 "Takeovers and Greenmail" remains section 15.2; section 15.3 "Market Microstructure and the Kyle Model" is now section 9.5; and section 15.4 "Rate-of-return Regulation and Government Procurement" is now section 10.4.

Topics that have been extensively reorganized or rewritten include 14.2 "Prices as Strategies"; 14.3 "Location Models"; the Mathematical Appendix, and the Bibliography. Section 4.5 "Discounting" is now in the Mathematical Appendix; 4.6 "Evolutionary Equilibrium: The Hawk–Dove Game" is now section 5.6; 7.5 "State-space Diagrams: Insurance Games I and II" is now section 8.5 and the sections in chapter 8 are reordered; 14.2 "Signal Jamming: Limit Pricing" is now section 11.6. I have recast 1.1 "Definitions," taking out the OPEC Game and using an entry deterrence game instead, to illustrate the difference between game theory and decision theory. Every other chapter has also been revised in minor ways.

Some readers preferred the First Edition to the Second because they thought the extra topics in the Second Edition made it more difficult to cover. To help with this problem, I have now starred the sections that I think are skippable. For reference, I continue to have those sections close to where the subjects are introduced.

The two most novel features of the book are not contained within its covers. One is the website, at http://rasmusen.org/GI/index.html

The website includes answers to the odd-numbered problems, new questions and answers, errata, files from my own teaching suitable for making overheads, and anything else I think might be useful to readers of this book.

The second new feature is a reader, Rasmusen (2001) – a prettified version of the course packet I use when I teach this material. This is available from Blackwell Publishing, and contains scholarly articles, news clippings, and cartoons arranged to correspond with the chapters of the book. I have tried especially to include material that is somewhat obscure or hard to locate, rather than just a collection of classic articles from leading journals.

If there is a fourth edition, three things I might add are (1) a long discussion of strategic complements and substitutes in chapter 14, or perhaps even as a separate chapter; (2) Holmstrom & Milgrom's 1987 article on linear contracts; and (3) Holmstrom & Milgrom's 1991 article on multitask agency. Readers who agree, let me know and perhaps I'll post notes on these topics on the website.

Changes in the Fourth Edition, 2006

Games and Information continues to do well despite the continued flow of books on game theory and industrial organization, and the arrival of a number of specialized books on topics such as contracting and auctions. I've had emails from readers in Canada, Chile, China, Dubai, Germany, Great Britain, India, Iran, Italy, Jamaica, Korea, Malaysia, Man, Mexico, Norway, Paraguay, Portugal, Spain, Taiwan, and the United States. This encourages me to think a new edition would be worthwhile, incorporating, especially, new models and ways to organize thoughts for the the material on asymmetric information in the second half of the book. I have also added more homework problems, and fourteen classroom games, one at the end of each chapter. Besides the specific changes mentioned below, I have made minor changes throughout the book.

The chapters that have been most changed are chapters 10 (Mechanisms), 13 (Auctions), and 14 (Pricing), but there is also new material in other chapters. Chapter 3 (Mixed Strategies) now has material on Bertrand equilibrium and strategic substitutes and complements formerly in chapter 14 and material on patent races formerly in chapter 15. It has a new section on existence of equilibrium, and an example of how a pure strategy can be strictly dominated by a mixed strategy.

Chapter 7 (Moral Hazard I) has a discussion of quasilinear utility functions and the effect of changes in bargaining power.

Chapter 8 (Moral Hazard II) has a new section on Holmstrom & Milgrom's 1991 idea of multitask agency, in which the agent uses more than one kind of effort and generates multiple outputs, only one of which can be well measured.

Chapter 9 (Adverse Selection) has a new version of the Production Game to illustrate the combination of moral hazard with adverse selection.

Chapter 10 (Mechanisms) also has a new version of the Production Game, used to illustrate mechanism design and the new topic of cross checking. I have added a section on the Sender–Receiver game of Crawford and Sobel. I've cut back on the treatment of Myerson's Trading Game, giving just one version instead of three. In general, I have tried to make the notation and analysis of this chapter more uniform, putting special emphasis on the standard outcome that the bad type's participation constraint and the good type's incentive compatibility constraints are binding. I have moved away from the term "moral hazard with hidden knowledge" in favor of the more direct "post-contractual hidden knowledge."

Chapter 11 (Signalling) contains the new topic of countersignalling (introduced in Feltovich, Harbaugh, & To [2002]), under which middle-quality types signal, but the best types deliberately do not, instead relying on other means of conveying their type. I have also replaced the 3rd edition's model of limit pricing as signal jamming with a new, simpler model.

Chapter 13 (Auctions) is the most drastically changed, by far. In earlier editions the treatment of auctions was relatively nontechnical because I wished to avoid the difficult task of trying to convey that intricate but unified literature in the simplified style of the rest of the book. By now, however, enough new treatments of the old material has appeared for the unities in auction theory to be presented more simply, and so I've made the chapter much longer, and technical. This allows me to add topics such as all-pay auctions, proof of the Revenue Equivalence Theorem, the marginal-revenue interpetation of reserve prices, a formal model comparing different auction rules in a common-value auction, Klemperer's Wallet Game, affiliation, and linkage.

Chapter 14 (Pricing) has a section on vertical quality differentiation, by a monopolist and by a duopoly, which also allows discussion of "crimping the product."

I have dropped Chapter 15 (Entry), though it remains available at the website. Its topics had no technical unity, and while they served well as examples of techniques from earlier chapters, I decided that they contained enough examples, especially as new editions have been increasing the number of models in those earlier chapters.

The book's website is at http://rasmusen.org/GI.
The answers to the odd-numbered homework problems, and teaching notes for the classroom games are at http://rasmusen.org/GI/funstuff.htm.

The classroom games are an innovation with this edition. I have found it helpful in MBA and undergraduate classes to have students take the parts of players in games. The greatest benefit is to force them to think about possible strategies and to realize that models are imperfect descriptions of the real world even in the controlled situation of a classroom – but that they do provide a starting point for thinking about the real world. Most of the games are less useful at teaching actual results because of the many outcomes that can happen, but they are useful as something like case studies, particular histories on which students and teacher can comment. Whether the games are useful for PhD students is less clear, but they, too, need to understand the link between models and reality, something hard to convey in lectures.

I am very interested in hearing feedback on how the classroom games work in particular situations. I have included detailed instructions on practical matters (e.g., what overheads to bring to class, what instructions the players are likely to get wrong), but I am sure I will hear of improvements in both implementation and explanation. I have included one game for each chapter, but some topics lend themselves to games more than others – mixed strategies, public good dilemmas, and backwards induction, in particular, with contracting being the least suited to games.

Readings in Games and Information continues to be available in hardback and paperback from Blackwell Publishing. Its website is at http://rasmusen.org/GI/reader/rcontents.htm.

Using the Book

The book is divided into three parts: part I on game theory; part II on information economics; and part III on applications to particular subjects. Parts I and II, but not part III, are ordered sets of chapters.

Part I by itself would be appropriate for a course on game theory, and sections from part III could be added for illustration. If students are already familiar with basic game theory, part II can be used for a course on information economics. The entire book would be useful as a secondary text for a course on industrial organization. I teach material from every chapter in a semester-long course for first- and second-year doctoral students at Indiana University's Kelley School of Business, including more or fewer chapter sections depending on the progress of the class.

Exercises and notes follow the chapters. It is useful to supplement a book like this with original articles, but I leave it to my readers or their instructors to follow up on the topics that interest them rather than recommending particular readings. I also recommend that readers try attending a seminar presentation of current research on some topic from the book; while most of the seminar may be incomprehensible, there is a real thrill in hearing someone attack the speaker with "Are you sure that equilibrium is perfect?" after just learning the previous week what "perfect" means.

Some of the exercises at the end of each chapter put slight twists on concepts in the text while others introduce new concepts. Answers to odd-numbered questions are given at the website. I particularly recommend working through the problems for those trying to learn this material without an instructor.

The endnotes to each chapter include substantive material as well as recommendations for further reading. Unlike the notes in many books, they are not meant to be skipped, since many of them are important but tangential, and some qualify statements in the main text. Less important notes supply additional examples or list technical results for reference. A mathematical appendix at the end of the book supplies technical references, defines certain mathematical terms, and lists some items for reference even though they are not used in the main text.

The Level of Mathematics

In surveying the prefaces of previous books on game theory, I see that advising readers how much mathematical background they need exposes an author to charges of being out of touch with reality. The mathematical level here is about the same as in Luce & Raiffa (1957), and I can do no better than to quote the advice on page 8 of their book:

> Probably the most important prerequisite is that ill-defined quality: mathematical sophistication. We hope that this is an ingredient not required in large measure, but that it is needed to some degree there can be no doubt. The reader must be able to accept conditional statements, even though he feels the suppositions to be false; he must be willing to make concessions to mathematical simplicity; he must be patient enough to follow along with the peculiar kind of construction that mathematics is; and, above all, he must have sympathy with the method – a sympathy based upon his knowledge of its past sucesses in various of the empirical sciences and upon his realization of the necessity for rigorous deduction in science as we know it.

If you do not know the terms "risk-averse," "first order condition," "utility function," "probability density," and "discount rate," you will not fully understand this book. Flipping through it, however, you will see that the equation density is much lower than in first-year graduate microeconomics texts. In a sense, game theory is less abstract than price theory, because it deals with individual agents rather than aggregate markets and it is oriented towards explaining stylized facts rather than supplying econometric specifications. Mathematics is nonetheless essential. Professor Wei puts this well in his informal unpublished class notes:

> My experience in learning and teaching convinces me that going through a proof (which does not require much mathematics) is *the most effective way in learning, developing intuition, sharpening technical writing ability, and improving creativity.* However it is an extremely painful experience for people with simple mind and narrow interests.
>
> Remember that a good proof should be *smooth* in the sense that any serious reader can read through it like the way we read *Miami Herald*; should be *precise* such that no one can add/delete/change a word – like the way we enjoy Robert Frost's poetry!

I wouldn't change a word of that.

Other Books

At the time of the first edition of this book, most of the topics covered were absent from existing books on either game theory or information economics. Noteworthy older books on game theory include Luce & Raiffa (1957), Moulin (1986), Ordeshook (1986), Rapoport (1960, 1970), and Shubik (1982). Books on information in economics were mainly concerned with decision making under uncertainty rather than asymmetric information. Since the First Edition, a spate of books on game theory has appeared. The stream of new books has become a flood, and one of the pleasing features of this literature is its variety. Each one is different, and both student and teacher can profit by owning an assortment of them, something one cannot say of many other subject areas. We have not converged, perhaps because teachers are still converting into books their own independent materials from courses not taught with texts. I only wish I could say I had been able to use all my competitors' good ideas in the present edition.

Why, you might ask in the spirit of game theory, do I conveniently list all my competitor's books here, giving free publicity to books that could substitute for mine? For an answer, you must buy this book and read chapter 11 on signalling. Then you will understand that only an author quite confident that his book compares well with possible substitutes would do such a thing, and you will be even more certain that your decision to buy the book was a good one.

Some Books on Game Theory and Its Applications

1988 **Tirole**, Jean, *The Theory of Industrial Organization*. MIT Press. 479 pages. Still the standard text for advanced industrial organization.

1989 **Eatwell**, John, Murray Milgate, & Peter Newman, eds., *The New Palgrave: Game Theory*. Norton. 264 pages. A collection of brief articles on topics in game theory by prominent scholars.
Rasmusen, Eric, *Games and Information*, 1st edition. Blackwell Publishing. 352 pages.
Schmalensee, Richard & Robert Willig, eds., *The Handbook of Industrial Organization*, in two volumes. North-Holland. A collection of not-so-brief articles on topics in industrial organization by prominent scholars.
Spulber, Daniel *Regulation and Markets*. MIT Press. 690 pages. Applications of game theory to rate of return regulation.

1990 **Banks**, Jeffrey, *Signalling Games in Political Science*. Harwood Publishers. 90 pages. Out of date by now, but worth reading anyway.
Friedman, James, *Game Theory with Applications to Economics*, 2nd edition. Oxford University Press (1st edition, 1986). 322 pages. By a leading expert on repeated games.
Kreps, David, *A Course in Microeconomic Theory*. Princeton University Press. 850 pages. A competitor to Varian's PhD micro text, in a more conversational style, albeit a conversation with a brilliant economist at a level of detail that scares some students.
Kreps, David, *Game Theory and Economic Modeling*. Oxford University Press. 195 pages. A discussion of Nash equilibrium and its problems.
Krouse, Clement, *Theory of Industrial Economics*. Blackwell Publishing. 602 pages. A good book on the same topics as Tirole's 1988 book, largely overshadowed by it.

1991 **Dixit**, Avinash K. & Barry J. Nalebuff, *Thinking Strategically: The Competitive Edge in Business, Politics, and Everyday Life*. Norton. 393 pages. A book in the tradition of popular science, full of fun examples but with serious ideas too. I use this for my MBA students' half-semester course, though newer books are offering competition for that niche.
Fudenberg, Drew & Jean Tirole, *Game Theory*. MIT Press. 579 pages. This has become the standard text for second-year PhD courses in game theory. (Though I hope the students are referring back to *Games and Information* for help in getting through the hard parts.)
Milgrom, Paul and John Roberts, *Economics of Organization and Management*. Prentice-Hall. 621 pages. A model for how to think about organization and management. The authors taught an MBA course from this, but I wonder whether that is feasible anywhere but Stanford Business School.
Myerson, Roger, *Game Theory: Analysis of Conflict*. Harvard University Press. 568 pages. At an advanced level. In revising for the third edition, I noticed how well

Myerson's articles are standing the test of time. There's even more Myerson in the fourth edition.

1992   **Aumann**, Robert & Sergiu Hart, eds., *Handbook of Game Theory with Economic Applications*, Volume 1. North-Holland. 733 pages. A collection of articles by prominent scholars on topics in game theory.

Binmore, Ken, *Fun and Games: A Text on Game Theory*. D.C. Heath. 642 pages. No pain, no gain; but pain and pleasure can be mixed even in the study of mathematics.

Gibbons, Robert, *Game Theory for Applied Economists*. Princeton University Press. 267 pages. Perhaps the main competitor to *Games and Information*. Shorter and less idiosyncratic.

Hirshleifer, Jack & John Riley, *The Economics of Uncertainty and Information*. Cambridge University Press. 465 pages. An underappreciated book that emphasizes information rather than game theory.

McMillan, John, *Games, Strategies, and Managers: How Managers Can Use Game Theory to Make Better Business Decisions*. Oxford University Press. 252 pages. Largely verbal, very well written, and an example of how clear thinking and clear writing go together.

Varian, Hal, *Microeconomic Analysis*, 3rd edition. Norton (1st edition, 1978; 2nd edition, 1984) 547 pages. Varian was the standard PhD micro text when I took the course in 1980. The third edition is much bigger, with lots of game theory and information economics concisely presented.

1993   **Basu**, Kaushik, *Lectures in Industrial Organization Theory*. Blackwell Publishing. 236 pages. Lots of game theory as well as I.O.

Laffont, Jean-Jacques & Jean Tirole, *A Theory of Incentives in Procurement and Regulation*. MIT Press. 705 pages. If you like section 10.6 of *Games and Information*, here is an entire book on the model.

Martin, Stephen, *Advanced Industrial Economics*. Blackwell Publishing. 660 pages. Detailed and original analysis of particular models, and much more attention to empirical articles than Krouse, Shy, and Tirole.

1994   **Aumann**, Robert & Sergiu Hart, eds., *Handbook of Game Theory with Economic Applications*, Volume 2. North-Holland. A collection of articles by prominent scholars on topics in game theory.

Baird, Douglas, Robert Gertner & Randal Picker, *Strategic Behavior and the Law: The Role of Game Theory and Information Economics in Legal Analysis*. Harvard University Press. 330 pages. A mostly verbal but not easy exposition of game theory using topics such as contracts, procedure, and tort.

Gardner, Roy, *Games for Business and Economics*. John Wiley and Sons. 480 pages. Indiana University has produced not one but two game theory texts.

Morris, Peter, *Introduction to Game Theory*. Springer-Verlag. 230 pages. Not in my library yet.

Morrow, James, *Game Theory for Political Scientists*. Princeton University Press. 376 pages. The usual topics, but with a political science slant, and especially good on things such as utility theory.

Osborne, Martin & Ariel Rubinstein, *A Course in Game Theory*. MIT Press. 352 pages. Similar in style to Eichberger's 1993 book. See their excellent "List of

Results" on pages 313-19 which summarizes the mathematical propositions without using specialized notation.

Rasmusen, Eric, *Games and Information*, 2nd edition. Blackwell Publishing.

1995   **Mas-Colell**, Andreu, Michael D. Whinston, & Jerry R. Green, *Microeconomic Theory*. Oxford University Press. 981 pages. This combines the topics of Varian's PhD micro text, those of *Games and Information*, and general equilibrium. Massive, and a good reference.

Owen, Guillermo, *Game Theory*. Academic Press, 3rd edition (1st edition, 1968; 2nd edition, 1982) This book clearly lays out the older approach to game theory, and holds the record for longevity in game theory books.

1996   **Besanko**, David, David Dranove, & Mark Shanley, *Economics of Strategy*. John Wiley and Sons. This actually can be used with Indiana M.B.A. students, and clearly explains some very tricky ideas such as strategic complements.

Shy, Oz, *Industrial Organization, Theory and Applications*. MIT Press. 466 pages. A new, somewhat easier competitor to Tirole's 1988 book.

1997   **Gates**, Scott & Brian Humes, *Games, Information, and Politics: Applying Game Theoretic Models to Political Science*. University of Michigan Press. 182 pages.

Ghemawat, Pankaj, *Games Businesses Play: Cases and Models*. MIT Press. 255 pages. Analysis of six cases from business using game theory at the MBA level. Good for the difficult task of combining theory with evidence.

Macho-Stadler, Ines, & J. David Perez-Castillo, *An Introduction to the Economics of Information: Incentives and Contracts*. Oxford University Press. 277 pages. Entirely on moral hazard, adverse selection, and signalling.

Romp, Graham, *Game Theory: Introduction and Applications*. Oxford University Press. 284 pages. With unusual applications (chapters on macroeconomics, trade policy, and environmental economics) and lots of exercises with answers.

Salanie, Bernard, *The Economics of Contracts: A Primer*. MIT Press. 232 pages. Specialized to a subject of growing importance.

1998   **Bierman**, H. Scott & Luis Fernandez, *Game Theory with Economic Applications*. Addison Wesley, 2nd edition (1st edition, 1993) 452 pages. A text for undergraduate courses, full of good examples.

Dugatkin, Lee & Hudson Reeve, ed., *Game Theory & Animal Behavior*. Oxford University Press. 320 pages. Just on biology applications.

1999   **Aliprantis**, Charalambos & Subir Chakrabarti, *Games and Decisionmaking*. Oxford University Press. 224 pages. An undergraduate text for game theory, decision theory, auctions, and bargaining, the third game theory text to come out of Indiana.

Basar, Tamar & Geert Olsder, *Dynamic Noncooperative Game Theory*, 2nd edition, revised. Society for Industrial and Applied Mathematics (1st edition, 1982; 2nd edition, 1995). This book is by and for mathematicians, with surprisingly little overlap between its bibliography and that of the present book. Suitable for people who like differential equations and linear algebra.

Dixit, Avinash & Susan Skeath, *Games of Strategy*. Norton. 600 pages. Nicely laid out with color and boldfacing. Game theory plus chapters on bargaining, auctions, voting, etc. Detailed verbal explanations of many games.

Dutta, Prajit, *Strategies and Games: Theory And Practice*. MIT Press. 450 pages.

Muthoo, Abhinay, *Bargaining Theory with Applications*. Cambridge University Press, 357 pages. As the title says: a place to go to look up bargaining models.

Stahl, Saul, *A Gentle Introduction to Game Theory*. American Mathematical Society. 176 pages. In the mathematics department tradition, with many exercises and numerical answers.

Wolfstetter, Elmar, *Topics in Microeconomics: Industrial Organization, Auctions, and Incentives*, Cambridge: Cambridge University Press. 370 pages. I like the chapter on auctions and stochastic dominance, in particular.

As I updated this to the 21st century for the Fourth Edition, I realized that I would have to be more selective. I've listed more books below, but have made less effort to be comprehensive. Mike Shor's website at http://www.gametheory.net/cgi-bin/viewbooks.pl is a good place to look for additional books.

2000   **Gintis**, Herbert, *Game Theory Evolving*. Princeton University Press. 531 pages. A wonderful book of problems and solutions, with much explanation and special attention to evolutionary biology.

Vives, Xavier, *Oligopoly Pricing: Old Ideas and New Tools*. MIT Press. 441 pages. The standard for that topic.

2001   **Laffont**, Jean-Jacques & David Martimort, *The Theory of Incentives: The Principal–Agent Model*. Princeton University Press. 421 pages. Special for its comments on historical development and for the perceptive intuitions mixed in among the equations.

Rasmusen, Eric, *Games and Information*. Blackwell Publishing, 3rd edition. 445 pages.

Rasmusen, Eric, ed. *Readings in Games and Information*. Blackwell Publishing. 427 pages. Journal and newspaper articles on game theory and information economics. A cartoon for each topic, too!

2002   **Aumann**, Robert & Sergiu Hart, eds., *Handbook of Game Theory with Economic Applications*, Volume 3. North-Holland. 733 pages. A collection of articles by prominent scholars on topics in game theory.

Krishna, Vijay, *Auction Theory*. Academic Press. 297 pages. The standard text for auction theory.

McAfee, R. Preston, *Competitive Solutions: The Strategist's Toolkit*. Princeton University Press. 404 pages. An excellent "strategy for managers" book that lays out ideas from game theory and information economics using words and business examples. It's as worth reading cover to cover for a professor as for an MBA student.

Watson, Joel. *Strategy: An Introduction to Game Theory*. W. W. Norton & Co. 334 pages. A book by a well-known contract theoriest that is similar in topics and level to *Games and Information*.

2003   **Milgrom**, Paul, *Putting Auction Theory to Work*. Cambridge University Press. 368 pages. Careful about the mathematical foundations, and covers many special cases (multiple objects, type correlations).

Osborne, Martin, *An Introduction to Game Theory*. Oxford University Press. 504 pages. His second game theory book, this one is for undergraduates, precise but with little calculus.

2004 **Klemperer**, Paul, *Auctions: Theory and Practice*. Princeton University Press. 246 pages. Mostly verbal, but especially good in the mathematics it does include.

2005 **Bolton**, Patrick & Mathias Dewatripont, *Contract Theory*. MIT Press. 688 pages. A detailed exposition of principal–agent models.

2006 **Rasmusen**, Eric, *Games and Information*. Blackwell Publishing, 4th edition (1st edition, 1989; 2nd edition, 1994; 3rd edition, 2001). Read on.

Contact Information

The website for the book is at

http://www.rasmusen.org/GI

The site has the answers to the odd-numbered problems at the end of the chapters, and has instructors' notes for the classroom games. For answers to even-numbered questions, instructors or others needing them for good reasons should email me at Erasmuse@Indiana.edu; send me snailmail at Eric Rasmusen, Department of Business Economics and Public Policy, Kelley School of Business, Indiana University, 1309 East 10th Street, Bloomington, Indiana, USA 47405-1701; or fax me at (812)855-3354.

If you wish to contact the publisher of this book, the addresses are Blackwell Publishing, 9600 Garsington Road, Oxford OX4 2DQ, UK; or 350 Main Street, Malden, Massachusetts 02148, U.S.A.

The text files on the website are two forms (1) *.tex, LaTeX, which uses only ASCII characters, but does not have the diagrams, and (2) *.pdf, Adobe Acrobat, which is formatted and can be read using a free reader program. I encourage readers to submit additional homework problems as well as errors and frustrations. They can be sent to me by e-mail at Erasmuse@Indiana.edu.

Acknowledgements

I would like to thank the many people who commented on clarity, suggested topics and references, or found mistakes. I've put affiliations next to their names, but remember that these change over time (A.B. was not a finance professor when he was my research assistant!).

First Edition: Dean Amel (Board of Governors, Federal Reserve), Dan Asquith (S.E.C.), Sushil Bikhchandani (UCLA business economics), Patricia Hughes Brennan (UCLA accounting), Paul Cheng, Luis Fernandez (Oberlin economics), David Hirshleifer (Ohio State finance), Jack Hirshleifer (UCLA economics), Steven Lippman (UCLA management science), Ivan Png (Singapore), Benjamin Rasmusen (Roseland Farm), Marilyn Rasmusen (Roseland Farm), Ray Renken (Central Florida physics), Richard Silver, Yoon Suh (UCLA accounting), Brett Trueman (Berkeley accounting), Barry Weingast (Hoover) and students in Management 200a made useful comments. D. Koh, Jeanne Lamotte, In-Ho Lee, Loi Lu, Patricia Martin, Timothy Opler (Ohio State finance), Sang Tran, Jeff Vincent, Tao Yang, Roy Zerner, and especially Emmanuel Petrakis (Crete economics) helped me with research assistance at one stage or another. Robert Boyd (UCLA anthropology), Mark Ramseyer (Harvard law), Ken Taymor, and John Wiley (UCLA law) made extensive comments in a reading group as each chapter was written.

Second Edition: Jonathan Berk (U. British Columbia commerce), Mark Burkey (Appalachian State economics), Craig Holden (Indiana finance), Peter Huang (Penn Law), Michael Katz (Berkeley business), Thomas Lyon (Indiana business economics), Steve Postrel (Northwestern business), Herman Quirmbach (Iowa State economics), H. Shifrin, George Tsebelis (UCLA poli sci), Thomas Voss (Leipzig sociology), and Jong-Shin Wei made useful comments, and Alexander Butler (Louisiana State finance) and An-Sing Chen provided research assistance. My students in Management 200 at UCLA and G601 at Indiana University provided invaluable help, especially in suffering through the first drafts of the homework problems.

Third Edition: Kyung-Hwan Baik (Sung Kyun Kwan), Patrick Chen, Robert Dimand (Brock economics), Mathias Erlei (Muenster), Francisco Galera, Peter-John Gordon (University of the West Indies), Erik Johannessen, Michael Mesterton-Gibbons (Pennsylvania), David Rosenbaum (Nebraska economics), Richard Tucker, Hal Wasserman (Berkeley), and Chad Zutter (Indiana finance) made comments that were helpful for the third edition. Blackwell supplied anonymous reviewers of superlative quality. Scott Fluhr, Pankaj Jain and John Spence provided research assistance and new generations of students in G601 were invaluable in helping to clarify my writing.

Fourth Edition: Abdullahi Abdulkadri (U. of the West Indies), Michael Alvarez (Bergen), Michael Baye (Indiana), David Collie (Cardiff), Bouwe Dijkstra (Nottingham), Yanqiong Ding (Shantung), Ralf Elsas (Goethe), Sean Gailmard (Chicago), Diego Garcia (Dartmouth), Richmond Harbaugh (Indiana), Paul Klemperer (Oxford), Bettina Kromen (Cologne), Eva Labro (LSE), Andrew Lilico (Europe Economics), Robert Losee (UNC-CH), Ron Mallon (Utah), Frank P. Maier-Rigaud (Friedrich Wilhelms U.), Ian McCarthy (Indiana), Alexandra Minicozzi (Texas), Luis Pacheco (Portucalense), Tommy Pousset (Louvain), Michael Rothkopf (Rutgers), Pedro Sousa (Portucalense), Charles Tharp, Randal Verbrugge (BLS),Victor Yip (Hong Kong), Lily Yu (Cornell), and especially Maria Arbatskaya (Emory), Kyung Baik (Sungkyunkwan), Martin Caley (Isle of Man Treasury) and Michael Rauh (Indiana) made useful comments. Lan Chang, Ariel Kemper, Manu Raghav, Michael Swetz, and Benjamin Warolin provided research assistance. As always, my students were an important part of writing this book.

Eric Rasmusen
Dan R. and Catherine M. Dalton Professor
Department of Business Economics and Public Policy
Kelley School of Business, Indiana University
Bloomington, Indiana

introduction

History

Not so long ago, the scoffer could say that econometrics and game theory were like Japan and Argentina. In the late 1940s both disciplines and both economies were full of promise, poised for rapid growth, and ready to make a profound impact on the world. We all know what happened to the economies of Japan and Argentina. Of the disciplines, econometrics became an inseparable part of economics, while game theory languished as a subdiscipline, interesting to its specialists but ignored by the profession as a whole. The specialists in game theory were generally mathematicians, who cared about definitions and proofs rather than applying the methods to economic problems. Game theorists took pride in the diversity of disciplines to which their theory could be applied, but in none had it become indispensable.

In the 1970s, the analogy with Argentina broke down. At the same time that Argentina was inviting back Juan Peron, economists were beginning to discover what they could achieve by combining game theory with the structure of complex economic situations. Innovation in theory and application was especially useful for situations with asymmetric information and a temporal sequence of actions, the two major themes of this book. During the 1980s, game theory became dramatically more important to mainstream economics. Indeed, it seemed to be swallowing up microeconomics just as econometrics had swallowed up empirical economics.

Game theory is generally considered to have begun with the publication of von Neumann & Morgenstern's *The Theory of Games and Economic Behaviour* in 1944. Although very little of the game theory in that thick volume is relevant to the present book, it introduced the idea that conflict could be mathematically analyzed and provided the terminology with which to do it. The development of the "Prisoner's Dilemma" (Tucker [unpub]) and Nash's papers on the definition and existence of equilibrium (Nash [1950b, 1951]) laid the foundations for modern noncooperative game theory. At the same time, cooperative game theory reached important results in papers by Nash (1950a) and Shapley (1953b) on bargaining games and Gillies (1953) and Shapley (1953a) on the core.

By 1953 virtually all the game theory that was to be used by economists for the next 20 years had been developed. Until the mid-1970s, game theory remained an autonomous field with little relevance to mainstream economics, important exceptions being Schelling's 1960 book, *The Strategy of Conflict*, which introduced the focal point, and a series of papers (of which Debreu & Scarf [1963] is typical) that showed the relationship of the core of a game to the general equilibrium of an economy.

In the 1970s, information became the focus of many models as economists started to put emphasis on individuals who act rationally but with limited information. When attention was given to individual agents, the time ordering in which they carried out actions began to be explicitly incorporated. With this addition, games had enough structure to reach interesting and nonobvious results. Important "toolbox" references include the earlier but long unapplied articles of Selten (1965) (on perfectness) and Harsanyi (1967) (on incomplete information), the papers by Selten (1975) and Kreps & Wilson (1982) extending perfectness, and the article by Kreps, Milgrom, Roberts, & Wilson (1982) on incomplete information in repeated games. Most of the applications in the present book were developed after 1975, and the flow of research shows no sign of diminishing.

Game Theory's Method

Game theory has been successful in recent years because it fits so well into the new methodology of economics. In the past, macroeconomists started with broad behavioral relationships like the consumption function, and microeconomists often started with precise but irrational behavioral assumptions such as sales maximization. Now all economists start with primitive assumptions about the utility functions, production functions, and endowments of the actors in the models (to which must often be added the available information). The reason is that it is usually easier to judge whether primitive assumptions are sensible than to evaluate high-level assumptions about behavior. Having accepted the primitive assumptions, the modeller figures out what happens when the actors maximize their utility subject to the constraints imposed by their information, endowments, and production functions. This is exactly the paradigm of game theory: the modeller assigns payoff functions and strategy sets to his players and sees what happens when they pick strategies to maximize their payoffs. The approach is a combination of the "Maximization Subject to Constraints" of MIT and the "No Free Lunch" of Chicago. We shall see, however, that game theory relies only on the spirit of these two approaches: it has moved away from maximization by calculus, and inefficient allocations are common. The players act rationally, but the consequences are often bizarre, which makes application to a world of intelligent men and ludicrous outcomes appropriate.

Exemplifying Theory

Along with the trend towards primitive assumptions and maximizing behavior has been a trend towards simplicity. I called this "no-fat modelling" in the first edition, but the term "exemplifying theory" from Fisher (1989) is more apt. This has also been called "modelling by example" or "MIT-style theory." A more smoothly flowing name, but immodest in its double meaning, is "exemplary theory." The heart of the approach is to discover the simplest assumptions needed to generate an interesting conclusion – the starkest, barest model that has the desired result. This desired result is the answer to some relatively narrow question.

Could education be just a signal of ability? Why might bid-ask spreads exist? Is predatory pricing ever rational?

The modeller starts with a vague idea such as "People go to college to show they're smart." He then models the idea formally in a simple way. The idea might survive intact; it might be found formally meaningless; it might survive with qualifications; or its opposite might turn out to be true. The modeller then uses the model to come up with precise propositions, whose proofs may tell him still more about the idea. After the proofs, he goes back to thinking in words, trying to understand more than whether the proofs are mathematically correct.

Good theory of any kind uses Occam's razor, which cuts out superfluous explanations, and the *ceteris paribus* assumption, which restricts attention to one issue at a time. Exemplifying theory goes a step further by providing, in the theory, only a narrow answer to the question. As Fisher says, "Exemplifying theory does not tell us what *must* happen. Rather it tells us what *can* happen."

In the same vein, at Chicago I have heard the style called "Stories That Might Be True." This is not destructive criticism if the modeller is modest, since there are also a great many "Stories That Can't Be True," which are often used as the basis for decisions in business and government. Just as the modeller should feel he has done a good day's work if he has eliminated most outcomes as equilibria in his model, even if multiple equilibria remain, so he should feel useful if he has ruled out certain explanations for how the world works, even if multiple plausible models remain. The aim should be to come up with one or more stories that might apply to a particular situation and then try to sort out which story gives the best explanation. In this, economics combines the deductive reasoning of mathematics with the analogical reasoning of law.

A critic of the mathematical approach in biology has compared it to an hourglass (Slatkin [1980]). First, a broad and important problem is introduced. Second, it is reduced to a very special but tractable model that hopes to capture its essence. Finally, in the most perilous part of the process, the results are expanded to apply to the original problem. Exemplifying theory does the same thing.

The process is one of setting up "If-Then" statements, whether in words or symbols. To apply such statements, their premises and conclusions need to be verified, either by casual or careful empiricism. If the required assumptions seem contrived or the assumptions and implications contradict reality, the idea should be discarded. If "reality" is not immediately obvious and data is available, econometric tests may help show whether the model is valid. Predictions can be made about future events, but that is not usually the primary motivation: most of us are more interested in explaining and understanding than predicting.

The method just described is close to how, according to Lakatos (1976), mathematical theorems are developed. It contrasts sharply with the common view that the researcher starts with a hypothesis and proves or disproves it. Instead, the process of proof helps show how the hypothesis should be formulated.

An important part of exemplifying theory is what Kreps & Spence (1985) have called "blackboxing": treating unimportant subcomponents of a model in a cursory way. The game "Entry for Buyout" (Rasmusen [1988a]), for example, asks whether a new entrant would be bought out by the industry's incumbent producer, something that depends on duopoly pricing and bargaining. Both pricing and bargaining are complicated games in themselves, but if the modeller does not wish to deflect attention to those topics he can use the simple Nash and Cournot solutions to those games and go on to analyze buyout. If the focus of the model were duopoly pricing, then using the Cournot solution would be open to attack, but as a simplifying assumption, rather than one that "drives" the model, it is acceptable.

Despite the style's drive towards simplicity, a certain amount of formalism and mathematics is required to pin down the modeller's thoughts. Exemplifying theory treads a middle path between mathematical generality and nonmathematical vagueness. Advocates of both alternatives will complain that exemplifying theory is too narrow. But beware of calls for more "rich," "complex," or "textured" descriptions; these often lead to theory either too incoherent or too incomprehensible to be applied to real situations. Richness in a model tends to make it flabby.

Some readers will think that exemplifying theory uses too little mathematical technique, but others, especially noneconomists, will think it uses too much. Intelligent laymen have objected to the amount of mathematics in economics since at least the 1880s, when George Bernard Shaw said that as a boy he (1) let someone assume that $a = b$, (2) permitted several steps of algebra, and (3) found he had accepted a proof that $1 = 2$. Forever after, Shaw distrusted assumptions and algebra. Despite the effort to achieve simplicity (or perhaps because of it), mathematics is essential to exemplifying theory. The conclusions can be retranslated into words, but rarely can they be found by verbal reasoning. The economist Wicksteed put this nicely in his reply to Shaw's criticism:

> Mr Shaw arrived at the sapient conclusion that there "was a screw loose somewhere" – not in his own reasoning powers, but – "in the algebraic art"; and thenceforth renounced mathematical reasoning in favour of the literary method which enables a clever man to follow equally fallacious arguments to equally absurd conclusions *without seeing that they are absurd.* This is the exact difference between the mathematical and literary treatment of the pure theory of political economy.   *(Wicksteed [1885] p. 732)*

In exemplifying theory, one can still rig a model to achieve a wide range of results, but it must be rigged by making strange primitive assumptions. Everyone familiar with the style knows that the place to look for the source of suspicious results is the description at the start of the model. If that description is not clear, the reader deduces that the model's counterintuitive results arise from bad assumptions concealed in poor writing. Clarity is therefore important, and the somewhat inelegant Players-Actions-Payoffs presentation used in this book is useful not only for helping the writer, but for persuading the reader.

This Book's Style

Substance and style are closely related. The difference between a good model and a bad one is not just whether the essence of the situation is captured, but also how much froth covers the essence. In this book, I have tried to make the games as simple as possible. They often, for example, allow each player a choice of only two actions. Our intuition works best with such models, and continuous actions are technically more troublesome. Other assumptions, such as zero production costs, rely on trained intuition. To the layman, the assumption that output is costless seems very strong, but a little experience with these models teaches that it is the constancy of the marginal cost that usually matters, not its level.

What matters more than what a model says is what we understand it to say. Just as an article written in Sanskrit is useless to me, so is one that is excessively mathematical or poorly written, no matter how rigorous it seems to the author. Such an article leaves me with some new belief about its subject, but that belief is not sharp, or precisely correct. Overprecision in sending a message creates imprecision when it is received, because precision is not clarity. The result of an attempt to be mathematically precise is sometimes to overwhelm the reader, in the same way that someone who requests the answer to a simple question in the discovery process of a lawsuit is overwhelmed when the other side responds with 70 boxes of tangentially related documents. The quality of the author's input should be judged not by some abstract standard but by the output in terms of reader processing cost and understanding.

In this spirit, I have tried to simplify the structure and notation of models while giving credit to their original authors, but I must ask pardon of anyone whose model has been oversimplified or distorted, or whose model I have inadvertently replicated without crediting them. In trying to be understandable, I have taken risks with respect to accuracy. My hope is that the impression left in the readers' minds will be more accurate than if a style more cautious and obscure had left them to devise their own errors. My major strength is in boiling down difficult models into simple games that still capture the essence of the models' ideas. My major weakness is in sliding past technical points, some unimportant, some important. I apologize in advance for the mistakes I am sure this book contains, but I hope that they are orthogonal to the mistakes of other books, and obvious enough not to lead the reader far astray.

Readers may be surprised to find occasional references to newspaper and magazine articles in this book. I hope these references will be reminders that models ought eventually to be applied to specific facts, and that a great many interesting situations are waiting for our analysis. The principal-agent problem is not found only in back issues of *Econometrica*: it can be found on the front page of today's *Wall Street Journal* if one knows what to look for.

I make the occasional joke here and there. Game theory is a subject intrinsically full of paradox and surprise. I want to emphasize, though, that I take game theory seriously, in the same way Chicago economists say that they take price theory seriously. It is not just an academic artform: people do choose actions deliberately and trade off one good against another, and game theory will help you understand how they do that. If it did not, I would not advise you to study such a difficult subject. There are much more elegant fields in mathematics from the aesthetic point of view. As it is, I think it is important that every educated person have some contact with the ideas in this book, just as they should have some contact with the basic principles of price theory.

I have been forced to exercise more discretion over definitions than I had hoped. Many concepts have been defined on an article-by-article basis in the literature, with no consistency and little attention to euphony or usefulness. Other concepts, such as "asymmetric information" and "incomplete information," have been considered so basic as to not need definition, and hence have been used in contradictory ways. I use existing terms whenever possible, and synonyms are listed.

I have often named the players Smith and Jones so that the reader's memory will be less taxed in remembering which is a player and which is a time period. I hope also to reinforce the idea that a model is a story made precise; we begin with Smith and Jones, even if we quickly descend to s and j. Keeping this in mind, the modeller is less likely to build mathematically correct models with absurd action sets, and his descriptions are more pleasant to read. In the same vein, labelling a curve "$U = 83$" sacrifices no generality: the phrase "$U = 83$ and $U = 66$" has virtually the same content as "$U = \alpha$ and $U = \beta$, where $\alpha > \beta$," but uses less short-term memory.

A danger of this approach is that readers may not appreciate the complexity of some of the material. While journal articles make the material seem harder than it is, this approach makes it seem easier (a statement that can be true even if readers find this book difficult). The better the author does his job, the worse this problem becomes. Keynes (1933) says of Alfred Marshall's *Principles*,

> The lack of emphasis and of strong light and shade, the sedulous rubbing away of rough edges and salients and projections, until what is most novel can appear as trite, allows the reader to pass too easily through. Like a duck leaving water, he can escape from this douche of ideas with scarce a wetting. The difficulties are concealed; the most ticklish problems are solved in footnotes; a pregnant and original judgement is dressed up as a platitude.

This book may well be subject to the same criticism, but I have tried to face up to difficult points, and the problems at the end of each chapter will help to avoid making the reader's progress too easy. Only a certain amount of understanding can be expected from a book, however. The efficient way to learn how to do research is to start doing it, not to read about it, and after reading this book, if not before, many readers will want to build their own models. My purpose here is to show them the big picture, to help them understand the models intuitively, and give them a feel for the modelling process.

Notes

- Perhaps the most important contribution of von Neumann & Morgenstern (1944) is the theory of expected utility (see section 2.3). Although they developed the theory because they needed it to find the equilibria of games, it is today heavily used in all branches of economics. In game theory proper, they contributed the framework to describe games, and the concept of mixed strategies (see section 3.1). A good historical discussion is Shubik (1992) in the Weintraub volume mentioned in the next note.
- A number of good books on the history of game theory have appeared in recent years. Norman Macrae's *John von Neumann* and Sylvia Nasar's *A Beautiful Mind* (on John Nash) are extraordinarily good biographies of founding fathers, while *Eminent Economists: Their Life Philosophies* and *Passion and Craft: Economists at Work*, edited by Michael Szenberg, and *Toward a History of Game Theory*, edited by Roy Weintraub, contain autobiographical essays by many scholars who use game theory, including Shubik, Riker, Dixit, Varian, and Myerson. Dimand & Dimand's *A History of Game Theory*, the first volume of which appeared in 1996, is a more intensive look at the intellectual history of the field. See also Myerson (1999).
- For articles from the history of mathematical economics, see the collection by Baumol & Goldfeld (1968), Dimand & Dimand's 1997 *The Foundations of Game Theory* in three volumes, and Kuhn (1997). Collections of more recent articles include Rasmusen (2001), Binmore & Dasgupta (1986), Diamond & Rothschild (1978) on information economics, Klemperer (2000) on auctions, and the immense Rubinstein (1990).
- On method, see the dialogue by Lakatos (1976), or Davis, Marchisotto, & Hersh (1981), chapter 6 of which is a shorter dialogue in the same style. Friedman (1953) is the classic essay on a different methodology: evaluating a model by testing its predictions. Kreps & Spence (1984) is a discussion of exemplifying theory.

- The mathematician Robert J. Kleinhenz is widely said to have likened proving a theorem to "seeing the peak of a mountain and trying to climb to the top. One establishes a base camp and begins scaling the mountain's sheer face, encountering obstacles at every turn, often retracing one's steps, and struggling every foot of the journey. Finally when the top is reached, one stands examining the peak, taking in the view of the surrounding countryside and then noting the automobile road up the other side!" (see e.g., http://users.characterlink.net/The-Cookie-Jar/math_jokes_10.html).

  In the spirit of Lakatos, I would agree except that usually halfway up you discover that what you thought was the peak is a mirage or a lower crest, so you have to change direction.

- Because style and substance are so closely linked, how one writes is important. For advice on writing, see McCloskey (1985, 1987) (on economics), Bowersock (1985) (on footnotes), Fowler (1931), Fowler & Fowler (1949), Halmos (1970) (on mathematical writing), Rasmusen (2000), Strunk & White (1959), Weiner (1984), and Wydick (1978).

- **A fallacious proof that $1 = 2$.** Suppose that $a = b$. Then $ab = b^2$ and $ab - b^2 = a^2 - b^2$. Factoring the last equation gives us $b(a - b) = (a + b)(a - b)$, which can be simplified to $b = a + b$. But then, using our initial assumption, $b = 2b$ and $1 = 2$. The fallacy is division by zero.

Part 1
game theory

Chapter 1
the rules of the game

1.1 Definitions

Game theory is concerned with the actions of decision makers who are conscious that their actions affect each other. When the only two publishers in a city choose prices for their newspapers, aware that their sales are determined jointly, they are players in a game with each other. They are not in a game with the readers who buy the newspapers, because each reader ignores his effect on the publisher. Game theory is not useful when decision makers ignore the reactions of others or treat them as impersonal market forces.

The best way to understand which situations can be modelled as games and which cannot, is to think about examples like the following:

1 OPEC members choosing their annual output;
2 General Motors purchasing steel from U.S. Steel;
3 two manufacturers, one of nuts and one of bolts, deciding whether to use metric or American standards;
4 a board of directors setting up a stock option plan for the chief executive officer;
5 the US Air Force hiring jet fighter pilots;
6 an electric company deciding whether to order a new power plant given its estimate of demand for electricity in ten years.

The first four examples are games. In (1), OPEC members are playing a game because Saudi Arabia knows that Kuwait's oil output is based on Kuwait's forecast of Saudi output, and the output from both countries matters to the world price. In (2), a significant portion of American trade in steel is between General Motors and U.S. Steel, companies which realize that the quantities traded by each of them affect the price. One wants the price low, the other high, so this is a game with conflict between the two players. In (3), the nut and bolt manufacturers are not in conflict, but the actions of one do affect the desired actions of the other, so the situation is a game nonetheless. In (4), the board of directors chooses a stock option plan anticipating the effect on the actions of the CEO.

Game theory is inappropriate for modelling the final two examples. In (5), each individual pilot affects the US Air Force insignificantly, and each pilot makes his employment decision without regard for the impact on the Air Force's policies. In (6), the electric company faces a complicated decision, but it does not face another rational agent. These situations are more appropriate for the use of **decision theory** than game theory, decision theory being the careful analysis of how one person makes a decision when he may be faced with uncertainty, or an entire sequence of decisions that interact with each other, but when he is not faced with having to interact strategically with other single decisionmakers. Changes in the important economic variables could, however, turn examples (5) and (6) into games. The appropriate model changes if the Air Force faces a pilots' union or if the public utility commission pressures the utility to change its generating capacity.

Game theory as it will be presented in this book is a modelling tool, not an axiomatic system. The presentation in this chapter is unconventional. Rather than starting with mathematical definitions or simple little games of the kind used later in the chapter, we will start with a situation to be modelled, and build a game from it step by step.

Describing a Game

The essential elements of a game are **players**, **actions**, **payoffs**, and **information** – PAPI, for short. These are collectively known as the **rules of the game**, and the modeller's objective is to describe a situation in terms of the rules of a game so as to explain what will happen in that situation. Trying to maximize their payoffs, the players will devise plans known as **strategies** that pick actions depending on the information that has arrived at each moment. The combination of strategies chosen by each player is known as the **equilibrium**. Given an equilibrium, the modeller can see what actions come out of the conjunction of all the players' plans, and this tells him the **outcome** of the game.

This kind of standard description helps both the modeller and his readers. For the modeller, the names are useful because they help ensure that the important details of the game have been fully specified. For his readers, they make the game easier to understand, especially if, as with most technical papers, the paper is first skimmed quickly to see if it is worth reading. The less clear a writer's style, the more closely he should adhere to the standard names, which means that most of us ought to adhere very closely indeed.

Think of writing a paper as a game between author and reader, rather than as a single-player production process. The author, knowing that he has valuable information but imperfect means of communication, is trying to convey the information to the reader. The reader does not know whether the information is valuable, and he must choose whether to read the paper closely enough to find out.[1]

To define the terms used above and to show the difference between game theory and decision theory, let us use the example of an entrepreneur trying to decide whether to start a dry cleaning store in a town already served by one dry cleaner. We will call the two firms "NewCleaner" and "OldCleaner." NewCleaner is uncertain about whether the economy will be in a recession or not, which will affect how much consumers pay for dry cleaning, and must also worry about whether OldCleaner will respond to entry with a price war, or by keeping its initial high prices. OldCleaner is a well-established firm, and it would survive

---

[1] Once you have read to the end of this chapter: What are the possible equilibria of this game?

any price war, though its profits would fall. NewCleaner must itself decide whether to initiate a price war or to charge high prices, and must also decide what kind of equipment to buy, how many workers to hire, and so forth.

Players *are the individuals who make decisions. Each player's goal is to maximize his utility by choice of actions.*

In the Dry Cleaners Game, let us specify the players to be NewCleaner and OldCleaner. Passive individuals like the customers, who react predictably to price changes without any thought of trying to change anyone's behavior, are not players, but environmental parameters. Simplicity is the goal in modelling, and the ideal is to keep the number of players down to the minimum that captures the essence of the situation.

Sometimes it is useful to explicitly include individuals in the model called **pseudo-players** whose actions are taken in a purely mechanical way.

Nature *is a pseudo-player who takes random actions at specified points in the game with specified probabilities.*

In the Dry Cleaners Game, we will model the possibility of recession as a move by Nature. With probability 0.3, Nature decides that there will be a recession, and with probability 0.7 there will not. Even if the players always took the same actions, this random move means that the model would yield more than just one prediction. We say that there are different **realizations** of a game depending on the results of random moves.

An **action** *or* **move** *by player i, denoted a_i, is a choice he can make.*

Player i's **action set**, *$A_i = \{a_i\}$, is the entire set of actions available to him.*

An **action profile** *is a list $a = \{a_i\}$, $(i = 1, \ldots, n)$ of one action for each of the n players in the game.*

Again, simplicity is our goal. We are trying to determine whether Newcleaner will enter or not, and for this it is not important for us to go into the technicalities of dry cleaning equipment and labor practices. Also, it will not be in Newcleaner's interest to start a price war, since it cannot possibly drive out Oldcleaners, so we can exclude that decision from our model. Newcleaner's action set can be modelled very simply as {*Enter*, *Stay Out*}. We will also specify Oldcleaner's action set to be simple: it is to choose price from {*Low*, *High*}.

By player i's **payoff** *$\pi_i(s_1, \ldots, s_n)$, we mean either:*

(1) The utility player i receives after all players and Nature have picked their strategies and the game has been played out; or

(2) The expected utility he receives as a function of the strategies chosen by himself and the other players.

For the moment, think of "strategy" as a synonym for "action." Definitions (1) and (2) are distinct and different, but in the literature and this book the term "payoff" is used for both the actual payoff and the expected payoff. The context will make clear which is meant.

Table 1.1 The Dry Cleaners Game

(a) Normal economy

		OldCleaner	
		Low price	*High price*
NewCleaner	*Enter*	−100, −50	100, 100
	Stay Out	0, 50	0, 300

(b) Recession

		OldCleaner	
		Low price	*High price*
NewCleaner	*Enter*	−160, −110	40, 40
	Stay Out	0, −10	0, 240

Payoffs to: (NewCleaner, OldCleaner) in thousands of dollars.

If one is modelling a particular real-world situation, figuring out the payoffs is often the hardest part of constructing a model. For this pair of dry cleaners, we will pretend we have looked over all the data and figured out that the payoffs are as given by table 1.1a (normal economy) if the economy is normal, and that if there is a recession the payoff of each player who operates in the market is 60,000 dollars lower, as shown in table 1.1b (recession).

Information is modelled using the concept of the **information set**, a concept which will be defined more precisely in section 2.2. For now, think of a player's information set as his knowledge at a particular time of the values of different variables. The elements of the information set are the different values that the player thinks are possible. If the information set has many elements, there are many values the player cannot rule out; if it has one element, he knows the value precisely. A player's information set includes not only distinctions between the values of variables such as the strength of oil demand, but also knowledge of what actions have previously been taken, so his information set changes over the course of the game.

Here, at the time that it chooses its price, OldCleaner will know NewCleaner's decision about entry. But what do the firms know about the recession? If both firms know about the recession we model that as Nature moving before NewCleaner; if only OldCleaner knows, we put Nature's move after NewCleaner; if neither firm knows whether there is a recession at the time they must make their decisions, we put Nature's move at the end of the game. Let us do this last.

It is convenient to lay out information and actions together in an **order of play**. Here is the order of play we have specified for the Dry Cleaners Game:

1 Newcleaner chooses its entry decision from {*Enter, Stay Out*}.
2 Oldcleaner chooses its price from {*Low, High*}.
3 Nature picks demand, D, to be *Recession* with probability 0.3 or *Normal* with probability 0.7.

The purpose of modelling is to explain how a given set of circumstances leads to a particular result. The result of interest is known as the outcome.

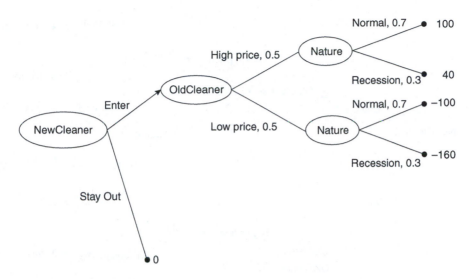

Figure 1.1 The Dry Cleaners Game as a decision tree.

> *The **outcome** of the game is a set of interesting elements that the modeller picks from the values of actions, payoffs, and other variables after the game is played out.*

The definition of the outcome for any particular model depends on what variables the modeller finds interesting. One way to define the outcome of the Dry Cleaners Game would be as either *Enter* or *Stay Out*. Another way, appropriate if the model is being constructed to help plan NewCleaner's finances, is as the payoff that NewCleaner realizes. From tables 1.1a and b, this is one element of the set {*0, 100, −100, 40, −160*}.

Having laid out the assumptions of the model, let us return to what is special about the way game theory models a situation. Decision theory sets up the rules of the game in much the same way as game theory, but its outlook is fundamentally different in one important way: there is only one player. Return to NewCleaner's decision about entry. In decision theory, the standard method is to construct a **decision tree** from the rules of the game, which is just a graphical way to depict the order of play.

Figure 1.1 shows a decision tree for the Dry Cleaners Game. It shows all the moves available to NewCleaner, the probabilities of states of nature (actions that NewCleaner cannot control), and the payoffs to NewCleaner depending on its choices and what the environment is like. Note that although we already specified the probabilities of Nature's move to be 0.7 for *Normal*, we also need to specify a probability for OldCleaner's move, which is set at probability 0.5 of *Low price* and probability 0.5 of *High price*.

Once a decision tree is set up, we can solve for the optimal decision which maximizes the expected payoff. Suppose NewCleaner has entered. If OldCleaner chooses a high price, then NewCleaner's expected payoff is 82, which is 0.7(100) + 0.3(40). If OldCleaner chooses a low price, then NewCleaner's expected payoff is −118, which is 0.7(−100) + 0.3(−160). Since there is a 50–50 chance of each move by OldCleaner, NewCleaner's overall expected payoff from *Enter* is −18. That is worse than the 0 which NewCleaner could get by choosing *stay out*, so the prediction is that NewCleaner will stay out.

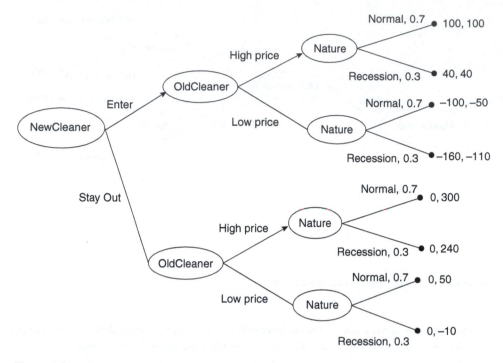

Figure 1.2   The Dry Cleaners Game as a game tree.

That, however, is wrong. This is a game, not just a decision problem. The flaw in the reasoning I just went through is the assumption that OldCleaner will choose *High price* with probability 0.5. If we use information about OldCleaner's payoffs and figure out what moves OldCleaner will take in solving its own profit maximization problem, we will come to a different conclusion.

First, let us depict the order of play as a **game tree** instead of a decision tree. Figure 1.2 shows our model as a game tree, with all of OldCleaner's moves and payoffs.

Viewing the situation as a game, we must think about both players' decision making. Suppose NewCleaner has entered. If OldCleaner chooses *High price*, OldCleaner's expected profit is 82, which is 0.7(100) + 0.3(40). If OldCleaner chooses *Low price*, OldCleaner's expected profit is −68, which is 0.7(−50) + 0.3(−110). Thus, OldCleaner will choose *High price*, and with probability 1.0, not 0.5. The arrow on the game tree for *High price* shows this conclusion of our reasoning. This means, in turn, that NewCleaner can predict an expected payoff of 82, which is 0.7(100) + 0.3(40), from *Enter*.

Suppose NewCleaner has not entered. If OldCleaner chooses *High price*, OldCleaner's expected profit is 282, which is 0.7(300) + 0.3(240). If OldCleaner chooses *Low price*, OldCleaner's expected profit is 32, which is 0.7(50) + 0.3(−10). Thus, OldCleaner will choose *High price*, as shown by the arrow on *High price*. If NewCleaner chooses *Stay out*, NewCleaner will have a payoff of 0, and since that is worse than the 82 which NewCleaner can predict from *Enter*, NewCleaner will in fact enter the market.

This switching back from the point of view of one player to the point of view of another is characteristic of game theory. The game theorist must practice putting himself in *everybody* else's shoes. (Does that mean we become kinder, gentler people? – Or do we just get trickier?)

Since so much depends on the interaction between the plans and predictions of different players, it is useful to go a step beyond simply setting out actions in a game. Instead, the modeller goes on to think about **strategies**, which are action plans.

Player i's **strategy** s_i *is a rule that tells him which action to choose at each instant of the game, given his information set.*

Player i's **strategy set** *or* **strategy space** $S_i = \{s_i\}$ *is the set of strategies available to him.*

A **strategy profile** $s = (s_1, \ldots, s_n)$ *is a list consisting of one strategy for each of the n players in the game.*[2]

Since the information set includes whatever the player knows about the previous actions of other players, the strategy tells him how to react to their actions. In the Dry Cleaners Game, the strategy set for NewCleaner is just {*Enter, Stay Out*}, since NewCleaner moves first and is not reacting to any new information. The strategy set for OldCleaner, though, is

$$\left\{ \begin{array}{l} \text{High Price if NewCleaner Entered, Low Price if NewCleaner Stayed Out} \\ \text{Low Price if NewCleaner Entered, High Price if NewCleaner Stayed Out} \\ \text{High Price No Matter What} \\ \text{Low Price No Matter What} \end{array} \right\}$$

The concept of the strategy is useful because the action a player wishes to pick often depends on the past actions of Nature and the other players. Only rarely can we predict a player's actions unconditionally, but often we can predict how he will respond to the outside world.

Keep in mind that a player's strategy is a complete set of instructions for him, which tells him what actions to pick in every conceivable situation, even if he does not expect to reach that situation. Strictly speaking, even if a player's strategy instructs him to commit suicide in 1989, it ought also to specify what actions he takes if he is still alive in 1990. This kind of care will be crucial in chapter 4's discussion of "subgame perfect" equilibrium. The completeness of the description also means that strategies, unlike actions, are unobservable. An action is physical, but a strategy is only mental.

Equilibrium

To predict the outcome of a game, the modeller focusses on the possible strategy profiles, since it is the interaction of the different players' strategies that determines what happens. The distinction between strategy profiles, which are sets of strategies, and outcomes, which are sets of values of whichever variables are considered interesting, is a common source of confusion. Often different strategy profiles lead to the same outcome. In the

---

[2] I used "strategy combination" instead of "strategy profile" in the third edition, but "profile" seems well enough established that I'm switching to it.

Dry Cleaners Game, the single outcome of *NewCleaner Enters* would result from either of the following two strategy profiles:

$$\left\{ \begin{array}{l} \textit{High Price if NewCleaner Enters, Low Price if NewCleaner Stays Out} \\ \textit{Enter} \end{array} \right\}$$

$$\left\{ \begin{array}{l} \textit{Low Price if NewCleaner Enters, High Price if NewCleaner Stays Out} \\ \textit{Enter} \end{array} \right\}$$

Predicting what happens consists of selecting one or more strategy profiles as being the most rational behavior by the players acting to maximize their payoffs.

An **equilibrium** $s^* = (s_1^*, \ldots, s_n^*)$ *is a strategy profile consisting of a best strategy for each of the n players in the game.*

The **equilibrium strategies** are the strategies players pick in trying to maximize their individual payoffs, as distinct from the many possible strategy profiles obtainable by arbitrarily choosing one strategy per player. Equilibrium is used differently in game theory than in other areas of economics. In a general equilibrium model, for example, an equilibrium is a set of prices resulting from optimal behavior by the individuals in the economy. In game theory, that set of prices would be the **equilibrium outcome**, but the equilibrium itself would be the strategy profile – the individuals' rules for buying and selling – that generated the outcome.

People often carelessly say "equilibrium" when they mean "equilibrium outcome," and "strategy" when they mean "action." The difference is not very important in most of the games that will appear in this chapter, but it is absolutely fundamental to thinking like a game theorist. Consider Germany's decision on whether to remilitarize the Rhineland in 1936. France adopted the strategy: *Do not fight*, and Germany responded by remilitarizing, leading to World War II a few years later. If France had adopted the strategy: *Fight if Germany remilitarizes; otherwise do not fight*, the outcome would still have been that France would not have fought. No war would have ensued, however, because Germany would not then remilitarize. Perhaps it was because he thought along these lines that John von Neumann was such a hawk in the Cold War, as MacRae describes in his biography (MacRae [1992]). This difference between actions and strategies, outcomes and equilibria, is one of the hardest ideas to teach in a game theory class, even though it is trivial to state.

To find the equilibrium, it is not enough to specify the players, strategies, and payoffs, because the modeller must also decide what "best strategy" means. He does this by defining an equilibrium concept.

An **equilibrium concept** *or* **solution concept** $F: \{S_1, \ldots, S_n, \pi_1, \ldots, \pi_n\} \rightarrow s^*$ *is a rule that defines an equilibrium based on the possible strategy profiles and the payoff functions.*

We have implicitly already used an equilibrium concept in the analysis above, which picked one strategy for each of the two players as our prediction for the game (what we implicitly used is the concept of **subgame perfectness** which will reappear in chapter 4). Only a few equilibrium concepts are generally accepted, and the remaining sections of this chapter are devoted to finding the equilibrium using the two best-known of them: dominant strategy equilibrium and Nash equilibrium.

Uniqueness

Accepted solution concepts do not guarantee uniqueness, and lack of a unique equilibrium is a major problem in game theory. Often the solution concept employed leads us to believe that the players will pick one of the two strategy profiles A or B, not C or D, but we cannot say whether A or B is more likely. Sometimes we have the opposite problem and the game has no equilibrium at all. Having no equilibrium means either that the modeller sees no good reason why one strategy profile is more likely than another, or that some player wants to pick an infinite value for one of his actions.

A model with no equilibrium or multiple equilibria is underspecified. The modeller has failed to provide a full and precise prediction for what will happen. One option is to admit that the theory is incomplete. This is not a shameful thing to do; an admission of incompleteness such as section 5.2's Folk Theorem is a valuable negative result. Or perhaps the situation being modelled really is unpredictable, in which case to make a prediction would be wrong. Another option is to renew the attack by changing the game's description or the solution concept. Preferably it is the description that is changed, since economists look to the rules of the game for the differences between models, and not to the solution concept. If an important part of the game is concealed under the definition of equilibrium, in fact, the reader is likely to feel tricked, and to charge the modeller with intellectual dishonesty.

1.2   Dominated and Dominant Strategies: The Prisoner's Dilemma

In discussing equilibrium concepts, it is useful to have shorthand for "all the other players' strategies."

For any vector $y = (y_1, \ldots, y_n)$, *denote by* y_{-i} *the vector* $(y_1, \ldots, y_{i-1}, y_{i+1}, \ldots, y_n)$, *which is the portion of* y *not associated with player* i.

Using this notation, s_{-Smith}, for instance, is the profile of strategies of every player except player *Smith*. That profile is of great interest to Smith, because he uses it to help choose his own strategy, and the new notation helps define his best response.

Player i's **best response** *or* **best reply** *to the strategies* s_{-i} *chosen by the other players is the strategy* s_i^* *that yields him the greatest payoff; that is,*

$$\pi_i(s_i^*, s_{-i}) \geq \pi_i(s_i', s_{-i}) \quad \forall s_i' \neq s_i^*. \tag{1.1}$$

The best response is strongly best if no other strategies are equally good, and weakly best otherwise.

The first important equilibrium concept is based on the idea of **dominance**.

*The strategy s_i^d is a **dominated strategy** if it is strictly inferior to some other strategy no matter what strategies the other players choose, in the sense that whatever strategies they pick, his payoff is lower with s_i^d. Mathematically, s_i^d is dominated if there exists a single s_i' such that*

$$\pi_i(s_i^d, s_{-i}) < \pi_i(s_i', s_{-i}) \quad \forall s_{-i}. \tag{1.2}$$

Note that s_i^d is not a dominated strategy if there is no s_{-i} to which it is the best response, but sometimes the better strategy is s_i' and sometimes it is s_i''. In that case, s_i^d could have the redeeming feature of being a good compromise strategy for a player who cannot predict what the other players are going to do. A dominated strategy is unambiguously inferior to some single other strategy.

There is usually no special name for the superior strategy that beats a dominated strategy. In unusual games, however, there is some strategy that beats *every* other strategy. We call that a "dominant strategy."

*The strategy s_i^* is a **dominant strategy** if it is a player's strictly best response to any strategies the other players might pick, in the sense that whatever strategies they pick, his payoff is highest with s_i^*. Mathematically,*

$$\pi_i(s_i^*, s_{-i}) > \pi_i(s_i', s_{-i}) \quad \forall s_{-i}, \ \forall s_i' \neq s_i^*. \tag{1.3}$$

*A **dominant-strategy equilibrium** is a strategy profile consisting of each player's dominant strategy.*

A player's dominant strategy is his strictly best response even to wildly irrational actions by the other players. Most games do not have dominant strategies, and the players must try to figure out each others' actions to choose their own.

The Dry Cleaners Game incorporated considerable complexity in the rules of the game to illustrate such things as information sets and the time sequence of actions. To illustrate equilibrium concepts, we will use simpler games, such as the Prisoner's Dilemma. In the Prisoner's Dilemma, two prisoners, Messrs. Row and Column, are being interrogated separately. If each tries to blame the other, each is sentenced to eight years in prison; if both remain silent, each is sentenced to one year.[3] If just one blames the other, he is released, but the silent prisoner is sentenced to ten years. The Prisoner's Dilemma is an example of a **2-by-2 game**, because each of the two players – Row and Column – has two possible actions in his action set: *Confess* and *Deny*. Table 1.2 gives the payoffs.

Each player has a dominant strategy. Consider Row. Row does not know which action Column is choosing, but if Column chooses *Deny*, Row faces a *Deny* payoff of -1, and a *Confess* payoff of 0, whereas if Column chooses *Confess*, Row faces a *Deny* payoff of -10, and a *Confess* payoff of -8. In either case Row does better with *Confess*. Since the game is symmetric, Column's incentives are the same. The dominant-strategy equilibrium

[3] Another way to tell the story is to say that if both are silent, then with probability 0.1 they are convicted anyway and serve ten years, for an expected payoff of $(-1, -1)$.

Table 1.2   The Prisoner's Dilemma

		Column	
		Deny	*Confess*
	Deny	−1, −1	−10, 0
Row			
	Confess	0, −10	**−8, −8**

Payoffs to: (Row, Column).

is (*Confess, Confess*), and the equilibrium payoffs are (−8, −8), which is worse for both players than (−1, −1). Sixteen, in fact, is the greatest possible combined total of years in prison.

The result is even stronger than it seems, because it is robust to substantial changes in the model. Because the equilibrium is a dominant-strategy equilibrium, the information structure of the game does not matter. If Column is allowed to know Row's move before taking his own, the equilibrium is unchanged. Row still chooses *Confess*, knowing that Column will surely choose *Confess* afterwards.

The Prisoner's Dilemma crops up in many different situations, including oligopoly pricing, auction bidding, salesman effort, political bargaining, and arms races. Whenever you observe individuals in a conflict that hurts them all, your first thought should be of the Prisoner's Dilemma.

The game seems perverse and unrealistic to many people who have never encountered it before (although friends who are prosecutors assure me that it is a standard crime-fighting tool). If the outcome does not seem right to you, you should realize that very often the chief usefulness of a model is to induce discomfort. Discomfort is a sign that your model is not what you think it is – that you left out something essential to the result you expected and didn't get. Either your original thought or your model is mistaken; and finding such mistakes is a real if painful benefit of model building. To refuse to accept surprising conclusions is to reject logic.

Cooperative and Noncooperative Games

What difference would it make if the two prisoners could talk to each other before making their decisions? It depends on the strength of promises. If promises are not binding, then although the two prisoners might agree to *Deny*, they would *Confess* anyway when the time came to choose actions.

*A **cooperative game** is a game in which the players can make binding commitments, as opposed to a **noncooperative game**, in which they cannot.*

This definition draws the usual distinction between the two theories of games, but the real difference lies in the modelling approach. Both theories start off with the rules of the game, but they differ in the kinds of solution concepts employed. Cooperative game theory is axiomatic, frequently appealing to Pareto-optimality,[4] fairness, and equity. Noncooperative game theory is economic in flavor, with solution concepts based on players maximizing their

---

[4] If outcome X **strongly Pareto-dominates** outcome Y, then all players have higher utility under outcome X. If outcome X **weakly Pareto-dominates** outcome Y, some player has higher utility under X, and no

own utility functions subject to stated constraints. Or, from a different angle: cooperative game theory is a reduced-form theory, which focusses on properties of the outcome rather than on the strategies that achieve the outcome, a method which is appropriate if modelling the process is too complicated. Except for the discussion of the Nash Bargaining Solution in chapter 12, this book is concerned exclusively with noncooperative games. (For an argument that cooperative game theory is more important than I think, see Aumann [1997].)

In applied economics, the most commonly encountered use of cooperative games is to model bargaining. The Prisoner's Dilemma is a noncooperative game, but it could be modelled as cooperative by allowing the two players not only to communicate but to make binding commitments. Cooperative games often allow players to split the gains from cooperation by making **side-payments** – transfers between themselves that change the prescribed payoffs. Cooperative game theory generally incorporates commitments and side-payments via the solution concept, which can become very elaborate, while noncooperative game theory incorporates them by adding extra actions. The distinction between cooperative and noncooperative games does *not* lie in conflict or absence of conflict, as is shown by the following examples of situations commonly modelled one way or the other:

A *cooperative game without conflict.* Members of a workforce choose which of equally arduous tasks to undertake to best coordinate with each other.

A *cooperative game with conflict.* Bargaining over price between a monopolist and a monopsonist.

A *noncooperative game with conflict.* The Prisoner's Dilemma.

A *noncooperative game without conflict.* Two companies set a product standard without communication.

1.3   Iterated Dominance: The Battle of the Bismarck Sea

Very few games have a dominant-strategy equilibrium, but sometimes dominance can still be useful even when it does not resolve things quite so neatly as in the Prisoner's Dilemma. The Battle of the Bismarck Sea, a game I found in Haywood (1954), is set in the South Pacific in 1943. General Imamura has been ordered to transport Japanese troops across the Bismarck Sea to New Guinea, and General Kenney wants to bomb the troop transports. Imamura must choose between a shorter northern route or a longer southern route to New Guinea, and Kenney must decide where to send his planes to look for the Japanese. If Kenney sends his planes to the wrong route he can recall them, but the number of days of bombing is reduced.

The players are Kenney and Imamura, and they each have the same action set, {*North, South*}, but their payoffs, given by table 1.3, are never the same. Imamura loses exactly

player has lower utility. A zero sum game does not have outcomes that even weakly Pareto-dominate other outcomes. All of its equilibria are Pareto-efficient because no player gains without another player losing.

It is often said that strategy profile x "Pareto dominates" or "dominates" strategy profile y. Taken literally, this is meaningless, since strategies do not necessarily have any ordering at all – one could define *Deny* as being bigger than *Confess*, but that would be arbitrary. The statement is really shorthand for "the payoff profile resulting from strategy profile x Pareto-dominates the payoff profile resulting from strategy y."

Table 1.3   The Battle of the Bismarck Sea

		Imamura	
		North	*South*
	North	**2, −2**	2, −2
Kenney			
	South	1, −1	3, −3

Payoffs to: (Kenney, Imamura).

what Kenney gains. Because of this special feature, the payoffs could be represented using just four numbers instead of eight, but listing all eight payoffs in table 1.3 saves the reader a little thinking. The 2-by-2 form with just four entries is a **matrix game**, while the equivalent table with eight entries is a **bimatrix game**. Games can be represented as matrix or bimatrix games even if they have more than two moves, as long as the number of moves is finite.

Strictly speaking, neither player has a dominant strategy. Kenney would choose *North* if he thought Imamura would choose *North*, but *South* if he thought Imamura would choose *South*. Imamura would choose *North* if he thought Kenney would choose *South*, and he would be indifferent between actions if he thought Kenney would choose *North*. This is what the arrows are showing. But we can still find a plausible equilibrium, using the concept of "weak dominance."

*Strategy s_i' is **weakly dominated** if there exists some other strategy s_i'' for player i which is possibly better and never worse, yielding a higher payoff in some strategy profile and never yielding a lower payoff. Mathematically, s_i' is weakly dominated if there exists s_i'' such that*

$$\pi_i(s_i'', s_{-i}) \geq \pi_i(s_i', s_{-i}) \quad \forall s_{-i}, \quad \text{and} \quad \pi_i(s_i'', s_{-i}) > \pi_i(s_i', s_{-i}) \quad \text{for some } s_{-i}. \tag{1.4}$$

Similarly, we call a strategy that is always at least as good as every other strategy and better than some a **weakly dominant strategy**.

One might define a **weak-dominance equilibrium** as the strategy profile found by deleting all the weakly dominated strategies of each player. Eliminating weakly dominated strategies does not help much in the Battle of the Bismarck Sea, however. Imamura's strategy of *South* is weakly dominated by the strategy *North* because his payoff from *North* is never smaller than his payoff from *South*, and it is greater if Kenney picks *South*. For Kenney, however, neither strategy is even weakly dominated. The modeller must therefore go a step further, to the idea of the iterated dominance equilibrium.

*An **iterated-dominance equilibrium** is a strategy profile found by deleting a weakly dominated strategy from the strategy set of one of the players, recalculating to find which remaining strategies are weakly dominated, deleting one of them, and continuing the process until only one strategy remains for each player.*

Applied to the Battle of the Bismarck Sea, this equilibrium concept implies that Kenney decides that Imamura will pick *North* because it is weakly dominant, so Kenney eliminates "Imamura chooses *South*" from consideration. Having deleted one column of table 1.3, Kenney has a strongly dominant strategy: he chooses *North*, which achieves payoffs strictly greater than *South*. The strategy profile (*North, North*) is an iterated dominance equilibrium, and indeed (*North, North*) was the outcome in 1943.

It is interesting to consider modifying the order of play or the information structure in the Battle of the Bismarck Sea. If Kenney moved first, rather than simultaneously with Imamura (*North, North*), would remain an equilibrium, but (*North, South*) would also become one. The payoffs would be the same for both equilibria, but the outcomes would be different.

If Imamura moved first (*North, North*), would be the only equilibrium. What is important about a player moving first is that it gives the other player more information before he acts, not the literal timing of the moves. If Kenney has cracked the Japanese code and knows Imamura's plan, then it does not matter that the two players move literally simultaneously; it is better modelled as a sequential game. Whether Imamura literally moves first or whether his code is cracked, Kenney's information set becomes either {Imamura moved *North*} or {Imamura moved *South*} after Imamura's decision, so Kenney's equilibrium strategy is specified as (*North* if Imamura moved *North*, *South* if Imamura moved *South*).

Game theorists often differ in their terminology, and the terminology applied to the idea of eliminating dominated strategies is particularly diverse. The equilibrium concept used in the Battle of the Bismarck Sea might be called **iterated-dominance equilibrium**, or **iterated-dominant-strategy equilibrium**, or one might say that the game is **dominance solvable**, that it can be **solved by iterated dominance**, or that the equilibrium strategy profile is **serially undominated**. Often the terms are used to mean deletion of strictly dominated strategies, and sometimes to mean deletion of weakly dominated strategies. Iteration of strictly dominated strategies is, of course, a more appealing idea, but one which more rarely is applicable. For a 3-by-3 example in which iterated elimination of strictly dominated strategies does reach a unique equilibrium despite no strategy being dominant for the game as a whole, see Ratliff (1997a, p. 7).

The significant difference is between strong and weak dominance. Everyone agrees that no rational player would use a strictly dominated strategy, but it is harder to argue against weakly dominated strategies. In economic models, firms and individuals are often indifferent about their behavior in equilibrium. In standard models of perfect competition, firms earn zero profits but it is crucial that some firms be active in the market and some stay out and produce nothing. If a monopolist knows that customer Smith is willing to pay up to ten dollars for a widget, the monopolist will charge exactly ten dollars to Smith in equilibrium, which makes Smith indifferent about buying and not buying, yet there is no equilibrium unless Smith buys. It is impractical, therefore, to rule out equilibria in which a player is indifferent about his actions. This should be kept in mind later when we discuss the "open-set problem" in section 4.3.

Another difficulty is multiple equilibria. The dominant-strategy equilibrium of any game is unique if it exists. Each player has at most one strategy whose payoff in any strategy profile is strictly higher than the payoff from any other strategy, so only one strategy profile can be formed out of dominant strategies. A strong iterated-dominance equilibrium is unique if it exists. A weak iterated-dominance equilibrium may not be, because the order in which strategies are deleted can matter to the final solution. If all the weakly dominated strategies are eliminated simultaneously at each round of elimination, the resulting equilibrium is unique, if it exists, but possibly no strategy profile will remain.

Consider table 1.4's Iteration Path Game. The strategy profiles (r_1, c_1) and (r_1, c_3) are both iterated dominance equilibria because each of those strategy profiles can be found

Table 1.4 The Iteration Path Game

Column

		c_1	c_2	c_3
	r_1	**2, 12**	1, 10	**1, 12**
Row	r_2	0, 12	0, 10	0, 11
	r_3	0, 12	1, 10	0, 13

Payoffs to: (Row, Column).

by iterated deletion. The deletion can proceed in the order (r_3, c_3, c_2, r_2), or in the order (r_2, c_2, c_1, r_3).

Despite these problems, deletion of weakly dominated strategies is a useful tool, and it is part of more complicated equilibrium concepts such as section 4.1's "subgame perfectness."

Zero-sum Games

The Iteration Path Game is like the typical game in economics in that if one player gains, the other player does not necessarily lose. The outcome (2, 12) is better for both players than the outcome (0, 10), for example. Since economics is largely about the gains from trade, it is not surprising that win–win outcomes are possible, even if the players are each trying to maximize only their own payoffs. Some games, however, such as the Battle of Bismarck Sea, are different, because the payoffs of the players always sum to zero. This feature is important enough to have acquired a name early in the history of game theory.

> A **zero-sum game** *is a game in which the sum of the payoffs of all the players is zero whatever strategies they choose. A game which is not zero-sum is* **nonzero-sum game** *or* **variable-sum.**

In a zero-sum game, what one player gains, another player must lose. The Battle of the Bismarck Sea is thus a zero-sum game, but the Prisoner's Dilemma and the Dry Cleaners Game are not. There is no way that the payoffs in those two games can be rescaled to make them zero-sum without changing the essential character of the games.

If a game is zero-sum the utilities of the players can be represented so as to sum to zero under any outcome. Since utility functions are to some extent arbitrary, the sum can also be represented to be nonzero even if the game is zero-sum. Often modellers will refer to a game as zero-sum even when the payoffs do not add up to zero, so long as the payoffs add up to some constant amount. The difference is a trivial normalization.

Although zero-sum games have fascinated game theorists for many years, they are uncommon in economics. One of the few examples is the bargaining game between two players who divide a surplus, but even this is often modelled nowadays as a nonzero-sum game in which the surplus shrinks as the players spend more time deciding how to divide it. In reality, even simple division of property can result in loss – just think of how much the lawyers take out when a divorcing couple bargain over dividing their possessions.

Although the 2-by-2 games in this chapter may seem facetious, they are simple enough for use in modelling economic situations. The Battle of the Bismarck Sea, for example, can be turned into a game of corporate strategy. Two firms, Kenney Company and Imamura

Table 1.5   Boxed Pigs

		Small Pig			
		Press		*Wait*	
	Press	5, 1	→	4, 4	
Big Pig		↓		↑	
	Wait	9, −1	→	0, 0	

Payoffs to: (Big Pig, Small Pig). Arrows show how a player can increase his payoff. Best-response payoffs are boxed.

Incorporated, are trying to maximize their shares of a market of constant size by choosing between the two product designs *North* and *South*. Kenney has a marketing advantage, and would like to compete head-to-head, while Imamura would rather carve out its own niche. The equilibrium is (*North, North*).

1.4   Nash Equilibrium: Boxed Pigs, the Battle of the Sexes, and Ranked Coordination

For the vast majority of games, which lack even iterated dominance equilibria, modellers use Nash equilibrium, the most important and widespread equilibrium concept. To introduce Nash equilibrium we will use the game Boxed Pigs from Baldwin & Meese (1979).

Two pigs are put in a box with a special control panel at one end and a food dispenser at the other end. When a pig presses the panel, at a utility cost of 2 units, 10 units of food are dispensed at the dispenser. One pig is "dominant" (let us assume he is bigger), and if he gets to the dispenser first, the other pig will only get his leavings, worth 1 unit. If, instead, the small pig is at the dispenser first, he eats 4 units, and even if they arrive at the same time the small pig gets 3 units. Thus, for example, the strategy profile (*Press, Press*) would yield a payoff of 5 for the big pig (10 units of food, minus 3 that the small pig eats, minus an effort cost of 2) and of 1 for the little pig (3 units of food, minus an effort cost of 2). Table 1.5 summarizes the payoffs for the strategies *Press* the panel and *Wait* by the dispenser at the other end.

Boxed Pigs has no dominant-strategy equilibrium, because what the big pig chooses depends on what he thinks the small pig will choose. If he believed that the small pig would press the panel, the big pig would wait by the dispenser, but if he believed that the small pig would wait, the big pig would press the panel. There does exist an iterated-dominance equilibrium (*Press, Wait*), but we will use a different line of reasoning to justify that outcome: Nash equilibrium.

Nash equilibrium is the standard equilibrium concept in economics. It is less obviously correct than dominant-strategy equilibrium but more often applicable. Nash equilibrium is so widely accepted that the reader can assume that if a model does not specify which equilibrium concept is being used, it is Nash or some refinement of Nash.

*The strategy profile s^* is a **Nash equilibrium** if no player has incentive to deviate from his strategy given that the other players do not deviate. Formally,*

$$\forall i, \quad \pi_i(s_i^*, s_{-i}^*) \geq \pi_i(s_i', s_{-i}^*), \quad \forall s_i'. \tag{1.5}$$

The strategy profile (*Press*, *Wait*) is a Nash equilibrium. The way to approach Nash equilibrium is to propose a strategy profile and test whether each player's strategy is a best response to the others' strategies. If the big pig picks *Press*, the small pig, who faces a choice between a payoff of 1 from pressing and 4 from waiting, is willing to wait. If the small pig picks *Wait*, the big pig, who has a choice between a payoff of 4 from pressing and 0 from waiting, is willing to press. This confirms that (*Press*, *Wait*) is a Nash equilibrium, and in fact it is the unique Nash equilibrium.[5]

It is useful to draw arrows in the tables when trying to solve for the equilibrium, since the number of calculations is great enough to soak up quite a bit of mental RAM. Another solution tip, illustrated in Table 1.5, is to circle payoffs that dominate other payoffs (or box, them, as is especially suitable here). Double arrows or dotted circles indicate weakly dominant payoffs. Any payoff profile in which every payoff is circled, or which has arrows pointing towards it from every direction, is a Nash equilibrium. I like using arrows better in 2-by-2 games, but circles are better for bigger games, since arrows become confusing when payoffs are not lined up in order of magnitude in the table (see chapter 2's table 2.2).

The pigs in this game have to be smarter than the players in the Prisoner's Dilemma. They have to realize that the only set of strategies supported by self-consistent beliefs is (*Press*, *Wait*). The definition of Nash equilibrium lacks the "$\forall s_{-i}$" of dominant-strategy equilibrium, so a Nash strategy need only be a best response to the other Nash strategies, not to all possible strategies. And although we talk of "best responses," the moves are actually simultaneous, so the players are predicting each others' moves. If the game were repeated or the players communicated, Nash equilibrium would be especially attractive, because it is even more compelling that beliefs should be consistent.

Like a dominant-strategy equilibrium, a Nash equilibrium can be either weak or strong. The definition above is for a weak Nash equilibrium. To define strong Nash equilibrium, make the inequality strict; that is, require that no player be indifferent between his equilibrium strategy and some other strategy.

Every dominant-strategy equilibrium is a Nash equilibrium, but not every Nash equilibrium is a dominant-strategy equilibrium. If a strategy is dominant it is a best response to *any* strategies the other players pick, including their equilibrium strategies. If a strategy is part of a Nash equilibrium, it need only be a best response to the other players' *equilibrium* strategies.

The Modeller's Dilemma of table 1.6 illustrates this feature of Nash equilibrium. The situation it models is the same as the Prisoner's Dilemma, with one major exception: although the police have enough evidence to arrest the prisoners as the "probable cause" of the crime, they will not have enough evidence to convict them of even a minor offense if neither prisoner confesses. The northwest payoff profile becomes (0, 0) instead of (−1, −1).

The Modeller's Dilemma does not have a dominant-strategy equilibrium. It does have what might be called a weak dominant-strategy equilibrium, because *Confess* is still a weakly dominant strategy for each player. Moreover, using this fact, it can be seen that (*Confess*, *Confess*) is an iterated dominance equilibrium, and it is a strong Nash equilibrium

[5] This game, too, has its economic analog. If Bigpig, Inc. introduces granola bars, at considerable marketing expense in educating the public, then Smallpig Ltd. can imitate profitably without ruining Bigpig's sales completely. If Smallpig introduces them at the same expense, however, an imitating Bigpig would hog the market.

Table 1.6   The Modeller's Dilemma

Column

		Deny	Confess
	Deny	0, 0 $\leftrightarrow$	-10, 0
Row		$\updownarrow$	$\downarrow$
	Confess	0, -10 $\rightarrow$	$\boxed{-8}$, $\boxed{-8}$

Payoffs to: (Row, Column). Arrows show how a player can increase his payoff.

as well. So the case for (*Confess, Confess*) still being the equilibrium outcome seems very strong.

There is, however, another Nash equilibrium in the Modeller's Dilemma: (*Deny, Deny*), which is a weak Nash equilibrium. This equilibrium is weak and the other Nash equilibrium is strong, but (*Deny, Deny*) has the advantage that its outcome is Pareto-superior: (0, 0) is uniformly greater than $(-8, -8)$. This makes it difficult to know which behavior to predict.

The Modeller's Dilemma illustrates a common difficulty for modellers: what to predict when two Nash equilibria exist. The modeller could add more details to the rules of the game, or he could use an **equilibrium refinement**, adding conditions to the basic equilibrium concept until only one strategy profile satisfies the refined equilibrium concept. There is no single way to refine Nash equilibrium. The modeller might insist on a strong equilibrium, or rule out weakly dominated strategies, or use iterated dominance. All of these lead to (*Confess, Confess*) in the Modeller's Dilemma. Or he might rule out Nash equilibria that are Pareto-dominated by other Nash equilibria, and end up with (*Deny, Deny*). Neither approach is completely satisfactory. In particular, do not be misled into thinking that weak Nash equilibria are to be despised. Often, no Nash equilibrium at all will exist unless the players have the expectation that player B chooses X when he is indifferent between X and Y. It is not that we are picking the equilibrium in which it is assumed B does X when he is indifferent. Rather, we are finding the *only* set of consistent expectations about behavior. (You will read more about this in connection with the "open-set problem" of section 4.2.)

The Battle of the Sexes

The third game we will use to illustrate Nash equilibrium is the Battle of the Sexes, a conflict between a man who wants to go to a prize fight and a woman who wants to go to a ballet. While selfish, they are deeply in love, and would, if necessary, sacrifice their preferences to be with each other. Less romantically, their payoffs are given by table 1.7.

The Battle of the Sexes does not have an iterated dominance equilibrium. It has two Nash equilibria, one of which is the strategy profile (*Prize Fight, Prize Fight*). Given that the man chooses *Prize Fight*, so does the woman; given that the woman chooses *Prize Fight*, so does the man. The strategy profile (*Ballet, Ballet*) is another Nash equilibrium by the same line of reasoning.

How do the players know which Nash equilibrium to choose? Going to the fight and going to the ballet are both Nash strategies, but for different equilibria. Nash equilibrium assumes correct and consistent beliefs. If they do not talk beforehand, the man might go

Table 1.7   The Battle of the Sexes[6]

		Woman		
		Prize Fight		*Ballet*
	Prize Fight	**2, 1**	←	0, 0
Man		↑		↓
	Ballet	0, 0	→	**1, 2**

Payoffs to: (Man, Woman). Arrows show how a player can increase his payoff.

to the ballet and the woman to the fight, each mistaken about the other's beliefs. But even if the players do not communicate, Nash equilibrium is sometimes justified by repetition of the game. If the couple do not talk, but repeat the game night after night, one may suppose that eventually they settle on one of the Nash equilibria.

Each of the Nash equilibria in the Battle of the Sexes is Pareto-efficient; no other strategy profile increases the payoff of one player without decreasing that of the other. In many games the Nash equilibrium is not Pareto-efficient: (*Blame, Blame*), for example, is the unique Nash equilibrium of the Prisoner's Dilemma, although its payoffs of $(-8, -8)$ are Pareto-inferior to the $(-1, -1)$ generated by (*Deny, Deny*).

Who moves first is important in the Battle of the Sexes, unlike any of the three previous games we have looked at. If the man could buy the fight ticket in advance, his commitment would induce the woman to go to the fight. In many games, but not all, the player who moves first (which is equivalent to commitment) has a **first-mover advantage.**

The Battle of the Sexes has many economic applications. One is the choice of an industry-wide standard when two firms have different preferences but both want a common standard to encourage consumers to buy the product. A second is to the choice of language used in a contract when two firms want to formalize a sales agreement but they prefer different terms. Both sides might, for example, want to add a "liquidated damages" clause which specifies damages for breach rather than trust the courts to estimate a number later, but one firm might want a value of $10,000 and the other firm, $12,000.

Coordination Games

Sometimes one can use the size of the payoffs to choose between Nash equilibria. In the following game, players Smith and Jones are trying to decide whether to design the computers they sell to use large, or small floppy disks. Both players will sell more computers if their disk drives are compatible, as shown in table 1.8.

The strategy profiles (*Large, Large*) and (*Small, Small*) are both Nash equilibria, but (*Large, Large*) Pareto-dominates (*Small, Small*). Both players prefer (*Large, Large*), and most modellers would use the Pareto-efficient equilibrium to predict the actual outcome. We could imagine that it arises from pregame communication between Smith and Jones taking place outside of the specification of the model, but the interesting question is what happens if communication is impossible. Is the Pareto-efficient equilibrium still more plausible? The question is really one of psychology rather than economics.

---

[6] Political correctness has led to bowdlerized versions of this game being presented in many game theory books. This is the original, unexpurgated game.

Table 1.8   Ranked Coordination

		Jones		
		Large		*Small*
Smith	*Large*	**2, 2**	←	−1, −1
		↑		↓
	Small	−1,−1	→	**1, 1**

Payoffs to: (Smith, Jones). Arrows show how a player can increase his payoff.

Table 1.9   Dangerous Coordination

		Jones		
		Large		*Small*
Smith	*Large*	**2, 2**	←	−1000, −1
		↑		↓
	Small	−1, −1	→	**1, 1**

Payoffs to: (Smith, Jones). Arrows show how a player can increase his payoff.

Ranked Coordination is one of a large class of games called **coordination games**, which share the common feature that the players need to coordinate on one of multiple Nash equilibria. Ranked Coordination has the additional feature that the equilibria can be Pareto ranked. Section 3.2 will return to problems of coordination to discuss the concepts of "correlated strategies" and "cheap talk." These games are of obvious relevance to analyzing the setting of standards; see, for example, Michael Katz & Carl Shapiro (1985) and Joseph Farrell & Garth Saloner (1985) . They can be of great importance to the wealth of economies – just think of the advantages of standard weights and measures (or read Charles Kindleberger [1983] on their history). Note, however, that not all apparent situations of coordination on Pareto-inferior equilibria turn out to be so. One oft-cited coordination problem is that of the QWERTY typewriter keyboard, developed in the 1870s when typing had to proceed slowly to avoid jamming. QWERTY became the standard, although it has been claimed that the faster speed possible with the Dvorak keyboard would amortize the cost of retraining full-time typists within ten days (David [1985]). Why large companies would not retrain their typists is difficult to explain under this story, and Liebowitz & Margolis (1990) show that economists have been too quick to accept claims that QWERTY is inefficient. English language spelling is a better example.

Table 1.9 shows another coordination game, Dangerous Coordination, which has the same equilibria as Ranked Coordination, but differs in the out-of-equilibrium payoffs. If an experiment were conducted in which students played Dangerous Coordination against each other, I would not be surprised if (*Small, Small*), the Pareto-dominated equilibrium, were the one that was played out. This is true even though *(Large, Large)* is still a Nash equilibrium; if Smith thinks that Jones will pick *Large*, Smith is quite willing to pick *Large* himself. The problem is that if the assumptions of the model are weakened, and Smith cannot trust Jones to be rational, well-informed about the payoffs of the game, and unconfused, then Smith will be reluctant to pick *Large* because his payoff if Jones picks *Small* is then −1,000. He would play it safe instead, picking *Small*, and ensuring a payoff of at least −1. In reality, people do make mistakes, and with such an extreme difference in payoffs, even a small probability of a mistake is important, so (*Large*, *Large*) would be a bad prediction.

Games like Dangerous Coordination are a major concern in the 1988 book by Harsanyi and Selten, two of the giants in the field of game theory. I will not try to describe their approach here, except to say that it is different from my own. I do not consider the fact that one of the Nash equilibria of Dangerous Coordination is a bad prediction as a heavy blow against Nash equilibrium. The bad prediction is based on two things: using the Nash equilibrium concept, and using the game Dangerous Coordination. If Jones might be confused about the payoffs of the game, then the game actually being played out is not Dangerous Coordination, so it is not surprising that it gives poor predictions. The rules of the game ought to describe the probabilities that the players are confused, as well as the payoffs if they take particular actions. If confusion is an important feature of the situation, then the two-by-two game of table 1.9 is the wrong model to use, and a more complicated game of incomplete information of the kind described in chapter 2 is more appropriate. Again, as with the Prisoner's Dilemma, the modeller's first thought on finding that the model predicts an odd result should not be "Game theory is bunk," but the more modest "Maybe I'm not describing the situation correctly" (or even "Maybe I should not trust my 'common sense' about what will happen").

Nash equilibrium is more complicated but also more useful than it looks. Jumping ahead a bit, consider a game slightly more complex than the ones we have seen so far. Two firms are choosing outputs Q_1 and Q_2 simultaneously. The Nash equilibrium is a pair of numbers (Q_1^*, Q_2^*) such that neither firm would deviate unilaterally. This troubles the beginner, who says to himself, "Sure, Firm 1 will pick Q_1^* if it thinks Firm 2 will pick Q_2^*. But Firm 1 will realize that if it makes Q_1 bigger, then Firm 2 will react by making Q_2 smaller. So the situation is much more complicated, and (Q_1^*, Q_2^*) is not a Nash equilibrium. Or, if it is, Nash equilibrium is a bad equilibrium concept."

But if there is a problem in this model, it is not Nash equilibrium but the model itself. Nash equilibrium makes perfect sense as a stable outcome in this model. The beginner's hypothetical is false because if Firm 1 chooses something other than Q_1^*, Firm 2 would not observe the deviation till it was too late to change Q_2 – remember, this is a simultaneous move game. The beginner's worry is really about the rules of the game, not the equilibrium concept. He seems to prefer a game in which the firms move sequentially, or maybe a repeated version of the game. If Firm 1 moved first, and then Firm 2, then Firm 1's strategy would still be a single number, Q_1, but Firm 2's strategy – its action rule – would have to be a function, $Q_2(Q_1)$. A Nash equilibrium would then consist of an equilibrium number, Q_1^{**}, and an equilibrium function, $Q_2^{**}(Q_1)$. The two outputs actually chosen, Q_1^{**} and $Q_2^{**}(Q_1^{**})$, will be different from the Q_1^* and Q_2^* in the original game. And they should be different – the new model represents a very different real-world situation. Look ahead, and you will see that these are the Cournot and Stackelberg models of chapter 3.

One lesson to draw from this is that it is essential to figure out the mathematical form the strategies take before trying to figure out the equilibrium. In the simultaneous move game, the strategy profile is a pair of nonnegative numbers. In the sequential game, the strategy profile is one nonnegative number and one function defined over the nonnegative numbers. Students invariably make the mistake of specifying Firm 2's strategy as a number, not a function. This is a far more important point than any beginner realizes. Trust me – you're going to make this mistake sooner or later, so it's worth worrying about.

1.5   Focal Points

Thomas Schelling's 1960 book, *The Strategy of Conflict*, is a classic in game theory, even though it contains no equations or Greek letters. Although it was published more than 40 years ago, it is surprisingly modern in spirit. Schelling is not a mathematician but a strategist, and he examines such things as threats, commitments, hostages, and delegation that we will examine in a more formal way in the remainder of this book. He is perhaps best known for his coordination games. Take a moment to decide on a strategy in each of the following games, adapted from Schelling, which you win by matching your response to those of as many of the other players as possible.

1   Circle one of the following numbers: 100, 14, 15, 16, 17, 18.
2   Circle one of the following numbers 7, 100, 13, 261, 99, 666.
3   Name Heads or Tails.
4   Name Tails or Heads.
5   You are to split a pie, and get nothing if your proportions add to more than 100 percent.
6   You are to meet somebody in New York City. When? Where?

Each of the games above has many Nash equilibria. In example (1), if each player thinks every other player will pick 14, he will too, and this is self-confirming; but the same is true if each player thinks every other player will pick 15. But to a greater or lesser extent they also have Nash equilibria that seem more likely. Certain of the strategy profiles are **focal points:** Nash equilibria which for psychological reasons are particularly compelling.

Formalizing what makes a strategy profile a focal point is hard, and depends on the context. In example (1), 100 is a focal point, because it is a number clearly different from all the others – it is biggest, and it is first in the listing. In example (2), Schelling found 7 to be the most common strategy, but in a group of Satanists, 666 might be the focal point. In repeated games, focal points are often provided by past history. Examples (3) and (4) are identical except for the ordering of the choices, but that ordering might make a difference. In (5), if we split a pie once, we are likely to agree on 50:50. But if last year we split a pie in the ratio 60:40, that provides a focal point for this year. Example (6) is the most interesting of all. Schelling found surprising agreement in independent choices, but the place chosen depended on whether the players knew New York well, or were unfamiliar with the city.

The **boundary** is a particular kind of focal point. If player Russia chooses the action of putting his troops anywhere from one inch to 100 miles away from the Chinese border, player China does not react. If he chooses to put troops from one inch to 100 miles *beyond* the border, China declares war. There is an arbitrary discontinuity in behavior at the boundary. Another example, quite vivid in its arbitrariness, is the rallying cry, "Fifty-four Forty or Fight!," which refers to the geographic parallel claimed as the boundary by jingoist Americans in the Oregon dispute between Britain and the United States in the 1840s.[7]

Once the boundary is established it takes on additional significance because behavior with respect to the boundary conveys information. When Russia crosses an established boundary, that tells China that Russia intends to make a serious incursion further into China. Boundaries must be sharp, and well known if they are not to be violated, and

---

[7] The threat was not credible: that parallel is now deep in British Columbia.

a large part of both law and diplomacy is devoted to clarifying them. Boundaries can also arise in business: two companies producing an unhealthful product might agree not to mention relative healthfulness in their advertising, but a boundary rule like "Mention unhealthfulness if you like, but don't stress it," would not work.

Mediation and **communication** are both important in the absence of a clear focal point. If players can communicate, they can tell each other what actions they will take, and sometimes, as in Ranked Coordination, this works, because they have no motive to lie. If the players cannot communicate, a mediator may be able to help by suggesting an equilibrium to all of them. They have no reason not to take the suggestion, and they would use the mediator even if his services were costly. Mediation in cases like this is as effective as arbitration, in which an outside party imposes a solution.

One disadvantage of focal points is that they lead to inflexibility. Suppose the Pareto-superior equilibrium (*Large*, *Large*) were chosen as a focal point in Ranked Coordination, but the game was repeated over a long interval of time. The numbers in the payoff matrix might slowly change until (*Small*, *Small*) and (*Large*, *Large*) both had payoffs of, say, 1.6, and (*Small*, *Small*) started to dominate. When, if ever, would the equilibrium switch?

In Ranked Coordination, we would expect that after some time one firm would switch and the other would follow. If there were communication, the switch point would be at the payoff of 1.6. But what if the first firm to switch is penalized more? Such is the problem in oligopoly pricing. If costs rise, so should the monopoly price, but whichever firm raises its price first suffers a loss of market share.

Notes

N1.2   Dominant strategies: The Prisoner's Dilemma

- Many economists are reluctant to use the concept of cardinal utility (see Starmer [2000]), and even more reluctant to compare utility across individuals (see Cooter & Rappoport [1984]). Noncooperative game theory never requires interpersonal utility comparisons, and only ordinal utility is needed to find the equilibrium in the Prisoner's Dilemma. So long as each player's rank ordering of payoffs in different outcomes is preserved, the payoffs can be altered without changing the equilibrium. In general, the dominant strategy and pure strategy Nash equilibria of games depend only on the ordinal ranking of the payoffs, but the mixed strategy equilibria depend on the cardinal values. Compare section 3.2's Chicken game with section 5.6's Hawk–Dove.
- If we consider only the ordinal ranking of the payoffs in 2-by-2 games, there are 78 distinct games in which each player has strict preference ordering over the four outcomes and 726 distinct games if we allow ties in the payoffs. Rapoport, Guyer, & Gordon's 1976 book, *The 2 × 2 Game*, contains an exhaustive description of the possible games.
- If we allow players to randomize their action choices (the "mixed strategies" of chapter 3), it can happen that some action is strictly dominated by a randomized strategy, even though it is not dominated by any nonrandom strategy. An example is in chapter 3. Jim Ratliff's web notes are good on this topic; see Ratliff (1997a, 1997b). If random strategies are allowed, it becomes much more difficult to check for dominance and to use the iterative dominance ideas of section 1.3.
- The Prisoner's Dilemma was so named by Albert Tucker in an unpublished paper, although the particular 2-by-2 matrix, discovered by Dresher and Flood, was already well known. Tucker was asked to give a talk on game theory to the psychology department at Stanford, and invented a story to go with the matrix, as recounted in Straffin (1980), Poundstone (1992, pp. 101–18), and Raiffa (1992, pp. 171–3).

Table 1.10   A general Prisoner's Dilemma

Column

		Silence		*Blame*
	Silence	R, R	$\rightarrow$	S, T
Row		$\downarrow$		$\downarrow$
	Blame	T, S	$\rightarrow$	**P, P**

Payoffs to: (Row, Column). Arrows show how a player can increase his payoff.

- In the Prisoner's Dilemma the notation *cooperate* and *defect* is often used for the moves. This is bad terminology, because it is easy to confuse with *cooperative* games, with *deviations* . It is also often called the Prisoners' Dilemma (rs', not r's). Whether one looks at from the point of the individual or the group, the prisoners have a problem.

- The Prisoner's Dilemma is not always defined the same way. If we consider just ordinal pay-offs, then the game in table 1.10 is a prisoner's dilemma if T (*temptation*) $>$ R(*revolt*) $>$ P(*punishment*) $>$ S(*Sucker*), where the terms in parentheses are mnemonics. This is standard notation; see, for example, Rapoport, Guyer, & Gordon (1976, p. 400). If the game is repeated, the cardinal values of the payoffs can be important. The requirement $2R > T + S > 2P$ should be added if the game is to be a standard Prisoner's Dilemma, in which (*Silence, Silence*) and (*Blame, Blame*) are the best and worst possible outcomes in terms of the sum of payoffs. Section 5.3 will show that an asymmetric game called the One-Sided Prisoner's Dilemma has properties similar to the standard Prisoner's Dilemma, but does not fit this definition.

  Sometimes the game in which $2R < T + S$ is also called a "Prisoner's Dilemma," but in it the sum of the players' payoffs is maximized when one blames the other and the other is silent. If the game were repeated or the prisoners could use the correlated equilibria defined in section 3.2, they would prefer taking turns being silent, which would make the game a coordination game similar to the Battle of the Sexes. David Shimko has suggested the name "Battle of the Prisoners" for this (or, perhaps, "The Sex Prisoners' Dilemma").

- Herodotus (429 BC, III-71) describes an early example of the reasoning in the Prisoner's Dilemma in a conspiracy against the Persian emperor. A group of nobles met and decided to overthrow the emperor, and it was proposed to adjourn till another meeting. One of them named Darius then spoke up and said that if they adjourned, he knew that one of them would go straight to the emperor and reveal the conspiracy, because if nobody else did, he would himself. Darius also suggested a solution – that they immediately go to the palace and kill the emperor.

  The conspiracy also illustrates a way out of coordination games. After killing the emperor, the nobles wished to select one of themselves as the new emperor. Rather than fight, they agreed to go to a certain hill at dawn, and whoever's horse neighed first would become emperor. Herodotus tells how Darius's groom manipulated this randomization scheme to make him the new emperor.

- Philosophers are intrigued by the Prisoner's Dilemma: see Campbell & Sowden (1985), a collection of articles on the Prisoner's Dilemma and the related Newcombe's paradox. Game theory has even been applied to theology: if one player is omniscient or omnipotent, what kind of equilibrium behavior can we expect? See Steven Brams's 1980 and 1983 books, *Biblical Games: A Strategic Analysis of Stories from the Old Testament* and *Superior Beings*.

N1.4   Nash equilibrium: Boxed Pigs, the Battle of the Sexes, and Ranked Coordination

- For a history of the idea of Nash equilibrium, see Roger Myerson's 1999 article, "Nash Equilibrium and the History of Game Theory." E. Roy Weintraub's 1992 collection of essays, *Toward a*

History of Game Theory, Norman Macrae's 1992 *John von Neumann*, William Poundstone's 1992 *Prisoner's Dilemma: John von Neumann, Game Theory, and the Puzzle of the Bomb*, Sylvia Nasar's 1998 *A Beautiful Mind*, and Mary and Robert Dimand's 1996 *A History of Game Theory* are other places to learn about the history of game theory. Good profiles of economists can be found in Michael Szenberg's 1992 *Eminent Economists: Their Life Philosophies* and 1998 *Passion and Craft: Economists at Work*. Sergiu Hart's 2005 "An Interview with Robert Aumann," http://www.ma.huji.ac.il/hart/abs/aumann.html, is also illuminating. Leonard (1995) discusses the "pre-history" from 1928 to 1944.

- I invented the payoffs for Boxed Pigs from the description of one of the experiments in Baldwin & Meese (1979). They do *not* think of this as an experiment in game theory, and they describe the result in terms of "reinforcement." The Battle of the Sexes is taken from p. 90 of Luce & Raiffa (1957). I have changed their payoffs of $(-1, -1)$ to $(-5, -5)$ to fit the story.

- Some people prefer the term "equilibrium point" to "Nash equilibrium," but the latter is more euphonious, since the discoverer's name is "Nash" and not "Mazurkiewicz."

- Bernheim (1984a) and Pearce (1984) use the idea of mutually consistent beliefs to arrive at a different equilibrium concept than Nash. They define a **rationalizable strategy** to be a strategy which is a best response for some set of rational beliefs in which a player believes that the other players choose their best responses. The difference from Nash is that not all players need have the same beliefs concerning which strategies will be chosen, nor need their beliefs be consistent. Every Nash equilibrium is rationalizable, but not every rationalizable equilibrium is Nash. Thus, the idea provides an argument for why Nash equilibria might be played, but not for why *just* Nash equilibria would be played. In a two-player game, the set of rationalizable strategies is the set which survives iterated deletion of strictly dominated strategies, but in a game with three or more players the set might be smaller. Ratliff (1997a) has an excellent discussion with numerical examples.

- Jack Hirshleifer (1982) uses the name "The Tender Trap" for a game essentially the same as Ranked Coordination. It has also been called the "Assurance Game."

- O. Henry's story, "The Gift of the Magi" is about a coordination game noteworthy for the reason communication is ruled out. A husband sells his watch to buy his wife combs for Christmas, while she sells her hair to buy him a watch fob. Communication would spoil the surprise, a worse outcome than discoordination.

- Macroeconomics has more game theory in it than is readily apparent. The macroeconomic concept of *rational expectations* faces the same problems of multiple equilibria and consistency of expectations as Nash equilibrium. Game theory is now often explicitly used in macroeconomics; see the books by Canzoneri & Henderson (1991) and Cooper (1999) .

N1.5   Focal points

- Besides his 1960 book, Schelling has written books on diplomacy (1966) and the oddities of aggregation (1978). Political scientists are now looking at the same issues more technically; see Brams & Kilgour (1988) and Ordeshook (1986). Douglas Muzzio's 1982 *Watergate Games*, Thomas Flanagan's 1998 *Game Theory and Canadian Politics*, and especially William Riker's 1986 *The Art of Political Manipulation* are absorbing examples of how game theory can be used to analyze specific historical episodes.

- In chapter 12 of *The General Theory*, Keynes (1936) suggests that the stock market is a game with multiple equilibria, like a contest in which a newspaper publishes the faces of 20 girls, and contestants submit the name of the one they think most people would submit as the prettiest. When the focal point changes, big swings in predictions about beauty and value result.

- Not all of what we call boundaries have an arbitrary basis. If the Chinese cannot defend themselves as easily once the Russians cross the boundary at the Amur River, they have a clear reason to fight there.

- Crawford & Haller (1990) take a careful look at focalness in repeated coordination games by asking which equilibria are objectively different from other equilibria, and how a player can learn through repetition which equilibrium the other players intend to play. If on the first repetition the players choose strategies that are Nash with respect to each other, it seems focal for them to continue playing those strategies, but what happens if they begin in disagreement?

Problems

1.1:   Nash and iterated dominance (medium)

(a)   Show that every iterated dominance equilibrium s^* is Nash.
(b)   Show by counterexample that not every Nash equilibrium can be generated by iterated dominance.
(c)   Is every iterated dominance equilibrium made up of strategies that are not weakly dominated?

1.2:   2-by-2 Games (easy)

Find or create examples of 2-by-2 games with the following properties:

(a)   No Nash equilibrium (you can ignore mixed strategies).
(b)   No weakly Pareto-dominant strategy profile.
(c)   At least two Nash equilibria, including one equilibrium that Pareto-dominates all other strategy profiles.
(d)   At least three Nash equilibria.

1.3:   Pareto dominance (medium) (from notes by Jong-Shin Wei)

(a)   If a strategy profile s^* is a dominant-strategy equilibrium, does that mean it weakly Pareto-dominates all other strategy profiles?
(b)   If a strategy profile s strongly Pareto-dominates all other strategy profiles, does that mean it is a dominant-strategy equilibrium?
(c)   If s weakly Pareto-dominates all other strategy profiles, then must it be a Nash equilibrium?

1.4:   Discoordination (easy)

Suppose that a man and a woman each choose whether to go to a prize fight or a ballet. The man would rather go to the prize fight, and the woman to the ballet. What is more important to them, however, is that the man wants to show up to the same event as the woman, but the woman wants to avoid him.

(a)   Construct a game matrix to illustrate this game, choosing numbers to fit the preferences described verbally.
(b)   If the woman moves first, what will happen?
(c)   Does the game have a first-mover advantage?
(d)   Show that there is no Nash equilibrium if the players move simultaneously.

1.5:   Drawing outcome matrices (easy)

It can be surprisingly difficult to look at a game using new notation. In this exercise, redraw the outcome matrix in a different form than in the main text. In each case, read the description of the game and draw the outcome matrix as instructed. You will learn more if you do this from the description, without looking at the conventional outcome matrix.

(a)   The Battle of the Sexes (table 1.7). Put (*Prize Fight, Prize Fight*) in the northwest corner, but make the woman the row player.
(b)   The Prisoner's Dilemma (table 1.2). Put (*Confess, Confess*) in the northwest corner.
(c)   The Battle of the Sexes (table 1.7). Make the man the row player, but put (*Ballet, Prize Fight*) in the northwest corner.

1.6:   Finding Nash equilibria (medium)

Find the Nash equilibria of the game illustrated in table 1.11. Can any of them be reached by iterated dominance?

Table 1.11   An abstract game

		Column Left	Middle	Right
	Up	10, 10	0, 0	−1, 15
Row	*Sideways*	−12, 1	8, 8	−1, −1
	Down	15, 1	8, −1	0, 0

Payoffs to: (Row, Column).

1.7:   Finding more Nash equilibria (medium)

Find the Nash equilibria of the game illustrated in table 1.12. Can any of them be reached by iterated dominance?

Table 1.12   Flavor and texture

		Brydox Flavor	Texture
	Flavor	−2, 0	0, 1
Apex	*Texture*	−1, −1	0, −2

Payoffs to: (Apex, Brydox).

1.8:   Which game? (medium)

Table 1.13 is like the payoff matrix for what game that we have seen? (1) A version of the Battle of the Sexes, (2) a version of the Prisoner's Dilemma, (3) a version of Pure Coordination, (4) a version of the Legal Settlement Game, (5) none of the above.

1.9:   Choosing computers (easy)

The problem of deciding whether to adopt IBM or HP computers by two offices in a company is most like which game that we have seen?

Table 1.13   Which game?

		Column	
		A	B
Row	A	3, 3	0, 1
	B	5, 0	−1, −1

1.10:   Campaign contributions (easy)

The large Wall Street investment banks have recently agreed not to make campaign contributions to state treasurers, which uptil now has been a common practice. What was the game in the past, and why can the banks expect this agreement to hold fast?

1.11:   A sequential Prisoner's Dilemma (hard)

Suppose Row moves first, then Column, in the Prisoner's Dilemma. What are the possible actions? What are the possible strategies? Construct a normal form, showing the relationship between strategy profiles and payoffs.

Hint: The normal form is *not* a two-by-two matrix here.

1.12:   Three-by-Three equilibria (medium)

Identify any dominated strategies and any Nash equilibria in pure strategies in the game of table 1.14.

Table 1.14   A three-by-three game

		Column		
		Left	Middle	Right
	Up	1, 4	5, −1	0, 1
Row	Sideways	−1, 0	−2, −2	−3, 4
	Down	0, 3	9, −1	5, 0

Payoffs to: (Row, Column).

Fisheries: A Classroom Game for Chapter 1

Each of eight countries in a fishery decides how many fish to catch each decade. Each country picks an integer number X_t as its fishing catch for decade t. The country's profit for decade t is

$$20X_t - X_t^2. \tag{1.6}$$

Thus, diminishing returns set in after a certain point and the marginal cost is too high for further fishing to be profitable.

The fish population starts at 112 (14 per country) and the game continues for 5 decades. Let Q_1 denote the fish population at the start of Decade 1. In Decade 2, the population is

$$1.5 * (Q_1 - (X_{1t} + X_{2t} + X_{3t} + \cdots)), \text{rounded up}, \tag{1.7}$$

where X_{it} is Country i's catch in Decade t.

If $X_{11} = 30$ and $X_{21} = X_{31} = \cdots = X_{81} = 3$, then the first country's profit is $20 * 30 - 30^2 = 600 - 900 = -300$, and each other country earns $20 * 3 - 3^2 = 60 - 6 = 54$. The second-year fish population would be $Q_2 = 1.5 * (112 - 30 - 7[3]) = 1.5(82 - 21) = 1.5(61) = 92$.

1   In the first scenario, one fishing authority chooses the catch for all eight countries to try to maximize the catch over all five decades. Each country will propose quotas for all eight countries for the first year. The class will discuss the proposals and the authority will deliberate and make its choice. Once the catch is finalized, the instructor calculates the next year's fish population, and the process repeats to pick the next year's catch.

2   The countries choose independently. Each country writes down its catch on a piece of paper, which it hands in to the instructor. The instructor opens them up as he receives them. He does not announce each country's catch until the end of this scenario's five decades, but he does announce the total catch. If the attempted catch exceeds the total fish population, those countries which handed in their catches first get priority, and a country's payoff is $20Z_t - X_t^2$, where Z_t is its actual catch and X_t is its attempted catch, what it wrote down on its paper. Do this for five decades.

3   Repeat Scenario 2, but with each country's actual (not attempted) catch announced at the end of each decade.

4   Repeat Scenario 3, but this time countries that so wish can form a binding treaty and submit their catches jointly, on one piece of paper.

Chapter 2
information

2.1 The Strategic and Extensive Forms of a Game

If half of strategic thinking is predicting what the other player will do, the other half is figuring out what he knows. Most of the games in chapter 1 assumed that the moves were simultaneous, so the players did not have a chance to learn each other's private information by observing each other. Information becomes central as soon as players move in sequence. The important difference, in fact, between simultaneous-move games and sequential-move games is that in sequential-move games the second player acquires the information on how the first player moved before he must make his own decision.

Section 2.1 shows how to use the strategic form and the extensive form to describe games with sequential moves. Section 2.2 shows how the extensive form, or game tree, can be used to describe the information available to a player at each point in the game. Section 2.3 classifies games based on the information structure. Section 2.4 shows how to redraw games with incomplete information so that they can be analyzed using the Harsanyi transformation, and derives Bayes' Rule for combining a player's prior beliefs with information which he acquires in the course of the game. Section 2.5 concludes the chapter with the Png Settlement Game, an example of a moderately complex sequential-move game.

The Strategic Form and the Outcome Matrix

Games with moves in sequence require more care in presentation than single-move games. In section 1.4 we used the 2-by-2 form, which for the game Ranked Coordination is shown in table 2.1.

Because strategies are the same as actions in Ranked Coordination and the outcomes are simple, the 2-by-2 form in table 2.1 accomplishes two things: it relates strategy profiles to payoffs, and action profiles to outcomes. These two mappings are called the strategic form and the outcome matrix, and in more complicated games they are distinct from each other. The strategic form shows what payoffs result from each possible strategy profile, while the outcome matrix shows what outcome results from each possible action profile.

Table 2.1   Ranked Coordination

		Jones		
		Large		*Small*
	Large	**2, 2**	←	−1, −1
Smith		↑		↓
	Small	−1, −1	→	**1, 1**

Payoffs to: (Smith, Jones). Arrows show how a player can increase his payoff.

The definitions below use n to denote the number of players, k the number of variables in the outcome vector, p the number of strategy profiles, and q the number of action profiles.

The **strategic form** *(or* **normal form***) consists of*

1   *All possible strategy profiles $s^1, s^2, \ldots, s^p$.*
2   *Payoff functions mapping s^i onto the payoff n-vector π^i ($i = 1, 2, \ldots, p$).*

The **outcome matrix** *consists of*

1   *All possible action profiles $a^1, a^2, \ldots, a^q$.*
2   *Outcome functions mapping a^i onto the outcome k-vector z^i ($i = 1, 2, \ldots, q$).*

Consider the following game based on Ranked Coordination, which we will call Follow-the-Leader I since we will create several variants of the game. The difference from Ranked Coordination is that Smith moves first, committing himself to a certain disk size no matter what size Jones chooses. The new game has an outcome matrix identical to Ranked Coordination, but its strategic form is different because Jones's strategies are no longer single actions. Jones's strategy set has four elements,

$$\left\{ \begin{array}{l} \text{(If Smith chose } Large, \text{ choose } Large; \text{ if Smith chose } Small, \text{ choose } Large), \\ \text{(If Smith chose } Large, \text{ choose } Large; \text{ if Smith chose } Small, \text{ choose } Small), \\ \text{(If Smith chose } Large, \text{ choose } Small; \text{ if Smith chose } Small, \text{ choose } Large), \\ \text{(If Smith chose } Large, \text{ choose } Small; \text{ if Smith chose } Small, \text{ choose } Small) \end{array} \right\}$$

which we will abbreviate as

$$\left\{ \begin{array}{l} (L|L, L|S), \\ (L|L, S|S), \\ (S|L, L|S), \\ (S|L, S|S) \end{array} \right\}$$

Follow-the-Leader I illustrates how adding a little complexity can make the strategic form too obscure to be very useful. The strategic form is shown in table 2.2, with equilibria

Table 2.2   Follow-the-Leader I

	Jones			
	J_1	J_2	J_3	J_4
	L/L, L/S	L/L, S/S	S/L, L/S	S/L, S/S
Smith S_1:Large	$\boxed{2}$, $\boxed{2}$ (E_1)	$\boxed{2}$, $\boxed{2}$ (E_2)	$\boxed{-1}$, -1	$-1, -1$
S_2:Small	$-1, -1$	$1, \boxed{1}$	$\boxed{-1}$, -1	$\boxed{1}$, $\boxed{1}$ (E_3)

Payoffs to: (Smith, Jones). Best-response payoffs are boxed (with dashes, if weak).

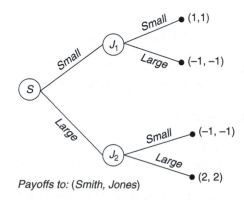

Payoffs to: (Smith, Jones)

Figure 2.1   Follow-the-Leader I in extensive form.

boldfaced and labelled E_1, E_2, and E_3.

Equilibrium	Strategies	Outcome
E_1	{*Large, (L|L, L|S)*}	Both pick *Large*
E_2	{*Large, (L|L, S|S)*}	Both pick *Large*
E_3	{*Small, (S|L, S|S)*}	Both pick *Small*

Consider why E_1, E_2, and E_3 are Nash equilibria. In Equilibrium E_1, Jones will respond with *Large* regardless of what Smith does, so Smith quite happily chooses *Large*. Jones would be irrational to choose *Large* if Smith chose *Small* first, but that event never happens in equilibrium. In Equilibrium E_2, Jones will choose whatever Smith chose, so Smith chooses *Large* to make the payoff 2 instead of 1. In Equilibrium E_3, Smith chooses *Small* because he knows that Jones will respond with *Small* whatever he does, and Jones is willing to respond with *Small* because Smith chooses *Small* in equilibrium. Equilibria E_1 and E_3 are not completely sensible because the choices *Large|Small* (as specified in E_1) and *Small|Large* (as specified in E_3) would reduce Jones's payoff if the game ever reached a point where he had to actually play them. Except for a little discussion in connection with figure 2.1, however, we will defer to chapter 4 the discussion of how to redefine the equilibrium concept to rule them out.

The Order of Play

The "normal form" is rarely used in modelling games of any complexity. Already, in section 1.1, we have seen an easier way to model a sequential game: the *order of play*. For Follow-the-Leader I, this would be:

1   Smith chooses his disk size to be either *Large* or *Small*.
2   Jones chooses his disk size to be either *Large* or *Small*.

The reason I have retained the concept of the normal form in this edition is that it reinforces the idea of laying out all the possible strategies and comparing their payoffs. The order of play, however, gives us a better way to describe games, as I will explain next.

The Extensive Form and the Game Tree

Two other ways to describe a game are the extensive form and the game tree. First we need to define their building blocks. As you read the definitions, you may wish to refer to figure 2.1 as an example.

A **node** *is a point in the game at which some player or Nature takes an action, or the game ends.*
A **successor** *to node X is a node that may occur later in the game if X has been reached.*
A **predecessor** *to node X is a node that must be reached before X can be reached.*
A **starting node** *is a node with no predecessors.*
An **end node** *or* **end point** *is a node with no successors.*
A **branch** *is one action in a player's action set at a particular node.*
A **path** *is a sequence of nodes and branches leading from the starting node to an end node.*

These concepts can be used to define the extensive form and the game tree.

The **extensive form** *is a description of a game consisting of*

1   *A configuration of nodes and branches running without any closed loops from a single starting node to its end nodes.*
2   *An indication of which node belongs to which player.*
3   *The probabilities that Nature uses to choose different branches at its nodes.*
4   *The information sets into which each player's nodes are divided.*
5   *The payoffs for each player at each end node.*

The **game tree** *is the same as the extensive form except that (5) is replaced with*

5'   *The outcomes at each end node.*

"Game tree" is a looser term than "extensive form." If the outcome is defined as the payoff profile, one payoff for each player, then the extensive form is the same as the game tree.

The extensive form for Follow-the-Leader I is shown in figure 2.1. We can see why Equilibria E_1 and E_3 of table 2.2 are unsatisfactory even though they are Nash equilibria. If

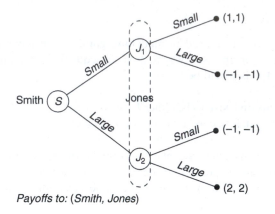

Payoffs to: (Smith, Jones)

Figure 2.2   Ranked Coordination in extensive form.

the game actually reached nodes J_1 or J_2, Jones would have dominant actions, *Small* at J_1 and *Large* at J_2, but E_1 and E_3 specify other actions at those nodes. In chapter 4 we will return to this game and show how the Nash concept can be refined to make E_2 the only equilibrium.

The extensive form for *Ranked Coordination*, shown in figure 2.2, adds dotted lines to the extensive form for *Follow-the-Leader I*. Each player makes a single decision between two actions. The moves are simultaneous, which we show by letting Smith move first, but not letting Jones know how he moved. The dotted line shows that Jones's knowledge stays the same after Smith moves. All Jones knows is that the game has reached some node within the information set defined by the dotted line; he does not know the exact node reached.

The Time Line

The **time line**, a line showing the order of events, is another way to describe games. Time lines are particularly useful for games with continuous strategies, exogenous arrival of information, and multiple periods, games that are frequently used in the accounting and finance literature. A typical time line is shown in figure 2.3a, which represents a game that will be described in section 11.5.

The time line illustrates the order of actions and events, not necessarily the passage of time. Certain events occur in an instant, others over an interval. In figure 2.3a, events 2 and 3 occur immediately after event 1, but events 4 and 5 might occur ten years later. We sometimes refer to the sequence in which decisions are made as **decision time** and the interval over which physical actions are taken as **real time**. A major difference is that players put higher value on payments received earlier in real time because of time preference (on which see the appendix).

A common and bad modelling habit is to restrict the use of the dates on the time line to separating events in real time. Events 1 and 2 in figure 2.3a are not separated by real time: as soon as the entrepreneur learns the project's value, he offers to sell stock. The modeller might foolishly decide to depict his model by a picture like figure 2.3b in which both events happen at date 1. Figure 2.3b is badly drawn, because readers might wonder which event occurs first or whether they occur simultaneously. In more than one seminar, 20 minutes of

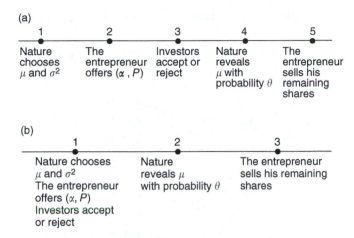

Figure 2.3   The time line for stock underpricing: (a) a good time line (b) a bad time line.

heated and confusing debate could have been avoided by 10 seconds care to delineate the order of events.

2.2   Information Sets

A game's information structure, like the order of its moves, is often obscured in the strategic form. During the Watergate affair, Senator Baker became famous for the question "How much did the President know, and when did he know it?" In games, as in scandals, these are the big questions. To make this precise, however, requires technical definitions so that one can describe who knows what, and when. This is done using the "information set," the set of nodes a player thinks the game might have reached, as the basic unit of knowledge.

> Player i's **information set** ω_i at any particular point of the game is the set of different nodes in the game tree that he knows might be the actual node, but between which he cannot distinguish by direct observation.

As defined here, the information set for player i is a set of nodes belonging to one player but on different paths. This captures the idea that player i knows whose turn it is to move, but not the exact location the game has reached in the game tree. Historically, player i's information set has been defined to include only nodes at which player i moves, which is appropriate for single-person decision theory, but leaves a player's knowledge undefined for most of any game with two or more players. The broader definition allows comparison of information across players, which under the older definition is a comparison of apples and oranges.

In the game in figure 2.4, Smith moves at node S_1 in 1984 and Jones moves at nodes J_1, J_2, J_3, and J_4 in 1985 or 1986. Smith knows his own move, but Jones can tell only whether Smith has chosen the moves which lead to J_1, J_2, or "other"; he cannot distinguish between J_3 and J_4. If Smith has chosen the move leading to J_3, his own information set is simply $\{J_3\}$, but Jones's information set is $\{J_3, J_4\}$.

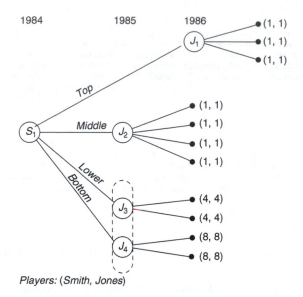

Figure 2.4   Information sets and information partitions.

One way to show information sets on a diagram is to put dashed lines around or between nodes in the same information set. The resulting diagrams can be very cluttered, so it is often more convenient to draw dashed lines around the information set of just the player making the move at a node. The dashed lines in figure 2.4 show that J_3 and J_4 are in the same information set for Jones, even though they are in different information sets for Smith. An expressive synonym for information set which is based on the appearance of these diagrams is "**cloud**": one would say that nodes J_3 and J_4 are in the same cloud, so that while Jones can tell that the game has reached that cloud, he cannot pierce the fog to tell exactly which node has been reached.

One node cannot belong to two different information sets of a single player. If node J_3 belonged to information sets $\{J_2, J_3\}$ and $\{J_3, J_4\}$ (unlike in figure 2.4), then if the game reached J_3, Jones would not know whether he was at a node in $\{J_2, J_3\}$ or a node in $\{J_3, J_4\}$ – which would imply that they were really the same information set.

If the nodes in one of Jones's information sets are nodes at which he moves, his action set must be the same at each node, because he knows his own action set (though his actions might differ later on in the game depending on whether he advances from J_3 or J_4). Jones has the same action sets at nodes J_3 and J_4, because if he had some different action available at J_3 he would know he was there and his information set would reduce to just $\{J_3\}$. For the same reason, nodes J_1 and J_2 could not be put in the same information set; Jones must know whether he has three or four moves in his action set. We also require end nodes to be in different information sets for a player if they yield him different payoffs.

With these exceptions, we do not include in the information structure of the game any information acquired by a player's rational deductions. In figure 2.4, for example, it seems clear that Smith would choose *Bottom*, because that is a dominant strategy – his payoff is 8 instead of the 4 from *Lower*, regardless of what Jones does. Jones should be able to deduce this, but even though this is an uncontroversial deduction, it is none the less a deduction, not an observation, so the game tree does not split J_3 and J_4 into separate information sets.

Table 2.3   Information partitions

Nodes	I	II	III	IV
J_1	$\{J_1\}$	$\{J_1\}$	$\left.\begin{matrix} J_1 \\ J_2 \\ J_3 \\ J_4 \end{matrix}\right]$	$\left.\begin{matrix} J_1 \\ J_2 \\ J_3 \end{matrix}\right\}$
J_2	$\{J_2\}$	$\{J_2\}$		
J_3	$\{J_3\}$	$\left.\begin{matrix} J_3 \\ J_4 \end{matrix}\right\}$		
J_4	$\{J_4\}$			$\{J_4\}$

Information sets also show the effects of unobserved moves by Nature. In figure 2.4, if the initial move had been made by Nature instead of by Smith, Jones's information sets would be depicted the same way.

Player i's **information partition** *is a collection of his information sets such that*

1   Each path is represented by one node in a single information set in the partition, and

2   The predecessors of all nodes in a single information set are in one information set.

The information partition represents the different positions that the player knows he will be able to distinguish from each other at a given stage of the game, carving up the set of all possible nodes into the subsets called information sets. One of Smith's information partitions is $(\{J_1\}, \{J_2\}, \{J_3\}, \{J_4\})$. The definition rules out information set $\{S_1\}$ being in that partition, because the path going through S_1 and J_1 would be represented by two nodes. Instead, $\{S_1\}$ is a separate information partition, all by itself. The information partition refers to a stage of the game, not chronological time. The information partition $(\{J_1\}, \{J_2\}, \{J_3, J_4\})$ includes nodes in both 1985 and 1986, but they are all immediate successors of node S_1.

Jones has the information partition $(\{J_1\}, \{J_2\}, \{J_3, J_4\})$. There are two ways to see that his information is worse than Smith's. First is the fact that one of his information *sets*, $\{J_3, J_4\}$, contains *more* elements than Smith's, and second, that one of his information *partitions*, $(\{J_1\}, \{J_2\}, \{J_3, J_4\})$, contains *fewer* elements.

Table 2.3 shows a number of different information partitions for this game. Partition I is Smith's partition and partition II is Jones's partition. We say that partition II is **coarser**, and partition I is **finer**. A profile of two or more of the information sets in a partition, which reduces the number of information sets and increases the numbers of nodes in one or more of them is a **coarsening**. A splitting of one or more of the information sets in a partition, which increases the number of information sets and reduces the number of nodes in one or more of them, is a **refinement**. Partition II is thus a coarsening of partition I, and partition I is a refinement of partition II. The ultimate refinement is for each information set to be a **singleton**, containing one node, as in the case of partition I. As in bridge, having a singleton can either help or hurt a player. The ultimate coarsening is for a player not to be able to distinguish between any of the nodes, which is partition III in table 2.3.[1]

---

[1] Note, however, that partitions III and IV are not really allowed in this game because Jones could tell the node from the actions available to him, as explained earlier.

A finer information partition is the formal definition for "better information." Not all information partitions are refinements or coarsenings of each other, however, so not all information partitions can be ranked by the quality of their information. In particular, just because one information partition contains more information sets does not mean it is a refinement of another information partition. Consider partitions II and IV in figure 2.3. Partition II separates the nodes into three information sets, while partition IV separates them into just two information sets. Partition IV is not a coarsening of partition II, however, because it cannot be reached by combining information sets from partition II, and one cannot say that a player with partition IV has worse information. If the node reached is J_1, partition II gives more precise information, but if the node reached is J_4, partition IV gives more precise information.

Information quality is defined independently of its utility to the player: it is possible for a player's information to improve, and for his equilibrium payoff to fall as a result. Game theory has many paradoxical models in which a player prefers having worse information, not a result of wishful thinking, escapism, or blissful ignorance, but of cold rationality. Coarse information can have a number of advantages. (a) It may permit a player to engage in trade because other players do not fear his superior information. (b) It may give a player a stronger strategic position because he usually has a strong position and is better off not knowing that in a particular realization of the game his position is weak. Or, (c) as in the more traditional economics of uncertainty, poor information may permit players to insure each other.

I will wait till later chapters to discuss points (a) and (b), the strategic advantages of poor information (go to section 6.3 on entry deterrence and chapter 9 on used cars if you feel impatient), but it is worth pausing here to think about point (c), the insurance advantage. Consider the following example which will illustrate that even when information is symmetric and behavior is nonstrategic, better information in the sense of a finer information partition, can actually reduce everybody's utility.

Suppose Smith and Jones, both risk averse, work for the same employer, and both know that one of them chosen randomly will be fired at the end of the year while the other will be promoted. The one who is fired will end with a wealth of 0 and the one who is promoted will end with 100. The two workers will agree to insure each other by pooling their wealth: they will agree that whoever is promoted will pay 50 to whoever is fired. Each would then end up with a guaranteed utility of U(50). If a helpful outsider offers to tell them who will be fired before they make their insurance agreement, they should cover their ears and refuse to listen. Such a refinement of their information would make both worse off, in expectation, because it would wreck the possibility of the two of them agreeing on an insurance arrangement. It would wreck the possibility because if they knew who would be promoted, the lucky worker would refuse to pool with the unlucky one. Each worker's expected utility with no insurance but with someone telling them what will happen is $.5 * U(0) + .5 * U(100)$, which is less than $1.0 * U(50)$ if they are risk averse. They would prefer not to know because better information would reduce the expected utility of both of them.

Common Knowledge

We have been implicitly assuming that the players know what the game tree looks like. In fact, we have assumed that the players also know that the other players know what the game tree looks like. The term "common knowledge" is used to avoid spelling out the infinite recursion to which this leads.

> *Information is* **common knowledge** *if it is known to all the players, if each player knows that all the players know it, if each player knows that all the players know that all the players know it, and so forth ad infinitum.*

Because of this recursion (the importance of which will be seen in section 6.3), the assumption of common knowledge is stronger than the assumption that players have the same beliefs about where they are in the game tree. Hirshleifer & Riley (1992, p. 169) use the term **concordant beliefs** to describe a situation where players share the same belief about the probabilities that Nature has chosen different states of the world, but where they do not necessarily know they share the same beliefs. (Brandenburger [1992] uses the term **mutual knowledge** for the same idea.)

For clarity, models are set up so that information partitions are common knowledge. Every player knows how precise the other players' information is, however ignorant he himself may be as to which node the game has reached. Modelled this way, the information partitions are independent of the equilibrium concept. Making the information partitions common knowledge is important for clear modelling, and restricts the kinds of games that can be modelled less than one might think. This will be illustrated in section 2.4 when the assumption will be imposed on a situation in which one player does not even know which of three games he is playing.

2.3   Perfect, Certain, Symmetric, and Complete Information

We categorize the information structure of a game in four different ways, so a particular game might have perfect, complete, certain, and symmetric information. The categories are summarized in table 2.4.

The first category divides games into those with perfect and those with imperfect information.

> *In a game of* **perfect information** *each information set is a singleton. Otherwise the game is one of* **imperfect information**.

Table 2.4   Information categories

Information category	Meaning
Perfect	Each information set is a singleton
Certain	Nature does not move after any player moves
Symmetric	No player has information different from other players when he moves, or at the end nodes
Complete	Nature does not move first, or her initial move is observed by every player

The strongest informational requirements are met by a game of perfect information, because in such a game each player always knows exactly where he is in the game tree. No moves are simultaneous, and all players observe Nature's moves. Ranked Coordination is a game of imperfect information because of its simultaneous moves, but Follow-the-Leader I is a game of perfect information. Any game of incomplete or asymmetric information is also a game of imperfect information.

> A game of **certainty** has no moves by Nature after any player moves. Otherwise the game is one of **uncertainty**.

The moves by Nature in a game of uncertainty may or may not be revealed to the players immediately. A game of certainty can be a game of perfect information if it has no simultaneous moves. The notion "game of uncertainty" is new with this book, but I doubt it would surprise anyone. The only quirk in the definition is that it allows an initial move by Nature in a game of certainty, because in a game of incomplete information Nature moves first to select a player's "type." Most modellers do not think of this situation as uncertainty.

We have already talked about information in Ranked Coordination, a game of imperfect, complete, and symmetric information with certainty. The Prisoner's Dilemma falls into the same categories. Follow-the-Leader I, which does not have simultaneous moves, is a game of perfect, complete, and symmetric information with certainty.

We can easily modify Follow-the-Leader I to add uncertainty, creating the game Follow-the-Leader II (figure 2.5). Imagine that if both players pick *Large* for their disks, the market yields either zero profits, or very high profits, depending on the state of demand, but demand would not affect the payoffs in any other strategy profile. We can quantify this by saying that if (*Large*, *Large*) is picked, the payoffs are (10, 10) with probability 0.2, and (0, 0) with probability 0.8, as shown in figure 2.5.

When players face uncertainty, we need to specify how they evaluate their uncertain future payoffs. The obvious way to model their behavior is to say that the players maximize the expected values of their utilities. Players who behave in this way are said to have

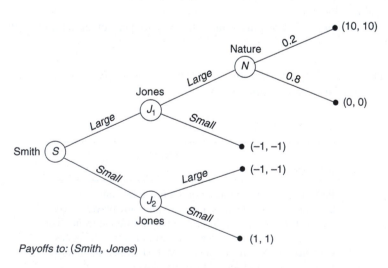

Payoffs to: (Smith, Jones)

Figure 2.5   Follow-the-Leader II.

von Neumann–Morgenstern utility functions, a name chosen to underscore von Neumann & Morgenstern's (1944) development of a rigorous justification of such behavior.

Maximizing their expected utilities, the players would behave exactly the same as in Follow-the-Leader I. Often, a game of uncertainty can be transformed into a game of certainty without changing the equilibrium, by eliminating Nature's moves and changing the payoffs to their expected values based on the probabilities of Nature's moves. Here we could eliminate Nature's move and replace the payoffs 10 and 0 with the single payoff 2 (=0.2[10] + 0.8[0]). This cannot be done, however, if the actions available to a player depend on Nature's moves, or if information about Nature's move is asymmetric.

The players in figure 2.5 might be either risk averse or risk neutral. Risk aversion is implicitly incorporated in the payoffs because they are in units of utility, not dollars. When players maximize their expected utility, they are not necessarily maximizing their expected dollars. Moreover, the players can differ in how they map money to utility. It could be that (0, 0) represents ($0, $5,000), (10, 10) represents ($100,000, $100,000), and (2, 2), the expected utility, could here represent a nonrisky ($3,000, $7,000).

In a game of **symmetric information**, *a player's information set at*

1 any node where he chooses an action, or
2 an end node

contains at least the same elements as the information sets of every other player. Otherwise the game is one of **asymmetric information.**

In a game of asymmetric information, the information sets of players differ in ways relevant to their behavior, or differ at the end of the game. Such games have imperfect information, since information sets which differ across players cannot be singletons. The definition of "asymmetric information" which is used in the present book for the first time is intended for capturing a vague meaning commonly used today. The essence of asymmetric information is that some player has useful **private information**: an information partition that is different and not worse than another player's.

A game of symmetric information can have moves by Nature or simultaneous moves, but no player ever has an informational advantage. The one point at which information may differ is when the player *not* moving has superior information because he knows what his own move *was*; for example, if the two players move simultaneously. Such information does not help the informed player, since by definition it cannot affect his move.

A game has asymmetric information if information sets differ at the end of the game because we conventionally think of such games as ones in which information differs, even though no player takes an action after the end nodes. The principal–agent model of chapter 7 is an example. The principal moves first, then the agent, and finally Nature. The agent observes the agent's move, but the principal does not, although he may be able to deduce it. This would be a game of symmetric information except for the fact that information continues to differ at the end nodes.

In a game of **incomplete information**, *Nature moves first and is unobserved by at least one of the players. Otherwise the game is one of* **complete information.**

A game with incomplete information also has imperfect information, because some player's information set includes more than one node. Two kinds of games have complete but imperfect information: games with simultaneous moves, and games where, late in the game, Nature makes moves not immediately revealed to all players.

Many games of incomplete information are games of asymmetric information, but the two concepts are not equivalent. If there is no initial move by Nature, but Smith takes a move unobserved by Jones, and Smith moves again later in the game, the game has asymmetric but complete information. The principal–agent games of chapter 7 are again examples: the agent knows how hard he worked, but his principal never learns, not even at the end nodes. A game can also have incomplete but symmetric information: let Nature, unobserved by either player, move first and choose the payoffs for (*Confess, Confess*) in the Prisoner's Dilemma to be either $(-6, -6)$ or $(-100, -100)$.

Harris & Holmstrom (1982) have a more interesting example of incomplete but symmetric information: Nature assigns different abilities to workers, but when workers are young their ability is known neither to employers nor to themselves. As time passes, the abilities become common knowledge, and if workers are risk averse, and employers are risk neutral, the model shows that equilibrium wages are constant, or rising over time.

Poker Examples of Information Classification

In the game of poker, the players make bets on who will have the best hand of cards at the end, where a ranking of hands has been pre-established. How would the following rules for behavior before betting be classified? (Answers are in note N2.3.)

1   All cards are dealt face up.
2   All cards are dealt face down, and a player cannot look even at his own cards before he bets.
3   All cards are dealt face down, and a player can look at his own cards.
4   All cards are dealt face up, but each player then scoops up his hand and secretly discards one card.
5   All cards are dealt face up, the players bet, and then each player receives one more card face up.
6   All cards are dealt face down, but then each player scoops up his cards without looking at them and holds them against his forehead so all the *other* players can see them (Indian poker).

2.4   The Harsanyi Transformation and Bayesian Games

The Harsanyi Transformation: Follow-the-Leader III

The term "incomplete information" is used in two quite different senses in the literature, usually without explicit definition. The definition in section 2.3 is what economists commonly *use*, but if asked to *define* the term, they might come up with the following, older definition.

Old definition

> In a game of **complete information**, *all players know the rules of the game. Otherwise the game is one of* **incomplete information.**

The old definition is not meaningful, since the game itself is ill defined if it does not specify exactly what the players' information sets are. Until 1967, game theorists spoke of games of incomplete information only to say that they could not be analyzed. Then John Harsanyi pointed out that any game that had incomplete information under the old definition could be remodelled as a game of complete but imperfect information without changing its essentials, simply by adding an initial move in which Nature chooses between different sets of rules. In the transformed game, all players know the new meta-rules, including the fact that Nature has made an initial move unobserved by them. Harsanyi's suggestion trivialized the definition of incomplete information, and people began using the term to refer to the transformed game instead. Under the old definition, a game of incomplete information was transformed into a game of complete information. Under the new definition, the original game is ill defined, and the transformed version is a game of incomplete information.

Follow-the-Leader III serves to illustrate the Harsanyi transformation. Suppose that Jones does not know the game's payoffs precisely. He does have some idea of the payoffs, and we represent his beliefs by a subjective probability distribution. He places a 70 percent probability on the game being game (A) in figure 2.6 (which is the same as Follow-the-Leader I), a 10 percent chance on game (B), and a 20 percent on game (C). In reality the game has a particular set of payoffs, and Smith knows what they are. This is a game of incomplete information (Jones does not know the payoffs), asymmetric information (when Smith moves, Smith knows something Jones does not), and certainty. (Nature does not move after the players do.)

The game cannot be analyzed in the form shown in figure 2.6. The natural way to approach such a game is to use the Harsanyi transformation. We can remodel the game to look like figure 2.7, in which Nature makes the first move and chooses the payoffs of game (A), (B), or (C), in accordance with Jones's subjective probabilities. Smith observes Nature's move, but Jones does not. Figure 2.7 depicts the same game as figure 2.6, but now we can analyze it. Both Smith and Jones know the rules of the game, and the difference between them is that Smith has observed Nature's move. Whether Nature actually makes the moves with the indicated probabilities, or Jones just imagines them, is irrelevant, so long as Jones's initial beliefs or fantasies are common knowledge.

Often what Nature chooses at the start of a game is the strategy set, information partition, and payoff function of one of the players. We say that the player can be any of several "types," a term to which we will return in later chapters. When Nature moves, especially if she affects the strategy sets and payoffs of both players, it is often said that Nature has chosen a particular "state of the world." In figure 2.7 Nature chooses the state of the world to be (A), (B), or (C).

> A player's **type** is the strategy set, information partition, and payoff function which Nature chooses for him at the start of a game of incomplete information.
>
> A **state of the world** is a move by Nature.

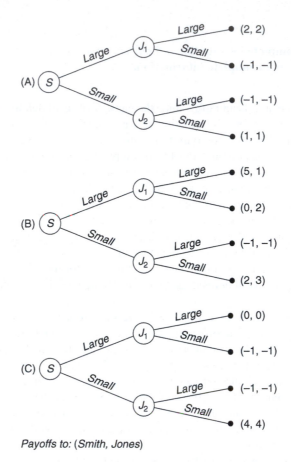

Payoffs to: (Smith, Jones)

Figure 2.6   Follow-the-Leader III: original.

As I have already said, it is good modelling practice to assume that the structure of the game is common knowledge, so that though Nature's choice of Smith's type may really just represent Jones's opinions about Smith's possible type, Smith knows what Jones's possible opinions are, and Jones knows that they are just opinions. The players may have different beliefs, but that is modelled as the effect of their observing different moves by Nature. All players begin the game with the same beliefs about the probabilities of the moves Nature will make – the same priors, to use a term that will shortly be introduced. This modelling assumption is known as the **Harsanyi doctrine**. If the modeller is following it, his model can never reach a situation where two players possess exactly the same information but disagree as to the probability of some past or future move of Nature. A model cannot, for example, begin by saying that Germany believes its probability of winning a war against France is 0.8, and France believes it is 0.4, so they are both willing to go to war. Rather, he must assume that beliefs begin the same but diverge because of private information. Both players initially think that the probability of a German victory is 0.4, but that if General Schmidt is a genius the probability rises to 0.8, and then Germany discovers that Schmidt is indeed a genius. If it is France that has the initiative to declare war, France's mistaken

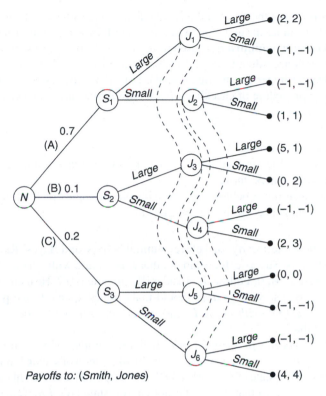

Figure 2.7   Follow-the-Leader III: after the Harsanyi transformation.

beliefs may lead to a conflict that would be avoidable if Germany could credibly reveal its private information about Schmidt's genius.

An implication of the Harsanyi doctrine is that players are at least slightly open-minded about their opinions. If Germany indicates that it is willing to go to war, France must consider the possibility that Germany has discovered Schmidt's genius, and update the probability that Germany will win (keeping in mind that Germany might be bluffing). Our next topic is how a player updates his beliefs upon receiving new information, whether it be by direct observation of Nature, or by observing the moves of another player who might be better informed.

Updating Beliefs with Bayes' Rule

When we classify a game's information structure we do not try to decide what a player can deduce from the other players' moves. Player Jones might deduce, upon seeing Smith choose *Large*, that Nature has chosen state (A), but we do not draw Jones's information set in figure 2.7 to take this into account. In drawing the game tree we want to illustrate only the exogenous elements of the game, uncontaminated by the equilibrium concept. But to find the equilibrium we do need to think about how beliefs change over the course of the game.

One part of the rules of the game is the collection of **prior beliefs** (or **priors**) held by the different players, beliefs that they update in the course of the game. A player holds prior beliefs concerning the types of the other players, and as he sees them take actions he updates his beliefs under the assumption that they are following equilibrium behavior.

The term **Bayesian equilibrium** is used to refer to a Nash equilibrium in which players update their beliefs according to Bayes' Rule. Since Bayes' Rule is the natural and standard way to handle imperfect information, the adjective, "Bayesian," is really optional. But the two-step procedure of checking a Nash equilibrium has now become a three-step procedure:

1   Propose a strategy profile.
2   See what beliefs the strategy profile generates when players update their beliefs in response to each others' moves.
3   Check that given those beliefs together with the strategies of the other players each player is choosing a best response for himself.

The rules of the game specify each player's initial beliefs, and Bayes' Rule is the rational way to update beliefs. Suppose, for example, that Jones starts with a particular prior belief, *Prob(Nature chose (A))*. In Follow-the-Leader III, this equals 0.7. He then observes Smith's move – *Large*, perhaps. Seeing *Large* should make Jones update to the **posterior** belief, *Prob(Nature chose (A)|Smith chose Large)*, where the symbol "|" denotes "conditional upon" or "given that."

Bayes' Rule shows how to revise the prior belief in the light of new information such as Smith's move. It uses two pieces of information, the likelihood of seeing Smith choose *Large* given that Nature chose state of the world (A), *Prob(Large|(A))*, and the likelihood of seeing Smith choose *Large* given that Nature did not choose state (A), *Prob(Large|(B) or (C))*. From these numbers, Jones can calculate *Prob(Smith chooses Large)*, the **marginal likelihood** of seeing *Large* as the result of one or another of the possible states of the world that Nature might choose.

$$Prob(Smith\ chooses\ Large) = Prob(Large|A)Prob(A) + Prob(Large|B)Prob(B)$$
$$+ Prob(Large|C)Prob(C). \tag{2.1}$$

To find his posterior, *Prob(Nature chose (A)|Smith chose Large)*, Jones uses the likelihood and his priors. The joint probability of both seeing Smith choose *Large* and Nature having chosen (A) is

$$Prob(Large, A) = Prob(A|Large)Prob(Large) = Prob(Large|A)Prob(A). \tag{2.2}$$

Since what Jones is trying to calculate is *Prob(A|Large)*, rewrite the last part of (2.2) as follows:

$$Prob(A|Large) = \frac{Prob(Large|A)Prob(A)}{Prob(Large)}. \tag{2.3}$$

Jones needs to calculate his new belief – his posterior – using *Prob(Large)*, which he calculates from his original knowledge using (2.1). Substituting the expression for *Prob(Large)*

Table 2.5 Bayesian terminology

Name	Meaning
Likelihood	*Prob(data|event)*
Marginal likelihood	*Prob(data)*
Conditional Likelihood	*Prob(data X|data Y, event)*
Prior	*Prob(event)*
Posterior	*Prob(event|data)*

from (2.1) into equation (2.3) gives the final result, a version of Bayes' Rule.

Prob(A|Large)

$$= \frac{Prob(Large|A)Prob(A)}{Prob(Large|A)Prob(A) + Prob(Large|B)Prob(B) + Prob(Large|C)Prob(C)}. \quad (2.4)$$

More generally, for Nature's move x and the observed data,

$$Prob(x|data) = \frac{Prob(data|x)Prob(x)}{Prob(data)} \quad (2.5)$$

Equation (2.6) is a verbal form of Bayes' Rule, which is useful for remembering the terminology, summarized in table 2.5.[2]

(Posterior for Nature's Move)

$$= \frac{(Likelihood\ of\ Player's\ Move) \cdot (Prior\ for\ Nature's\ Move)}{(Marginal\ likelihood\ of\ Player's\ Move)}. \quad (2.6)$$

Bayes' Rule is not purely mechanical. It is the only way to rationally update beliefs. The derivation is worth understanding, because Bayes' Rule is hard to memorize but easy to rederive.

Updating Beliefs in Follow-the-Leader III

Let us now return to the numbers in Follow-the-Leader III to use the belief-updating rule just derived. Jones has a prior belief that the probability of event "Nature picks state (A)" is 0.7 and he needs to update that belief on seeing the data "Smith picks *Large*." His prior is *Prob(A)* = 0.7, and we wish to calculate *Prob(A|Large)*.

To use Bayes' Rule from equation (2.4), we need the values of *Prob(Large|A)*, *Prob(Large|B)*, and *Prob(Large|C)*. These values depend on what Smith does in equilibrium, so Jones's beliefs cannot be calculated independently of the equilibrium. This is

[2] The name "marginal likelihood" may seem strange to economists since it is an unconditional likelihood and when economists use "marginal" they mean "an increment conditional on starting from a particular level." The statisticians defined marginal likelihood this way because they start with *Prob(a, b)*, and then derive *Prob(b)*. That is like going to the margin of a graph in (a, b)-space, the b-axis, and asking how probable the value of b is integrating over all possible a's.

the reason for the three-step procedure suggested above, for what the modeller must do is propose an equilibrium and then use it to calculate the beliefs. Afterwards, he must check that the equilibrium strategies are indeed the best responses given the beliefs they generate.

A candidate for equilibrium in Follow-the-Leader III is for Smith to choose *Large* if the state is (A) or (B) and *Small* if it is (C), and for Jones to respond to *Large* with *Large* and to *Small* with *Small*. This can be abbreviated as $(L|A, L|B, S|C; L|L, S|S)$. Let us test that this is an equilibrium, starting with the calculation of $Prob(A|Large)$.

If Jones observes *Large*, he can rule out state (C), but he does not know whether the state is (A) or (B). Bayes' Rule tells him that the posterior probability of state (A) is

$$Prob(A|Large) = \frac{(1)(0.7)}{(1)(0.7) + (1)(0.1) + (0)(0.2)}$$
$$= 0.875. \tag{2.7}$$

The posterior probability of state (B) must then be $1 - 0.875 = 0.125$, which could also be calculated from Bayes' Rule, as follows:

$$Prob(B|Large) = \frac{(1)(0.1)}{(1)(0.7) + (1)(0.1) + (0)(0.2)}$$
$$= 0.125. \tag{2.8}$$

Figure 2.8 shows a graphic intuition for Bayes' Rule. The first line shows the total probability, 1, which is the sum of the prior probabilities of states (A), (B), and (C). The second line shows the probabilities, summing to 0.8, which remain after *Large* is observed, and state (C) is ruled out. The third line shows that state (A) represents an amount 0.7 of that probability, a fraction of 0.875. The fourth line shows that state (B) represents an amount 0.1 of that probability, a fraction of 0.125.

Jones must use Smith's strategy in the proposed equilibrium to find numbers for $Prob(Large|A)$, $Prob(Large|B)$, and $Prob(Large|C)$. As always in Nash equilibrium, the

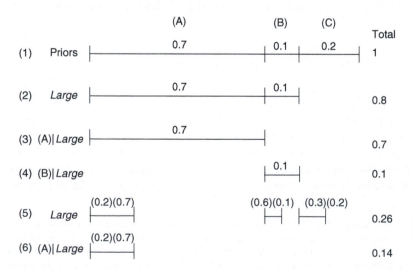

Figure 2.8 Bayes' Rule.

modeller assumes that the players know which equilibrium strategies are being played out, even though they do not know which particular actions are being chosen.

Given that Jones believes that the state is (A) with probability 0.875, and state (B) with probability 0.125, his best response is *Large*, even though he knows that if the state were actually (B) the better response would be *Small*. Given that he observes *Large*, Jones's expected payoff from *Small* is -0.625 $(=0.875[-1] + 0.125[2])$, but from *Large* it is 1.875 $(=0.875[2] + 0.125[1])$. The strategy profile $(L|A, L|B, S|C; L|L, S|S)$ is a Bayesian equilibrium.

A similar calculation can be done for *Prob(A|Small)*. Using Bayes' Rule, equation (2.4) becomes

$$Prob(A|Small) = \frac{(0)(0.7)}{(0)(0.7) + (0)(0.1) + (1)(0.2)} = 0. \tag{2.9}$$

Given that he believes the state is (C), Jones's best response to *Small* is *Small*, which agrees with our proposed equilibrium.

Smith's best responses are much simpler. Given that Jones will imitate his action, Smith does best by following his equilibrium strategy of $(L|A, L|B, S|C)$.

The calculations are relatively simple because Smith uses a nonrandom strategy in equilibrium, so, for instance, *Prob(Small|A)* $= 0$ in equation (2.9). Consider what happens if Smith uses a random strategy of picking *Large* with probability 0.2 in state (A), 0.6 in state (B), and 0.3 in state (C) (we will analyze such "mixed" strategies in chapter 3). The equivalent of equation (2.7) is

$$Prob(A|Large) = \frac{(0.2)(0.7)}{(0.2)(0.7) + (0.6)(0.1) + (0.3)(0.2)} = 0.54 \quad (rounded). \tag{2.10}$$

If he sees *Large*, Jones's best guess is still that Nature chose state (A), even though in state (A) Smith has the smallest probability of choosing *Large*, but Jones's subjective posterior probability, $Pr(A|Large)$, has fallen to 0.54 from his prior of $Pr(A) = 0.7$.

The last two lines of figure 2.8 illustrate this case. The second-to-last line shows the total probability of *Large*, which is formed from the probabilities in all three states and sums to 0.26 $(=0.14 + 0.06 + 0.06)$. The last line shows the component of that probability arising from state (A), which is the amount 0.14, and fraction 0.54 (rounded).

Regression to the Mean, the Two-armed Bandit, and Cascades

Bayesian learning is important not just in modelling Bayesian games, but in explaining behavior that is nonstrategic, in the sense that although players may learn from the moves of other players, their payoffs are not directly affected by those moves. I will discuss three phenomena that give us useful explanations for behavior: regression to the mean, the bandit problem, and cascades.

Regression to the mean is an old statistical idea that has a Bayesian interpretation. Suppose that each student's performance on a test results partly from his ability and partly from random error because of his mood the day of the test. The teacher does not know the individual student's ability, but does know that the average student will score 70 out of 100. If a student scores 40, what should the teacher's estimate of his ability be?

It should not be 40. A score of 30 points below the average score could be the result of two things: (1) the student's ability is below average, or (2) the student was in a bad mood the day of the test. Only if mood is completely unimportant should the teacher use 40 as his estimate. More likely, both ability and luck matter to some extent, so the teacher's best guess is that the student has an ability below average, but was also unlucky. The best estimate lies somewhere between 40 and 70, reflecting the influence of both ability, and luck. Of the students who score 40 on the test, more than half can be expected to score above 40 on the next test. Since the scores of these poorly performing students tend to float up towards the mean of 70, this phenomenon is called "regression to the mean." Similarly, students who score 90 on the first test will tend to score less well on the second test.

This is "regression to the mean" ("toward" would be more precise) not "regression beyond the mean." A low score does indicate low ability, on average, so the predicted score on the second test is still below average. Regression to the mean merely recognizes that both luck and ability are at work.

In Bayesian terms, the teacher in this example has a prior mean of 70, and is trying to form a posterior estimate using the prior and one piece of data, the score on the first test. For typical distributions, the posterior mean will lie between the prior mean, and the data point, so the posterior mean will be between 40 and 70.

In a business context, regression to the mean can be used to explain business conservatism, as I do in Rasmusen (1992b). It is sometimes claimed that businesses pass up profitable investments because they have an excessive fear of risk. Let us suppose that the business is risk neutral, because the risk associated with the project and the uncertainty over its value are nonsystematic – that is, they are risks that a widely held corporation can distribute in such a way that each shareholder's risk is trivial. Suppose that the firm will not spend $100,000 on an investment with a present value of $105,000. This is easily explained if the $105,000 is an estimate and the $100,000 is cash. If the average value of a new project of this kind is less than $100,000 – as is likely to be the case since profitable projects are not easy to find – the best estimate of the value will lie between the measured value of $105,000 and that average value, unless the staffer who came up with the $105,000 figure has already adjusted his estimate. Regressing the $105,000 to the mean may regress it past $100,000. Put a bit differently, if the prior mean is, let us say, $80,000, and the data point is $105,000, the posterior may well be less than $100,000. Regression to the mean is an alternative to strategic behavior in explaining certain odd phenomena. In analyzing test scores, one might try to explain the rise in the scores of poor students by changes in their effort level in an attempt to achieve a target grade in the course with minimum work. In analyzing business decisions, one might try to explain why apparently profitable projects are rejected because of managers' dislike for innovations that would require them to work harder.

Bayesian learning also explains apparently suboptimal behavior in the "Two-Armed Bandit" model of Rothschild (1974). In each of a sequence of periods, a person chooses to play slot machine A, or slot machine B. Slot machine A pays out $1 with known probability 0.5 in exchange for the person putting in $0.25 and pulling its arm. Slot machine B pays out $1 with an unknown probability which has a prior probability density centered on 0.5. The optimal strategy is to begin by playing machine B, since not only does it have the same expected payout per period, but also playing it improves the player's information, whereas playing machine A leaves his information unchanged. The player will switch to machine A if machine B pays out $0 often enough relative to the number of times it pays out $1, where "often enough" depends on the particular prior beliefs he has. If the first 1,000 plays all result in a payout of $1, he will keep playing machine B, but if the next 9,000 plays all result in a payout of $0, he should become very sure that machine B's payout rate is less than

0.5 and he should switch to machine A. But he will never switch back. Once he is playing machine A, he is learning nothing new as a result of his wins and losses, and even if he gets a payout of $0 ten thousand times in a row, that gives him no reason to change machines. As a result, it can happen that even if machine B actually is better, a player following the ex ante optimal strategy can end up playing machine A an infinite number of times.

Another model with a similar flavor is the **cascade model**. Consider a simplified version of the first example of a cascade in Bikhchandani, Hirshleifer & Welch (1992) (who with Bannerjee [1992] originated the idea; see also Hirshleifer [1995]). A sequence of people must decide whether to Adopt at cost 0.5 or Reject a project worth either 0 or 1 with equal prior probabilities, having observed the decisions of people ahead of them in the sequence plus an independent private signal that takes the value High with probability $p > 0.5$ if the project's value is 1 and with probability $(1 - p)$ if it is 0, and otherwise takes the value Low.

The first person will simply follow his signal, choosing Adopt if the signal is High and Reject if it is Low. The second person uses the information of the first person's decision plus his own signal. One Nash equilibrium is for the second person to always imitate the first person. It is easy to see that he should imitate the first person if the first person chose Adopt and the second signal is High. What if the first person chose Adopt and the second signal is Low? Then the second person can deduce that the first signal was High, and choosing on the basis of a prior of 0.5 and two contradictory signals of equal accuracy, he is indifferent – and so will not deviate from an equilibrium in which his assigned strategy is to imitate the first person when indifferent. The third person, having seen the first two choose Adopt, will also deduce that the first person's signal was High. He will ignore the second person's decision, knowing that in equilibrium that person just imitates, but he, too will imitate. Thus, even if the sequence of signals is (High, Low, Low, Low, Low, ...), everyone will choose Adopt. A "cascade" has begun, in which players later in the sequence ignore their own information and rely completely on previous players. Thus, we have a way to explain fads and fashions as Bayesian updating under incomplete information, without any strategic behavior.

2.5   An Example: The Png Settlement Game

The Png (1983) model of out-of-court settlement is an example of a game with a fairly complicated extensive form.[3] The plaintiff alleges that the defendant was negligent in providing safety equipment at a chemical plant, a charge which is true with probability q. The plaintiff files suit, but the case is not decided immediately. In the meantime, the defendant and the plaintiff can settle out of court.

What are the moves in this game? It is really made up of two games: the one in which the defendant is liable for damages, and the one in which he is blameless. We therefore start the game tree with a move by Nature, who makes the defendant either liable or blameless. At the next node, the plaintiff takes an action: *Sue* or *Grumble*. If he decides on *Grumble* the game ends with zero payoffs for both players. If he decides to *Sue*, we go to the next node. The defendant then decides whether to *Resist* or *Offer* to settle. If the defendant chooses

---

[3] "Png," by the way, is pronounced the same way it is spelt.

Offer, then the plaintiff can *Settle* or *Refuse*; if the defendant chooses to *Resist*, the plaintiff can *Try* the case or *Drop* it. The following description adds payoffs to this model.

The Png Settlement Game

PLAYERS
The plaintiff and the defendant.

THE ORDER OF PLAY
0 Nature chooses the defendant to be Liable for injury to the plaintiff with probability $q = 0.13$ and Blameless otherwise. The defendant observes this but the plaintiff does not.

1   The plaintiff decides to Sue or just to Grumble.
2   The defendant Offers a settlement amount of $S = 0.15$ to the plaintiff, or Resist, setting $S = 0$.
3a If the defendant offered $S = 0.15$, the plaintiff agrees to Settle or he Refuses and goes to trial.
3b If the defendant offered $S = 0$, the plaintiff Drops the case, for legal costs of $P = 0$ and $D = 0$ for himself and the defendant, or chooses to Try it, creating legal costs of $P = 0.1$ and $D = 0.2$.
4   If the case goes to trial, the plaintiff wins damages of $W = 1$ if the defendant is Liable and $W = 0$ if the defendant is Blameless. If the case is dropped, $W = 0$.

PAYOFFS
The plaintiff's payoff is $(S + W - P)$. The defendant's payoff is $(-S - W - D)$.

We can also depict this on a game tree, as in figure 2.9.

This model assumes that the settlement amount, $S = 0.15$, and the amounts spent on legal fees are exogenous. Except in the infinitely long games without end nodes that will appear in chapter 5, an extensive form should incorporate all costs and benefits into the payoffs at the end nodes, even if costs are incurred along the way. If the court required a $100 filing fee (which it does not in this game, although a fee will be required in the similar game of Nuisance Suits in section 4.3), it would be subtracted from the plaintiff's payoffs at every end node except those resulting from his choice of *Grumble*. Such consolidation makes it easier to analyze the game and would not affect the equilibrium strategies unless payments along the way revealed information, in which case what matters is the information, not the fact that payoffs change.

We assume that if the case reaches the court, justice is done. In addition to his legal fees D, the defendant pays damages $W = 1$ only if he is liable. We also assume that the players are risk neutral, so they only care about the expected dollars they will receive, not the variance. Without this assumption we would have to translate the dollar payoffs into utility, but the game tree would be unaffected.

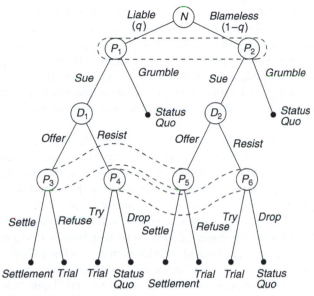

Figure 2.9 The game tree for the Png Settlement Game.

This is a game of certain, asymmetric, imperfect, and incomplete information. We have assumed that the defendant knows whether he is liable, but we could modify the game by assuming that he has no better idea than the plaintiff of whether the evidence is sufficient to prove him so. The game would become one of symmetric information and we could reasonably simplify the extensive form by eliminating the initial move by Nature and setting the payoffs equal to the expected values. We cannot perform this simplification in the original game, because the fact that the defendant, and only the defendant, knows whether he is liable strongly affects the behavior of both players.

Let us now find the equilibrium. Using dominance we can rule out one of the plaintiff's strategies immediately – *Grumble* – which is dominated by (*Sue, Settle, Drop*).

Whether a strategy profile is a Nash equilibrium depends on the parameters of the model – S, W, P, D, and q, which are the settlement amount, the damages, the court costs for the plaintiff and defendant, and the probability the defendant is liable. Depending on the parameter values, three outcomes are possible: settlement (if the settlement amount is low), trial (if expected damages are high and the plaintiff's court costs are low), and the plaintiff dropping the action (if expected damages minus court costs are negative). Here, I have inserted the parameter values $S = 0.15, D = 0.2, W = 1, q = 0.13$, and $P = 0.1$. Two Nash equilibria exist for this set of parameter values, both weak.

One equilibrium is the strategy profile {(*Sue, Settle, Try*), (*Offer, Offer*)}. The plaintiff sues, the defendant offers to settle (whether liable or not), and the plaintiff agrees to settle. Both players know that if the defendant did not offer to settle, the plaintiff would go to court and try the case. Such **out-of-equilibrium** behavior is specified by the equilibrium, because the threat of trial is what induces the defendant to offer to settle, even though trials never occur in equilibrium. This is a Nash equilibrium because given that the plaintiff chooses

(*Sue, Settle, Try*), the defendant can do no better than (*Offer, Offer*), settling for a payoff of
−0.15 whether he is liable or not; and, given that the defendant chooses (*Offer, Offer*), the
plaintiff can do no better than the payoff of 0.15 from (*Sue, Settle, Try*).

The other equilibrium is {(*Sue, Refuse, Try*), (*Resist, Resist*)}. The plaintiff sues, the
defendant resists and makes no settlement offer, the plaintiff would refuse any offer
that was made, and goes to trial. Since he foresees the plaintiff will refuse a settlement offer of $S = 0.15$, the defendant is willing to resist, because his action makes no
difference.

One final observation on the Png Settlement Game: the game illustrates the Harsanyi
doctrine in action, because while the plaintiff and defendant differ in their beliefs as to the
probability the plaintiff will win, they do so because the defendant has different information,
not because the modeller assigns them different beliefs at the start of the game. This seems
awkward compared to the everyday way of approaching this problem in which we simply
note that potential litigants have different beliefs, and will go to trial if they both think
they can win. It is very hard to make the story consistent, however, because if the differing
beliefs are common knowledge, both players know that one of them is wrong, and each has
to believe that he is correct. This may be fine as a "reduced form," in which the attempt is
to simply describe what happens without explaining it in any depth. After all, even in the
Png Settlement Game, if a trial occurs it is because the players differ in their beliefs, so
one could simply chop off the first part of the game tree. But that is also the problem with
violating the Harsanyi doctrine: one cannot analyze how the players react to each other's
moves if the modeller simply assigns them inflexible beliefs. In the Png Settlement Game,
a settlement is rejected and a trial can occur under certain parameters because the plaintiff
weighs the probability that the defendant knows he will win versus the probablility that he
is bluffing, and sometimes decides to risk a trial. Without the Harsanyi doctrine it is very
hard to evaluate such an explanation for trials.

Notes

N2.1   The strategic and extensive forms of a game

* The term "outcome matrix" is used in Shubik (1982, p. 70), but never formally defined there.
* The term "node" is sometimes defined to include only points at which a player or Nature makes
  a decision, which excludes the end points.

N2.2   Information sets

* If you wish to depict a situation in which a player does not know whether the game has reached
  node A_1 or A_2 and he has different action sets at the two nodes, restructure the game. If you wish
  to say that he has action set (X, Y, Z) at A_1 and (X, Y) at A_2, first add action Z to the information
  set at A_2. Then specify that at A_2, action Z simply leads to a new node, A_3, at which the choice
  is between X and Y.
* The term "common knowledge" comes from Lewis (1969). Discussions include Brandenburger
  (1992) and Geanakoplos (1992). For rigorous but nonintuitive definitions of common knowledge,
  see Aumann (1976) (for two players) and Milgrom (1981a) (for n players).

N2.3   Perfect, certain, symmetric, and complete information

- Tirole (1988, p. 431) (and more precisely Fudenberg & Tirole [1991a, p. 82]) have defined games of *almost perfect* information. They use this term to refer to repeated simultaneous-move games (of the kind studied here in chapter 5) in which at each repetition all players know the results of all the moves, including those of Nature, in previous repetitions. It is a pity they use such a general-sounding term to describe so narrow a class of games; it could be usefully extended to cover all games which have perfect information except for simultaneous moves.
- **Poker classifications:** (1) Perfect, certain. (2) Incomplete, symmetric, certain. (3) Incomplete, asymmetric, certain. (4) Complete, asymmetric, certain. (5) Perfect, uncertain. (6) Incomplete, asymmetric, certain.
- For explanation of von Neumann–Morgenstern utility, see Varian (1992, chapter 11) or Kreps (1990a, chapter 3). For other approaches to utility, see Starmer (2000). Expected utility and Bayesian updating are the two foundations of standard game theory, partly because they seem realistic but more because they are so simple to use. Sometimes they do not explain people's behavior well, and there exist extensive literatures (a) pointing out anomalies, and (b) suggesting alternatives. So far no alternatives have proven to be big enough improvements to justify replacing the standard techniques, given the tradeoff between descriptive realism and added complexity in modelling. The standard response is to admit and ignore the anomalies in theoretical work, and to not press any theoretical models too hard in situations where the anomalies are likely to make a significant difference. On anomalies, see Kahneman, Slovic, & Tversky (1982) (an edited collection); Thaler (1992) (essays from his *Journal of Economic Perspectives* column); and Dawes (1988) (a good mix of psychology and business).
- Mixed strategies (to be described in section 3.1) are allowed in a game of perfect information because they are an aspect of the game's equilibrium, not of its exogenous structure.
- Although the word "perfect," appears in both "perfect information" (section 2.3) and "perfect equilibrium" (section 4.1), the concepts are unrelated.
- An unobserved move by Nature in a game of symmetric information can be represented in any of three ways: (1) as the last move in the game; (2) as the first move in the game; or (3) by replacing the payoffs with the expected payoffs and not using any explicit moves by Nature.

N2.4   The Harsanyi transformation and Bayesian games

- Mertens & Zamir (1985) probes the mathematical foundations of the Harsanyi transformation. The transformation requires the extensive form to be common knowledge, which raises subtle questions of recursion.
- A player always has some idea of what the payoffs are, so we can always assign him a subjective probability for each possible payoff. What would happen if he had no idea? Such a question is meaningless, because people always have some notion, and when they say they do not, they generally mean that their prior probabilities are low but positive for a great many possibilities. You, for instance, probably have as little idea as I do of how many cups of coffee I have consumed in my lifetime, but you would admit it to be a nonnegative number less than 3,000,000, and you could make a much more precise guess than that. On the topic of subjective probability, the classic reference is Savage (1954).
- If two players have common priors and their information partitions are finite, but they each have private information, iterated communication between them will lead to the adoption of a common posterior. This posterior is not always the posterior they would reach if they directly pooled their information, but it is almost always that posterior (Geanakoplos & Polemarchakis [1982]).

Problems

2.1:   The Monty Hall problem (easy)

You are a contestant on the TV show, "Let's Make a Deal." You face three curtains, labelled A, B, and C. Behind two of them are toasters, and behind the third is a Mazda Miata car. You choose A, and the TV showmaster says, pulling curtain B aside to reveal a toaster, "You're lucky you didn't choose B, but before I show you what is behind the other two curtains, would you like to change from curtain A to curtain C?" Should you switch? What is the exact probability that curtain C hides the Miata?

2.2:   Elmer's Apple Pie (hard)

Mrs Jones has made an apple pie for her son, Elmer, and she is trying to figure out whether the pie tasted divine, or merely good. Her pies turn out divinely a third of the time. Elmer might be ravenous, or merely hungry, and he will eat either 2, 3, or 4 pieces of pie. Mrs Jones knows he is ravenous half the time (but not which half). If the pie is divine, then, if Elmer is hungry, the probabilities of the three consumptions are (0, 0.6, 0.4), but if he is ravenous the probabilities are (0, 0, 1). If the pie is just good, then the probabilities are (0.2, 0.4, 0.4) if he is hungry and (0.1, 0.3, 0.6) if he is ravenous.

   Elmer is a sensitive, but useless, boy. He will always say that the pie is divine and his appetite weak, regardless of his true inner feelings.

(a)   What is the probability that he will eat four pieces of pie?
(b)   If Mrs Jones sees Elmer eat four pieces of pie, what is the probability that he is ravenous and the pie is merely good?
(c)   If Mrs Jones sees Elmer eat four pieces of pie, what is the probability that the pie is divine?

2.3:   Cancer tests (easy) (adapted from McMillan [1992, p. 211])

Imagine that you are being tested for cancer, using a test that is 98 percent accurate. If you indeed have cancer, the test shows positive (indicating cancer) 98 percent of the time. If you do not have cancer, it shows negative 98 percent of the time. You have heard that 1 in 20 people in the population actually have cancer. Now your doctor tells you that you tested positive, but you should not worry because his last 19 patients all died. How worried should you be? What is the probability you have cancer?

2.4:   The Battleship Problem (hard) (adapted from Barry Nalebuff, "Puzzles," *Journal of Economic Perspectives*, 2: 181–2 [Fall 1988])

The Pentagon has the choice of building one battleship or two cruisers. One battleship costs the same as two cruisers, but a cruiser is sufficient to carry out the navy's mission – if the cruiser survives to get close enough to the target. The battleship has a probability of p of carrying out its mission, whereas a cruiser only has probability $p/2$. Whatever the outcome, the war ends and any surviving ships are scrapped. Which option is superior?

2.5:   Joint ventures (medium)

Software Inc. and Hardware Inc. have formed a joint venture. Each can exert either high or low effort, which is equivalent to costs of 20 and 0. Hardware moves first, but Software cannot observe his effort.

Revenues are split equally at the end, and the two firms are risk neutral. If both firms exert low effort, total revenues are 100. If the parts are defective, the total revenue is 100; otherwise, if both exert high effort, revenue is 200, but if only one player does, revenue is 100 with probability 0.9 and 200 with probability 0.1. Before they start, both players believe that the probability of defective parts is 0.7. Hardware discovers the truth about the parts by observation before he chooses effort, but Software does not.

(a)   Draw the extensive form and put dotted lines around the information sets of Software at any nodes at which he moves.
(b)   What is the Nash equilibrium?
(c)   What is Software's belief, in equilibrium, as to the probability that Hardware chooses low effort?
(d)   If Software sees that revenue is 100, what probability does he assign to defective parts if he himself exerted high effort and he believes that Hardware chose low effort?

2.6:   California drought (hard)

California is in a drought and the reservoirs are running low. The probability of rainfall in 1991 is 1/2, but with probability 1 there will be heavy rainfall in 1992 and any saved water will be useless. The state uses rationing rather than the price system, and it must decide how much water to consume in 1990, and how much to save till 1991. Each Californian has a utility function of $U = log(w_{90}) + log(w_{91})$. Show that if the discount rate is zero the state should allocate twice as much water to 1990 as to 1991.

2.7:   Smith's energy level (easy)

The boss is trying to decide whether Smith's energy level is high or low. He can only look in on Smith once during the day. He knows if Smith's energy is low, he will be yawning with a 50 percent probability, but if it is high, he will be yawning with a 10 percent probability. Before he looks in on him, the boss thinks that there is an 80 percent probability that Smith's energy is high, but then he sees him yawning. What probability of high energy should the boss now assess?

2.8:   Two games (medium)

Suppose that Column gets to choose which of the two payoff structures in tables 2.6 and 2.7 applies to the simultaneous-move game he plays with Row. Row does not know which of these Column has chosen.

(a)   What is one example of a strategy for each player?
(b)   Find a Nash equilibrium. Is it unique? Explain your reasoning.
(c)   Is there a dominant strategy for Column? Explain why or why not.
(d)   Is there a dominant strategy for Row? Explain why or why not.
(e)   Does Row's choice of strategy depend on whether Column is rational or not? Explain why or why not.

Table 2.6   Payoffs (A), The Prisoner's Dilemma

		Column	
		Deny	*Confess*
	Deny	−1, −1	−10, 0
Row			
	Confess	0, −10	−8, −8

Payoffs to: (Row, Column).

Table 2.7   Payoffs (B), A Confession Game

		Column	
		Deny	*Confess*
	Deny	−4, −4	−12, −200
Row			
	Confess	−200, −12	−10, −410

Payoffs to: (Row, Column).

Bayes' Rule at the Bar: A Classroom Game for Chapter 2

I have wandered into a dangerous bar in Jersey City. There are six people in there. Based on past experience, I estimate that three are cold-blooded killers and three are cowardly bullies. I know that 2/3 of killers are aggressive and 1/3 reasonable; but 1/3 of cowards are aggressive and 2/3 are reasonable. Unfortunately, I spill my drink on a mean-looking rascal, who asks me if I want to die.

In crafting my response in the two seconds I have to think, I would like to know the probability I have offended a killer. Give me your estimate.

The story continues. A friend of the wet rascal comes in from the street outside the bar and learns what happened. He, too, turns aggressive. I know that the friend is just like the first rascal – a killer if the first one was a killer, a coward otherwise. Does this extra trouble change your estimate that the two of them are killers?

This game is a descendant of the game in Charles Holt & Lisa R. Anderson. "Classroom Games: Understanding Bayes Rule," *Journal of Economic Perspectives*, 10: 179–87 (Spring [1996]), but I use a different heuristic for the rule and a barroom story instead of urns. Psychologists have found that people can solve logical puzzles better if the puzzles are associated with a story involving social interactions. See chapter 7 of Robin Dunbar's *The Trouble with Science*, which explains experiments and ideas from Cosmides & Toobey (1993).

Chapter 3
mixed and continuous strategies

3.1 Mixed Strategies: The Welfare Game

The games we have looked at so far have been simple in at least one respect: the number of moves in the action set has been finite. In this chapter we allow a continuum of moves, such as when a player chooses a price between 10 and 20 or a purchase probability between 0 and 1. Chapter 3 begins by showing how to find mixed-strategy equilibria for a game with no pure-strategy equilibria. In section 3.2 the mixed-strategy equilibria are found by the payoff-equating method, and mixed strategies are applied to two dynamic games, the War of Attrition and Patent Race for a New Market. Section 3.3 takes a more general look at mixed strategy equilibria and extends the analysis to three or more players. Section 3.4 distinguishes between mixed strategies and random actions in the important class of "auditing games." Section 3.5 switches from the continuous strategy spaces of mixed strategies to strategy spaces that are continuous even with pure strategies, using the Cournot duopoly model, in which two firms choose output on the continuum between zero and infinity. Section 3.6 looks at the Bertrand model and strategic substitutes. Section 3.7 switches gears a bit and talks about four reasons why a Nash equilibrium might not exist. These last sections introduce a number of ideas besides simply how to find equilibria, ideas that will be built upon in later chapters – dynamic games in chapter 4, auditing and agency in chapters 7 and 8, and Cournot oligopoly in chapter 14.

We invoked the concept of Nash equilibrium to provide predictions of outcomes without dominant strategies, but some games lack even a Nash equilibrium. It is often useful and realistic to expand the strategy space to include random strategies, in which case a Nash equilibrium almost always exists. These random strategies are called "mixed strategies."

A **pure strategy** *maps each of a player's possible information sets to one action.* $s_i : \omega_i \to a_i.$

A **mixed strategy** *maps each of a player's possible information sets to a probability distribution over actions.*

$$s_i : \omega_i \to m(a_i), \quad \text{where } m \geq 0 \quad \text{and} \quad \int_{A_i} m(a_i) da_i = 1.$$

*A **completely mixed** strategy puts positive probability on every action, so m > 0.*

*The version of a game expanded to allow mixed strategies is called the **mixed extension** of the game.*

A pure strategy constitutes a rule that tells the player what action to choose, while a mixed strategy constitutes a rule that tells him what dice to throw in order to choose an action. If a player pursues a mixed strategy, he might choose any of several different actions in a given situation, an unpredictability which can be helpful to him. Mixed strategies occur frequently in the real world. In American football games, for example, the offensive team has to decide whether to pass or to run. Passing generally gains more yards, but what is most important is to choose an action not expected by the other team. Teams decide to run part of the time and pass part of the time in a way that seems random to observers but rational to game theorists.

The Welfare Game

The Welfare Game models a government that wishes to aid a pauper if he searches for work but not otherwise, and a pauper who searches for work only if he cannot depend on government aid.

Table 3.1 shows payoffs which represent the situation."Work" represents trying to find work, and "Loaf" represents not trying. The government wishes to help a pauper who is trying to find work, but not one who does not try. Neither player has a dominant strategy, and with a little thought we can see that no Nash equilibrium exists in pure strategies either.

Each strategy profile must be examined in turn to check for Nash equilibria.

1   The strategy profile (*Aid, Work*) is not a Nash equilibrium, because the pauper would respond with *Loaf* if the government picked *Aid*.
2   (*Aid, Loaf*) is not Nash, because the government would switch to *No Aid*.
3   (*No Aid, Loaf*) is not Nash, because the pauper would switch to *Work*.
4   (*No Aid, Work*) is not Nash, because the government would switch to *Aid*, which brings us back to (1).

The Welfare Game does have a mixed-strategy Nash equilibrium, which we can calculate. The players' payoffs are the expected values of the payments from table 3.1. If the government plays *Aid* with probability θ_a and the pauper plays *Work* with probability γ_w,

Table 3.1   The Welfare Game

		Pauper		
		Work (γ_w)		Loaf ($1 - \gamma_w$)
	Aid (θ_a)	3, 2	$\rightarrow$	$-1, 3$
Government		$\uparrow$		$\downarrow$
	No Aid ($1 - \theta_a$)	$-1, 1$	$\leftarrow$	0, 0

Payoffs to: (Government, Pauper). Arrows show how a player can increase his payoff.

the government's expected payoff is

$$\pi_{Government} = \theta_a[3\gamma_w + (-1)(1 - \gamma_w)] + [1 - \theta_a][-1\gamma_w + 0(1 - \gamma_w)],$$
$$= \theta_a[3\gamma_w - 1 + \gamma_w] - \gamma_w + \theta_a\gamma_w,$$
$$= \theta_a[5\gamma_w - 1] - \gamma_w. \tag{3.1}$$

If only pure strategies are allowed, θ_a equals zero or one, but in the mixed extension of the game, the government's action of θ_a lies on the continuum from zero to one, the pure strategies being the extreme values. If we followed the usual procedure for solving a maximization problem, we would differentiate the payoff function with respect to the choice variable to obtain the first-order condition. That procedure is actually not the best way to find mixed-strategy equilibria, which is the "payoff-equating method" I will describe in the next section. Let us use the maximization approach here, though, because it will help you understand how mixed strategies work. The first-order condition for the government would be

$$0 = \frac{d\pi_{Government}}{d\theta_a} = 5\gamma_w - 1,$$
$$\Rightarrow \gamma_w = 0.2. \tag{3.2}$$

In the mixed-strategy equilibrium, the pauper selects *Work* 20 percent of the time. This is a bit strange, though: we obtained the pauper's strategy by differentiating the government's payoff! That is because we have not used maximization in the standard way. The problem has a corner solution, because depending on the pauper's strategy, one of three strategies maximizes the government's payoff: (1) Do not aid ($\theta_a = 0$) if the pauper is unlikely enough to try to work; (2) Definitely aid ($\theta_a = 1$) if the pauper is likely enough to try to work; (3) any probability of aid, if the government is indifferent because the pauper's probability of work is right on the border line of $\gamma_w = 0.2$.

It is possibility (3) which allows a mixed strategy equilibrium to exist. To see this, go through the following four steps:

1   I assert that an optimal mixed strategy exists for the government.
2   If the pauper selects *Work* more than 20 percent of the time, the government always selects *Aid*. If the pauper selects *Work* less than 20 percent of the time, the government never selects *Aid*.
3   If a mixed strategy is to be optimal for the government, the pauper must therefore select *Work* with probability exactly 20 percent.

To obtain the probability of the government choosing *Aid*, we must turn to the pauper's payoff function, which is

$$\pi_{Pauper} = \gamma_w(2\theta_a + 1[1 - \theta_a]) + (1 - \gamma_w)(3\theta_a + [0][1 - \theta_a]),$$
$$= 2\gamma_w\theta_a + \gamma_w - \gamma_w\theta_a + 3\theta_a - 3\gamma_w\theta_a,$$
$$= -\gamma_w(2\theta_a - 1) + 3\theta_a. \tag{3.3}$$

The first-order condition is

$$\frac{d\pi_{Pauper}}{d\gamma_w} = -(2\theta_a - 1) = 0,$$

$$\Rightarrow \theta_a = 1/2. \tag{3.4}$$

If the pauper selects *Work* with probability 0.2, the government is indifferent among selecting *Aid* with probability 100 percent, 0 percent, or anything in between. If the strategies are to form a Nash equilibrium, however, the government must choose $\theta_a = 0.5$. In the mixed-strategy Nash equilibrium, the government selects *Aid* with probability 0.5 and the pauper selects *Work* with probability 0.2. The equilibrium outcome could be any of the four entries in the outcome matrix. The entries having the highest probability of occurence are (*No Aid, Loaf*) and (*Aid, Loaf*), each with probability 0.4 (=0.5[1 − 0.2]).

Interpreting Mixed Strategies

Mixed strategies are not as intuitive as pure strategies, and many modellers prefer to restrict themselves to pure-strategy equilibria in games which have them. One objection to mixed strategies is that people in the real world do not take random actions. That is not a compelling objection, because all that a model with mixed strategies requires to be a good description of the world is that the actions appear random to observers, even if the player himself has always been sure what action he would take. Even explicitly random actions are not uncommon, however – the Internal Revenue Service randomly selects which tax returns to audit, and telephone companies randomly monitor their operators' conversations to discover whether they are being polite.

A more troubling objection is that a player who selects a mixed strategy is always indifferent between two pure strategies. In the Welfare Game, the pauper is indifferent between his two pure strategies and a whole continuum of mixed strategies, given the government's mixed strategy. If the pauper were to decide not to follow the particular mixed strategy $\gamma_w = 0.2$, the equilibrium would collapse because the government would change its strategy in response. Even a small deviation in the probability selected by the pauper, a deviation that does not change his payoff if the government does not respond, destroys the equilibrium completely because the government does respond. A mixed-strategy Nash equilibrium is weak in the same sense as the (*North, North*) equilibrium in the Battle of the Bismarck Sea: to maintain the equilibrium a player who is indifferent between strategies must pick a particular strategy from out of the set of strategies.

One way to reinterpret the Welfare Game is to imagine that instead of a single pauper there are many, with identical tastes and payoff functions, all of whom must be treated alike by the government. In the mixed-strategy equilibrium, each of the paupers chooses *Work* with probability 0.2, just as in the one-pauper game. But the many-pauper game has a pure-strategy equilibrium: 20 percent of the paupers choose the pure strategy *Work* and 80 percent choose the pure strategy *Loaf*. The problem persists of how an individual pauper, indifferent between the pure strategies, chooses one or the other, but it is easy to imagine that individual characteristics outside the model could determine which actions are chosen by which paupers.

The number of players needed so that mixed strategies can be interpreted as pure strategies in this way depends on the equilibrium probability γ_w, since we cannot speak of a fraction of a player. The number of paupers must be a multiple of five in the Welfare Game in order to use this interpretation, since the equilibrium mixing probability is a multiple of $\frac{1}{5}$. For the interpretation to apply no matter how we vary the parameters of a model we would need a *continuum* of players.

Another interpretation of mixed strategies, which works even in the single-pauper game, assumes that the pauper is drawn from a population of paupers, and the government does not know his characteristics. The government only knows that there are two types of paupers, in the proportions (0.2, 0.8): those who pick *Work* if the government picks $\theta_a = 0.5$, and those who pick *Loaf*. A pauper drawn randomly from the population might be of either type. Harsanyi (1973) gives a careful interpretation of this situation.

Mixed Strategies Can Dominate Otherwise Undominated Pure Strategies

Before we continue with methods of calculating mixed strategies, it is worth taking a moment to show how they can be used to simplify the set of rational strategies players might use in a game. Chapter 1 talked about using the ideas of dominated strategies and iterated dominance as an alternative to Nash equilibrium, but it ignored the possibility of mixed strategies. That is a meaningful omission, because some pure strategy in a game may be strictly dominated by a mixed strategy, even if it is not dominated by any of the other pure strategies. The example in table 3.2 illustrates this.

In the zero-sum game of table 3.2, Row's army can attack in the North, attack in the South, or remain on the defensive. Column can respond by preparing to defend in the North or in the South. If Row attacks Column and Column has chosen to defend the other direction, Row's payoff is 4, but if Column defends the same direction, Row's payoff is 0. Defense yields Row a payoff of 1 regardless of what Column does.

Thus, Row can guarantee himself a payoff of 1 if he chooses *Defense*, which neither *North* nor *South* dominates. But suppose he plays *North* with probability 0.5 and *South* with probability 0.5. His expected payoff from this mixed strategy if Column plays *North* with probability N is

$$0.5(N)(0) + 0.5(1-N)(4) + 0.5(N)(4) + 0.5(1-N)(0) = 2, \qquad (3.5)$$

so whatever response Column picks, Row's expected payoff is higher from the mixed strategy than his payoff of 1 from *Defense*. For Row, *Defense* is strictly dominated by (0.5 *North*, 0.5 *South*).

"What if Row is risk-averse?" you may ask. "Might he not prefer the sure payoff of 1 from playing *Defense*?" No. Payoffs are specified in units of utility, not of money or some other input into a utility function. In table 3.2, it might be that Row's payoff of 0 represents

Table 3.2 Pure strategies dominated by a mixed strategy

		Column	
		North	*South*
	North	0, 0	4, −9
Row	*South*	4, −6	0, 0
	Defense	1, −1	1, −1

Payoffs to: (Row, Column).

gaining no territory, 1 represents 100 square miles, and 4 represents 800 square miles, so the marginal payoff of territory acquisition is declining. When using mixed strategies it is particularly important to keep track of the difference between utility and the inputs into utility.

Thus, regardless of risk aversion, in the unique Nash equilibrium of Pure Strategies Dominated by a Mixed Strategy, Row and Column would both choose *North* with probability $N = 0.5$ and *South* with probability 0.5. This is a player's unique equilibrium action because any other choice would cause the other player to deviate to whichever direction was not being guarded as often.

3.2   The Payoff-equating Method and Games of Timing

The next game illustrates why we might decide that a mixed-strategy equilibrium is best even if pure-strategy equilibria also exist. In the game of Chicken, the players are two Malibu teenagers, Smith and Jones. Smith drives a hot rod south down the middle of Route 1, and Jones drives north. As collision threatens, each decides whether to *Continue* in the middle or *Swerve* to the side. If a player is the only one to *Swerve*, he loses face, but if neither player picks *Swerve* they are both killed, which has an even lower payoff. If a player is the only one to *Continue*, he is covered with glory, and if both *Swerve* they are both embarassed. (We will assume that to *Swerve* means by convention to *Swerve* right; if one swerved to the left and the other to the right, the result would be both death and humiliation.) Table 3.3 assigns numbers to these four outcomes.

Chicken has two pure-strategy Nash equilibria, (*Swerve*, *Continue*) and (*Continue*, *Swerve*), but they have the defect of asymmetry. How do the players know which equilibrium is the one that will be played out? Even if they talk before the game started, it is not clear how they could arrive at an asymmetric result. We encountered the same dilemma in choosing an equilibrium for the Battle of the Sexes. As in that game, the best prediction in Chicken is perhaps the mixed-strategy equilibrium, because its symmetry makes it a focal point of sorts, and does not require any differences between the players.

The **payoff-equating** method used here to calculate the mixing probabilities for Chicken will be based on the logic followed in section 3.1, but it does not use the calculus of maximization. The basis of the payoff-equating method is that **when a player uses a mixed strategy in equilibrium, he must be getting the same payoff from each of the pure strategies used in the mixed strategy**. If one of his mixing strategies has a higher payoff, he should deviate to use just that one instead of mixing. If one has a lower payoff, he should deviate by dropping it from his mixing.

Table 3.3   Chicken

		Jones		
		Continue (θ)		*Swerve* $(1-\theta)$
	Continue (θ)	$-3, -3$	$\rightarrow$	**2, 0**
Smith		$\downarrow$		$\uparrow$
	Swerve $(1-\theta)$	**0, 2**	$\leftarrow$	1, 1

Payoffs to: (Smith, Jones). Arrows show how a player can increase his payoff.

In Chicken, therefore, Smith's payoffs from the pure strategies of *Swerve* and *Continue* must be equal. Moreover, Chicken, unlike the Welfare Game, is a symmetric game, so we can guess that in equilibrium each player will choose the same mixing probability. If that is the case, then, since the payoffs from each of Jones' pure strategies must be equal in a mixed-strategy equilibrium, it is true that

$$\pi_{Jones}(Swerve) = (\theta_{Smith}) \cdot (0) + (1 - \theta_{Smith}) \cdot (1)$$

$$= (\theta_{Smith}) \cdot (-3) + (1 - \theta_{Smith}) \cdot (2) = \pi_{Jones}(Continue). \quad (3.6)$$

From equation (3.6) we can conclude that $1 - \theta_{Smith} = 2 - 5\theta_{Smith}$, so $\theta_{Smith} = 0.25$. In the symmetric equilibrium, both players choose the same probability, so we can replace θ_{Smith} with simply θ. As for the question of the greatest interest to their mothers, the two teenagers will survive with probability $1 - (\theta \cdot \theta) = 0.9375$.

The payoff-equating method is easier to use than the calculus method if the modeller is sure which strategies will be mixed, and it can also be used in asymmetric games. In the Welfare Game, it would start with $V_g(Aid) = V_g(No\ Aid)$ and $V_p(Loaf) = V_p(Work)$, yielding two equations for the two unknowns, θ_a and γ_w, which when solved give the same mixing probabilities as were found earlier for that game. The reason why the payoff-equating and calculus maximization methods reach the same result is that the expected payoff is linear in the possible payoffs, so differentiating the expected payoff equalizes the possible payoffs. The only difference from the symmetric-game case is that two equations are solved for two different mixing probabilities instead of a single equation for the one mixing probability that both players use.

It is interesting to see what happens if the payoff of -3 in the northwest corner of table 3.3 is generalized to x. Solving the analog of equation (3.6) then yields

$$\theta = \frac{1}{1 - x}. \quad (3.7)$$

If $x = -3$, this yields $\theta = 0.25$, as was just calculated, and if $x = -9$, it yields $\theta = 0.10$. This makes sense; increasing the loss from crashes reduces the equilibrium probability of continuing down the middle of the road. But what if $x = 0.5$? Then the equilibrium probability of continuing appears to be $\theta = 2$, which is impossible; probabilities are bounded by zero and one.

When a mixing probability is calculated to be greater than one or less than zero, the implication is either that the modeller has made an arithmetic mistake or, as in this case, that he is wrong in thinking that the game has a mixed-strategy equilibrium. If $x = 0.5$, one can still try to solve for the mixing probabilities, but, in fact, the only equilibrium is in pure strategies – (*Continue, Continue*) (the game has become a Prisoner's Dilemma). The absurdity of probabilities greater than one or less than zero is a valuable aid to the fallible modeller because such results show that he is wrong about the qualitative nature of the equilibrium – it is pure, not mixed. Or, if the modeller is not sure whether the equilibrium is mixed or not, he can use this approach to prove that the equilibrium is not in mixed strategies.

The War of Attrition

After the start of the book with the Dry Cleaners Game, we have been looking at games that are either simultaneous or have the players move in sequence. Some situations, however, are naturally modelled as flows of time during which players repeatedly choose their moves. The War of Attrition is one of these. It is a game something like Chicken stretched out over time, where both players start with *Continue*, and the game ends when the first one picks *Swerve*. Until the game ends, both earn a negative amount per period, and when one exits, he earns zero and the other player earns a reward for outlasting him.

We will look at a war of attrition in discrete time. We will continue with Smith and Jones, who have both survived to maturity and now play games with more expensive toys: they control two firms in an industry which is a natural monopoly, with demand strong enough for one firm to operate profitably, but not two. The possible actions are to *Exit* or to *Continue*. In each period that both *Continue*, each earns −1. If a firm exits, its losses cease and the remaining firm obtains the value of the market's monopoly profit, which we set equal to 3. We will set the discount rate equal to $r > 0$, although that is inessential to the model, even if the possible length of the game is infinite (discount rates will be discussed in detail in section 4.3).

The War of Attrition has a continuum of Nash equilibria. One simple equilibrium is for Smith to choose (*Continue* regardless of what Jones does) and for Jones to choose (*Exit* immediately), which are best responses to each other. But we will solve for a symmetric equilibrium in which each player chooses the same mixed strategy: a constant probability θ that the player picks *Exit* given that the other player has not yet exited.

We can calculate θ as follows, adopting the perspective of Smith. Denote the expected discounted value of Smith's payoffs by V_{stay} if he stays and V_{exit} if he exits immediately. These two pure strategy payoffs must be equal in a mixed strategy equilibrium (which was the basis for the payoff-equating method). If Smith exits, he obtains $V_{exit} = 0$. If Smith stays in, his payoff depends on what Jones does. If Jones stays in too, which has probability $(1 - \theta)$, Smith gets −1 currently and his expected value for the following period, which is discounted using r, is unchanged. If Jones exits immediately, which has probability θ, then Smith receives a payment of 3. In symbols,

$$V_{stay} = \theta \cdot (3) + (1 - \theta) \left(-1 + \left[\frac{V_{stay}}{1 + r} \right] \right),$$ (3.8)

which, after a little manipulation, becomes

$$V_{stay} = \left(\frac{1 + r}{r + \theta} \right) (4\theta - 1).$$ (3.9)

Once we equate V_{stay} to V_{exit}, which equals zero, equation (3.9) tells us that $\theta = 0.25$ in equilibrium, and that this is independent of the discount rate r.

Returning from arithmetic to ideas, why does Smith *Exit* immediately with positive probability, given that Jones will exit first if Smith waits long enough? The reason is that Jones might choose to continue for a long time and both players would earn −1 each period until Jones exited. The equilibrium mixing probability is calculated so that both of them are likely to stay in long enough so that their losses soak up the gain from being the survivor. Papers on the war of attrition include Fudenberg & Tirole (1986b), Ghemawat & Nalebuff (1985), Maynard Smith (1974), Nalebuff & Riley (1985), and Riley (1980). All are examples of "rent-seeking" welfare losses. As Posner (1975) and Tullock (1967) have pointed out, the real costs of acquiring rents can be much bigger than the second-order triangle losses from allocative distortions, and the war of attrition shows that the big loss from a natural monopoly might be not the reduced trade that results from higher prices, but the cost of the battle to gain the monopoly.

We are likely to see wars of attrition in business when new markets open up, either new geographic markets for old goods or new goods, especially when it appears the market may be a natural monopoly, as in situations of network externalities. McAfee (2002, p. 76, 364) cites as examples the fight between Sky Television and British Satellite Broadcasting for the British satellite TV market; Amazon versus Barnes and Noble for the Internet book market; and Windows CE versus Palm in the market for handheld computers. Wars of attrition can also arise in declining industries, as a contest for which firm can exit the latest. In the United States, for example, the number of firms making rockets declined from six in 1990 to two by 2002 (McAfee [2002, p. 104]).

In the War of Attrition, the reward goes to the player who does not choose the move which ends the game, and a cost is paid each period that both players refuse to end it. Various other **timing games** also exist. The opposite of a war of attrition is a **preemption game**, in which the reward goes to the player who chooses the move which ends the game, and a cost is paid if both players choose that move, but no cost is incurred in a period when neither player chooses it. The game of **Grab the Dollar** is an example. A dollar is placed on the table between Smith and Jones, who each must decide whether to grab for it or not. If both grab, both are fined one dollar. This could be set up as a one-period game, a T-period game, or an infinite-period game, but the game definitely ends when someone grabs the dollar. Table 3.4 shows the payoffs.

Like the War of Attrition, Grab the Dollar has asymmetric equilibria in pure strategies, and a symmetric equilibrium in mixed strategies. In the infinite-period version, the equilibrium probability of grabbing is 0.5 per period in the symmetric equilibrium.

Still another class of timing games are duels, in which the actions are discrete occurrences which the players locate at particular points in continuous time. Two players with guns approach each other and must decide when to shoot. In a **noisy duel**, if a player shoots and misses, the other player observes the miss and can kill the first player at his leisure. An equilibrium exists in pure strategies for the noisy duel. In a **silent duel**, a player does not know when the other player has fired, and the equilibrium is in mixed strategies. Karlin (1959) has details on duelling games, and chapter 4 of Fudenberg & Tirole (1991a) has an excellent discussion of games of timing in general. See also Shubik (1954) on the rather different problem of whom to shoot first in a battle with three or more sides.

We will go through one more game of timing to see how to derive a continuous mixed strategies probability distribution, instead of just the single number derived earlier. In presenting this game, a new presentation scheme will be useful. If a game has a continuous strategy set, it is harder or impossible to depict the payoffs using tables or the extensive

Table 3.4   Grab the Dollar

		Jones		
		Grab		*Don't Grab*
	Grab	$-1, -1$	$\rightarrow$	**1, 0**
Smith		$\downarrow$		$\uparrow$
	Don't Grab	**0, 1**	$\leftarrow$	0, 0

Payoffs to: (Smith, Jones). Arrows show how a player can increase his payoff.

form using a tree. Tables of the sort we have been using so far would require a continuum of rows and columns, and trees a continuum of branches. A new format for game descriptions of the players, actions, and payoffs will be used for the rest of the book. The new format will be similar to the way the rules of the Dry Cleaners Game were presented in section 1.1.

Patent Race for a New Market

PLAYERS
Three identical firms, Apex, Brydox, and Central.

THE ORDER OF PLAY
Each firm simultaneously chooses research spending $x_i \geq 0$ ($i = a, b, c$).

PAYOFFS
Firms are risk-neutral and the discount rate is zero. Innovation occurs at time $T(x_i)$ where $T' < 0$. The value of the patent is V, and if several players innovate simultaneously they share its value. Let us look at the payoff of firm $i = a, b, c$, with j and k indexing the other two firms:

$$\pi_i = \begin{cases} V - x_i & \text{if } T(x_i) < Min\{T(x_j), T(x_k))\} \quad \text{(Firm } i \text{ gets the patent)} \\ \dfrac{V}{2} - x_i & \text{if } T(x_i) = Min\{T(x_j), T(x_k)\} \quad \text{(Firm } i \text{ shares the patent with} \\ & \qquad\quad < Max\{T(x_j), T(x_k)\} \quad \text{1 other firm)} \\ \dfrac{V}{3} - x_i & \text{if } T(x_i) = T(x_j) = T(x_k) \quad \text{(Firm } i \text{ shares the patent with} \\ & \qquad\qquad\qquad\qquad\qquad\qquad\quad \text{2 other firms)} \\ -x_i & \text{if } T(x_i) > Min\{T(x_j), T(x_k)\} \quad \text{(Firm } i \text{ does not get the patent)} \end{cases}$$

The format first assigns the game a title, after which it lists the players, the order of play (together with who observes what), and the payoff functions. Listing the players is redundant, strictly speaking, since they can be deduced from the order of play, but it is useful for letting the reader know what kind of model to expect. The format includes very little explanation; that is postponed, lest it obscure the description. This exact format is not standard in the literature, but every good article begins its technical section by specifying the same information, if in a less structured way, and the novice is strongly advised to use all the structure he can.

The game Patent Race for a New Market does not have any pure strategy Nash equilibria, because the payoff functions are discontinuous. A slight difference in research by one player can make a big difference in the payoffs, as shown in figure 3.1 for fixed values of x_b and x_c. The research levels shown in figure 3.1 are not equilibrium values. If Apex chose any research level x_a less than V, Brydox would respond with $x_a + \varepsilon$ and win the patent. If Apex chose $x_a = V$, then Brydox and Central would respond with $x_b = 0$ and $x_c = 0$, which would make Apex want to switch to $x_a = \varepsilon$.

There does exist a symmetric mixed strategy equilibrium. Denote the probability that firm i chooses a research level less than or equal to x as $M_i(x)$. This function describes the firm's mixed strategy. In a mixed-strategy equilibrium a player is indifferent between

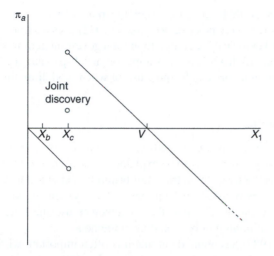

Figure 3.1   The payoffs in Patent Race for a New Market.

any of the pure strategies among which he is mixing (the basis of section 3.2's payoff-equating method). Since we know that the pure strategies $x_a = 0$ and $x_a = V$ yield zero payoffs, if Apex mixes over the support $[0, V]$ then the expected payoff for every strategy mixed between must also equal zero. The expected payoff from the pure strategy x_a is the expected value of winning minus the cost of research. Letting x stand for nonrandom and X for random variables, this is

$$\pi_a(x_a) = V \cdot Pr(x_a \geq X_b, x_a \geq X_c) - x_a = 0 = \pi_a(x_a = 0), \tag{3.10}$$

which can be rewritten as

$$V \cdot Pr(X_b \leq x_a)Pr(X_c \leq x_a) - x_a = 0, \tag{3.11}$$

or

$$V \cdot M_b(x_a)M_c(x_a) - x_a = 0. \tag{3.12}$$

We can rearrange equation (3.12) to obtain

$$M_b(x_a)M_c(x_a) = \frac{x_a}{V}. \tag{3.13}$$

If all three firms choose the same mixing distribution M, then

$$M(x) = \left(\frac{x}{V}\right)^{1/2} \quad \text{for } 0 \leq x \leq V. \tag{3.14}$$

What is noteworthy about a patent race is not the nonexistence of a pure-strategy equilibrium but the overexpenditure on research. All three players have expected payoffs of zero, because the patent value V is completely dissipated in the race. As in Brecht's *Threepenny Opera* (Act III, Scene 7), "When all race after happiness/Happiness comes in last." To be sure, the innovation is made earlier than it would have been by a monopolist, but hurrying the innovation is not worth the cost, from society's point of view, a result that would persist even if the discount rate were positive. Rogerson (1982) uses a game very similar to Patent Race for a New Market to analyze competition for a government monopoly franchise. Also, we will see in chapter 13 that this is an example of an "all-pay auction," and the techniques and findings of auction theory can be quite useful when modelling this kind of conflict.

Correlated Strategies

One example of a war of attrition is setting up a market for a new security, which may be a natural monopoly for reasons to be explained in section 8.5. Certain stock exchanges have avoided the destructive symmetric equilibrium by using lotteries to determine which of them would trade newly listed stock options under a system similar to the football draft.[1] Rather than waste resources fighting, these exchanges use the lottery as a coordinating device, even though it might not be a binding agreement.

Aumann (1974, 1987) has pointed out that it is often important whether players can use the same randomizing device for their mixed strategies. If they can, we refer to the resulting strategies as **correlated strategies**. Consider the game of Chicken. The only mixed-strategy equilibrium is the symmetric one in which each player chooses *Continue* with probability 0.25, and the expected payoff is 0.75. A correlated equilibrium would be for the two players to flip a coin, and for Smith to choose *Continue* if it comes up heads, and Jones if it comes up tails. Each player's strategy is a best response to the other's, the probability of each choosing *Continue* is 0.5, and the expected payoff for each is 1.0, which is better than the 0.75 achieved without correlated strategies.

Usually the randomizing device is not modelled explicitly when a model refers to correlated equilibrium. If it is, uncertainty over variables that do not affect preferences, endowments, or production is called **extrinsic uncertainty.** Extrinsic uncertainty is the driving force behind **sunspot models**, so called because the random appearance of sunspots might cause macroeconomic changes via correlated equilibria (Maskin & Tirole [1987]) or bets made between players (Cass & Shell [1983]).

One way to model correlated strategies is to specify a move in which Nature gives each player the ability to commit first to an action such as *Continue* with equal probability. This is often realistic because it amounts to a zero probability of both players entering the industry at exactly the same time without anyone knowing in advance who will be the lucky starter. Neither firm has an a priori advantage, but the outcome is efficient.

The population interpretation of mixed strategies cannot be used for correlated strategies. In ordinary mixed strategies, the mixing probabilities are statistically independent, whereas in correlated strategies they are not. In Chicken, the usual mixed strategy can be interpreted as populations of Smiths and Joneses, each population consisting of a certain proportion of pure swervers and pure stayers. The correlated equilibrium has no such interpretation.

Another coordinating device, useful in games that, like the Battle of the Sexes, have a coordination problem, is **cheap talk** (Crawford & Sobel [1982], Farrell [1987]). Cheap talk refers to costless communication before the game proper begins. In Ranked Coordination, cheap talk instantly allows the players to make the desirable outcome a focal

---

[1] "Big Board Will Begin Trading of Options on 4 Stocks IT Lists," *Wall Street Journal*, p. 15 (October 4, 1985).

point. In Chicken, cheap talk is useless, because it is dominant for each player to announce that he will choose *Continue*. But in the Battle of the Sexes, coordination and conflict are combined. Without communication, the only symmetric equilibrium is in mixed strategies. If both players know that making inconsistent announcements will lead to the wasteful mixed-strategy outcome, then they are willing to mix announcing whether they will go to the ballet or the prize fight. With many periods of announcements before the final decision, their chances of coming to an agreement are high. Thus communication can help reduce inefficiency even if the two players are in conflict.

*3.3   Mixed Strategies with General Parameters and N Players: The Civic Duty Game

Having looked at a number of specific games with mixed-strategy equilibria, let us now apply the method to the general game of table 3.5.

To find the game's equilibrium, equate the payoffs from the pure strategies. For Row, this yields

$$\pi_{Row}(Up) = \theta a + (1 - \theta)b \tag{3.15}$$

and

$$\pi_{Row}(Down) = \theta c + (1 - \theta)d. \tag{3.16}$$

Equating (3.15) and (3.16) gives us

$$\theta(a + d - b - c) + b - d = 0, \tag{3.17}$$

which yields

$$\theta^* = \frac{d - b}{(d - b) + (a - c)}. \tag{3.18}$$

Similarly, equating the payoffs for Column gives

$$\pi_{Column}(Left) = \gamma w + (1 - \gamma)y = \pi_{Column}(Right) = \gamma x + (1 - \gamma)z, \tag{3.19}$$

which yields

$$\gamma^* = \frac{z - y}{(z - y) + (w - x)}. \tag{3.20}$$

Table 3.5   The General 2-by-2 Game

		Column	
		Left (θ)	*Right* ($1 - \theta$)
	Up (γ)	a, w	b, x
Row			
	Down ($1 - \gamma$)	c, y	d, z

Payoffs to: (Row, Column).

The equilibrium represented by (3.18) and (3.20) illustrates a number of features of mixed strategies.

First, it is possible, but wrong, to follow the payoff-equating method for finding a mixed strategy even if no mixed strategy equilibrium actually exists. Suppose, for example, that *Down* is a strictly dominant strategy for Row, so $c > a$ and $d > b$. Row is unwilling to mix, so the equilibrium is not in mixed strategies. Equation (3.18) would be misleading, though some idiocy would be required to stay misled for very long since the equation implies that $\theta^* > 1$ or $\theta^* \leq 0$ in cases like that.

Second, the exact features of the equilibrium in mixed strategies depend heavily on the cardinal values of the payoffs, not just on their ordinal values like the pure strategy equilibria in other 2-by-2 games. Ordinal rankings are all that is needed to know that an equilibrium exists in mixed strategies, but cardinal values are needed to know the exact mixing probabilities. If the payoff to Column from (*Confess, Confess*) is changed slightly in the Prisoner's Dilemma it makes no difference at all to the equilibrium. If the payoff of z to Column from (*Down, Right*) is increased slightly in the General 2-by-2 Game, equation (3.20) says that the mixing probability γ^* will change also.

Third, the payoffs can be changed by affine transformations without changing the game substantively, even though cardinal payoffs do matter (which is to say that monotonic but non-affine transformations do make a difference). Let each payoff π in table 3.5 become $\alpha + \beta\pi$. Equation (3.20) then becomes

$$
\begin{aligned}
\gamma^* &= \frac{\alpha + \beta z - \alpha - \beta y}{(\alpha + \beta z - \alpha - \beta y) + (\alpha + \beta w - \alpha - \beta x)}, \\
&= \frac{z - y}{(z - y) + (w - x)}.
\end{aligned}
\tag{3.21}
$$

The affine transformation has left the equilibrium strategy unchanged.

Fourth, as was mentioned earlier in connection with the Welfare Game, each player's mixing probability depends only on the payoff parameters of the other player. Row's strategy γ^* in equation (3.20) depends on the parameters w, x, y, and z, which are the payoff parameters for Column, and have no direct relevance for Row.

Categories of Games with Mixed Strategies

Table 3.6 uses the players and actions of table 3.5 to depict three major categories of 2-by-2 games in which mixed-strategy equilibria are important. Some games fall in none of these categories – those with tied payoffs, such as the Swiss Cheese Game in which all eight payoffs equal zero – but the three games in table 3.6 encompass a wide variety of economic phenomena.

Discoordination games have a single equilibrium, in mixed strategies. The payoffs are such that either (1) $a > c, d > b, x > w$, and $y > z$, or (2) $c > a, b > d, w > x$, and $z > y$. The Welfare Game is a discoordination game, as are Auditing Game I in the next section and Matching Pennies in problem 3.3.

Coordination games have three equilibria: two symmetric equilibria in pure strategies and one symmetric equilibrium in mixed strategies. The payoffs are such that $a > c, d > b$,

Table 3.6   2-by-2 Games with mixed-strategy equilibria

$a,w \rightarrow b,x$ $\uparrow \qquad \downarrow$ $c,y \leftarrow d,z$	$a,w \leftarrow b,x$ $\downarrow \qquad \uparrow$ $c,y \rightarrow d,z$	$a,w \leftarrow b,x$ $\uparrow \qquad \downarrow$ $c,y \rightarrow d,z$	$a,w \rightarrow b,x$ $\downarrow \qquad \uparrow$ $c,y \leftarrow d,z$
Discoordination Games	Coordination Games		Contribution Games

Payoffs to: (Row, Column). Arrows show how a player can increase his payoff.

$w > x$, and $z > y$. Ranked Coordination and the Battle of the Sexes are two varieties of coordination games in which the players have the same and opposite rankings of the pure-strategy equilibria.

Contribution games have three equilibria: two asymmetric equilibria in pure strategies and one symmetric equilibrium in mixed strategies. The payoffs are such that $c > a, b > d$, $x > w$, and $y > z$. Also, it must be true that ($c < b$ and $y > x$) or ($c > b$ and $y < x$).

I have used the name "contribution game" because the type of game described by this term is often used to model a situation in which two players each have a choice of taking some action that contributes to the public good, but would each like the other player to bear the cost. The difference from the Prisoner's Dilemma is that each player in a contribution game is willing to bear the cost alone if necessary.

Contribution games appear to be quite different from the Battle of the Sexes, but they are essentially the same. Both of them have two pure-strategy equilibria, ranked oppositely by the two players. In mathematical terms, the fact that contribution games have the equilibria in the southwest and northeast corners of the outcome matrix whereas coordination games have them in the northwest and southeast, is unimportant; the location of the equilibria could be changed by just switching the order of Row's strategies. We do view real situations differently, however, depending on whether players choose the same actions or different actions in equilibrium.

Let us take a look at a particular contribution game to show how to extend two-player games to games with several players. A notorious example in social psychology is the murder of Kitty Genovese, who was killed in New York City in 1964 despite the presence of numerous neighbors. "For more than half an hour 38 respectable, law-abiding citizens in Queens watched a killer stalk and stab a woman in three separate attacks in Kew Gardens. . . . Twice the sound of their voices and the sudden glow of their bedroom lights interrupted him and frightened him off. Each time he returned, sought her out, and stabbed her again. Not one person telephoned the police during the assault; one witness called after the woman was dead" (Martin Gansberg, "38 Who Saw Murder Didn't Call Police," *The New York Times*, March 27, 1964, p. 1). Even as hardened an economist as myself finds it somewhat distasteful to call this a "game," but game theory does explain what happened.

I will use a less appalling story for our model. In the Civic Duty Game of table 3.7, Smith and Jones observe a burglary taking place. Each would like someone to call the police and stop the burglary because having it stopped adds 10 to his payoff, but neither wishes to make the call himself because the effort subtracts 3. If Smith can be assured that Jones will call, Smith himself will ignore the burglary. Table 3.7 shows the payoffs.

The Civic Duty Game has two asymmetric pure-strategy equilibria and a symmetric mixed-strategy equilibrium. In solving for the mixed-strategy equilibrium, let us move from two players to N players. In the N-player version of the game, the payoff to Smith is 0

Table 3.7   The Civic Duty Game

		Jones	
		Ignore (γ)	Telephone ($1 - \gamma$)
	Ignore (γ)	0, 0 $\rightarrow$	**10, 7**
Smith		$\downarrow$	$\uparrow$
	Telephone ($1 - \gamma$)	**7, 10** $\leftarrow$	7, 7

Payoffs to:(Row, Column). Arrows show how a player can increase his payoff.

if nobody calls, 7 if he himself calls, and 10 if one or more of the other $(N - 1)$ players calls. This game also has asymmetric pure-strategy and a symmetric mixed-strategy equilibrium. If all players use the same probability γ of *Ignore*, the probability that the other $(N - 1)$ players besides Smith all choose *Ignore* is γ^{N-1}, so the probability that one or more of them chooses *Telephone* is $(1 - \gamma^{N-1})$. Thus, equating Smith's pure-strategy payoffs using the payoff-equating method of equilibrium calculation yields

$$\pi_{Smith}(Telephone) = 7 = \pi_{Smith}(Ignore) = \gamma^{N-1}(0) + (1 - \gamma^{N-1})(10). \tag{3.22}$$

Equation (3.22) tells us that

$$\gamma^{N-1} = 0.3 \tag{3.23}$$

and

$$\gamma^* = 0.3^{1/(N-1)}. \tag{3.24}$$

If $N = 2$, Smith chooses *Ignore* with a probability of 0.30. As N increases, Smith's expected payoff remains equal to 7 whether $N = 2$ or $N = 38$, since his expected payoff equals his payoff from the pure strategy of *Telephone*. The probability of *Ignore*, however, (γ^*) increases with N. If $N = 38$, the value of γ^* is about 0.97. When there are more players, each player relies more on somebody else calling.

The probability that nobody calls is γ^{*N}. Equation (3.23) shows that $\gamma^{*N-1} = 0.3$, so $\gamma^{*N} = 0.3\gamma^*$, which is increasing in N because γ^* is increasing in N. If $N = 2$, the probability that neither player phones the police is $\gamma^{*2} = 0.09$. When there are 38 players, the probability rises to γ^{*38}, about 0.29. The more people that watch a crime, the less likely it is to be reported.

As in the Prisoner's Dilemma, the disappointing result in the Civic Duty Game suggests a role for active policy. The mixed-strategy outcome is clearly bad. The expected payoff per player remains equal to 7 whether there is 1 player or 38, whereas if the equilibrium played out was the equilibrium in which one and only one player called the police, the average payoff would rise from 7 with 1 player to about 9.9 with 38 $(=[1(7) + 37(10)]/38)$. A situation like this requires something to make one of the pure-strategy equilibria a focal point. The problem is divided responsibility. One person must be made responsible for calling the police, whether by tradition (e.g., the oldest person on the block always calls the police), or direction (e.g., Smith shouts to Jones: "Call the police!").

*3.4 Randomizing Is Not Always Mixing: The Auditing Game

The next three games will illustrate the difference between mixed strategies and random actions, a subtle but important distinction. In all three games, the Internal Revenue Service must decide whether to audit a certain class of suspect tax returns to discover whether they are accurate or not. The goal of the IRS is to either prevent or catch cheating at minimum cost. The suspects want to cheat only if they will not be caught. Let us assume that the benefit of preventing or catching cheating is 4, the cost of auditing is C, where $C < 4$, the cost to the suspects of obeying the law is 1, and the cost of being caught is the fine $F > 1$.

Even with all of this information, there are several ways to model the situation. Table 3.8 shows one way: a 2-by-2 simultaneous-move game.

Auditing Game I is a discoordination game, with only a mixed strategy equilibrium. Equations (3.18) and (3.20), or the payoff-equating method tell us that

$$Probability(Cheat) = \theta^* = \frac{4 - (4 - C)}{(4 - (4 - C)) + ((4 - C) - 0)},$$

$$= \frac{C}{4} \tag{3.25}$$

and

$$Probability(Audit) = \gamma^* = \frac{-1 - 0}{(-1 - 0) + (-F - (-1))},$$

$$= \frac{1}{F}. \tag{3.26}$$

Using (3.25) and (3.26), the payoffs are

$$\pi_{IRS}(Audit) = \pi_{IRS}(Trust) = \theta^*(0) + (1 - \theta^*)(4),$$

$$= 4 - C \tag{3.27}$$

and

$$\pi_{Suspect}(Obey) = \pi_{Suspect}(Cheat) = \gamma^*(-F) + (1 - \gamma^*)(0),$$

$$= -1. \tag{3.28}$$

A second way to model the situation is as a sequential game. Let us call this Auditing Game II. The simultaneous game implicitly assumes that both players choose their actions

Table 3.8 Auditing Game I

		Suspects	
		Cheat (θ)	Obey ($1 - \theta$)
	Audit (γ)	$4 - C, -F$ →	$4 - C, -1$
IRS		↑	↓
	Trust ($1 - \gamma$)	$0, 0$ ←	$4, -1$

Payoffs to: (IRS, Suspects). Arrows show how a player can increase his payoff.

without knowing what the other player has decided. In the sequential game, the IRS chooses government policy first, and the suspects react to it. The equilibrium in Auditing Game II is in pure strategies, a general feature of sequential games of perfect information. In equilibrium, the IRS chooses *Audit*, anticipating that the suspect will then choose *Obey*. The payoffs are $(4 - C)$ for the IRS and -1 for the suspects, the same for both players as in Auditing Game I, although now there is more auditing and less cheating and fine-paying.

We can go a step further. Suppose the IRS does not have to adopt a policy of auditing or trusting every suspect, but instead can audit a random sample. This is not necessarily a mixed strategy. In Auditing Game I, the equilibrium strategy was to audit all suspects with probability $1/F$ and none of them otherwise. That is different from announcing in advance that the IRS will audit a random sample of $1/F$ of the suspects. For Auditing Game III, suppose the IRS move first, but let its move consist of the choice of the proportion α of tax returns to be audited.

We know that the IRS is willing to deter the suspects from cheating, since it would be willing to choose $\alpha = 1$ and replicate the result in Auditing Game II if it had to. It chooses α so that

$$\pi_{suspect}(Obey) \geq \pi_{suspect}(Cheat), \tag{3.29}$$

that is,

$$-1 \geq \alpha(-F) + (1 - \alpha)(0). \tag{3.30}$$

In equilibrium, therefore, the IRS chooses $\alpha = 1/F$ and the suspects respond with *Obey*. The IRS payoff is $(4 - \alpha C)$, which is better than the $(4 - C)$ in the other two games, and the suspect's payoff is -1, exactly the same as before.

The equilibrium of Auditing Game III is in pure strategies, even though the IRS's action is random. It is different from Auditing Game I because the IRS must go ahead with the costly audit even if the suspect chooses *Obey*. Auditing Game III is different in another way also: its action set is continuous. In Auditing Games I and Auditing Game II the action set is {*Audit, Trust*}, although the strategy set becomes $\gamma \in [0, 1]$ once mixed strategies are allowed. In Auditing Game III, the action set is $\alpha \in [0, 1]$, and the strategy set would allow mixing of any of the elements in the action set, although mixed strategies are pointless for the IRS because the game is sequential.

Games with mixed strategies are like games with continuous strategies since a probability is drawn from the continuum between zero and one. Auditing Game III also has a strategy drawn from the interval between zero and one, but it is not a mixed strategy to pick an audit probability of, say, 70 percent. An example of a mixed strategy would be the choice of a probability 0.5 of an audit probability of 60 percent and 0.5 of 80 percent. The big difference between the pure strategy choice of an audit probability of 0.70 and the mixed strategy choice of (0.5–60% audit, 0.5–80% audit), both of which yield an audit probability of 70 percent, is that the pure strategy is an irreversible choice that might be used even when the player is not indifferent between pure strategies, but the mixed strategy is the result of a player who in equilibrium is indifferent as to what he does. The next section will show another difference between mixed strategies and continuous strategies: the payoffs are linear in the mixed-strategy probability, as is evident from payoff equations (3.15) and (3.16), but they can be nonlinear in continuous strategies generally.

I have used auditing here mainly to illustrate what mixed strategies are and are not, but auditing is interesting in itself and optimal auditing schemes have many twists to them. An example is the idea of **cross-checking**. Suppose an auditor is supposed to check the value of some variable $x \in [0, 1]$, but his employer is worried that he will not report the true value. This might be because the auditor will be lazy and guess rather than go to the effort of finding x, or because some third party will bribe him, or that certain values of x will trigger punishments or policies the auditor dislikes (this model applies even if x is the auditor's own performance on some other task). The idea of cross-checking is to hire a second auditor and ask him to simultaneously report x. If both auditors report the same x, they are both rewarded, but if they report different values they are both punished. There will still be multiple equilibria, because anything in which they report the same value is an equilibrium. But at least truthful reporting becomes a possible equilibrium. See Kandori & Matsushima (1998) for details (and the further discussion of cross-checking in chapter 10).

3.5   Continuous Strategies: The Cournot Game

Most of the games so far in the book have had discrete strategy spaces: *Aid* or *No Aid*, *Confess* or *Deny*. Quite often when strategies are discrete and moves are simultaneous, no pure-strategy equilibrium exists. The only sort of compromise possible in the Welfare Game, for instance, is to choose *Aid* sometimes and *No Aid* sometimes, a mixed strategy. If "*A Little Aid*" were a possible action, maybe there would be a pure-strategy equilibrium. The simultaneous-move game we discuss next, the Cournot Game, has a continuous strategy space even without mixing. It models a duopoly in which two firms choose output levels in competition with each other.

The Cournot Game

PLAYERS
Firms Apex and Brydox

THE ORDER OF PLAY
Apex and Brydox simultaneously choose quantities q_a and q_b from the set $[0, \infty)$.

PAYOFFS
Marginal cost is constant at $c = 12$. Demand is a function of the total quantity sold, $Q = q_a + q_b$, and we will assume it to be linear (for generalization see chapter 14), and, in fact, will use the following specific function:

$$p(Q) = 120 - q_a - q_b. \tag{3.31}$$

Payoffs are profits, which are given by a firm's price times its quantity minus its costs, that is,

$$\pi_{Apex} = (120 - q_a - q_b)q_a - cq_a = (120 - c)q_a - q_a^2 - q_aq_b;$$
$$\pi_{Brydox} = (120 - q_a - q_b)q_b - cq_b = (120 - c)q_b - q_aq_b - q_b^2. \tag{3.32}$$

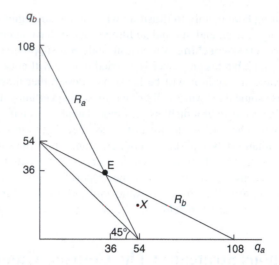

Figure 3.2   Reaction curves in the Cournot Game.

If this game were cooperative (see section 1.2), firms would end up producing somewhere on the 45° line in figure 3.2, where total output is the monopoly output and maximizes the sum of the payoffs. The monopoly output maximizes $pQ - cQ = (120 - Q - c)Q$ with respect to the total output of Q, resulting in the first-order condition

$$120 - c - 2Q = 0, \tag{3.33}$$

which implies a total output of $Q = 54$ and a price of 66. Deciding how much of that output of 54 should be produced by each firm – where the firm's output should be located on the 45° line – would be a zero-sum cooperative game, an example of bargaining. But since the Cournot Game is noncooperative, the strategy profiles such that $q_a + q_b = 54$ are not necessarily equilibria despite their Pareto optimality (where Pareto optimality is defined from the point of view of the two players, not of consumers, and under the implicit assumption that price discrimination cannot be used).

Cournot noted in chapter 7 of his 1838 book that this game has a unique equilibrium when demand curves are linear. To find that "Cournot–Nash" equilibrium, we need to refer to the **best-response functions** for the two players. If Brydox produced 0, Apex would produce the monopoly output of 54. If Brydox produced $q_b = 108$ or greater, the market price would fall to 12 and Apex would choose to produce zero. The best response function is found by maximizing Apex's payoff, given in equation (3.32), with respect to his strategy, q_a. This generates the first-order condition $120 - c - 2q_a - q_b = 0$, or

$$q_a = 60 - \left(\frac{q_b + c}{2}\right) = 54 - \left(\frac{1}{2}\right) q_b. \tag{3.34}$$

Another name for the best response function, the name usually used in the context of the Cournot Game, is the **reaction function**. Both names are somewhat misleading since the players move simultaneously with no chance to reply or react, but they are useful in imagining what a player would do if the rules of the game did allow him to move second.

The reaction functions of the two firms are labelled R_a and R_b in figure 3.2. Where they cross, point E, is the **Cournot–Nash equilibrium**, which is simply the Nash equilibrium when the strategies consist of quantities. Algebraically, it is found by solving the two reaction functions for q_a and q_b, which generates the unique equilibrium, $q_a = q_b = 40 - c/3 = 36$. The equilibrium price is then 48 ($= 120 - 36 - 36$).

In the Cournot Game, the Nash equilibrium has the particularly nice property of **stability**: we can imagine how starting from some other strategy profile the players might reach the equilibrium. If the initial strategy profile is point X in figure 3.2, for example, Apex's best response is to decrease q_a and Brydox's is to increase q_b, which moves the profile closer to the equilibrium. But this is special to the Cournot Game, and Nash equilibria are not always stable in this way.

Stackelberg Equilibrium

There are many ways to model duopoly. The three most prominent are Cournot, Stackelberg, and Bertrand. Stackelberg equilibrium differs from Cournot in that one firm gets to choose its quantity first. If Apex moved first, what output would it choose? Apex knows how Brydox will react to its choice, so it picks the point on Brydox's reaction curve that maximizes Apex's profit (see figure 3.3).

The Stackelberg Game

PLAYERS
Firms Apex and Brydox

THE ORDER OF PLAY
1   Apex chooses quantity q_a from the set $[0, \infty)$.
2   Brydox chooses quantity q_b from the set $[0, \infty)$.

PAYOFFS
Marginal cost is constant at $c = 12$. Demand is a function of the total quantity sold, $Q = q_a + q_b$:

$$p(Q) = 120 - q_a - q_b. \tag{3.35}$$

Payoffs are profits, which are given by a firm's price times its quantity minus its costs, that is,

$$\pi_{Apex} = (120 - q_a - q_b)q_a - cq_a = (120 - c)q_a - q_a^2 - q_a q_b;$$
$$\tag{3.36}$$
$$\pi_{Brydox} = (120 - q_a - q_b)q_b - cq_b = (120 - c)q_b - q_a q_b - q_b^2.$$

Apex, moving first, is called the **Stackelberg leader** and Brydox is the **Stackelberg follower**. The distinguishing characteristic of a Stackelberg equilibrium is that one player gets

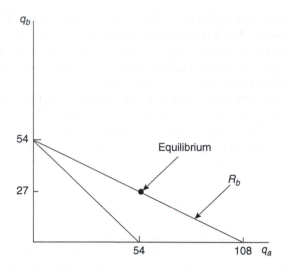

Figure 3.3   Stackelberg equilibrium.

to commit himself first. In figure 3.3, Apex moves first intertemporally. If moves were simultaneous but Apex could commit himself to a certain strategy, the same equilibrium would be reached as long as Brydox was not able to commit himself. Algebraically, since Apex forecasts Brydox's output to be $q_b = 60 - (q_a + c)/2$ from the analog of equation (3.34), Apex can substitute this into his payoff function in (3.32) to obtain

$$\pi_a = (120 - c)q_a - q_a^2 - q_a \left(60 - \frac{q_a + c}{2} \right).$$ (3.37)

Maximizing his payoff with respect to q_a yields the first-order condition

$$(120 - c) - 2q_a - 60 + q_a + \frac{c}{2} = 0,$$ (3.38)

which generates Apex's reaction function, $q_a = 60 - c/2 = 54$ (which only equals the monopoly output by coincidence, due to the particular numbers in this example). Once Apex chooses this output, Brydox chooses his output to be $q_b = 27$. (That Brydox chooses exactly half the monopoly output is also accidental.) The market price is $120 - 54 - 27 = 39$ for both firms, so Apex has benefited from his status as Stackelberg leader, but industry profits have fallen compared to the Cournot equilibrium.

3.6   Continuous Strategies: The Bertrand Game, Strategic Complements, and Strategic Substitutes

A natural alternative to a duopoly model in which the two firms pick outputs simultaneously is a model in which they pick prices simultaneously. This is known as **Bertrand equilibrium**, because the difficulty of choosing between the two models was stressed in Bertrand (1883), a review discussion of Cournot's book. We will use the same two-player linear-demand world as before, but now the strategy spaces will be the prices, not the quantities.

We will also use the same demand function, equation (3.31), which implies that if p is the lowest price, $q = 120 - p$. In the Cournot model, firms chose quantities but allowed the market price to vary freely. In the Bertrand model, they choose prices and sell as much as they can.

The Bertrand Game

PLAYERS
Firms Apex and Brydox

THE ORDER OF PLAY
Apex and Brydox simultaneously choose prices p_a and p_b from the set $[0, \infty)$.

PAYOFFS
Marginal cost is constant at $c = 12$. Demand is a function of the total quantity sold, $Q(p) = 120 - p$. The payoff function for Apex (Brydox's would be analogous) is

$$\pi_a = \begin{cases} (120 - p_a)(p_a - c) & \text{if } p_a \leq p_b, \\ \dfrac{(120 - p_a)(p_a - c)}{2} & \text{if } p_a = p_b, \\ 0 & \text{if } p_a > p_b. \end{cases}$$

The Bertrand Game has a unique Nash equilibrium: $p_a = p_b = c = 12$, with $q_a = q_b = 54$. That this is a weak Nash equilibrium is clear: if either firm deviates to a higher price, it loses all its customers and so fails to increase its profits to above zero. In fact, this is an example of a Nash equilibrium in weakly dominated strategies. That the equilibrium is unique is less clear. To see why it is, divide the possible strategy profiles into four groups:

$p_a < c$ or $p_b < c$. In either of these cases, the firm with the lowest price will earn negative profits, and could profitably deviate to a price high enough to reduce its demand to zero.

$p_a > p_b > c$ or $p_b > p_a > c$. In either of these cases the firm with the higher price could deviate to a price below its rival and increase its profits from zero to some positive value.

$p_a = p_b > c$. In this case, Apex could deviate to a price ϵ less than Brydox and its profit would rise, because it would go from selling half the market quantity to selling all of it with an infinitesimal decline in profit per unit sale.

$p_a > p_b = c$ or $p_b > p_a = c$. In this case, the firm with the price of c could move from zero profits to positive profits by increasing its price slightly while keeping it below the other firm's price.

This proof is a good example of one common method of proving uniqueness of equilibrium in game theory: partition the strategy profile space and show area by area that deviations would occur. It is such a good example that I recommend it to anyone teaching from this book as a good test question.[2]

Like the surprising outcome of Prisoner's Dilemma, the Bertrand equilibrium is less surprising once one thinks about the model's limitations. What it shows is that duopoly profits do not arise just because there are two firms. Profits arise from something else, such as multiple periods, incomplete information, or differentiated products.

Both the Bertrand and Cournot models are in common use. The Bertrand model can be awkward mathematically because of the discontinuous jump from a market share of 0 to 100 percent after a slight price cut. The Cournot model is useful as a simple model that avoids this problem and which predicts that the price will fall gradually as more firms enter the market. There are also ways to modify the Bertrand model to obtain intermediate prices and gradual effects of entry. Let us proceed to look at one such modification.

The Differentiated Bertrand Game

The Bertrand model generates zero profits because only slight price discounts are needed to bid away customers. The assumption behind this is that the two firms sell identical goods, so if Apex's price is slightly higher than Brydox's all the customers go to Brydox. If customers have brand loyalty or poor price information, the equilibrium is different. Let us now move to a different duopoly market, where the demand curves facing Apex and Brydox are

$$q_a = 24 - 2p_a + p_b \tag{3.39}$$

and

$$q_b = 24 - 2p_b + p_a, \tag{3.40}$$

and they have constant marginal costs of $c = 3$.

The greater the difference in the coefficients on prices in a demand curve like (3.39) or (3.40), the less substitutable are the products. As with standard demand functions such as equation (3.31), we have made implicit assumptions about the extreme points of equations (3.39) and (3.40). These equations only apply if the quantities demanded turn out to be nonnegative, and we might also want to restrict them to prices below some ceiling, since otherwise the demand facing one firm becomes infinite as the other's price rises to infinity. A sensible ceiling here is 12, since if $p_a > 12$ and $p_b = 0$, equation (3.39) would yield a negative quantity demanded for Apex. Keeping in mind these limitations, the payoffs are

$$\pi_a = (24 - 2p_a + p_b)(p_a - c) \tag{3.41}$$

and

$$\pi_b = (24 - 2p_b + p_a)(p_b - c). \tag{3.42}$$

[2] Is it still a good question given that I have just provided a warning to the students? Yes. First, it will prove a filter for discovering which students have even skimmed the assigned reading. Second, questions like this are not always easy even if one knows they are on the test. Third, and most important, even if in equilibrium every student answers the question correctly, that very fact shows that the incentive to learn this particular item has worked – and that is our main goal, is it not?

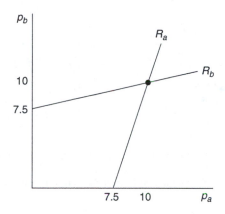

Figure 3.4   Bertrand reaction functions with differentiated products.

The order of play is the same as in the Bertrand Game (or Undifferentiated Bertrand Game, as we will call it when that is necessary to avoid confusion): Apex and Brydox simultaneously choose prices p_a and p_b from the set $[0, \infty)$.

Maximizing Apex's payoff by choice of p_a, we obtain the first-order condition,

$$\frac{d\pi_a}{dp_a} = 24 - 4p_a + p_b + 2c = 0, \tag{3.43}$$

and the reaction function,

$$p_a = 6 + \left(\frac{1}{2}\right)c + \left(\frac{1}{4}\right)p_b = 7.5 + \left(\frac{1}{4}\right)p_b. \tag{3.44}$$

Since Brydox has a parallel first-order condition, the equilibrium occurs where $p_a = p_b = 10$. The quantity each firm produces is 14, which is below the 21 each would produce at prices of $p_a = p_b = c = 3$. Figure 3.4 shows that the reaction functions intersect. Apex's demand curve has the elasticity

$$\left(\frac{\partial q_a}{\partial p_a}\right) \cdot \left(\frac{p_a}{q_a}\right) = -2\left(\frac{p_a}{q_a}\right), \tag{3.45}$$

which is finite even when $p_a = p_b$, unlike in the undifferentiated-goods Bertrand model.

The differentiated-good Bertrand model is important because it is often the most descriptively realistic model of a market. A basic idea in marketing is that selling depends on "The Four P's": Product, Place, Promotion, and Price. Economists have concentrated heavily on price differences between products, but we realize that differences in product quality and characteristics, where something is sold, and how the sellers get information about it to the buyers also matter. Sellers use their prices as control variables more often than their quantities, but the seller with the lowest price does not get all the customers.

Why, then, did I bother to even describe the Cournot and undifferentiated Bertrand models? Aren't they obsolete? No, because descriptive realism is not the *summum bonum* of modelling. Simplicity matters a lot too. The Cournot and undifferentiated Bertrand models are simpler, especially when we go to three or more firms, so they are better models in many applications.

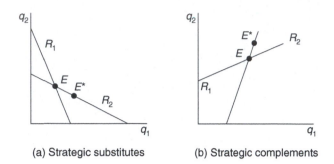

Figure 3.5   Cournot versus Differentiated Bertrand reaction functions (strategic substitutes versus strategic complements).

Strategic Substitutes and Strategic Complements

You may have noticed an interesting difference between the Cournot and Differentiated Bertrand reaction curves in figures 3.2 and 3.4: the reaction curves have opposite slopes. Figure 3.5 puts the two together for easier comparison.

In both models, the reaction curves cross once, so there is a unique Nash equilibrium. Off the equilibrium path, though, there is an interesting difference. If a Cournot firm increases its output, its rival will do the opposite and reduce its output. If a Bertrand firm increases its price, its rival will do the same thing, and increase its price too.

We can ask of any game: "If the other players do more of their strategy, will I do more of my own strategy, or less?" In some games, the answer is "do more" and in others it is "do less." Jeremy Bulow, John Geanakoplos, & Paul Klemperer (1985) apply the term "strategic complements" to the strategies in the "do more" kind of game, because when Player 1 does more of his strategy that increases Player 2's marginal payoff from 2's strategy, just as when I buy more bread it increases my marginal utility from buying more butter. If strategies are strategic complements, their reaction curves are upward sloping, as in the Differentiated Bertrand Game.

On the other hand, in the "do less" kind of game, when Player 1 does more of his strategy that *reduces* Player 2's marginal payoff from 2's strategy, just as my buying potato chips reduces my marginal utility from buying more corn chips. The strategies are therefore "strategic substitutes" and their reaction curves are downward sloping, as in the Cournot Game.

Which way the reaction curves slope also affects whether a player wants to move first or second. Esther Gal-Or (1985) notes that if reaction curves slope down (as with strategic substitutes and Cournot) there is a first-mover advantage, whereas if they slope upwards (as with strategic complements and Differentiated Bertrand) there is a second-mover advantage.

We can see that in figure 3.5 the Cournot Game in which Player 1 moves first is simply the Stackelberg Game, which we have already analyzed using figure 3.3. The equilibrium moves from E to E^* in figure 3.5a, Player 1's payoff increases, and Player 2's payoff falls. Note, too, that the total industry payoff is lower in Stackelberg than in Cournot − not only does one player lose, but he loses more than the other player gains.

We have not analyzed the Differentiated Bertrand Game when Player 1 moves first, but since price is a strategic complement, the effect of sequentiality is very different from in the Cournot Game (and, actually, from the sequential undifferentiated Bertrand Game – see the end-of-chapter notes). We cannot tell what Player 1's optimal strategy is from the diagram alone, but figure 3.5 illustrates one possibility. Player 1 chooses a price p^* higher than he would in the simultaneous-move game, predicting that Player 2's response will be a price somewhat lower than p^* but still greater than the simultaneous Bertrand price at E. The result is that Player 2's payoff is higher than Player 1's – a second-mover advantage. Note, however, that both players are better off at E^* than at E, so both players would favor converting the game to be sequential.

Both sequential games could be elaborated further by adding moves beforehand which would determine which player would choose his price or quantity first, but I will leave that to you. The important point for now is that whether a game has strategic complements or strategic substitutes is hugely important to the incentives of the players.

The point is simple enough and important enough that I devote an entire session of my MBA game theory course to strategic complements and strategic substitutes. In the practical game theory that someone with a Master of Business Administration degree ought to know, the most important thing is to learn how to describe a situation in terms of players, actions, information, and payoffs. Often there is not enough data to use a specific functional form, but it is possible to figure out with a mixture of qualitative and quantitative information whether the relation between actions and payoffs is one of strategic substitutes or strategic complements. The businessman then knows whether, for example, he should try to be a first mover or a second mover, and whether he should keep his action secret or proclaim his action to the entire world.

To understand the usefulness of the idea of strategic complements and substitutes, think about how you would model situations like the following (note that there is no universally right answer for any of them):

1   Two firms are choosing their research and development budgets. Are the budgets strategic complements or strategic substitutes?
2   Smith and Jones are both trying to be elected President of the United States. Each must decide how much he will spend on advertising in California. Are the advertising budgets strategic complements or strategic substitutes?
3   Seven firms are each deciding whether to make their products more special, or more suited to the average consumer. Is the degree of specialness a strategic complement or a strategic substitute?
4   India and Pakistan are each deciding whether to make their armies larger or smaller. Is army size a strategic complement or a strategic substitute?

Economists have a growing appreciation of how powerful the ideas of substitution and complementarity can be in thinking about the deep structure of economic behavior. The mathematical idea of supermodularity, to be discussed in chapter 14, is all about complementarity. For an inspiring survey, see Vives (2005).

*3.7   Existence of Equilibrium

One of the strong points of Nash equilibria is that they exist in practically every game one is likely to encounter. There are four common reasons why an equilibrium might not exist or might only exist in mixed strategies.

(1) An unbounded strategy space

Suppose in a stock market game that Smith can borrow money and buy as many shares x of stock as he likes, so his strategy set, the amount of stock he can buy, is $[0, \infty)$, a set which is unbounded above. (Note, by the way, that we thus assume that he can buy fractional shares, e.g., $x = 13.4$, but cannot sell short, e.g., $x = -100$.)

If Smith knows that the price is lower today than it will be tomorrow, his payoff function will be $\pi(x) = x$ and he will want to buy an infinite number of shares, which is not an equilibrium purchase. If the amount he buys is restricted to be less than or equal to 1,000, however, then the strategy set is bounded (by 1,000), and an equilibrium exists, $-x = 1,000$.

Sometimes, as in the Cournot Game discussed earlier in this chapter, the unboundedness of the strategy sets does not matter because the optimum is an interior solution. In other games, though, it is important, not just to get a determinate solution but because the real world is a rather bounded place. The solar system is finite in size, as is the amount of human time past and future.

(2) An open strategy space

Again consider Smith. Let his strategy be $x \in [0, 1,000)$, which is the same as saying that $0 \le x < 1,000$, and his payoff function be $\pi(x) = x$. Smith's strategy set is bounded (by 0 and 1,000), but it is open rather than closed, because he can choose any number less than 1,000, but not 1,000 itself. This means no equilibrium will exist, because he wants to buy 999.999... shares. This is just a technical problem; we ought to have specified Smith's strategy space to be $[0, 1,000]$, and then an equilibrium would exist, at $x = 1,000$.

(3) A discrete strategy space (or, more generally, a nonconvex strategy space)

Suppose we start with an arbitrary pair of strategies s_1 and s_2 for two players. If the players' strategies are strategic complements, then if Player 1 increases his strategy in response to s_2, Player 2 will increase his strategy in response to that. An equilibrium will occur where the players run into diminishing returns or increasing costs, or where they hit the upper bounds of their strategy sets. If, on the other hand, the strategies are strategic substitutes, then if Player 1 increases his strategy in response to s_2, Player 2 will in turn want to reduce his strategy. If the strategy spaces are continuous, this can lead to an equilibrium, but if they are discrete, Player 2 cannot reduce his strategy just a little bit – he has to jump down a discrete level. That could then induce Player 1 to increase his strategy by a discrete amount. This jumping of responses can be never-ending – there is no equilibrium.

That is what is happening in the Welfare Game of table 3.1 in this chapter. No compromise is possible between a little aid and no aid, or between working and not working – until we introduce mixed strategies. That allows for each player to choose a continuous amount of his strategy.

This problem is not limited to games such as 2-by-2 games that have discrete strategy spaces. Rather, it is a problem of "gaps" in the strategy space. Suppose we had a game in which the government was not limited to amount 0 or 100 of aid, but could choose any amount in the space $\{[0, 10], [90, 100]\}$. That is a continuous, closed, and bounded strategy space, but it is non convex – there is gap in it. (For a space $\{x\}$ to be convex, it must be true that if x_1 and x_2 are in the space, so is $\theta x_1 + (1 - \theta)x_2$ for any $\theta \in [0, 1]$.) Without mixed strategies, an equilibrium to the game might well not exist.

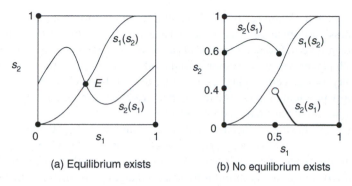

(a) Equilibrium exists   (b) No equilibrium exists

Figure 3.6   Continuous and discontinuous reaction functions.

(4) A discontinuous reaction function arising from nonconcave or discontinuous payoff functions

Even if the strategy spaces are closed, bounded, and convex, a problem remains. For a Nash equilibrium to exist, we need for the reaction functions of the players to intersect. If the reaction functions are discontinuous, they might not intersect.

Figure 3.6 shows this for a two-player game in which each player chooses a strategy from the interval between 0 and 1. Player 1's reaction function, $s_1(s_2)$, must pick one or more value of s_1 for each possible value of s_2, so it must cross from the bottom to the top of the diagram. Player 2's reaction function, $s_2(s_1)$, must pick one or more value of s_2 for each possible value of s_1, so it must cross from the left to the right of the diagram. If the strategy sets were unbounded or open, the reaction functions might not exist, but that is not a problem here: they do exist. And in Panel (a) a Nash equilibrium exists, at the point, E, where the two reaction functions intersect.

In Panel (b), however, no Nash equilibrium exists. The problem is that Firm 2's reaction function $s_2(s_1)$ is discontinuous at the point $s_1 = 0.5$. It jumps down from $s_2(0.5) = 0.6$ to $s_2(0.50001) = 0.4$. As a result, the reaction curves never intersect, and no equilibrium exists.

If the two players can use mixed strategies, then an equilibrium will exist even for the game in Panel (b), though I will not prove that here. I would, however, like to say why it is that the reaction function might be discontinuous. A player's reaction functions, remember, is derived by maximizing his payoff as a function of his own strategy given the strategies of the other players.

Thus, a first reason why Player 1's reaction function might be discontinuous in the other players' strategies is that his payoff function is discontinuous in either his own or the other players' strategies. This is what happens in chapter 14's Hotelling Pricing Game, where if Player 1's price drops enough (or Player 2's price rises high enough), all of Player 2's customers suddenly rush to Player 1.

A second reason why Player 1's reaction function might be discontinuous in the other players' strategies is that his payoff function is not concave. The intuition is that if an objective function is not concave, then there might be a number of maxima that are local but not global, and as the parameters change, which maximum is the global one can suddenly change. This means that the reaction function will suddenly jump from one maximizing choice to another one that is far-distant, rather than smoothly changing as it would in a more nicely behaved problem.

Problems (1) and (2) are really problems in decision theory, not game theory, because unboundedness and openness lead to nonexistence of the solution to even a one-player maximization problem. Problems (3) and (4) are special to game theory. They arise because although each player has a best response to the other players, no profile of best choices is such that everybody has chosen his best response to everybody else. They are similar to the decision theory problem of nonexistence of an interior solution, but if only one player were involved, we would at least have a corner solution.

In this chapter, I have introduced a number of seemingly disparate ideas – mixed strategies, auditing, continuous strategy spaces, reaction curves, complentary substitutes and complements, existence of equilibrium… What ties them together? The unifying theme is the possibility of reaching equilibrium by small changes in behavior, whether that be by changing the probability in a mixed strategy or an auditing game or by changing the level of a continuous price or quantity. Continuous strategies free us from the need to use n-by-n tables to predict behavior in games, and with a few technical assumptions they guarantee we will find equilibria.

Notes

N3.1   Mixed strategies: the Welfare Game

- Waldegrave (1713) is a very early reference to mixed strategies.
- Mixed strategies come up constantly in recreational games. The Scissors-Paper-Stone choosing game, for example, has a unique mixed-strategy equilibrium, as shown in Fisher & Ryan (1992). There are usually analogs in other spheres; it turns out that three types of Californian side-blotched lizard males play the same game, as reported in Sinevero & Lively (1996). It is interesting to try to see how closely players come to the theoretically optimal mixing strategies. Chiappori, Levitt, & Groseclose (2002) conclude that players choosing whether to kick right or left in soccer penalty kicks are following optimal mixed strategies, but that kickers are heterogeneous in their abilities to kick in each direction.
- The January 1992 issue of *Rationality and Society* is devoted to attacks on and defenses of the use of game theory in the social sciences, with considerable discussion of mixed strategies and multiple equilibria. Contributors include Harsanyi, Myerson, Rapaport, Tullock, & Wildavsky. The Spring 1989 issue of the *The RAND Journal of Economics* also has an exchange on the use of game theory, between Franklin Fisher and Carl Shapiro. I recommend the Peltzman (1991) attack on the game theory approach to industrial organization in the spirit of the "Chicago School."
- In this book it will always be assumed that players remember their previous moves. Without this assumption of **perfect recall**, the definition in the text is not that for a mixed strategy, but for a **behavior strategy**. As historically defined, a player pursues a mixed strategy when he randomly chooses between pure strategies at the starting node, but he plays a pure strategy thereafter. Under that definition, the modeller cannot talk of random choices at any but the starting node. Kuhn (1953) showed that the definition of mixed strategy given in the text is equivalent to the original definition if the game has perfect recall. Since all important games have perfect recall and the new definition of mixed strategy is better in keeping with the modern spirit of sequential rationality, I have abandoned the old definition.

  The classic example of a game without perfect recall is **bridge**, where the four players of the actual game can be cutely modelled as two players who forget what half their cards look like at any one time in the bidding. A more useful example is a game that has been simplified by restricting players to Markov strategies (see section 5.4), but usually the modeller sets up such a game with perfect recall and then rules out non-Markov equilibria after showing that the Markov strategies form an equilibrium for the general game.

- It is *not* true that when two pure-strategy equilibria exist a player would be just as willing to use a strategy mixing the two even when the other player is using a pure strategy. In the Battle of the Sexes, for instance, if the man knows the woman is going to the ballet he is not indifferent between the ballet and the prize fight.

- A continuum of players is useful not only because the modeller need not worry about fractions of players, but because he can use more modelling tools from calculus – taking the integral of the quantities demanded by different consumers, for example, rather than the sum. But using a continuum is also mathematically more difficult: see Aumann (1964a, 1964b) .

- There is an entire literature on the econometrics of estimating game theory models. Suppose we would like to estimate the payoff numbers in a 2-by-2 game, where we observe the actions taken by each of the two players and various background variables. The two actions might be, for example, to enter or not enter, and the background variables might be such things as the size of the market or the cost conditions facing one of the players. We will of course need multiple repetitions of the situation to generate enough data to use econometrics. There is an identification problem, because there are eight payoffs in a 2-by-2 payoff matrix, but only four possible action profiles – and if mixed strategies are being used, the four mixing probabilities have to add up to one, so there are really only three independent observed outcomes. How can we estimate eight parameters with only three possible outcomes? For identification, it must be that some environmental variables affect only one of the players, as Bajari, Hong, & Ryan (2004) note. In addition, there is the problem that there may be multiple equilibria being played out, so that additional identifying assumptions are needed to help us know which equilibria are being played out in which observations. The foundational articles in this literature are Bresnahan & Reiss (1990, 1991a), and it is an active area of research.

N3.2   The Payoff-equating Method and games of timing

- The game of Chicken discussed in the text is simpler than the game acted out in the movie *Rebel Without a Cause,* in which the players race towards a cliff and the winner is the player who jumps out of his car last. The pure-strategy space in the movie game is continuous and the payoffs are discontinuous at the cliff's edge, which makes the game more difficult to analyze technically. (Recall, too, the importance in the movie of a disastrous mistake – the kind of "tremble" that section 4.1 will discuss.)

- Technical difficulties arise in some models with a continuum of actions and mixed strategies. In the Welfare Game, the government chose a single number, a probability, on the continuum from zero to one. If we allowed the government to mix over a continuum of aid levels, it would choose a function, a probability density, over the continuum. The original game has a finite number of elements in its strategy set, so its mixed extension still has a strategy space in $\mathbf{R}^n$. But with a continuous strategy set extended by a continuum of mixed strategies for each pure strategy, the mathematics become difficult.

    Games in continuous time frequently run into this problem. Sometimes it can be avoided by clever modelling, as in Fudenberg & Tirole's (1986b) continuous-time war of attrition with asymmetric information. They specify as strategies the length of time firms would proceed to *Continue* given their beliefs about the type of the other player, in which case there is a pure-strategy equilibrium.

- **Differential games** are played in continuous time. The action is a function describing the value of a state variable at each instant, so the strategy maps the game's past history to such a function. Differential games are solved using dynamic optimization. A book-length treatment is Bagchi (1984).

- Fudenberg & Levine (1986) show circumstances under which the equilibria of games with infinite strategy spaces can be found as the limits of equilibria of games with finite strategy spaces.
- Crawford and Sobel (1982) define cheap talk to include what I will call "expensive talk" in chapter 6. By their definition, any message whose cost is uncorrelated with its content is cheap talk, even if the sending of the message is extremely costly. It is "cheap" only in the sense that there is no penalty for lying. A third possibility is that the message has negative cost; the sender derives direct utility from sending it. We might call this "**fun talk**." Whether the message is costly or not matters because it affects whether a player is willing to send a message even if he expects to be disbelieved.

N3.4   Randomizing versus mixing: the Auditing Game

- Auditing Game I is similar to a game called the Police Game. Care must be taken in such games that one does not use a simultaneous-move game when a sequential game is appropriate. Also, discrete strategy spaces can be misleading. In general, economic analysis assumes that costs rise convexly in the amount of an activity and benefits rise concavely. Modelling a situation with a 2-by-2 game uses just two discrete levels of the activity, so the concavity or convexity is lost in the simplification. If the true functions are linear, as in auditing costs which rise linearly with the probability of auditing, this is no great loss. If the true costs rise convexly, as in the case where the hours a policeman must stay on the street each day are increased, then a 2-by-2 model can be misleading. Be especially careful not to press the idea of a mixed-strategy equilibrium too hard if a pure-strategy equilibrium would exist when intermediate strategies are allowed. See Tsebelis (1989) and the criticism of it in Jack Hirshleifer & Eric Rasmusen (1992).
- Douglas Diamond (1984) shows the implications of monitoring costs for the structure of financial markets. A fixed cost to monitoring investments motivates the creation of a financial intermediary to avoid repetitive monitoring by many investors.
- Baron & Besanko (1984) study auditing in the context of a government agency which can at some cost collect information on the true production costs of a regulated firm.
- Mookherjee & Png (1989) and Border & Sobel (1987) have examined random auditing in the context of taxation. They find that if a taxpayer is audited he ought to be more than compensated for his trouble if it turns out he was telling the truth. Under the optimal contract, the truthtelling taxpayer should be delighted to hear that he is being audited. The reason is that a reward for truthfulness widens the differential between the agent's payoff when he tells the truth and when he lies.

  Why is such a scheme not used? It is certainly practical, and one would think it would be popular with the voters. One reason might be the possibility of corruption; if being audited leads to a lucrative reward, the government might purposely choose to audit its friends. The current danger seems even worse, though, since the government can audit its enemies and burden them with the trouble of an audit even if they have paid their taxes properly.

- Government action strongly affects what information is available as well as what is contractible. In 1988, for example, the United States passed a law sharply restricting the use of lie detectors for testing or monitoring. Previous to the restriction, about two million workers had been tested each year. ("Law Limiting Use of Lie Detectors Is Seen Having Widespread Effect," *Wall Street Journal*, p. 13, July 1, 1988, "American Polygraph Association," http://www.polygraph.org/betasite/menu8.html, Eric Rasmusen, "Bans on Lie Detector Tests," http://www.rasmusen.org/x/2006/07/26/bans-on-lie-detector_tests/).
- Section 3.4 shows how random actions come up in auditing and in mixed strategies. Another use for randomness is to reduce transactions costs. In 1983, for example, Chrysler was bargaining over how much to pay Volkswagen for a Detroit factory. The two negotiators locked themselves into a hotel room and agreed not to leave till they had an agreement. When they narrowed the price gap from $100 million to $5 million, they agreed to flip a coin. Chrysler won.

How would you model that? "Chrysler Hits Brakes, Starts Saving Money after Shopping Spree," *Wall Street Journal*, p. 1, January 12, 1988. See also David Friedman's ingenious idea in chapter 15 of *Law's Order* of using a 10 percent probability of death to replace a 6-year prison term (http://www.daviddfriedman.com/laws_order/index.shtml).

N3.5   Continuous strategies: the Cournot Game

- An interesting class of simple continuous payoff games are the **Colonel Blotto games** (Tukey [1949], McDonald & Tukey [1949]). In these games, two military commanders allocate their forces to m different battlefields, and a battlefield contributes more to the payoff of the commander with the greater forces there. A distinguishing characteristic is that player i's payoff increases with the value of player i's particular action relative to player j's, and i's actions are subject to a budget constraint. Except for the budget constraint, this is similar to the tournaments of section 8.2.
- "Stability" is a word used in many different ways in game theory and economics. The natural meaning of a stable equilibrium is that it has dynamics which cause the system to return to that point after being perturbed slightly, and the discussion of the stability of Cournot equilibrium is in that spirit. The uses of the term by von Neumann & Morgenstern (1944) and Kohlberg & Mertens (1986) are entirely different.
- The term "Stackelberg equilibrium" is not clearly defined in the literature. It is sometimes used to denote equilibria in which players take actions in a given order, but since that is just the perfect equilibrium (see section 4.1) of a well-specified extensive form, I prefer to reserve the term for the Nash equilibrium of the duopoly quantity game in which one player moves first, which is the context of chapter 3 of Stackelberg (1934).

  An alternative definition is that a Stackelberg equilibrium is a strategy profile in which players select strategies in a given order and in which each player's strategy is a best response to the fixed strategies of the players preceding him and the yet-to-be-chosen strategies of players succeeding him, that is, a situation in which players precommit to strategies in a given order. Such an equilibrium would not generally be either Nash or perfect.
- Stackelberg (1934) suggested that sometimes the players are confused about which of them is the leader and which the follower, resulting in the disequilibrium outcome called **Stackelberg warfare**.
- With linear costs and demand, total output is greater in Stackelberg equilibrium than in Cournot. The slope of the reaction curve is less than one, so Apex's output expands more than Brydox's contracts. Total output being greater, the price is less than in the Cournot equilibrium.
- A useful application of Stackelberg equilibrium is to an industry with a dominant firm and a **competitive fringe** of smaller firms that sell at capacity if the price exceeds their marginal cost. These smaller firms act as Stackelberg leaders (not followers), since each is small enough to ignore its effect on the behavior of the dominant firm. The oil market could be modelled this way with OPEC as the dominant firm and producers such as Britain on the fringe.

N3.6   Continuous strategies: the Bertrand Game, strategic complements, and strategic substitutes

- The text analyzed the simultaneous undifferentiated Bertrand game but not the sequential one. $p_a = p_c = c$ remains an equilibrium outcome, but it is no longer unique. Suppose Apex moves first, then Brydox, and suppose, for a technical reason to be apparent shortly, that if $p_a = p_b$ Brydox captures the entire market. Apex cannot achieve more than a payoff of zero, because either $p_a = c$ or Brydox will choose $p_b = p_a$ and capture the entire market. Thus, Apex is indifferent between any $p_a \geq c$.

The game needs to be set up with this tiebreaking rule because if the market is split between Apex and Brydox when $p_a = p_b$, Brydox's best response to $p_a > c$ would be to choose p_b to be the biggest number less than p_a – but with a continuous space, no such number exists, so Brydox's best response is ill-defined. Giving all the demand to Brydox in case of price ties gets around this problem.

• The demand curves (3.39) and (3.40) can be generated by a quadratic utility function. Dixit (1979) tells us that with respect to three goods 0, 1, and 2, the utility function

$$U = q_0 + \alpha_1 q_1 + \alpha_2 q_2 - \frac{1}{2}\left(\beta_1 q_1^2 + 2\gamma q_1 q_2 + \beta_2 q_2^2\right) \tag{3.46}$$

(where the constants $\alpha_1, \alpha_2, \beta_1$, and β_2 are positive and $\gamma^2 \le \beta_1 \beta_2$) generates the inverse demand functions

$$p_1 = \alpha_1 - \beta_1 q_1 - \gamma q_2 \tag{3.47}$$

and

$$p_2 = \alpha_2 - \beta_2 q_2 - \gamma q_1. \tag{3.48}$$

• We can also work out the Cournot equilibrium for demand functions (3.39) and (3.40), but product differentiation does not affect it much. Start by expressing the price in the demand curve in terms of quantities alone, obtaining

$$p_a = 12 - \left(\frac{1}{2}\right) q_a + \left(\frac{1}{2}\right) p_b \tag{3.49}$$

and

$$p_b = 12 - \left(\frac{1}{2}\right) q_b + \left(\frac{1}{2}\right) p_a. \tag{3.50}$$

After substituting from (3.50) into (3.49) and solving for p_a, we obtain

$$p_a = 24 - \left(\frac{2}{3}\right) q_a - \left(\frac{1}{3}\right) q_b. \tag{3.51}$$

The first-order condition for Apex's maximization problem is

$$\frac{d\pi_a}{dq_a} = 24 - 3 - \left(\frac{4}{3}\right) q_a - \left(\frac{1}{3}\right) q_b = 0, \tag{3.52}$$

which gives rise to the reaction function

$$q_a = 15.75 - \left(\frac{1}{4}\right) q_b. \tag{3.53}$$

We can guess that $q_a = q_b$. It follows from (3.53) that $q_a = 12.6$ and the market price is 11.4. On checking, you would find this to indeed be a Nash equilibrium. But reaction function (3.53) has much the same shape as if there were no product differentiation, unlike when we moved from undifferentiated to differentiated Bertrand competition.

• For more on the technicalities of strategic complements and strategic substitutes, see Bulow, Geanakoplos, & Klemperer (1985) and Milgrom & Roberts (1990). If the strategies are strategic complements, Milgrom & Roberts (1990) and Vives (1990) show that pure-strategy equilibria exist. These models often explain peculiar economic phenomena nicely, as in Peter Diamond (1982) on search and business cycles and Douglas Diamond & Dybvig (1983) on bank runs. If the strategies are strategic substitutes, existence of pure-strategy equilibria is more troublesome; see Dubey, Haimanko, & Zapechelnyuk (2005).

Problems

3.1:   Presidential primaries (medium)

Smith and Jones are fighting it out for the Democratic nomination for President of the United States. The more months they keep fighting, the more money they spend, because a candidate must spend one million dollars a month in order to stay in the race. If one of them drops out, the other one wins the nomination, which is worth 11 million dollars. The discount rate is r per month. To simplify the problem, you may assume that this battle could go on forever if neither of them drops out. Let θ denote the probability that an individual player will drop out each month in the mixed-strategy equilibrium.

(a)   In the mixed-strategy equilibrium, what is the probability θ each month that Smith will drop out? What happens if r changes from 0.1 to 0.15?
(b)   What are the two pure-strategy equilibria?
(c)   If the game only lasts one period, and the Republican wins the general election if both Democrats refuse to give up (resulting in Democrat payoffs of zero), what is the probability γ with which each Democrat drops out in a symmetric equilibrium?

3.2:   Running from the police (medium)

Two risk-neutral men, Schmidt and Braun, are walking south along a street in Nazi Germany when they see a single policeman coming to check their papers. Only Braun has his papers (unknown to the policeman, of course). The policeman will catch both men if both or neither of them run north, but if just one runs, he must choose which one to stop – the walker or the runner. The penalty for being without papers is 24 months in prison. The penalty for running away from a policeman is 24 months in prison, on top of the sentences for any other charges, but the conviction rate for this offense is only 25 percent. The two friends want to maximize their joint welfare, which the policeman wants to minimize. Braun moves first, then Schmidt, then the policeman.

(a)   What is the outcome matrix for outcomes that might be observed in equilibrium? (Use θ for the probability that the policeman chases the runner and γ for the probability that Braun runs.)
(b)   What is the probability that the policeman chases the runner, (call it θ^*)?
(c)   What is the probability that Braun runs, (call it γ^*)?
(d)   Since Schmidt and Braun share the same objectives, is this a cooperative game?

3.3:   Uniqueness in matching pennies (easy)

In the game Matching Pennies, Smith and Jones each show a penny with either heads or tails up. If they choose the same side of the penny, Smith gets both pennies; otherwise, Jones gets them.

(a)   Draw the outcome matrix for Matching Pennies.
(b)   Show that there is no Nash equilibrium in pure strategies.
(c)   Find the mixed-strategy equilibrium, denoting Smith's probability of *Heads* by γ and Jones's by θ.
(d)   Prove that there is only one mixed-strategy equilibrium.

3.4:   Mixed strategies in the Battle of the Sexes (medium)

Refer back to the Battle of the Sexes and Ranked Coordination. Denote the probabilities that the man and woman pick *Prize Fight* by γ and θ.

(a)   Find an expression for the man's expected payoff.
(b)   What are the equilibrium values of γ and θ, and the expected payoffs?

(c)   Find the most likely outcome and its probability.
(d)   What is the equilibrium payoff in the mixed-strategy equilibrium for Ranked Coordination?
(e)   Why is the mixed-strategy equilibrium a better focal point in the Battle of the Sexes than in Ranked Coordination?

3.5:   A voting paradox (medium)

Adam, Karl, and Vladimir are the only three voters in Podunk. Only Adam owns property. There is a proposition on the ballot to tax property-holders 120 dollars and distribute the proceeds equally among all citizens who do not own property. Each citizen dislikes having to go to the polling place and vote (despite the short lines), and would pay 20 dollars to avoid voting. They all must decide whether to vote before going to work. The proposition fails if the vote is tied. Assume that in equilibrium Adam votes with probability θ and Karl and Vladimir each vote with the same probability γ, but they decide to vote independently of each other.

(a)   What is the probability that the proposition will pass, as a function of θ and γ?
(b)   What are the two possible equilibrium probabilities γ_1 and γ_2 with which Karl might vote? Why, intuitively, are there two symmetric equilibria?
(c)   What is the probability θ that Adam will vote in each of the two symmetric equilibria?
(d)   What is the probability that the proposition will pass?

3.6:   Rent seeking (hard)

I mentioned that Rogerson (1982) uses a game very similar to "Patent Race for a New Market" to analyze competition for a government monopoly franchise. See if you can do this too. What can you predict about the welfare results of such competition?

3.7:   Nash equilibrium (easy)

Find the unique Nash equilibrium of the game in table 3.9.

Table 3.9   A meaningless game

		Column		
		Left	Middle	Right
	Up	1, 0	10, −1	0, 1
Row	Sideways	−1, 0	−2, −2	−12, 4
	Down	0, 2	823, −1	2, 0

Payoffs to: (Row, Column).

3.8:   Triopoly (easy)

Three companies provide tires to the Australian market. The total cost curve for a firm making Q tires is $TC = 5 + 20Q$, and the demand equation is $P = 100 - N$, where N is the total number of tires on the market.

According to the Cournot model, in which the firms simultaneously choose quantities, what will the total industry output be?

3.9:   Cournot with heterogeneous costs (hard)

On a seminar visit, Professor Schaffer of Michigan told me that in a Cournot model with a linear demand curve $P = \alpha - \beta Q$ and constant marginal cost C_i for firm i, the equilibrium industry output

Q depends on $\Sigma_i C_i$, but not on the individual levels of C_i. I may have misremembered. Prove or disprove this assertion. Would your conclusion be altered if we made some other assumption on demand? Discuss.

3.10: Alba and Rome: asymmetric information and mixed strategies (medium)

A Roman, Horatius, unwounded, is fighting the three Curiatius brothers from Alba, each of whom is wounded. If Horatius continues fighting, he wins with probability 0.1, and the payoffs are $(10, -10)$ for (Horatius, Curiatii) if he wins, and $(-10, 10)$ if he loses. With probability $\alpha = 0.5$, Horatius is panic-stricken and runs away. If he runs and the Curiatii do not chase him, the payoffs are $(-20, 10)$. If he runs and the Curiatius brothers chase and kill him, the payoffs are $(-21, 20)$. If, however, he is not panic-stricken, but he runs anyway and the Curiatii give chase, he is able to kill the fastest brother first and then dispose of the other two, for payoffs of $(10, -10)$. Horatius is, in fact, not panic-stricken.

(a)   With what probability θ would the Curiatii give chase if Horatius were to run?
(b)   With what probability γ does Horatius run?
(c)   How would θ and γ be affected if the Curiatii falsely believed that the probability of Horatius being panic-stricken was 1? What if they believed it was 0.9?

3.11: Finding Nash equilibria (easy)

Find all of the Nash equilibria for the game of table 3.10.

Table 3.10   A Takeover Game

		Hard	Target Medium	Soft
	Hard	-3, -3	-1, 0	4, 0
Raider	Medium	0, 0	2, 2	3, 1
	Soft	0, 0	2, 4	3, 3

Payoffs to: (Raider, Target).

3.12: Risky skating (hard)

Elena and Mary are the two leading figure skaters in the world. Each must choose during her training what her routine is going to look like. They cannot change their minds later and try to alter any details of their routines. Elena goes first in the Olympics, and Mary goes next. Each has five minutes for her performance. The judges will rate the routines on three dimensions, beauty, how high they jump, and whether they stumble after they jump. A skater who stumbles is sure to lose, and if both Elena and Mary stumble, one of the ten lesser skaters will win, though those ten skaters have no chance otherwise.

Elena and Mary are exactly equal in the beauty of their routines, and both of them know this, but they are not equal in their jumping ability. Whoever jumps higher without stumbling will definitely win. Elena's probability of stumbling is $P(h)$, where h is the height of the jump, and P is increasing smoothly and continuously in h. (In calculus terms, let P' and P'' both exist, and P' be positive) Mary's probability is $0.9P(h)$ – that is, it is 10 percent less for equal heights.

Let us define as $h = 0$ the maximum height that the lesser skaters can achieve, and assume that $P(0) = 0$.

(a)   Show that it cannot be an equilibrium for both Mary and Elena to choose the same value for h (Call them M and E).
(b)   Show for any pair of values (M, E) that it cannot be an equilibrium for Mary and Elena to choose those values.
(c)   Describe the optimal strategies to the best of your ability.
(d)   What is a business analogy? Find some situation in business or economics that could use this same model.

3.13:   The Kosovo War (easy)

Senator Robert Smith of New Hampshire said of the US policy in Serbia of bombing but promising not to use ground forces, "It's like saying we'll pass on you but we won't run the football." (*Human Events*, p. 1, April 16, 1999.) Explain what he meant, and why this is a strong criticism of U.S. policy, using the concept of a mixed strategy equilibrium. (Foreign students: in American football, a team can choose to throw the football (to pass it) or to hold it and run with it to move towards the goal.) Construct a numerical example to compare the U.S. expected payoff in (a) a mixed strategy equilibrium in which it ends up not using ground forces, and (b) a pure-strategy equilibrium in which the United States has committed not to use ground forces.

3.14:   IMF aid (easy)

Consider the game of table 3.11.

(a)   What is the exact form of every Nash equilibrium?
(b)   For what story would this matrix be a good model?

Table 3.11   IMF Aid

| | | **Debtor** | |
		Reform	*Waste*
IMF	*Aid*	3, 2	−1, 3
	No Aid	−1, 1	0, 0

Payoffs to: (IMF, Debtor).

3.15:   Coupon competition (hard)

Two marketing executives are arguing. Smith says that reducing our use of coupons will make us a less aggressive competitor, and that will hurt our sales. Jones says that reducing our use of coupons will make us a less aggressive competitor, but that will end up helping our sales.

Discuss, using the effect of reduced coupon use on your firm's reaction curve, under what circumstance each executive could be correct.

The War of Attrition: A Classroom Game for Chapter 3

Each firm consists of three students. Each year a firm must decide whether to stay in the industry or to exit. If it stays in, it incurs a fixed cost of 300 and a marginal cost of 2, and it chooses an integer price at which to sell. The firms can lose unlimited amounts of money; they are backed by large corporations who will keep supplying them with capital indefinitely.

Demand is inelastic at 60 up to a threshold price of $10/unit, above which the quantity demanded falls to zero.

Each firm writes down its price (or the word "EXIT") on a piece of paper and gives it to the instructor. The instructor then writes the strategies of each firm on the blackboard (EXIT or price). The firm charging the lowest price sells to all 60 consumers. If there is a tie for the lowest price, the firms charging that price split the consumers evenly.

The game then starts with a new year, but any firm that has exited is out permanently and cannot reenter. The game continues until only one firm is active, in which case it is awarded a prize of $2,000, the capitalized value of being a monopolist. This means the game can continue forever, in theory. The instructor may wish to cut it off at some point, however.

The game can be restarted and continued for as long as class time permits.

Chapter 4
dynamic games with symmetric information

4.1 Subgame Perfectness

In this chapter we will make heavy use of the extensive form to study games with moves that occur in sequence. We start in section 4.1 with a refinement of the Nash equilibrium concept called perfectness that incorporates sensible implications of the order of moves. Perfectness is illustrated in section 4.2 with a game of entry deterrence. Section 4.3 expands on the idea of perfectness using the example of nuisance suits, meritless lawsuits brought in the hopes of obtaining a settlement out of court. Nuisance suits show the importance of a threat being made credible and how sinking costs early or having certain nonmonetary payoffs can benefit a player. This example will also be used to discuss the open-set problem of weak equilibria in games with continuous strategy spaces, in which a player offering a contract chooses its terms to make the other player indifferent about accepting or rejecting. The last perfectness topic will be renegotiation: the idea that when there are multiple perfect equilibria, the players will coordinate on equilibria that are Pareto optimal in subgames but not in the game as a whole.

The Perfect Equilibrium of Follow-the-Leader I

Subgame perfectness is an equilibrium concept based on the ordering of moves and the distinction between an equilibrium path and an equilibrium. The **equilibrium path** is the path through the game tree that is followed in equilibrium, but the equilibrium itself is a strategy profile, which includes the players' responses to other players' deviations from the equilibrium path. These off-equilibrium responses are crucial to decisions on the equilibrium path. A threat, for example, is a promise to carry out a certain action if another player deviates from his equilibrium actions, and it has an influence even if it is never used.

Perfectness is best introduced with an example. In section 2.1, a flaw of Nash equilibrium was revealed in the game Follow-the-Leader I, which has three pure strategy Nash equilibria of which only one is reasonable. The players are Smith and Jones, who choose disk sizes. Both their payoffs are greater if they choose the same size and greatest if they coordinate on *Large*. Smith moves first, so his strategy set is {*Small, Large*}. Jones' strategy is more complicated, because it must specify an action for each information set, and Jones' information set depends on what Smith chose. A typical element of Jones' strategy set is (*Large, Small*), which specifies that he chooses *Large* if Smith chose *Large*, and *Small* if Smith chose *Small*. From the normal form we found the following three Nash equilibria.

Equilibrium	Strategies	Outcome
E_1	{*Large*, (*Large, Large*)}	Both pick *Large*.
E_2	{*Large*, (*Large, Small*)}	Both pick *Large*.
E_3	{*Small*, (*Small, Small*)}	Both pick *Small*.

Only Equilibrium E_2 is reasonable, because the order of the moves should matter to the decisions players make. The problem with the normal form, and thus with simple Nash equilibrium, is that it ignores who moves first. Smith moves first, and it seems reasonable that Jones should be allowed – in fact should be required – to rethink his strategy after Smith moves.

Consider Jones's strategy of (*Small, Small*) in equilibrium E_3. If Smith deviated from equilibrium by choosing *Large*, it would be unreasonable for Jones to stick to the response *Small*. Instead, he should also choose *Large*. But if Smith expected a response of *Large*, he would have chosen *Large* in the first place, and E_3 would not be an equilibrium. A similar argument shows that it would be irrational for Jones to choose (*Large, Large*), and we are left with E_2 as the unique equilibrium.

We say that equilibria E_1 and E_3 are Nash equilibria but not "perfect" Nash equilibria. A strategy profile is a perfect equilibrium if it remains an equilibrium on all possible paths, including not only the equilibrium path but all the other paths, which branch off into different "subgames." A player's perfect equilibrium strategy is thus a best response to the other players' equilibrium strategies not only on the equilibrium path, but **"out of equilibrium"** or **"off the equilibrium path."**

*A **subgame** is a game consisting of a node which is a singleton in every player's information partition, that node's successors, and the payoffs at the associated end nodes.*[1]

*A strategy profile is a **subgame perfect Nash equilibrium** if (a) it is a Nash equilibrium for the entire game; and (b) its relevant action rules are a Nash equilibrium for every subgame.*

The extensive form of Follow the Leader I in figure 4.1 (a reprise of figure 2.1) has three subgames: (a) the entire game, (b) the subgame starting at node J_1, and (c) the subgame starting at node J_2. Strategy profile E_1 is not a subgame perfect equilibrium because it is only Nash in subgames (a) and (c), not in subgame (b). Strategy profile E_3 is not a subgame perfect equilibrium because it is only Nash in subgames (a) and (b), not in subgame (c). Strategy profile E_2 is perfect because it is Nash in all three subgames.

---

[1] Technically, this is a *proper* subgame because of the information qualifier, but no economist is so ill-bred as to use any other kind of subgame.

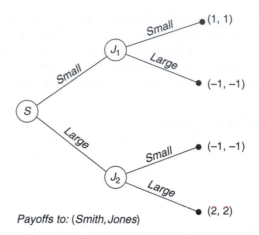

Figure 4.1   Follow-the-Leader I.

The term **sequential rationality** is often used to denote the idea that a player should maximize his payoffs at each point in the game, reoptimizing his decisions at each point and taking into account the fact that he will reoptimize in the future. This is a blend of the economic ideas of ignoring sunk costs and rational expectations. Sequential rationality is so standard a criterion for equilibrium now that often I will speak of "equilibrium" without the qualifier when I wish to refer to an equilibrium that satisfies sequential rationality in the sense of being a "subgame perfect equilibrium" or, in a game of asymmetric information, a "perfect Bayesian equilibrium."

One reason why perfectness (the word "subgame" is usually left off) is a good equilibrium concept is because it represents the idea of sequential rationality. A second reason is that a weak Nash equilibrium is not robust to small changes in the game. So long as he is certain that Smith will not choose *Large*, Jones is indifferent between the never-to-be-used responses (*Small* if *Large*) and (*Large* if *Large*). Equilibria E_1, E_2, and E_3 are all weak Nash equilibria because of this. But if there is even a small probability that Smith will choose *Large* – perhaps by mistake – then Jones would prefer the response (*Large* if *Large*), and equilibria E_1 and E_3 are no longer valid. Perfectness is a way to eliminate some of these less robust weak equilibria. The small probability of a mistake is called a **tremble**, and section 6.1 returns to this **trembling hand** approach as one way to extend the notion of perfectness to games of asymmetric information.

For the moment, however, the reader should note that the tremble approach is distinct from sequential rationality. Consider figure 4.2's Tremble Game. This game has three Nash equilibria, all weak: (*Out, Down*), (*Out, Up*), and (*In, Up*). Only (*Out, Up*) and (*In, Up*) are subgame perfect, because although *Down* is weakly Jones's best response to Smith's *Out*, it is inferior if Smith chooses *In*. In the subgame starting with Jones's move, the only subgame perfect equilibrium is for Jones to choose *Up*. The possibility of trembles, however, rules out (*In, Up*) as an equilibrium. If Jones has even an infinitesimal chance of trembling and choosing *Down*, Smith will choose *Out* instead of *In*. Also, Jones will choose *Up*, not *Down*, because if Smith trembles and chooses *In*, Jones prefers *Up* to *Down*. This leaves only (*Out, Up*) as an equilibrium, despite the fact that it is weakly Pareto dominated by ((*In, Up*).

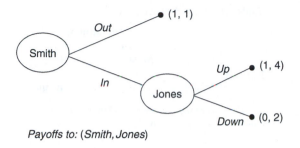

Payoffs to: (Smith, Jones)

Figure 4.2   The tremble game: trembling hand versus subgame perfectness.

4.2   An Example of Perfectness: Entry Deterrence I

We turn now to a game in which perfectness plays a role just as important as in Follow-the-Leader-I but in which the players are in conflict. An old question in industrial organization is whether an incumbent monopolist can maintain his position by threatening to wage a price war against any new firm that enters the market. This idea was heavily attacked by Chicago School economists such as McGee (1958) on the grounds that a price war would hurt the incumbent more than collusion with the entrant. Game theory can present this reasoning very cleanly. Let us consider a single episode of possible entry and price warfare, which nobody expects to be repeated. We will assume that even if the incumbent chooses to collude with the entrant, maintaining a duopoly is difficult enough that market revenue drops considerably from the monopoly level.

Entry Deterrence I

PLAYERS
Two firms, the entrant and the incumbent.

THE ORDER OF PLAY
1   The entrant decides whether to *Enter* or *Stay Out*.
2   If the entrant enters, the incumbent can *Collude* with him, or *Fight* by cutting the price drastically.

PAYOFFS
Market profits are 300 at the monopoly price and 0 at the fighting price. Entry costs are 10. Duopoly competition reduces market revenue to 100, which is split evenly.

The strategy sets can be discovered from the order of play. They are {*Enter*, *Stay Out*} for the entrant, and {*Collude* if entry occurs, *Fight* if entry occurs} for the incumbent. The game has the two Nash equilibria indicated in boldface in table 4.1, (*Enter*, *Collude*) and (*Stay Out*, *Fight*). The equilibrium (*Stay Out*, *Fight*) is weak, because the incumbent would just as soon *Collude* given that the entrant is staying out.

Table 4.1   Entry Deterrence I

		Incumbent		
		Collude		*Fight*
	Enter	**40, 50**	←	−10, 0
Entrant		↑		↓
	Stay Out	0, 300	↔	**0, 300**

Payoffs to: (Entrant, Incumbent). Arrows show how a player can increase his payoff.

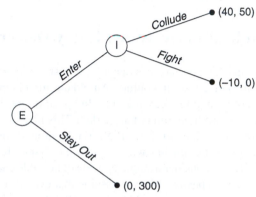

Payoffs to: (Entrant, Incumbent)

Figure 4.3   Entry deterrence I.

A piece of information has been lost by condensing from the extensive form, figure 4.3, to the normal form, table 4.1: the fact that the entrant gets to move first. Once he has chosen *Enter*, the incumbent's best response is *Collude*. The threat to fight is not credible and would be employed only if the incumbent could bind himself to fight, in which case he never does fight, because the entrant chooses to stay out. The equilibrium (*Stay Out*, *Fight*) is Nash but not subgame perfect, because if the game is started after the entrant has already entered, the incumbent's best response is *Collude*. This does not prove that collusion is inevitable in duopoly, but it is the equilibrium for Entry Deterrence I.

The trembling hand interpretation of perfect equilibrium can be used here. So long as it is certain that the entrant will not enter, the incumbent is indifferent between *Fight* and *Collude*, but if there were even a small probability of entry – perhaps because of a lapse of good judgement by the entrant – the incumbent would prefer *Collude* and the Nash equilibrium would be broken.

Perfectness rules out threats that are not credible. Entry Deterrence I is a good example because if a communication move were added to the game tree, the incumbent might tell the entrant that entry would be followed by fighting, but the entrant would ignore this noncredible threat. If, however, some means existed by which the incumbent could precommit himself to fight entry, the threat would become credible. The next section will look at one context, nuisance lawsuits, in which such precommitment might be possible.

Should the Modeller Ever Use Nonperfect Equilibria?

A game in which a player can commit himself to a strategy can be modelled in two ways:

1   As a game in which nonperfect equilibria are acceptable, or
2   By changing the game to replace the action *Do X* with *Commit To Do X* at an earlier node.

An example of (2) in Entry Deterrence I is to reformulate the game so the incumbent moves first, deciding in advance whether or not to choose *Fight* before the entrant moves. Approach (2) is better than (1) because if the modeller wants to let players commit to some actions and not to others, he can do this by carefully specifying the order of play. Allowing equilibria to be nonperfect forbids such discrimination and multiplies the number of equilibria. Indeed, the problem with subgame perfectness is not that it is too restrictive but that it still allows too many strategy profiles to be equilibria in games of asymmetric information. A subgame must start at a single node and not cut across any player's information set, so often the only subgame will be the whole game and subgame perfectness does not restrict equilibrium at all. Section 6.1 discusses perfect Bayesian equilibrium and other ways to extend the perfectness concept to games of asymmetric information.

4.3   Credible Threats, Sunks Costs, and the Open-set Problem in the Game of Nuisance Suits

Like the related concepts of sunks costs and rational expectations, sequential rationality is a simple idea with tremendous power. This section will show that power in another simple game, one which models nuisance suits. We have already come across one application of game theory to law, in the Png (1983) model of section 2.5. In some ways, law is particularly well suited to analysis by game theory because the legal process is so concerned with conflict and the provision of definite rules to regulate that conflict. In what other field could an article be titled "An Economic Analysis of Rule 68," as Miller (1986) does in his discussion of the federal rule of procedure that penalizes a losing litigant who had refused to accept a settlement offer. The growth in the area can be seen by comparing the overview in the Ayres's (1990) review of the first edition of the present book with the entire book by Baird, Gertner, & Picker (1994). In law, even more clearly than in business, a major objective is to avoid inefficient outcomes by restructuring the rules, and nuisance suits are one of the inefficiencies that a good policy maker hopes to eliminate.

Nuisance suits are lawsuits with little chance of success, whose only possible purpose seems to be the hope of a settlement out of court. In the context of entry deterrence people commonly think large size is an advantage and a large incumbent will threaten a small entrant, but in the context of nuisance suits people commonly think large size is a disadvantage and a wealthy corporation is vulnerable to extortionary litigation. Nuisance Suits I models the essentials of the situation: bringing suit is costly and has little chance of success, but because defending the suit is also costly the defendant might pay a generous amount to settle it out of court. The model is similar to the Png Settlement Game of chapter 2 in many respects, but here the model will be one of symmetric information and we will make explicit the sequential rationality requirement that was implicit in the discussion in chapter 2.

Nuisance Suits I: Simple Extortion

PLAYERS
A plaintiff and a defendant.

THE ORDER OF PLAY
1   The plaintiff decides whether to bring suit against the defendant at cost c.
2   The plaintiff makes a take-it-or-leave-it settlement offer of $s > 0$.
3   The defendant accepts or rejects the settlement offer.
4   If the defendant rejects the offer, the plaintiff decides whether to give up or go to trial at a cost p to himself and d to the defendant.
5   If the case goes to trial, the plaintiff wins amount x with probability γ and otherwise wins nothing.

PAYOFFS
Figure 4.4 shows the payoffs. Let $\gamma x < p$, so the plaintiff's expected winnings are less than his marginal cost of going to trial.

The perfect equilibrium is

Plaintiff: *Do nothing, Offer s, Give up*
Defendant: *Reject*
Outcome: The plaintiff does not bring a suit.

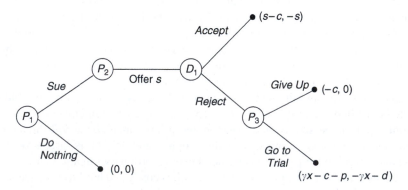

Payoffs to: (Plaintiff, Defendent)

Figure 4.4   The extensive form for Nuisance Suits.

The equilibrium settlement offer s can be any positive amount. Note that the equilibrium specifies actions at all four nodes of the game, even though only the first is reached in equilibrium.

To find a perfect equilibrium the modeller starts at the end of the game tree, following the advice of Dixit & Nalebuff (1991, p. 34) to "Look ahead and reason back." At node P_3, the plaintiff will choose *Give Up*, since by assumption $\gamma x - c - p < -c$. This is because the suit is brought only in the hope of settlement, not in the hope of winning at trial. At node D_1, the defendant, foreseeing that the plaintiff will give up, rejects any positive settlement offer. This makes the plaintiff's offer at P_2 irrelevant, and, looking ahead to a payoff of $-c$ from choosing *Sue* at P_1, the plaintiff chooses *Do Nothing*.

Thus, if nuisance suits are brought, it must be for some reason other than the obvious one, the plaintiff's hope of extracting a settlement offer from a defendant who wants to avoid trial costs. This is fallacious because the plaintiff himself bears trial costs and hence cannot credibly make the threat. It is fallacious even if the defendant's legal costs would be much higher than the plaintiff's (d much bigger than p), because the relative size of the costs does not enter into the argument.

One might wonder how risk aversion affects this conclusion. Might not the defendant settle because he is more risk-averse than the plaintiff? That is a good question, but Nuisance Suits I can be adapted to risk-averse players with very little change. Risk would enter at the trial stage, as a final move by Nature to decide who wins. In Nuisance Suits I, γx represented the expected value of the award. If both the defendant and the plaintiff are equally risk-averse, γx can still represent the expected payoff from the award – one simply interprets x and 0 as the utility of the cash award and the utility of an award of 0, rather than as the actual cash amounts. If the players have different degrees of risk aversion, the expected loss to the defendant is not the same as the expected gain to the plaintiff, and the payoffs must be adjusted. If the defendant is more risk-averse, the payoffs from *Go to trial* would change to $(-c - p + \gamma x, -\gamma x - y - d)$, where y represents the extra disutility of risk to the defendant. This, however, makes no difference to the equilibrium. The crux of the game is that the plaintiff is unwilling to go to trial because of the cost to himself, and the cost to the defendant, including the cost of bearing risk, is irrelevant.

If nuisance suits are brought, it must therefore be for some more complicated reason. Already, in chapter 2, we looked at one reason for litigation to reach trial in the Png Settlement Game: incomplete information. That is probably the most important explanation and it has been much studied, as can be seen from the surveys by Cooter & Rubinfeld (1989) and Kennan & R. Wilson (1993). In this section, though, let us confine ourselves to explanations where the probability of the suit's success is common knowledge. Even then, costly threats might be credible because of sinking costs strategically (Nuisance Suits II), or because of the nonmonetary payoffs resulting from going to trial (Nuisance Suits III).

Nuisance Suits II: Using Sunk Costs Strategically

Let us now modify the game, following the inspiration of Rosenberg & Shavell (1985), so that the plaintiff can pay his lawyer the amount p in advance, with no refund if the case settles. This inability to obtain a refund actually helps the plaintiff, by changing the payoffs from the game so his payoff from *Give Up* is $(-c - p)$, compared to $(-c - p + \gamma x)$ from *Go to Trial*. Having sunk the legal costs, he will go to trial if $\gamma x > 0$ – that is, if he has any chance of success at all.

This, in turn, means that the plaintiff would only prefer settlement to trial if $s > \gamma x$. The defendant would prefer settlement to trial if $s < \gamma x + d$, so there is a positive **settlement range** of $[\gamma x, \gamma x + d]$ within which both players are willing to settle. The exact amount of the settlement depends on the bargaining power of the parties, something to be examined in chapter 12. Here, allowing the plaintiff to make a take-it-or-leave-it offer means that $s = \gamma x + d$ in equilibrium, and if $\gamma x + d > p + c$, the nuisance suit will be brought even though $\gamma x < p + c$. Thus, the plaintiff is bringing the suit only because he can extort d, the amount of the defendant's legal costs.

Even though the plaintiff can now extort a settlement, he does it at some cost to himself, so an equilibrium with nuisance suits will require that

$$-c - p + \gamma x + d \geq 0. \tag{4.1}$$

If inequality (4.1) is false, then, even if the plaintiff could extract the maximum possible settlement of $s = \gamma x + d$, he would not do so, because he would then have to pay $c + p$ before reaching the settlement stage. This implies that a totally meritless suit (with $\gamma = 0$), would not be brought unless the defendant had higher legal costs than the plaintiff ($d > p$). If inequality (4.1) is satisfied, however, the following strategy profile is a perfect equilibrium:

Plaintiff: *Sue, Offer $s = \gamma x + d$, Go to Trial*

Defendant: *Accept $s \leq \gamma x + d$*

Outcome: Plaintiff sues and offers to settle, to which the defendant agrees.

An obvious counter to the plaintiff's ploy would be for the defendant to also sink his costs, by paying d before the settlement negotiations, or even before the plaintiff decides to file suit. Perhaps this is one reason why large corporations use in-house counsel, who are paid a salary regardless of how many hours they work, as well as outside counsel, hired by the hour. If so, nuisance suits cause a social loss – the wasted time of the lawyers, d – even if nuisance suits are never brought, just as aggressor nations cause social loss in the form of world military expenditure even if they never start a war.[2]

Two problems, however, face the defendant who tries to sink the cost d. First, although it saves him γx if it deters the plaintiff from filing suit, it also means the defendant must pay the full amount d. This is worthwhile if the plaintiff has all the bargaining power, as in Nuisance Suits II, but it might not be if s lay in the middle of the settlement range because the plaintiff was not able to make a take-it-or-leave-it offer. If settlement negotiations resulted in s lying exactly in the middle of the settlement range, so $s = \gamma x + (d/2)$, then it might not be worthwhile for the defendant to sink d to deter nuisance suits that would settle for $\gamma x + (d/2)$.

Second, there is an asymmetry in litigation: the plaintiff has the choice of whether to bring suit or not. Since it is the plaintiff who has the initiative, he can sink p and make

---

[2] Nonrefundable lawyers' fees, paid in advance, have traditionally been acceptable, but a New York court recently ruled they were unethical. The court thought that such fees unfairly restricted the client's ability to fire his lawyer, an example of how ignorance of game theory can lead to confused rule-making. See "Nonrefundable Lawyers' Fees, Paid in Advance, Are Unethical, Court Rules," *Wall Street Journal*, January 29, 1993, p. B3, citing *In the matter of Edward M. Cooperman, Appellate Division of the Supreme Court, Second Judicial Department, Brooklyn, 90-00429.*

the settlement offer before the defendant has the chance to sink d. The only way for the defendant to avoid this is to pay d well in advance, in which case the expenditure is wasted if no possible suits arise. What the defendant would like best would be to buy legal insurance which, for a small premium, would pay all defense costs in future suits that might occur. As we will see in chapters 8 and 9, however, insurance of any kind faces problems arising from asymmetric information. In this context, there is the "moral hazard" problem, in that once the defendant is insured he has less incentive to avoid causing harm to the plaintiff and provoking a lawsuit.

The Open-set Problem in Nuisance Suits II

Nuisance Suits II illustrates a technical point that arises in a great many games with continuous strategy spaces and causes great distress to novices in game theory. The equilibrium in Nuisance Suits II is only a weak Nash equilibrium. The plaintiff proposes $s = \gamma x + d$, and the defendant has the same payoff from accepting or rejecting, but in equilibrium the defendant accepts the offer with probability one, despite his indifference. This seems arbitrary, or even silly. Should not the plaintiff propose a slightly lower settlement to give the defendant a strong incentive to accept it and avoid the risk of having to go to trial? If the parameters are such that $s = \gamma x + d = 60$, for example, why does the plaintiff risk holding out for 60 when he might be rejected and most likely receive 0 at trial, when he could offer 59 and give the defendant a strong incentive to accept?

One answer is that no other equilibrium exists besides $s = 60$. Offering 59 cannot be part of an equilibrium because it is dominated by offering 59.9; offering 59.9 is dominated by offering 59.99, and so forth. This is known as the **open-set problem**, because the set of offers that the defendant strongly wishes to accept is open and has no maximum – it is bounded at 60, but a set must be bounded *and closed* to guarantee that a maximum exists. We are not just picking the Nash equilibrium in which the defendant accepts paying 60; we are picking the *only* Nash equilibrium.

A second answer is that under the assumptions of rationality and Nash equilibrium the objection's premise is false because the plaintiff bears no risk whatsoever in offering $s = 60$. It is fundamental to Nash equilibrium that each player believe that the others will follow equilibrium behavior. Thus, if the equilibrium strategy profile says that the defendant will accept $s \leq 60$, the plaintiff can offer 60 and believe it will be accepted. This is really just to say that a weak Nash equilibrium is still a Nash equilibrium, a point emphasized in chapter 3 in connection with mixed strategies.

A third answer is that the problem is an artifact of using a model with a continuous strategy space, and it disappears if the strategy space is made discrete. Assume that s can only take values in multiples of 0.01, so it could be 59.0, 59.01, 59.02, and so forth, but not 59.001 or 59.002. The settlement part of the game will now have two perfect equilibria. In the strong equilibrium E1, $s = 59.99$ and the defendant accepts any offer $s < 60$. In the weak equilibrium E2, $s = 60$ and the defendant accepts any offer $s \leq 60$. The difference is trivial, so the discrete strategy space has made the model more complicated without any extra insight.[3]

---

[3] A good example of the ideas of discrete money values and sequential rationality is in Robert Louis Stevenson's 1893 story, "The Bottle Imp" (Stevenson [1987]). The imp grants the wishes of the bottle's owner but will seize his soul if he dies in possession of it. Although the bottle cannot be given away, it can be sold, but only at a price less than that for which it was purchased.

One can also specify a more complicated bargaining game to avoid the issue of how exactly the settlement is determined. Here one could say that the settlement is not proposed by the plaintiff, but simply emerges with a value halfway through the settlement range, so $s = \gamma x + (d/2)$. This seems reasonable enough, and it adds a little extra realism to the model at the cost of a little extra complexity. It avoids the open-set problem, but only by avoiding being clear about how s is determined. I call this kind of modelling **blackboxing**, because it is as if at some point in the game, variables with certain values go into a black box and come out the other side with values determined by an exogenous process. Blackboxing is perfectly acceptable as long as it neither drives nor obscures the point the model is making. Nuisance Suits III will illustrate this method.

Fundamentally, however, the point to keep in mind is that games are models, not reality. They are meant to clear away the unimportant details of a real situation and simplify it down to the essentials. Since a model is trying to answer a question, it should focus on what answers that question. Here, the question is why nuisance suits might be brought, so it is proper to exclude details of the bargaining if they are irrelevant to the answer. Whether a plaintiff offers 59.99 or 60, and whether a rational person accepts an offer with probability 0.99 or 1.00, is part of the unimportant detail, and whatever approach is simplest should be used. If the modeller really thinks that these are important matters, they can indeed be modelled, but they are not important in this context.

One source of concern over the open-set problem, I think, is that perhaps that the pay-offs are not quite realistic, because the players should derive utility from hurting "unfair" players. If the plaintiff makes a settlement offer of 60, keeping the entire savings from avoiding the trial for himself, everyday experience tells us that the defendant will indig-nantly refuse the offer. Guth, Schmittberger, & Schwarze (1982) have found in experiments that people turn down bargaining offers they perceive as unfair, as one might expect. If indignation is truly important, it can be explicitly incorporated into the payoffs, and if that is done, the open-set problem returns. Indignation is not boundless, whatever people may say. Suppose that accepting a settlement offer that benefits the plaintiff more than the defendant gives a disutility of x to the defendant because of his indignation at his unjust treatment. The plaintiff will then offer to settle for exactly $60 - x$, so the equilibrium is still weak and the defendant is still indifferent between accepting and rejecting the offer. The open-set problem persists, even after realistic emotions are added to the model.

I have spent so much time on the open-set problem not because it is important but because it arises so often and is a sticking point for people unfamiliar with modelling. It is not a problem that disturbs experienced modellers, unlike other basic issues we have already encountered – for example, the issue of how a Nash equilibrium comes to be common knowledge among the players – but it is important to understand why it is not important.

Nuisance Suits III: Malice

One of the most common misconceptions about game theory, as about economics in general, is that it ignores nonrational and nonmonetary motivations. Game theory does take the basic motivations of the players to be exogenous to the model, but those motivations are crucial to the outcome and they often are not monetary, although payoffs are always given numerical values. Game theory does not call somebody irrational who prefers leisure to money or who is motivated by the desire to be world dictator. It does require the players' emotions to be carefully gauged to determine exactly how the actions and outcomes affect the players' utility.

Emotions are often important to lawsuits, and law professors tell their students that when the cases they study seem to involve disputes too trivial to be worth taking to court, they can guess that the real motivations are emotional. Emotions could enter in a variety of distinct ways. The plaintiff might simply like going to trial, which can be expressed as a value of $p < 0$. This would be true of many criminal cases, because prosecutors like news coverage and want credit with the public for prosecuting certain kinds of crime. The Rodney King trials of 1992 and 1993 were of this variety; regardless of the merits of the cases against the policemen who beat Rodney King, the prosecutors wanted to go to trial to satisfy the public outrage, and when the state prosecutors failed in the first trial, the federal government was happy to accept the cost of bringing suit in the second trial. A different motivation is that the plaintiff might derive utility from the fact of winning the case quite separately from the monetary award, because he wants a public statement that he is in the right. This is a motivation in bringing libel suits, or for a criminal defendant who wants to clear his good name.

A different emotional motivation for going to trial is the desire to inflict losses on the defendant, a motivation we will call "malice," although it might as inaccurately be called "righteous anger." In this case, d enters as a positive argument in the plaintiff's utility function. We will construct a model of this kind, called Nuisance Suits III, and assume that $\gamma = 0.1$, $c = 3$, $p = 14$, $d = 50$, and $x = 100$, and that the plaintiff receives additional utility of 0.1 times the defendant's disutility. Let us also adopt the blackboxing technique discussed earlier and assume that the settlement s is in the middle of the settlement range. The payoffs conditional on suit being brought are

$$\pi_{plaintiff}(\textit{Defendant accepts}) = s - c + 0.1s = 1.1s - 3 \qquad (4.2)$$

and

$$\begin{aligned}
\pi_{plaintiff}(\textit{Go to Trial}) &= \gamma x - c - p + 0.1(d + \gamma x) \\
&= 10 - 3 - 14 + 6 = -1.
\end{aligned} \qquad (4.3)$$

Now, working back from the end in accordance with sequential rationality, note that since the plaintiff's payoff from *Give Up* is -3, he will go to trial if the defendant rejects the settlement offer. The overall payoff from bringing a suit that eventually goes to trial is still -1, which is worse than the payoff of 0 from not bringing suit in the first place, but if s is high enough, the payoff from bringing suit and settling is higher still. If s is greater than 1.82 $(=(-1+3)/1.1$, rounded), the plaintiff prefers settlement to trial, and if s is greater than about 2.73 $(=(0+3)/1.1$, rounded), he prefers settlement to not bringing the suit at all.

In determining the settlement range, the relevant payoff is the expected incremental payoff since the suit was brought. The plaintiff will settle for any $s \geq 1.82$, and the defendant will settle for any $s \leq \gamma x + d = 60$, as before. The settlement range is $[1.82, 60]$, and $s = 30.91$. The settlement offer is no longer the maximizing choice of a player, and hence is moved to the outcome in the equilibrium description below.

Plaintiff: *Sue, Go to Trial*

Defendant: *Accept any $s \leq 60$*

Outcome: The plaintiff sues and offers $s = 30.91$, and the defendant accepts the settlement.

Perfectness is important here because the defendant would like to threaten never to settle and be believed. The plaintiff would not bring suit given his expected payoff of -1 from bringing a suit that goes to trial, so a believable threat would be effective. But such a threat is not believable. Once the plaintiff does bring suit, the only Nash equilibrium in the remaining subgame is for the defendant to accept his settlement offer. This is interesting because the plaintiff, despite his willingness to go to trial, ends up settling out of court. When information is symmetric, as it is here, there is a tendency for equilibria to be efficient. Although the plaintiff wants to hurt the defendant, he also wants to keep his expenses low. Thus, he is willing to hurt the defendant less if it enables him to save on his own legal costs.

One final point before leaving these models is that much of the value of modelling comes simply from setting up the rules of the game, which helps to show what is important in a situation. One problem that arises in setting up a model of nuisance suits is deciding what a "nuisance suit" really is. In the game of Nuisance Suits, it has been defined as a suit whose expected damages do not repay the plaintiff's costs of going to trial. But having to formulate a definition brings to mind another problem that might be called the problem of nuisance suits: that the plaintiff brings suits he knows will not win unless the court makes a mistake. Since the court might make a mistake with very high probability, the games above would not be appropriate models. The parameter γ would be high, and the problem is not that the plaintiff's expected gain from trial is low, but that it is high. This, too, is an important problem, but having to construct a model shows that it is different.

4.4   Recoordination to Pareto-dominant Equilibria in Subgames: Pareto Perfection

One simple refinement of equilibrium that was mentioned in chapter 1 is to rule out any strategy profiles that are Pareto dominated by Nash equilibria. Thus, in the game of Ranked Coordination, the inferior Nash equilibrium would be ruled out as an acceptable equilibrium. The idea behind this is that in some unmodelled way the players discuss their situation and coordinate to avoid the bad equilibria. Since only Nash equilibria are discussed, the players' agreements are self-enforcing and this is a more limited suggestion than the approach in cooperative game theory according to which the players make binding agreements.

The coordination idea can be taken further in various ways. One is to think about coalitions of players coordinating on favorable equilibria, so that two players might coordinate on an equilibrium even if a third player dislikes it. Bernheim, Peleg, & Whinston (1987), and Bernheim & Whinston (1987) define a Nash strategy profile as a **coalition-proof Nash equilibrium** if no coalition of players could form a self-enforcing agreement to deviate from it. They take the idea further by subordinating it to the idea of sequential rationality. The natural way to do this is to require that no coalition would deviate in future subgames, a notion called by various names, including **renegotiationproofness**, **recoordination** (e.g., Laffont & Tirole [1993], p. 460), and **Pareto perfection** (e.g., Fudenberg & Tirole [1991a], p. 175). The idea has been used extensively in the analysis of infinitely repeated games, which are particularly subject to the problem of multiple equilibria; Abreu, Pearce, &

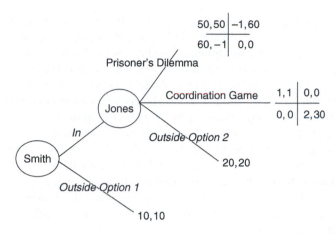

Figure 4.5   The Pareto Perfection Puzzle.

Stachetti (1986) is an example of this literature. Whichever name is used, the idea is distinct from the renegotiation problem in the principal–agent models to be studied in chapter 8, which involves the rewriting of earlier binding contracts to make new binding contracts.

The best way to demonstrate the idea of Pareto perfection is by an illustration, the Pareto Perfection Puzzle, whose extensive form is shown in figure 4.5. In this game Smith chooses *In* or *Outside Option 1*, which yields payoffs of 10 to each player. Jones then chooses *Outside Option 2*, which yields 20 to each player, or initiates either a coordination game or a prisoner's dilemma. Rather than draw the full subgames in extensive form, figure 4.5 inserts the payoff matrix for the subgames.

The Pareto Perfection Puzzle illustrates the complicated interplay between perfectness and Pareto dominance. The Pareto-dominant strategy profile is (In, Prisoner's Dilemma|In, any actions in the coordination subgame, the actions yielding (50, 50) in the Prisoner's Dilemma subgame). Nobody expects this strategy profile to be an equilibrium, since it is neither perfect nor Nash. Perfectness tells us that if the Prisoner's Dilemma subgame is reached, the payoffs will be (0, 0), and if the coordination subgame is reached they will be either (1, 1) or (2, 30). In light of this, the perfect equilibria of the Pareto Perfection Puzzle are

E1: (*In, Outside option 2|In*, the actions yielding (1, 1) in the coordination subgame, the actions yielding (0, 0) in the Prisoner's Dilemma subgame.) The payoffs are (20, 20).

E2: (*Outside Option 1*, coordination game|*In*, the actions yielding (2, 30) in the coordination subgame, the actions yielding (0, 0) in the Prisoner's Dilemma subgame.) The payoffs are (10, 10).

If one applies Pareto dominance without perfection, E1 will be the equilibrium, since both players prefer it. If the players can recoordinate at any point and change their expectations, however, then if play of the game reaches the coordination subgame, the players will recoordinate on the actions yielding (2, 30). Pareto perfection thus knocks out E1 as an equilibrium. Not only does it rule out the Pareto-dominant strategy profile that yields (50, 50) as an equilibrium, it also rules out the Pareto-dominant perfect strategy profile that yields

(20, 20) as an equilibrium. Rather, the payoff is (10, 10). Thus, Pareto perfection is not the same thing as simply picking the Pareto-dominant perfect strategy profile.

It is difficult to say which equilibrium is best here, since this is an abstract game and we cannot call upon details from the real world to refine the model. The approach of applying an equilibrium refinement is not as likely to yield results as using the intuition behind the refinement. The intuition here is that the players will somehow coordinate on Pareto-dominant equilibria, perhaps finding open discussion helpful. If we ran an experiment on student players using the Pareto Perfection Puzzle, I would expect to reach different equilibria depending on what communication is allowed. If the players are allowed to talk only before the game starts, it seems more likely that E1 would be the equilibrium, since players could agree to play it and would have no chance to explicitly recoordinate later. If the players could talk at any time as the game proceeded, E2 becomes more plausible. Real-world situations arise with many different communications technologies, so there is no one right answer.

Notes

N4.1   Subgame perfectness

- The terms "perfectness" and "perfection" are used synonymously. Selten (1965) proposed the equilibrium concept in an article written in German. "Perfectness" is used in Selten (1975) and conveys an impression of completeness more appropriate to the concept than the goodness implied by "perfection." "Perfection," however, is more common.
- It is debatable whether the definition of subgame ought to include the original game. Gibbon (1992, p. 122) does not, for example, and modellers usually do not in their conversation.
- Perfectness is not the only way to eliminate weak Nash equilibria like (*Stay Out, Collude*). In Entry Deterrence I, (*Enter, Collude*) is the only iterated dominance equilibrium, because *Fight* is weakly dominated for the incumbent.
- The distinction between perfect and nonperfect Nash equilibria is like the distinction between **closed loop** and **open loop** trajectories in dynamic programming. Closed loop (or **feedback**) trajectories can be revised after they start, like perfect equilibrium strategies, while open loop trajectories are completely prespecified (though they may depend on state variables). In dynamic programming the distinction is not so important, because prespecified strategies do not change the behavior of other players. No threat, for example, is going to alter the pull of the moon's gravity on a rocket.
- A subgame can be infinite in length, and infinite games can have nonperfect equilibria. The infinitely repeated Prisoner's Dilemma is an example; here every subgame looks exactly like the original game but begins at a different point in time.
- **Sequential rationality in macroeconomics.** In macroeconomics the requirement of **dynamic consistency** or **time consistency** is similar to perfectness. These terms are less precisely defined than perfectness, but they usually require that strategies need only be best responses in subgames starting from nodes on the equilibrium path, instead of all subgames. Under this interpretation, time consistency is a less stringent condition than perfectness.

  The Federal Reserve, for example, might like to induce inflation to stimulate the economy, but the economy is stimulated only if the inflation is unexpected. If the inflation is expected, its effects are purely bad. Since members of the public know that the Fed would like to fool them, they disbelieve its claims that it will not generate inflation (see Kydland & Prescott [1977]). Likewise, the government would like to issue nominal debt, and promises lenders that it will keep inflation low, but once the debt is issued, the government has an incentive to inflate its real value to zero. One reason the US Federal Reserve Board was established to be independent of Congress in the United States was to diminish this problem.

- Often, irrationality – behavior that is automatic rather than strategic – is an advantage. The Doomsday Machine in the movie *Dr Strangelove* is one example. The Soviet Union decides that it cannot win a rational arms race against the richer United States, so it creates a bomb which automatically blows up the entire world if anyone explodes a nuclear bomb. The movie also illustrates a crucial detail without which such irrationality is worse than useless: you have to tell the other side that you have the Doomsday Machine.

  President Nixon reportedly told his aide H. R. Haldeman that he followed a more complicated version of this strategy: "I call it the Madman Theory, Bob. I want the North Vietnamese to believe that I've reached the point where I might do *anything* to stop the war. We'll just slip the word to them that 'for God's sake, you know Nixon is obsessed about Communism. We can't restrain him when he's angry – and he has his hand on the nuclear button' – and Ho Chi Minh himself will be in Paris in two days begging for peace" (H. R. Haldeman & Joseph DiMona, *The Ends of Power*, 1978, p. 83). The Gang of Four model in section 6.4 tries to model a situation like that.

- The "lock-up agreement" is an example of a credible threat: in a takeover defense, the threat to destroy the firm is made legally binding. See Macey & McChesney (1985), p. 33.

- A famous paradox relating to sequential rationality is the "Quiz on Friday Paradox." You are going to have a quiz next week, but I am going to surprise you with my choice of day. If we reach Thursday without a quiz, however, you will know the quiz must be on Friday and not be surprised, so the quiz must be earlier. The same argument applies to looking ahead to Thursday on Wednesday, however, and by iteration all days can be ruled out. Philosophers from Quine (1953) to Schick (2003, ch. 5) have puzzled over this.

N4.3   An example of perfectness: Entry Deterrence I

- The Stackelberg equilibrium of a duopoly game (section 3.4) can be viewed as the perfect equilibrium of a Cournot game modified so that one player moves first, a game similar to Entry Deterrence I. The player moving first is the Stackelberg leader and the player moving second is the Stackelberg follower. The follower could threaten to produce a high output, but he will not carry out his threat if the leader produces a high output first.

- Perfectness is not so desirable a property of equilibrium in biological games. The reason the order of moves matters is because the rational best reply depends on the node at which the game has arrived. In many biological games the players act by instinct and unthinking behavior is not unrealistic.

- Reinganum & Stokey (1985) is a clear presentation of the implications of perfectness and commitment illustrated with the example of natural resource extraction.

Problems

4.1:   Repeated Entry Deterrence (easy)

Consider two repetitions without discounting of the game Entry Deterrence I from section 4.2. Assume that there is one entrant, who sequentially decides whether to enter two markets that have the same incumbent.

(a)   Draw the extensive form of this game.
(b)   What are the 16 elements of the strategy sets of the entrant?

(c)   What is the subgame perfect equilibrium?
(d)   What is one of the nonperfect Nash equilibria?

4.2:   The Three-way Duel (medium) (after Shubik [1954])

Three gangsters armed with pistols, Al, Bob, and Curly, are in a room with a suitcase containing 120,000 dollars. Al is the least accurate, with a 20 percent chance of killing his target. Bob has a 40 percent probability. Curly is slow but sure; he kills his target with 70 percent probability. For each, the value of his own life outweighs the value of any amount of money. Survivors split the money.

(a)   Suppose each gangster has one bullet and the order of shooting is first Al, then Bob, then Curly. Assume also that each gangster must try to kill another gangster when his turn comes. What is an equilibrium strategy profile and what is the probability that each of them dies in that equilibrium? Hint: Do not try to draw a game tree.
(b)   Suppose now that each gangster has the additional option of shooting his gun at the ceiling, which may kill somebody upstairs but has no direct effect on his payoff. Does the strategy profile that you found was an equilibrium in part (a) remain an equilibrium?
(c)   Replace the three gangsters with three companies, Apex, Brydox, and Costco, which are competing with slightly different products. What story can you tell about their advertising strategies?
(d)   In the United States, before the general election a candidate must win the nomination of his party. It is often noted that candidates are reluctant to be seen as the frontrunner in the race for the nomination of their party, Democrat or Republican. In the general election, however, no candidate ever minds being seen to be ahead of his rival from the other party. Why?
(e)   In the 1920s, several men vied for power in the Soviet Union after Lenin died. First Stalin and Zinoviev combined against Trotsky. Then Stalin and Bukharin combined against Zinoviev. Then Stalin turned on Bukharin. Relate this to Curly, Bob, and Al.

4.3:   Heresthetics in Pliny and the Freedmens' Trial (easy) (Pliny [105] "To Aristo," Riker [1986, pp. 78–88])

Afranius Dexter died mysteriously, perhaps dead by his own hand, perhaps killed by his freedmen (servants a step above slaves), or perhaps killed by his freedmen by his own orders. The freedmen went on trial before the Roman Senate. Assume that 45 percent of the senators favor acquittal, 35 percent favor banishment, and 20 percent favor execution, and that the preference rankings in the three groups are $A \succ B \succ E$, $B \succ A \succ E$, and $E \succ B \succ A$. Also assume that each group has a leader and votes as a bloc.

(a)   Modern legal procedure requires the court to decide guilt first and then assign a penalty if the accused is found guilty. Draw a tree to represent the sequence of events (this will not be a game tree, since it will represent the actions of groups of players, not of individuals). What is the outcome in a perfect equilibrium?
(b)   Suppose that the acquittal bloc can pre-commit to how they will vote in the second round if guilt wins in the first round. What will they do, and what will happen? What would the execution bloc do if they could control the second-period vote of the acquittal bloc?
(c)   The normal Roman procedure began with a vote on execution versus no execution, and then voted on the alternatives in a second round if execution failed to gain a majority. Draw a tree to represent this. What would happen in this case?

(d)   Pliny proposed that the Senators divide into three groups, depending on whether they supported acquittal, banishment, or execution, and that the outcome with the most votes should win. This proposal caused a roar of protest. Why did he propose it?

(e)   Pliny did not get the result he wanted with his voting procedure. Why not?

(f)   Suppose that personal considerations made it most important to a senator that he show his stand by his vote, even if he had to sacrifice his preference for a particular outcome. If there were a vote over whether to use the traditional Roman procedure or Pliny's procedure, who would vote with Pliny, and what would happen to the freedmen?

4.4:   Garbage entry (medium)

Mr Turner is thinking of entering the garbage collection business in a certain large city. Currently, Cutright Enterprises has a monopoly, earning 40 million dollars from the 40 routes the city offers up for bids. Turner thinks he can take away as many routes as he wants from Cutright, at a profit of 1.5 million per route for him. He is worried, however, that Cutright might resort to assassination, killing him to regain their lost routes. He would be willing to be assassinated for profit of 80 million dollars, and assassination would cost Cutright 6 million dollars in expected legal costs and possible prison sentences.

How many routes should Turner try to take away from Cutright?

4.5:   Voting cycles (medium)

Uno, Duo, and Tres are three people voting on whether the budget devoted to a project should be Increased, kept the Same, or Reduced. Their payoffs from the different outcomes, given in table 4.2, are not monotonic in budget size. Uno thinks the project could be very profitable if its budget were increased, but will fail otherwise. Duo mildly wants a smaller budget. Tres likes the budget as it is now.

Table 4.2   Payoffs from different policies

	Uno	Duo	Tres
Increase	100	2	4
Same	3	6	9
Reduce	9	8	1

Each of the three voters writes down his first choice. If a policy gets a majority of the votes, it wins. Otherwise, *Same* is the chosen policy.

(a)   Show that (*Same, Same, Same*) is a Nash equilibrium. Why does this equilibrium seem unreasonable to us?

(b)   Show that (*Increase, Same, Same*) is a Nash equilibrium.

(c)   Show that if each player has an independent small probability ϵ of "trembling" and choosing each possible wrong action by mistake, (*Same, Same, Same*) and (*Increase, Same, Same*) are no longer equilibria.

(d)   Show that (*Reduce, Reduce, Same*) is a Nash equilibrium that survives each player has an independent small probability ϵ of "trembling" and choosing each possible wrong action by mistake.

(e)   Part (d) showed that if Uno and Duo are expected to choose *Reduce*, then Tres would choose *Same* if he could hope they might tremble – not *Increase*. Suppose, instead, that Tres votes first, and publicly. Construct a subgame perfect equilibrium in which Tres chooses *Increase*. You need not worry about trembles now.

(f) Consider the following voting procedure. First, the three voters vote between *Increase* and *Same*. In the second round, they vote between the winning policy and *Reduce*. If, at that point, *Increase* is not the winning policy, the third vote is between *Increase* and whatever policy won in the second round.

What will happen? (Watch out for the trick in this question!)

(g) Speculate about what would happen if the payoffs are in terms of dollar willingness to pay by each player and the players could make binding agreements to buy and sell votes. What, if anything, can you say about which policy would win, and what votes would be bought at what price?

US Air for Sale: A Classroom Game for Chapter 4

On October 2, 1995, US Air, at the time the nation's fifth largest airline, announced that it had approached United Airlines and American Airlines about a possible buyout. United and American are the two largest U.S. airlines, and both are interested in growth in the highly competitive airline market. United and American must now consider what to do.

Financial analysts for both United and American have made projections for all the possible scenarios, on the request of the strategic bidding consultants. They say that United and American start in equally strong positions, but that can change depending on who wins the auction.

The three possible outcomes for an airline are:

Neither firm bids enough for US Air to accept. Both United and American will maintain their strong positions, and they can expect future profits of $50 billion each.

Our airline wins. The winning airline will become the dominant firm in the market, and can expect future profits of $80 billion. The purchase cost of US Air, however, must be subtracted from this in order to calculate net profit. Therefore, the payoff for the firm with the winning bid is

$$Payoff_{Winner} = 80 - B_{winning}. \tag{4.4}$$

The minimum price US Air will accept is $10 billion.

Our airline loses. The losing firm may have trouble competing with the larger network of the winner because of the greater variety of flights a large airline can offer. The more, however, that the winner pays for US Air, the better off is the loser, because the cash flow the winner uses to pay for the acquisition is no longer available for other investments in new equipment and lenders will be more reluctant to lend to the newly enlarged firm. The analysts suggest that a good approximation to the payoff of the losing firm will be

$$Payoff_{Loser} = 30 + 0.25 * B_{winning}. \tag{4.5}$$

US Air for Sale: A Classroom Game for Chapter 4 (Continued)

In particular, if the winner pays just $10 billion for US Air, the loser's profit will be $32.5 billion.

We will look at two kinds of auction rules: ascending, and first price.

First-price Auction Rules: US Air will solicit bids in writing from anyone who cares to bid. Once all bids are received, they will be announced publicly. If there is just one bid, it wins if it is $10 billion or above. If there are no bids, US Air will continue as an independent firm. If there are two bids, and at least one is $10 billion or above, the winner has purchased US Air, ties being broken by the flip of a coin.

Ascending Auction Rules: US Air will solicit initial bids in writing from United and American, choosing the first bidder randomly and announcing its bid publicly before asking the other for a written bid. If there are no written bids of at least 10 billion dollars, US Air will continue as an independent firm. If there is at least one bid of 10 billion dollars or above, US Air will allow counteroffers, and an ascending auction commences. The winner has purchased US Air.

Students playing the game will be put into groups of three representing either United or American. Groups will be paired up to play out the auction under the ascending or first-price rules. First, play all the pairs by the first-price rules, then by the ascending rules.

Chapter 5
reputation and repeated games
with symmetric information

5.1 Finitely Repeated Games and the Chainstore Paradox

Chapter 4 showed how to refine the concept of Nash equilibrium to find sensible equilibria in games with moves in sequence over time, so-called dynamic games. An important class of dynamic games is repeated games, in which players repeatedly make the same decision in the same environment. Chapter 5 will look at such games, in which the rules of the game remain unchanged with each repetition and all that changes is the "history" which grows as time passes, and, if the number of repetitions is finite, the approach of the end of the game. It is also possible for asymmetry of information to change over time in a repeated game since players' moves may convey their private information, but chapter 5 will confine itself to games of symmetric information.

Section 5.1 will show the perverse unimportance of repetition for the games of Entry Deterrence and the Prisoner's Dilemma, a phenomenon known as the Chainstore Paradox. Neither discounting, probabilistic end dates, infinite repetitions, nor precommitment are satisfactory escapes from the Chainstore Paradox. This is summarized in the Folk Theorem in section 5.2. Section 5.2 will also discuss strategies which punish players who fail to cooperate in a repeated game – strategies such as the Grim Strategy, Tit-for-Tat, and Minimax. Section 5.3 builds a framework for reputation models based on the Prisoner's Dilemma, and section 5.4 presents one particular reputation model, the Klein–Leffler model of product quality. Section 5.5 concludes the chapter with an overlapping generations model of consumer switching costs which uses the idea of Markov strategies to narrow down the number of equilibria.

The Chainstore Paradox

Suppose that we repeat Entry Deterrence I 20 times in the context of a chainstore that is trying to deter entry into 20 markets where it has outlets. We have seen that entry into just one market would not be deterred, but perhaps with 20 markets the outcome is different because the chainstore would fight the first entrant to deter the next 19.

The repeated game is much more complicated than the **one-shot game**, as the unrepeated version is called. A player's action is still to *Enter* or *Stay Out*, to *Fight* or *Collude*, but his strategy is a potentially very complicated rule telling him what action to choose depending on what actions both players took in each of the previous periods. Even the five-round repeated Prisoner's Dilemma has a strategy set for each player with over two billion strategies, and the number of strategy profiles is even greater (Sugden [1986, p. 108]).

The obvious way to solve the game is from the beginning, where there is the least past history on which to condition a strategy, but that is not the easy way. We have to follow Kierkegaard, who said, "Life can only be understood backwards, but it must be lived forwards" (Kierkegaard [1938, p. 465]). In picking his first action, a player looks ahead to its implications for all the future periods, so it is easiest to start by understanding the end of a multiperiod game, where the future is shortest.

Consider the situation in which 19 markets have already been invaded (and maybe the chainstore fought, or maybe not). In the last market, the subgame in which the two players find themselves is identical to the one-shot Entry Deterrence I, so the entrant will *Enter* and the chainstore will *Collude*, regardless of the past history of the game. Next, consider the next-to-last market. The chainstore can gain nothing from building a reputation for ferocity, because it is common knowledge that he will *Collude* with the last entrant anyway. So he might as well *Collude* in the nineteenth market. But we can say the same of the eighteenth market and – by continuing backward induction – of every market, including the first. This result is called the **Chainstore Paradox** after Selten (1978).

Backward induction ensures that the strategy profile is a subgame perfect equilibrium. There are other Nash equilibria – (*Always Fight, Never Enter*), for example – but because of the Chainstore Paradox they are not perfect.

The Repeated Prisoner's Dilemma

The Prisoner's Dilemma is similar to Entry Deterrence I. Here the prisoners would like to commit themselves to *Deny*, but, in the absence of commitment, they *Confess*. The Chainstore Paradox can be applied to show that repetition does not induce cooperative behavior. Both prisoners know that in the last repetition, both will *Confess*. After 18 repetitions, they know that no matter what happens in the nineteenth, both will *Confess* in the twentieth, so they might as well *Confess* in the nineteenth too. Building a reputation is pointless, because in the twentieth period it is not going to matter. Proceeding inductively, both players *Confess* in every period, the unique perfect equilibrium outcome.

In fact, as a consequence of the fact that the one-shot Prisoner's Dilemma has a dominant-strategy equilibrium, confessing is the only Nash outcome for the repeated Prisoner's Dilemma, not just the only perfect outcome. The argument of the previous paragraph did not show that confessing was the unique Nash outcome. To show subgame perfectness, we worked back from the end using longer and longer subgames. To show that confessing is the only Nash outcome, we do not look at subgames, but instead rule out successive classes of strategies from being Nash. Consider the portions of the strategy which apply to the equilibrium path (i.e., the portions directly relevant to the payoffs). No strategy in the class that calls for *Deny* in the last period can be a Nash strategy, because the same strategy with *Confess* replacing *Deny* would dominate it. But if both players have strategies calling for confessing in the last period, then no strategy that does not call for confessing in the next-to-last period is Nash, because a player should deviate by replacing *Deny* with *Confess* in the next-to-last period. The argument can be carried back to the first period, ruling out any class of strategies that does not call for confessing everywhere along the equilibrium path.

The strategy of always confessing is not a dominant strategy, as it is in the one-shot game, because it is not the best response to various suboptimal strategies such as (*Deny until the other player Confesses, then Deny for the rest of the game*). Moreover, the uniqueness is only on the equilibrium path. Nonperfect Nash strategies could call for cooperation at nodes far away from the equilibrium path, since that action would never have to be taken. If Row has chosen (*Always Confess*), one of Column's best responses is (*Always Confess unless Row has chosen Deny ten times; then always Deny*).

5.2   Infinitely Repeated Games, Minimax Punishments, and the Folk Theorem

The contradiction between the Chainstore Paradox and what many people think of as real world behavior has been most successfully resolved by adding incomplete information to the model, as will be seen in chapter 6. Before we turn to incomplete information, however, we will explore certain other modifications. One idea is to repeat the Prisoner's Dilemma an infinite number of times instead of a finite number (after all, few economies have a known end date). Without a last period, the inductive argument in the Chainstore Paradox fails.

In fact, we can find a simple perfect equilibrium for the infinitely repeated Prisoner's Dilemma in which both players cooperate – a game in which both players adopt the Grim Strategy.

The Grim Strategy

1   Start by choosing Deny.
2   Continue to choose Deny unless some player has chosen Confess, in which case choose Confess forever.

Notice that the Grim Strategy says that even if a player is the first to deviate and choose *Confess*, he continues to choose *Confess* thereafter.

If Column uses the Grim Strategy, the Grim Strategy is weakly Row's best response. If Row cooperates, he will continue to receive the high (*Deny, Deny*) payoff forever. If he confesses, he will receive the higher (*Confess, Deny*) payoff once, but the best he can hope for thereafter is the (*Confess, Confess*) payoff.

Even in the infinitely repeated game, cooperation is not immediate, and not every strategy that punishes confessing is perfect. A notable example is the strategy of Tit-for-Tat.

Tit-for-Tat

1   Start by choosing Deny.
2   Thereafter, in period n choose the action that the other player chose in period (n − 1).

If Column uses Tit-for-Tat, Row does not have an incentive to *Confess* first, because if Row cooperates he will continue to receive the high (*Deny, Deny*) payoff, but if he confesses and then returns to Tit-for-Tat, the players alternate (*Confess, Deny*) with (*Deny, Confess*) forever. Row's average payoff from this alternation would be lower than if he had stuck to (*Deny, Deny*), and would swamp the one-time gain. But Tit-for-Tat is almost never perfect in the infinitely repeated Prisoner's Dilemma without discounting, because it is not rational for Column to punish Row's initial *Confess*. Adhering to Tit-for-Tat's punishments results in a miserable alternation of *Confess* and *Deny*, so Column would rather ignore Row's first *Confess*. The deviation is not from the equilibrium path action of *Deny*, but from the off-equilibrium action rule of *Confess in response to a Confess*. Thus, Tit-for-Tat, unlike the Grim Strategy, is not subgame perfect. (See Kalai, Samet, & Stanford [1988] and problem 5.5 for more on this point.)

Theorem 5.1 (The Folk Theorem)

In an infinitely repeated n-person game with finite action sets at each repetition, any profile of actions observed in any finite number of repetitions is the unique outcome of some subgame perfect equilibrium given

Condition 1: *The rate of time preference is zero, or positive and sufficiently small;*

Condition 2: *The probability that the game ends at any repetition is zero, or positive and sufficiently small; and*

Condition 3: *The set of payoff profiles that strictly Pareto dominate the minimax payoff profiles in the mixed extension of the one-shot game is n-dimensional.*

What the Folk Theorem tells us is that claiming that particular behavior arises in a perfect equilibrium is meaningless in an infinitely repeated game. This applies to any game that meets conditions 1 to 3, not just to the Prisoner's Dilemma. If an infinite amount of time always remains in the game, a way can always be found to make one player willing to punish some other player for the sake of a better future, even if the punishment currently hurts the punisher as well as the punished. Any finite interval of time is insignificant compared to eternity, so the threat of future reprisal makes the players willing to carry out the punishments needed.

We will next discuss conditions 1 to 3.

Condition 1: Discounting

The Folk Theorem helps answer the question of whether discounting future payments lessens the influence of the troublesome Last Period. Quite to the contrary, with discounting, the present gain from confessing is weighted more heavily and future gains from cooperation more lightly. If the discount rate is very high the game almost returns to being one-shot. When the real interest rate is a thousand percent, a payment next year is little better than a payment a hundred years hence, so next year is practically irrelevant. Any model that relies on a large number of repetitions also assumes that the discount rate is not too high.

Allowing a little discounting is nonetheless important to show there is no discontinuity at the discount rate of zero. If we come across an undiscounted, infinitely repeated game with many equilibria, the Folk Theorem tells us that adding a low discount rate will not reduce the number of equilibria. This contrasts with the effect of changing the model by having a large but finite number of repetitions, a change which often eliminates all but one outcome by inducing the Chainstore Paradox.

A discount rate of zero supports many perfect equilibria, but if the rate is high enough, the only equilibrium outcome is eternal confessing. We can calculate the critical value for given parameters. The Grim Strategy imposes the heaviest possible punishment for deviant behavior. Using the payoffs for the Prisoner's Dilemma from table 5.2a in the next section, the equilibrium payoff from the Grim Strategy is the current payoff of five plus the value of the rest of the game, which from table 4.2 is $5/r$. If Row deviated by confessing, he would receive a current payoff of 10, but the value of the rest of the game would fall to 0. The critical value of the discount rate is found by solving the equation $5 + 5/r = 10 + 0$, which yields $r = 1$, a discount rate of 100 percent or a discount factor of $\delta = 0.5$. Unless the players are extremely impatient, confessing is not much of a temptation.

Condition 2: A probability of the game ending

Time preference is fairly straightforward, but what is surprising is that assuming that the game ends in each period with probability θ does not make a drastic difference. In fact, we could even allow θ to vary over time, so long as it never became too large. If $\theta > 0$, the game ends in finite time with probability one; or, put less dramatically, the expected number of repetitions is finite, but it still behaves like a discounted infinite game, because the expected number of future repetitions is always large, no matter how many have already occurred. The game still has no Last Period, and it is still true that imposing one, no matter how far beyond the expected number of repetitions, would radically change the results.

The following two situations are different from each other.

"1   The game will end at some uncertain date before T."

"2   There is a constant probability of the game ending."

In situation (1), the game is like a finite game, because, as time passes, the maximum length of time still to run shrinks to zero. In situation (2), even if the game will end by T with high probability, if it actually lasts until T the game looks exactly the same as at time zero. The fourth verse from the hymn "Amazing Grace" puts this "stationarity" very nicely (though I expect it is supposed to apply to a game with $\theta = 0$).

When we've been there ten thousand years,
Bright shining as the sun,
We've no less days to sing God's praise
Than when we'd first begun.

Condition 3: Dimensionality

The "minimax payoff" mentioned in theorem 5.1 is the payoff that results if all the other players pick strategies solely to punish player i, and he protects himself as best he can.

The set of strategies s^*_{-i} is a set of $(n-1)$ **minimax strategies** *chosen by all the players except i to keep i's payoff as low as possible, no matter how he responds. s^*_{-i} solves*

$$\underset{s_{-i}}{\text{Minimize}}\ \underset{s_i}{\text{Maximum}}\ \pi_i(s_i, s_{-i}). \tag{5.1}$$

Player i's **minimax payoff**, **minimax value**, *or* **security value** *is his payoff from the solution of (5.1).*

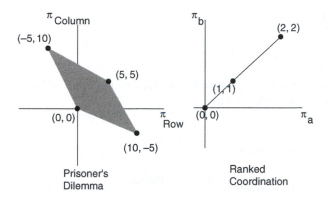

Figure 5.1   The dimensionality condition.

The dimensionality condition is needed only for games with three or more players. It is satisfied if there is some payoff profile for each player in which his payoff is greater than his minimax payoff but still different from the payoff of every other player. Figure 5.1 shows how this condition is satisfied for the two-person Prisoner's Dilemma of table 5.2a a few pages beyond this paragraph, but not for the two-person Ranked Coordination game. It is also satisfied by the n-person Prisoner's Dilemma in which a solitary confessor gets a higher payoff than his cooperating fellow-prisoners, but not by the n-person Ranked Coordination game, in which all the players have the same payoff. The condition is necessary because establishing the desired behavior requires some way for the other players to punish a deviator without punishing themselves.

An alternative to the dimensionality condition in the Folk Theorem is

Condition 3′

The repeated game has a "desirable" subgame-perfect equilibrium in which the strategy profile $\bar{s}$ played each period gives player i a payoff that exceeds his payoff from some other "punishment" subgame-perfect equilibrium in which the strategy profile $\underline{s}^i$ is played each period:

$$\exists \bar{s} : \forall i, \ \exists \underline{s}^i : \pi_i(\underline{s}^i) < \pi_i(\bar{s}).$$

Condition 3′ is useful because sometimes it is easy to find a few perfect equilibria. To enforce the desired pattern of behavior, use the "desirable" equilibrium as a carrot and the "punishment" equilibrium as a self-enforcing stick (see Rasmusen [1992a]).

Minimax and Maximin

In discussions of strategies which enforce cooperation, the question of the maximum severity of punishment strategies frequently arises. Thus, the idea of the minimax strategy – the most severe sanction possible if the offender does not cooperate in his own punishment – entered into the statement of the Folk Theorem. The corresponding strategy for an offender trying to protect himself from punishment, is the maximin strategy.

*The strategy s_i^* is a **maximin strategy** for player i if, given that the other players pick strategies to make i's payoff as low as possible, s_i^* gives i the highest possible payoff.*

In our notation, s_i^* solves

$$\underset{s_i}{Maximize}\ \underset{s_{-i}}{Minimum}\ \pi_i(s_i, s_{-i}).\tag{5.2}$$

The following formulas show how to calculate the minimax and maximin strategies for a two-player game with Player 1 as i.

Player 1's maximin strategy: $\underset{s_1}{Maximize}\ \underset{s_2}{Minimum}\ \pi_1(s_1, s_2)$

Player 2's minimax strategy: $\underset{s_2}{Minimize}\ \underset{s_1}{Maximum}\ \pi_1(s_1, s_2)$

In the Prisoner's Dilemma, the minimax and maximin strategies are both *Confess*. Although the Welfare Game (table 3.1) has only a mixed strategy Nash equilibrium, if we restrict ourselves to the pure strategies (just for illustration here) the Pauper's maximin strategy is *Try to Work*, which guarantees him at least 1, and his strategy for minimaxing the Government is *Be Idle*, which prevents the Government from getting more than zero.

Under minimax, Player 2 is purely malicious but must move first (at least in choosing a mixing probability) in his attempt to cause Player 1 the maximum pain. Under maximin, Player 1 moves first, in the belief that Player 2 is out to get him. In variable-sum games, minimax is for sadists and maximin for paranoids. In zero-sum games, the players are merely neurotic. Minimax is for optimists, and maximin is for pessimists.

The maximin strategy need not be unique, and it can be in mixed strategies. Since maximin behavior can also be viewed as minimizing the maximum loss that might be suffered, decision theorists refer to such a policy as a **minimax criterion**, a catchier phrase (Luce & Raiffa [1957], p. 279).

It is tempting to use maximin strategies as the basis of an equilibrium concept. A **maximin equilibrium** is made up of a maximin strategy for each player. Such a strategy might seem reasonable because each player then has protected himself from the worst harm possible. Maximin strategies have very little justification, however, for a rational player. They are not simply the optimal strategies for risk-averse players, because risk aversion is accounted for in the utility payoffs. The players' implicit beliefs can be inconsistent in a maximin equilibrium, and a player must believe that his opponent would choose the most harmful strategy out of spite rather than self-interest if maximin behavior is to be rational.

The usefulness of minimax and maximin strategies is not in directly predicting the best strategies of the players, but in setting the bounds of how their strategies affect their payoffs, as in condition 3 of theorem 5.1.

It is important to remember that minimax and maximin strategies are not always pure strategies. In the Minimax Illustration Game of table 5.1, which I take from Fudenberg & Tirole (1991a, p. 150), Row can guarantee himself a payoff of 0 by choosing *Down*, so that is his maximin strategy. Column cannot hold Row's payoff down to 0, however, by using a pure minimax strategy. If Column chooses *Left*, Row can choose *Middle* and get a payoff of 1; if Column chooses *Right*, Row can choose *Up* and get a payoff of 1. Column can, however, hold Row's payoff down to 0 by choosing a mixed minimax strategy of

Table 5.1   The Minimax Illustration Game

		Column	
		Left	*Right*
	Up	− 2, ②	① , − 2
Row	*Middle*	① , −2	− 2, ②
	Down	0, ①	0, ①

Payoffs to: (Row, Column) Best response payoffs are boxed.

(*Probability 0.5 of Left, Probability 0.5 of Right*). Row would then respond with *Down*, for a minimax payoff of 0, since either *Up*, *Middle*, or a mixture of the two would give him a payoff of $-0.5\ (= 0.5(-2) + 0.5(1))$.

Column's maximin and minimax strategies can also be computed. The strategy for Row minimaxing Column is (*Probability 0.5 of Up, Probability 0.5 of Middle*), Column's maximin strategy is (*Probability 0.5 of Left, Probability 0.5 of Right*), and Column's minimax payoff is 0.

In two-person zero-sum games, minimax and maximin strategies are more directly useful, because when Player 1 reduces Player 2's payoff, he increases his own payoff. Punishing the other player is equivalent to rewarding yourself. This is the origin of the celebrated **Minimax Theorem** (von Neumann [1928]), which says that a minimax equilibrium exists in pure or mixed strategies for every two-person zero-sum game and is identical to the maximin equilibrium. Unfortunately, the games that come up in applications are usually not zero-sum games, so the Minimax Theorem usually cannot be applied.

Precommitment

What if we use metastrategies, abandoning the idea of perfectness by allowing players to commit at the start to a strategy for the rest of the game? We would still want to keep the game noncooperative by disallowing binding promises, but we could model it as a game with simultaneous choices by both players, or with one move each in sequence.

If precommitted strategies are chosen simultaneously, the equilibrium outcome of the finitely repeated Prisoner's Dilemma calls for always confessing, because allowing commitment is the same as allowing equilibria to be nonperfect, in which case, as was shown earlier, the unique Nash outcome is always confessing.

A different result is achieved if the players precommit to strategies in sequence. The outcome depends on the particular values of the parameters, but one possible equilibrium is the following: Row moves first and chooses the strategy (*Deny* until Column *Confesses*; thereafter always *Confess*), and Column chooses (*Deny* until the last period; then *Confess*). The observed outcome would be for both players to choose *Deny* until the last period, and then for Row to again choose *Deny*, but for Column to choose *Confess*. Row would submit to this because if he chose a strategy that initiated confessing earlier, Column would choose a strategy of starting to confess earlier too. The game has a second-mover advantage.

5.3   Reputation: The One-sided Prisoner's Dilemma

Part II of this book will analyze moral hazard and adverse selection. Under moral hazard, a player wants to commit to high effort, but he cannot credibly do so. Under adverse selection, a player wants to convey his high ability, but he cannot. In both, the problem is that the penalties for lying are insufficient. Reputation seems to offer a way out of the problem. If the relationship is repeated, perhaps a player is willing to be honest in early periods in order to establish a reputation for honesty which will be valuable to himself later.

Reputation seems to play a similar role in making threats to punish credible. Usually punishment is costly to the punisher as well as the punished, and it is not clear why the punisher should not let bygones be bygones. Yet in 1988 the Soviet Union paid off 70-year-old debt to dissuade the Swiss authorities from blocking a mutually beneficial new bond issue ("Soviets Agree To Pay Off Czarist Debt to Switzerland," *Wall Street Journal*, January 19, 1988, p. 60). Why were the Swiss so vindictive towards Lenin?

The questions of why players do punish and do not cheat are really the same questions that arise in the repeated Prisoner's Dilemma, where the fact of an infinite number of repetitions allows cooperation. That is the great problem of reputation. Since everyone knows that a player will *Confess*, choose low effort, or default on debt in the last period, why do they suppose he will bother to build up a reputation in the present? Why should past behavior be any guide to future behavior?

Not all reputation problems are quite the same as the Prisoner's Dilemma, but they have much the same flavor. Some games, like duopoly or the original Prisoner's Dilemma, are **two-sided** in the sense that each player has the same strategy set and the payoffs are symmetric. Others, such as the game of Product Quality (see below), are what we might call **one-sided Prisoner's Dilemmas**, which have properties similar to the Prisoner's Dilemma, but do not fit the usual definition because they are asymmetric. Table 5.2 shows the normal forms for both the original Prisoner's Dilemma and the one-sided version.[1] The important difference is that in the one-sided Prisoner's Dilemma at least one player really does prefer the outcome equivalent to (*Deny, Deny*), which is (*High Quality, Buy*) in table 5.2b, to anything else. He confesses defensively, rather than both offensively and defensively. The payoff (0, 0) can often be interpreted as the refusal of one player to interact with the other, for example, the motorist who refuses to buy cars from Chrysler because he knows they once falsified odometers. Table 5.3 lists examples of both one-sided and two-sided games.

The Nash and iterated dominance equilibria in the one-sided Prisoner's Dilemma are still (*Confess, Confess*), but it is not a dominant-strategy equilibrium. Column does not have a dominant strategy, because if Row were to choose *Deny*, Column would also choose *Deny*, to obtain the payoff of 5; but if Row were to chooses *Confess*, Column would choose *Confess*, for a payoff of zero. *Confess* is however, weakly dominant for Row, which makes (*Confess, Confess*) the iterated dominant strategy equilibrium. In both games, the players would like to persuade each other that they will cooperate, and devices that induce cooperation in the one-sided game will usually obtain the same result in the two-sided game.

---

[1] The exact numbers are different from the Prisoner's Dilemma in table 1.1, but the ordinal rankings are the same. Numbers such as those in table 5.2 are more commonly used, because it is convenient to normalize the (*Confess, Confess*) payoffs to (0, 0) and to make most of the numbers positive rather than negative.

Table 5.2 Prisoner's Dilemmas

(a) Two-sided (conventional)

	Column		
	Deny		*Confess*
Deny	5, 5	→	−5, 10
Row	↓		↓
Confess	10, −5	→	**0, 0**

Payoffs to: (Row, Column). Arrows show how a player can increase his payoff.

(b) One-sided

	Consumer (Column)		
	Buy		*Boycott*
High quality	5, 5	←	0, 0
Seller (Row)	↓		↕
Low quality	10, −5	→	**0,0**

Payoffs to: (Seller, Consumer). Arrows show how a player can increase his payoff.

Table 5.3 Some repeated games in which reputation is important

Application	Sidedness	Players	Actions
Prisoner's Dilemma	Two-sided	Row	*Deny/Confess*
		Column	*Deny/Confess*
Duopoly	Two-sided	Firm	*High price/Low price*
		Firm	*High price/Low price*
Employment	Two-sided	Employer	*Bonus/No bonus*
		Employee	*Work/Shirk*
Product quality	One-sided	Consumer	*Buy/Boycott*
		Seller	*High quality/Low quality*
Entry deterrence	One-sided	Incumbent	*Low price/High price*
		Entrant	*Enter/Stay out*
Financial disclosure	One-sided	Corporation	*Truth/Lies*
		Investor	*Invest/Refrain*
Borrowing	One-sided	Lender	*Lend/Refuse*
		Borrower	*Repay/Default*

5.4 Product Quality in an Infinitely Repeated Game

The Folk Theorem tells us that some perfect equilibrium of an infinitely repeated game – sometimes called an **infinite horizon model** – can generate any pattern of behavior observed over a finite number of periods. But since the Folk Theorem is no more than a mathematical result, the strategies that generate particular patterns of behavior may be unreasonable. The theorem's value is in provoking close scrutiny of infinite horizon models so that the modeller must show why his equilibrium is better than a host of others. He must go beyond satisfaction of the technical criterion of perfectness and justify the strategies on other grounds.

In the simplest model of product quality, a seller can choose between producing costly high quality or costless low quality, and the buyer cannot determine quality before he purchases. If the seller would produce high quality under symmetric information, we have a one-sided Prisoner's Dilemma, as in table 5.2b. Both players are better off when the seller produces high quality and the buyer purchases the product, but the seller's weakly dominant strategy is to produce low quality, so the buyer will not purchase. This is also an example of moral hazard, the topic of chapter 7.

A potential solution is to repeat the game, allowing the firm to choose quality at each repetition. If the number of repetitions is finite, however, the outcome stays the same because of the Chainstore Paradox. In the last repetition, the subgame is identical to the one-shot game, so the firm chooses low quality. In the next-to-last repetition, it is foreseen that the last period's outcome is independent of current actions, so the firm also chooses low quality, an argument that can be carried back to the first repetition.

If the game is repeated an infinite number of times, the Chainstore Paradox is inapplicable and the Folk Theorem says that a wide range of outcomes can be observed in equilibrium. Klein & Leffler (1981) construct a plausible equilibrium for an infinite period model. Their original article, in the traditional verbal style of UCLA, does not phrase the result in terms of game theory, but we will recast it here, as I did in Rasmusen (1989b). In equilibrium, the firm is willing to produce a high quality product because it can sell at a high price for many periods, but consumers refuse to ever buy again from a firm that has once produced low quality. The equilibrium price is high enough that the firm is unwilling to sacrifice its future profits for a one-time windfall from deceitfully producing low quality and selling it at a high price. Although this is only one of a large number of subgame perfect equilibria, the consumers' behavior is simple and rational: no consumer can benefit by deviating from the equilibrium.

Product Quality

PLAYERS
An infinite number of potential firms and a continuum of consumers.

THE ORDER OF PLAY
1   An endogenous number n of firms decide to enter the market at cost F.
2   A firm that has entered chooses its quality to be *High* or *Low*, incurring the constant marginal cost c if it picks *High* and zero if it picks *Low*. The choice is unobserved by consumers. The firm also picks a price p.
3   Consumers decide which firms (if any) to buy from, choosing firms randomly if they are indifferent. The amount bought from firm i is denoted q_i.
4   All consumers observe the quality of all goods purchased in that period.
5   The game returns to (2) and repeats.

PAYOFFS
The consumer benefit from a product of low quality is zero, but consumers are willing to buy quantity $q(p) = \sum_{i=1}^{n} q_i$ for a product believed to be high quality, where $dq/dp < 0$.
If a firm stays out of the market, its payoff is zero.
If firm i enters, it receives $-F$ immediately. Its current end-of-period payoff is $q_i p$ if it produces *Low* quality and $q_i(p - c)$ if it produces *High* quality. The discount rate is $r > 0$.

That the firm can produce low quality items at zero marginal cost is unrealistic, but it is only a simplifying assumption. By normalizing the cost of producing low quality to zero, we avoid having to carry an extra variable through the analysis without affecting the result.

The Folk Theorem tells us that this game has a wide range of perfect outcomes, including a large number with erratic quality patterns like (*High, High, Low, High, Low, Low, . . .*). If we confine ourselves to pure-strategy equilibria with the stationary outcome of constant quality and identical behavior by all firms in the market, then the two outcomes are low quality and high quality. Low quality is always an equilibrium outcome, since it is an equilibrium of the one-shot game. If the discount rate is low enough, high quality is also an equilibrium outcome, and this will be the focus of our attention. Consider the following strategy profile:

Firms: $\tilde{n}$ firms enter. Each produces high quality and sells at price $\tilde{p}$. If a firm ever deviates from this, it thereafter produces low quality (and sells at the same price $\tilde{p}$). The values of $\tilde{p}$ and $\tilde{n}$ are given by equations (5.4) and (5.8) below.

Buyers: Buyers start by choosing randomly among the firms charging $\tilde{p}$. Thereafter, they remain with their initial firm unless it changes its price or quality, in which case they switch randomly to a firm that has not changed its price or quality.

This strategy profile is a perfect equilibrium. Each firm is willing to produce high quality and refrain from price-cutting because otherwise it would lose all its customers. If it has deviated, it is willing to produce low quality because the quality is unimportant, given the absence of customers. Buyers stay away from a firm that has produced low quality because they know it will continue to do so, and they stay away from a firm that has cut the price because they know it will produce low quality. For this story to work, however, the equilibrium must satisfy three constraints that will be explained in more depth in section 7.3: incentive compatibility, competition, and market clearing.

The **incentive compatibility** constraint says that the individual firm must be willing to produce high quality. Given the buyers' strategy, if the firm ever produces low quality it receives a one-time windfall profit, but loses its future profits. The tradeoff is represented by constraint (5.3), which is satisfied if the discount rate is low enough.

$$\frac{q_i p}{1 + r} \leq \frac{q_i(p - c)}{r} \quad \text{(incentive compatibility)}. \tag{5.3}$$

Inequality (5.3) determines a lower bound for the price, which must satisfy

$$\tilde{p} \geq (1 + r)c. \tag{5.4}$$

Condition (5.4) will be satisfied as an equality, because any firm trying to charge a price higher than the quality-guaranteeing $\tilde{p}$ would lose all its customers.

The second constraint is that competition drives profits to zero, so firms are indifferent between entering and staying out of the market.

$$\frac{q_i(p - c)}{r} = F \quad \text{(competition)}. \tag{5.5}$$

Treating (5.3) as an equation and using it to replace p in equation (5.5) gives

$$q_i = \frac{F}{c}. \tag{5.6}$$

We have now determined p and q_i, and only n remains, which is determined by the equality of supply and demand. The market does not always clear in models of asymmetric information (see Stiglitz [1987]), and in this model each firm would like to sell more than its equilibrium output at the equilibrium price, but the market output must equal the quantity demanded by the market.

$$nq_i = q(p) \quad (market\ clearing). \tag{5.7}$$

Combining equations (5.3), (5.6), and (5.7) yields

$$\tilde{n} = \frac{cq([1+r]c)}{F}. \tag{5.8}$$

We have now determined the equilibrium values, the only difficulty being the standard existence problem caused by the requirement that the number of firms be an integer (see note N5.4).

The equilibrium price is fixed because F is exogenous and demand is not perfectly inelastic, which pins down the size of firms. If there were no entry cost, but demand were still elastic, then the equilibrium price would still be the unique p that satisfied constraint (5.3), and the market quantity would be determined by $q(p)$, but F and q_i would be undetermined. If consumers believed that any firm which might possibly produce high quality paid an exogenous dissipation cost F, the result would be a continuum of equilibria. The firms' best response would be for $\tilde{n}$ of them to pay F and produce high quality at price $\tilde{p}$, where $\tilde{n}$ is determined by the zero profit condition as a function of F. Klein & Leffler note this indeterminacy and suggest that the profits might be dissipated by some sort of brand-specific capital. This is especially plausible when there is asymmetric information, so firms might wish to use capital spending to signal that they intend to be in the business for a long time; Rasmusen & Perri (2001) shows a way to model this. Another good explanation for which firms enjoy the high profits of good reputation is simply the history of the industry. Schmalensee (1982) shows how a pioneering brand can retain a large market share because consumers are unwilling to investigate the quality of new brands.

The repeated-game model of reputation for product quality can be used to model many other kinds of reputation too. Even before Klein & Leffler (1981), Telser titled his 1980 article "A Theory of Self-Enforcing Agreements," and looked at a number of situations in which repeated play balanced the short-run gain from cheating against the long-run gain from cooperation. We will see the idea later in this book in section 8.1 as part of the idea of the "efficiency wage."

Keep in mind, however, that "reputation" can be modelled in two distinct ways. In our model here, a firm with a good reputation is one which produces high quality to avoid losing that reputation, a "moral hazard" model because the focus is on the player's choice of actions. An alternative is a model in which the firm with a good reputation is one which has shown that it would not produce low quality even if there were no adverse consequences from doing so, an "adverse selection" model because the focus is on the player's type. One kind of reputation is for deciding to be good; the other is for Nature having chosen the player to be good. As you will see, the Gang of Four model of chapter 6 mixes the two.

*5.5   Markov Equilibria and Overlapping Generations: Customer Switching Costs

The next model demonstrates a general modelling technique, the **overlapping genera-tions model**, in which different cohorts of otherwise identical players enter and leave the game with overlapping "lifetimes," and a new equilibrium concept, "Markov equilibrium." The best-known example of an overlapping-generations model is the original consumption-loans model of Samuelson (1958). The models are most often used in macroeconomics, but they can also be useful in microeconomics. Klemperer (1987) stimulated considerable interest in customers who incur costs in moving from one seller to another. The model used here will be that of Farrell & Shapiro (1988).

Customer Switching Costs

PLAYERS
Firms Apex and Brydox, and a series of customers, each of whom is first called a youngster and then an oldster.

THE ORDER OF PLAY
1a   Brydox, the initial incumbent, picks the incumbent price p_1^i.
1b   Apex, the initial entrant, picks the entrant price p_1^e.
1c   The oldster picks a firm.
1d   The youngster picks a firm.
1e   Whichever firm attracted the youngster becomes the incumbent.
1f   The oldster dies and the youngster becomes an oldster.
2a   Return to (1a), possibly with new identities for entrant and incumbent.

PAYOFFS
The discount factor is δ. The customer reservation price is R and the switching cost is c. The per period payoffs in period t are, for $j = (i, e)$,

$$\pi_{firm\ j} = \begin{cases} 0 & \text{if no customers are attracted.} \\ p_t^{\ j} & \text{if just oldsters or just youngsters are attracted.} \\ 2p_t^j & \text{if both oldsters and youngsters are attracted.} \end{cases}$$

$$\pi_{oldster} = \begin{cases} R - p_t^i & \text{if he buys from the incumbent.} \\ R - p_t^e - c & \text{if he switches to the entrant.} \end{cases}$$

$$\pi_{youngster} = \begin{cases} R - p_t^i & \text{if he buys from the incumbent.} \\ R - p_t^e & \text{if he buys from the entrant.} \end{cases}$$

Finding all the perfect equilibria of an infinite game like this one is difficult, so we will follow Farrell and Shapiro in limiting ourselves to the much easier task of finding the perfect Markov equilibrium, which is unique.

A **Markov strategy** *is a strategy that, at each node, chooses the action independently of the history of the game except for the immediately preceding action (or actions, if they were simultaneous).*

Here, a firm's Markov strategy is its price as a function of whether the particular is the incumbent or the entrant, and not a function of the entire past history of the game.

There are two ways to use Markov strategies: (1) just look for equilibria that use Markov strategies, and (2) disallow non-Markov strategies and then look for equilibria. Because the first way does not disallow non-Markov strategies, the equilibrium must be such that no player wants to deviate by using any other strategy, whether Markov or not. This is just a way of eliminating possible multiple equilibria by discarding ones that use non-Markov strategies. The second way is much more dubious, because it requires the players not to use non-Markov strategies, even if they are best responses. A **perfect Markov equilibrium** uses the first approach: it is a perfect equilibrium that happens to use only Markov strategies.

Brydox, the initial incumbent, moves first and chooses p^i low enough that Apex is not tempted to choose $p^e < p^i - c$ and steal away the oldsters. Apex's profit is p^i if it chooses $p^e = p^i$ and serves just youngsters, and $2(p^i - c)$ if it chooses $p^e = p^i - c$ and serves both oldsters and youngsters. Brydox chooses p^i to make Apex indifferent between these alternatives, so

$$p^i = 2(p^i - c), \tag{5.9}$$

and

$$p^i = p^e = 2c. \tag{5.10}$$

In equilibrium, Apex and Brydox take turns being the incumbent and charge the same price.

Because the game lasts forever and the equilibrium strategies are Markov, we can use a trick from dynamic programming to calculate the payoffs from being the entrant versus being the incumbent. The equilibrium payoff of the current entrant is the immediate payment of p^e plus the discounted value of being the incumbent in the next period:

$$\pi_e^* = p^e + \delta\pi_i^*. \tag{5.11}$$

The incumbent's payoff can be similarly stated as the immediate payment of p^i plus the discounted value of being the entrant next period:

$$\pi_i^* = p^i + \delta\pi_e^*. \tag{5.12}$$

We could use equation (5.10) to substitute for p^e and p^i, which would leave us with the two equations (5.11) and (5.12) for the two unknowns π_i^* and π_e^*, but an easier way to compute the payoff is to realize that in equilibrium the incumbent and the entrant sell the same amount at the same price, so $\pi_i^* = \pi_e^*$ and equation (5.12) becomes

$$\pi_i^* = 2c + \delta\pi_i^*. \tag{5.13}$$

It follows that

$$\pi_i^* = \pi_e^* = \frac{2c}{1 - \delta}. \tag{5.14}$$

Prices and total payoffs are increasing in the switching cost c, because that is what gives the incumbent market power and prevents ordinary competition of the ordinary Bertrand kind. The total payoffs are increasing in δ for the usual reason that future payments increase in value as δ approaches one.

*5.6   Evolutionary Equilibrium: The Hawk–Dove Game

For most of this book we have been using the Nash equilibrium concept or refinements of it based on information and sequentiality, but in biology such concepts are often inappropriate. The lower animals are less likely than humans to think about the strategies of their opponents at each stage of a game. Their strategies are more likely to be preprogrammed and their strategy sets more restricted than the businessman's, if perhaps not more so than his customer's. In addition, behavior evolves, and any equilibrium must take account of the possibility of odd behavior caused by the occasional mutation. That the equilibrium is common knowledge, or that players cannot precommit to strategies, are not compelling assumptions. Thus, the ideas of Nash equilibrium and sequential rationality are much less useful than when game theory is modelling rational players.

Game theory has grown to some importance in biology, but the style is different than in economics. The goal is not to explain how players would rationally pick actions in a given situation, but to explain how behavior evolves or persists over time under exogenous shocks. Both approaches end up defining equilibria to be strategy profiles that are best responses in some sense, but biologists care much more about the stability of the equilibrium and how strategies interact over time. In section 3.5, we touched briefly on the stability of the Cournot equilibrium, but economists view stability as a pleasing by-product of the equilibrium rather than its justification. For biologists, stability is the point of the analysis.

Consider a game with identical players who engage in pairwise contests. In this special context, it is useful to think of an equilibrium as a strategy profile such that no player with a new strategy can enter the environment (**invade**) and receive a higher expected payoff than the old players. Moreover, the invading strategy should continue to do well even if it plays itself with finite probability, or its invasion could never grow to significance. In the commonest model in biology, all the players adopt the same strategy in equilibrium, called an evolutionarily stable strategy. John Maynard Smith originated this idea, which is somewhat confusing because it really aims at an equilibrium concept, which involves a strategy profile, not just one player's strategy. For games with pairwise interactions and identical players, however, the evolutionarily stable strategy can be used to define an equilibrium concept.

*A strategy s^* is an **evolutionarily stable strategy**, or **ESS**, if, using the notation $\pi(s_i, s_{-i})$ for player i's payoff when his opponent uses strategy s_{-i}, for every other strategy s' either*

$$\pi(s^*, s^*) > \pi(s', s^*) \tag{5.15}$$

or

$$(a) \quad \pi(s^*, s^*) = \pi(s', s^*)$$

and $\tag{5.16}$

$$(b) \quad \pi(s^*, s') > \pi(s', s').$$

Table 5.4   The Utopian Exchange Economy game

		Jones		
		Low Output		*High Output*
	Low Output	**1, 1**	↔	1, 1
Smith		↕		↓
	High Output	1, 1	→	**2, 2**

Payoffs to: (Smith, Jones). Arrows show how a player can increase his payoff.

If condition (5.15) holds, then a population of players using s^* cannot be invaded by a deviant using s'. If condition (5.16) holds, then s' does well against s^*, but badly against itself, so that if more than one player tried to use s' to invade a population using s^*, the invaders would fail.

We can interpret ESS in terms of Nash equilibrium. Condition (5.15) says that s^* is a strong Nash equilibrium (although not every strong Nash strategy is an ESS). Condition (5.16) says that if s^* is only a weak Nash strategy, the weak alternative s' is not a best response to itself. ESS is a refinement of Nash, narrowed by the requirement that ESS not only be a best response, but that (a) it have the highest payoff of any strategy used in equilibrium (which rules out equilibria with asymmetric payoffs), and (b) it be a strictly best response to itself.

The motivations behind the two equilibrium concepts are quite different, but the similarities are useful because even if the modeller prefers ESS to Nash, he can start with the Nash strategies in his efforts to find an ESS.

As an example of (a), consider the Battle of the Sexes. In it, the mixed strategy equilibrium is an ESS, because a player using it has as high a payoff as any other player. The two pure strategy equilibria are not made up of ESS's, though, because in each of them one player's payoff is higher than the other's. Compare with Ranked Coordination, in which the two pure strategy equilibria and the mixed strategy equilibrium are all made up of ESSs. (The dominated equilibrium strategy is nonetheless an ESS, because given that the other players are using it, no player could do as well by deviating.)

As an example of (b), consider the Utopian Exchange Economy game in table 5.4, adapted from problem 7.5 of Gintis (2000). In Utopia, each citizen can produce either one or two units of individualized output. He will then go into the marketplace and meet another citizen. If either of them produced only one unit, trade cannot increase their payoffs. If both of them produced two, however, they can trade one unit for one unit, and both end up happier with their increased variety of consumption.

This game has three Nash equilibria, one of which is in mixed strategies. Since all strategies but *High Output* are weakly dominated, that alone is an ESS. *Low Output* fails to meet condition (5.16b), because it is not the strictly best response to itself. If the economy began with all citizens choosing *Low Output*, then if Smith deviated to *High Output* he would not do any better, but if *two* people deviated to *High Output*, they would do better in expectation because they might meet each other and receive the payoff of (2, 2).

An Example of ESS: Hawk–Dove

The best-known illustration of the ESS is the game of Hawk–Dove. Imagine that we have a population of birds, each of whom can behave as an aggressive Hawk or a pacific Dove.

Table 5.5   Hawk–Dove: economics notation

		Bird Two		
		Hawk		*Dove*
Bird One	*Hawk*	$-1, -1$	$\rightarrow$	**2, 0**
		$\downarrow$		$\uparrow$
	Dove	**0, 2**	$\leftarrow$	1, 1

Payoffs to: (Bird One, Bird Two). Arrows show how a player can increase his payoff.

Table 5.6   Hawk–Dove: biology notation

		Bird Two	
		Hawk	*Dove*
Bird One	*Hawk*	-1	2
	Dove	0	1

Payoffs to: (Bird One).

We will focus on two randomly chosen birds, Bird One and Bird Two. Each bird has a choice of what behavior to choose on meeting another bird. A resource worth $V = 2$ "fitness units" is at stake when the two birds meet. If they both fight, the loser incurs a cost of $C = 4$, which means that the expected payoff when two Hawks meet is -1 $(=0.5[2] + 0.5[-4])$ for each of them. When two Doves meet, they split the resource, for a payoff of 1 apiece. When a Hawk meets a Dove, the Dove flees for a payoff of 0, leaving the Hawk with a payoff of 2. Table 5.5 summarizes this.

These payoffs are often depicted differently in biology games. Since the two players are identical, one can depict the payoffs by using a table showing the payoffs only of the row player. Applying this to Hawk–Dove generates table 5.6.

Hawk–Dove is Chicken with new feathers. The two games have the same ordinal ranking of payoffs, as can be seen by comparing table 5.5 with table 3.2, and their equilibria are the same except for the mixing parameters. Hawk–Dove has no symmetric pure-strategy Nash equilibrium, and hence no pure-strategy ESS, since in the two asymmetric Nash equilibria, *Hawk* gives a bigger payoff than *Dove*, and the doves would disappear from the population. In the ESS for this game, neither hawks nor doves completely take over the environment. If the population consisted entirely of hawks, a dove could invade and obtain a one-round payoff of 0 against a hawk, compared to the -1 that a hawk obtains against itself. If the population consisted entirely of doves, a hawk could invade and obtain a one-round payoff of 2 against a dove, compared to the 1 that a dove obtains against a dove.

In the mixed-strategy ESS, the equilibrium strategy is to be a hawk with probability 0.5 and a dove with probability 0.5, which can be interpreted as a population 50 percent hawks and 50 percent doves. As in the mixed-strategy equilibria in chapter 3, the players are indifferent as to their strategies. The expected payoff from being a hawk is the 0.5(2) from meeting a dove plus the $0.5(-1)$ from meeting another hawk, a sum of 0.5. The expected payoff from being a dove is the 0.5(1) from meeting another dove plus the 0.5(0) from meeting a hawk, also a sum of 0.5. Moreover, the equilibrium is stable in a sense similar to the Cournot equilibrium. If 60 percent of the population were hawks, a bird would have a higher fitness level as a dove. If "higher fitness" means being able to reproduce faster, the number of doves increases and the proportion returns to 50 percent over time.

The ESS depends on the strategy sets allowed the players. If two birds can base their behavior on commonly observed random events such as which bird arrives at the resource first, and $V < C$ (as specified above), then the strategy called the **bourgeois strategy** in Maynard Smith & Parker (1976) is an ESS. Under this strategy, the bird respects property rights like a good bourgeois; it behaves as a hawk if it arrives first, and a dove if it arrives second, where we assume the order of arrival is random. The bourgeois strategy has an expected payoff of 1 from meeting itself, and behaves exactly like a 50:50 randomizer when it meets a strategy that ignores the order of arrival, so it can successfully invade a population of 50:50 randomizers. But the bourgeois strategy is a correlated strategy (see section 3.3), and requires something like the order of arrival to decide which of two identical players will play *Hawk*.

The ESS is suited to games in which all the players are identical and interacting in pairs. It does not apply to games with nonidentical players – wolves who can be wily or big and deer who can be fast or strong – although other equilibrium concepts of the same flavor can be constructed. The approach follows three steps, specifying (a) the initial population proportions and the probabilities of interactions, (b) the pairwise interactions, and (c) the dynamics by which players with higher payoffs increase in number in the population. Economics games generally use only the second step, which describes the strategies and payoffs from a single interaction.

The third step, the evolutionary dynamics, is especially foreign to economics. In specifying dynamics, the modeller must specify a difference equation (for discrete time) or differential equation (for continuous time) that describes how the strategies employed change over iterations, whether because players differ in the number of their descendants or because they learn to change their strategies over time. In economics games, the adjustment process is usually degenerate: the players jump instantly to the equilibrium. In biology games, the adjustment process is slower and cannot be derived from theory. How quickly the population of hawks increases relative to doves depends on the metabolism of the bird and the length of a generation.

Slow dynamics also makes the starting point of the game important, unlike the case when adjustment is instantaneous. Figure 5.2, taken from David Friedman (1991), shows a way to graphically depict evolution in a game in which all three strategies of *Hawk*, *Dove*, and *Bourgeois* are used. A point in the triangle represents a proportion of the three strategies in the population. At point E_3, for example, half the birds play *Hawk*, half play *Dove*, and none play *Bourgeois*, while at E_4 all the birds play *Bourgeois*.

Figure 5.2 shows the result of dynamics based on a function specified by Friedman that gives the rate of change of a strategy's proportion based on its payoff relative to the other two strategies. Points E_1, E_2, E_3, and E_4 are all fixed points in the sense that the proportions do not change no matter which of these points the game starts from. Only point E_4 represents an evolutionarily stable equilibrium, however, and if the game starts with any positive proportion of birds playing *Bourgeois*, the proportions tend towards E_4. The original Hawk–Dove which excluded the bourgeois strategy can be viewed as the HD line at the bottom of the triangle, and E_3 is evolutionarily stable in that restricted game.

Figure 5.2 also shows the importance of mutation in biological games. If the population of birds is 100 percent dove, as at E_2, it stays that way in the absence of mutation, since if there are no hawks to begin with, the fact that they would reproduce at a faster rate than

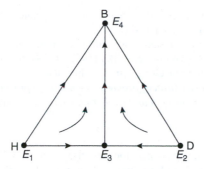

Figure 5.2   Evolutionary Dynamics in the Hawk–Dove – Bourgeois game.

doves becomes irrelevant. If, however, a bird could mutate to play *Hawk* and then pass this behavior on to his offspring, then eventually some bird would do so and the mutant strategy would be successful. The technology of mutations can be important to the ultimate equilibrium. In more complicated games than Hawk–Dove, it can matter whether mutations happen to be small, accidental shifts to strategies similar to those that are currently being played, or can be of arbitrary size, so that a superior strategy quite different from the existing strategies might be reached.

The idea of mutation is distinct from the idea of evolutionary dynamics, and it is possible to use one without the other. In economics models, a mutation would correspond to the appearance of a new action in the action set of one of the players in a game. This is one way to model innovation: not as research followed by stochastic discoveries, but as accidental learning. The modeller might specify that the discovered action becomes available to players slowly through evolutionary dynamics, or instantly, in the usual style of economics. This style of research has promise for economics, but since the technologies of dynamics and mutation are important there is a danger of simply multiplying models without reliable results unless the modeller limits himself to a narrow context and bases his technology on empirical measurements.

Notes

N5.1   Finitely repeated games and the Chainstore Paradox

- The Chainstore Paradox does not apply to all games as neatly as to Entry Deterrence and the Prisoner's Dilemma. If the one-shot game has only one Nash equilibrium, the perfect equilibrium of the finitely repeated game is unique and has that same outcome. But if the one-shot game has multiple Nash equilibria, the perfect equilibrium of the finitely repeated game can have not only the one-shot outcomes, but others besides. See Benoit & Krishna (1985), Harrington (1987), and Moreaux (1985).
- John Heywood is Bartlett's source for the term "tit-for-tat," from the French "tant pour tant."
- A realistic expansion of a game's strategy space may eliminate the Chainstore Paradox. Hirshleifer & Rasmusen (1989), for example, show that allowing the players in a multi-person finitely repeated Prisoner's Dilemma to ostracize offenders can enforce cooperation even if there

are economies of scale in the number of players who cooperate and are not ostracized. Similarly, a little altruism can eliminate the paradox.

- The peculiarity of the unique Nash equilibrium, for the repeated Prisoner's Dilemma was noticed long before Selten (1978) (see Luce & Raiffa [1957], p. 99), but the term Chainstore Paradox is now generally used for all unravelling games of this kind.

- An **epsilon-equilibrium** *is a strategy profile s* such that no player has more than an ε incentive to deviate from his strategy given that the other players do not deviate. Formally,*

$$\forall i, \quad \pi_i(s_i^*, s_{-i}^*) \geq \pi_i(s_i', s_{-i}^*) - \epsilon, \quad \forall s_i' \in S_i. \tag{5.17}$$

Radner (1980) has shown that cooperation can arise as an ε-equilibrium of the finitely repeated Prisoner's Dilemma. Fudenberg & Levine (1986) compare the ε-equilibria of finite games with the Nash equilibria of infinite games. Other concepts besides Nash can also use the ε-equilibrium idea.

- A general way to decide whether a mathematical result is a trick of infinity is to see if the same result is obtained as the limit of results for longer and longer finite models. Applied to games, a good criterion for picking among equilibria of an infinite game is to select one which is the limit of the equilibria for finite games as the number of periods gets longer. Fudenberg & Levine (1986) show under what conditions one can find the equilibria of infinite-horizon games by this process. For the Prisoner's Dilemma, (*Always Confess*) is the only equilibrium in all finite games, so it uniquely satisfies the criterion.

- Defining payoffs in games that last an infinite number of periods presents the problem that the total payoff is infinite for any positive payment per period. Ways to distinguish one infinite amount from another include the following.

1   Use an **overtaking criterion**. Payoff stream π is preferred to $\tilde{\pi}$ if there is some time T^* such that for every $T \geq T^*$,

$$\sum_{t=1}^{T} \delta^t \pi_t > \sum_{t=1}^{T} \delta^t \tilde{\pi}_t.$$

2   Specify that the discount rate is strictly positive, and compare the present values of π and $\tilde{\pi}$. Since payments in distant periods count for less, the discounted value is finite unless the payments are growing faster than the discount rate. Equivalently, compare the **average discounted payoffs**, defined as $\rho/(1 + \rho)$ times the total payoffs. If the payoff is x/ρ because x is a perpetuity then the average discounted payoff is

$$\left(\frac{\rho}{1 + \rho}\right)\left(\frac{x}{\rho}\right) = \frac{x}{1 + \rho}.$$

3   Compare the average payments per period of π and $\tilde{\pi}$, a tricky method since some sort of limit needs to be taken as the number of periods averaged goes to infinity.

Whatever the approach, game theorists assume that the payoff function is **additively separable** over time, which means that the total payoff is based on the sum or average, possibly discounted, of the one-shot payoffs. Macroeconomists worry about this assumption, which rules out, for example, a player whose payoff is very low if any of his one-shot payoffs dips below a certain subsistence level. The issue of separability will arise again in chapter 14 when we discuss durable monopoly.

- Ending in finite time with probability one means that the limit of the probability the game has ended by date t approaches one as t tends to infinity; the probability that the game lasts till infinity is zero. Equivalently, the expectation of the end date is finite, which it could not be were there a positive probability of an infinite length.

N5.2   Infinitely repeated games, minimax punishments, and the Folk Theorem

- Aumann (1981), Fudenberg & Maskin (1986), Fudenberg & Tirole (1991a, pp. 152–62), and Rasmusen (1992a) tell more about the Folk Theorem. The most commonly cited version of the Folk Theorem says that if conditions 1 to 3 are satisfied, then:

  Any payoff profile that strictly Pareto-dominates the minimax payoff profiles in the mixed extension of an n-person one-shot game with finite action sets is the average payoff in some perfect equilibrium of the infinitely repeated game.

- The evolutionary approach can also be applied to the repeated Prisoner's Dilemma. Boyd & Lorberbaum (1987) show that no pure strategy, including Tit-for-Tat, is evolutionarily stable in a population-interaction version of the Prisoner's Dilemma. Hirshleifer & Martinez-Coll (1988) have found that Tit-for-Tat is no longer part of an ESS in an evolutionary Prisoner's Dilemma if (a) more complicated strategies have higher computation costs; or (b) sometimes a *Deny* is observed to be a *Confess* by the other player. Yet biologists have found animals playing tit-for-tat – notably the sticklebacks in Milinski (1987) who can choose whether to shirk or not in investigating predator fish.
- **Trigger strategies** or *trigger-price strategies* are an important kind of strategies for repeated games. Consider the oligopolist facing uncertain demand (as in Stigler [1964]). He cannot tell whether the low demand he observes facing him is due to Nature or to price cutting by his fellow oligopolists. Two things that could trigger him to cut his own price in retaliation are a series of periods with low demand or one period of especially low demand. Finding an optimal trigger strategy is a difficult problem (see Porter [1983a]). Trigger strategies are usually not subgame perfect unless the game is infinitely repeated, in which case they are a subset of the equilibrium strategies. Recent work has looked carefully at what trigger strategies are possible and optimal for players in infinitely repeated games; see Abreu, Pearce, & Stacchetti (1990). Many theorists have studied what happens when players can imperfectly observe each others' actions. For a survey, see Kandori (2002).

  Empirical work on trigger strategies includes Porter (1983b), who examines price wars between railroads in the 19th century, and Slade (1987), who concluded that price wars among gas stations in Vancouver used small punishments for small deviations rather than big punishments for big deviations.
- A macroeconomist's technical note related to the similarity of infinite games and games with a constant probability of ending is Blanchard (1979), which discusses speculative bubbles.
- In the repeated Prisoner's Dilemma, if the end date is infinite with positive probability and only one player knows it, cooperation is possible by reasoning similar to that of the Gang of Four theorem in section 6.4.
- Any Nash equilibrium of the one-shot game is also a perfect equilibrium of the finitely or infinitely repeated game.
- What happens if one player is long lived and the other player is a sequence of short-lived players? See Fudenberg & Tirole (1989).

N5.3   Reputation: the one-sided Prisoner's Dilemma

- *A game that is repeated an infinite number of times without discounting is called a* **supergame**. There is no connection between the terms "supergame" and "subgame."

- The terms, "one-sided" and "two-sided" Prisoner's Dilemma, are my inventions. Only the two-sided version is a true Prisoner's Dilemma according to the definition of note N1.2.
- Empirical work on reputation is scarce. One worthwhile effort is Jarrell & Peltzman (1985), which finds that product recalls inflict costs greatly in excess of the measurable direct costs of the operations. The investigations into actual business practice of Macaulay (1963) is much cited and little imitated. He notes that reputation seems to be more important than the written details of business contracts.
- **Vengeance and gratitude:** Most models have excluded these feelings (although see Jack Hirshleifer [1987]), which can be modelled in two ways.

  1   A player's current utility from *Confess* or *Deny* depends on what the other player has played in the past; or
  2   A player's current utility depends on current actions and the other players' current utility in a way that changes with past actions of the other player.

The two approaches are subtly different in interpretation. In (1), the joy of revenge is in the action of confessing. In (2), the joy of revenge is in the discomfiture of the other player. Especially if the players have different payoff functions, these two approaches can lead to different results.

N5.4   Product Quality in an infinitely repeated game

- The Product Quality Game may also be viewed as a principal–agent model of moral hazard (see chapter 7). The seller (an agent), takes the action of choosing quality that is unobserved by the buyer (the principal), but which affects the principal's payoff, an interpretation used in much of the Stiglitz (1987) survey of the links between quality and price.

  The intuition behind the Klein & Leffler model is similar to the explanation for high wages in the Shapiro & Stiglitz (1984) model of involuntary unemployment (section 8.1). Consumers, seeing a low price, realize that with a price that low the firm cannot resist lowering quality to make short-term profits. A large margin of profit is needed for the firm to decide on continuing to produce high quality.
- A paper related to Klein & Leffler (1981) is Shapiro (1983), which reconciles a high price with free entry by requiring that firms price under cost during the early periods to build up a reputation. If consumers believe, for example, that any firm charging a high price for any of the first five periods has produced a low quality product, but any firm charging a high price thereafter has produced high quality, then firms behave accordingly and the beliefs are confirmed. That the beliefs are self-confirming does not make them irrational; it only means that many different beliefs are rational in the many different equilibria.
- An equilibrium exists in the Product Quality model only if the entry cost F is just the right size to make n an integer in equation (5.8). Any of the usual assumptions to get around the integer problem could be used: allowing potential sellers to randomize between entering and staying out; assuming that for historical reasons, n firms have already entered; or assuming that firms lie on a continuum and the fixed cost is a uniform density across firms that have entered.

N5.5   Markov equilibria and overlapping generations in the game of Customer Switching Costs

- We assumed that the incumbent chooses its price first, but the alternation of incumbency remains even if we make the opposite assumption. The natural assumption is that prices are chosen simultaneously, but because of the discontinuity in the payoff function, that subgame has no equilibrium in pure strategies.

N5.6   Evolutionary equilibrium: the Hawk–Dove Game

- Dugatkin & Reeve (1998) is an edited volume of survey articles on different applications of game theory to biology. Dawkins (1989) is a good verbal introduction to evolutionary conflict. See also Axelrod & Hamilton (1981) for a short article on biological applications of the Prisoner's Dilemma, Hines (1987) for a survey, and Maynard Smith (1982) for a book. Jack Hirshleifer (1982) compares the approaches of economists and biologists. Boyd & Richerson (1985) uses evolutionary game theory to examine cultural transmission, which has important differences from purely genetic transmission.

Problems

5.1:   Overlapping generations (see Samuelson [1958]) medium)

There is a long sequence of players. One player is born in each period t, and he lives for periods t and $t + 1$. Thus, two players are alive in any one period, a youngster and an oldster. Each player is born with one unit of chocolate, which cannot be stored. Utility is increasing in chocolate consumption, and a player is very unhappy if he consumes less than 0.3 units of chocolate in a period: the per-period utility functions are $U(C) = -1$ for $C < 0.3$ and $U(C) = C$ for $C \geq 0.3$, where C is consumption. Players can give away their chocolate, but, since chocolate is the only good, they cannot sell it. A player's action is to consume X units of chocolate as a youngster and give away $1 - X$ to some oldster. Every person's actions in the previous period are common knowledge, and so can be used to condition strategies upon.

(a)   If there is finite number of generations, what is the unique Nash equilibrium?
(b)   If there are an infinite number of generations, what are two Pareto-ranked perfect equilibria?
(c)   If there is a probability θ at the end of each period (after consumption takes place) that barbarians will invade and steal all the chocolate (leaving the civilized people with payoffs of -1 for any X), what is the highest value of θ that still allows for an equilibrium with $X = 0.5$?

5.2:   Product Quality with lawsuits (medium)

Modify the Product Quality game of section 5.4 by assuming that if the seller misrepresents his quality he must, as a result of a class-action suit, pay damages of x per unit sold, where $x \in (0, c]$ and the seller becomes liable for x at the time of sale.

(a)   What is $\tilde{p}$ as a function of x, F, c, and r? Is $\tilde{p}$ greater than when $x = 0$?
(b)   What is the equilibrium output per firm? Is it greater than when $x = 0$?
(c)   What is the equilibrium number of firms? Show that a rise in x has an ambiguous effect on the number of firms.
(d)   If, instead of x per unit, the seller pays X to a law firm to successfully defend him, what is the incentive compatibility constraint?

5.3:   Repeated games (see Benoit & Krishna [1985]) (hard)

Players Benoit and Krishna repeat the game in table 5.7 three times, with discounting:

Table 5.7   A Benoit–Krishna Game

		Krishna		
		Deny	*Waffle*	*Confess*
	Deny	10, 10	−1, −12	−1, 15
Benoit	*Waffle*	−12, −1	8, 8	−1, −1
	Confess	15, −1	−1, −1	0, 0

Payoffs to: (Benoit, Krishna).

(a)   Why is there no equilibrium in which the players play *Deny* in all three periods?
(b)   Describe a perfect equilibrium in which both players pick *Deny* in the first two periods.
(c)   Adapt your equilibrium to the twice-repeated game.
(d)   Adapt your equilibrium to the T-repeated game.
(e)   What is the greatest discount rate for which your equilibrium still works in the three-period game?

5.4:   Repeated Entry Deterrence (medium)

Assume that Entry Deterrence I is repeated an infinite number of times, with a tiny discount rate and with payoffs received at the start of each period. In each period, the entrant chooses *Enter* or *Stay Out*, even if he entered previously.

(a)   What is a perfect equilibrium in which the entrant enters each period?
(b)   Why is (*Stay Out, Fight*) not a perfect equilibrium?
(c)   What is a perfect equilibrium in which the entrant never enters?
(d)   What is the maximum discount rate for which your strategy profile in part (c) is still an equilibrium?

5.5:   The Repeated Prisoner's Dilemma (medium)

Set $P = 0$ in the general Prisoner's Dilemma in table 1.9, and assume that $2R > S + T$.

(a)   Show that the Grim Strategy, when played by both players, is a perfect equilibrium for the infinitely repeated game. What is the maximum discount rate for which the Grim Strategy remains an equilibrium?
(b)   Show that Tit-for-Tat is not a perfect equilibrium in the infinitely repeated Prisoner's Dilemma with no discounting.

5.6:   Evolutionarily stable strategies (medium)

A population of scholars are playing the following coordination game over their two possible conversation topics over lunch, football and economics. Let $N_t(F)$ and $N_t(E)$ be the numbers who talk football and economics in period t, and let θ be the percentage who talk football, so $\theta = N(football)/(N(football) + N(economics))$. Government regulations requiring lunchtime attendance and stipulating the topics of conversation have maintained the values $\theta = 0.5, N_t(F) = 50,000$, and $N_t(E) = 50{,}000$ up to this year's deregulatory reform. In the future, some people may decide to go home for lunch instead, or change their conversation. Table 5.8 shows the payoffs.

Table 5.8   Evolutionarily stable strategies

		Scholar 2	
		Football (θ)	Economics $(1-\theta)$
	Football (θ)	1, 1	0, 0
Scholar 1			
	Economics $(1-\theta)$	0, 0	5, 5

Payoffs to: (Scholar 1, Scholar 2).

(a) There are three Nash equilibria: (*Football, Football*), (*Economics, Economics*), and a mixed-strategy equilibrium. What are the evolutionarily stable strategies?

(b) Let $N_t(s)$ be the number of scholars playing a particular strategy in period t and let $\pi_t(s)$ be the payoff. Devise a Markov difference equation to express the population dynamics from period to period: $N_{t+1}(s) = f(N_t(s), \pi_t(s))$. Start the system with a population of 100,000, half the scholars talking football and half talking economics. Use your dynamics to finish table 5.9.

Table 5.9   Conversation dynamics

t	$N_t(F)$	$N_t(E)$	θ	$\pi_t(F)$	$\pi_t(E)$
-1	50,000	50,000	0.5	0.5	2.5
0					
1					
2					

(c) Repeat part (b), but specifying non-Markov dynamics, in which $N_{t+1}(s) = f(N_t(s), \pi_t(s), \pi_{t-1}(s))$.

5.7:   Grab the Dollar (medium)

Table 5.10 shows the payoffs for the simultaneous-move game of Grab the Dollar. A silver dollar is put on the table between Smith and Jones. If one grabs it, he keeps the dollar, for a payoff of 4 utils. If both grab, then neither gets the dollar, and both feel bitter. If neither grabs, each gets to keep something.

Table 5.10   Grab the dollar

		Jones	
		Grab (θ)	Wait $(1-\theta)$
	Grab (θ)	$-1, -1$	4, 0
Smith			
	Wait $(1-\theta)$	0, 4	1, 1

Payoffs to: (Smith, Jones).

(a) What are the evolutionarily stable strategies?

(b) Suppose each player in the population is a point on a continuum, and that the initial amount of players is 1, evenly divided between *Grab* and *Wait*. Let $N_t(s)$ be the amount of players playing a particular strategy in period t and let $\pi_t(s)$ be the payoff. Let the population dynamics be

$$N_{t+1}(i) = (2N_t(i)) \left(\frac{\pi_t(i)}{\sum_j \pi_t(j)} \right).$$

Find the missing entries in table 5.11.

Table 5.11   Grab the Dollar dynamics

t	$N_t(G)$	$N_t(W)$	$N_t(total)$	θ	$\pi_t(G)$	$\pi_t(w)$
0	0.5	0.5	1	0.5	1.5	0.5
1						
2						

(c)   Repeat part (b), but with the dynamics

$$N_{t+t}(s) = \left[1 + \frac{\pi_t(s)}{\sum_j \pi_t(j)} \right] [2N_t(s)].$$

(d)   Which three games that have appeared so far in the book resemble Grab the Dollar?

5.8:   Minimaxing (easy)

Table 5.12 shows the payoffs for the simultaneous-move game of Mixed Minimaxing. Use θ for the probability that Row chooses *North* when mixing, and γ for the probability that Column chooses *West*. *Payoffs to: (Row, Column)*.

Table 5.12   Mixed Minimaxing

		Column	
		West (γ)	East $(1-\gamma)$
Row	North (θ)	1, 1	0, −2
	South $(1-\theta)$	−2, 0	1, 1

(a)   What are the three Nash equilibria?
(b)   What is Column's payoff in the three Nash equilibria?
(c)   What would Column's strategy be for minimaxing Row if both were restricted to pure strategies, and what would Row's minimax payoff then be?
(d)   What is Column's strategy for minimaxing Row if mixed strategies are allowed? What is Row's minimax payoff?
(e)   What would Row's maximin strategy be if both players were restricted to pure strategies, and what would his maximin payoff then be?
(f)   What is Row's maximin strategy if mixed strategies are allowed? What is Row's maximin payoff?

The Repeated Prisoner's Dilemma: A Classroom Game for Chapter 5

Consider the following Prisoner's Dilemma, obtained by adding 8 to each payoff in table 1.2 (table 5.13):

Table 5.13   The Prisoner's Dilemma

		Column	
		Deny	*Confess*
	Deny	7, 7	−2, 8
Row			
	Confess	8, −2	**0, 0**

Payoffs to: (Row,Column).

Students will pair up to repeat this game ten times in the same pair. The objective is to get as high a summed, undiscounted, payoff as possible (*not* just to get a higher summed payoff than any other person in the class).

Chapter 6
dynamic games with incomplete information

6.1 Perfect Bayesian Equilibrium: Entry Deterrence II and III

Asymmetric information, and, in particular, incomplete information, is enormously important in game theory. This is particularly true for dynamic games, since when the players have several moves in sequence, their earlier moves may convey private information that is relevant to the decisions of players moving later on. Revealing and concealing information are the basis of much of strategic behavior and are especially useful as ways of explaining actions that would be irrational in a nonstrategic world.

Chapter 4 showed that even if there is symmetric information in a dynamic game, Nash equilibrium may need to be refined using subgame perfectness if the modeller is to make sensible predictions. Asymmetric information requires a somewhat different refinement to capture the idea of sunk costs and credible threats, and section 6.1 sets out the standard refinement of perfect Bayesian equilibrium. Section 6.2 shows that even this may not be enough refinement to guarantee uniqueness and discusses further refinements based on out-of-equilibrium beliefs. Section 6.3 uses the idea to show that a player's ignorance may work to his advantage, and to explain how even when all players know something, lack of common knowledge still affects the game. Section 6.4 introduces incomplete information into the repeated Prisoner's Dilemma and shows the Gang of Four solution to the Chainstore Paradox of chapter 5. Section 6.5 describes the celebrated Axelrod tournament, an experimental approach to the same paradox. Section 6.6 applies the idea of a dynamic game of incomplete information to the evolution of creditworthiness using the model of Diamond (1989).

Subgame Perfectness Is Not Enough

In games of asymmetric information, we will still require that an equilibrium be subgame perfect, but the mere forking of the game tree might not be relevant to a player's decision, because with asymmetric information he does not know which fork the game has taken. Smith might know he is at one of two different nodes depending on whether Jones has high or low production costs, but if he does not know the exact node, the "subgames"

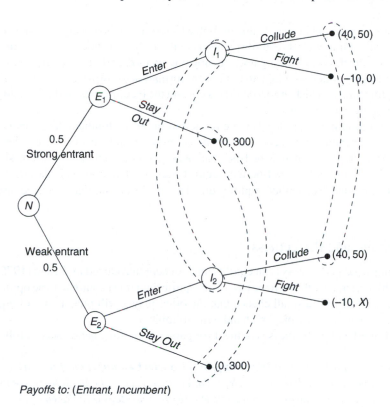

Figure 6.1   Entry Deterrence II, III, and IV.

starting at each node are irrelevant to his decisions. In fact, they are not even subgames as we have defined them, because they cut across Smith's information sets. This can be seen in an asymmetric information version of Entry Deterrence I (section 4.2). In Entry Deterrence I, the incumbent colluded with the entrant because fighting him was more costly than colluding once the entrant had entered. Now, let us set up the game to allow some entrants to be *Strong* and some *Weak* in the sense that it is more costly for the incumbent to choose *Fight* against a *Strong* entrant than a *Weak* one. The incumbent's payoff from *Fight|Strong* will be 0, as before, but his payoff from *Fight|Weak* will be X, where X will take values ranging from 0 (Entry Deterrence I) to 300 (Entry Deterrence IV and V) in different versions of the game.

Entry Deterrence II, III, and IV will all have the extensive form shown in figure 6.1. With 50 percent probability, the incumbent's payoff from *Fight* is X rather than the 0 in Entry Deterrence I, but the incumbent does not know which payoff is the correct one in the particular realization of the game. This is modelled as an initial move by Nature, who chooses between the entrant being *Weak* or *Strong*, unobserved by the incumbent.

Entry Deterrence II: Fighting Is Never Profitable

In Entry Deterrence II, $X = 1$, so information is not very asymmetric. It is common knowledge that the incumbent never benefits from *Fight*, even though his exact payoff might be zero or might be one. Unlike in Entry Deterrence I, however, subgame perfectness does not rule out any Nash equilibria, because the only subgame is the subgame starting at node N, which is the entire game. A subgame cannot start at nodes E_1 or E_2, because neither of those nodes are singletons in the information partitions. Thus, the implausible Nash equilibrium in which the entrant stays out and the incumbent would Fight entry escapes elimination by a technicality.

The equilibrium concept needs to be refined in order to eliminate the implausible equilibrium. Two general approaches can be taken: either introduce small "trembles" into the game, or require that strategies be best responses given rational beliefs. The first approach takes us to the "trembling hand-perfect" equilibrium, while the second takes us to the "perfect Bayesian" and "sequential" equilibrium. The results are similar whichever approach is taken.

Trembling-hand Perfectness

Trembling-hand perfectness is an equilibrium concept introduced by Selten (1975) according to which a strategy that is to be part of an equilibrium must continue to be optimal for the player even if there is a small chance that the other player will pick an out-of-equilibrium action (i.e., that the other player's hand will "tremble").

Trembling-hand perfectness is defined for games with finite action sets as follows.

The strategy profile s^* is a **trembling-hand perfect** *equilibrium if for any ϵ there is a vector of positive numbers $\delta_1, \ldots, \delta_n \in [0, 1]$ and a vector of completely mixed strategies $\sigma_1, \ldots, \sigma_n$ such that the perturbed game where every strategy is replaced by $(1-\delta_i)s_i+\delta_i\sigma_i$ has a Nash equilibrium in which every strategy is within distance ϵ of s^*.*

Every trembling-hand perfect equilibrium is subgame perfect; indeed, section 4.1 justified subgame perfectness using a tremble argument. Unfortunately, it is often hard to tell whether a strategy profile is trembling-hand perfect, and the concept is undefined for games with continuous strategy spaces because it is hard to work with mixtures of a continuum (see note N3.1). Moreover, the equilibrium depends on which trembles are chosen, and deciding why one tremble should be more common than another may be difficult.

Perfect Bayesian Equilibrium and Sequential Equilibrium

The second approach to asymmetric information, introduced by Kreps & Wilson (1982) in the spirit of Harsanyi (1967), is to start with prior beliefs, common to all players, that specify the probabilities with which Nature chooses the types of the players at the beginning of the game. Some of the players observe Nature's move and update their beliefs, while other players can update their beliefs only by deductions they make from observing the actions of the informed players.

The deductions used to update beliefs are based on the actions specified by the equilibrium. When players update their beliefs, they assume that the other players are following the equilibrium strategies, but since the strategies themselves depend on the beliefs, an equilibrium can no longer be defined based on strategies alone. Under asymmetric information, an equilibrium is a strategy profile and a set of beliefs such that the strategies are best responses.

On the equilibrium path, all that the players need to update their beliefs are their priors and Bayes' Rule, but off the equilibrium path this is not enough. Suppose that in equilibrium, the entrant always stays out. If for whatever reason the impossible happens and the entrant enters, what is the incumbent to think about the probability that the entrant is weak? Bayes' Rule does not help, because when $Prob(data) = 0$, which is the case for data such as *Enter* that is never observed in equilibrium, the posterior belief cannot be calculated using Bayes' Rule. From section 2.4, Bayes' Rule says

$$Prob(Weak|Enter) = \frac{Prob(Enter|Weak)Prob(Weak)}{Prob(Enter)}. \tag{6.1}$$

The posterior $Prob(Weak|Stay\ Out)$ is undefined, because (6.1) requires dividing by zero. (It does not help that 0 is in the numerator too – see note N6.1.)

A natural way to define equilibrium is as a strategy profile consisting of best responses given that equilibrium beliefs follow Bayes' Rule and out-of-equilibrium beliefs follow a specified pattern that does not contradict Bayes' Rule.

A **perfect Bayesian equilibrium** *is a strategy profiles and a set of beliefs μ such that at each node of the game:*

(1)   The strategies for the remainder of the game are Nash given the beliefs and strategies of the other players.

(2)   The beliefs at each information set are rational given the evidence appearing thus far in the game (meaning that they are based, if possible, on priors updated by Bayes' Rule, given the observed actions of the other players under the hypothesis that they are in equilibrium).

Perfect Bayesian equilibria are always subgame perfect (condition (1) takes care of that), and every trembling-hand perfect equilibrium is a perfect Bayesian equilibrium.

Back to Entry Deterrence II

Armed with the concept of the perfect Bayesian equilibrium, we can find a sensible equilibrium for Entry Deterrence II .

Entrant: *Enter|Weak, Enter|Strong*

Incumbent: *Collude*

Beliefs: $Prob(Strong|Stay\ Out) = 0.4$

In this equilibrium the entrant enters whether he is *Weak* or *Strong*. The incumbent's strategy is *Collude*, which is not conditioned on Nature's move, since he does not observe it. Because the entrant enters regardless of Nature's move, an out-of-equilibrium belief for the incumbent if he should observe *Stay Out* must be specified, and this belief is arbitrarily chosen to be that the incumbent's subjective probability that the entrant is *Strong* is 0.4 given his observation that the entrant deviated by choosing *Stay Out*. Given this strategy profile and out-of-equilibrium belief, neither player has incentive to change his strategy.

There is no perfect Bayesian equilibrium in which the entrant chooses *Stay Out*. *Fight* is a bad response even under the most optimistic possible belief, that the entrant is *Weak* with probability 1. Notice that perfect Bayesian equilibrium is not defined structurally, like subgame perfectness, but rather in terms of optimal responses. This enables it to come closer to the economic intuition which we wish to capture by an equilibrium refinement.

Finding the perfect Bayesian equilibrium of a game, like finding the Nash equilibrium, requires intelligence. Algorithms are not useful. To find a Nash equilibrium, the modeller thinks about his game, picks a plausible strategy profile, and tests whether the strategies are best responses to each other. To make it a perfect Bayesian equilibrium, he notes which actions are never taken in equilibrium and specifies the beliefs that players use to interpret those actions. He then tests whether each player's strategies are best responses given his beliefs at each node, checking in particular whether any player would like to take an out-of-equilibrium action in order to set in motion the other players' out-of-equilibrium beliefs and strategies. This process does not involve testing whether a player's beliefs are beneficial to the player, because players do not choose their own beliefs; the priors and out-of-equilibrium beliefs are exogenously specified by the modeller.

One might wonder why the beliefs have to be specified in Entry Deterrence II. Does not the game tree specify the probability that the entrant is *Weak*? What difference does it make if the entrant stays out? Admittedly, Nature does choose each type with probability 0.5, so if the incumbent had no other information than this prior, that would be his belief. But the entrant's action might convey additional information. The concept of perfect Bayesian equilibrium leaves the modeller free to specify how the players form beliefs from that additional information, so long as the beliefs do not violate Bayes' Rule. (A technically valid choice of beliefs by the modeller might still be met with scorn, though, as with any silly assumption.) Here, the equilibrium says that if the entrant stays out, the incumbent believes he is *Strong* with probability 0.4 and *Weak* with probability 0.6, beliefs that are arbitrary but do not contradict Bayes' Rule.

In Entry Deterrence II the out-of-equilibrium beliefs do not and should not matter. If the entrant chooses *Stay Out*, the game ends, so the incumbent's beliefs are irrelevant. Perfect Bayesian equilibrium was only introduced as a way out of a technical problem. In the next section, however, the precise out-of-equilibrium beliefs will be crucial to which strategy profiles are equilibria.

6.2   Refining Perfect Bayesian Equilibrium in the Entry Deterrence and PhD Admissions Games

Entry Deterrence III: Fighting Is Sometimes Profitable

In Entry Deterrence III, assume that $X = 60$, not $X = 1$. This means that fighting is more profitable for the incumbent than collusion if the entrant is *Weak*. As before, the entrant knows if he is *Weak*, but the incumbent does not. Retaining the prior after observing out-of-equilibrium actions, a prior here of $Prob(Strong) = 0.5$, is a convenient way to form beliefs that is called **passive conjectures**. The following is a perfect Bayesian equilibrium which uses passive conjectures.

A plausible pooling equilibrium for Entry Deterrence III

Entrant: *Enter|Weak, Enter|Strong*

Incumbent: *Collude*

Out-of-equilibrium beliefs: *Prob(Strong|Stay Out)* = 0.5

In choosing whether to enter, the entrant must predict the incumbent's behavior. If the probability that the entrant is *Weak* is 0.5, the expected payoff to the incumbent from choosing *Fight* is 30 (=0.5[0] + 0.5[60]), which is less than the payoff of 50 from *Collude*. The incumbent will collude, so the entrant enters. The entrant may know that the incumbent's payoff is actually 60, but that is irrelevant to the incumbent's behavior.

The out-of-equilibrium belief does not matter to this first equilibrium, although it will in other equilibria of the same game. Although beliefs in a perfect Bayesian equilibrium must follow Bayes' Rule, that puts very little restriction on how players interpret out-of-equilibrium behavior. Out-of-equilibrium behavior is "impossible," so when it does occur there is no obvious way the player should react. Some beliefs may seem more reasonable than others, however, and Entry Deterrence III has another equilibrium that requires less plausible beliefs off the equilibrium path.

An implausible pooling equilibrium for Entry Deterrence III

Entrant: *Stay Out|Weak, Stay Out|Strong*

Incumbent: *Fight*

Out-of-equilibrium beliefs: *Prob(Strong|Enter)* = 0.1

This is an equilibrium because if the entrant were to deviate and enter, the incumbent would calculate his payoff from fighting to be 54 (=0.1[0] + 0.9[60]), which is greater than the *Collude* payoff of 50. The entrant would therefore stay out.

The beliefs in the implausible equilibrium are different and less reasonable than in the plausible equilibrium. Why should the incumbent believe that weak entrants would enter mistakenly nine times as often as strong entrants? The beliefs do not violate Bayes' Rule, but they have no justification.

The reasonableness of the beliefs is important because if the incumbent uses passive conjectures, the implausible equilibrium breaks down. With passive conjectures, the incumbent would want to change his strategy to *Collude*, because the expected payoff from *Fight* would be less than 50. The implausible equilibrium is less robust with respect to beliefs than the plausible equilibrium, and it requires beliefs that are harder to justify.

Even though dubious outcomes may be perfect Bayesian equilibria, the concept does have some bite, ruling out other dubious outcomes. There does not, for example, exist an equilibrium in which the entrant enters only if he is *Strong* and stays out if he is *Weak* (called a "separating equilibrium" because it separates out different types of players). Such an equilibrium would have to look like this:

A conjectured separating equilibrium for Entry Deterrence III

Entrant: *Stay Out|Weak, Enter|Strong*

Incumbent: *Collude*

No out-of-equilibrium beliefs are specified for the conjectures in the separating equilibrium because there is no out-of-equilibrium behavior about which to specify them. Since the incumbent might observe either *Stay Out* or *Enter* in equilibrium, the incumbent will always use Bayes' Rule to form his beliefs. He will believe that an entrant who stays out must be weak and an entrant who enters must be strong. This conforms to the idea behind Nash equilibrium that each player assumes that the other follows the equilibrium strategy, and then decides how to reply. Here, the incumbent's best response, given his beliefs, is *Collude|Enter*, so that is the second part of the proposed equilibrium. But this cannot be an equilibrium, because the entrant would want to deviate. Knowing that entry would be followed by collusion, even the weak entrant would enter. So there cannot be an equilibrium in which the entrant enters only when strong. We have rejected the conjecture.

The PhD Admissions Game

Passive conjectures may not always be the most satisfactory belief, as the next example shows. Suppose that a university knows that 90 percent of the population hate economics and would be unhappy in its PhD program, and 10 percent love economics and would do well. In addition, it cannot observe the applicant's type. If the university rejects an application, its payoff is 0 and the applicant's is −1 because of the trouble needed to apply. If the university accepts the application of someone who hates economics, the payoffs of both university and student are −10, but if the applicant loves economics, the payoffs are +20 for each player.

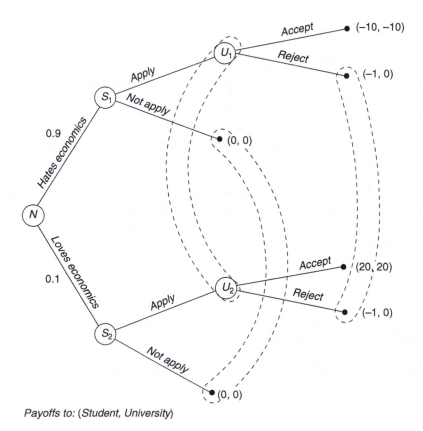

Payoffs to: (Student, University)

Figure 6.2   The PhD Admissions Game.

Figure 6.2 shows this game in extensive form. The population proportions are represented by a node at which Nature chooses the student to be a *Lover* or *Hater* of economics.

The PhD Admissions Game is a signalling game of the kind we will look at in chapter 11. It has various perfect Bayesian equilibria that differ in their out-of-equilibrium beliefs, but the equilibria can be divided into two distinct categories, depending on the outcome: the **separating equilibrium**, in which the lovers of economics apply and the haters do not, and the **pooling equilibrium**, in which neither type of student applies.

A separating equilibrium for the PhD Admissions Game

Student: *Apply|Lover, Do Not Apply|Hater*

University: *Admit*

The separating equilibrium does not need to specify out-of-equilibrium beliefs, because Bayes' Rule can always be applied whenever both of the two possible actions *Apply* and *Do Not Apply* can occur in equilibrium.

A pooling equilibrium for the PhD Admissions Game

Student: *Do Not Apply|Lover, Do Not Apply|Hater*

University: *Reject*

Out-of-equilibrium beliefs: $Prob(Hater|Apply) = 0.9$ (passive conjectures)

The pooling equilibrium is supported by passive conjectures. Both types of students refrain from applying because they believe correctly that they would be rejected and receive a payoff of -1; and the university is willing to reject any student who foolishly applied, believing that he is a *Hater* with 90 percent probability.

Because the perfect Bayesian equilibrium concept imposes no restrictions on out-of-equilibrium beliefs, economists have come up with a variety of exotic refinements of the equilibrium concept. Let us consider whether various alternatives to passive conjectures would support the pooling equilibrium in PhD Admissions.

Passive Conjectures. $Prob(Hater|Apply) = 0.9$
This is the belief specified above, under which out-of-equilibrium behavior leaves beliefs unchanged from the prior. The argument for passive conjectures is that the student's application is a mistake, and that both types are equally likely to make mistakes, although *Haters* are more common in the population. This supports the pooling equilibrium.

The Intuitive Criterion. $Prob(Hater|Apply) = 0$
Under the Intuitive Criterion or ("equilibrium dominance") of Cho & Kreps (1987), if there is a type of informed player who would be hurt by the out-of-equilibrium action no matter what beliefs were held by the uninformed player, the uninformed player's belief must put zero probability on that type. Here, the *Hater* would be hurt by applying under any possible beliefs of the university, so the university puts zero probability on an applicant being a *Hater*. This argument will not support the pooling equilibrium, because if the university holds this belief, it will want to admit anyone who applies.

Complete Robustness. Prob(Hater|Apply) = m, 0 ≤ m ≤ 1

Under this approach, the equilibrium strategy profile must consist of responses that are best, given any and all out-of-equilibrium beliefs. Our equilibrium for Entry Deterrence II satisfied this requirement. Complete robustness rules out a pooling equilibrium in the PhD Admissions Game, because a belief like $m = 0$ makes accepting applicants a best response, in which case only the *Lover* will apply. A useful first step in analyzing conjectured pooling equilibria is to test whether they can be supported by extreme beliefs such as $m = 0$ and $m = 1$.

An ad hoc specification. Prob(Hater|Apply) = 1

Sometimes the modeller can justify beliefs by the circumstances of the particular game. Here, one could argue that anyone so foolish as to apply knowing that the university would reject them could not possibly have the good taste to love economics. This supports the pooling equilibrium also.

An alternative approach to the problem of out-of-equilibrium beliefs is to remove its origin by building a model in which every outcome is possible in equilibrium because different types of players take different equilibrium actions. In the PhD Admissions Game, we could assume that there are a few students who both love economics and actually enjoy writing applications. Those students would always apply in equilibrium, so there would never be a pure pooling equilibrium in which nobody applied, and Bayes' Rule could always be used. In equilibrium, the university would always accept someone who applied, because applying is never out-of-equilibrium behavior and it always indicates that the applicant is a *Lover*. This approach is especially attractive if the modeller takes the possibility of trembles literally, instead of just using it as a technical tool.

The arguments for different kinds of beliefs can also be applied to Entry Deterrence III, which had two different pooling equilibria and no separating equilibrium. We used passive conjectures in the "plausible" equilibrium. The intuitive criterion would not restrict beliefs at all, because both types would enter if the incumbent's beliefs were such as to make him collude, and both would stay out if they made him fight. Complete robustness would rule out as an equilibrium the strategy profile in which the entrant stays out regardless of type, because the optimality of staying out depends on the beliefs. It would support the strategy profile in which the entrant enters and out-of-equilibrium beliefs do not matter.

6.3   The Importance of Common Knowledge: Entry Deterrence IV and V

To demonstrate the importance of common knowledge, let us consider two more versions of Entry Deterrence. We will use passive conjectures in both. In Entry Deterrence III, the incumbent was hurt by his ignorance. Entry Deterrence IV will show how he can benefit from it, and Entry Deterrence V will show what can happen when the incumbent has the same information as the entrant but the information is not common knowledge.

Entry Deterrence IV: The Incumbent Benefits from Ignorance

To construct Entry Deterrence IV, let $X = 300$ in figure 6.1, so fighting is even more profitable than in Entry Deterrence III but the game is otherwise the same: the entrant knows his type, but the incumbent does not. The following is the unique perfect Bayesian equilibrium in pure strategies.[1]

Equilibrium for Entry Deterrence IV

Entrant: *Stay Out|Weak, Stay Out|Strong*

Incumbent: *Fight,*

Out-of-equilibrium beliefs: *Prob(Strong|Enter)* = 0.5 (passive conjectures)

This equilibrium can be supported by other out-of-equilibrium beliefs, but no equilibrium is possible in which the entrant enters. There is no pooling equilibrium in which both types of entrant enter, because then the incumbent's expected payoff from *Fight* would be 150(=0.5[0] + 0.5[300]), which is greater than the *Collude* payoff of 50. There is no separating equilibrium, because if only the strong entrant entered and the incumbent always colluded, the weak entrant would be tempted to imitate him and enter as well.

In Entry Deterrence IV, unlike Entry Deterrence III, the incumbent benefits from his own ignorance, because he would always fight entry, even if the payoff were (unknown to himself) just zero. The entrant would very much like to communicate the costliness of fighting, but the incumbent would not believe him, so entry never occurs.

Entry Deterrence V: Lack of Common Knowledge of Ignorance

In Entry Deterrence V, it may happen that both the entrant and the incumbent know the payoff from (*Enter, Fight*), but the entrant does not know whether the incumbent knows. The information is known to both players, but is not common knowledge.

Figure 6.3 depicts this somewhat complicated situation. The game begins with Nature assigning the entrant a type, *Strong* or *Weak* as before. This is observed by the entrant but not by the incumbent. Next, Nature moves again and either tells the incumbent the entrant's type or remains silent. This is observed by the incumbent, but not by the entrant. The four games starting at nodes G_1 to G_4 represent different profiles of payoffs from (*Enter, Fight*) and knowledge of the incumbent. The entrant does not know how well informed the incumbent is, so the entrant's information partition is ($\{G_1, G_2\}, \{G_3, G_4\}$).

Equilibrium for Entry Deterrence V

Entrant: *Stay Out|Weak, Stay Out|Strong*

Incumbent: *Fight|Nature said "Weak," Collude|Nature said "Strong," Fight|Nature said nothing,*

Out-of-equilibrium beliefs: *Prob(Strong|Enter, Nature said nothing)* = 0.5 (passive conjectures)

Since the entrant puts a high probability on the incumbent not knowing, the entrant should stay out. The incumbent will probably fight, for one of two reasons. First, with probability 0.9 Nature has said nothing and the incumbent calculates his expected payoff from *Fight*

---

[1] There exists a plausible mixed-strategy equilibrium too: *Entrant: Enter if Strong, Enter with probability m = 0.2 if Weak; Incumbent: Collude with probability n = 0.2.* The payoff from this is only 150, so if the equilibrium were one in mixed strategies, ignorance would *not* help.

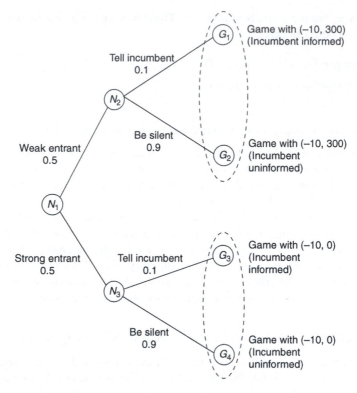

Figure 6.3 Entry Deterrence V.

to be 150, high enough to choose *Fight*. Second, with probability 0.05 (=0.1[0.5]) Nature has told the incumbent that the entrant is weak and the payoff from *Fight* is 300. Only with probability 0.05 will the incumbent choose *Collude* because the entrant is strong and the incumbent knows it. Even then, the entrant would choose *Stay Out*, because he does not know that the incumbent knows, and from his point of view his expected payoff from *Enter* is −5 (=[0.9][−10] + 0.1[40]).

If it were common knowledge that the entrant was strong, the entrant would enter and the incumbent would collude. If it is known by both players, but not common knowledge, the entrant stays out, even though the incumbent would collude if he entered. Such is the importance of common knowledge.

6.4   Incomplete Information in the Repeated Prisoner's Dilemma: The Gang of Four Model

Chapter 5 explored various ways to steer between the Scylla of the Chainstore Paradox and the Charybdis of the Folk Theorem to find a resolution to the problem of repeated games. In the end, uncertainty turned out to make little difference to the problem, but incomplete information was left unexamined in chapter 5. One might imagine that if the players did not know each others' types, the resulting confusion might allow cooperation. Let us investigate this by adding incomplete information to the finitely repeated Prisoner's Dilemma (whose payoffs are repeated in table 6.1) and finding the perfect Bayesian equilibria.

Table 6.1   The Prisoner's Dilemma

		Column	
		Deny	*Confess*
	Deny	5, 5	−5, 10
Row			
	Confess	10, −5	**0, 0**

Payoffs to: (Row, Column).

One way to incorporate incomplete information would be to assume that a large number of players are irrational, but that a given player does not know whether any other player is of the irrational type or not. In this vein, one might assume that with high probability Row is a player who blindly follows the strategy of Tit-for-Tat. If Column thinks he is playing against a Tit-for-Tat player, his optimal strategy is to *Deny* until near the last period (how near depending on the parameters), and then *Confess*. If he were not certain of this, but the probability were high that he faced a Tit-for-Tat player, Row would choose that same strategy. Such a model begs the question, because it is not the incompleteness of the information that drives the model, but the high probability that one player blindly uses Tit-for-Tat. Tit-for-Tat is not a rational strategy, and to assume that many players use it is to assume away the problem. A more surprising result is that a small amount of incomplete information can make a big difference to the outcome.[2]

The Gang of Four Model

One of the most important explanations of reputation is that of Kreps, Milgrom, Roberts, & Wilson (1982), hereafter referred to as the Gang of Four. In their model, a few players are genuinely unable to play any strategy but Tit-for-Tat, and many players pretend to be of that type. The beauty of the model is that it requires only a small amount of incomplete information, and a low probability γ that player Row is a Tit-for-Tat player. It is not unreasonable to suppose that the world contains a few mildly irrational Tit-for-Tat players, and such behavior is especially plausible among consumers, who are subject to less evolutionary pressure than firms.

It may even be misleading to call Tit-for-Tat "irrational" because they may just have unusual payoffs, particularly since we will assume that they are rare. The unusual players have a small direct influence, but they matter because other players imitate them. Even if Column knows that with high probability Row is just pretending to be a Tit-for-Tat player, Column does not care what the truth is so long as Row keeps on pretending. Hypocrisy is not only the tribute vice pays to virtue; it can be just as good for detering misbehavior.

This observational equivalence of true altruism and reciprocal altruism when everyone behaves well has been known for millenia, as we can see from *Matthew* 5: 44–8:

> But I say unto you, Love your enemies, bless them that curse you, do good to them that hate you, and pray for them which despitefully use you, and persecute you; That ye may be the children of your Father which is in heaven: for he maketh his sun to rise on the evil and on the good, and sendeth rain on the just and on the unjust. For if ye love them which love you, what reward

---

[2] Begging the question is not as illegitimate in modelling as in rhetoric, however, because it may indicate that the question is a vacuous one in the first place. If the payoffs of the Prisoner's Dilemma are not those of most of the people one is trying to model, the Chainstore Paradox becomes irrelevant.

have ye? do not even the publicans the same? And if ye salute your brethren only, what do ye more? do not even the publicans so? Be ye therefore perfect, even as your Father which is in heaven is perfect.

The Gang of Four formalize this, noting, however, the important point that the publicans will start choosing *Confess* as the end of the world approaches.

Theorem 6.1 (The Gang of Four Theorem)

Consider a T-stage, repeated Prisoner's Dilemma, without discounting but with a probability γ of a Tit-for-Tat player. In any perfect Bayesian equilibrium, the number of stages in which either player chooses Confess *is less than some number M that depends on γ but not on T.*

The significance of the Gang of Four theorem is that while the players do resort to *Confess* as the last period approaches, the number of periods during which they *Confess* is independent of the total number of periods. Suppose $M = 2,500$. If $T = 2,500$, we might see *Confess* every period. But if $T = 10,000$, 7,500 periods pass without a *Confess* move. For reasonable probabilities of the unusual type, the number of periods of cooperation can be much larger. Wilson (unpublished) has set up an entry deterrence model in which the incumbent fights entry (the equivalent of *Deny* above) up to seven periods from the end, although the probability the entrant is of the unusual type is only 0.008.

The Gang of Four Theorem characterizes the equilibrium outcome rather than the equilibrium. Finding perfect Bayesian equilibria is difficult and tedious, since the modeller must check all the out-of-equilibrium subgames, as well as the equilibrium path. Modellers usually content themselves with describing important characteristics of the equilibrium strategies and payoffs.

To get a feeling for why theorem 6.1 is correct, consider what would happen in a 10,001 period game with a probability of 0.01 that Row is playing the Grim Strategy of *Deny* until the first *Confess*, and *Confess* every period thereafter. Using table 6.1's payoffs, a best response for Column to a known Grim player is (*Confess* only in the last period, unless Row chooses *Confess* first, in which case respond with *Confess*). Both players will choose *Deny* until the last period, and Column's payoff will be 50,010 (=(10,000)(5)+10). Suppose for the moment that if Row is not Grim, he is highly aggressive, and will choose *Confess* every period. If Column follows the strategy just described, the outcome will be (*Confess, Deny*) in the first period and (*Confess, Confess*) thereafter, for a payoff to Column of $-5(=-5 + (10,000)(0))$. If the probabilities of the two outcomes are 0.01 and 0.99, Column's expected payoff from the strategy described is 495.15. If instead he follows a strategy of (*Confess* every period), his expected payoff is just 0.1 (= 0.01(10) + 0.99(0)). It is clearly in Column's advantage to take a chance by cooperating with Row, even if Row has a 0.99 probability of following a very aggressive strategy.

The aggressive strategy, however, is not Row's best response to Column's strategy. A better response is for Row to choose *Deny* until the second-to-last period, and then to choose *Confess*. Given that Column is cooperating in the early periods, Row will cooperate also. This argument has not described the true Nash equilibrium, since the iteration back and forth between Row and Column can be continued, but it does show why Column chooses *Deny* in the first period, which is the leverage the argument needs: the payoff is so great if Row is actually the Grim player that it is worthwhile for Column to risk a low payoff for one period.

The Gang of Four Theorem provides a way out of the Chainstore Paradox, but it creates a problem of multiple equilibria in much the same way as the infinitely repeated game. For one thing, if the asymmetry is two-sided, so both players might be unusual types, it becomes much less clear what happens in threat games such as Entry Deterrence. Also, what happens depends on which unusual behaviors have positive, if small, probability. Theorem 6.2 says that the modeller can make the average payoffs take any particular values by making the game last long enough and choosing the form of the irrationality carefully.

Theorem 6.2 (The Incomplete Information Folk Theorem [Fudenberg & Maskin [1986] p. 547])

For any two-person repeated game without discounting, the modeller can choose a form of irrationality so that for any probability $\epsilon > 0$ there is some finite number of repetitions such that with probability $(1 - \epsilon)$ a player is rational and the average payoffs in some sequential equilibrium are closer than ϵ to any desired payoffs greater than the minimax payoffs.

6.5   The Axelrod Tournament

Another way to approach the repeated Prisoner's Dilemma is through experiments, such as the round robin tournament described by political scientist Robert Axelrod in his 1984 book. Contestants submitted strategies for a 200-repetition Prisoner's Dilemma. Since the strategies could not be updated during play, players could precommit, but the strategies could be as complicated as they wished. If a player wanted to specify a strategy which simulated subgame perfectness by adapting to past history just as a noncommitted player would, he was free to do so, but he could also submit a nonperfect strategy such as Tit-for-Tat or the slightly more forgiving Tit-for-Two-Tats. Strategies were submitted in the form of computer programs that were matched with each other and played automatically. In Axelrod's first tournament, 14 programs were submitted as entries. Every program played every other program, and the winner was the one with the greatest sum of payoffs over all the plays. The winner was Anatol Rapoport, whose strategy was Tit-for-Tat.

The tournament helps to show which strategies are robust against a variety of other strategies in a game with given parameters. It is quite different from trying to find a Nash equilibrium, because it is not common knowledge what the equilibrium is in such a tournament. The situation could be viewed as a game of incomplete information in which Nature chooses the number and cognitive abilities of the players and their priors regarding each other.

After the results of the first tournament were announced, Axelrod ran a second tournament, adding a probability $\theta = 0.00346$ that the game would end each round so as to avoid the Chainstore Paradox. The winner among the 62 entrants was again Anatol Rapoport, and again he used Tit-for-Tat.

Before choosing his tournament strategy, Rapoport had written an entire book on the Prisoner's Dilemma in analysis, experiment, and simulation (Rapoport & Chammah [1965]). Why did he choose such a simple strategy as Tit-for-Tat? Axelrod points out that Tit-for-Tat has three strong points.

1   It never initiates confessing (**niceness**);
2   It retaliates instantly against confessing (**provocability**);

3   It forgives someone who plays *Confess* but then goes back to cooperating (it is **forgiving**).

Despite these advantages, care must be taken in interpreting the results of the tournament. It does not follow that Tit-for-Tat is the best strategy, or that cooperative behavior should always be expected in repeated games.

First, Tit-for-Tat never beats any other strategy in a one-on-one contest. It won the tournament by piling up points through cooperation, having lots of high-score plays and very few low-score plays. In an elimination tournament, Tit-for-Tat would be eliminated very early, because it scores *high* payoffs but never the *highest* payoff.

Second, the other players' strategies matter to the success of Tit-for-Tat. In neither tournament were the strategies submitted a Nash equilibrium. If a player knew what strategies he was facing, he would want to revise his own. Some of the strategies submitted in the second tournament would have won the first, but they did poorly because the environment had changed. Other programs, designed to try to probe the strategies of their opposition, wasted too many (*Confess*, *Confess*) episodes on the learning process, but if the games had lasted a thousand repetitions they would have done better.

Third, in a game in which players occasionally confessed because of trembles, two Tit-for-Tat players facing each other would do very badly. The strategy instantly punishes a confessing player, and it has no provision for ending the punishment phase.

Optimality depends on the environment. When information is complete and the payoffs are all common knowledge, confessing is the only equilibrium outcome. In practically any real-world setting, however, information is slightly incomplete, so cooperation becomes more plausible. Tit-for-Tat is suboptimal for any given environment, but it is robust across environments, and that is its advantage.

*6.6   Credit and the Age of the Firm: The Diamond Model

An example of another way to look at reputation is Douglas Diamond's model of credit terms, which seeks to explain why older firms get cheaper credit using a game similar to the Gang of Four model. Telser (1966) suggested that predatory pricing would be a credible threat if the incumbent had access to cheaper credit than the entrant, and so could hold out for more periods of losses before going bankrupt. While one might wonder whether this is effective protection against entry – what if the entrant is a large old firm from another industry? – we shall focus on how better-established firms might get cheaper credit.

Diamond (1989) aims to explain why old firms are less likely than young firms to default on debt. His model has both adverse selection, because firms differ in type, and moral hazard, because they take hidden actions. The three types of firms, R, S, and RS, are "born" at time zero and borrow to finance projects at the start of each of T periods. We must imagine that there are overlapping generations of firms, so that at any point in time a variety of ages are coexisting, but the model looks at the lifecycle of only one generation. All the players are risk neutral. Type RS firms can choose independently risky projects with negative expected values or safe projects with low but positive expected values. Although the risky projects are worse in expectation, if they are successful the return is much higher than from safe projects. Type R firms can only choose risky projects, and type S firms only safe projects.

At the end of each period the projects bring in their profits and loans are repaid, after which new loans and projects are chosen for the next period. Lenders cannot tell which project is chosen or what a firm's current profits are, but they can seize the firm's assets if a loan is not repaid, which always happens if the risky project was chosen and turned out unsuccessfully.

This game foreshadows two other models of credit that will be described in this book, the Repossession Game of section 8.4 and the Stiglitz–Weiss model of section 9.6. Both will be one-shot games in which the bank worried about not being repaid; in the Repossession Game because the borrower did not exert enough effort, and in the Stiglitz–Weiss model because he was of an undesirable type that could not repay. The Diamond model is a mixture of adverse selection and moral hazard: the borrowers differ in type, but some borrowers have a choice of action.

The equilibrium path has three parts. The RS firms start by choosing risky projects. Their downside risk is limited by bankruptcy, but if the project is successful the firm keeps large residual profits after repaying the loan. Over time, the number of firms with access to the risky project (the RS's and R's) diminishes through bankruptcy, while the number of S's remains unchanged. Lenders can therefore maintain zero profits while lowering their interest rates. When the interest rate falls, the value of a stream of safe investment profits minus interest payments rises relative to the expected value of the few periods of risky returns minus interest payments before bankruptcy. After the interest rate has fallen enough, the second phase of the game begins when the RS firms switch to safe projects at a period we will call t_1. Only the tiny and diminishing group of type R firms continue to choose risky projects. Since the lenders know that the RS firms switch, the interest rate can fall sharply at t_1. A firm that is older is less likely to be a type R, so it is charged a lower interest rate. Figure 6.4 shows the path of the interest rate over time.

Towards period T, the value of future profits from safe projects declines and even with a low interest rate the RS's are again tempted to choose risky projects. They do not all switch at once, however, unlike in period t_1. In period t_1, if a few RS's had decided to

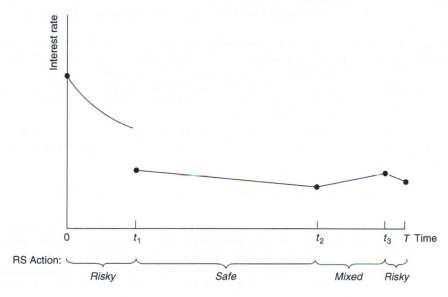

Figure 6.4 The interest rate over time.

switch to safe projects, the lenders would have been willing to lower the interest rate, which would have made switching even more attractive. If a few firms switch to risky projects at some time t_2, on the other hand, the interest rate rises and switching to risky projects becomes more attractive – a result that will also be seen in the Lemons model in chapter 9. Between t_2 and t_3, the RS's follow a mixed strategy, an increasing number of them choosing risky projects as time passes. The increasing proportion of risky projects causes the interest rate to rise. At t_3, the interest rate is high enough and the end of the game is close enough that the RS's revert to the pure strategy of choosing risky projects. The interest rate declines during this last phase as the number of RS's diminishes because of failed risky projects.

One might ask, in the spirit of modelling by example, why the model contains three types of firms rather than two. Types S and RS are clearly needed, but why type R? The little extra detail in the game description allows simplification of the equilibrium, because with three types bankruptcy is never out-of-equilibrium behavior, since the failing firm might be a type R. Bayes' Rule can therefore always be applied, eliminating the problem of ruling out peculiar beliefs and absurd perfect Bayesian equilibria.

This is a Gang of Four model but differs from previous examples in an important respect: the Diamond model is not stationary, and as time progresses, some firms of types R and RS go bankrupt, which changes the lenders' payoff functions. Thus, it is not, strictly speaking, a repeated game.

Notes

N6.1   Perfect Bayesian equilibrium: Entry Deterrence I and II

- Section 4.1 showed that even in games of perfect information, not every subgame perfect equilibrium is trembling-hand perfect. In games of perfect information, however, every subgame perfect equilibrium is a perfect Bayesian equilibrium, since no out-of-equilibrium beliefs need to be specified.
- Suppose $y > 0$ and $x = (0 \cdot y)/0$, as in equation (6.1), and we accept this as valid, concluding that $(0 \cdot y)/0 = y$. By ordinary arithmetic, $x \cdot 0 = ((0 \cdot y)/0) \cdot 0$, but then $0 = (0^2 \cdot y)/0 = (0 \cdot y)/0 = y$, a contradiction. Thus, we cannot cancel out zeroes in fractions.
- Kreps & Wilson (1982) used the same idea as perfect Bayesian equilibrium to form their equilibrium concept of sequential equilibrium, but they impose a third condition, defined only for games with discrete strategies, to restrict beliefs a little further:

    (3) The beliefs are the limit of a sequence of rational beliefs, that is, if (μ^*, s^*) is the equilibrium assessment, then some sequence of rational beliefs and completely mixed strategies converges to it:

$$(\mu^*, s^*) = Lim_{n \to \infty}(\mu^n, s^n) \quad \text{for some sequence } (\mu^n, s^n) \text{ in } \{\mu, s\}.$$

    Condition (3) is quite reasonable and makes sequential equilibrium close to trembling-hand perfect equilibrium, but it adds more to the concept's difficulty than to its usefulness. If players are using the sequence of completely mixed strategies s^n, then every action is taken with some positive probability, so Bayes' Rule can be applied to form the beliefs μ^n after any action is observed. Condition (3) says that the equilibrium belief has to be the limit of some such sequence (though not of every such sequence).

N6.2   Refining perfect Bayesian equilibrium: the PhD Admissions Game

- Fudenberg & Tirole (1991b) is a careful analysis of the issues involved in defining perfect Bayesian equilibrium.
- Section 6.2 is about debatable ways of restricting beliefs such as passive conjectures or equilibrium dominance, but less controversial restrictions are sometimes useful. In a three-player game, consider what happens when Smith and Jones have incomplete information about Brown, and then Jones deviates. If it was Brown himself who had deviated, one might think that the other players might deduce something about Brown's type. But should they update their priors on Brown because Jones has deviated? Especially, should Jones updated his beliefs, just because he himself deviated? Passive conjectures seems much more reasonable.

  If, to take a second possibility, Brown himself does deviate, is it reasonable for the out-of-equilibrium beliefs to specify that Smith and Jones update their beliefs about Brown in different ways? This seems dubious in light of the Harsanyi doctrine that everyone begins with the same priors.

  On the other hand, consider a tremble interpretation of out-of-equilibrium moves. Maybe if Jones trembles and picks the wrong strategy, that really does say something about Brown's type. Jones might tremble more often, for example, if Brown's type is strong than if it is weak. Jones himself might learn from his own trembles. Once we are in the realm of non-Bayesian beliefs, it is hard to know what to do without a real-world context.

  Dominance and tremble arguments used to rule out Nash equilibria apply to past, present (in simultaneous move games), and future actions of the other player. Belief arguments only depend on past actions, because they rely on the uninformed player observing behavior and interpreting it. Thus, for example, a tremble or weak dominance argument might say a player should take action 1 instead of 2 because although their payoffs are equal, action 2 would lead to a very low payoff if the other player later trembled and chose an unintended action that hurt both of them. An argument based on beliefs would not work in such a game.

- For discussions of the appropriateness of different equilibrium concepts in actual economic models see Rubinstein (1985b) on bargaining, Shleifer & Vishny (1986) on greenmail and D. Hirshleifer & Titman (1990) on tender offers.
- **Exotic refinements.** Perfect Bayesian equilibrium is the logical extension of Nash equilibrium, combining the ideas of best responses, backwards induction, and rational beliefs. There are perhaps further refinements that would be uncontroversial, such as requiring that identical players update their beliefs in the same way when they observe an out-of-equilibrium move, but the added complexity has not been useful enough for such refinements to become standard. Many more controversial ways to rule out out-of-equilibrium beliefs thought unreasonable have been proposed (e.g., the intuitive criterion), but none of them have been generally accepted. Binmore (1990) and Kreps (1990b) are booklength treatments of rationality and equilibrium concepts. See also Van Damme (2002), a chapter in the *Handbook of Game Theory*.
- See Kohlberg & Mertens (1986) or Van Damme (1989) on the curious idea of "**burning money**" or "**forward induction.**"

  The Forward-Induction Requirement: *A self-enforcing outcome must remain self-enforcing when a strategy is deleted which is inferior (i.e., not a best reply) at every equilibrium with that outcome.*

  Here is the logic. Consider a two-player game with multiple equilibria in which Player 1 likes Equilibrium X best and in which he may burn a five-dollar bill if he wishes before the rest of the game is played out. There is no reason for him to burn the money unless he could thereby influence Player 2 to play out Equilibrium X, so if Player 2 sees him do it, forward induction says that Player 2 should think that Player 1 thinks they will play X. In that case Player 1 will play X, and Player 2's best response is to play X also, so Player 1's money-burning ploy as worked.

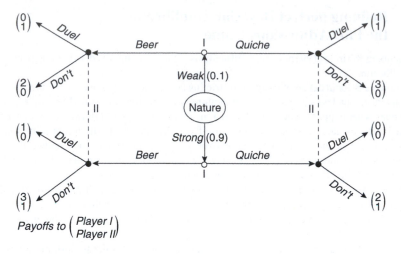

Figure 6.5   The Beer–Quiche Game.

The weird twist is that if Player 1 could do this and get his preferred equilibrium, X, then if Player 1 does *not* burn the money Player 2 should think that Player 1 thinks they will play out X anyway, and Player 2 will therefore play X himself. Thus, *not* burning the money also can change beliefs. The key to the success of the "strong, silent type" is that Player 1 have the the *option* of sending a costly message; It's not what you say; it's whether you can say it.

Note that forward induction has an impact even in games of symmetric information.

- **The Beer–Quiche Game** of Cho & Kreps (1987). To illustrate their "intuitive criterion," Cho and Kreps use the Beer–Quiche Game. In this game, Player I might be either weak or strong in his duelling ability, but he wishes to avoid a duel even if he thinks he can win. Player II wishes to fight a duel only if player I is weak, which has a probability of 0.1. Player II does not know player I's type, but he observes what player I has for breakfast. He knows that weak players prefer quiche for breakast, while strong players prefer beer. The payoffs are shown in figure 6.5.

Figure 6.5 illustrates a few twists on how to draw an extensive form. It begins with Nature's choice of *Strong* or *Weak* in the middle of the diagram. Player I then chooses whether to breakfast on *beer* or *quiche*. Player II's nodes are connected by a dotted line if they are in the same information set. Player II chooses *Duel* or *Don't*, and payoffs are then received.

This game has two perfect Bayesian equilibrium outcomes, both of which are pooling. In E_1, player I has beer for breakfast regardless of type, and Player II chooses not to duel. This is supported by the out-of-equilibrium belief that a quiche-eating player I is weak with probability over 0.5, in which case player II would choose to duel on observing quiche. In E_2, player I has quiche for breakfast regardless of type, and player II chooses not to duel. This is supported by the out-of-equilibrium belief that a beer-drinking player I is weak with probability greater than 0.5, in which case player II would choose to duel on observing beer.

Passive conjectures and the intuitive criterion both rule out equilibrium E_2. According to the reasoning of the intuitive criterion, player I could deviate without fear of a duel by giving the following convincing speech,

> "I am having beer for breakfast, which ought to convince you I am strong. The only conceivable benefit to me of breakfasting on beer comes if I am strong. I would never wish to have beer for breakfast if I were weak, but if I am strong and this message is convincing, then I benefit from having beer for breakfast."

N6.5   The Axelrod tournament

- Hofstadter (1983) is a nice discussion of the Prisoner's Dilemma and the Axelrod tournament by an intelligent computer scientist who came to the subject untouched by the preconceptions or training of economics. It is useful for elementary economics classes. Axelrod's 1984 book provides a fuller treatment.

Problems

6.1:   Cournot duopoly under incomplete information about costs (hard)

This problem introduces incomplete information into the Cournot model of chapter 3 and allows for a continuum of player types.

(a)   Modify the Cournot Game of chapter 3 by specifying that Apex's average cost of production be c per unit, while Brydox's remains zero. What are the outputs of each firm if the costs are common knowledge? What are the numerical values if $c = 10$?

(b)   Let Apex's cost c be c_{max} with probability θ and 0 with probability $1 - \theta$, so Apex is one of two types. Brydox does not know Apex's type. What are the outputs of each firm?

(c)   Let Apex's cost c be drawn from the interval $[0, c_{max}]$ using the uniform distribution, so there is a continuum of types. Brydox does not know Apex's type. What are the outputs of each firm?

(d)   Outputs were 40 for each firm in the zero-cost game in chapter 3. Check your answers in parts (b) and (c) by seeing what happens if $c_{max} = 0$.

(e)   Let $c_{max} = 20$ and $\theta = 0.5$, so the expectation of Apex's average cost is 10 in parts (a), (b), and (c). What are the average outputs for Apex in each case?

(f)   Modify the model of part (b) so that $c_{max} = 20$ and $\theta = 0.5$, but somehow $c = 30$. What outputs do your formulas from part (b) generate? Is there anything this could sensibly model?

6.2:   Limit pricing (medium) (see Milgrom & Roberts [1982a])

An incumbent firm operates in the local computer market, which is a natural monopoly in which only one firm can survive. The incumbent knows his own operating cost c, which is 20 with probability 0.2 and 30 with probability 0.8.

In the first period, the incumbent can price *Low*, losing 40 in profits, or *High*, losing nothing if his cost is $c = 20$. If his cost is $c = 30$, however, then pricing *Low* he loses 180 in profits. (You might imagine that all consumers have a reservation price that is *High*, so a static monopolist would choose that price whether marginal cost was 20 or 30.)

A potential entrant knows those probabilities, but not the incumbent's exact cost. In the second period, the entrant can enter at a cost of 70, and his operating cost of 25 is common knowledge. If there are two firms in the market, each incurs an immediate loss of 50, but one then drops out and the survivor earns the monopoly revenue of 200 and pays his operating cost. There is no discounting: $r = 0$.

(a)   In a perfect Bayesian equilibrium in which the incumbent prices *High* regardless of its costs (a pooling equilibrium), about what do out-of-equilibrium beliefs have to be specified?

(b) Find a pooling perfect Bayesian equilibrium, in which the incumbent always chooses the same price no matter what his costs may be.
(c) What is a set of out-of-equilibrium beliefs that do not support a pooling equilibrium at a *High* price?
(d) What is a separating equilibrium for this game?

6.3:   Symmetric information and prior beliefs (medium)

In the Expensive-Talk Game of table 6.2, the Battle of the Sexes is preceded by a communication move in which the man chooses *Silence* or *Talk*. *Talk* costs 1 payoff unit, and consists of a declaration by the man that he is going to the prize fight. This declaration is just talk; it is not binding on him.

(a) Draw the extensive form for this game, putting the man's move first in the simultaneous-move subgame.
(b) What are the strategy sets for the game? (Start with the woman's.)
(c) What are the three perfect pure-strategy equilibrium outcomes in terms of observed actions? (Remember: strategies are not the same thing as outcomes.)
(d) Describe the equilibrium strategies for a perfect equilibrium in which the man chooses to talk.
(e) The idea of "forward induction" says that an equilibrium should remain an equilibrium even if strategies dominated in that equilibrium are removed from the game and the procedure is iterated. Show that this procedure rules out *Silence* and both players choosing *Ballet* as an equilibrium outcome.

6.4:   Lack of common knowledge (medium)

This problem looks at what happens if the parameter values in Entry Deterrence V are changed.

(a) Why does $Pr(Strong|Enter, Nature\ said\ nothing) = 0.95$ not support the equilibrium in section 6.3?
(b) Why is the equilibrium in section 6.3 not an equilibrium if 0.7 is the probability that Nature tells the incumbent?
(c) Describe the equilibrium if 0.7 is the probability that Nature tells the incumbent. For what out-of-equilibrium beliefs does this remain the equilibrium?

Table 6.2   Subgame payoffs in the Expensive-Talk Game

| | | **Woman** | |
		Fight	*Ballet*
Man	*Fight*	3, 1	0, 0
	Ballet	0, 0	1, 3

Payoffs to: (Man, Woman).

The Repeated Prisoner's Dilemma under Incomplete Information: A Classroom Game for Chapter 6

Consider the Prisoner's Dilemma in table 6.3, obtained by adding 8 to each payoff in table 1.2, and identical to table 5.10:

Table 6.3   The Prisoner's Dilemma

		Column		
		Deny		*Confess*
	Deny	7, 7	→	−2, 8
Row		↓		↓
	Confess	8, −2	→	**0, 0**

Payoffs to: (Row, Column).

This game will be repeated five times, and your objective is to get as high a summed, undiscounted, payoff as possible (*not* just to get a higher summed payoff than anybody else). Remember, too, that there are lots of pairing of Row and Column in the class, so to just beat your immediate opponent would not even be the right tournament strategy.

The instructor will form groups of three students each to represent *Row*, and groups of one student each to represent *Column*. Each *Row* group will play against multiple *Columns*.

The five-repetition games will be different in how *Column* behaves.

Game (i) Complete Information: Column will seek to maximize his payoff according to table 6.3.

Game (ii) 80 percent Tit-for-Tat: With 20 percent probability, Column will seek to maximize his payoff according to table 6.3. With 80 percent probability, Column is a "Tit-for-Tat Player" and must use the strategy of "Tit-for-Tat," starting with *Silence* in Round 1 and after that imitating what Row did in the previous round.

Game (iii) 10 percent Tit-for-Tat: With 90 percent probability, Column will seek to maximize his payoff according to table 6.3. With 10% probability, Column is a "Tit-for-Tat Player" and must use the strategy of "Tit-for-Tat," starting with *Silence* in Round 1 and after that imitating what Row did in the previous round. The identities of the Game (ii).

The probabilities are independent, so although in Game (ii) the most likely outcome is that 8 of 10 Column players use tit-for-tat, it is possible that 7 or 9 do, or even (improbably) 0 or 10.

Part 2
asymmetric information

Chapter 7
moral hazard: hidden actions

7.1 Categories of Asymmetric Information Models

It used to be that the economist's first response to peculiar behavior which seemed to contradict basic price theory was "It must be some kind of price discrimination." Today, we have a new answer: "It must be some kind of asymmetric information." In a game of asymmetric information, player Smith knows something that player Jones does not. This covers a broad range of models (including price discrimination itself), so it is not surprising that so many situations come under its rubric. We will look at them in five chapters.

Moral Hazard with Hidden Actions (chapters 7 and 8)

Smith and Jones begin with symmetric information and agree to a contract, but then Smith takes an action unobserved by Jones. Information is complete.

Adverse Selection (chapter 9)

Nature begins the game by choosing Smith's type, unobserved by Jones. Smith and Jones then agree to a contract. Information is incomplete.

Mechanism Design in Adverse Selection and Postcontractual Hidden Knowledge (chapter 10)

Jones is designing a contract for Smith designed to elicit Smith's private information. This may happen under adverse selection – in which case Smith knows the information prior to contracting – or postcontractual hidden knowledge (also called moral hazard with hidden information) – in which case Smith will learn it after contracting.

Signalling and Screening (chapter 11)

Nature begins the game by choosing Smith's type, unobserved by Jones. To demonstrate his type, Smith takes actions that Jones can observe. If Smith takes the action before they agree to a contract, he is signalling. If he takes it afterwards, he is being screened. Information is incomplete.

The important distinctions to keep in mind are whether or not the players agree to a contract before or after information becomes asymmetric, and whether their own actions are common knowledge. Not all the terms I used above are firmly established. In particular, some people would say that information *becomes* incomplete in a model of postcontractual hidden knowledge, even though it is complete at the start of the game. That statement runs contrary to the definition of complete information in chapter 2, however.

We will make heavy use of the principal–agent model. Usually this term is applied to moral hazard models, since the problems studied in the law of agency usually involve an employee who disobeys orders by choosing the wrong actions, but the paradigm is useful in all four contexts listed above. The two players are the principal and the agent, who are usually representative individuals. The principal hires an agent to perform a task, and the agent acquires an informational advantage about his type, his actions, or the outside world at some point in the game. It is usually assumed that the players can make a binding **contract** at some point in the game, which is to say that the principal can commit to paying the agent an agreed sum if he observes a certain outcome. In the background of such models are courts, which will punish any player who breaks a contract in a way that can be proven with public information.

> The **principal** *(or **uninformed player**)* is the player who has the coarser information partition.
>
> The **agent** *(or **informed player**)* is the player who has the finer information partition.

Figure 7.1 shows the game trees for five principal–agent models. In each model, the principal (P) offers the agent (A) a contract, which he accepts or rejects. In some, Nature (N) makes a move or the agent chooses an effort level, message, or signal. The moral hazard models are games of complete information with uncertainty. The principal offers a contract, and after the agent accepts, Nature adds noise to the task being performed. In moral hazard with hidden actions, figure 7.1a, the agent moves before Nature and in postcontractual hidden knowledge, figure 7.1b, the agent moves after Nature and conveys a "message" to the principal about Nature's move.

Adverse selection models have incomplete information, so Nature moves first and picks the type of the agent, generally on the basis of his ability to perform the task. In the simplest model, figure 7.1c, the agent simply accepts or rejects the contract. If the agent can send a "signal" to the principal, as in figures 7.1d and 7.1e, the model is signalling if he sends the signal before the principal offers a contract, and screening otherwise. A "signal" is different from a "message" because it is not a costless statement, but a costly action. Some adverse selection models include uncertainty and some do not.

A problem we will consider in detail arises when an employer (the principal) hires a worker (the agent). If the employer knows the worker's ability but not his effort level, the problem is moral hazard with hidden actions. If neither player knows the worker's ability at first, but the worker discovers it once he starts working, the problem is postcontractual hidden knowledge. If the worker knows his ability from the start, but the employer does not, the problem is adverse selection. If, in addition to the worker knowing his ability from the start he can acquire credentials before he makes a contract with the employer, the problem

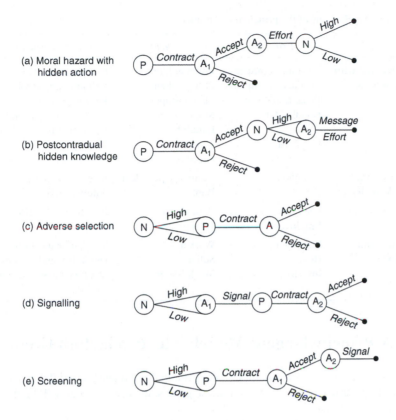

Figure 7.1   Categories of asymmetric information models.

is signalling. If the worker acquires his credentials in response to a wage offer made by the employer, the problem is screening.

The five categories are not uniformly recognized, and in particular, some would argue that what I have called "postcontractual hidden knowledge" and "screening" are essentially the same as adverse selection. Myerson (1991, p. 263), for example, suggests calling the problem of players taking the wrong action "moral hazard" and the problem of misreporting information "adverse selection." Or, the two problems can be called "hidden actions" versus "hidden knowledge." (The separation of asymmetric information into hidden actions and hidden knowledge is suggested in Arrow [1985] and commented on in Hart & Holmstrom [1987].) Many economists do not realize that screening and signalling are different and use the terms interchangeably. "Signal" is such a useful word that it is often used simply to indicate any variable conveying information. Most people have not thought very hard about any of the definitions, but the importance of the distinctions will become clear as we explore the properties of the models. For readers whose minds are more synthetic than analytic, table 7.1 may be as helpful as anything in clarifying the categories.

Section 7.2 discusses the roles of uncertainty and asymmetric information in a principal–agent model of moral hazard with hidden actions, called the Production Game, and section 7.3 shows how various constraints are satisfied in equilibrium. Section 7.4 collects several unusual contracts produced under moral hazard and discusses the properties of optimal contracts using the example of the Broadway Game.

Table 7.1 Applications of the principal–agent model

	Principal	Agent	Effort or type and signal
Moral hazard with hidden actions	Insurance company	Policyholder	Care to avoid theft
	Insurance company	Policyholder	Drinking and smoking
	Plantation owner	Sharecropper	Farming effort
	Bondholders	Stockholders	Riskiness of corporate projects
	Tenant	Landlord	Upkeep of the building
	Landlord	Tenant	Upkeep of the building
	Society	Criminal	Number of robberies
Postcontractual hidden knowledge	Shareholders	Company president	Investment decision
	FDIC	Bank	Safety of loans
Adverse selection	Insurance company	Policyholder	Infection with HIV virus
	Employer	Worker	Skill
Signalling and screening	Employer	Worker	Skill and education
	Buyer	Seller	Durability and warranty
	Investor	Stock issuer	Stock value and percentage retained

7.2 A Principal–agent Model: The Production Game

In the archetypal principal–agent model, the principal is a manager and the agent a worker. In this section we will devise a series of these games, the last of which will be the standard principal–agent model.

Denote the monetary value of output by $q(e)$, which is increasing in effort, e. The agent's utility function $U(e, w)$ is decreasing in effort and increasing in the wage, w, while the principal's utility $V(q - w)$ is increasing in the difference between output and the wage.

The Production Game

PLAYERS
The principal and the agent.

THE ORDER OF PLAY
1 The principal offers the agent a wage w.
2 The agent decides whether to accept or reject the contract.
3 If the agent accepts, he exerts effort e.
4 Output equals $q(e)$, where $q' > 0$.

PAYOFFS
If the agent rejects the contract, then $\pi_{agent} = \overline{U}$ and $\pi_{principal} = 0$.
If the agent accepts the contract, then $\pi_{agent} = U(e, w)$ and $\pi_{principal} = V(q - w)$.

An assumption common to most principal–agent models is that either the principal or the agent is one of many perfect competitors. In the background, either (1) other principals compete to employ the agent, so the principal's equilibrium profit equals zero; or (2) many agents compete to work for the principal, so the agent's equilibrium utility equals the minimum for which he will accept the job, called the **reservation utility**, $\overline{U}$. There is some reservation utility level even if the principal is a monopolist, however, because the agent has the option of remaining unemployed if the wage is too low.

One way of viewing the assumption in the Production Game that the principal moves first is that many agents compete for one principal. The order of moves allows the principal to make a take-it-or-leave-it offer, leaving the agent with as little bargaining room as if he had to compete with a multitude of other agents. This is really just a modelling convenience, however, since the agent's reservation utility, $\overline{U}$, can be set at the level a principal would have to pay the agent in competition with other principals. This level of $\overline{U}$ can even be calculated, since it is the level at which the principal's payoff from profit maximization using the optimal contract is driven down to the principal's reservation utility by competition with other principals. Here the principal's reservation utility is zero, but that too can be chosen to fit the situation being modelled. As in section 4.3's game of Nuisance Suits, the main concern in choosing who makes the offer is to avoid the distraction of more complicated modelling of the bargaining subgame.

Refinements of the equilibrium concept will not be important in this chapter. Information is complete, and the concerns of perfect Bayesian equilibrium will not arise. Subgame perfectness will be required, since otherwise the agent might commit to reject any contract that does not give him all of the gains from trade, but it will not drive the important results.

We will go through a series of eight versions of the Production Game in various chapters.

Production Game I: Full Information

In the first version of the game, every move is common knowledge and the contract is a function $w(e)$.

Finding the equilibrium involves finding the best possible contract from the point of view of the principal, given that he must make the contract acceptable to the agent and that he foresees how the agent will react to the contract's incentives. The principal must decide what he wants the agent to do and what incentive to give him to do it.

The agent must be paid some amount $\widetilde{w}(e)$ to exert effort e, where $\widetilde{w}(e)$ is the function that makes him just willing to accept the contract, so

$$U(e, w(e)) = \overline{U}. \tag{7.1}$$

Thus, the principal's problem is

$$\underset{e}{Maximize}\ V(q(e) - \widetilde{w}(e)). \tag{7.2}$$

The first-order condition for this problem is

$$V'(q(e) - \widetilde{w}(e)) \left(\frac{\partial q}{\partial e} - \frac{\partial \widetilde{w}}{\partial e} \right) = 0, \tag{7.3}$$

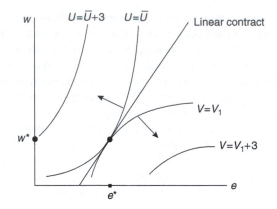

Figure 7.2   The efficient effort level in Production Game I.

which implies that

$$\frac{\partial q}{\partial e} = \frac{\partial \tilde{w}}{\partial e}. \tag{7.4}$$

From condition (7.1), using the implicit function theorem (see section 13.4), we get

$$\frac{\partial \tilde{w}}{\partial e} = -\left(\frac{\partial U/\partial e}{\partial U/\partial \tilde{w}}\right). \tag{7.5}$$

Combining equations (7.4) and (7.5) yields

$$\left(\frac{\partial U}{\partial \tilde{w}}\right)\left(\frac{\partial q}{\partial e}\right) = -\left(\frac{\partial U}{\partial e}\right). \tag{7.6}$$

Equation (7.6) says that at the optimal effort level, e^*, the marginal utility to the agent which would result if he kept all the marginal output from extra effort equals the marginal disutility to him of that effort.

Figure 7.2 shows this graphically. The agent has indifference curves in effort-wage space that slope upwards, since if his effort rises his wage must increase also to keep his utility the same. The principal's indifference curves also slope upwards, because although he does not care about effort directly, he does care about output, which rises with effort. The principal might be either risk-averse or risk-neutral; his indifference curve is concave rather than linear in either case because figure 7.2 shows a technology with diminishing returns to effort (i.e., concave, with $q''(e) < 0$). If effort starts out being higher, extra effort yields less additional output so the wage cannot rise as much without reducing profits.

Under perfect competition among the principals the profits are zero, so the reservation utility, $\overline{U}$, will be at the level such that at the profit-maximizing effort e^*, $\tilde{w}(e^*) = q(e^*)$, or

$$U(e^*, q(e^*)) = \overline{U}. \tag{7.7}$$

The principal selects the point on the $U = \overline{U}$ indifference curve that maximizes his profits, at effort e^* and wage w^*. He must then design a contract that will induce the agent to choose

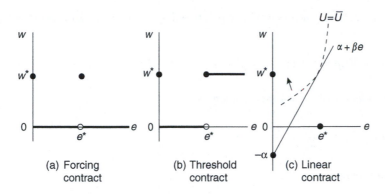

Figure 7.3   Three contracts that induce effort e^* for wage w^*.

this effort level. The following three contracts, shown in figure 7.3, are equally effective under full information.

1   The **forcing contract** sets $w(e^*) = w^*$ and $w(e \neq e^*) = 0$. This is certainly a strong incentive for the agent to choose exactly $e = e^*$.
2   The **threshold contract** sets $w(e \geq e^*) = w^*$ and $w(e < e^*) = 0$. This can be viewed as a flat wage for low effort levels, equal to 0 in this contract, plus a bonus if effort reaches e^*. Since the agent dislikes effort, the agent will choose exactly $e = e^*$.
3   The **linear contract**, shown in both figures 7.2 and 7.3c, sets $w(e) = \alpha + \beta e$, where α and β are chosen so that $w^* = \alpha + \beta e^*$ and the contract line is tangent to the indifference curve $U = \overline{U}$ at e^*. In figure 7.3c, the most northwesterly of the agent's indifference curves that touch this contract line touches it at e^*.

Let's now fit out Production Game I with specific functional forms. Suppose the agent exerts effort $e \in [0, \infty)$, and output equals

$$q(e) = 100 * log(1 + e), \tag{7.8}$$

so $q' = 100/(1 + e) > 0$ and $q'' = -100/(1 + e)^2 < 0$. If the agent rejects the contract, let $\pi_{agent} = \overline{U} = 3$ and $\pi_{principal} = 0$, whereas if the agent accepts the contract, let $\pi_{agent} = U(e, w) = log(w) - e^2$ and $\pi_{principal} = q(e) - w(e)$.

The agent must be paid some amount $\tilde{w}(e)$ to exert effort e, where $\tilde{w}(e)$ is defined to be the wage that makes the agent willing to participate, that is, as in equation (7.1),

$$U(e, w(e)) = \overline{U}, \quad \text{so } log(\tilde{w}(e)) - e^2 = 3. \tag{7.9}$$

Knowing the particular functional form as we do, we can solve (7.9) for the wage function:

$$\tilde{w}(e) = Exp(3 + e^2), \tag{7.10}$$

where we use $Exp(x)$ to mean Euler's constant (about 2.718) to the power x, since the conventional notation of e^x would be confused with e as effort.

Equation (7.10) makes sense. As effort rises, the wage must rise to compensate, and rise more than exponentially if utility is to be kept equal to 3.

Now that we have a necessary-wage function $\widetilde{w}(e)$, we can attack the principal's problem, which is

$$\underset{e}{Maximize}\ V(q(e) - \widetilde{w}(e)) = 100 * log(1 + e) - Exp(3 + e^2). \tag{7.11}$$

The first-order condition for this problem is

$$V'(q(e) - \widetilde{w}(e))\left(\frac{\partial q}{\partial e} - \frac{\partial \widetilde{w}}{\partial e}\right) = 0, \tag{7.12}$$

so for our problem,

$$\left(\frac{100}{1 + e}\right) - 2e(Exp(3 + e^2)) = 0, \tag{7.13}$$

which cannot be solved analytically.[1] Using the computer program Mathematica, I found that $e^* \approx 0.77$, from which, using the formulas above, we get $q^* \approx 57$ and $w^* \approx 37$. The payoffs are $\pi_{agent} = 3$ and $\pi_{principal} \approx 20$.

If $\overline{U}$ were high enough, the principal's payoff would be zero. If the market for agents were competitive, this is what would happen, since the agent's reservation payoff would be the utility of working for another principal instead of $\overline{U} = 3$.

To obtain $e^* = 0.77$, a number of styles of contract could be used, as shown in figure 7.3.

1   The **forcing contract** sets $w(e^*) = w^*$ and $w(e \neq 0.77) = 0$. Here, $w(0.77) = 37$ (rounding up) and $w(e \neq e^*) = 0$.
2   The **threshold contract** sets $w(e \geq e^*) = w^*$ and $w(e < e^*) = 0$. Here, $w(e \geq 0.77) = 37$ and $w(e < 0.77) = 0$.
3   The **linear contract** sets $w(e) = \alpha + \beta e$, where α and β are chosen so that $w^* = \alpha + \beta e^*$ and the contract line is tangent to the indifference curve $U = \overline{U}$ at e^*. The slope of that indifference curve is the derivative of the $\widetilde{w}(e)$ function, which is

$$\frac{\partial \widetilde{w}(e)}{\partial e} = 2e * Exp(3 + e^2). \tag{7.14}$$

At $e^* = 0.77$, this takes the value 56 (which only coincidentally is near the value of $q^* = 57$). That is the β for the linear contract. The α must solve $w(e^*) = 37 = \alpha + 56(0.77)$, so $\alpha = -7$.

We ought to be a little concerned as to whether the agent will choose the effort we hope for if he is given the linear contract. We constructed it so that he would be willing to accept the contract, because if he chooses $e = 0.77$, his utility will be 3. But might he prefer to choose some larger or smaller e and get even more utility? No, because his utility is concave. That makes the indifference curve convex, so its slope is always increasing and no preferable indifference curve touches the equilibrium contract line.

---

[1] Note that we did not need to use the principal's risk-neutrality – that $V' = 1$ – to get to equation (7.13). The optimal effort does not depend on the principal's degree of risk aversion in this certainty model.

Quasilinearity and Alternative Functional Forms for the Production Game

Consider the following three functional forms for utility:

$$U(e, w) = log(w) - e^2 \tag{7.15a}$$

$$U(e, w) = w - e^2 \tag{7.15b}$$

$$U(e, w) = log(w - e^2) \tag{7.15c}$$

Utility function (7.15a) is what we just used in Production Game I. Utility function (7.15b) is an example of **quasilinear preferences**, because utility is separable in one good – money, here – and linear in that good. This kind of utility function is commonly used to avoid wealth effects that would otherwise occur in the interactions among the various goods in the utility function. Separability means that giving an agent a higher wage does not, for example, increase his marginal disutility of effort. Linearity means furthermore that giving an agent a higher wage does not change his trade-off between money and effort, his marginal rate of substitution, as it would in function (7.15a), where a richer agent is less willing to accept money for higher effort. In effort-wage diagrams, quasilinearity implies that the indifference curves are parallel along the effort axis (which they are *not* in figure 7.2).

Quasilinear utility functions most often are chosen to look like (7.15b), but my colleague Michael Rauh points out that what quasilinearity really requires is just linearity in the special good (w here) for some monotonic transformation of the utility function. Utility function (7.15c) is a logarithmic transformation of (7.15b), which is a monotonic transformation, so it too is quasilinear. That is because marginal rates of substitution, which is what matters here, are a feature of general utility functions, not the Von Neumann–Morgenstern functions we typically use. Thus, utility function (7.15c) is also a quasilinear function, because it is just a monotonic function of (7.15b). This is worth keeping in mind because utility function (7.15c) is concave in w, so it represents a risk-averse agent.

Returning to the solution of Production Game I, let us now use a different approach to get to the same answer as we did using the principal's maximization problem (7.11). Instead, we will return to the general optimality condition (7.6), here repeated.

$$\left(\frac{\partial U}{\partial \tilde{w}}\right) \left(\frac{\partial q}{\partial e}\right) = -\frac{\partial U}{\partial e}. \tag{7.6}$$

For any of our three utility functions we will continue using the same output function $q(e) = 100 * log(1 + e)$ from (7.8), which has the first derivative $q' = 100/(1 + e)$.

Using utility function (a), $\partial U/\partial \tilde{w} = 1/w$, and $\partial U/\partial e = -2e$, so equation (7.6) becomes

$$\left(\frac{1}{w}\right) \left(\frac{100}{1 + e}\right) = -(-2e). \tag{7.16}$$

If we substitute for w using the function $\tilde{w}(e) = Exp(3 + e^2)$ that we found in equation (7.10), we get essentially the same equation as (7.13), and so outcomes are the same: $e^* \approx 0.77$, $q^* \approx 57$, and $w^* \approx 37$, $\pi_{agent} = 3$, and $\pi_{principal} \approx 20$.

Using utility function (7.15b), $\partial U/\partial \tilde{w} = 1$ and $\partial U/\partial e = -2e$, so equation (7.6) becomes

$$(1) \left(\frac{100}{1 + e}\right) = -(-2e) \tag{7.17}$$

Notice that w has disappeared. The optimal effort no longer depends on the agent's wealth. Thus, we don't need to use the wage function to solve for the optimal effort. Solving directly, we get $e^* \approx 6.59$ and $q^* \approx 203$. The wage function will be different now, solving $w - e^2 = 3$, so $w^* \approx 43$, $\pi_{agent} = 3$, and $\pi_{principal} \approx 160$. (These numbers are not really comparable to when we used utility function (7.15a), but they will be useful in Production Game II.)

Using utility function (7.15c), $\partial U / \partial \widetilde{w} = 1/(w - e^2)$ and $\partial U / \partial e = -2e/(w - e^2)$, so equation (7.6) becomes

$$\left(\frac{1}{w - e^2} \right) \left(\frac{100}{1 + e} \right) = - \left(\frac{-2e}{w - e^2} \right) \tag{7.18}$$

and with a little simplification,

$$\frac{100}{1 + e} = 2e. \tag{7.19}$$

The variable w has again disappeared, so as with utility function (7.15b) the optimal effort does not depend on the agent's wealth. Solving for the optimal effort yields $e^* \approx 6.59$ and $q^* \approx 203$, the same as with utility function (7.15b). The wage function is different, however. Now it solves $log(w - e^2) = 3$, so $w = e^2 + exp(3)$ and $w^* \approx 63$, $\pi_{agent} = 3$, and $\pi_{principal} \approx 140$.

Before going on to versions of the game with asymmetric information, it will be useful to look at another version of the game with full information, Production Game II, in which the agent, not the principal, proposes the contract.

Production Game II: Full Information. Agent Moves First

In this version, every move is common knowledge and the contract is a function $w(e)$. The order of play, however, is now as follows.

The order of play

1   The agent offers the principal a contract $w(e)$.
2   The principal decides whether to accept or reject the contract.
3   If the principal accepts, the agent exerts effort e.
4   Output equals $q(e)$, where $q' > 0$.

Now the agent has all the bargaining power, not the principal. Thus, instead of requiring that the contract be at least barely acceptable to the agent, our concern is that the contract be at least barely acceptable to the principal, who must earn zero profits so $q(e) - w(e) \geq 0$. The agent will maximize his own payoff by driving the principal to exactly zero profits, so $w(e) = q(e)$. Substituting $q(e)$ for $w(e)$ to account for this constraint, the maximization problem for the agent in proposing an effort level e at a wage $w(e)$ can therefore be written as

$$\underset{e}{Maximize} \ U(e, q(e)) \tag{7.20}$$

The first-order condition is

$$\frac{\partial U}{\partial e} + \left(\frac{\partial U}{\partial q}\right)\left(\frac{\partial q}{\partial e}\right) = 0. \tag{7.21}$$

Since $\partial U/\partial q = \partial U/\partial w$ when the wages equals output, equation (7.21) implies that

$$\left(\frac{\partial U}{\partial w}\right)\left(\frac{\partial q}{\partial e}\right) = -\left(\frac{\partial U}{\partial e}\right). \tag{7.22}$$

Compare this with equation (7.6), the optimization condition in Production Game I, when the principal had the bargaining power. The optimality equation is identical in Production Games I and II. The intuition is the same in both too: since the player who proposes the contract captures all the gains from trade (for a given reservation payoff of the other player), he will choose an efficient effort level. This requires that the marginal utility of the money derived from marginal effort equal the marginal disutility of effort.

Although the form of the optimality equation is the same, however, the optimal effort might not be, because except in the special case in which the agent's reservation payoff in Production Game I equals his equilibrium payoff in Production Game II, the agent ends up with higher wealth if he has all the bargaining power. If the utility function is not quasilinear, the wealth effect will change the optimal effort.

We can see the wealth effect by solving out optimality equation (7.22) for the specific functional forms of Production Game I from expression (7.15).

Using utility function (a) from expression (7.15)

$$\left(\frac{1}{w}\right)\left(\frac{100}{1+e}\right) = -(-2e). \tag{7.23}$$

That is the same as in Production Game I, equation (7.16), but now w is different. It is not found by driving the agent to his reservation payoff, but by driving the principal to zero profits: $w = q$. Since $q = 100 * log(1 + e)$, we can substitute that in for w to get

$$\left(\frac{1}{100 * log(1+e)}\right)\left(\frac{100}{1+e}\right) = 2e. \tag{7.24}$$

When solved numerically, this yields $e^* \approx 0.63$, and thus $q = w \approx 49$, and $\pi_{principal} = 0$ and $\pi_{agent} \approx 3.49$. In Production Game I, the optimal effort using this utility function was 0.77 and the agent's payoff was 3. The difference arises because there the agent's wealth was lower because the principal had the bargaining power. In Production Game II the agent is, in effect, wealthier, and since his marginal utility of money is lower, he chooses to convert some (but not all) of that extra wealth into what we might call leisure – working less hard.

Using the quasilinear utility functions (7.15b) and (7.15c) from expression (7.15), recall that both have the same optimality condition, the one we found in equations (7.17) and (7.19):

$$\frac{100}{1+e} = 2e \tag{7.19}$$

As we observed before, w does not appear in equation (7.19), so the wage equation does not matter to e^*. But that means that in Production Game II, $e^* \approx 6.59$ and $q^* \approx 203$, just as in Production Game I. With quasilinear utility, the efficient action does not depend on bargaining power. Of course, the wage and payoffs do depend on who has the bargaining power. In Production Game II, $w^* = q^* \approx 203$, and $\pi_{principal} = 0$. The agent's payoff is higher than in Production Game I, but it differs, of course, depending on the payoff function. For utility function (7.15b) it is $\pi_{agent} \approx 160$ and for utility function (7.15c) it is $\pi_{agent} \approx 5.08$.

If utility is quasilinear, the efficient effort level is independent of which side has the bargaining power because the gains from efficient production are independent of how those gains are distributed so long as each party has no incentive to abandon the relationship. This is the same lesson as the Coase Theorem's: under general conditions the activities undertaken will be efficient and independent of the distribution of property rights (Coase [1960]). This property of the efficient effort level means that the modeller is free to make the assumptions on bargaining power that help to focus attention on the information problems he is studying.

There are thus three reasons why modellers so often use take-it-or-leave-it offers. The first two reasons were discussed earlier in the context of Production Game I: (1) such offers are a good way to model competitive markets, and (2) if the reservation payoff of the player without the bargaining power is set high enough, such offers lead to the same outcome as would be reached if that player had more bargaining power. Quasilinear utility provides a third reason: (3) if utility is quasilinear, the optimal effort level does not depend on who has the bargaining power, so the modeller is justified in choosing the simplest model of bargaining.

Production Game III: A Flat Wage under Certainty

In this version of the game, the principal can condition the wage neither on effort nor on output. This is modelled as a principal who observes neither effort nor output, so information is asymmetric.

That a principal cannot observe effort is often realistic, but it seems less usual that he cannot observe output, since that directly affects the value of his payoff. It is not ridiculous that he cannot base wages on output, however, because a contract must be enforceable by some third party such as a court. Law professors complain about economists who speak of "unenforceable contracts." In law school, a contract is defined as an enforceable agreement, and most of a contracts class is devoted to discovering which agreements are contracts. A court cannot in practice enforce a contract in which a client agrees to pay a barber \$50 "if the haircut is especially good," but just \$10 otherwise. Similarly, an employer may be able to tell that a worker's slacking is hurting output, but that does not mean he can prove it in court. A court can only enforce contingencies it can observe. In the extreme, Production Game III is appropriate. Either output is not **contractible** (the court will not enforce a contract) or it is not **verifiable** (the court cannot observe output), which usually leads to the same outcome as when output is unobservable to the principal.

The outcome of Production Game III is simple and inefficient. If the wage is nonnegative, the agent accepts the job and exerts zero effort, so the principal offers a wage of zero.

In Production Game III, we have finally reached "moral hazard," the problem of the agent choosing the wrong action because the principal cannot use the contract to punish him. The term "moral hazard" is an old insurance term, as we will see later. A good way to think of it is that it is the danger to the principal that the agent, constrained only by his morality, not punishments, cannot be trusted to behave as he ought. Or, you might think of the situation as a temptation for the agent, a hazard to his morals.

Sometimes, as we will soon see, a clever contract can overcome moral hazard by conditioning the wage on something that is observable and correlated with effort, such as output. If there is nothing on which to condition the wage, however, the agency problem cannot be solved by designing the contract carefully. If it is to be solved at all, it will be by some other means such as reputation or repetition of the game, the solutions of chapter 5, or by morality – which might be modelled as a part of the agent's utility function which causes him disutility if he secretly breaks an agreement. Typically, however, there is some contractible variable such as output upon which the principal can condition the wage. Such is the case in Production Game IV.

Production Game IV: An Output-based Wage under Certainty

In this version, the principal cannot observe effort but he can observe output and specify the contract to be $w(q)$.

Unlike in Production Game III, the principal now picks not a number w but a function $w(q)$. His problem is not quite so straightforward as in Production Game I, where he picked the function $w(e)$, but here, too, it is possible to achieve the efficient effort level e^* despite the unobservability of effort. The principal starts by finding the optimal effort level e^*, as in Production Game I. That effort yields the efficient output level $q^* = q(e^*)$. To give the agent the proper incentives, the contract must reward him when output is q^*. Again, a variety of contracts could be used. The forcing contract, for example, would be any wage function such that $U(e^*, w(q^*)) = \overline{U}$ and $U(e, w(q)) < \overline{U}$ for $e \neq e^*$.

Production Game IV shows that the unobservability of effort is not a problem in itself, if the contract can be conditioned on something which is observable and perfectly correlated with effort. The true agency problem occurs when that perfect correlation breaks down, as in Production Game V.

Production Game V: An Output-based Wage under Uncertainty

In this version, the principal cannot observe effort but can observe output and specify the contract to be $w(q)$. Output, however, is a function $q(e, \theta)$ both of effort and the state of the world $\theta \in \mathbf{R}$, which is chosen by Nature according to the probability density $f(\theta)$ as a new move (5) of the game. Move (5) comes just after the agent chooses effort, so the agent cannot choose a low effort knowing that Nature will take up the slack. (If the agent can observe Nature's move before his own, the game becomes "moral hazard with hidden knowledge and hidden actions.")

Because of the uncertainty about the state of the world, effort does not map cleanly onto observed output in Production Game V. A given output might have been produced by any of several different effort levels, so a forcing contract based on output will not necessarily achieve the desired effort. Unlike in Production Game IV, here the principal cannot deduce $e \neq e^*$ from $q \neq q^*$. Moreover, even if the contract does induce the agent to choose e^*, if it does so by penalizing him heavily when $q \neq q^*$ it will be expensive for the principal. The agent's expected utility must be kept equal to $\overline{U}$ so he will accept the contract, and if he is sometimes paid a low wage because output happens not to equal q^* despite his correct effort, he must be paid more when output does equal q^* to make up for it. If the agent is risk-averse, this variability in his wage requires that his expected wage be higher than the w^* found earlier, because he must be compensated for the extra risk. There is a tradeoff between incentives and insurance against risk.

Put more technically, moral hazard is a problem when $q(e)$ is not a one-to-one function and a single value of e might result in any of a number of values of q, depending on the value of θ. In this case the output function is not invertible; knowing q, the principal cannot deduce the value of e perfectly without assuming equilibrium behavior on the part of the agent.

The combination of unobservable effort and lack of invertibility in Production Game V means that no contract can induce the agent to put forth the efficient effort level without incurring extra costs, which usually take the form of extra risk imposed on the agent. In some situations this is not actually a cost, because the agent is risk-neutral, but more often the best the principal can do is balance the benefit of extra incentive for effort against the cost of extra risk for a risk-average agent. We will still try to find a contract that is efficient in the sense of maximizing welfare given the informational constraints. The terms "first-best" and "second-best" are used to distinguish these two kinds of optimality.

A **first-best contract** *achieves the same allocation as the contract that is optimal when the principal and the agent have the same information set and all variables are contractible.*

A **second-best contract** *is Pareto optimal given information asymmetry and constraints on writing contracts.*

The difference in welfare between the first-best and the second-best is the cost of the agency problem.

So how do we find a second-best contract? Even to define the strategy space in a game like Production Game V is tricky, because the principal may wish to choose a very complicated function for $w(q)$. It is not very useful, for example, simply to maximize profit over all possible linear contracts, because the best contract may well not be linear. Because of the tremendous variety of possible contracts, finding the optimal contract when a forcing contract cannot be used is a hard problem without general answers. The rest of the chapter will show how the problem may be approached, if not actually solved.

7.3   The Incentive Compatibility and Participation Constraints

The principal's objective in Production Game V is to maximize his utility knowing that the agent is free to reject the contract entirely and that the contract must give the agent an incentive to choose the desired effort. These two constraints arise in every moral hazard problem, and they are named the **participation constraint** and the **incentive compatibility contraint**. Mathematically, the principal's problem is

$$\underset{w(\cdot)}{Maximize}\ EV(q(\tilde{e},\theta) - w(q(\tilde{e},\theta))) \tag{7.25a}$$

subject to

$$\tilde{e} = \overset{argmax}{e} \; EU(e, w(q(e, \theta))) \quad \text{(incentive compatibility constraint)} \qquad (7.25b)$$

$$EU(\tilde{e}, w(q(\tilde{e}, \theta))) \geq \overline{U} \qquad \text{(participation constraint)} \qquad (7.25c)$$

The incentive-compatibility constraint takes account of the fact that the agent moves second, so the contract must induce him to voluntarily pick the desired effort. The participation constraint, also called the **reservation utility** or **individual rationality** constraint, requires that the worker prefer the contract to leisure, home production, or alternative jobs.

Expression (7.25a) is the way an economist instinctively sets up the problem, but setting it up is often as far as he can get with the **first-order condition approach**. The difficulty is not just that the maximizer is choosing a wage function instead of a number, because control theory or the calculus of variations can solve such problems. Rather, it is that the constraints are nonconvex – they do not rule out a nice convex set of points in the space of wage functions such as the constraint "$w \geq 4$" would, but rather rule out a very complicated set of possible wage functions.

A different approach, developed by Grossman & Hart (1983) and called the **three-step procedure** by Fudenberg & Tirole (1991a), is to focus on contracts that induce the agent to pick a particular action rather than to directly attack the problem of maximizing profits. The first step is to find for each possible effort level the set of wage contracts that induce the agent to choose that effort level. The second step is to find the contract which supports that effort level at the lowest cost to the principal. The third step is to choose the effort level that maximizes profits, given the necessity to support that effort with the costly wage contract from the second step.

To support the effort level e, the wage contract $w(q)$ must satisfy the incentive compatibility and participation constraints. Mathematically, the problem of finding the least cost $C(\tilde{e})$ of supporting the effort level $\tilde{e}$ combines steps one and two.

$$C(\tilde{e}) = \underset{w(\cdot)}{Minimum} \, Ew(q(\tilde{e}, \theta)) \qquad (7.26)$$

subject to constraints (7.25b) and (7.25c).

Step three takes the principal's problem of maximizing his payoff, expression (7.25a), and restates it as

$$\underset{\tilde{e}}{Maximize} \; EV(q(\tilde{e}, \theta) - C(\tilde{e})). \qquad (7.27)$$

After finding which contract most cheaply induces each effort, the principal discovers the optimal effort by solving problem (7.27).

Breaking the problem into parts makes it easier to solve. Perhaps the most important lesson of the three-step procedure, however, is to reinforce the points that the goal of the contract is to induce the agent to choose a particular effort level and that asymmetric information increases the cost of the inducements.

7.4   Optimal Contracts: The Broadway Game

The next game, inspired by Mel Brooks's offbeat film *The Producers*, illustrates a peculiarity of optimal contracts: sometimes the agent's reward should not increase with his output.

Investors advance funds to the producer of a Broadway show that might succeed or might fail. The producer has the choice of embezzling or not embezzling the funds advanced to him, with a direct gain to himself of 50 if he embezzles. If the show is a success, the revenue is 500 if he did not embezzle and 100 if he did. If the show is a failure, revenue is -100 in either case, because extra expenditure on a fundamentally flawed show is useless.

Broadway Game I

PLAYERS
Producer and investors.

THE ORDER OF PLAY
1   The investors offer a wage contract $w(q)$ as a function of revenue q.
2   The producer accepts or rejects the contract.
3   The producer chooses: *Embezzle* or *Do not embezzle*.
4   Nature picks the state of the world to be *Success* or *Failure* with equal probability. Table 7.2 shows the resulting revenue q.

PAYOFFS
The producer is risk-averse and the investors are risk-neutral. The producer's payoff is $U(100)$ if he rejects the contract, where $U' > 0$ and $U'' < 0$, and the investors' payoff is 0. Otherwise,

$$\pi_{producer} = \begin{cases} U(w(q) + 50) & \textit{if he embezzles} \\ U(w(q)) & \textit{if he is honest} \end{cases}$$

$$\pi_{investors} = q - w(q)$$

Another way to tabulate outputs, shown in table 7.3, is to put the probabilities of outcomes in the boxes, with effort in the rows and output in the columns.

The investors will observe q to equal either $-100, +100,$ or $+500$, so the producer's contract will specify at most three different wages: $w(-100), w(+100),$ and $w(+500)$. The producer's expected payoffs from his two possible actions are

$$\pi(Do\ not\ embezzle) = 0.5U(w(-100)) + 0.5U(w(+500)) \tag{7.28}$$

Table 7.2   Profits in Broadway Game I

		State of the World	
		Failure (0.5)	*Success (0.5)*
	Embezzle	-100	$+100$
Effort			
	Do not embezzle	-100	$+500$

Table 7.3 Probabilities of Profits in Broadway Game I

		Profit			
		-100	$+100$	$+500$	*Total*
	Embezzle	0.5	0.5	0	1
Effort					
	Do not embezzle	0.5	0	0.5	1

and

$$\pi(Embezzle) = 0.5U(w(-100)+50) + 0.5U(w(+100)+50). \tag{7.29}$$

The incentive compatibility constraint is $\pi(Do\ not\ embezzle) \geq \pi(Embezzle)$, so

$$0.5U(w(-100)) + 0.5U(w(+500)) \geq 0.5U(w(-100)+50) + 0.5U(w(+100)+50), \tag{7.30}$$

and the participation constraint is

$$\pi(Do\ not\ embezzle) = 0.5U(w(-100)) + 0.5U(w(+500)) \geq U(100). \tag{7.31}$$

The investors want the participation constraint (7.31) to be satisfied at as low a dollar cost as possible. This means they want to impose as little risk on the producer as possible, since he requires a higher expected wage for higher risk. Ideally, $w(-100) = w(+500)$, which provides full insurance. The usual agency trade-off is between smoothing out the agent's wage and providing him with incentives. Here, no trade-off is required, because of a special feature of the problem: there exists an outcome that could not occur unless the producer chooses the undesirable action. That outcome is $q = +100$, and it means that the following **boiling-in-oil contract** provides both riskless wages and effective incentives.

$w(+500) = 100.$

$w(-100) = 100.$

$w(+100) = -\infty.$

Under this contract, the producer's wage is a flat 100 when he does not embezzle. Thus, the participation constraint is satisfied. It is also binding, because it is satisfied as an equality, and the investors would have a higher payoff if the constraint were relaxed. If the producer does embezzle, he faces a payoff of $-\infty$ with probability 0.5, so the incentive compatibility constraint is satisfied, but it is nonbinding, because it is satisfied as a strong inequality and the investors' equilibrium payoff does not fall if the constraint is tightened a little by making the producer's earnings from embezzlement slightly higher. The cost of the contract to the investors is 100 in equilibrium, so their overall expected payoff is $0.5(-100)+0.5(+500) - 100 = 100$, an amount greater than zero and thus yielding enough return for the show to be profitable.

The boiling-in-oil contract is an application of the **sufficient statistic condition**, which says that for incentive purposes, if the agent's utility function is separable in effort and

money, wages should be based on whatever evidence best indicates effort, and only inci-
dentally on output (see Holmstrom [1979] and note N7.2). In the spirit of the three-step
procedure, what the principal wants is to induce the agent to choose the appropriate effort,
Do not embezzle, and his data on what the agent chose is the output. In equilibrium
(though not out of it), the datum $q = +500$ contains exactly the same information as
the datum $q = -100$. Both lead to the same posterior probability that the agent chose
Do not embezzle, so the wages conditioned on each datum should be the same. We need to
insert the qualifier "in equilibrium," because to form the posterior probabilities the principal
needs to have some beliefs as to the agent's behavior. Otherwise, the principal could not
interpret $q = -100$ at all.

Milder contracts would also be effective. Two wages will be used in equilibrium, a
low wage $\underline{w}$ for an output of $q = 100$ and a high wage $\overline{w}$ for any other output. The
participation and incentive compatibility constraints provide two equations to solve for
these two unknowns. To find the mildest possible contract, the modeller must also specify
a function for utility $U(w)$, something which, interestingly enough, was unnecessary for
finding the first boiling-in-oil contract. Let us specify that

$$U(w) = 100w - 0.1w^2. \tag{7.32}$$

A quadratic utility function like this is only increasing if its argument is not too large, but
since the wage will not exceed $w = 1000$, it is a reasonable utility function for this model.
Substituting (7.32) into the participation constraint (7.31) and solving for the full-insurance
high wage $\overline{w} = w(-100) = w(+500)$ yields $\overline{w} = 100$ and a reservation utility of 9,000.
Substituting into the incentive compatibility constraint, (7.30), yields

$$9,000 \geq 0.5U(100 + 50) + 0.5U(\underline{w} + 50). \tag{7.33}$$

When (7.33) is solved using the quadratic equation, it yields (with rounding error), $\underline{w} \leq 5.6$.
A low wage of $-\infty$ is far more severe than what is needed.

If both the producer and the investors were risk-averse, risk-sharing would change the
part of the contract that applied in equilibrium. The optimal contract would then provide for
$w(-100) < w(+500)$ to share the risk. The principal would have a lower marginal utility
of wealth when output was $+500$, so he would be better able to pay an extra dollar of wages
in that state than when output was -100.

One of the oddities of Broadway Game I is that the wage is higher for an output of -100
than for an output of $+100$. This illustrates the idea that the principal's aim is to reward
input, not output. If the principal pays more simply because output is higher, he is rewarding
Nature, not the agent. People usually believe that higher pay for higher output is "fair," but
Broadway Game I shows that this ethical view is too simple. Higher effort usually leads to
higher output, but not always. Thus, higher pay is usually a good incentive, but not always,
and sometimes low pay for high output actually punishes slacking.

The decoupling of reward and result has broad applications. Becker (1968) in criminal
law and Polinsky & Che (1991) in tort law note that if society's objective is to keep the
amount of enforcement costs and harmful behavior low, the penalty applied should not
simply be matched to the harm. Very high penalties seldom inflicted will provide the proper
incentives and keep enforcement costs low, even though a few unlucky offenders will receive
penalties out of proportion to the harm they caused.

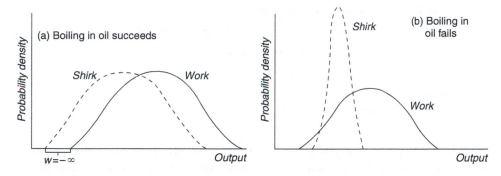

Figure 7.4   Shifting supports in an agency model.

A less gaudy name for a boiling-in-oil contract is the alliterative "**shifting support scheme**," so named because the contract depends on the support of the output distribution being different when effort is optimal than when effort is other than optimal. The set of possible outcomes under optimal effort must be different from the set of possible outcomes under any other effort level. As a result, particular outputs show without doubt that the producer embezzled. Very heavy punishments inflicted only for those outputs achieve the first-best because a nonembezzling producer has nothing to fear.

Figure 7.4a shows shifting supports in a model where output can take not three but a continuum of values. If the agent shirks instead of working, certain low outputs become possible and certain high outputs become impossible. In a case like this, where the support of the output shifts when behavior changes, boiling-in-oil contracts are useful: the wage is $-\infty$ for the low outputs possible only under shirking. In figure 7.4b, on the other hand, the support just shrinks under shirking, so boiling-in-oil is inappropriate. When there is a limit to the amount the agent can be punished, or the support under shirking is a subset of the first-best support, the threat of boiling-in-oil might not achieve the first-best. Sometimes, however, similar contracts can still be used. The conditions favoring such contracts are

1 The agent is not very risk-averse.
2 There are outcomes with high probability under shirking that have low probability under optimal effort.
3 The agent can be severely punished.
4 It is credible that the principal will carry out the severe punishment.

Selling the Store

Another first-best contract that can sometimes be used is **selling the store**. Under this arrangement, the agent buys the entire output for a flat fee paid to the principal, becoming the **residual claimant**, since he keeps every additional dollar of output that his extra effort produces. This is equivalent to fully insuring the principal, since his payoff becomes independent of the moves of the agent and of Nature.

In Broadway Game I, selling the store takes the form of the producer paying the investors $100 \,(=0.5[-100]+0.5[+500]-100)$ and keeping all the profits for himself. The drawbacks

Table 7.4   Profits in Broadway Game II

		State of the World		
		Failure (0.5)	*Minor Success (0.3)*	*Major Success (0.2)*
	Embezzle	−100	−100	+400
Effort				
	Do not embezzle	−100	+450	+575

are that (1) the producer might not be able to afford to pay the investors the flat price of 100; and (2) the producer might be risk-averse and incur a heavy utility cost in bearing the entire risk. These two drawbacks are why producers go to investors in the first place.

Public Information That Hurts the Principal and the Agent

We can modify Broadway Game I to show how having more public information available can hurt both players. This will also provide a little practice in using information sets. Let us split *Success* into two states of the world, *Minor Success* and *Major Success*, which have probabilities 0.3 and 0.2 as shown in table 7.4.

Under the optimal contract,

$$w(-100) = w(+450) = w(+575) > w(+400) + 50. \tag{7.34}$$

This is so because the producer is risk-averse and only the datum $q = +400$ is proof that the producer embezzled. The optimal contract must do two things: deter embezzlement and pay the producer as predictable a wage as possible. For predictability, the wage is made constant unless $q = +400$. To deter embezzlement, the producer must be punished if $q = +400$. As in Broadway Game I, the punishment would not have to be infinitely severe, and the minimum effective punishment could be calculated in the same way as in that game. The investors would pay the producer a wage of 100 in equilibrium and their expected payoff would be 100 ($=0.5(-100)+0.3(450)+0.2(575)-100$). Thus, a contract can be found for Broadway Game II such that the agent would not embezzle.

But consider what happens when the information set is refined so that before the agent takes his action both he and the principal can tell whether the show will be a major success or not. Let us call this Broadway Game III. Under the refinement, each player's information partition is

({*Failure, Minor Success*}, {*Major Success*}),

instead of Broadway Game I and II's coarse partition

({*Failure, Minor Success, Major Success*}).

If the information sets were refined all the way to singletons, this would be very useful to the investors, because they could abstain from investing in a failure and they could easily determine whether the producer embezzled or not. As it is, however, the refinement does not help the investors decide when to finance the show. If they could still hire the producer and prevent him from embezzling at a cost of 100, the payoff from investing in a major success would be 475 (=575 − 100). But the payoff from investing in a show given the information set {*Failure, Minor Success*} would be about 6.25, which is still positive (it is $(0.5/(0.5 + 0.3))(-100) + (0.3/(0.5 + 0.3))(450) - 100$). So the improvement in information is no help with respect to the decision of when to invest.

The refinement does, however, ruin the producer's incentives. If he observes {*Failure, Minor Success*}, he is free to embezzle without fear of the oil-boiling output of +400. He would still refrain from embezzling if he observed {*Major Success*}, but no contract that does not impose risk on a nonembezzling producer can stop him from embezzling if he observes {*Failure, Minor Success*}. Whether a risky contract can be found that would prevent the producer from embezzling at a cost of less than 6.25 to the investors depends on the producer's risk aversion. If he is very risk-averse, the cost of the incentive is more than 6.25, and the investors will give up investing in shows that might be minor successes. Better information reduces welfare, because it increases the producer's temptation to misbehave.

Notes

N7.1 Categories of asymmetric information models

- Three books that cover the theory of contracts are Macho-Stadler and Perez-Castillo's 1997 *An Introduction to the Economics of Information: Incentives and Contracts*, Salanie's 1997 *The Economics of Contracts: A Primer* and Bolton and Dewatripont's 2005 *Contract Theory*. For a survey of recent empirical work on contracts, see Chiappori & Salanie (2003).

- A large literature of nonmathematical theoretical papers looks at organizational structure in the light of the agency problem. See Alchian & Demsetz (1972), Fama (1980), and Klein, Crawford, & Alchian (1978). Milgrom & Roberts (1992) have written a book on organization theory that describes what has been learned about the principal–agent problem at a technical level that MBA students can understand. There may be much to be learned from intelligent economists of the past also; note that part III, chapter 8, section 12 of Pigou's *Economics of Welfare* (1932/1920) has an interesting discussion of the advantage of piece-rate work, which can more easily induce each worker to choose the correct effort when abilities differ as well as efforts. I recommend chapter 1 ("Incentives in Economic Thought") of Laffont & Martimort (2002) as a short survey of the history of incentives in economic theory.

- An important consideration in real-world contracts is manipulation and fraud by the agent. If an executive is rewarded for higher earnings per share, and he controls the accountants who measure earnings, for example, he may tell them to measure them so that they surpass the threshold in his threshold contract. Even worse, he might cut prices so as to speed up sales before January 1 and meet his yearly target. Jensen's 2003 "Paying People to Lie: The Truth about the Budgeting Process," points this out and notes that linear contracts are less vulnerable to this type of manipulation.

- We have lots of "prinsipuls"in economics. I find this paradigm helpful for remembering spelling: "The principal's principal principle was to preserve his principal." More simply, "The principal is my pal," takes care of the "al" case.

- "Principal" and "Agent" are legal terms, and agency is an important area of the law. Economists have focused on quite different questions than lawyers. Economists focus on effort: how the principal induces the agent to do things. Lawyers focus on malfeasance and third parties: how the principal stops the agent from doing the wrong things and who bears the burden if he fails. If, for example, the manager of a tavern enters into a supply contract against the express command of the owner, who must be disappointed – the owner or the third party supplier?

- *Double-sided moral hazard.* The text described one-sided moral hazard. Moral hazard can also be double-sided, as when each player takes actions unobservable by the other that affect the payoffs of both of them. An example is tort negligence by both plaintiff and defendant: if a careless auto driver hits a careless pedestrian, and they go to court, then the court must try to allocate blame, and the legislature must try to set up laws to induce the proper amount of care. Landlords and tenants also face double moral hazard, as implied in table 7.1.

- A common convention in principal–agent models is to make one player male and the other female, so that "his" and "her" can be used to distinguish between them. I find this distracting, since gender is irrelevant to most models and adds one more detail for the reader to keep track of. If readers naturally thought "male" when they saw "principal," this would not be a problem – but they do not.

N7.2　A principal–agent model: the Production Game

- The model in the text uses "effort" as the action taken by the agent, but effort is used to represent a variety of real-world actions. The cost of pilferage by employees is an estimated $8 billion a year in the United States. Employers have offered rewards for detection, one even offering the option of a year of twice-weekly lottery tickets instead of a lump sum. The Chicago department store Marshall Field's, with 14,000 workers, in one year gave out 170 rewards of $500 each, catching almost 500 dishonest employees. ("Hotlines and Hefty Rewards: Retailers Step Up Efforts to Curb Employee Theft," *Wall Street Journal*, September 17, 1987, p. 37.)

  For an illustration of the variety of kinds of "low effort," see "Hermann Hospital Estate, Founded for the Poor, Has Benefited the Wealthy, Investigators Allege," *Wall Street Journal*, March 13, 1985, p. 4, which describes such forms of misbehavior as pleasure trips on company funds, high salaries, contracts for redecorating awarded to girlfriends, phony checks, kicking back real estate commissions, and investing in friendly companies. Nonprofit enterprises, often lacking both principles and principals, are especially vulnerable, as are governments, for the same reason.

- The Production Game assumes that the agent dislikes effort. Is this realistic? People differ. My father tells of his experience in the navy when the sailors were kept busy by being ordered to scrape loose paint. My father found it a way to pass the time but says that other sailors would stop chipping when they were not watched, preferring to stare into space. *De gustibus non est disputandum* ("About tastes there can be no arguing"). But even if effort has positive marginal utility at low levels, it has negative marginal utility at high enough levels – including, perhaps, at the efficient level. This is as true for professors as for sailors.

- Suppose that the principal does not observe the variable θ (which might be effort), but he does observe t and x (which might be output and profits). From Holmstrom (1979) and Shavell (1979) we have, restated in my words,

  The Sufficient Statistic Condition. *If t is a sufficient statistic for θ relative to x, then the optimal contract needs to be based only on t if both principal and agent have separable utility functions.*

  The variable t is a **sufficient statistic** *for θ relative to x if, for all t and x,*

  $$Prob(\theta|t,x) = Prob(\theta|t). \tag{7.35}$$

This implies, from Bayes' Rule, that $Prob(t,x|\theta) = Prob(x|t)Prob(t|\theta)$; that is, x depends on θ only because x depends on t and t depends on θ.

The sufficient statistic condition is closely related to the Rao–Blackwell Theorem (see Cox & Hinkley [1974], p. 258), which says that the decision rule for nonstrategic decisions ought not to be random.

Gjesdal (1982) notes that if the utility functions are not separable, the theorem does not apply and randomized contracts may be optimal. Suppose there are two actions the agent might take. The principal prefers action X, which reduces the agent's risk aversion, to action Y, which increases it. The principal could offer a randomized wage contract, so the agent would choose action X and make himself less risk-averse. This randomization is not a mixed strategy. The principal is not indifferent to high and low wages; he prefers to pay a low wage, but we allow him to commit to a random wage earlier in the game.

N7.3   The incentive compatibility and participation constraints

- The term, "individual rationality constraint," is perhaps more common, but "participation constraint" is more sensible. Since in modern modelling every constraint requires individuals to be rational, the name is ill-chosen.
- **Paying the agent more than his reservation wage**. If agents compete to work for principals, the participation constraint is binding whenever there are only two possible outcomes or whenever the agent's utility function is separable in effort and wages. Otherwise, it might happen that the principal picks a contract giving the agent more expected utility than is necessary to keep him from quitting. The reason is that the principal not only wants to keep the agent working, but to choose a high effort.
- If the distribution of output satisfies the **monotone likelihood ratio property** (MLRP), the optimal contract specifies higher pay for higher output. Let $f(q|e)$ be the probability density of output. The MLRP is satisfied if

$$\forall e' > e, \quad \text{and} \quad q' > q, \quad f(q'|e')f(q|e) - f(q'|e)f(q|e') > 0, \tag{7.36}$$

or, in other words, if when $e' > e$, the ratio $f(q|e')/f(q|e)$ is increasing in q. Alternatively, f satisfies the MLRP if $q' > q$ implies that q' is a more favorable message than q in the sense of Milgrom (1981b). Less formally, the MLRP is satisfied if the ratio of the likelihood of a high effort to a low effort rises with observed output. The distributions in the Broadway Game of section 7.4 violate the MLRP, but the normal, exponential, Poisson, uniform, and chi-square distributions all satisfy it. Stochastic dominance does not imply the MLRP. If effort of 0 produces outputs of 10 or 12 with equal probability, and effort of 1 produces outputs of 11 or 13 also with equal probability, the second distribution is stochastically dominant, but the MLRP is not satisfied. See chapter 13 (Auctions) for more on the MLRP.

N7.4   Optimal contracts: the Broadway Game

- Daniel Asquith suggested the idea behind Broadway Game II.
- Franchising is one compromise between selling the store and paying a flat wage. See Mathewson & Winter (1985), Rubin (1978), and Klein & Saft (1985).
- Mirrlees (1974) is an early reference on the idea of the boiling-in-oil contract.
- Broadway Game II shows that improved information could reduce welfare by increasing a player's incentive to misbehave. This is distinct from the nonstrategic insurance reason why improved information can be harmful. Suppose that Smith is insuring Jones against hail ruining Jones' wheat crop during the next year, increasing Jones' expected utility and giving a profit to Smith. If someone comes up with a way to forecast the weather before the insurance contract is agreed upon, both players will be hurt. Insurance will break down, because if it is known that hail will

ruin the crop, Smith will not agree to share the loss, and if it is known there will be no hail, Jones will not pay a premium for insurance. Both players prefer not knowing the outcome in advance.

Problems

7.1:   First-best solutions in a principal–agent model (easy)

Suppose an agent has the utility function of $U = \sqrt{w} - e$, where e can assume the levels 0 or 1. Let the reservation utility level be $\overline{U} = 3$. The principal is risk-neutral. Denote the agent's wage, conditioned on output, as $\underline{w}$ if output is 0 and $\overline{w}$ if output is 100. Table 7.5 shows the outputs.

Table 7.5   A moral hazard game

Effort	Probability of output of		Total
	0	*100*	
Low ($e = 0$)	0.3	0.7	1
High ($e = 1$)	0.1	0.9	1

(a)   What would the agent's effort choice and utility be if he owned the firm?
(b)   If agents are scarce and principals compete for them, what will the agent's contract be under full information? His utility?
(c)   If principals are scarce and agents compete to work for them, what would the contract be under full information? What will the agent's utility and the principal's profit be in this situation?
(d)   Suppose that $U = w - e$. If principals are the scarce factor and agents compete to work for principals, what would the contract be when the principal cannot observe effort? (Negative wages are allowed.) What will be the agent's utility and the principal's profit be in this situation?

7.2:   The principal–agent problem (medium)

Suppose the agent has a utility function of $U = \sqrt{w} - e$, where e can assume the levels 0 or 7, and a reservation utility of $\overline{U} = 4$. The principal is risk-neutral. Denote the agent's wage, conditioned on output, as $\underline{w}$ if output is 0 and $\overline{w}$ if output is 1,000. Only the agent observes his effort. Principals compete for agents. Table 7.6 shows the output.

Table 7.6   Output from low and high effort

Effort	Probability of output of		Total
	0	*1,000*	
Low ($e = 0$)	0.9	0.1	1
High ($e = 7$)	0.2	0.8	1

(a)   What are the incentive compatibility, participation, and zero-profit constraints for obtaining high effort?

(b)   What would utility be if the wage were fixed and could not depend on output or effort?
(c)   What is the optimal contract? What is the agent's utility?
(d)   What would the agent's utility be under full information? Under asymmetric information, what is the agency cost (the lost utility) as a percentage of the utility the agent receives?

7.3:   Why entrepreneurs sell out (medium)

Suppose an agent has a utility function of $U = \sqrt{w} - e$, where e can assume the levels 0 or 2.4, and his reservation utility is $\overline{U} = 7$. The principal is risk-neutral. Denote the agent's wage, conditioned on output, as $w(0)$, $w(49)$, $w(100)$, or $w(225)$. Table 7.7 shows the output.

Table 7.7   Entrepreneurs selling out

Method	Probability of output of				Total
	0	49	100	225	
Safe (e = 0)	0.1	0.1	0.8	0	1
Risky (e = 2.4)	0	0.5	0	0.5	1

(a)   What would the agent's effort choice and utility be if he owned the firm?
(b)   If agents are scarce and principals compete for them, what will the agent's contract be under full information? His utility?
(c)   If principals are scarce and agents compete to work for principals, what will the contract be under full information? What will the agent's utility and the principal's profit be in this situation?
(d)   If agents are the scarce factor, and principals compete for them, what will the contract be when the principal cannot observe effort? What will the agent's utility and the principal's profit be in this situation?

7.4:   Authority (medium)

A salesman must decide how hard to work on his own time on getting to know a potential customer. If he exerts effort X, he incurs a utility cost $X^2/2$. With probability X, he can then go to the customer and add V to his own earnings. With probability $(1 - X)$, he offends the customer, and on going to him would subtract L from his earnings. The boss will receive benefit B from the sale in either case. The ranking of these numbers is $V > L > B > 0$. The boss and the salesman have equal bargaining power, and are free to make side payments to each other.

(a)   What is the first-best level of effort, X_a?
(b)   If the boss has the authority to block the salesman from selling to this customer, but cannot force him to sell, what value will X take?
(c)   If the salesman has the authority over the decision on whether to sell to this customer, and can bargain for higher pay, what will his effort be?
(d)   Rank the effort levels X_a, X_b, and X_c in the previous three sections.

7.5:   Worker effort (easy)

A worker can be *Careful* or *Careless*, efforts which generate mistakes with probabilities 0.25 and 0.75. His utility function is $U = 100 - 10/w - x$, where w is his wage and x takes the value 2 if he is careful, and 0 otherwise. Whether a mistake is made is contractible, but effort is not. Risk-neutral employers compete for the worker, and his output is worth 0 if a mistake is made and 20 otherwise. No computation is needed for any part of this problem.

(a)   Will the worker be paid anything if he makes a mistake?
(b)   Will the worker be paid more if he does not make a mistake?
(c)   How would the contract be affected if employers were also risk-averse?
(d)   What would the contract look like if a third category, "slight mistake," with an output of 19, occurs with probability 0.1 after *Careless* effort and with probability zero after *Careful* effort?

7.6:   The supercomputer salesman (medium)

If a salesman exerts high effort, he will sell a supercomputer this year with probability 0.9. If he exerts low effort, he will succeed with probability 0.5. The company will make a profit of 2 million dollars if the sale is made. The salesman would require a wage of $50,000 if he had to exert low effort, but $70,000 if he had to exert high effort, he is risk-neutral, and his utility is separable in effort and money. (Let's just use payoffs in thousands of dollars, so 70,000 dollars will be written as 70, and 2 million dollars will be 2000.)

(a)   Prove that high effort is first-best efficient.
(b)   How high would the probability of success with low effort have to be for high effort to be inefficient?
(c)   If you cannot monitor the programmer and cannot pay him a wage contingent on success, what should you do?
(d)   Now suppose you can make the wage contingent on success. Let the wage be S if he makes a sale and F if he does not. S and F will have to satisfy two conditions: a participation constraint and an incentive compatibility constraint. What are they?
(e)   What is a contract that will achieve the first best?
(f)   Now suppose the salesman is risk-averse, and his utility from money is $log(w)$. Set up the participation and incentive compatibility constraints again.
(g)   You do not need to solve for the optimal contract. Using the $log(w)$ utility function assumption, however, will the expected payment by the firm in the optimal contract rise, fall, or stay the same, compared with what it was in part (e) for the risk-neutral salesman?
(h)   You do not need to solve for the optimal contract. Using the $log(w)$ utility function assumption, however, will the gap between S and F in the optimal contract rise, fall, or stay the same, compared with what it was in part (e) for the risk-neutral salesman?

7.7:   Optimal compensation (easy)

An agent's utility function is $U = (log(wage) - effort)$. What should his compensation scheme be if different (output, effort) pairs have the probabilities in table 7.8?

(a)   The agent should be paid exactly his output.
(b)   The same wage should be paid for outputs of 1 and 100.
(c)   The agent should receive more for an output of 100 than of 1, but should receive still lower pay if output is 2.
(d)   None of the above.

Table 7.8 Effort and output

		Output		
		1	*2*	*100*
	High	0.5	0	0.5
Effort				
	Low	0.1	0.8	0.1

7.8: Effort and output, multiple choices (easy)

The utility function of the agents whose situation is depicted in table 7.9 is $U = w + \sqrt{w} - \alpha e$, and his reservation utility is 0. Principals compete for agents, and have reservation profits of zero. Principals are risk-neutral.

Table 7.9 Output and effort

		Effort	
		Low (e = 0)	*High (e = 5)*
	$y = 0$	0.9	0.5
Output			
	$y = 100$	0.1	0.5

1   If $\alpha = 2$, then if the agent's action can be observed by the principal, his equilibrium utility is in the interval
   (a) $[-\infty, 0.5]$
   (b) $[0.5, 5]$
   (c) $[5, 10]$
   (d) $[10, 40]$
   (e) $[40, \infty]$

2   If $\alpha = 10$, then if the agent's action can be observed by the principal, his equilibrium utility is in the interval
   (a) $[-\infty, 0.5]$
   (b) $[0.5, 5]$
   (c) $[5, 10]$
   (d) $[10, 40]$
   (e) $[40, \infty]$

3   If $\alpha = 5$, then if the agent's action can be observed by the principal, his equilibrium effort level is
   (a)   Low
   (b)   High
   (c)   A mixed strategy effort, sometimes low and sometimes high

4   If $\alpha = 2$, then if the agent's action cannot be observed by the principal, and he must be paid a flat wage, his wage will be in the interval
   (a) $[-\infty, 2]$
   (b) $[2, 5]$
   (c) $[5, 8]$
   (d) $[8, 12]$
   (e) $[12, \infty]$

5   If the agent owns the firm, and $\alpha = 2$, will his utility be higher or lower than in the case where he works for the principal and his action can be observed?
   (a)   Higher
   (b)   Lower
   (c)   Exactly the same

6   If the agent owns the firm, and $\alpha = 2$, his equilibrium utility is in the interval
   (a) $[-\infty, 0.5]$
   (b) $[0.5, 5]$
   (c) $[5, 10]$
   (d) $[10, 40]$
   (e) $[40, \infty]$

7   If the agent owns the firm, and $\alpha = 8$, his equilibrium utility is in the interval
   (a) $[-\infty, 0.5]$
   (b) $[0.5, 5]$
   (c) $[5, 10]$
   (d) $[10, 40]$
   (e) $[40, \infty]$

7.9:   Hiring a lawyer (easy)

A one-man firm with concave utility function $U(X)$ hires a lawyer to sue a customer for breach of contract. The lawyer is risk-neutral and effort averse, with a convex disutility of effort. What can you say about the optimal contract? What would be the practical problem with such a contract, if it were legal?

7.10:   Constraints (medium)

An agent has the utility function $U = log(w) - e$, where e can take the levels 0 and 4, and his reservation utility is $\overline{U} = 4$. His principal is risk-neutral. Denote the agent's wage conditioned on output as $\underline{w}$ if output is 0 and $\overline{w}$ if output is 10. Only the agent observes his effort. Principals compete for agents. Output is as shown in table 7.10.

   What are the incentive compatibility and participation constraints for obtaining high effort?

Table 7.10   Output function I

Effort	Probability of outputs		Total
	0	10	
Low ($e = 0$)	0.9	0.1	1
High ($e = 4$)	0.2	0.8	1

7.11:   Constraints again (medium)

Suppose an agent has the utility function $U = log(w) - e$, where e can take the levels 1 or 3, and a reservation utility of $\overline{U}$. The principal is risk-neutral. Denote the agent's wage conditioned on output

Table 7.11   Output function II

Effort	Probability of outputs	
	0	*100*
Low ($e = 1$)	0.9	0.1
High ($e = 3$)	0.5	0.5

as $\underline{w}$ if output is 0 and $\overline{w}$ if output is 100. Only the agent observes his effort. Principals compete for agents, and outputs occur according to table 7.11.

What conditions must the optimal contract satisfy, given that the principal can only observe output, not effort? You do not need to solve out for the optimal contract – just provide the equations which would have to be true. Do not just provide inequalities – if the condition is a binding constraint, state it as an equation.

Moral Hazard: A Classroom Game for Chapter 7

Each student works as a salesman for Apex, Brydox, or neither firm, choosing anew each year. Each year you also pick your effort level, which is unobserved by the firms. Your sales equal

$$Q = 2 + e + u,$$

where u takes the values -2 and $+2$ with equal probability.

Your payoff is 600 if you work for neither firm and otherwise is a function of your wage and effort:

$$Payoff = V(w) - e^2, \tag{7.37}$$

where $V(w)$ is shown in the following table:

w	<0	0	1	2	3	4	5	6	7	8	9	10	11	12	13	≥ 14
$V(w)$	0	0	100	190	370	540	690	830	930	1000	1020	1030	1038	1044	1046	1046

You will have limited time to make your choices of contract and effort. If you do not hand in a card with your choice by the deadline, your default choices are to work for neither firm (if you fail to choose an employer) and $e = 0$ (if you don't choose your effort).

A **linear contract** takes the form,

$$w(Q) = \alpha + \beta Q, \tag{7.38}$$

where if the value of w from the equation is not an integer it is rounded up.

A **threshold contract** takes the form

$$w(Q) = \alpha \text{ if } Q \geq \beta; \quad w = 0 \text{ otherwise.} \tag{7.39}$$

A **monitoring contract** takes the form

$$w(Q) = \alpha \text{ unless you are caught with } e < \beta;$$

$$w = 0 \text{ otherwise; probability of monitoring} = \gamma. \tag{7.40}$$

Chapter 8
further topics in moral hazard

Moral hazard deserves two chapters. As we will see, adverse selection will sneak two in also, since signalling is really just an elaboration of the adverse selection model, but moral hazard is perhaps even more important, as being the study of incentives, one of the central concepts of economics. In this chapter we will be going through a hodge-podge of special situations in which chapter 7's paradigm of providing the right incentives for effort by satisfying a participation constraint and an incentive compatibility constraint do not apply so straightforwardly.

The chapter begins with efficiency wages – high wages provided when incentive compatibility is so important that the principal is willing to abandon a tight participation constraint. Section 8.2 will be about tournaments – situations where competition between two agents can be used to simplify the optimal contract. After an excursion into various institutions, we will go to a big problem for incentive contracts: how does the principal restrain himself from being too merciful to a wayward agent when mercy is not only kind but profitable? Section 8.3 looks at some of the institutions that solve agency problems, and section 8.4 shows that one institution, contractual punishment, often fails because both parties are willing to renegotiate the contract. Section 8.5 abandons the algebraic paradigm to pursue a diagrammatic approach to the classic problem of moral hazard in insurance, and section 8.6 looks at another special case: the teams problem, in which the unobservable efforts of many agents produce one observable output. Section 8.7 concludes with the multitask agency problem, in which the agent allocates his effort among more than one task.

8.1   Efficiency Wages

Is the aim of an incentive contract to punish the agent if he chooses the wrong action? Not exactly. Rather, it is to create a difference between the agent's expected payoff from right and wrong actions, something which can be done either with the stick of punishment or the carrot of reward. It is important to keep this in mind, because sometimes punishments are simply not available. Consider the following game.

The Lucky Executive Game

PLAYERS
A corporation and an executive.

THE ORDER OF PLAY
1   The corporation offers the executive a contract which pays $w(q) \geq 0$ depending on profit, q.
2   The executive accepts the contract, or rejects it and receives his reservation utility of $\overline{U} = 5$.
3   The executive exerts effort e of either 0 or 10.
4   Nature chooses profit according to table 8.1.

PAYOFFS
Both players are risk-neutral. The corporation's payoff is $(q - w)$. The executive's payoff is $(w - e)$ if he accepts the contract.

Table 8.1   Output in the Lucky Executive Game

Effort	Probability of outputs		
	0	400	Total
Low ($e = 0$)	0.5	0.5	1
High ($e = 10$)	0.1	0.9	1

Since both players are risk-neutral, you might think that the first-best can be achieved by selling the store, putting the entire risk on the agent. The participation constraint if the executive exerts high effort is

$$0.1[w(0) - 10] + 0.9[w(400) - 10] \geq 5, \tag{8.1}$$

so his expected wage must equal 15. The incentive compatibility constraint is

$$0.5w(0) + 0.5w(400) \leq 0.1w(0) + 0.9w(400) - 10, \tag{8.2}$$

which can be rewritten as $w(400) - w(0) \geq 25$, so the gap between the executive's wage for high output and low output must equal at least 25.

A contract that satisfies both constraints is $\{w(0) = -345, w(400) = 55\}$. But this contract is not feasible, because the game requires $w(q) \geq 0$. This is an example of the common and realistic **bankruptcy constraint**; the principal cannot punish the agent by taking away more than the agent owns in the first place – zero in the Lucky Executive Game. (If the executive's initial wealth were positive that would help a little, and perhaps that is a reason why a company should prefer hiring rich people to poor people.) The worst the principal can do is fire the agent. So what can be done?

What can be done is to use the carrot instead of the stick and abandon satisfying the participation constraint as an equality. All that is needed for constraint (8.2) is a gap of 25 between the high wage and the low wage. Setting the low wage as low as is feasible, the corporation can use the contract $\{w(0) = 0, w(400) = 25\}$ and induce high effort. The executive's expected utility, however, will be $0.1(0) + 0.9(25) - 10 = 12.5$, more than double his reservation utility of 5. He is very happy in this equilibrium – but the corporation is reasonably happy, too. The corporation's payoff is 337.5 ($=0.1(0-0)+0.9(400-25)$), compared with the 195 ($=0.5(0-5)+0.5(400-5)$) it would get if it paid a lower expected wage. Since high enough punishments are infeasible, the corporation has to use higher rewards.

Executives, of course, will be lining up to work for this corporation, since they can get an expected utility of 12.5 there and only 5 elsewhere. If there was some chance of the current executive dying and his job opening up, potential successors would be willing to pass up alternative jobs in order to be in position to get this unusually attractive job. Thus, the model generates unemployment. These are the two parts of the idea of the **efficiency wage**: the employer pays a wage higher than that needed to attract workers, and workers are willing to be unemployed in order to get a chance at the efficiency-wage job.

Shapiro & Stiglitz (1984) show in more detail how involuntary unemployment can be explained by a principal–agent model. When all workers are employed at the market wage, a worker who is caught shirking and fired can immediately find another job just as good. Firing is ineffective, and effective penalties like boiling-in-oil are excluded from the strategy spaces of legal businesses. Becker & Stigler (1974) suggest that workers post performance bonds, and Gaver & Zimmerman (1977) describe how a performance bond of 100 percent was required for contractors building the BART subway system in San Francisco. "Surety companies" generally bond a contractor for 5 to 20 times his net worth, at a charge of 0.6 percent of the bond per year, and absorption of their bonding capacity is a serious concern for contractors in accepting jobs. If workers are poor, though, bonds are impractical, and without bonds or boiling-in-oil, the worker chooses low effort and receives a low wage.

To induce a worker not to shirk, the firm can offer to pay a premium over the market-clearing wage, which he loses if he is caught shirking and fired. If one firm finds it profitable to raise the wage, however, so do all firms. One might think that after the wages equalized, the incentive not to shirk would disappear. But when a firm raises its wage, its demand for labor falls, and when all firms raise their wages, the market demand for labor falls, creating unemployment. Even if all firms pay the same wage, a worker has an incentive not to shirk, because if he were fired he would stay unemployed, and even if there is a random chance of leaving the unemployment pool, the unemployment rate rises sufficiently high that workers choose not to risk being caught shirking. The equilibrium is not first-best efficient, because even though the marginal revenue of labor equals the wage, it exceeds the marginal disutility of effort, but it is efficient in the second-best sense. By deterring shirking, the hungry workers hanging around the factory gates are performing a socially valuable function (but they mustn't be paid for it!). While the efficiency wage model does explain involuntary unemployment, though, it does not explain cyclical changes in unemployment. There is no reason for the unemployment needed to control moral hazard to fluctuate widely and create a business cycle.

The idea of paying high wages to increase the threat of dismissal is old, and can even be found in *The Wealth of Nations* (Smith [1776], p. 207). What is new in Shapiro & Stiglitz (1984) is the observation that unemployment is generated by these "efficiency wages."

The firms behave paradoxically. They pay workers more than necessary to attract them, and outsiders who offer to work for less are turned away. Can this explain why "overqualified" jobseekers are unsuccessful and mediocre managers are retained? Employers are unwilling to hire someone talented, because he could find another job after being fired for shirking, and trustworthiness matters more than talent in some jobs. The idea also explains the paradoxical phenomenon of slaveowners paying wages to their slaves, as happened sometimes in the American South. The slaveowner had no legal obligation to pay his slave anything, but if he wanted careful effort from the slave – something important not so much for picking cotton as for such things as carpentry – the slaveowner had to provide positive incentives.

This discussion should remind you of section 5.4's Product Quality Game. There too, purchasers paid more than the reservation price in order to give the seller an incentive to behave properly, because a seller who misbehaved could be punished by termination of the relationship. The key characteristics of such models are a constraint on the amount of contractual punishment for misbehavior and a participation constraint that is not binding in equilibrium. In addition, although the Lucky Executive Game works even with just one period, many versions, including the Product Quality Game, rely on there being a repeated game (infinitely repeated, or otherwise avoiding the Chainstore Paradox). Repetition allows for a situation in which the agent could considerably increase his payoff in one period by misbehavior such as stealing or low quality, but refrains because he would lose his position and lose all the future efficiency wage payments.

8.2   Tournaments

Games in which relative performance is important are called **tournaments**. Tournaments are similar to auctions, the difference being that the actions of the losers have real rather than just pecuniary effects; even the effort of an agent who loses a tournament benefits the principal, but the losing bids in an auction don't enrich the seller. (As we will see in chapter 13, though, the "all-pay" auction is one way to model a tournament.) Like auctions, tournaments are especially useful when the principal wants to elicit information from the agents. A principal-designed tournament is sometimes called a **yardstick competition** because the agents provide the measure for their wages.

Farrell (2001) uses a tournament to explain how "slack" might be the major source of welfare loss from monopoly, an old idea usually prompted by faulty reasoning. The usual claim is that monopolists are inefficient because unlike competitive firms, they do not have to maximize profits to survive. This relies on the dubious assumption that firms care about survival, not profits. Farrell makes a subtler point: although the shareholders of a monopoly maximize profit, the managers maximize their own utility, and moral hazard is severe without the benchmark of other firms' performances.

Let firm Apex have two possible production techniques, *Fast* and *Careful*. Independently for each technique, Nature chooses production cost $c = 1$ with probability θ and $c = 2$ with probability $(1 - \theta)$. The manager can either choose a technique at random or investigate the costs of both techniques at a utility cost to himself of α. The shareholders can observe the resulting production cost, but not whether the manager investigates. If they see the manager pick *Fast* and a cost of $c = 2$, they do not know whether he chose it without investigating, or investigated both techniques and found they were both costly. The wage contract is based on what the shareholders can observe, so it takes the form (w_1, w_2), where w_1 is the wage if $c = 1$ and w_2 if $c = 2$. The manager's utility is $log(w)$ if he does not investigate and $(log(w) - \alpha)$ if he does, or the reservation utility of $log(\overline{w})$ if he quits.

If the shareholders want the manager to investigate, the contract must satisfy the self-selection constraint

$$U(\text{not investigate}) \leq U(\text{investigate}). \tag{8.3}$$

If the manager investigates, he still fails to find a low-cost technique with probability $(1-\theta)^2$, so inequality (8.3) is equivalent to

$$\theta log(w_1) + (1 - \theta)log(w_2) \leq [1 - (1 - \theta)^2]log(w_1) + (1 - \theta)^2 log(w_2) - \alpha. \tag{8.4}$$

The self-selection constraint is binding, since the shareholders want to keep the manager's compensation to a minimum. Turning inequality (8.4) into an equality and simplifying yields

$$\theta(1 - \theta)log\left(\frac{w_1}{w_2}\right) = \alpha. \tag{8.5}$$

The participation constraint, which is also binding, is $U(\overline{w}) = U(\text{investigate})$, or

$$log(\overline{w}) = [1 - (1 - \theta)^2]log(w_1) + (1 - \theta)^2 log(w_2) - \alpha. \tag{8.6}$$

Solving equations (8.5) and (8.6) together for w_1 and w_2 yields

$$w_1 = \overline{w}e^{\alpha/\theta},$$
$$w_2 = \overline{w}e^{-\alpha/(1-\theta)}, \tag{8.7}$$

where e does not here denote effort, but the constant $e \approx 2.72$ in natural logarithms. The expected cost to the firm is

$$[1 - (1 - \theta)^2]\overline{w}e^{\alpha/\theta} + (1 - \theta)^2\overline{w}e^{-\alpha/(1-\theta)}. \tag{8.8}$$

If the parameters are $\theta = 0.1$, $\alpha = 1$, and $\overline{w} = 1$, the rounded values are $w_1 = 22,026$ and $w_2 = 0.33$, and the expected cost is 4,185. Quite possibly, the shareholders decide it is not worth making the manager investigate.

But suppose that Apex has a competitor, Brydox, in the same situation. The shareholders of Apex can threaten to boil their manager in oil if Brydox adopts a low-cost technology and Apex does not. If Brydox does the same, the two managers are in a Prisoner's Dilemma, both wishing not to investigate, but each investigating from fear of the other. Apex's forcing contract specifies $w_1 = w_2$ to fully insure the manager, and boiling-in-oil if Brydox has lower costs than Apex. The contract need satisfy only the participation constraint that $log(w - \alpha) = log(\overline{w})$, so $w = 2.72$ and Apex's cost of extracting the manager's information is only 2.72, not 4,185. Competition raises efficiency, not through the threat of firms going bankrupt but through the threat of managers being fired.

*8.3   Institutions and Agency Problems

Ways to Alleviate Agency Problems

Usually when agents are risk-averse, the first-best cannot be achieved, because some trade-off must be made between providing the agent with incentives and keeping his compensation from varying too much for reasons not under his control such as between states of the world, or because it is not possible to punish him sufficiently. We have looked at a number of different ways to solve the problem, and at this point a listing might be useful. Each method is illustrated by application to the particular problem of executive compensation, which is empirically important, and interesting both because explicit incentive contracts are used and because they are not used more often (see Baker, Jensen, & Murphy [1988]).

1   **Reputation** (sections 5.3, 5.4, 6.4, 6.6): Managers are promoted on the basis of past effort or truthfulness.

2   **Risk-sharing contracts** (sections 7.2, 7.3, 7.4): The executive receives not only a salary, but call options on the firm's stock. If he reduces the stock value, his options fall in value.

3   **Boiling-in-oil** (section 7.4): If the firm would only become unable to pay dividends if the executive shirked and was unlucky, the threat of firing him when the firm skips a dividend will keep him working hard.

4   **Selling the store** (section 7.4): The managers buy the firm in a leveraged buyout.

5   **Efficiency wages** (section 8.1): To make him fear losing his job, the executive is paid a higher salary than his ability warrants (cf. Rasmusen [1988b] on mutual banks).

6   **Tournaments** (section 8.2): Several vice-presidents compete and the winner succeeds the president.

7   **Monitoring** (section 3.4): The directors hire a consultant to evaluate the executive's performance.

8   **Repetition**: Managers are paid less than their marginal products for most of their career, but are rewarded later with higher salaries or generous pensions if their career record has been good.

9   **Changing the type of the agent**: Older executives encourage the younger ones by praising ambition and hard work.

We have talked about all but the last two solutions. Repetition enables the contract to come closer to the first-best if the discount rate is low (Radner [1985]). Production Game V failed to attain the first-best in section 7.2 because output depended on both the agent's effort and random noise. If the game were repeated 50 times with independent drawings of the noise, the randomness would average out and the principal could form an accurate estimate of the agent's effort. This is, in a sense, begging the question, by saying that in the long run effort can be deduced after all.

Changing the agent's type by increasing the direct utility of desirable or reducing the utility of undesirable behavior is a solution that has received little attention from economists, who have focused on changing the utility by changing monetary rewards. Akerlof (1983), one of the few papers on the subject of changing type, points out that the moral education of children, not just their intellectual education, affects their productivity and success. The attitude of economics, however, has been that while virtuous agents exist, the rules of an organization need to be designed with the unvirtuous agents in mind. As the Chinese thinker Han Fei Tzu said some two thousand years ago,

"Hardly ten men of true integrity and good faith can be found today, and yet the offices of the state number in the hundreds. If they must be filled by men of integrity and good faith, then there will never be enough men to go around; and if the offices are left unfilled, then those whose business it is to govern will dwindle in numbers while disorderly men increase. Therefore the way of the enlightened ruler is to unify the laws instead of seeking for wise men, to lay down firm policies instead of longing for men of good faith." *(Han Fei Tzu [1964], p. 109 from his chapter, "The Five Vermin")*

The number of men of true integrity has probably not increased as fast as the size of government, so Han Fei Tzu's observation remains valid, but it should be kept in mind that honest men do exist and honesty can enter into rational models. There are trade-offs between spending to foster honesty and spending for other purposes, and there may be trade-offs between using the second-best contracts designed for agents indifferent about the truth and using the simpler contracts appropriate for honest agents.

Government Institutions and Agency Problems

The field of law is well suited to analysis by principal–agent models. Even in the nineteenth century, Holmes (1881, p. 31) conjectured in *The Common Law* that the reason why sailors at one time received no wages if their ship was wrecked was to discourage them from taking to the lifeboats too early instead of trying to save it. As is typical, incentive compatibility and insurance work in opposite directions here. If sailors are more risk-averse than ship owners, and pecuniary advantage would not add much to their effort during storms, then the owner ought to provide insurance to the sailors by guaranteeing them wages whether the voyage succeeds or not. If not, the old rule could be efficient.

Another legal question is who should bear the cost of an accident, the victim (e.g., a pedestrian hit by a car) or the person who caused it (the driver). The economist's answer is that it depends on who has the most severe moral hazard. If the pedestrian could have prevented the accident at the lowest cost, he should pay; otherwise, the driver. Indeed, as Coase (1960) points out, the term "cause" can be misleading: both driver and victim cause the accident, in the sense that either of them could prevent it, though at different costs. This **least-cost avoider principle** is extremely useful in the economic analysis of law and a major theme of Posner's classic treatise (Posner [1992]).

Criminal law is also concerned with trade-offs between incentives and insurance. Holmes (1881, p. 40) notes approvingly that Macaulay's draft of the Indian Penal Code made breach of contract for the carriage of passengers a criminal offense. Palanquin-bearers were too poor to pay damages for abandoning their passengers in desolate regions, so the power of the state was needed to provide for heavier punishments than bankruptcy. In general, however, the legal rules actually used seem to diverge more from optimality in criminal law than civil law. If, for example, there is no chance that an innocent man can be convicted of embezzlement, boiling embezzlers in oil might be good policy, but most countries would not allow this. Taking the example a step further, if the evidence for murder is usually less convincing than for embezzling, our analysis could easily indicate that the penalty for murder should be less, but such reasoning offends the common notion that the severity of punishment should be matched with the harm from the crime.

Private Institutions and Agency Problems

While agency theory can be used to explain and perhaps improve government policy, it also helps explain many curious private institutions. Agency problems are an important hindrance to economic development, and may explain a number of apparently irrational practices. Popkin (1979, pp. 66, 73, 157) notes a variety of these. In Vietnam, for example, absentee landlords were more lenient than local landlords, but improved the land less, as one would expect of principals who suffer from informational disadvantages *vis-à-vis* their agents. Along the pathways in the fields, farmers would plant early-harvesting rice that the farmer's family could harvest by itself in advance of the regular crop, so that hired labor could not grab handfuls as they travelled. In thirteenth-century England, beans were seldom grown, despite their nutritional advantages, because they were too easy to steal. Some villages tried to solve the problem by prohibiting anyone from entering the beanfields except during certain hours marked by the priest's ringing the church bell, so everyone could tend and watch their beans at the same official time.

In less exotic settings, moral hazard provides another reason besides tax advantages for why employees take some of their compensation in fringe benefits. Professors are granted some of their wages in university computer time because this induces them to do more research. Having a zero marginal cost of computer time is a way around the moral hazard of slacking on research, despite being a source of moral hazard in wasting computer time. A less typical example is the bank in Minnesota which, concerned about its image, gave each employee $100 in credit at certain clothing stores to upgrade their style of dress. By compromising between paying cash and issuing uniforms the bank could hope to raise both profits and employee happiness. ("The $100 Sounds Good, but What Do They Wear on the Second Day?" *The Wall Street Journal*, October 16, 1987, p. 17.)

Longterm contracts are an important occasion for moral hazard, since so many variables are unforeseen, and hence noncontractible. The term **opportunism** has been used to describe the behavior of agents who take advantage of noncontractibility to increase their payoff at the expense of the principal (see Williamson [1975] and Tirole [1986]). Smith may be able to extract a greater payment from Jones than was agreed upon in their contract because Smith can threaten to harm Jones by failing to perform his contractual duties unless the contract is renegotiated. This is called **hold-up potential** (Klein, Crawford, & Alchian [1978]), often modelled in the style of Hart and Moore's seminal 1990 article on who should own assets. Hold-up potential can even make an agent introduce competing agents into the game, if competition is not so extreme as to drive rents to zero. Someone told me that Fairchild once developed a new patent on a component of electronic fuel injection systems that it sought to sell to another firm, TRW. TRW offered a much higher price if Fairchild would license its patent to other producers, fearing the hold-up potential of buying from just one supplier. TRW could have tried writing a contract to prevent hold-up, but knew that it would be difficult to prespecify all the ways that Fairchild could cause harm, including not only slow delivery, poor service, and low quality, but also sins of omission like failing to sufficiently guard the plant from shutdown due to accidents and strikes.

It should be clear from the variety of these examples that moral hazard is a common problem. Now that the first flurry of research on the principal–agent problem has finished, researchers are beginning to use the new theory to study specific institutions and practices like these that were formerly relegated to descriptive "soft" scholarly work in management, law, and anthropology.

*8.4   Renegotiation: The Repossession Game

Renegotiation comes up in two very different contexts in game theory. Chapter 4 looked at when players can coordinate in Pareto-superior subgame equilibria that might be Pareto inferior for the entire game, an idea linked to the problem of selecting among multiple equilibria. This section looks at a different context, in which the players have signed a binding contract, but in a subsequent subgame both might agree to scrap the old contract and write a new one, using the old contract as the starting point in their negotiations. Here, the questions are not about equilibrium selection but about which strategies should be part of the game. The issue frequently arises in principal–agent models, especially in the hidden knowledge literature starting from Dewatripont (1989) and Hart & Moore (1990). Here we will use a model of hidden actions to illustrate renegotiation, a model in which a bank that wants to lend money to a consumer to buy a car must worry about whether he will work hard enough to repay the loan.

The Repossession Game

PLAYERS
A bank and a consumer.

THE ORDER OF PLAY
1 The bank can do nothing or it can at cost 11 offer the consumer an auto loan which allows him to buy a car that costs 11 but requires him to pay back L or lose possession of the car to the bank.
2 The consumer accepts the loan and buys the car, or rejects it.
3 The consumer chooses to *Work*, for an income of 15, or *Play*, for an income of 8. The disutility of work is 5.
4 The consumer repays the loan or defaults.
4a In one version of the game, the bank offers to settle for an amount S and leave possession of the car to the consumer.
4b The consumer accepts or rejects the settlement S.
5 If the bank has not been paid L or S, it repossesses the car.

PAYOFFS
If the bank does not make any loan or the consumer rejects it, both players' payoffs are zero. The value of the car is 12 to the consumer and 7 to the bank, so the bank's payoff if the loan is made is

$$\pi_{bank} = \begin{cases} L - 11 & \text{if the original loan is repaid,} \\ S - 11 & \text{if a settlement is made,} \\ 7 - 11 & \text{if the car is repossessed.} \end{cases}$$

If the consumer chooses *Work*, his income is $W = 15$ and his disutility of effort is $D = 5$. If he chooses *Play*, then $W = 8$ and $D = 0$. His payoff is

$$\pi_{consumer} = \begin{cases} W + 12 - L - D & \text{if the original loan is repaid,} \\ W + 12 - S - D & \text{if a settlement is made,} \\ W - D & \text{if the car is repossessed or he rejects the loan.} \end{cases}$$

We will consider two versions of the game which differ in whether they allow the renegotiation moves (4a) and (4b). As we will see, the outcome is Pareto superior if renegotiation is not possible.

Repossession Game I

The first version of the game does not allow renegotiation, so moves (4a) and (4b) are omitted. In equilibrium, the bank will make the loan at a rate of $L = 12$, and the consumer will choose *Work* and repay the loan. Working back from the end of the game in accordance with sequential rationality, the consumer is willing to repay because by repaying 12 he receives a car worth 12.[1] He will choose *Work* because he can then repay the loan and his payoff will be 10 ($=15+12-12-5$), but if he chooses *Play* he will not be able to repay and the bank will repossess the car, reducing his payoff to 8 ($=8-0$). The bank will offer a loan at $L = 12$ because the consumer will repay it and that is the maximum repayment to which the consumer will agree. The bank's equilibrium payoff is 1 ($=12-11$). This outcome is efficient because the consumer does buy the car, which he values at more than its cost to the car dealer. The bank ends up with the surplus, however, because of our assumption that the bank has all the bargaining power.

In equilibrium, the bank's strategy is to offer $L = 12$; and the consumer's strategy is to *Accept* if $L \leq 12$; to *Work* if $L \leq 12$ and he has accepted the loan or if he has rejected the loan (for a payoff of $15 - 5 = 10$); and to *Repay* if $W + 12 - L - D \geq W - D$ so $L \leq 12$. The equilibrium outcome is that the bank offers $L = 12$, the consumer accepts, he works, and he repays the loan.

Repossession Game II

The second version of the game does allow renegotiation, so moves (4a) and (4b) are included in the game. Renegotiation turns out to be harmful, because it results in an equilibrium in which the bank refuses to make the loan, reducing the payoffs of bank and consumer to (0, 10) instead of (1, 10). The gains from trade vanish.

The equilibrium in Repossession Game I breaks down in Repossession Game II because the consumer would deviate by choosing *Play*. In Repossession Game I the consumer would not do that, because the bank would repossess the car. In Repossession Game II, the bank still has the right to repossess it, for a payoff of -4 ($=7-11$). The bank now has the alternative to renegotiate and offer $S = 8$, on the other hand, and the offer will be accepted by the consumer since in exchange he gets to keep a car worth 12. The payoffs of bank and consumer would be -3 ($=8-11$) and 12 ($=8 + 12 - 8$). Since the bank prefers -3 to -4 it will renegotiate and the consumer will have increased his payoff from 10 to 12 by choosing *Play*. Looking ahead to this from move (1), however, the bank will see that it can do better by refusing to make the loan, resulting in the payoffs (0, 10). One might think the bank could adjust by raising the the loan

[1] As usual, we could change the model slightly to make the consumer strongly desire to repay the loan, by substituting a bargaining subgame that splits the gains from trade between bank and consumer rather than specifying that the bank make a take-it-or-leave-it offer (see section 4.3). We could also change the game to give all the bargaining power to the agent, and the outcomes of the two versions of the game would remain similar.

rate L, but that is no help. Even if $L = 30$, for instance, the consumer will still happily accept, knowing that when he chooses *Play* and defaults the ultimate amount he will pay will be just $S = 8$. Since both parties know there will be renegotiation later, the contract amount L is meaningless, the first, empty, offer in a bargaining game.

In equilibrium, the bank's strategy is to not offer a loan at all, but if it did offer a loan and the consumer accepted and defaulted, to offer $S = 8$ or $S = 12$ depending on whether the consumer chose *Work* or *Play*. The consumer's strategy is to *Accept* any loan made, whatever the value of L; to *Work* only if he rejected the loan (for a payoff of $15 - 5 = 10$) and otherwise to *Play* and *Default*; and to accept a settlement offer of $S = 8$ if he chose *Play* and $S = 12$ if he chose *Work*. The equilibrium outcome is that the bank does not offer a loan and the consumer chooses *Work*.

Renegotiation is paradoxical. In the subgame starting with consumer default it increases efficiency, by allowing the players to make a Pareto improvement over an inefficient punishment. In the game as a whole, however, it reduces efficiency by preventing players from using punishments to deter inefficient actions. This is true of any situation in which punishment imposes a deadweight loss instead of being simply a transfer from punished to punisher. This may be why American judges are less willing than the general public to impose punishments on criminals. By the time a criminal reaches the courtroom, extra years in jail have no deterrent effect for that crime and impose real costs on both criminal and society. For every particular case, viewed in isolation, the sentences are inefficient, retribution aside.

The renegotiation problem also comes up in principal–agent models because of risk bearing by a risk-averse agent when the principal is risk-neutral. Optimal contracts impose risk on risk-averse agents to provide incentives for high effort or self selection. If at some point in the game it is common knowledge that the agent has chosen his action, but Nature has not yet moved, the agent bears needless risk. The principal knows the agent has already moved, so the two of them are willing to recontract to shift the risk from Nature's move back on the principal. But the expected future recontracting makes a joke of the original contract and reduces the agent's incentives for effort or truthfulness.

The Repossession Game illustrates other ideas too. It is a game of perfect information, but it has the feel of a game of moral hazard with hidden actions. This is because it has an implicit bankruptcy constraint, so the contract cannot sufficiently punish the consumer for an inefficient choice of effort. Restricting the strategy space has the same effect as restricting the information available to a player. It is another example of the distinction between observability and contractibility – the consumer's effort is observable, but it is not really contractible, because the bankruptcy constraint prevents him from being punished for his low effort.

Both models allow commitment in the sense of legally binding agreements over transfers of money and wealth but they do not allow the consumer to commit directly to *Work*. Also, if the consumer does not repay the loan, the bank has the legal right to repossess the car, but the bank cannot have the consumer thrown into prison for breaking a promise to choose *Work*.

This game illustrates the difficulty of deciding what "bargaining power" means. This is a term that is very important to how many people think about law and public policy but which they define hazily. The natural way to think of bargaining power is to treat it as the ability to get a bigger share of the surplus from a bargaining interaction. Here, there is a surplus of 1 from the consumer's purchase of a car that costs 11 and yields 12 in utility. Both versions of the Repossession Game give all the bargaining power to the bank in the sense that where there is a surplus to be split, the bank gets 100 percent of it. But this does not help the bank in Repossession Game II, because the consumer can put himself in a position where the bank ends up a loser from the transaction despite its bargaining power.

*8.5 State-space Diagrams: Insurance Games I and II

An approach to principal–agent problems, especially useful when the strategy space is continuous, is to use diagrams. The term "moral hazard" comes from the insurance industry, where it refers to the idea that if a person is insured he will be less careful and the danger from accidents will rise. Suppose Smith (the agent) is considering buying theft insurance for a car with a value of 12. Figure 8.1, which illustrates his situation, is an example of a **state-space diagram**, a diagram whose axes measure the values of one variable in two different states of the world. Before Smith buys insurance, his dollar wealth is 0 if there is a theft and 12 otherwise, depicted as his endowment, $\omega = (12, 0)$. The point $(12, 0)$ indicates a wealth of 12 in one state and 0 in the other, while the point $(6, 6)$ indicates a wealth of 6 in each state.

One cannot tell the probabilities of each state just by looking at the state-space diagram. Let us specify that if Smith is careful where he parks, the state *Theft* occurs with probability 0.5, but if he is careless the probability rises to 0.75. He is risk-averse, and, other things equal, he has a mild preference to be careless, a preference worth only some small amount ϵ to him. Other things are not equal, however, and he would choose to be careful were he uninsured, because of the high correlation of carelessness with carlessness.

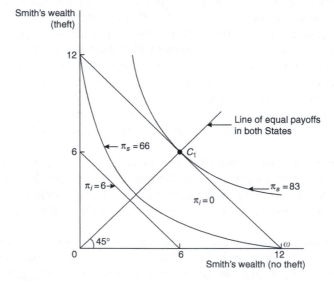

Figure 8.1 Insurance Game I.

The insurance company (the principal) is risk-neutral, perhaps because it is owned by diversified shareholders. We assume that no transaction costs are incurred in providing insurance and that the market is competitive, a switch from Production Game V, where the principal collected all the gains from trade. If the insurance company can require Smith to park carefully, it offers him insurance at a premium of 6, with a payout of 12 if theft occurs, leaving him with an allocation of $C_1 = (6, 6)$. This satisfies the competition constraint because it is the most attractive contract any company can offer without making losses. Smith, whose allocation is 6 no matter what happens, is **fully insured**. In state-space diagrams, allocations which like C_1 fully insure one player are on the 45° line through the origin, the line along which his allocations in the two states are equal.

The game is described below in a specification that includes two insurance companies to simulate a competitive market. For Smith, who is risk-averse, we must distinguish between dollar *allocations* such as (12, 0) and utility *payoffs* such as $0.5U(12) + 0.5U(0)$. The curves in figure 8.1 are labelled in units of utility for Smith and dollars for the insurance company.

Insurance Game I: Observable Care

PLAYERS
Smith and two insurance companies.

THE ORDER OF PLAY
1   Smith chooses to be either *Careful* or *Careless*, observed by the insurance company.
2   Insurance company 1 offers a contract (x, y), in which Smith pays premium x and receives compensation y if there is a theft.
3   Insurance company 2 also offers a contract of the form (x, y).
4   Smith picks a contract.
5   Nature chooses whether there is a theft, with probability 0.5 if Smith is *Careful* or 0.75 if Smith is *Careless*.

PAYOFFS
Smith is risk-averse and the insurance companies are risk-neutral. The insurance company not picked by Smith has a payoff of zero.

Smith's utility function U is such that $U' > 0$ and $U'' < 0$. If Smith picks contract (x, y), the payoffs are:
If Smith chooses *Careful*,

$$\pi_{Smith} = 0.5U(12 - x) + 0.5U(0 + y - x)$$

$$\pi_{company} = 0.5x + 0.5(x - y), \quad \text{for his insurer.}$$

If Smith chooses *Careless*,

$$\pi_{Smith} = 0.25U(12 - x) + 0.75U(0 + y - x) + \epsilon$$

$$\pi_{company} = 0.25x + 0.75(x - y), \quad \text{for his insurer.}$$

In equilibrium, Smith chooses to be *Careful* because he foresees that otherwise his insurance will be more expensive. Figure 8.1 is the corner of an Edgeworth box which shows the indifference curves of Smith and his insurance company given that Smith's care keeps the probability of a theft down to 0.5. The company is risk-neutral, so its indifference curve, $\pi_i = 0$, is a straight line with slope $-1/1$. Its payoffs are higher on indifference curves such as $\pi_i = 6$ that are closer to the origin and thus have smaller expected payouts to Smith. The insurance company is indifferent between points ω and C_1, at both of which its profits are zero. Smith is risk-averse, so if he is *Careful* his indifference curves are closest to the origin on the 45° line, where his wealth in the two states is equal. Picking the numbers 66 and 83 for concreteness, I have labelled his original indifference curve $\pi_s = 66$ and drawn the preferred indifference curve $\pi_s = 83$ through the equilibrium contract C_1. The equilibrium contract is C_1, which satisfies the competition constraint by generating the highest expected utility for Smith that allows nonnegative profits to the company.

Insurance Game I is a game of symmetric information. Insurance Game II changes that. Suppose that

1 the company cannot observe Smith's action (care is *unobservable*); or
2 the state insurance commission does not allow contracts to require Smith to be careful (care is *noncontractible*); or
3 a contract requiring Smith to be careful is impossible to enforce because of the cost of proving carelessness (care is *nonverifiable* in a court of law).

In each case Smith's action is a noncontractible variable, so we model all three the same way, by putting Smith's move second. The new game is like Production Game V, with uncertainty, unobservability, and two levels of output, *Theft* and *No Theft*. The insurance company may not be able to directly observe Smith's action, but his dominant strategy is to be *Careless*, so the company knows the probability of a theft is 0.75. Insurance Game II is the same as Insurance Game I except for the following.

Insurance Game II: Unobservable Care

THE ORDER OF PLAY
1 Insurance company 1 offers a contract of form (x, y), under which Smith pays premium x and receives compensation y if there is a theft.
2 Insurance company 2 offers a contract of form (x, y).
3 Smith picks a contract.
4 Smith chooses either *Careful* or *Careless*.
5 Nature chooses whether there is a theft, with probability 0.5 if Smith is *Careful* or 0.75 if Smith is *Careless*.

Smith's dominant strategy is *Careless* in Insurance Game II, so in contrast to Insurance Game I the insurance company must offer a contract with a premium of 9 and a payout of 12 to prevent losses, which leaves Smith with an allocation $C_2 = (3, 3)$. Making thefts more probable reduces the slopes of both players' indifference curves, because it decreases the utility of points to the southeast of the 45° line and increases utility to the northwest.

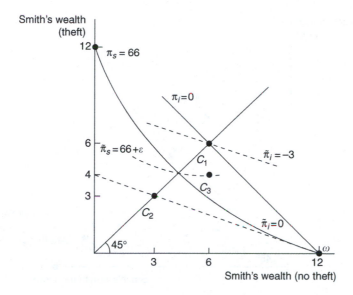

Figure 8.2   Insurance Game II with full and partial insurance.

In figure 8.2, the insurance company's isoprofit curve swivels from the solid line $\pi_i = 0$ to the dotted line $\tilde{\pi}_i = 0$. It swivels around ω because that is the point at which the company's profit is independent of how probable it is that Smith's car will be stolen (at point ω the company is not insuring him at all). Smith's indifference curve also swivels, from the solid curve $\pi_s = 66$ to the dotted curve $\tilde{\pi}_s = 66 + \epsilon$. It swivels around the intersection of the $\pi_s = 66$ curve with the $45°$ line, because on that line the probability of theft does not affect his payoff. The ϵ difference appears because Smith gets to choose the action *Careless*, which he slightly prefers.

Figure 8.2 shows that no full-insurance contract will be offered. The contract C_1 is acceptable to Smith, but not to the insurance company, because it earns negative profits, and the contract C_2 is acceptable to the insurance company, but not to Smith, who prefers ω. Smith would like to commit himself to being careful, but he cannot make his commitment credible. If the means existed to prove his honesty, he would use them even if they were costly. He might, for example, agree to buy off-street parking even though locking his car would be cheaper, if verifiable.

Although no full-insurance contract such as C_1 or C_2 is mutually agreeable, other contracts can be used. Consider the partial-insurance contract C_3 in figure 8.2, which has a premium of 6 and a payout of 8. Smith would prefer C_3 to his endowment of $\omega = (12, 0)$ whether he chooses *Careless* or *Careful*. We can think of C_3 in two ways:

1   Full insurance except for a **deductible** of four. The insurance company pays for all losses in excess of four.
2   Insurance with a **coinsurance** rate of one-third. The insurance company pays two-thirds of all losses.

The outlook is bright because Smith chooses *Careful* if he only has partial insurance, as with contract C_3. The moral hazard is "small" in the sense that Smith barely prefers *Careless*.

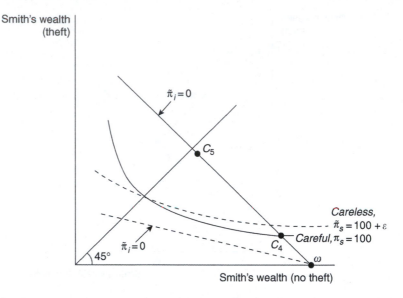

Figure 8.3 More on partial insurance in Insurance Game II.

With even a small deductible, Smith would choose *Careful* and the probability of theft would fall to 0.5, allowing the company to provide much more generous insurance. The solution of full insurance is "almost" reached. In reality, we rarely observe truly full insurance, because insurance contracts repay only the price of the car and not the bother of replacing it, a bother big enough to deter owners from leaving their cars unlocked.

Figure 8.3 illustrates effort choice under partial insurance. Smith has a choice between dashed indifference curves (*Careless*) and solid ones (*Careful*). To the southeast of the 45° line, the dashed indifference curve for a particular utility level is always above that utility's solid indifference curve. Offered contract C_4, Smith chooses *Careful*, remaining on the solid indifference curve, so C_4 yields zero profit to the insurance company. In fact, the competing insurance companies will offer contract C_5 in equilibrium, which is almost full insurance, but just almost, so that Smith will choose *Careful* to avoid the small amount of risk he still bears.

Thus, as in the principal–agent model there is a trade-off between efficient effort and efficient risk allocation. Even when the ideal of full insurance and efficient effort cannot be reached, there exists some best choice like C_5 in the set of feasible contracts, a second-best insurance contract that recognizes the constraints of informational asymmetry.

The idea of "care" as effort in a moral hazard model comes up in many contexts. Two of the most important are in tort law, and in the law and the economics of renting and leasing. The great problem of tort law is how to create the correct incentives for care by the various people who can act to prevent an accident by the way the law allocates liability when an accident occurs, or by regulation to directly require care. One of the biggest problem in rentals, whether of cars, apartments, or tuxedos is that the renters lack efficient incentives to take care. As P. J. O'Rourke says (as attributed by McAfee [2002, p. 189] and others):

> There's a lot of debate on this subject – about what kind of car handles best. Some say a a front-engined car, some say a rear-engined car. I say a rented car. Nothing handles better than a

rented car. You can go faster, turn corners sharper, and put the transmission into reverse while going forward at a higher rate of speed in a rented car than in any other kind.

*8.6   Joint Production by Many Agents: The Holmstrom Teams Model

To conclude this chapter, let us switch our focus from the individual agent to a group of agents. We have already looked at tournaments, which involve more than one agent, but a tournament still takes place in a situation where each agent's output is distinct. The tournament is a solution to the standard problem, and the principal could always fall back on other solutions such as individual risk-sharing contracts. In this section, the existence of a group of agents results in destroying the effectiveness of the individual risk-sharing contracts, because observed output is a joint function of the unobserved effort of many agents. Even though there is a group, a tournament is impossible, because only one output is observed. The situation has much of the flavor of the Civic Duty Game of chapter 3: the actions of a group of players produce a joint output, and each player wishes that the others would carry out the costly actions. A teams model is defined as follows.

*A **team** is a group of agents who independently choose effort levels that result in a single output for the entire group.*

We will look at teams using the following game (Holmstrom [1982]).

Teams

PLAYERS
A principal and n agents.

THE ORDER OF PLAY
1   The principal offers a contract to each agent i of the form $w_i(q)$, where q is total output.
2   The agents decide whether or not to accept the contract.
3   The agents simultaneously pick effort levels e_i, $(i = 1, \ldots, n)$.
4   Output is $q(e_1, \ldots, e_n)$.

PAYOFFS
If any agent rejects the contract, all payoffs equal zero. Otherwise,

$$\pi_{principal} = q - \sum_{i=1}^{n} w_i;$$

$$\pi_i = w_i - v_i(e_i), \quad \text{where } v_i' > 0 \text{ and } v_i'' > 0.$$

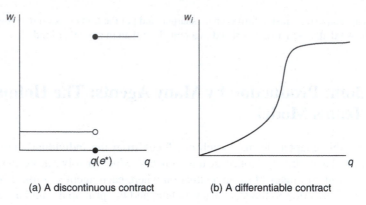

(a) A discontinuous contract   (b) A differentiable contract

Figure 8.4   Contracts in the Holmstrom Teams Model.

Despite the risk neutrality of the agents, "selling the store" fails to work here, because the team of agents still has the same problem as the employer had. The team's problem is cooperation between agents, and the principal is peripheral.

Denote the efficient vector of actions by e^*. An efficient contract, illustrated in figure 8.4a, is

$$w_i(q) = \begin{cases} b_i & \text{if } q \geq q(e^*), \\ 0 & \text{if } q < q(e^*), \end{cases} \quad \text{where } \sum_{i=1}^{n} b_i = q(e^*) \text{ and } b_i > v_i(e_i^*). \tag{8.9}$$

Contract (8.9) gives agent i the wage b_i if all agents pick the efficient effort, and nothing if any of them shirks (in which case the principal keeps the output). The teams model gives one reason to have a principal: he is the residual claimant who keeps the forfeited output. Without him, it is questionable whether the agents would carry out the threat to discard all the output if, say, output were 99 instead of the efficient 100. There is a problem of dynamic consistency or renegotiation similar to the problem in the Repossession Game earlier in this chapter. The agents would like to commit in advance to throw away output, but only because they never have to do so in equilibrium. If the modeller wishes to disallow discarding output, he imposes the **budget-balancing constraint** that the sum of the wages exactly equal the output, no more and no less. But budget balancing creates a problem for the team that is summarized in proposition 8.1. (The proof is simplest for differentiable contracts such as that in figure 8.4b but the intuition applies to nondifferentiable contracts too.)

Proposition 8.1   *If there is a budget-balancing constraint, no differentiable wage contract $w_i(q)$ generates an efficient Nash equilibrium.*

Agent i's problem is

$$\underset{e_i}{Maximize}\ w_i(q(e)) - v_i(e_i). \tag{8.10}$$

His first-order condition is

$$\left(\frac{dw_i}{dq}\right)\left(\frac{\partial q}{\partial e_i}\right) - \frac{dv_i}{de_i} = 0. \tag{8.11}$$

With budget balancing and a linear utility function, the Pareto optimum maximizes the sum of utilities (something not generally true), so the optimum solves

$$\text{Maximize}_{e_1, \dots, e_n} \ q(e) - \sum_{i=1}^{n} v_i(e_i) \tag{8.12}$$

The first-order condition is that the marginal dollar contribution to output equal the marginal disutility of effort:

$$\frac{\partial q}{\partial e_i} - \frac{dv_i}{de_i} = 0. \tag{8.13}$$

Equation (8.13) contradicts equation (8.11), the agent's first-order condition, because dw_i/dq is not equal to one. If it were, agent i would be the residual claimant and receive the entire marginal increase in output – but under budget balancing, not every agent can do that. Because each agent bears the entire burden of his marginal effort and only part of the benefit, the contract does not achieve the first-best. Without budget balancing, on the other hand, if the agent shirked a little he would gain the entire leisure benefit from shirking, but he would lose his entire wage under the optimal contract in equation (8.9).

Discontinuities in Public Good Payoffs

Ordinarily, there is a free rider problem if several players each pick a level of effort which increases the level of some public good whose benefits they share. Noncooperatively, they choose effort levels lower than if they could make binding promises. Mathematically, let identical risk-neutral players indexed by i choose effort levels e_i to produce amount $q(e_1, \dots, e_n)$ of the public good, where q is a continuous function. Player i's problem is

$$\text{Maximize}_{e_i} \ q(e_1, \dots, e_n) - e_i, \tag{8.14}$$

which has first-order condition

$$\frac{\partial q}{\partial e_i} - 1 = 0, \tag{8.15}$$

whereas the greater, first-best effort n-vector e^* is characterized by

$$\sum_{i=1}^{n} \frac{\partial q}{\partial e_i} - 1 = 0. \tag{8.16}$$

If the function q were discontinuous at e^* (e.g., $q = 0$ if $e_i < e_i^*$ and $q = e_i$ if $e_i \geq e_i^*$ for any i), the strategy profile e^* could be a Nash equilibrium. In the game of Teams, the same effect is at work. Although output is not discontinuous, contract (8.9) is constructed as if it were (as if $q=0$ if $e_i \neq e_i^*$ for any i), in order to obtain the same incentives.

The first-best can be achieved because the discontinuity at e^* makes every player the marginal, decisive player. If he shirks a little, output falls drastically and with certainty.

Either of the following two modifications restores the free rider problem and induces shirking:

1   Let q be a function not only of effort but of random noise – Nature moves after the players. Uncertainty makes the *expected* output a continuous function of effort.
2   Let players have incomplete information about the critical value – Nature moves before the players and chooses e^*. Incomplete information makes the estimated output a continuous function of effort.

The discontinuity phenomenon is common. Examples include:

1   Effort in teams (Holmstrom [1982], Rasmusen [1987])
2   Entry deterrence by an oligopoly (Bernheim [1984b], Waldman [1987])
3   Output in oligopolies with trigger strategies (Porter [1983a])
4   Patent races
5   Tendering shares in a takeover (Grossman & Hart [1980])
6   Preferences for levels of a public good

*8.7   The Multitask Agency Problem

Holmstrom & Milgrom (1991) point out an omission in the standard principal–agent model: often the principal wants the agent to split his time among several tasks, each with a separate output, rather than just working on one of them. If the principal uses one of the incentive contracts we have described in these chapters to incentivize just one of the tasks, this "high-powered incentive" can result in the agent completely neglecting his other tasks and leave the principal worse off than under a flat wage. We will see that in the next two models, in which the principal can observe the output from one of the agent's tasks (q_1) but not from the other (q_2).

Multitasking I: Two Tasks, No Leisure

PLAYERS
A principal and an agent.

THE ORDER OF PLAY
1   The principal offers the agent either an incentive contract of the form $w(q_1)$ or a monitoring contract that pays m under which he pays the agent a base wage of $\overline{m}$ plus m_1 if he observes him working on Task 1 and m_2 if he observes him working on Task 2 (the $\overline{m}$ base is superfluous notation in Multitasking I, but is used in Multitasking II).
2   The agent decides whether or not to accept the contract.
3   The agent picks efforts e_1 and e_2 for the two tasks such that $e_1 + e_2 = 1$, where 1 denotes the total time available.
4   Outputs are $q_1(e_1)$ and $q_2(e_2)$, where $dq_1/de_1 > 0$ and $dq_2/de_2 > 0$ but we do not require decreasing returns to effort.

PAYOFFS
If any agent rejects the contract, all payoffs equal zero. Otherwise,

$$\pi_{principal} = q_1 + \beta q_2 - m - w - C,$$
$$\pi_{agent} = m + w - e_1^2 - e_2^2,$$

(8.17)

where C, the cost of monitoring, is $\overline{C}$ if a monitoring contract is used and zero otherwise.

Let's start with the first best. This can be found by choosing e_1 and e_2 (subject to $e_1 + e_2 = 1$) and C to maximize the sum of the payoffs,

$$\pi_{principal} + \pi_{agent} = q_1(e_1) + \beta q_2(e_2) - C - e_1^2 - e_2^2. \tag{8.18}$$

In the first-best, $C = 0$ of course – no costly monitoring is needed. Substituting $e_2 = 1 - e_1$ and using the first-order condition for e_1 yields

$$C^* = 0 \quad e_1^* = \frac{1}{2} + \left(\frac{dq_1/de_1 - \beta(dq_2/de_2)}{4}\right) \quad e_2^* = \frac{1}{2} - \left(\frac{dq_1/de_1 - \beta(dq_2/de_2)}{4}\right). \tag{8.19}$$

Thus, which effort should be bigger depends on β (a measure of the relative value of Task 2) and the diminishing returns to effort in each task. If, for example, $\beta > 1$ so Task 2's output is more valuable and the functions $q_1(e_1)$ and $q_2(e_2)$ produce the same output for the same effort, then from (8.19) we can see that $e_1^* < e_2^*$, as one would expect.

Can an incentive contract achieve the first best? Let's define q_1^*, q_2^*, e_1^*, and e_2^* as the first-best levels of those variables and define the minimum wage payment that would induce the agent to accept a contract requiring the first-best effort as

$$w^* \equiv (e_1^*)^2 + (e_2^*)^2. \tag{8.20}$$

Next, let's think about what happens with the profit-maximizing flat-wage contract, which could be either the incentive contract $w(q_1) = w^*$ or the monitoring contract $\{w^*, w^*\}$. The agent's effort choice would then be to split his effort equally between the two tasks, so $e_1 = e_2 = 0.5$. To satisfy the participation constraint it would be necessary that $\pi_{agent} = w^* + w - e_1^2 - e_2^2 \geq 0$, so $\pi_{agent} = w^* - 0.25 - 0.25 = 0$ and $w^* = 0.5$. The principal would prefer to use an "incentive contract," rather than a monitoring contract, of course, if the wage is going to be the same regardless of what costly monitoring would discover.

What about a sharing-rule incentive contract, in which the wage rises with output (i.e., $dw/dq_1 > 0$)? The problem is not quite the principal's accustomed difficulty of inducing high effort as cheaply as possible without paying for effort whose marginal disutility exceeds the value of the extra output. That difficulty is still present, but in addition the principal must worry about an externality of sorts: the greater the agent's effort on Task 1, the less will be his effort on Task 2. Even if extra e_1 could be achieved for free, the principal might not want it – and, in fact, might be willing to pay to stop it.

Consider the simplest sharing-rule contract, the linear one with $dw/dq_1 = b$, so $w(q_1) = a + bq_1$. The agent will pick e_1 and e_2 to maximize

$$\pi_{agent} = a + bq_1(e_1) - e_1^2 - e_2^2, \tag{8.21}$$

subject to $e_1 + e_2 = 1$ (which allows us to rewrite the maximand in terms of just e_1, since $e_2 = 1 - e_1$). The first-order condition is

$$\frac{d\pi_{agent}}{de_1} = b\left(\frac{dq_1}{de_1}\right) - 2e_1^* - 2(1 - e_1^*)(-1) = 0, \tag{8.22}$$

so

$$e_1^* = \frac{1}{2} + \left(\frac{b}{4}\right)\left(\frac{dq_1}{de_1}\right). \tag{8.23}$$

If $e_1^* \geq 0.5$, the linear contract will work just fine. The contract parameters a and b can be chosen so that the linear-contract effort in equation (8.23) is the same as the first-best effort in equation (8.19), with a taking a value to extract all the surplus so the participation constraint is barely satisfied.

If $e_1^* < 0.5$, though, the linear contract cannot achieve the first best with a positive value for b. Even under a flat wage ($b = 0$), the agent will choose $e_1 = 0.5$, which is too high. If the principal rewards the agent for more of the observable output q_1, the principal will get too little of the unobservable output q_2. Instead, the contract must actually punish the agent for high output! It must have at least a slightly negative value for b, so as to defeat the agent's preferred allocation of effort evenly across the tasks.

One context for this is sales jobs, where it is easy for the firm to measure the orders a salesmen takes down from customers, but hard to observe how much good feeling he leaves behind, how much he helps other salesmen, or how much care he takes to obey laws against bribery and fraud. If the firm rewards orders alone, the salesman will maximize orders. If the salesman actually likes spending his time on the other efforts enough, this does not necessarily lead to inefficiency, but it could also happen that the unrewarded efforts are slighted more than they should be.

Chapter 7 compared three contracts: linear, threshold, and forcing contracts. The threshold contract will work as well or better than the linear contract in Multitasking I. It at least does not provide incentive to go above the threshold, which is positively bad in this model. The forcing contract is even better, because the principal positively dislikes having e_1 be too great. In chapter 7, the forcing contract's low wage for an output that was too high seemed unrealistic, and forcing contracts were used for simplicity rather than realism; here, it makes intuitive sense. Perhaps this is one way to look at the common fear that winning high ratings from students will hurt a professor's tenure chances because it indicates that he is not spending enough time on his research.

Thus, in equilibrium the principal chooses some contract that elicits the first-best effort e^*, such as the forcing contract,

$$
\begin{aligned}
w(q_1 = q_1^*) &= w^*, \\
w(q_1 \neq q_1^*) &= 0.
\end{aligned}
\tag{8.24}
$$

A monitoring contract, which would incur monitoring cost $\overline{C}$, is suboptimal, since an incentive contract can achieve the first-best anyway, but let's see how the optimal monitoring contract would work. Let us set $\overline{m} = 0$ in Multitasking I, since we can add the constant part of the wage to m_1 and m_2 anyway. The agent will choose his effort to maximize

$$
\begin{aligned}
\pi_{agent} &= e_1 m_1 + e_2 m_2 - e_1^2 - e_2^2, \\
&= e_1 m_1 + (1 - e_1) m_2 - e_1^2 - (1 - e_1)^2,
\end{aligned}
\tag{8.25}
$$

since with probability e_1 the monitoring finds him working on Task 1 and with probability e_2 it finds him on Task 2. Maximizing by choice of e_1 yields

$$
\frac{d\pi_{agent}}{de_1} = m_1 - m_2 - 2e_1 - 2(-1)(1 - e_1) = 0,
\tag{8.26}
$$

so if the principal wants the agent to pick the particular effort $e_1 = e_1^*$ that we found in equation (8.19) he should choose m_1^* and m_2^* so that

$$m_1^* = 4e_1^* + m_2^* - 2. \tag{8.27}$$

Note that if $e_1^* > e_2^*$, which means that $e_1^* > 0.5$, equation (8.27) tells us that $m_1^* > m_2^*$, just as we would expect.

We have one equation for the two unknowns of m_1^* and m_2^* in (8.27), so we need to add some information. Let us use the fact that if the participation constraint is satisfied exactly then we can set the agent's payoff from (8.25) equal to zero, which is a second equation for our two unknowns. After going through the algebra to solve (8.27) together with the binding participation constraint, we get

$$m_1^* = 4e_1^* - 2(e_1^*)^2 - 1 \tag{8.28}$$

from which we can find, using (8.27),

$$
\begin{aligned}
m_2^* &= [4e_1^* - 2(e_1^*)^2 - 1] + 2 - 4e_1^*, \\
&= 1 - 2(e_1^*)^2.
\end{aligned} \tag{8.29}
$$

These have the expected property that $dm_1^*/de_1^* = -4e_1^* + 4 > 0$ and $dm_2^*/de_1^* = -4e_1^* < 0$.

In this risk-neutral model, occasional errorless monitoring is just as good as the principal being able to observe effort 100 percent of the time. Indeed, if we changed the model description to say that the principal could at a cost of $\overline{C}$ observe the levels of e_1 and e_2 rather than just a snapshot of what the agent is doing at some random time, the mathematics could stay exactly the same. Risk aversion of the principal or agent would complicate things, of course, since then the randomness of the principal's monitoring would create risk that was costly. What about if the agent's time was not split between just the two tasks, but between the two tasks and shirking? That will be our next model.

Multitasking II: Two Tasks Plus Leisure

This game is the same as Multitasking I, except that now the agent's effort budget constraint is not $e_1 + e_2 = 1$, but $e_1 + e_2 \leq 1$. The amount $(1 - e_1 - e_2)$ represents leisure, whose value we set equal to zero in the agent's utility function (compared to effort, which enters in negatively and with increasing marginal disutility). This is not the typical use of leisure in an economic model: here leisure represents not time off the job, but time on the job (a total timespan of 1) spent shirking rather than working.

Again let us begin with the first-best. This can be found by choosing e_1 and e_2 and C to maximize the sum of the payoffs:

$$q_1(e_1) + \beta q_2(e_2) - C - e_1^2 - e_2^2, \tag{8.30}$$

subject to $e_1 + e_2 \leq 1$, the only change in the optimization problem from Multitasking I.

We now cannot use the trick of substituting for e_2 using the constraint $e_2 = 1 - e_1$, since it might happen that the effort budget constraint is not binding at the optimum. Solving the two first-order conditions for e_1 and e_2 for those two unknowns is straightforward but messy, so we will not do it here. We will just represent the solutions by e_1^*, e_2^*, q_1^*, and q_2^*

and the payment necessary to give the agent a payoff of zero by w^*, just as in Multitasking I, with the understanding that the values of those solutions will be the same if it is efficient for the agent to have zero leisure and smaller otherwise.

It might happen that $e_1^* + e_2^* = 1$, as in Multitasking I, so that the first-best effort levels are the same as in that game. Positive leisure for the agent in the first-best, i.e., the effort budget constraint being nonbinding, is a realistic case. It means that paying the agent enough to work on the two tasks every minute of the day is inefficient. Instead, it might be profit-maximizing to give the agent a coffee break, or time off for lunch, or permission to talk to his wife if she telephones.

Next, let's think about a flat-wage contract. In Multitasking I, a flat wage led to $e_1 = e_2 = 0.5$. In Multitasking II, it would lead to $e_1 = e_2 = 0$, quite a different result. Now the agent has the option of leisure, which he prefers to either task. Even if the first-best effort levels are identical in Multitasking I and II, with zero leisure, we cannot expect the second-best contracts to be the same. A low-powered incentive contract is disastrous, because pulling the agent away from high effort on Task 1 does not leave him working harder on Task 2.

A high-powered sharing-rule incentive contract in which the wage rises with output performs much better, even though we cannot reach the first-best as we did in Multitasking I. Since the flat wage leads to $e_2 = 0$ anyway, adding incentives for the agent to increase e_1 cannot do any harm. Effort on Task 2 will remain zero – so the first-best is unreachable – but a suitable sharing rule can lead to $e_1 = e_1^*$.

The combination $(e_1 = e_1^*, e_2 = 0)$ is the second-best incentive-contract solution in Multitasking II, since at e_1^* the marginal disutility of effort equals the marginal utility of the marginal product of effort. That conclusion might be misleading, though. We have assumed that the disutility of effort on Task I is separable from the disutility of effort on Task II. That is why even if the agent is devoting no effort to Task II he should not work any harder on Task I. More realistically, the disutility of effort would be some nonseparable function $f(e_1, e_2)$ such that the efforts are "substitute bads" and $\partial^2 f / (\partial e_1 \partial e_2) > 0$. In that case, in the second-best the principal, unable to induce e_2 to be positive, would push e_1 above the first-best level, since the agent's marginal disutility of e_1 would be less at $(e_1^*, 0)$ than at (e_1^*, e_2^*).

Thus, one lesson of Multitasking II is that if an agent has a strong temptation to spend his time on tasks which have no benefit for the principal, the situation is much closer to the conventional agency models than to Multitasking I. The agent does not substitute between the task with easy-to-measure output and the task with hard-to-measure output, but between each task and leisure. The best the principal can do may be to ignore the multitasking feature of the problem and just get the incentives right for the task whose output he can measure.

Things are not quite so bleak, though. The first-best effort levels *can* be attained, but it requires a monitoring contract instead of an incentive contract. Monitoring is costly, so this is not quite the first best, and it might not even be superior to the second-best incentive contract if the monitoring cost $\overline{C}$ were too big, but monitoring can induce any level of e_2 the principal desires.

The agent will choose his effort to maximize

$$\pi_{agent} = \overline{m} + e_1 m_1 + e_2 m_2 - e_1^2 - e_2^2, \tag{8.31}$$

subject to $e_1 + e_2 \leq 1$. Unlike in Multitasking I, the base wage $\overline{m}$ matters, since it may happen that the principal monitors the agent and finds him working on neither Task 1 nor Task 2. The base wage may even be negative, which can be interpreted as a bond for good effort posted by the agent or as a fee he pays for the privilege of filling the job and possibly earning m_1 or m_2.

The principal will pick m_1 and m_2 to induce the agent to choose e_1^* and e_2^*, so he will pick them to solve the first-order conditions of the agent's problem for e_1^* and e_2^*:

$$\frac{\partial \pi_{agent}}{\partial e_1} = m_1 - 2e_1 = 0,$$
$$\frac{\partial \pi_{agent}}{\partial e_2} = m_2 - 2e_2 = 0. \tag{8.32}$$

These can be solved to yield $m_1 = e_1^*/2$ and $m_2 = e_2^*/2$. We still need to determine the base wage, $\overline{m}$. Substituting into the participation constraint, which will be binding, and recalling that we defined the agent's reservation expected wage as $w^* = e_1^2 + e_2^2$,

$$\pi_{agent} = \overline{m} + e_1 m_1 + e_2 m_2 - e_1^2 - e_2^2 = 0,$$
$$= \overline{m} + e_1^* \left(\frac{e_1^*}{2}\right) + e_2^* \left(\frac{e_2^*}{2}\right) - w^* = 0,$$
$$= \overline{m} + \left(\frac{1}{2}\right) w^* - w^* = 0, \tag{8.33}$$

so $\overline{m} = w^*/2$.

The base wage is thus positive; even if the principal finds the agent shirking when he monitors, he will pay him more than zero. That is intuitive when $e_1^* + e_2^* < 1$, because then the principal wants the agent to take some leisure in equilibrium, rather than have to pay him more for a leisureless job. It is more surprising that the base wage is positive when $e_1^* + e_2^* = 1$; that is, when efficiency requires zero leisure. Why pay the agent anything at all for inefficient behavior?

The answer is that the base wage is important only for inducing the agent to take the job and has no influence whatsoever on the agent's choice of effort. Increasing the base wage does not make the agent more likely to take leisure, because he gets the base wage regardless of how much time he spends on each activity. If $e_1^* + e_2^* = 1$, then the agent chooses zero leisure despite knowing that he would still receive his base pay for doing nothing, because the incentive of m_1 and m_2 is great enough that he does not want to waste any opportunity to get that incentive pay.

Thus, we end our two chapters on moral hazard on a happy note: the agent whose work is so valuable and whose pay is so good that he willingly works just as the principal wants him to.

Notes

N8.1 Efficiency wages

- Which is the better, the carrot or the stick? I will mention two other considerations besides the bankruptcy constraint. First, if the agent is risk-averse, equal dollar punishments and rewards lead to the punishment disutility being greater than the reward utility. Second, regression to the mean can easily lead a principal to think sticks work better than carrots in practice. Suppose a teacher assigns equal utility rewards and punishments to a student depending on his performance on tests, and that the student's effort is, in fact, constant. If the student is lucky on a test, he will do well and be rewarded, but will probably do worse on the next test. If the student is unlucky, he will be punished, and will do better on the next test. The naive teacher will think that rewards hurt performance and punishments help it. See Robyn Dawes's 1988 book, *Rational Choice in an Uncertain World* (especially pp. 84–7) for a good exposition of this and other pitfalls of reasoning. Kahneman, Slovic, & Tversky (1982) cover similar material.

- For surveys of the efficiency wage literature, see the article by L. Katz (1986), the book of articles edited by Akerlof & Yellen (1986), and the book-length survey by Weiss (1990).
- The efficiency wage idea is essentially the same idea as in the Klein & Leffler (1981) model of product quality formalized in section 5.3. If no punishment is available for player who is tempted to misbehave, a punishment can be created by giving him something to take away. This "something" can be a high-paying job or a loyal customer. It is also similar to the idea of **co-opting** opponents familiar in politics and university administration. To tame the radical student association, give them an office of their own which can be taken away if they seize the dean's office. Rasmusen (1988b) shows yet another context: when depositors do not know which investments are risky and which are safe, mutual bank managers can be highly paid to deter them from making risky investments that might cost them their jobs.
- Adverse selection can also drive an efficiency wage model. We will see in chapter 9 that a customer might be willing to pay a high price to attract sellers of high-quality cars when he cannot detect quality directly.

N8.2   Tournaments

- An article which stimulated much interest in tournaments is Lazear & Rosen (1981), which discusses in detail the importance of risk aversion and adverse selection. Antle & Smith (1986) is an empirical study of tournaments in managers' compensation. Rosen (1986) is a theoretical model of a labor tournament in which the prize is promotion.
- One example of a tournament is the two-year, three-man contest for the new chairman of Citicorp. The company named three candidates as vice-chairmen: the head of consumer banking, the head of corporate banking, and the legal counsel. Earnings reports were even split into three components, two of which were the corporate and consumer banking (the third was the "investment" bank, irrelevant to the tournament). See "What Made Reed Wriston's Choice at Citicorp," *Business Week*, July 2, 1984, p. 25.
- General Motors has tried a tournament among its production workers. During a depressed year, management credibly threatened to close down the auto plant with the lowest productivity. Reportedly, this did raise productivity. Such a tournament is interesting because it helps explain why a firm's supply curve could be upward sloping even if all its plants are identical, and why it might hold excess capacity. Should information on a plant's current performance have been released to other plants? See "Unions Say Auto Firms Use Interplant Rivalry to Raise Work Quotas," *Wall Street Journal*, November 8, 1983, p. 1.
- Under adverse selection, tournaments must be used differently than under moral hazard because agents cannot control their effort. Instead, tournaments are used to deter agents from accepting contracts in which they must compete for a prize with other agents of higher ability.
- Interfirm management tournaments run into difficulties when shareholders want managers to cooperate in some arenas. If managers collude in setting prices, for example, they can also collude to make life easier for each other.

- Suppose a firm conducts a tournament in which the best-performing of its vice- presidents becomes the next president. Should the firm fire the most talented vice-president before it starts the tournament? The answer is not obvious. Maybe in the tournament's equilibrium, Mr Talent works less hard because of his initial advantage, so that all of the vice-presidents retain the incentive to work hard.

- A tournament can reward the winner, or shoot the loser. Which is better? Nalebuff & Stiglitz (1983) say to shoot the loser, and Rasmusen (1987) finds a similar result for teams, but for a different reason. Nalebuff & Stiglitz's result depends on uncertainty and a large number of agents in the tournament, while Rasmusen's depends on risk aversion. If a utility function is concave because the agent is risk-averse, the agent is hurt more by losing a given sum than he would benefit by gaining it. Hence, for incentive purposes the carrot is inferior to the stick, a result unfortunate for efficiency since penalties are often bounded by bankruptcy or legal constraints.

- Using a tournament, the equilibrium effort might be greater in a second-best contract than in the first-best, even though the second-best is contrived to get around the problem of inducing sufficient effort. An agent-by-agent contract might lead to zero effort, for example, but a tournament, while better, might overshoot and lead to inefficiently high effort. Also, a pure tournament, in which the prizes are distributed solely according to the ordinal ranking of output by the agents, is often inferior to a tournament in which an agent must achieve a significant margin of superiority over his fellows in order to win (Nalebuff & Stiglitz [1983]). Companies using sales tournaments sometimes have prizes for record yearly sales besides ordinary prizes, and some long distance athletic races have nonordinal prizes to avoid dull events in which the best racers run "tactical races." Ehrenberg & Bognanno (1990) find that professional golfers' scores are not as good if the prize money is lower, especially for scores in later rounds of the tournament when they are tired. Duggan & Levitt (2002) find evidence that Japanese sumo wrestlers purposely lose if they are above the threshold number of victories to maintain their status but their opponent badly needs a victory.

- Organizational slack of the kind described in the Farrell model has important practical implications. In dealing with bureaucrats, one must keep in mind that they are usually less concerned with the organization's prosperity than with their own. In complaining about bureaucratic ineptitude, it may be much more useful to name particular bureaucrats and send them copies of the complaint than to stick to the issues at hand. Private firms, at least, are well aware that customers help monitor agents.

- The idea that an uninformed player can design a scheme to extract information from two or more informed players by having them make independent reports and punishing them for discrepancies has other applications. The tournament in the Farrell model is similar to the cross-checking that will be discussed in chapter 10 on mechanism design, where an uninformed court punishes two players if they give different reports of the same private information.

N8.3   Institutions and agency problems

- Even if a product's quality need not meet government standards, the seller may wish to bind himself to them voluntarily. Stroh's *Erlanger* beer proudly announced on every bottle that although it is American, "Erlanger is a special beer brewed to meet the stringent requirements of Reinheitsgebot, a German brewing purity law established in 1516." Inspection of household electrical appliances by an independent lab to get the "U_L" listing is a similarly voluntary adherence to standards.

- The stock price is a way of using outside analysts to monitor an executive's performance. When General Motors bought EDS, they created a special class of stock, GM-E, which varied with EDS performance and could be used to monitor it.

*N8.6   Joint production by many agents: the Holmstrom Teams model

- **Team theory**, as developed by Marschak & Radner (1972) is an older mathematical approach to organization. In the old usage of "team" (different from the current, Holmstrom [1982] usage), several agents who have different information but cannot communicate it must pick decision rules. The payoff is the same for each agent, and their problem is coordination, not motivation.

- The efficient contract (8.9) supports the efficient Nash equilibrium, but it also supports a continuum of inefficient Nash equilibria. Suppose that in the efficient equilibrium all workers work equally hard. Another Nash equilibrium is for one worker to do no work and the others to work inefficiently hard to make up for him.

- **A teams' contract with hidden knowledge:** In the 1920s, National City Co. assigned 20 percent of profits to compensate management as a group. A management committee decided how to share it, after each officer submitted an unsigned ballot suggesting the share of the fund that Chairman Mitchell should have, and a signed ballot giving his estimate of the worth of each of the other eligible officers, himself excluded (Galbraith [1954], p. 157).

- **A first-best, budget-balancing contract when agents are risk-averse:** Proposition 8.1 can be shown to hold for any contract, not just for differentiable sharing rules, but it does depend on risk-neutrality and separability of the utility function. Consider the following contract from Rasmusen (1987):

$$
w_i = \begin{cases} b_i & \text{if } q \geq q(e^*). \\ \begin{cases} 0 & \text{with probability } (n-1)/n \\ q & \text{with probability } 1/n \end{cases} & \text{if } q < q(e^*) \end{cases} \tag{8.34}
$$

  If the worker shirks, he enters a lottery. If his risk aversion is strong enough, he prefers the riskless return b_i, so he does not shirk. If agents' wealth is unlimited, then for any positive risk aversion we could construct such a contract, by making the losers in the lottery accept negative pay.

- A teams contract such as (8.9) is not a tournament. Only absolute performance matters, even though the level of absolute performance depends on what all the players do.

- **The budget-balancing constraint:** The legal doctrine of "consideration" makes it difficult to make binding, Pareto-suboptimal promises. An agreement is not a legal contract unless it is more than a promise: both parties have to receive something valuable for the courts to enforce the agreement.

- Adverse selection can be incorporated into a teams model. A team of workers who may differ in ability produce a joint output, and the principal tries to ensure that only high-ability workers join the team. (See Rasmusen & Zenger [1990].

Problems

8.1:   Monitoring with error (easy)

An agent has a utility function $U = \sqrt{w} - \alpha e$, where $\alpha = 1$ and e is either 0 or 5. His reservation utility level is $\overline{U} = 9$, and his output is 100 with low effort and 250 with high effort. Principals are risk-neutral and scarce, and agents compete to work for them. The principal cannot condition the wage on effort or output, but he can, if he wishes, spend five minutes of his time, worth 10 dollars, to drop in and watch the agent. If he does that, he observes the agent *Daydreaming* or *Working*, with probabilities that differ depending on the agent's effort. He can condition the wage on those two things, so the contract will be $\{\underline{w}, \overline{w}\}$. The probabilities are given by table 8.2.

Table 8.2 Monitoring with error

Effort	Probability of	
	Daydreaming	Working
Low ($e = 0$)	0.6	0.4
High ($e = 5$)	0.1	0.9

(a) What are profits in the absence of monitoring, if the agent is paid enough to make him willing to work for the principal?
(b) Show that high effort is efficient under full information.
(c) If $\alpha = 1.2$, is high effort still efficient under full information?
(d) Under asymmetric information, with $\alpha = 1$, what are the participation and incentive compatibility constraints?
(e) Under asymmetric information, with $\alpha = 1$, what is the optimal contract?

8.2: Monitoring with error: second offenses (medium) (see Rubinstein [1979])

Individuals who are risk-neutral must decide whether to commit zero, one, or two robberies. The cost to society of robbery is 10, and the benefit to the robber is 5. No robber is ever convicted and jailed, but the police beat up any suspected robber they find. They beat up innocent people mistakenly sometimes, as shown by table 8.3, which shows the probabilities of zero or more beatings for someone who commits zero, one, or two robberies.

Table 8.3 Crime

Robberies	Beatings		
	0	1	2
0	0.81	0.18	0.01
1	0.60	0.34	0.06
2	0.49	0.42	0.09

(a) How big should p^*, the disutility of a beating, be made to deter crime completely while inflicting a minimum of punishment on the innocent?
(b) In equilibrium, what percentage of beatings are of innocent people? What is the payoff of an innocent man?
(c) Now consider a more flexible policy, which inflicts heavier beatings on repeat offenders. If such flexibility is possible, what are the optimal severities for first- and second-time offenders? (call these p_1 and p_2). What is the expected utility of an innocent person under this policy?
(d) Suppose that the probabilities are as given in table 8.4. What is an optimal policy for first and second offenders?

Table 8.4   More crime

Robberies	Beatings		
	0	1	2
0	0.9	0.1	0
1	0.6	0.3	0.1
2	0.5	0.3	0.2

8.3:   Bankruptcy constraints (hard)

A risk-neutral principal hires an agent with utility function $U = w - e$ and reservation utility $\overline{U} = 5$. Effort is either 0 or 10. There is a bankruptcy constraint: $w \geq 0$. Output is given by table 8.5.

Table 8.5   Bankruptcy

Effort	Probability of output of		
	0	400	Total
Low ($e = 0$)	0.5	0.5	1
High ($e = 10$)	0.2	0.8	1

(a)   What would be the agent's effort choice and utility if he owned the firm?
(b)   If agents are scarce and principals compete for them what will be the agent's contract under full information? His utility?
(c)   If principals are scarce and agents compete to work for them, what will the contract be under full information? What will the agent's utility be?
(d)   If principals are scarce and agents compete to work for them, what will the contract be when the principal cannot observe effort? What will the payoffs be for each player?
(e)   Suppose there is no bankruptcy constraint. If principals are the scarce factor and agents compete to work for them, what will the contract be when the principal cannot observe effort? What will the payoffs be for principal and agent?

8.4:   Teams (medium)

A team of two workers produces and sells widgets for the principal. Each worker chooses high or low effort. An agent's utility is $U = w - 20$ if his effort is high, and $U = w$ if it is low, with a reservation utility of $\overline{U} = 0$. Nature chooses business conditions to be excellent, good, or bad, with probabilities θ_1, θ_2, and θ_3. The principal observes output but not business conditions, as shown in table 8.6.

(a)   Suppose $\theta_1 = \theta_2 = \theta_3$. Why is $\{(w(100) = 30, w(not\ 100) = 0), (High, High)\}$ not an equilibrium?
(b)   Suppose $\theta_1 = \theta_2 = \theta_3$. Is it optimal to induce high effort? What is an optimal contract with nonnegative wages?
(c)   Suppose $\theta_1 = 0.5, \theta_2 = 0.5$, and $\theta_3 = 0$. Is it optimal to induce high effort? What is an optimal contract (possibly with negative wages)?
(d)   Should the principal stop the agents from talking to each other?

Table 8.6   Team output

	Excellent (θ_1)	Good (θ_2)	Bad (θ_3)
High, High	100	100	60
High, Low	100	50	20
Low, Low	50	20	0

8.5:   Efficiency wages and risk aversion (medium) (see Rasmusen [1992c])

In each of two periods of work, a worker decides whether to steal amount v, and is detected with probability α and suffers legal penalty p if he, in fact, did steal. A worker who is caught stealing can also be fired, after which he earns the reservation wage w_0. If the worker does not steal, his utility in the period is $U(w)$; if he steals, it is $U(w+v) - \alpha p$, where $U(w_0+v) - \alpha p > U(w_0)$. The worker's marginal utility of income is diminishing: $U' > 0$, $U'' < 0$, and $lim_{x\to\infty} U'(x) = 0$. There is no discounting. The firm definitely wants to deter stealing in each period, if at all possible.

(a)   Show that the firm can indeed deter theft, even in the second period, and, in fact, do so with a second-period wage w_2^* that is higher than the reservation wage w_0.
(b)   Show that the equilibrium second-period wage w_2^* is higher than the first- period wage w_1^*.

8.6:   The Game Wizard (medium)

A high-tech firm is trying to develop the game Wizard 1.0. It will have revenues of $200,000 if it succeeds, and $0 if it fails. Success depends on the programmer. If he exerts high effort, the probability of success is 0.8. If he exerts low effort, it is 0.6. The programmer requires wages of at least $50,000 if he can exert low effort, but $70,000 if he must exert high effort. (Let's just use payoffs in thousands of dollars, so 70,000 dollars will be written as 70.)

(a)   Prove that high effort is first-best efficient.
(b)   Explain why high effort would be inefficient if the probability of success when effort is low were 0.75.
(c)   Let the probability of success with low effort go back to 0.6 for the remainder of the problem. If you cannot monitor the programmer and cannot pay him a wage contingent on success, what should you do?
(d)   Now suppose you can make the wage contingent on success. Let the wage be S if Wizard is successful, and F if it fails. S and F will have to satisfy two conditions: a participation constraint and an incentive compatibility constraint. What are they?
(e)   What is a contract that will achieve the first best?
(f)   What is the optimal contract if you cannot pay a programmer a negative wage?

8.7:   Machinery (medium)

Mr Smith is thinking of buying a custom-designed machine from either Mr Jones or Mr Brown. This machine costs 5,000 dollars to build, and it is useless to anyone but Smith. It is common knowledge that with 90 percent probability the machine will be worth 10,000 dollars to Smith at the time of delivery, one year from today, and with 10 percent probability it will only be worth 2,000 dollars. Smith owns assets of 1,000 dollars. At the time of contracting, Jones and Brown believe there is a

20 percent chance that Smith is actually acting as an "undisclosed agent" for Anderson, who has assets of 50,000 dollars.

Find the price be under the following two legal regimes: (1) An undisclosed principal is not responsible for the debts of his agent; and (2) even an undisclosed principal is responsible for the debts of his agent. Also, explain (as part [3]) which rule a moral hazard model like this would tend to support.

Lobbying Teams: A Classroom Game for Chapter 8

Some of you will be manufacturing firms and some agricultural firms. Each firm will consist of two people.

The president of the United States is deciding between two policies. Free Trade will yield $10 million in benefit to each agricultural firm. Protectionism will yield $10 million in benefit to each manufacturing firm.

In each year, each firm will write down its favored policy and its lobbying expenditure, amount X, on a notecard and hand it in.

Whichever policy gets the most lobbying expenditure wins. If your favored policy wins, your payoff is $10 - X$. If it loses, your payoff is $-X$.

Each round the rules will variously allow communication and agreements of different kinds.

Chapter 9
adverse selection

9.1   Introduction: Production Game VI

In chapter 7, games of asymmetric information were divided between games with moral hazard, in which agents are identical, and games with adverse selection, in which agents differ. In moral hazard with hidden knowledge and adverse selection, the principal tries to sort out agents of different types. In moral hazard with hidden knowledge, the emphasis is on the agent's action rather than his choice of contract because agents accept contracts before acquiring information. Under adverse selection, the agent has private information about his type or the state of the world before he agrees to a contract, which means that the emphasis is on which contract he will accept.

For comparison with moral hazard, let us consider still another version of the Production Game of chapters 7 and 8.

Production Game VI: Adverse Selection

PLAYERS
The principal and the agent.

THE ORDER OF PLAY
0   Nature chooses the agent's ability a, observed by the agent but not by the principal, according to distribution $F(a)$.
1   The principal offers the agent one or more wage contracts $w_1(q), w_2(q), \ldots$.
2   The agent accepts one contract or rejects them all.
3   Nature chooses a value for the state of the world, θ, according to distribution $G(\theta)$. Output is then $q = q(a, \theta)$.

PAYOFFS
If the agent rejects all contracts, then $\pi_{agent} = \overline{U}(a)$, which might or might not vary with his type, a; and $\pi_{principal} = 0$.
Otherwise, $\pi_{agent} = U(w, a)$ and $\pi_{principal} = V(q - w)$.

Under adverse selection, it is not the worker's effort, but his ability, that is noncontractible. Without uncertainty (move [3]), the principal would provide a single contract specifying high wages for high output and low wages for low output, but either high or low output might be observed in equilibrium, unlike under moral hazard – if both types of agents accepted the contract. Also, under adverse selection, unlike moral hazard, offering multiple contracts can be an improvement over offering a single contract. The principal might, for example, provide a flat-wage contract for low-ability agents and an incentive contract for high-ability agents.

Production Game VIa puts specific functional forms into the game to illustrate how to find an equilibrium.

Production Game VIa: Adverse Selection with Particular Parameters

PLAYERS
The principal and the agent.

THE ORDER OF PLAY
0   Nature chooses the agent's ability a, unobserved by the principal, according to distribution $F(a)$, which puts probability 0.9 on low ability, $a = 0$, and probability 0.1 on high ability, $a = 10$.
1   The principal offers the agent one or more wage contracts
    $W_1 = (w_1(q = 0), w_1(q = 10)), W_2 = (w_2(q = 0), w_2(q = 10)) \ldots$.
2   The agent accepts one contract or rejects them all.
3   Nature chooses a value for the state of the world, θ, according to distribution $G(\theta)$, which puts equal weight on 0 and 10. Output is then $q = Min(a + \theta, 10)$.

PAYOFFS
If the agent rejects all contracts, then depending on his type his reservation payoff is either $\overline{U}_{Low} = 3$ or $\overline{U}_{High} = 2$ and the principal's payoff is $\pi_{principal} = 0$.
Otherwise, $U_{agent} = w$ and $V_{principal} = q - w$.

Thus, in Production Game VIa, output is 0 or 10 for the low-ability type of agent, depending on the state of the world, but always 10 for the high-ability agent. The agent types also differ in their reservation payoffs: the low-ability agent would work for an expected wage of 3, but the high-ability agents would require just 2. More realistically the high-ability agent would have a higher reservation wage (his ability might be recognizeable in some alternative job), but I have chosen $\overline{U}_{High} = 2$ to illustrate an interesting feature of the equilibrium.

A separating equilibrium is

Principal: Offer $W_1 = \{w_1(q = 0) = 3, w_1(q = 10) = 3\}$,
$W_2 = \{w_2(q = 0) = 0, w_2(q = 10) = 3\}$.

Low agent: Accept W_1.

High agent: Accept W_2.

As usual, this is a weak equilibrium. Both Low and High agents are indifferent about whether they accept or reject their contract. The equilibrium indifference of the agents arises from the open-set problem; if the principal were to specify a wage of 3.01 for W_2, for example, the high-ability agent would no longer be indifferent about accepting it instead of W_1.

Let us go through how I came up with the equilibrium contracts above. First, what action does the principal desire from each type of agent? The agents do not choose effort, but they do choose whether or not to work for the principal, and which contract to accept. The low-ability agent's expected output is $0.5(0) + 0.5(10) = 5$, compared to a reservation payoff of 3, so the principal will want to hire the low-ability agent if he can do it at an expected wage of 5 or less. The high-ability agent's expected output is $0.5(10) + 0.5(10) = 10$, compared to a reservation payoff of 2, so the principal will want to hire the high-ability agent if he can do it at an expected wage of 10 or less.

In hidden-action models, the principal tries to construct a contract which will induce the agent to take the single appropriate action. In hidden-knowledge models, the principal tries to make different actions attractive to different types of agent, so the agent's choice depends on the hidden information. The principal's problem, as in Production Game V with its moral hazard and hidden actions, is to maximize his profit subject to

1 **Incentive compatibility** (the agent picks the desired contract and actions).
2 **Participation** (the agent prefers the contract to his reservation utility).

In a model with hidden knowledge, the incentive compatibility constraint is customarily called the **self-selection constraint**, because it induces the different types of agents to pick different contracts. A big difference from moral hazard is that in a separating equilibrium there will be an entire set of self-selection constraints, one for each type of agent, since the appropriate contract depends on the hidden information. A second big difference is that the incentive compatibility constraint could vanish, instead of multiplying. The principal might decide to give up on separating the types of agent, in which case all he must do is make sure they all participate.

Here, the participation constraints are, letting $\pi_i(W_j)$ denote the expected payoff an agent of type i gets from contract j,

$$\pi_L(W_1) \geq \overline{U}_{Low}; \quad 0.5w_1(0) + 0.5w_1(10) \geq 3,$$
$$\pi_H(W_2) \geq \overline{U}_{High}; \quad 0.5w_2(10) + 0.5w_2(10) \geq 2. \tag{9.1}$$

Clearly the contracts in our conjectured equilibrium, $W_1 = (3, 3)$ and $W_2 = (0, 3)$, satisfy the participation constraints. In the equilibrium, the low- and the high-output wages both matter to the low-ability agent, but only the high-output wage matters to the high-ability agent. Both agents, however, end up earning a wage of 3 in each state of the world, the only difference being that contract W_2 would be a very risky contract for the low-ability agent despite being riskless for the high-ability agent. The principal would like to make W_1 risk-free, with the same wage in each state of the world.

In our separating equilibrium, the participation constraint is binding for the "bad" type but not for the "good" type, who would accept a wage as low as 2 if nothing better were available. This is typical of adverse selection models (if there are more than two types it is the participation constraint of the worst type that is binding, and no other). The principal makes the bad type's contract unattractive for two reasons. First, if he pays less, he keeps more. Second, when the bad type's contract is less attractive, the good type can be more cheaply lured away to a different contract. The principal allows the good type to earn more than his reservation payoff, on the other hand, because the good type always has the option of lying about his type and choosing the bad type's contract, and the good type, with his greater skill, could earn a positive payoff from the bad type's contract. Thus, the principal can never extract all the gains from trade from the good type unless he gives up on making either of his contracts acceptable to the bad type.

Another typical feature of this equilibrium is that the low-ability agent's contract not only drives him down to his participation constraint, but is riskless. An alternative would be to offer the low-ability agent a contract of the form $W_1' = (w_l, w_h)$, where it still satisfies the participation constraint because $0.5U(w_l) + 0.5U(w_h) \geq 3$. That is easy enough to do in Production Game VIa, because the agents are risk-neutral, and when $U(w) = w$, the low-ability agent would be as happy with $W_1' = (0, 6)$ as with $W_1 = (3, 3)$. But W_1' would create a big problem for self-selection, because the high-ability agent would get an expected payoff of 6 from it, since his output is always high. Also, if the agents were risk-averse, the risky contract would have to have a higher expected wage than W_1, to make up for the risk, and thus would be more expensive for the principal.

Next, look at the self-selection constraints, which are

$$\pi_L(W_1) \geq \pi_L(W_2); \quad 0.5w_1(0) + 0.5w_1(10) \geq 0.5w_2(0) + 0.5w_2(10),$$

$$\pi_H(W_2) \geq \pi_H(W_1); \quad 0.5w_2(10) + 0.5w_2(10) \geq 0.5w_1(10) + 0.5w_1(10). \tag{9.2}$$

The first inequality in (9.2) says that the contract W_2 has to have a low enough expected return for the low-ability agent to deter him from accepting it. The second inequality says that the wage contract W_1 must be less attractive than W_2 to the high-ability agent. The conjectured equilibrium contracts $W_1 = (3, 3)$ and $W_2 = (0, 3)$ do this, as can be seen by substituting their values into the constraints:

$$\pi_L(W_1) \geq \pi_L(W_2); \quad 0.5(3) + 0.5(3) \geq 0.5(0) + 0.5(3)$$

$$\pi_H(W_2) \geq \pi_H(W_1); \quad 0.5(3) + 0.5(3) \geq 0.5(3) + 0.5(3). \tag{9.3}$$

The self-selection constraint is binding for the good type but not for the bad type. This, too, is typical of adverse selection models. The principal wants the good type to reveal his type so he makes the appropriate contract as attractive to the good type as the bad type's contract. It does not have to be *more* attractive though (here notice the open-set problem), so the principal will minimize his salary expenditures and choose two contracts equally attractive to the good type. In so doing, the principal will have chosen a contract for the good type that is strictly worse for the bad type, who cannot achieve a high output so easily.

It is to show how the participation constraint does not have to be binding for the good type that I assumed $\overline{U}_{High} = 2$ for Production Game VIa. If I had assumed $\overline{U}_{High} = 3$, then we would still have $W_2 = (0, 3)$, but the fact that the "3" came from the self-selection constraint would be obscured. And although it is typical that the good agent's participation constraint is nonbinding and his incentive compatibility constraint is not, it is by no means necessary. If I had assumed $\overline{U}_{High} = 4$, then we would need $W_2 = (0,4)$ to satisfy the participation constraint as cheaply as possible, so it would be binding, and then the self-selection constraint would not be binding. Despite all this, modellers most often expect to find the bad type's participation constraint and the good type's self-selection constraint binding in a two-type model, and the worst agent's participation constraint and all other agents' self-selection constraints in a multitype model.

Once the self-selection and participation constraints are satisfied, weakly or strictly, the agents will not deviate from their equilibrium actions. All that remains to be checked is whether the principal could increase his payoff. He cannot, because he makes a profit from either contract, and having driven the low-ability agent down to his reservation payoff and the high-ability agent down to the minimum payoff needed to achieve separation, he cannot further reduce their pay.

Competition and Pooling

As with hidden actions, if principals compete in offering contracts under hidden information, a **competition constraint** would be added: the equilibrium contract must be as attractive as possible to the agent, since otherwise another principal could profitably lure him away. An equilibrium may also need to satisfy a part of the competition constraint not found in hidden actions models: either a **nonpooling constraint** or a **nonseparating constraint**. If one of several competing principals wishes to construct a pair of separating contracts C_1 and C_2, he must construct it so that not only do agents choose C_1 and C_2 depending on the state of the world (to satisfy incentive compatibility), but also they prefer (C_1, C_2) to a pooling contract C_3 (to satisfy nonpooling). We only have one principal in Production Game VI, though, so competition constraints are irrelevant.

Although it is true that the participation constraints must be satisfied for agents who accept the contracts, it is not always the case that they accept different contracts in equilibrium, and if they do not, they do not need to satisfy self-selection constraints.

If all types of agents choose the same strategy in all states, the equilibrium is **pooling**. *Otherwise, it is* **separating**.

The distinction between pooling and separating is different from the distinction between equilibrium concepts. A model might have multiple Nash equilibria, some pooling and some separating. Moreover, a single equilibrium – even a pooling one – can include several contracts, but if it is pooling the agent always uses the same strategy, regardless of type. If the agent's equilibrium strategy is mixed, the equilibrium is pooling if the agent always picks the same mixed strategy, even though the messages and efforts would differ across realizations of the game.

These two terms came up in section 6.2 in the game of PhD Admissions. Neither type of student applied in the pooling equilibrium, but one type did in the separating equilibrium. In a principal–agent model, the principal tries to design the contract to achieve separation unless the incentives turn out to be too costly. In Production Game VI, the equilibrium was separating, since the two types of agents choose different contracts.

A separating contract need not be fully separating. If agents who observe a state variable $\theta \leq 4$ accept contract C_1 but other agents accept C_2, then the equilibrium is separating but it does not separate out every type. We say that the equilibrium is **fully revealing** if the agent's choice of contract always conveys his private information to the principal. Between pooling and fully revealing equilibria are the **imperfectly separating** equilibria synonymously called **semi-separating**, **partially separating**, **partially revealing**, or **partially pooling** equilibria.

The possibility of a pooling equilibrium reveals one more step we need to take to establish that the proposed separating equilibrium in Production Game VIa is really an equilibrium: would the principal do better by offering a pooling contract instead, or a separating contract under which one type of agent does not participate? All of my derivation above was to show that the agents would not deviate from the proposed equilibrium, but it might still be that the principal would deviate.

First, would the principal prefer pooling? Then all that is necessary is that the contract as cheaply as possible induce both types of agent to participate. Here, that would require that we make the contract barely acceptable to the type with the lowest ability and highest reservation payoff, the low-ability agent. The contract $(3,3)$ offered by itself would do that, but it would not increase profits over W_1 and W_2 in our equilibrium above. Either pooling or separating would yield profits of $0.9(0.5(0-3)+0.5(10-3))+0.1(0.5(10-3)+0.5(10-3)) = 2.5$.

Second, would the principal prefer a separating contract that "gave up" on one type of agent? The principal would not want to drive away the high-ability agent, of course, though he could do so by offering a high wage for $q = 0$ and a low wage for $q = 10$, because the high-ability agent has both greater output and a lower reservation payoff (if we had $\overline{U}_{High} = 11$ then the outcome would be different). But if the principal did not have to offer a contract that gave the low-ability agent his reservation payoff of 3, he could be more stingy towards the high-ability agent. If there were no low-ability agent, the principal would offer a contract such as $(0,2)$ to the high-ability agent, driving him down to his reservation payoff and increasing the profits from hiring him. Here, however, there are not enough high-ability agents for that to be a good strategy for the principal. His payoff would decline to $0.9(0)+0.1(0.5(10-2)+0.5(10-2)) = 0.8$, a big decline from 2.5. If 99 percent of the agents were high-ability, instead of 10 percent, things would have turned out differently, but there are too many agents who have low-ability yet can be efficiently hired for the principal to give up on them.

The Production Game is one setting for adverse selection, and is a good foundation for modelling it, but the best-known setting, and one which well illustrates the power of the idea in explaining everyday phenomenon, is the used-car market. We will look at that market in the next few sections. All adverse selection games are games of incomplete information, but they might or might not contain uncertainty, moves by Nature occuring after the agents take their first actions. We will continue using games of certainty in sections 9.2 and 9.3, and wait to look at the effect of uncertainty in section 9.4. The first game will model a used car market in which the quality of the car is known to the seller but not the buyer, and the various versions of the game will differ in the types and numbers of the buyers and sellers. Section 9.4 will return to models with uncertainty, in a model of adverse selection in insurance. One result there will be that a Nash equilibrium in pure strategies fails to exist for certain parameter values. Section 9.5 applies the idea of adverse selection to explain the magnitude of the bid-ask spread in financial markets, and section 9.6 touches on a variety of other applications.

9.2   Adverse Selection under Certainty: Lemons I and II

Akerlof stimulated an entire field of research with his 1970 model of the market for shoddy used cars ("lemons"), in which adverse selection arises because car quality is better known to the seller than to the buyer. In agency terms, the principal contracts to buy from the agent a car whose quality, which might be high or low, is noncontractible despite the lack of uncertainty.

We will spend considerable time adding twists to a model of the market in used-cars. The game will have one buyer and one seller, but this will simulate competition between buyers, as discussed in section 7.2, because the seller moves first. If the model had symmetric information there would be no consumer surplus. It will often be convenient to discuss the game as if it had many sellers, interpreting one seller to whom Nature randomly assigns a type to be a population of sellers of different types, one of whom is drawn by Nature to participate in the game.

The Basic Lemons Model

PLAYERS
A buyer and a seller.

THE ORDER OF PLAY
0   Nature chooses quality type θ for the seller according to the distribution $F(\theta)$. The seller knows θ, but while the buyer knows F, he does not know the θ of the particular seller he faces.
1   The buyer offers a price P.
2   The seller accepts or rejects.

PAYOFFS
If the buyer rejects the offer, both players receive payoffs of zero.
Otherwise, $\pi_{buyer} = V(\theta) - P$ and $\pi_{seller} = P - U(\theta)$, where V and U will be defined later.

The payoffs of both players are normalized to zero if no transaction takes place. (A normalization is part of the notation of the model rather than a substantive assumption.) The model assigns the players' utility a base value of zero when no transaction takes place, and the payoff functions show changes from that base. The seller, for instance, gains P if the sale takes place but loses $U(\theta)$ from giving up the car.

The functions $F(\theta)$, $U(\theta)$, and $V(\theta)$ will be specified differently in different versions of the game. We start with identical tastes and two types (Lemons I), and generalize to a continuum of types (Lemons II). Section 9.3 specifies first that the sellers are identical and value cars more than buyers (Lemons III), next that the sellers have heterogeneous tastes (Lemons IV). We will look less formally at other modifications involving risk aversion and the relative numbers of buyers and sellers.

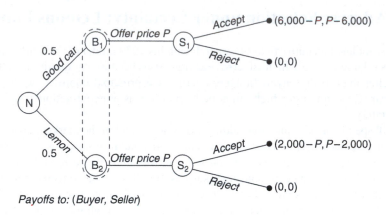

Payoffs to: *(Buyer, Seller)*

Figure 9.1   An extensive form for Lemons I.

Lemons I: Identical Tastes, Two Types of Sellers

Let good cars have quality 6,000 and bad cars (lemons) quality 2,000, so $\theta \in \{2,000, 6,000\}$, and suppose that half the cars in the world are of the first type and the other half of the second type. A payoff profile of $(0,0)$ will represent the status quo, in which the buyer has $50,000 and the seller has the car. Assume that both players are risk-neutral and they value quality at one dollar per unit, so after a trade the payoffs are $\pi_{buyer} = \theta - P$ and $\pi_{seller} = P - \theta$. Figure 9.1 shows the extensive form.

If he could observe quality at the time of his purchase, the buyer would be willing to accept a contract to pay $6,000 for a good car and $2,000 for a lemon. He cannot observe quality, however, and we assume that he cannot enforce a contract based on his discovery once the purchase is made. Given these restrictions, if the seller offers $4,000, a price equal to the average quality, the buyer will deduce that the car is a lemon. The very fact that the car is for sale demonstrates its low quality. Knowing that for $4,000 he would be sold only lemons, the buyer would refuse to pay more than $2,000. Let us assume that an indifferent seller sells his car, in which case half of the cars are traded in equilibrium, all of them lemons.

A friendly advisor might suggest to the owner of a good car that he wait until all the lemons have been sold and then sell his own car, since everyone knows that only good cars have remained unsold. But allowing for such behavior changes the model by adding a new action. If it were anticipated, the owners of lemons would also hold back and wait for the price to rise. Such a game could be formally analyzed as a war of attrition (section 3.2).

The outcome that half the cars are held off the market is interesting, though not startling, since half the cars do have genuinely higher quality. It is a formalization of Groucho Marx's wisecrack that he would refuse to join any club that would accept him as a member. Lemons II will have a more dramatic outcome.

Lemons II: Identical Tastes, a Continuum of Types of Sellers

One might wonder whether the outcome of Lemons I was an artifact of the assumption of just two types. Lemons II generalizes the game by allowing the seller to be any of a continuum of types. We will assume that the quality types are uniformly distributed

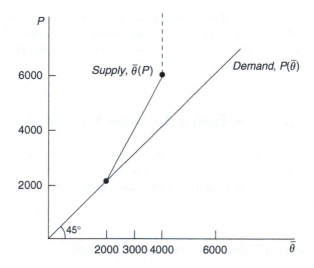

Figure 9.2 Lemons II: identical tastes.

between 2,000 and 6,000. The average quality is $\overline{\theta} = 4,000$, which is therefore the price the buyer would be willing to pay for a car of unknown quality if all cars were on the market. The probability density is zero except on the support [2,000, 6,000], where it is $f(\theta) = 1/(6,000 - 2,000)$, and the cumulative density is

$$F(\theta) = \int_{2,000}^{\theta} f(x)dx,$$

$$= \int_{2,000}^{\theta} \frac{1}{4,000}dx = \left.\frac{x}{4,000}\right|_{x=2,000}^{\theta},$$

$$= \frac{\theta}{4,000} - 0.5. \tag{9.4}$$

The payoff functions are the same as in Lemons I.

The equilibrium price must be less than \$4,000 in Lemons II because, as in Lemons I, not all cars are put on the market at that price. Owners are willing to sell only if the quality of their cars is less than 4,000, so while the average quality of all used cars is 4,000, the average quality offered for sale is 3,000. The price cannot be \$4,000 when the average quality is 3,000, so the price must drop at least to \$3,000.

If that happens, the owners of cars with values from 3,000 to 4,000 pull their cars off the market and the average of those remaining is 2,500. The acceptable price falls to \$2,500, and the unravelling continues until the price reaches its equilibrium level of \$2,000. But at $P = 2,000$ the number of cars on the market is infinitesimal. The market has completely collapsed!

Figure 9.2 puts the price of used-cars on one axis and the average quality of cars offered for sale on the other. Each price leads to a different average quality, $\overline{\theta}(P)$, and the slope of $\overline{\theta}(P)$ is greater than one because average quality does not rise proportionately with price. If the price rises, the quality of the *marginal* car offered for sale equals the new price, but the quality of the *average* car offered for sale is much lower. In equilibrium, the average quality must equal the price, so the equilibrium lies on the 45° line through the origin. That line is a demand schedule of sorts, just as $\overline{\theta}(P)$ is a supply schedule. The only intersection is the point (2,000, 2,000).

9.3   Heterogeneous Tastes: Lemons III and IV

The outcome that no cars are traded is extreme, but there is no efficiency loss in either Lemons I or Lemons II. Since all the players have identical tastes, it does not matter who ends up owning the cars. But the players of the next game, whose tastes differ, have real need of a market.

Lemons III : Buyers Value Cars More than Sellers

Assume that sellers value their cars at exactly their qualities θ but that buyers have valuations 20 percent greater, and, moreover, outnumber the sellers. The payoffs if trade occurs are $\pi_{buyer} = 1.2\theta - P$ and $\pi_{seller} = P - \theta$. In equilibrium, the sellers will capture the gains from trade.

In figure 9.3, the curve $\overline{\theta}(P)$ is much the same as in Lemons II, but the equilibrium condition is no longer that price and average quality lie on the 45° line, but that they lie on the demand schedule $P(\overline{\theta})$, which has a slope of 1.2 instead of 1.0. The demand and supply schedules intersect only at $(P = 3,000, \overline{\theta}(P) = 2,500)$. Because buyers are willing to pay a premium, we only see **partial adverse selection;** the equilibrium is partially pooling. The outcome is inefficient, because in a world of perfect information all the cars would be

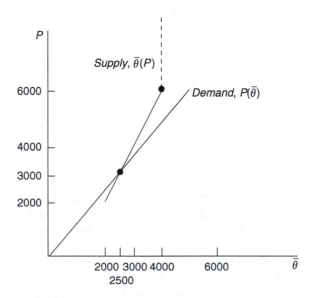

Figure 9.3   Buyers value cars more than sellers: Lemons III.

owned by the "buyers," who value them more, but under adverse selection they only end up owning the low-quality cars.

Lemons IV: Sellers' Valuations Differ

In Lemons IV, we dig a little deeper to explain why trade occurs, and we model sellers as consumers whose valuations of quality have changed since they bought their cars. For a particular seller, the valuation of one unit of quality is $(1+\varepsilon)$, where the random disturbance ε can be either positive or negative and has an expected value of zero. The disturbance could arise because of the seller's mistake – he did not realize how much he would enjoy driving when he bought the car – or because conditions changed – he switched to a job closer to home. Payoffs if a trade occurs are $\pi_{buyer} = \theta - P$ and $\pi_{seller} = P - (1+\varepsilon)\theta$.

If $\varepsilon = -0.15$ and $\theta = 2{,}000$ for a particular seller, then \$1,700 is the lowest price at which he would resell his car. The average quality of cars offered for sale at price P is the expected quality of cars valued by their owners at less than P, that is,

$$\overline{\theta}(P) = E(\theta|(1+\varepsilon)\theta \le P). \tag{9.5}$$

Suppose that a large number of new buyers, greater in number than the sellers, appear in the market, and let their valuation of one unit of quality be \$1. The demand schedule, shown in figure 9.4, is the 45° line through the origin. Figure 9.4 shows one possible shape for the supply schedule $\overline{\theta}(P)$, although to specify it precisely we would have to specify the distribution of the disturbances.

In contrast to Lemons I, II, and III, here if $P \ge \$6{,}000$ some car owners would be reluctant to sell, because they received positive disturbances to their valuations. The average quality of cars on the market is less than 4,000 even at $P = \$6{,}000$. On the other hand, even if

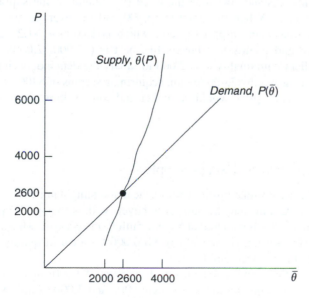

Figure 9.4   Lemons IV: sellers' valuations differ.

$P = \$2,000$ some sellers with low-quality cars *and* negative realizations of the disturbance do sell, so the average quality remains above 2,000. Under some distributions of ε, a few sellers hate their cars so much they would pay to have them taken away.

The equilibrium drawn in figure 9.4 is $(P = \$2,600, \ \bar{\theta} = 2,600)$. Some used cars are sold, but the number is inefficiently low. Some of the sellers have high-quality cars but negative disturbances, and although they would like to sell their cars to someone who values them more, they will not sell at a price of $2,600.

A theme running through all four Lemons models is that when quality is unknown to the buyer, less trade occurs. Lemons I and II show how trade diminishes, while Lemons III and IV show that the disappearance can be inefficient because some sellers value cars less than some buyers. Next we will use Lemons III, the simplest model with gains from trade, to look at various markets with more sellers than buyers, excess supply, and risk-averse buyers.

More Sellers than Buyers

In analyzing Lemons III we assumed that buyers outnumbered sellers. As a result, the sellers earned producer surplus. In the original equilibrium, all the sellers with quality less than 3,000 offered a price of $3,000 and earned a surplus of up to $1,000. There were more buyers than sellers, so every seller who wished to sell was able to do so, but the price equalled the buyers' expected utility, so no buyer who failed to purchase was dissatisfied. The market cleared.

If, instead, sellers outnumber buyers, what price should a seller offer? At $3,000, not all would-be sellers can find buyers. A seller who proposed a lower price would find willing buyers despite the somewhat lower expected quality. The buyer's trade-off between lower price and lower quality is shown in figure 9.3, in which the expected consumer surplus is the vertical distance between the price (the height of the supply schedule) and the demand schedule. When the price is $3,000 and the average quality is 2,500, the buyer expects a consumer surplus of zero, which is $3,000 − \$1.2 \cdot 2,500$. The combination of price and quality that buyers like best is ($2,000, 2,000), because if there were enough sellers with quality $\theta = 2,000$ to satisfy the demand, each buyer would pay $P = \$2,000$ for a car worth $2,400 to him, acquiring a surplus of $400. If there were fewer sellers, the equilibrium price would be higher and some sellers would receive producer surplus.

Heterogeneous Buyers: Excess Supply

If buyers have different valuations for quality, the market might not clear, as Charles Wilson (1980) points out. Assume that the number of buyers willing to pay $1.2 per unit of quality exceeds the number of sellers, but that buyer Smith is an eccentric whose demand for high quality is unusually strong. He would pay $100,000 for a car of quality 5,000 or greater, and $0 for a car of any lower quality.

In Lemons III without Smith, the outcome is a price of $3,000, an average market quality of 2,500, and a market quality range between 2,000 and 3,000. Smith would be unhappy with this, since he has zero probability of finding a car he likes. In fact, he would be willing to accept a price of $6,000, so that all the cars, from quality 2,000 to 6,000, would be offered for sale and the probability that he buys a satisfactory car would rise from 0 to 0.25. But Smith would not want to buy all the cars offered to him, so the equilibrium has two prices, $3,000 and $6,000, with excess supply at the higher price.

Strangely enough, Smith's demand function is upward sloping. At a price of $3,000, he is unwilling to buy; at a price of $6,000, he is willing, because expected quality rises with price. This does not contradict basic price theory, for the standard assumption of *ceteris paribus* is violated. As the price increases, the quantity demanded would fall if all else stayed the same, but all else does not – quality rises.

Risk Aversion

We have implicitly assumed, by the choice of payoff functions, that the buyers and sellers are both risk-neutral. What happens if they are risk-averse – that is, if the marginal utilities of wealth and car quality are diminishing? Again we will use Lemons III and the assumption of many buyers.

On the seller's side, risk aversion changes nothing. The seller runs no risk because he knows exactly the price he receives and the quality he surrenders. But the buyer does bear risk, because he buys a car of uncertain quality. Although he would pay $3,600 for a car he knows has quality 3,000, if he is risk-averse he will not pay that much for a car with expected quality 3,000 but actual quality of possibly 2,500 or 3,500: he would obtain less utility from adding 500 quality units than from subtracting 500. The buyer would pay perhaps $2,900 for a car whose expected quality is 3,000 where the demand schedule is nonlinear, lying everywhere below the demand schedule of the risk-neutral buyer. As a result, the equilibrium has a lower price and average quality.

9.4   Adverse Selection under Uncertainty: Insurance Game III

The term "adverse selection," like "moral hazard," comes from insurance. Insurance pays more if there is an accident than otherwise, so it benefits accident-prone customers more than safe ones and a firm's customers are "adversely selected" to be accident-prone. The classic article on adverse selection in insurance markets is Rothschild & Stiglitz (1976), which begins, "Economic theorists traditionally banish discussions of information to footnotes." How things have changed! Within ten years, information problems came to dominate research in both microeconomics and macroeconomics.

We will follow Rothschild & Stiglitz in using state-space diagrams, and we will use a version of section 8.5's Insurance Game. Under moral hazard, Smith chose whether to be *Careful* or *Careless*. Under adverse selection, Smith cannot affect the probability of a theft, which is chosen by Nature. Rather, Smith is either *Safe* or *Unsafe*, and while he cannot affect the probability that his car will be stolen, he does know what the probability is.

Insurance Game III

PlAYERS
Smith and two insurance companies.

THE ORDER OF PLAY

0 Nature chooses Smith to be either *Safe*, with probability 0.6, or *Unsafe*, with probability 0.4. Smith knows his type, but the insurance companies do not.

1 Each insurance company offers its own contract (x, y) under which Smith pays premium x unconditionally and receives compensation y if there is a theft.

2 Smith picks a contract.

3 Nature chooses whether there is a theft, using probability 0.5 if Smith is *Safe* and 0.75 if he is *Unsafe*.

PAYOFFS
Smith's payoff depends on his type and the contract (x, y) that he accepts. Let $U' > 0$ and $U'' < 0$.

$$\pi_{Smith}(Safe) = 0.5U(12 - x) + 0.5U(0 + y - x).$$

$$\pi_{Smith}(Unsafe) = 0.25U(12 - x) + 0.75U(0 + y - x).$$

The companies' payoffs depend on what types of customers accept their contracts, as shown in table 9.1.

Table 9.1   Insurance Game III payoffs

Company payoff	Types of customers
0	No customers
$0.5x + 0.5(x - y)$	Just *Safe*
$0.25x + 0.75(x - y)$	Just *Unsafe*
$0.6[0.5x + 0.5(x - y)] + 0.4[0.25x + 0.75(x - y)]$	*Unsafe* and *Safe*

Smith is *Safe* with probability 0.6 and *Unsafe* with probability 0.4. Without insurance, Smith's dollar wealth is 12 if there is no theft and 0 if there is, depicted in figure 9.5 as his endowment in state space, $\omega = (12, 0)$. If Smith is *Safe*, a theft occurs with probability 0.5, but if he is *Unsafe* the probability is 0.75. Smith is risk-averse (because $U'' < 0$) and the insurance companies are risk-neutral.

If an insurance company knew that Smith was *Safe*, it could offer him insurance at a premium of 6 with a payout of 12 after a theft, leaving Smith with an allocation of $(6, 6)$. This is the most attractive contract that is not unprofitable, because it fully insures Smith. Whatever the state, his allocation is 6.

Figure 9.5 shows the indifference curves of Smith and an insurance company, with the no-insurance starting point at $\omega = (12, 0)$. A higher insurance premium reduces Smith's

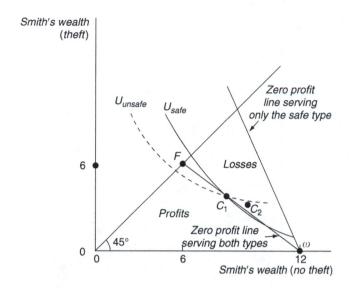

Figure 9.5   Insurance Game III: nonexistence of a pooling equilibrium.

wealth in both states of the world; a higher theft insurance payout increases Smith's wealth in the state of the world in which there is a theft. The insurance company is risk-neutral, so its indifference curve is a straight line with negative slope, since to keep the company's profit constant, the decrease in profit from a rise in Smith's wealth if there is no theft must be balanced by an increase in profit from a fall in Smith's wealth if there is a theft.

If Smith will be a customer regardless of his type, the company's indifference curve based on its expected profits is ωF (although if the company knew that Smith was *Safe*, the indifference curve would be steeper, and if it knew he was Unsafe, the curve would be less steep). The insurance company is indifferent between ω and C_1, at both of which its expected profits are zero. Smith is risk-averse, so his indifference curves are convex, and closest to the origin along the 45° line if the probability of *Theft* is 0.5. He has two sets of indifference curves, solid if he is *Safe* and dotted if he is *Unsafe*.

Figure 9.5 shows why no Nash pooling equilibrium exists. To make zero profits, the equilibrium must lie on the line ωF. It is easiest to think about these problems by imagining an entire population of Smiths, whom we will call "customers." Pick a contract C_1 anywhere on ωF and think about drawing the indifference curves for the *Unsafe* and *Safe* customers that pass through C_1. *Safe* customers are always willing to trade *Theft* wealth for *No Theft* wealth at a higher rate than *Unsafe* customers. At any point, therefore, the slope of the solid (*Safe*) indifference curve is steeper than that of the dashed (*Unsafe*) curve. Since the slopes of the dashed and solid indifference curves differ, we can insert another contract, C_2, between them and just barely to the right of ωF. The *Safe* customers prefer contract C_2 to C_1, but the *Unsafe* customers stay with C_1, so C_2 is profitable – since C_2 only attracts *Safe*s, it need not be to the left of ωF to avoid losses. But then the original contract C_1 was not a Nash equilibrium, and since our argument holds for any pooling contract, no pooling equilibrium exists.

The attraction of the *Safe* customers away from pooling is referred to as **cream skimming**, although profits are still zero when there is competition for the cream. We next consider

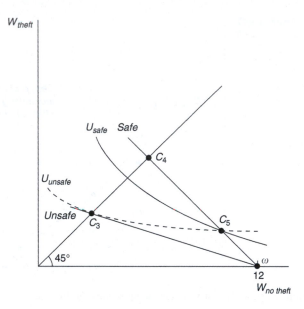

Figure 9.6   A separating equilibrium for Insurance Game III.

whether a separating equilibrium exists, using figure 9.6. The zero-profit condition requires that the *Safe* customers take contracts on ωC_4 and the *Unsafe*s on ωC_3.

The *Unsafe*s will be completely insured in any equilibrium, albeit at a high price. On the zero-profit line ωC_3, the contract they like best is C_3, which the *Safe*s are not tempted to take. The *Safe*s would prefer contract C_4, but C_4 uniformly dominates C_3, so it would attract *Unsafe*s too, and generate losses. To avoid attracting *Unsafe*s, the *Safe* contract must be below the *Unsafe* indifference curve. Contract C_5 is the fullest insurance the *Safe*s can get without attracting *Unsafe*s: it satisfies the self-selection and competition constraints.

Contract C_5, however, might not be an equilibrium either. Figure 9.7 is the same as figure 9.6 with a few additional points marked. If one firm offered C_6, it would attract both types, *Unsafe* and *Safe*, away from C_3 and C_5, because it is to the right of the indifference curves passing through those points. Would C_6 be profitable? That depends on the proportions of the different types. The assumption on which the equilibrium of figure 9.6 is based is that the proportion of *Safe*s is 0.6, so the zero-profit line for pooling contracts is ωF and C_6 would be unprofitable. In figure 9.7 it is assumed that the proportion of *Safe*s is higher, so the zero-profit line for pooling contracts would be $\omega F'$ and C_6, lying to its left, is profitable. But we already showed that no pooling contract is Nash, so C_6 cannot be an equilibrium. Since neither a separating pair like (C_3, C_5) nor a pooling contract like C_6 is an equilibrium, no equilibrium whatsoever exists.

The essence of nonexistence here is that if separating contracts are offered, some company is willing to offer a superior pooling contract; but if a pooling contract is offered, some company is willing to offer a separating contract that makes it unprofitable. A monopoly would have a pure-strategy equilibrium, but in a competitive market only a mixed-strategy Nash equilibrium exists (see Dasgupta & Maskin [1986]).

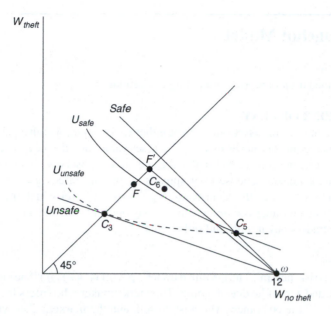

Figure 9.7   Curves for which there is no equilibrium in Insurance Game III.

*9.5   Market Microstructure

The prices of securities such as stocks depend on what investors believe is the value of the assets that underlie them. The values are highly uncertain, and new information about them is constantly being generated. The market microstructure literature is concerned with how new information enters the market. In the paradigmatic situation, an informed trader has private information about the asset value that he hopes to use to make profitable trades, but other traders know that someone might have private information. This is adverse selection, because the informed trader has better information on the value of the stock, and no uninformed trader wants to trade with an informed trader – the informed trade is a "bad type" from the point of view of the other side of the market. An institution that many markets have developed is the "marketmaker" or "specialist," a trader in a particular stock who is always willing to buy or sell to keep the market going. Other traders feel safer in trading with the marketmaker than with a potentially informed trader, but this just transfers the adverse selection problem to the marketmaker, who always loses when he trades with someone who is informed.

The two models in this section will look at how a marketmaker deals with the problem of informed trading. Both are descendants of the verbal model in Bagehot (1971). ("Bagehot," pronounced "badget," is a pseudonym for Jack Treynor. See Glosten & Milgrom [1985] for a formalization.) In the Bagehot model, there may or may not be one or more informed traders, but the informed traders as a group have a trade of fixed size if they are present. The marketmaker must decide how big a bid-ask spread to charge. In the Kyle (1985) model, there is one informed trader, who decides how much to trade. On observing the imbalance of orders, the marketmaker decides what price to offer.

The Bagehot Model

PLAYERS
The informed trader and two competing marketmakers.

THE ORDER OF PLAY
0   Nature chooses the asset value v to be either $p_0 - \delta$ or $p_0 + \delta$ with equal probability. The marketmakers never observe the asset value, nor do they observe whether anyone else observes it, but the "informed" trader observes v with probability θ.
1   The marketmakers choose their spreads s, offering prices $p_{bid} = p_0 - s/2$ at which they will buy the security and $p_{ask} = p_0 + s/2$ for which they will sell it.
2   The informed trader decides whether to buy one unit, sell one unit, or do nothing.
3   Noise traders buy n units and sell n units.

PAYOFFS
Everyone is risk-neutral. The informed trader's payoff is $(v - p_{ask})$ if he buys, $(p_{bid} - v)$ if he sells, and zero if he does nothing. The marketmaker who offers the highest p_{bid} trades with all the customers who wish to sell, and the marketmaker who offers the lowest p_{ask} trades with all the customers who wish to buy. If the marketmakers set equal prices, they split the market evenly. A marketmaker who sells x units gets a payoff of $x(p_{ask} - v)$, and a marketmaker who buys x units gets a payoff of $x(v - p_{bid})$.

Optimal strategies are simple. Competition between the marketmakers will make their prices identical and their profits zero. The informed trader should buy if $v > p_{ask}$ and sell if $v < p_{bid}$. He has no incentive to trade if $v \in [p_{bid}, p_{ask}]$.

A marketmaker will always lose money trading with the informed trader, but if $s > 0$, so $p_{ask} > p_0$ and $p_{bid} < p_0$, he will earn positive expected profits in trading with the noise traders. Since a marketmaker could specialize in either sales or purchases, he must earn zero expected profits overall from either type of trade. Centering the bid-ask spread on the expected value of the stock, p_0, ensures this. Marketmaker sales will be at the ask price of $(p_0 + s/2)$. With probability 0.5, this is above the true value of the stock, $(p_0 - \delta)$, in which case the informed trader will not buy but the marketmakers will earn a total profit of $n[(p_0 + s/2) - (p_0 - \delta)]$ from the noise traders. With probability 0.5, the ask price of $(p_0 + s/2)$ is below the true value of the stock, $(p_0 + \delta)$, in which case the informed trader will be informed with probability θ and buy one unit and the noise traders will buy n more in any case, so the marketmakers will earn a total expected profit of $(n + \theta)[(p_0 + s/2) - (p_0 + \delta)]$, a negative number. For marketmaker profits from sales at the ask price to be zero overall, this expected profit must be zero:

$$0.5n[(p_0 + s/2) - (p_0 - \delta)] + 0.5(n + \theta)[(p_0 + s/2) - (p_0 + \delta)] = 0. \qquad (9.6)$$

Equation (9.6) implies that $n[s/2 + \delta] + (n + \theta)[s/2 - \delta] = 0$, so

$$s^* = \frac{2\delta\theta}{2n + \theta}. \qquad (9.7)$$

The profit from marketmaker purchases must similarly equal zero, and will for the same spread s^*, though we will not go through the algebra here.

Equation (9.7) has a number of implications. First, the spread s^* is positive. Even though marketmakers compete and have zero transactions costs, they charge a different price to buy and to sell. They make money dealing with the noise traders but lose money with the informed trader, if he is present. The comparative statics reflect this. The spread s^* rises in δ, the dispersion of the true value, because divergent true values increase losses from trading with the informed trader, and s^* falls in n, which reflects the number of noise traders relative to informed traders, because when there are more noise traders, the profits from trading with them are greater. The spread s^* rises in θ, the probability that the informed trader really has inside information, which is also intuitive but requires a little calculus to demonstrate, using equation (9.7):

$$\frac{\partial s^*}{\partial \theta} = \frac{2\delta}{2n+\theta} - \frac{2\delta\theta}{(2n+\theta)^2} = \left(\frac{1}{(2n+\theta)^2}\right)(4\delta n + 2\delta\theta - 2\delta\theta) > 0. \qquad (9.8)$$

The second model of market microstructure, important because it is commonly used as a foundation for more complicated models, is the Kyle model. It focuses on the decision of the informed trader, not the marketmaker. The Kyle model is set up so that marketmaker observes the trade volume before he chooses the price.

The Kyle Model (Kyle [1985])

PLAYERS
The informed trader and two competing marketmakers.

THE ORDER OF PLAY
0   Nature chooses the asset value v from a normal distribution with mean p_0 and variance σ_v^2, observed by the informed trader but not by the marketmakers.
1   The informed trader offers a trade of size $x(v)$, which is a purchase if positive and a sale if negative, unobserved by the marketmaker.
2   Nature chooses a trade of size u by noise traders, unobserved by the marketmaker, where u is distributed normally with mean zero and variance σ_u^2.
3   The marketmakers observe the total market trade offer $y = x + u$, and choose prices $p(y)$.
4   Trades are executed. If y is positive (the market wants to purchase, in net), whichever marketmaker offers the lowest price executes the trades; if y is negative (the market wants to sell, in net), whichever marketmaker offers the highest price executes the trades. The value v is then revealed to everyone.

PAYOFFS
All players are risk-neutral. The informed trader's payoff is $(v - p)x$. The marketmaker's payoff is zero if he does not trade and $(p - v)y$ if he does.

An equilibrium for this game is the strategy profile

$$x(v) = (v - p_0)\left(\frac{\sigma_u}{\sigma_v}\right) \tag{9.9}$$

and

$$p(y) = p_0 + \left(\frac{\sigma_v}{2\sigma_u}\right)y. \tag{9.10}$$

This is reasonable. It says that the informed trader will increase the size of his trade as v gets bigger relative to p_0 (and he will sell, not buy, if $v - p_0 < 0$), and the marketmaker will increase the price he charges if y is bigger and more people want to sell, which is an indicator that the informed trader might be trading heavily. The variances of the asset value (σ_v^2) and the noise trading (σ_u^2) enter as one would expect, and they matter only in their relation to each other. If σ_v^2/σ_u^2 is large, then the asset value fluctuates more than the amount of noise trading, and it is difficult for the informed trader to conceal his trades under the noise. The informed trader will trade less, and a given amount of trading will cause a greater response from the marketmaker. One might say that the market is less "liquid": a trade of given size will have a greater impact on the price.

I will not (and cannot) prove uniqueness of the equilibrium, since it is very hard to check all possible profiles of nonlinear strategies, but I will show that {(9.9), (9.10)} is Nash and is the unique linear equilibrium. To start, hypothesize that the informed trader uses a linear strategy, so

$$x(v) = \alpha + \beta v, \tag{9.11}$$

for some constants α and β. Competition between the marketmakers means that their expected profits will be zero, which requires that the price they offer be the expected value of v. Thus, their equilibrium strategy $p(y)$ will be an unbiased estimate of v given their data y, where they know that y is normally distributed and that

$$y = x + u,$$
$$= \alpha + \beta v + u. \tag{9.12}$$

This means that their best estimate of v given the data y is, following the usual regression rule (which readers unfamiliar with statistics must accept on faith),

$$E(v|y) = E(v) + \left(\frac{cov(v, y)}{var(y)}\right)y,$$
$$= p_0 + \left(\frac{\beta\sigma_v^2}{\beta^2\sigma_v^2 + \sigma_u^2}\right)y,$$
$$= p_0 + \lambda y, \tag{9.13}$$

where λ is a new shorthand variable to save writing out the term in parentheses.

The function $p(y)$ will be a linear function of y under our assumption that x is a linear function of v. Given that $p(y) = p_0 + \lambda y$, what must next be shown is that x will indeed be a linear function of v. Start by writing the informed trader's expected payoff, which is

$$
\begin{aligned}
E\pi_i &= E([v - p(y)]x), \\
&= E([v - p_0 - \lambda(x + u)]x), \\
&= [v - p_0 - \lambda(x + 0)]x,
\end{aligned}
\tag{9.14}
$$

since $E(u) = 0$. Maximizing the expected payoff with respect to x yields the first-order condition

$$
v - p_0 - 2\lambda x = 0,
\tag{9.15}
$$

which on rearranging becomes

$$
x = -\frac{p_0}{2\lambda} + \left(\frac{1}{2\lambda}\right) v.
\tag{9.16}
$$

Equation (9.16) establishes that $x(v)$ is linear, given that $p(y)$ is linear. All that is left is to find the value of λ. By comparing (9.16) and (9.11) we can see that $\beta = 1/2\lambda$. Substituting this β into the value of λ from (9.13) leads to

$$
\lambda = \frac{\beta \sigma_v^2}{\beta^2 \sigma_v^2 + \sigma_u^2} = \frac{\sigma_v^2/2\lambda}{\sigma_v^2/(4\lambda^2) + \sigma_u^2},
\tag{9.17}
$$

which upon solving for λ yields $\lambda = \sigma_v/2\sigma_u$. Since $\beta = 1/2\lambda$, it follows that $\beta = \sigma_u/\sigma_v$. These values of λ and β together with equation (9.16) give the strategies asserted at the start in equations (9.9) and (9.10).

The Bagehot model is perhaps a better explanation of why marketmakers might charge a bid/ask spread even under competitive conditions and with zero transactions costs. Its assumption is that the marketmaker cannot change the price depending on volume, but must instead offer a price, and then accept whatever order comes along – a buy order, or a sell order.

The two main divisions of the field of finance are corporate finance and asset pricing. Corporate finance, the study of such things as project choice, capital structure, and mergers has the most obvious applications of game theory, but the Bagehot and Kyle models show that the same techniques are also important in asset pricing. For more, I recommend Harris & Raviv (1995).

*9.6   A Variety of Applications

Price Dispersion

Usually the best model for explaining price dispersion is a search model – Salop & Stiglitz (1977), for example, which is based on buyers whose search costs differ. But although we passed over it quickly in section 9.3, the Lemons model with Smith, the quality-conscious consumer, generated not only excess supply, but price dispersion as well. Cars of the same average quality were sold for $3,000 and $6,000.

Similarly, while the most obvious explanation for why brands of stereo amplifiers sell at different prices is that customers are willing to pay more for higher quality, adverse selection contributes another explanation. Consumers might be willing to pay high prices because they know that high-priced brands could include both high-quality and low-quality amplifiers, whereas low-priced brands are invariably low quality. The low-quality amplifier ends up selling at two prices: a high price in competition with high-quality amplifiers, and, in different stores or under a different name, a low price aimed at customers less willing to trade dollars for quality.

This explanation does depend on sellers of amplifiers incurring a large enough fixed set-up or operating cost. Otherwise, too many low-quality brands would crowd into the market, and the proportion of high-quality brands would be too small for consumers to be willing to pay the high price. The low-quality brands would benefit as a group from entry restrictions: too many of them spoil the market, not through price competition but through degrading the average quality.

Health Insurance

Medical insurance is subject to adverse selection because some people are healthier than others. The variance in health is particularly high among old people, who sometimes have difficulty in obtaining insurance at all. Under basic economic theory this is a puzzle: the price should rise until supply equals demand. The problem is pooling: when the price of insurance is appropriate for the average old person, healthier ones stop buying. The price must rise to keep profits nonnegative, and the market disappears, just as in Lemons II.

If the facts indeed fit this story, adverse selection is an argument for government-enforced pooling. If all old people are required to purchase government insurance, then while the healthier of them may be worse off, the vast majority could be helped.

Using adverse selection to justify medicare, however, points out how dangerous many of the models in this book can be. For policy questions, the best default opinion is that markets are efficient. On closer examination, we have found that many markets are inefficient because of strategic behavior or information asymmetry. It is dangerous, however, to immediately conclude that the government should intervene, because the same arguments applied to government show that the cure might be worse than the disease. The analyst of health-care needs to take seriously the moral hazard and rent seeking that arise from government insurance. Doctors and hospitals will increase the cost and amount of treatment if the government pays for it, and the transfer of wealth from young people to the elderly, which is likely to swamp the gains in efficiency, might distort the shape of the government program from the economist's ideal.

Henry Ford's Five-dollar Day

In 1914 Henry Ford made a much-publicized decision to raise the wage of his auto workers to $5 a day, considerably above the market wage. This pay hike occurred without pressure from the workers, who were nonunionized. Why did Ford do it?

The pay hike could be explained by either moral hazard or adverse selection. In accordance with the idea of efficiency wages (section 8.1), Ford might have wanted workers who worried about losing their premium job at his factory, because they would work harder and refrain from shirking. Adverse selection could also explain the pay hike: by raising his wage Ford attracted a mixture of low- and high-quality workers, rather than low-quality alone (see Raff & Summers [1987]).

Bank Loans

Suppose that two people come to you for an unsecured loan of $10,000. One offers to pay an interest rate of 10 percent and the other offers 200 percent. Who do you accept? Like Charles Wilson's car buyer in section 9.3 who chose to buy at a high price, you may choose to lend at a low interest rate.

If a lender raises his interest rate, both his pool of loan applicants and their behavior change because adverse selection and moral hazard contribute to a rise in default rates. Borrowers who expect to default are less concerned about the high interest rate than dependable borrowers, so the number of loans shrinks and the default rate rises (see Stiglitz & Weiss [1981]). In addition, some borrowers shift to higher-risk projects with greater chance of default but higher yields when they are successful. In section 6.6 we went through the model of Diamond (1989) which looks at the evolution of this problem as firms age.

Whether because of moral hazard or adverse selection, asymmetric information can also result in excess demand for bank loans. The savers who own the bank do not save enough at the equilibrium interest rate to provide loans to all the borrowers who want loans. Thus, the bank makes a loan to John Smith, while denying one to Joe, his observationally equivalent twin. Policymakers should carefully consider any laws that rule out arbitrary loan criteria or require banks to treat all customers equally. A bank might wish to restrict its loans to left-handed people, neither from prejudice nor because it is useful to ration loans according to some criterion arbitrary enough to avoid the moral hazard of favoritism by loan officers.

Bernanke (1983) suggests adverse selection in bank loans as an explanation for the Great Depression in the United States. The difficulty in explaining the Depression is not so much the initial stock market crash as the persistence of the unemployment that followed. Bernanke notes that the crash wiped out local banks and dispersed the expertise of the loan officers. After the loss of this expertise, the remaining banks were less willing to lend because of adverse selection, and it was difficult for the economy to recover.

Solutions to Adverse Selection

Even in markets where it apparently does not occur, the threat of adverse selection, like the threat of moral hazard, can be an important influence on market institutions. Adverse selection can be circumvented in a number of ways besides the contractual solutions we have been analyzing. I will mention some of them in the context of the used-car market.

One set of solutions consists of ways to make car quality contractible. Buyers who find that their car is defective may have recourse to the legal system if the sellers were fraudulent, although in the United States the courts are too slow and costly to be fully effective. Other government bodies such as the Federal Trade Commission may do better by issuing regulations particular to the industry. Even without regulation, private warranties – promises to repair the car if it breaks down – may be easier to enforce than oral claims, by dispelling ambiguity about what level of quality is guaranteed.

Testing (the equivalent of moral hazard's monitoring) is always used to some extent. The prospective driver tries the car on the road, inspects the body, and otherwise tries to reduce information asymmetry. At a cost, he could even reverse the asymmetry by hiring mechanics who can tell him more about the car than the owner himself knows. The rule is not always *caveat emptor*; what should one's response be to an antique dealer who offers to pay $500 for an apparently worthless old chair?

Reputation can solve adverse selection, just as it can solve moral hazard, but only if the transaction is repeated and the other conditions of the models in chapters 5 and 6 are met. An almost opposite solution is to show that there are innocent motives for a sale; that the owner of the car has gone bankrupt, for example, and his creditor is selling the car cheaply to avoid the holding cost.

Penalties not strictly economic are also important. One example is the social ostracism inflicted by the friend to whom a lemon has been sold; the seller is no longer invited to dinner. Or, the seller might have moral principles that prevent him from defrauding buyers. Such principles, provided they are common knowledge, would help him obtain a higher price in the used-car market. Akerlof himself has worked on the interaction between social custom and markets in his 1980 and 1983 articles. The second of these articles looks directly at the value of inculcating moral principles, using theoretical examples to show that parents might wish to teach their children principles, and that society might wish to give hiring preference to students from elite schools.

It is by violating the assumptions needed for perfect competition that asymmetric information enables government and social institutions to raise efficiency. This points to a major reason for studying asymmetric information: where it is important, noneconomic interference can be helpful instead of harmful. I find the social solutions particularly interesting since, as mentioned earlier in connection with health care, government solutions introduce agency problems as severe as the information problems they solve. Noneconomic behavior is important under adverse selection, in contrast to perfect competition, which allows an "Invisible Hand" to guide the market to efficiency, regardless of the moral beliefs of the traders. If everyone were honest, the lemons problem would disappear because the sellers would truthfully disclose quality. If some fraction of the sellers were honest, but buyers could not distinguish them from the dishonest sellers, the outcome would presumably be somewhere between the outcomes of complete honesty and complete dishonesty. The subject of market ethics is important, and would profit from investigation by scholars trained in economic analysis.

9.7   Adverse Selection and Moral Hazard Combined: Production Game VII

What happens when adverse selection and moral hazard combine, so that agents begin the game with private information but then also take unobserved actions in the course of the game? Production Game VII shows one possibility, in a model that will also be used at the start of chapter 10.

Production Game VII: Adverse Selection and Moral Hazard

PLAYERS
The principal and the agent.

THE ORDER OF PLAY
0   Nature chooses the state of the world s, observed by the agent but not by the principal, according to distribution $F(s)$, where the state s is Good with probability 0.5 and Bad with probability 0.5.
1   The principal offers the agent a wage contract $w(q)$.
2   The agent accepts or rejects the contract.
3   The agent chooses effort level e.
4   Output is $q = q(e, s)$, where $q(e, good) = 3e$ and $q(e, bad) = e$.

PAYOFFS
If the agent rejects all contracts, then $\pi_{agent} = \overline{U} = 0$ and $\pi_{principal} = 0$.
Otherwise, $\pi_{agent} = U(e, w, s) = w - e^2$ and $\pi_{principal} = V(q - w) = q - w$.

Thus, there is no uncertainty, both principal and agent are risk-neutral in money, and effort is increasingly costly.

In this model, the first-best effort depends on the state of the world. The two social surplus maximization problems are

$$\underset{e_g}{Maximize}\ 3e_g - e_g^2, \tag{9.18}$$

which is solved by the optimal effort $e_g = 1.5$ (and $q_g = 4.5$) in the good state, and

$$\underset{e_g}{Maximize}\ e_b - e_b^2, \tag{9.19}$$

which is solved by the optimal effort $e_b = 0.5$ (and $q_b = 0.5$) in the bad state.

The problem is that the principal does not know what level of effort and output are appropriate. He does not want to require high output in both states, because if he does, he will have to pay too high a salary to the agent to compensate for the difficulty of attaining that output in the bad state. Rather, he must solve the following problem:

$$\underset{q_g,q_b,w_g,w_b}{Maximize}\ [0.5(q_g - w_g) + 0.5(q_b - w_b)], \tag{9.20}$$

where the agent has a choice between two forcing contracts, (q_g, w_g) and (q_b, w_b), and the contracts must induce participation and self selection.

The self-selection constraints are based on efforts of $e = q/3$ for the good state and $e = q$ for the bad state. In the good state, the agent must choose the good-state contract, so

$$\pi_{agent}(q_g, w_g|good) = w_g - \left(\frac{q_g}{3}\right)^2 \geq \pi_{agent}(q_b, w_b|good) = w_b - \left(\frac{q_b}{3}\right)^2 \tag{9.21}$$

and in the bad state he must choose the bad-state contract, so

$$\pi_{agent}(q_b, w_b | bad) = w_b - q_b^2 \geq \pi_{agent}(q_g, w_g | bad) = w_g - q_g^2. \tag{9.22}$$

The participation constraints are

$$\pi_{agent}(q_g, w_g | good) = w_g - \left(\frac{q_g}{3}\right)^2 \geq 0 \tag{9.23}$$

and

$$\pi_{agent}(q_b, w_b | bad) = w_b - q_b^2 \geq 0. \tag{9.24}$$

The bad state's participation constraint will be binding, since in the bad state the agent will not be tempted by the good-state contract's higher output and wage. Thus, we can conclude from constraint (9.24) that

$$w_b = q_b^2. \tag{9.25}$$

The good state's participation constraint will not be binding, since there the agent will be left with an informational rent – the principal must leave the agent some surplus to induce him to reveal the good state.

The good state's self-selection constraint will be binding, since in the good state the agent *will* be tempted to take the easier contract appropriate for the bad state. Thus, we can conclude from constraint (9.21) that

$$\begin{aligned}
w_g &= \left(\frac{q_g}{3}\right)^2 + w_b - \left(\frac{q_b}{3}\right)^2, \\
&= \left(\frac{q_g}{3}\right)^2 + q_b^2 - \left(\frac{q_b}{3}\right)^2,
\end{aligned} \tag{9.26}$$

where the second step substitutes for w_b from equation (9.25). The bad state's self-selection constraint will not be binding, since the agent would then not be tempted to produce a large amount for a large wage.

Now let's return to the principal's maximization problem. Having found expressions for w_b and w_g we can rewrite (9.20) as

$$\underset{q_g, q_b}{Maximize} \left[0.5 \left(q_g - \left(\frac{q_g}{3}\right)^2 - q_b^2 + \left(\frac{q_b}{3}\right)^2 \right) + 0.5(q_b - q_b^2) \right] \tag{9.27}$$

with no constraints. The first-order conditions are

$$0.5 \left(1 - \frac{2q_g}{9} \right) = 0, \tag{9.28}$$

so $q_g = 4.5$, and

$$0.5 \left(-2q_b + \frac{2q_b}{9} \right) + 0.5(1 - 2q_b) = 0, \tag{9.29}$$

so $q_b \approx 0.26$. We can then find the wages that satisfy the constraints, which are $w_g \approx 2.32$ and $w_b \approx 0.07$.

Thus, in the second-best world of information asymmetry, the effort in the good state remains the first-best effort, but second-best effort in the bad state is lower than first-best. This results from the principal's need to keep the bad-state contract from being too attractive in the good state. Bad-state output and compensation must be suppressed. Good-state output, on the other hand, should be left at the first-best level, since the agent will not be tempted by that contract in the bad state.

Also, observe that in the good state the agent earns an informational rent. As explained earlier, this is because the good-state agent could always earn a positive payoff by pretending the state was bad and taking that contract, so any contract that separates out the good-state agent (while leaving some contract acceptable to the bad-state agent) must also have a positive payoff.

Notes

N9.1   Introduction: Production Game VI

- In moral hazard with hidden knowledge, the contract must ordinarily satisfy only one participation constraint, whereas in adverse selection problems there is a different participation constraint for each type of agent. An exception is if there are constraints limiting how much an agent can be punished in different states of the world. If, for example, there are bankruptcy constraints, then, if the agent has different wealths across the N possible states of the world, there will be N constraints for how negative his wage can be, in addition to the single participation constraint. These can be looked at as **interim** participation constraints, since they represent the idea that the agent wants to get out of the contract once he observes the state of the world midway through the game.

- Gresham's Law ("Bad money drives out good") is a statement of adverse selection. Only debased money will be circulated if the payer knows the quality of his money better than the receiver. The same result occurs if quality is common knowledge, but for legal reasons the receiver is obligated to take the money, whatever its quality. An example of the first is Roman coins with low silver content; and of the second, Zambian currency with an overvalued exchange rate.

- Most adverse selection models have types that could be called "good" and "bad," because one type of agent would like to pool with the other, who would rather be separate. It is also possible to have a model in which both types would rather separate – types of workers who prefer night shifts versus those who prefer day shifts, for example – or two types who both prefer pooling – male and female college students.

- Two curious features of labor markets is that workers of widely differing outputs seem to be paid identical wages and that tests are not used more in hiring decisions. Schmidt and Judiesch (as cited in Seligman [1992], p. 145) have found that in jobs requiring only unskilled and semi-skilled blue-collar workers, the top 1 percent of workers, as defined by performance on ability tests not directly related to output, were 50 percent more productive than the average. In jobs defined as "high complexity" the difference was 127 percent.

  At about the same time as Akerlof (1970), another seminal paper appeared on adverse selection, Mirrlees (1971), although the relation only became clear later. Mirrlees looked at optimal taxation and the problem of how the government chooses a tax schedule given that it cannot observe the abilities of its citizens to earn income, and this began the literature on mechanism design. Used cars and income taxes do not appear similar, but in both situations an uninformed player must decide how to behave to another player whose type he does not know. Section 10.4 sets out a descendant of Mirrlees (1971) in a model of government procurement: much of government policy is motivated by the desire to create incentives for efficiency at minimum cost while eliciting information from individuals with superior information.

N9.2   Adverse selection under certainty: Lemons I and II

- Suppose that the cars of Lemons II lasted two periods and did not physically depreciate. A naive economist looking at the market would see new cars selling for $6,000 (twice $3,000) and old cars selling for $2,000 and conclude that the service stream had depreciated by 33 percent. Depreciation and adverse selection are hard to untangle using market data.
- Lemons II uses a uniform distribution. For a general distribution F, the average quality $\bar{\theta}(P)$ of cars with quality P or less is

$$\bar{\theta}(P) = E(\theta | \theta \leq P) = \frac{\int_{-\infty}^{P} x F'(x) dx}{F(P)}. \tag{9.30}$$

Equation (9.30) also arises in physics (the equation for the center of gravity) and nonlinear econometrics (the likelihood equation). Think of $\bar{\theta}(P)$ as a weighted average of the values of θ up to P, the weights being densities. Having multiplied by all these weights in the numerator, we have to divide by their "sum," $F(P) = \int_{-\infty}^{P} F'(x) dx$, in the denominator, giving rise to equation (9.30).

N9.3   Heterogeneous tastes: Lemons III and IV

- You might object to a model in which the buyers of used cars value quality more than the sellers, since the sellers are often richer people. Remember that quality here is "quality of used cars," which is different from "quality of cars." The utility functions could be made more complicated without abandoning the basic model. We could specify something like $\pi_{buyer} = \theta + k/\theta - P$, where $\theta^2 > k$. Such a specification implies that the lower is the quality of the car, the greater the difference between the valuations of buyer and seller.
- In the original article, Akerlof (1970), the quality of new cars is uniformly distributed between 0 and 2, and the model is set up differently, with the demand and supply curves offered by different types of traders and net supply and gross supply presented rather confusingly. Usually the best way to model a situation in which traders sell some of their endowment and consume the rest is to use only gross supplies and demands. Each old owner supplies his car to the market, but in equilibrium he might buy it back, having better information about his car than the other consumers. Otherwise, it is easy to count a given unit of demand twice, once in the demand curve and once in the net supply curve.
- See Stiglitz (1987) for a good survey of the relation between price and quality. Leibenstein (1950) uses diagrams to analyze the implications of individual demand being linked to the market price of quantity in markets for "bandwagon," "snob," and "Veblen" goods.
- Risk aversion is concerned only with variability of outcomes, not their level. If the quality of used cars ranges from 2,000 to 6,000, buying a used car is risky. If all used cars are of quality 2,000, buying a used car is riskless, because the buyer knows exactly what he is getting.

  In Insurance Game III in section 9.4, the separating contract for the *Unsafe* consumer fully insures him: he bears no risk. But in constructing the equilibrium, we had to be very careful to keep the *Unsafes* from being tempted by the risky contract designed for the *Safes*. Risk is a bad thing, but as with old age, the alternative is worse. If Smith were certain his car would be stolen, he would bear no risk, because he would be certain to have low utility.
- To the buyers in Lemons IV, the average quality of cars for a given price is stochastic because they do not know which values of ε were realized. To them, the curve $\bar{\theta}(P)$ is only the *expectation* of the average quality.
- **Lemons III′: minimum quality of zero:** If the minimum quality of car in Lemons III were 0, not 2,000, the resulting game (Lemons III′) would be close to the original Akerlof (1970) specification. As figure 9.8 shows, the supply schedule and the demand schedule intersect at the origin, so that

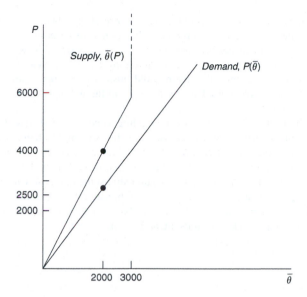

Figure 9.8   Lemons III′ when buyers value cars more and the minimum quality is zero.

the equilibrium price is zero and no cars are traded. The market has shut down entirely because of the unravelling effect described in Lemons II. Even though the buyers are willing to accept a quality lower than the dollar price, the price that buyers are willing to pay does not rise with quality as fast as the price needed to extract that average quality from the sellers, and a car of minimum quality is valued exactly the same by buyers and sellers. A 20 percent premium on zero is still zero. The efficiency implications are even stronger than before, because at the optimum all the old cars are sold to new buyers, but in equilibrium, none are.

N9.4   Adverse selection under uncertainty: Insurance Game III

- Markets with two types of customers are very common in insurance, because it is easy to distinguish male from female, both those types are numerous, and the difference between them is important. Males under age 25 pay almost twice the auto insurance premiums of females, and females pay 10–30 percent less for life insurance. The difference goes both ways, however: Aetna charges a 35-year-old woman 30–50 percent more than a man for medical insurance. One market in which rates do not differ much is disability insurance. Women do make more claims, but the rates are the same because relatively few women buy the product (*Wall Street Journal*, August 27, 1987, p. 21).

N9.6   A variety of applications

- Economics professors sometimes make use of self-selection for student exams. One of my colleagues put the following instructions on an MBA exam, after stating that either Question 5 or 6 must be answered. "The value of Question 5 is less than that of Question 6. Question 5, however, is straightforward and the average student may expect to answer it correctly. Question 6 is more tricky: only those who have understood and absorbed the content of the course well will be able to answer it correctly ... . For a candidate to earn a final course grade of A or higher, it will be *necessary* for him to answer Question 6 successfully." Making the question even more self-referential, he asked the students for an explanation of its purpose.

Another of my colleagues tried asking who in his class would be willing to skip the exam and settle for an A−. Those students who were willing received an A−. The others got A's. But nobody had to take the exam. (This method did upset a few people.) More formally, Guasch & Weiss (1980) have looked at adverse selection and the willingess of workers with different abilities to take tests.

- Nalebuff & Scharfstein (1987) have written on testing, generalizing Mirrlees (1974), who showed how a forcing contract in which output is costlessly observed might attain efficiency by punishing only for very low output. In Nalebuff & Scharfstein, testing is costly and agents are risk-averse. They develop an equilibrium in which the employer tests workers with small probability, using high-quality tests and heavy punishments to attain almost the first-best. Under a condition which implies that large expenditures on each test can eliminate false accusations, they show that the principal will test workers with small probability, but use expensive, accurate tests when he does test a worker, and impose a heavy punishment for lying.

Problems

9.1: Insurance with equations and diagrams (easy)

The text analyzes Insurance Game III using diagrams. Here, let us use equations too. Let $U(t) = log(t)$.

(a) Give the numeric values (x, y) for the full-information separating contracts C_3 and C_4 from figure 9.6. What are the coordinates for C_3 and C_4?

(b) Why is it not necessary to use the $U(t) = log(t)$ function to find the values?

(c) At the separating contract under incomplete information, C_5, $x = 2.01$. What is y? Justify the value 2.01 for x. What are the coordinates of C_5?

(d) What is a contract C_6 that might be profitable and that would lure both types away from C_3 and C_5?

9.2: Testing and commitment (medium)

Fraction β of workers are talented, with output $a_t = 5$, and fraction $(1-\beta)$ are untalented, with output $a_u = 0$. Both types have a reservation wage of 1 and are risk-neutral. At a cost of 2 to itself and 1 to the job applicant, employer Apex can test a job applicant and discover his true ability with probability θ, which takes a value of something over 0.5. There is just one period of work. Let $\beta = 0.001$. Suppose that Apex can commit itself to a wage schedule before the workers take the test, and that Apex must test all applicants and pay all the workers it hires the same wage, to avoid grumbling among workers and corruption in the personnel division.

(a) What is the lowest wage, w_t, that will induce talented workers to apply? What is the lowest wage, w_u, that will induce untalented workers to apply? Which is greater?

(b) What is the minimum accuracy value θ that will induce Apex to use the test? What are the firm's expected profits per worker who applies?

(c) Now suppose that Apex can pay w_p to workers who pass the test and w_f to workers who flunk. What are w_p and w_f? What is the minimum accuracy value θ that will induce Apex to use the test? What are the firm's expected profits per worker who applies?

(d)   What happens if Apex cannot commit to paying the advertised wage, and can decide each applicant's wage individually?

(e)   If Apex cannot commit to testing every applicant, why is there no equilibrium in which either untalented workers do not apply or the firm tests every applicant?

9.3:   Finding the mixed-strategy equilibrium in a testing game (medium)

Half of high school graduates are talented, producing output $a = x$, and half are untalented, producing output $a = 0$. Both types have a reservation wage of 1 and are risk-neutral. At a cost of 2 to himself and 1 to the job applicant, an employer can test a graduate and discover his true ability. Employers compete with each other in offering wages but they cooperate in revealing test results, so an employer knows if an applicant has already been tested and failed. There is just one period of work. The employer cannot commit to testing every applicant or any fixed percentage of them.

(a)   Why is there no equilibrium in which either untalented workers do not apply or the employer tests every applicant?

(b)   In equilibrium, the employer tests workers with probability γ and pays those who pass the test w, the talented workers all present themselves for testing, and the untalented workers present themselves with probability α, where possibly $\gamma = 1$ or $\alpha = 1$. Find an expression for the equilibrium value of α in terms of w. Explain why α is not directly a function of x in this expression, even though the employer's main concern is that some workers have a productivity advantage of x.

(c)   If $x = 9$, what are the equilibrium values of α, γ, and w?

(d)   If $x = 8$, what are the equilibrium values of α, γ, and w?

9.4:   Two-time losers (easy)

Some people are strictly principled and will commit no robberies, even if there is no penalty. Others are incorrigible criminals and will commit two robberies, regardless of the penalty. Society wishes to inflict a particular penalty on criminals as retribution. Retribution requires an expected penalty of 15 per crime (15 if detection is sure, 150 if it has probability 0.1, etc.). Innocent people are sometimes falsely convicted, as shown in table 9.2.

Table 9.2   Two-time losers

Robberies	Convictions		
	0	1	2
0	0.81	0.18	0.01
1	0.60	0.34	0.06
2	0.49	0.42	0.09

Two systems are proposed: (1) a penalty of X for each conviction, and (2) a penalty of 0 for the first conviction, and some amount P for the second conviction.

(a)   What must X and P be to achieve the desired amount of retribution?

(b)   Which system inflicts the smaller cost on innocent people? How much is the cost in each case?

(c)   Compare this with problem 8.2. How are they different?

9.5:   Insurance and state-space diagrams (medium)

Two types of risk-averse people, clean-living and dissolute, would like to buy health insurance. Clean-living people become sick with probability 0.3, and dissolute people with probability 0.9. In state-space diagrams with the person's wealth if he is healthy on the vertical axis and if he is sick on the horizontal, every person's initial endowment is (5, 10), because his initial wealth is 10 and the cost of medical treatment is 5.

(a)   What is the expected wealth of each type of person?

(b)   Draw a state-space diagram with the indifference curves for a risk-neutral insurance company that insures each type of person separately. Draw in the post-insurance allocations C_1 for the dissolute and C_2 for the clean-living under the assumption that a person's type is contractible.

(c)   Draw a new state-space diagram with the initial endowment and the indifference curves for the two types of people that go through that point.

(d)   Explain why, under asymmetric information, no pooling contract C_3 can be part of a Nash equilibrium.

(e)   If the insurance company is a monopoly, can a pooling contract be part of a Nash equilibrium?

Adverse Selection in Stock Sales: A Classroom Game for Chapter 9

This is a game modelling a financial market in which sellers of stock know the value of the stock better than buyers do, but buyers get more utility than sellers from a given asset.

There are two kinds of people: buyers and sellers. Each buyer starts with a checking account with $200. Each seller starts with 4 stock certificates from 4 different companies. Stock face values are $90, $70, $30, and $10 in equal proportions.

Buyers value stocks more than cash, because they wish to save. Each buyer has the following payoff function, where payoff is measured in utils.

$$\pi(buyer) = cash + 1.5 * (stock\ value). \tag{9.31}$$

The initial payoff of a buyer is 200 utils from his $200 in cash, but it would rise to 300 utils if the buyer could convert his $200 in cash to $200 in stocks.

Sellers value cash more than stocks, because they wish to consume now. Each seller has payoff function

$$\pi(seller) = 1.5 * cash + (stock\ value). \tag{9.32}$$

In the game, buyers and sellers buy and sell stock. The buyers pay with checks registered on the blackboard. If buyer Smith buys a stock certificate for $40 from Jones, he writes "Smith" on the board, and under it writes "Owes $40 to Jones." If Smith then buys a certificate for $90 from Lee, he writes "Owes $90 to Lee" under the first entry.

The game is repeated with different features. Each time, sellers start with 4 new shares, and buyers start with $200. Players do *not* keep their earnings from previous rounds. (Think of the 1993 movie, *Groundhog Day*, http://www.imdb.com/title/tt0107048.)

1 Symmetric information: The instructor writes the value of each company on the board.
2 Asymmetric information – decentralized: The instructor tells the sellers, but not the buyers, the value of each company.
3 The same as round 2, but starting over with different shares.
4 Asymmetric information – centralized: Partial regulation: Sellers must disclose if their stock is worth less than 50. The instructor tells the sellers, but not the buyers, the value of each company.
5 Asymmetric information – centralized: Truth regulation: Sellers *may* guarantee their stock value. The instructor tells the sellers, but not the buyers, the value of each company.

Chapter 10
mechanism design and postcontractual hidden knowledge

10.1 Mechanisms, Unravelling, Cross Checking, and the Revelation Principle

This chapter looks at mechanism design. A mechanism is a set of rules that one player constructs and another freely accepts in order to convey information from the second player to the first. The mechanism contains an information report by the second player and a mapping from each possible report to some action by the first.

Adverse selection models can be viewed as problems of mechanism design. Insurance Game III was about an insurance company which wanted to know whether a customer was safe or not. In equilibrium it offers two contracts, an expensive full-insurance contract preferred by the safe customers and a cheap partial-insurance contract preferred by the unsafe. In the language of mechanism design, the insurance company sets up a game in which a customer reports his type as Safe or Unsafe, whichever he prefers to report, and the company then assigns him either partial or full insurance as a consequence. The contract offers are a mechanism for getting the agents to truthfully report their types.

Mechanism design goes beyond simple adverse selection. It can be useful even when players begin a game with symmetric information or when both players have hidden information that they would like to exchange.

Section 10.1 introduces moral hazard with hidden knowledge using Production Game VIII. It shows how to construct an optimal mechanism, how cross checking can attain the first-best when information is observable by the players but unverifiable by courts, and how "unravelling" can reveal private information if lying can be prevented but silence cannot. Section 10.2 designs a mechanism for a product quality game invented by Roger Myerson. Section 10.3 uses diagrams to apply the model to sales quotas. Section 10.4 introduces a mechanism that is multi-player and "dominant-strategy," the Groves Mechanism, for use when the problem is to elicit truthful reports from not one but N agents who need to decide whether to invest in a public good. Section 10.5 applies the principles of mechanism design to price discrimination. Section 10.6 lays out a more complicated model, of rate-of-return regulation by a government that constructs a mechanism to induce a regulated company to reveal how easily it could reduce its costs.

Postcontractual Hidden Knowledge

Information is complete in moral hazard games, but in **moral hazard with hidden knowledge**, also called **postcontractual adverse selection**, the agent, but not the principal, observes a move of Nature after the game begins, but before he takes his action. Information is symmetric at the time of contracting – thus the "moral hazard" – but becomes asymmetric later – thus the "hidden knowledge." From the principal's point of view, agents are identical at the beginning of the game but develop private types midway through. His chief concern is to give them incentives to disclose their types later, which gives the games a flavor close to that of adverse selection. The agent might also have to exert effort in the game, but effort's contractibility is less important when the principal does not know which effort is appropriate because he is ignorant of the state of the world chosen by Nature. The main difference technically is that if information is symmetric at the start and only becomes asymmetric after a contract is signed, the participation constraint is based on the agent's expected payoffs across the different types of agent he might become. Thus, there is just one participation constraint even if there are eventually n possible types of agents in the model, rather than the n participation constraints that would be required in a standard adverse selection model.

What makes postcontractual hidden knowledge an ideal setting for the paradigm of mechanism design is that the problem is to set up a contract that (1) induces the agent to make a truthful report to the principal, and (2) is acceptable to both principal and agent. There is more hope for obtaining efficient outcomes than in adverse selection. The advantage is that information is symmetric at the time of contracting, so neither player can use private information to extract surplus from the other by choosing inefficient contract terms.

For a comparison between the two types of moral hazard, let us modify Production Game VII from chapter 9 and turn it into a slightly different game of hidden knowledge.

Production Game VIII: Mechanism Design

PLAYERS
The principal and the agent.

THE ORDER OF PLAY
1   The principal offers the agent a wage contract of the form $w(q, m)$, where q is output and m is a message to be sent by the agent.
2   The agent accepts or rejects the principal's offer.
3   Nature chooses the state of the world s, according to probability distribution $F(s)$, where the state s is *good* with probability 0.5 and *bad* with probability 0.5. The agent observes s, but the principal does not.
4   If the agent accepted, he exerts effort e unobserved by the principal, and sends message $m \in \{good, bad\}$ to him.
5   Output is $q(e, s)$, where $q(e, good) = 3e$ and $q(e, bad) = e$, and the wage is paid.

PAYOFFS
If the agent rejects the contract, $\pi_{agent} = \overline{U} = 0$ and $\pi_{principal} = 0$.
If the agent accepts the contract, $\pi_{agent} = U(e, w, s) = w - e^2$ and $\pi_{principal} = V(q - w) = q - w$.

This game is almost the same as Production Game VII. The big difference is that now the agent does not know his type at the point in time at which he must accept or reject the contract. A smaller difference is that we have added the message m which the agent sends to the principal. This message is cheap talk – it does not affect payoffs directly and there is no penalty for lying. It is useful as a modelling convenience, to indicate which output-wage combination the agent chooses.

The principal would like to know s so he can tell which effort level is appropriate. In an ideal world he would employ an honest agent who always chose $m = s$, but in noncooperative games we ordinarily assume that agents have no moral sense. Since the agent's words are worthless, the principal must try to design a contract that either provides incentive for truth-telling or takes lying into account. He **implements** a **mechanism** to extract the agent's information.

In Production Game VII, the adverse selection version of the game, the optimal contracts had to satisfy two participation constraints and two incentive compatibility constraints.

In Production Game VIII, the moral hazard with hidden information version, the optimal contract must satisfy just one participation constraint, with the same two incentive compatibility constraints.

The first-best is unchanged from Production Game VII. The optimal effort and output in the good state of the world are $e_g = 1.5$ and $q_g = 4.5$, and in the bad state they are $e_b = 0.5$ and $q_b = 0.5$. Also unchanged is that the principal must solve the problem:

$$\underset{q_g, q_b, w_g, w_b}{Maximize} \, [0.5(q_g - w_g) + 0.5(q_b - w_b)], \tag{10.1}$$

where the agent is paid under one of two forcing contracts, (q_g, w_g) if he reports $m = good$ and (q_b, w_b) if he reports $m = bad$, where producing the wrong output for a given contract results in boiling in oil.

The contracts must induce participation and self-selection. We can write the constraints in terms of the agent's payoff function from in effect choosing one of the two (q, w) contracts by his choice of the report $good$ or bad. The effort he will choose under those contracts will be $e = q/3$ for the good state and $e = q$ for the bad state, the same as in Production Game VII.

The self-selection constraints are the same as in Production Game VII. In the good state, the agent must choose the good-state contract, so

$$\pi_{agent}(q_g, w_g | good) = w_g - \left(\frac{q_g}{3}\right)^2 \geq \pi_{agent}(q_b, w_b | good) = w_b - \left(\frac{q_b}{3}\right)^2 \tag{10.2}$$

and in the bad state he must choose the bad-state contract, so

$$\pi_{agent}(q_b, w_b | bad) = w_b - q_b^2 \geq \pi_{agent}(q_g, w_g | bad) = w_g - q_g^2. \tag{10.3}$$

The participation constraints of Production Game VII now merge, though, because at the time of contracting the agent does not know what the state will be. The single participation constraint is therefore

$$0.5\pi_{agent}(q_g, w_g | good) + 0.5\pi_{agent}(q_b, w_b | bad) = 0.5\left(w_g - \left(\frac{q_g}{3}\right)^2\right) + 0.5(w_b - q_b^2) \geq 0. \tag{10.4}$$

This single participation constraint is binding, since the principal wants to pay the agent as little as possible. The good state's self-selection constraint will be binding. In the good state the agent will be tempted to take the easier contract appropriate for the bad state (due to the "single-crossing property" to be discussed in a later section) and so the principal has to increase the agent's payoff from the good-state contract to yield him at least as much as in the bad state. He does not want to increase the surplus any more than necessary, though, so the good state's self-selection constraint will be exactly satisfied. This gives us two equations,

$$0.5\left(w_g - \left(\frac{q_g}{3}\right)^2\right) + 0.5(w_b - q_b^2) = 0,$$

$$w_g - \left(\frac{q_g}{3}\right)^2 = w_b - \left(\frac{q_b}{3}\right)^2.$$

(10.5)

Solving them out yields $w_b = (5/9)q_b^2$ and $w_g = (1/9)q_g^2 + (4/9)q_b^2$.

Returning to the principal's maximization problem in (10.1) and substituting for w_b and w_g, we can rewrite it as

$$\underset{q_g,q_b}{Maximize}\ \pi_{principal} = \left[0.5\left(q_g - \frac{q_g^2}{9} - \frac{4q_b^2}{9}\right) + 0.5\left(q_b - \frac{5q_b^2}{9}\right)\right]$$

(10.6)

with no constraints. The first-order conditions are

$$\frac{\partial \pi_{principal}}{\partial q_g} = 0.5\left(1 - \left[\frac{2}{9}\right]q_g\right) = 0,$$

(10.7)

so $q_g = 4.5$, and

$$\frac{\partial \pi_{principal}}{\partial q_b} = 0.5\left(-\frac{8q_b}{9}\right) + 0.5\left(1 - \frac{10q_b}{9}\right) = 0,$$

(10.8)

so $q_b = 9/18 = 0.5$. We can then find the wages that satisfy the constraints, which are $w_g \approx 2.36$ and $w_b \approx 0.14$.

As in Production Game VII, in the good state effort is at the first-best level while in the bad state it is less. Unlike in Production Game VII the agent does not earn informational rents, because at the time of contracting he has no private information. In Production Game VII the wages were $w'_g \approx 2.32$ and $w'_b \approx 0.07$. Both wages are higher in Production Game VIII, but so is the effort and output required of the agent in the bad state. The principal in Production Game VIII is less constrained, and thus able to (1) come closer to the first-best when the state is bad, and (2) reduce the rents to the agent. Those are general features of moral hazard with hidden knowledge.

Observable but Nonverifiable Information and the Maskin Matching Scheme

If the state or type is public information, then it is straightforward to obtain the first-best using forcing contracts. What if the state is observable by both principal and agent, but is not public information?

The problem is that there are really three players involved in the contracting situation: the principal who offers the contract, the agent who accepts it – and the court that enforces it. If the courts cannot observe the state, a contract conditioning the wage on the state is unenforceable, no better than having no contract at all. We say that the variable s is **nonverifiable** if contracts based on it cannot be enforced. Most simply, the variable would one whose value the court cannot measure accurately enough to be useful – a worker's intensity of effort, for example, as opposed to the number of hours he was on the job. Or, the variable could be one which the court could observe but which for some reason it will not allow to be used in a legal contract – the amount of cocaine in a package, for example.

It does seem, however, that even if the courts will not enforce a contract based on a variable, if both the principal and the agent observe it they should be able to come up with a more efficient contract than if just the agent observes it. And indeed, mutual observability can help. Maskin (1977) suggested **cross checking**, as idea which would take the following two-part form for Production Game VIII:

1   Principal and agent simultaneously send messages m_p and m_a to the court saying whether the state is good or bad. If $m_p \neq m_a$, then no contract is chosen and both players earn zero payoffs. If $m_p = m_a$, the court enforces part (2) of the scheme.
2   The agent is paid the wage $(w|q)$ with either the good-state forcing contract $(2.25|4.5)$ or the bad-state forcing contract $(0.25|0.5)$, depending on his report m_a, or is boiled in oil if the output is inappropriate to his report.

There exists an equilibrium in which both players are willing to send truthful messages, because a deviation would result in zero payoffs. The agent earns a payoff of zero anyway (the numbers in the forcing contract come from making his participation constraint binding), but that is due to the open-set problem and to our assumption that the principal has all of the bargaining power. The principal's payoff is positive and efforts are at the first-best level.

Usually this kind of scheme has multiple equilibria, however, perverse ones in which both players send false messages which match and inefficient actions result. Here, in a perverse equilibrium the principal and agent would always send the message $m_p = m_a = bad$. Even when the state was actually good, the payoffs would be $\pi_{principal}(good) = 0.5 - 0.25 > 0$ and $\pi_{agent}(good) = 0.25 - (0.5)^2 = 0$, so neither player would have incentive to deviate unilaterally and drive payoffs to zero.[1]

Perhaps a bigger problem than the multiplicity of equilibria is renegotiation due to players' inability to commit to the mechanism. Suppose the equilibrium says that both players will send truthful messages, but the agent deviates and reports $m_a = bad$ even though the state is good. The court will say that the contract is void. I told you that the payoffs would be zero is that case, but the court's decision is not really the end of the story. The agent could negotiate a new contract with the principal, something the principal would be willing to do rather than give up the gains from trade. In cross checking the punishment for deviation is costly to both players, and so they will agree to bypass the scheme rather than inflict the punishment.

---

[1] By the way, "$m_p = m_a = good$ always" could not happen in equilibrium because the agent would prefer the zero payoff from mismatching to being forced by the threat of boiling oil to try to attain q_g when the state is bad.

In this, cross checking is like the Holmstrom Teams contract, where if output was even a little too small, it was destroyed rather than divided among the team members. There, a solution was to have a third party who would receive the output if it was slightly too small, and so would refuse to renegotiate it. The analogy here would be to write a contract in which both principal and agent paid a third party if their announcements disagreed. This sounds possible, yet we rarely observe this in practice.

Or do we? In his book *Wise Guys* (p. 57), Nicholas Pileggi quotes low-level gangster Henry Hill as saying that criminals need the protection of mafia "wiseguys" because they can't go to the police when they have a dispute over illegal activities: "For instance, say I've got a fifty-thousand-dollar hijack load, and when I make my delivery, instead of getting paid, I get stuck up. What am I supposed to do? Go to the cops? Not likely. Shoot it out? I'm a hijacker, not a cowboy. No. The only way to guarantee that I'm not going ripped off by anybody is to be established with a member, like Paulie. Somebody who is a made man. A member of a crime family. A soldier. Then … that's the end of the ball game. Goodbye. They're dead … Of course, problems can arise when the guys sticking you up are associated with wiseguys too. Then there has to be a sit-down between your wiseguys and their wiseguys. What usually happens then is that the wiseguys divide whatever you stole for their own pocket, send you and the guy who robbed you home with nothing. And if you complain, you're dead." The low-level gangsters have a strong incentive to report the same story, or the higher-ups take away the property under dispute. This may sound familiar to parents too – "If we can't resolve this, the toy is going in the closet for a whole week." It is perhaps even the wisdom of Solomon – see Glazer & Ma (1989) or Baliga (2002) (which also has a nice exposition of mechanism design using the author's own work to illustrate).

Unravelling: Information Disclosure When Lying Is Prohibited

There is another special case in which hidden information can be forced into the open: when the agent is prohibited from lying and only has a choice between telling the truth or remaining silent.

In Production Game VIII, this set-up would give the agent two possible message sets. If the state were good, the agent's message would be taken from $m \in \{good, silent\}$. If the state were *bad*, the agent's message would be taken from $m \in \{bad, silent\}$.

The agent would have no reason to be silent if the true state were bad (which means low output would be excusable), so his message then would be *bad*. But then if the principal hears the message *silent* he knows the state must be good – *good* and *silent* both would occur only when the state was good. So the option to remain silent is worthless to the agent.

This can be generalized. Suppose Nature uses the uniform distribution to assign the variable s some value in the interval $[0, 10]$ and the agent's payoff is increasing in the principal's estimate of s. Usually we assume that the agent can lie freely, sending a message m taking any value in $[0, 10]$, but let us assume instead that he cannot lie but he can conceal information. Thus, if $s = 2$, he can send the uninformative message $m \geq 0$ (equivalent to no message), or the message $m \geq 1$, or $m = 2$, but not the lie that $m \geq 4.36$.

When $s = 2$ the agent might as well send a message that is the exact truth: "$m = 2$." Loosely speaking, if he were to choose the message "$m \geq 1$" instead, the principal's first thought might be to estimate s as the average value in the interval $[1, 10]$, which is 5.5. But the principal would realize that no agent with a value of s greater than 5.5 would want to send the message "$m \geq 1$" if 5.5 was the resulting deduction. This realization restricts the possible interval to [1, 5.5], which in turn has an average of 3.25. But then no agent with $s > 3.25$ would send the message "$m \geq 1$." The principal would continue this process of logical **unravelling** to conclude that $s = 1$. The message "$m \geq 0$" would be even worse, making the principal believe that $s = 0$. In this model, no news is bad news. The agent would therefore not send the message "$m \geq 1$" and he would be indifferent between "$m = 2$" and "$m \geq 2$" because the principal would make the same deduction from either message.

More precisely, and perhaps more simply, use the Nash equilibrium approach of looking for profitable deviations. The equilibrium is either fully separating or it has some pooling. If it is fully separating, the agent's type is revealed, so he might as well send $m = s$. If it has some pooling, there exists some type s_{best} which is the best in the pool that sends a given signal $\tilde{m}$. The principal's estimate of s on observing $\tilde{m}$ would be the average in the pool, which is less than s_{best}. Agent type s_{best} would therefore deviate to $m = s_{best}$ and reveal his type. Thus, somebody would deviate from any partially pooling equilibrium. The unique equilibrium must be fully separating.

Perfect unravelling is paradoxical, but that is because the assumptions behind the last paragraph's reasoning are rarely satisfied in the real world. In particular, either unpunishable lying or genuine ignorance allow information to be concealed. If the seller is free to lie without punishment then in the absence of other incentives he always pretends that his information is extremely favorable, so nothing he says conveys any information, good or bad. If he really is ignorant in some states of the world, then his silence could mean either that he has nothing to say or that he has nothing favorable to report. The unravelling argument fails because if he sends an uninformative message the buyers will attach some probability to "I don't know" instead of "unfavorable news." Problem 10.1 explores unravelling further. For a careful discussion of the idea, see Milgrom (1981b).

The Revelation Principle

A principal might choose to offer a contract that induces his agent to lie in equilibrium, since he can take lying into account when he designs the contract, but this complicates the analysis. Each state of the world has a single truth, but a continuum of lies. Generically speaking, almost everything is false. The following principle helps us simplify contract design. Recall that w is the wage, q is output, m is the message, and s is the agent type.

The Revelation Principle: *For every contract $w(q, m)$ that leads to lying (i.e., to $m \neq s$), there is a contract $w^*(q, m)$ with the same payoff for every s but no incentive for the agent to lie.*

Many possible contracts make false messages profitable for the agent because when the state of the world is a he receives a reward of x_1 for the true report of a and $x_2 > x_1$ for the false report of b. A contract which gives the agent the same reward of x_2 regardless of whether he reports a or b would lead to exactly the same payoffs for each player while giving the agent no incentive to lie. The revelation principle notes that a truth-telling contract like this can always be found by imitating the relation between states of the world and payoffs in the equilibrium of a contract with lying. There are two levels of simplification in mechanism design problems. First, if there are n possible types of agent, we can restrict the agent's message to take only n values (or, similarly, if the type is a value t on an interval $[a, b]$, we can restrict messages to that interval). If we do so, it is called a **direct mechanism**; if we allow more possible messages than types, it is an **indirect mechanism**. Second, we can require the mechanism to be constructed to elicit truthful messages from the agent. The revelation principle says that this requirement does not change the payoffs a mechanism might achieve.

In Production Game VIII, the revelation principle is not very useful since there are only two possible states and the equilibrium is perfectly separating – agents get different rewards in each state. Where the principle has bite is when the equilibrium involves some pooling. Suppose we are trying to design a mechanism to make people with higher incomes pay higher taxes, but anyone who makes $70,000 a year can claim he makes $50,000 and we do not have the resources to catch him, or any other variables to use for leverage to end up with a fully separating equilibrium. We could design a mechanism in which higher reported incomes pay higher taxes, but reports of $50,000 would come both from people who truly have that income and people whose income is $70,000. The revelation principle says that we can rewrite the tax code to set the tax to be the same for taxpayers earning $70,000 and for those earning $50,000, and the same amount of taxes will be collected without anyone having incentive to lie. This would be better if we are concerned with the effect on the moral climate of cheating on income taxes. Similarly, applied to children's education, the principle says that the mother who agrees never to punish her daughter if she tells her all her escapades will never hear any untruths. That is fine for deterring lying, but not very useful for deterring other misbehavior.

Clearly, the principle's usefulness is not so much to improve outcomes as to simplify contracts. The principal (and the modeller) need only look at contracts which induce truth-telling instead of more complex schemes in which the principal knows lying is going on but adjusts rewards accordingly. Thus, the relevant strategy space is shrunk, and we can add a third constraint to the incentive compatibility and participation constraints to help calculate the equilibrium:

Truth-telling: *The equilibrium contract makes the agent willing to choose $m = s$.*

The revelation principle says that a truth-telling equilibrium exists, but not that it is unique. It may well happen that the equilibrium is a weak Nash equilibrium in which the optimal contract gives the agent no incentive to lie but also no incentive to tell the truth. This is similar to section 4.3's open-set problem; the optimal contract satisfies the agent's participation constraint but makes him indifferent between accepting and rejecting the contract. If agents derive the slightest utility from telling the truth, then truth-telling becomes a strong equilibrium, but if their utility from telling the truth is really significant, it should be made an explicit part of the model. If the utility of truth-telling is strong enough, in fact, agency problems and the costs associated with them disappear. This is one reason why morality is useful to business.

The revelation principle does depend heavily on an implicit assumption we have made: the principal cannot breach his contract. In the example of tax design, for example, if the government can freely modify the tax schedule after the agents report their incomes, the direct mechanism under which agents pay the same tax for income of either $50,000 or $70,000 will break down, because the rich agents know that if they report their incomes of $70,000 truthfully, the government will change the tax schedule ex post and make them pay more. Instead, the government will have to use an indirect mechanism in which taxes are always higher for higher incomes and those people with incomes of $70,000 untruthfully report $50,000. Thus, throughout this chapter we will be assuming that the principal can commit to his mechanism – can commit to not using all the information he receives from the agent.

The Sender–Receiver Game of Crawford and Sobel: Coarse Information Transmission

Even if the informed and uninformed players have different incentives, can lie, and can't commit to a mechanism, if their incentives are close enough, truthful if imperfect messages can be sent in equilibrium – unlike in the unravelling games, where incentives are entirely divergent. Let us call the informed player "the sender" and the uninformed player "the receiver." That is common in this kind of model, instead of calling the two players the agent and the principal. Let the sender's type, t, be uniformly distributed on $[0, 10]$. The sender sends a message, m, and the receiver chooses an action, a, in response, where a and m are also in $[0, 10]$. At the extremes of payoff function similarity, it is clear what happens. Suppose the sender wants a to be as close to t as possible. If the sender also wants a to be close to t, he will tell the truth: $m = t$. If he wants a to be as big as possible regardless of t, on the other hand, because his ideal action is $a = 10$, then he will lie and the receiver will ignore any message.

But what happens if, say, the sender's ideal action is $(t + 1)$, so he doesn't want a to be too large, but he does want a to be bigger than a fully-informed receiver would choose? Crawford & Sobel (1982) discovered the answer in a famous article titled "Strategic Information Transmission." We will see what happens in the game below, which I adapted from Gibbons (1992, section 4.3.A), a good place to go if you want to learn more.

The Crawford–Sobel Sender–Receiver Game

PLAYERS
The sender and the receiver.

THE ORDER OF PLAY
0   Nature chooses the sender's type to be $t \sim U[0, 10]$.
1   The sender chooses message $m \in [0, 10]$.
2   The receiver chooses action $a \in [0, 10]$.

PAYOFFS
The payoffs are quadratic loss functions in which each player has an ideal point and wants a to be close to that ideal point.

$$\pi_{sender} = \alpha - (a - [t + 1])^2,$$

$$\pi_{receiver} = \alpha - (a - t)^2. \tag{10.9}$$

First, let's see why perfect truthtelling cannot happen in equilibrium. Suppose the receiver believed that the sender always sent $m = t$ and so chooses $a = m$. Would the sender indeed be willing to tell the truth?

He would not. The sender would not always report $m = 10$, because his ideal point is $a = t + 1$, rather than a being as big as possible. If, however, the sender thinks the receiver will believe him, he will deviate to reporting $m = t + 1$, always exaggerating his type slightly.

What if the receiver adapts to this, and chooses $a = m - 1$? Then the sender would change too, and send $m = t + 2$, exaggerating more. This unravelling away from the truth (as opposed to the unravelling *toward* the truth when outright lying is forbidden) continues until the only message the sender reports is $m = 10$, regardless of his type and the receiver ignores it. This explanation is heuristic, and does not prove that there is no fully separating equilibrium, in which each type of sender reports a different message, but Crawford & Sobel (1982) prove that this is the case.

Thus, one equilibrium is the pooling equilibrium in which the sender's message is ignored and the receiver chooses $a = Et = 5$. This equilibrium could take either of two forms:

Pooling Equilibrium 1

Sender: Send $m = 10$ regardless of t.

Receiver: Choose $a = 5$ regardless of m.

Out-of-equilibrium belief: If the sender sends $m < 10$, the receiver uses passive conjectures and still believes that $t \sim U[0, 10]$.

Pooling Equilibrium 2

Sender: Send m using a mixed-strategy distribution independent of t that has the support $[0, 10]$ with positive density everywhere.

Receiver: Choose $a = 5$ regardless of m.

Out-of-equilibrium belief: Unnecessary, since any message might be observed in equilibrium.

In each of these two equilibria, the sender's action conveys no information and is ignored by the receiver. The sender is happy about this if it happens that $t = 4$, and the receiver is if $t = 5$, but averaging over all possible t, both their payoffs are lower than if the sender could commit to truthtelling. There also, however, exists a partial pooling equilibrium in which the sender truthfully reports whether his type is in the low interval $[0, x]$ or the high interval $[x, 10]$, with $x = 3$.

Partial Pooling Equilibrium 3

Sender: Send $m = 0$ if $t \in [0, 3]$ or $m = 10$ if $t \in [3, 10]$.

Receiver: Choose $a = 1.5$ if $m < 3$ and $a = 6.5$ if $m \geq 3$.

Out-of-equilibrium belief: If m is something other than 0 or 10, then $t \sim U[0, 3]$ if $m \in [0, 3)$ and $t \sim U[3, 10]$ if $a \in [3, 10]$.

In effect, the Sender has reduced his message space to two messages, LOW (=0) and HIGH (=10), in Equilibrium 3. Rather than just testing that this is an equilibrium, let us derive it, to show why the equilibrium interval-splitting type is $x = 3$.

First, note that the receiver's optimal strategy in a a partially pooling equilibrium is to choose his action to equal the expected value of the type in the interval the sender has chosen. Thus, if $m = 0$, the receiver will choose $a = x/2$ and if $m = 10$ he will choose $a = (x + 10)/2$.

The receiver's equilibrium response determines the sender's payoffs from his two messages. The payoffs between which he chooses are:

$$\pi_{sender, \, m=0} = \alpha - \left([t + 1] - \frac{x}{2}\right)^2,$$

$$\pi_{sender, \, m=10} = \alpha - \left(\frac{10 + x}{2} - [t + 1]\right)^2.$$

(10.10)

There exists a value x such that if $t = x$, the sender is indifferent between $m = 0$ and $m = 10$, but if t is lower he prefers $m = 0$ and if t is higher he prefers $m = 10$. To find x, equate the two payoffs in expression (10.10) and simplify to obtain

$$[t + 1] - \frac{x}{2} = \frac{10 + x}{2} - [t + 1].$$

(10.11)

We set $t = x$ at the point of indifference, and solving for x yields $x = 3$.

Thus, the divergence in preferences of the sender and receiver coarsens the message space, in effect. The sender will not send a truthful precise message, but if expectations are right (so we have the partially pooling equilibrium) he will send a truthful coarse message. If the true value of t is small, the sender will report the fairly precise information that t lies in [0,3]. If t is larger, it is harder to induce a truthful report, since the sender has a tendency to exaggerate and report t larger than it is, but the message can at least rule out the interval [0,3).

If instead of wanting $(t + 1)$ to be the action, the preferences of sender and receiver diverged more – say, to $(t + 8)$ – then there would only be the uninformative pooling equilibrium. If they diverged less – say, to $(t + 0.1)$ – then there would exist other partially pooling equilibria that had more than just two effective messages and would distinguish between three or more intervals instead of between just two.

In the Sender–Receiver Game, the receiver cannot commit to the way he reacts to the message, so this is not a mechanism design problem. The sender is not punished for lying, so the unravelling argument for truthtelling does not apply. Nor do the players' payoffs depend directly on the message, which might permit the signalling we will study in chapter 11 to operate. Instead, this is a **cheap-talk game**, so called because of these absences: m does not affect the payoff directly, the players cannot commit to future actions, and lying brings no direct penalty. In chapter 3 I alluded to how cheap talk might help select among equilibria in the Battle of the Sexes. In particular, knowing what the other player was thinking of doing would help to avoid the mixed-strategy equilibrium, with its low payoff. Our sender and receiver are in a similar situation here: their interests are similar but not identical, and they could both benefit from some transfer of information. If expectations are appropriate, they do so, in the partially pooling equilibrium. If they do not expect the cheap talk to be informative, however, it will not be, and coordination will fail.

10.2   Myerson Mechanism Design

The classic example of mechanism design is Roger Myerson's, who uses a version of it in sections 6.4 and 10.3 of his 1991 book. A seller has 100 units of a good. If it is high quality, he values it at 40 dollars per unit; if it is low quality, at 20 dollars. The buyer, who cannot observe quality before purchase, values high quality at 50 dollars per unit and low quality at 30 dollars. For efficiency, all of the good should be transferred from the seller to the buyer. The only way to get the seller to truthfully reveal the quality of the good, however, is for the buyer to say that if the seller admits the quality is bad, he will buy more units than if the seller claims it is good. Let us see how this works out.

Depending on who offers the contract and when it is offered, various games result. We will look at one in which the seller makes the offer, and does so before he knows whether his quality is high or low.

The Myerson Trading Game: Postcontractual Hidden Knowledge

PLAYERS
A buyer and a seller.

THE ORDER OF PLAY
1   The seller offers the buyer a contract $\{q_h, p_h, q_l, p_l\}$ under which the seller will declare his quality m to be high or low, and the buyer will then buy q_l or q_h units of the 100 the seller has available, at price p_l or p_h. The contract is $\{w(m) = q(m)p(m), q(m)\}$. Zero is paid if the wrong output is delivered.
2   The buyer accepts or rejects the contract.
3   Nature chooses whether the type of the seller's good, s, is High quality (probability 0.2) or Low (probability 0.8), unobserved by the buyer.
4   If the contract was accepted by both sides, the seller declares his type to be L or H and sells at the appropriate quantity and price as stated in the contract.

PAYOFFS
If the buyer rejects the contract, $\pi_{buyer} = 0$, $\pi_{seller\,H} = 40 * 100$, and $\pi_{seller\,L} = 20 * 100$.
If the buyer accepts the contract and the seller declares a type that has price p and quantity q then

$$\pi_{buyer|L} = (30 - p)q \quad \text{and} \quad \pi_{buyer|H} = (50 - p)q \tag{10.12}$$

and

$$\pi_{seller\,H} = 40(100 - q) + pq \quad \text{and} \quad \pi_{seller\,L} = 20(100 - q) + pq. \tag{10.13}$$

because the seller has an opportunity cost (a personal value or production cost) of 40 per high-quality unit and 20 per low-quality unit.

The seller wants to design a contract subject to two sets of constraints. First, the buyer must accept the contract. Thus, the participation constraint is[2]

$$(0.8)\pi_{buyer|seller\ L} + (0.2)\pi_{buyer|seller\ H} \geq 0,$$

$$0.8[(30 - p_l)q_l] + 0.2[(50 - p_h)q_h] \geq 0. \tag{10.14}$$

This constraint will be binding, since the seller has no reason to leave the buyer any surplus. Notice, however, that if it is binding and both q_l and q_h are positive, we can conclude that $p_l = 30$ and $p_h = 50$.

There might also be a participation constraint for the seller himself, because it might be that even when he designs the contract that maximizes his payoff, his payoff is no higher than when he refuses to offer a contract. He can always offer the acceptable (if vacuous) null contract ($q_l = 0, p_l = 0, q_h = 0, p_h = 0$), however, so we do not need to write out the seller's participation constraint separately.

Second, the seller must design a contract that will induce himself to tell the truth later once he discovers his type. This is, of course a bit unusual – the seller is like a principal designing a contract for himself as agent. That is why things are different in this chapter than in the chapters on moral hazard. What is happening is that the seller is trying to sell not just a good, but a contract, and so he must make the contract attractive to the buyer. Thus, he faces two incentive compatibility constraints: one for when he is low quality,

$$\pi_{seller\ L}(q_l, p_l) \geq \pi_{seller\ L}(q_h, p_h),$$

$$20(100 - q_l) + p_l q_l \geq 20(100 - q_h) + p_h q_h,$$

$$20(100 - q_l) + 30 q_l \geq 20(100 - q_h) + 50 q_h, \tag{10.15}$$

$$q_l \geq 3q_h.$$

and one for when he has high quality,

$$\pi_{seller\ H}(q_h, p_h) \geq \pi_{seller\ H}(q_l, p_l),$$

$$40(100 - q_h) + p_h q_h \geq 40(100 - q_l) + p_l q_l,$$

$$40(100 - q_h) + 50 q_h \geq 40(100 - q_l) + 30 q_l, \tag{10.16}$$

$$q_h \geq -q_l.$$

The low-quality incentive compatibility constraint, inequality (10.15), tells us that $q_l > q_h$. The price of 50 that comes from claiming to have high quality dominates the price of 30 that comes from claiming to have low quality. If the seller cannot sell as great a quantity when he claims the quality is high, though, he might admit to low quality (think of an extreme case such as $q_l = 100, q_h = 5$).

On the other hand, the high-quality incentive compatibility constraint is satisfied for all possible q_l and q_h, because the high-quality seller's opportunity cost of 40 is greater than the price of 30 he could get by pretending to have low quality.

---

[2] Another kind of participation constraint would apply if the buyer had the option to reject purchasing anything, after accepting the contract and hearing the seller's type announcement. That would not make a difference here.

Thus, we know from the low-quality incentive compatibility constraint that we need $q_l > q_h$, and in fact that $q_l = 3q_h$ at the optimum. The seller's payoff function is

$$\pi_s = 0.8\pi_{seller\ L}(q_l, p_l) + 0.2\pi_{seller\ H}(q_h, p_h),$$

$$= 0.8[(20)(100 - q_l) + p_l q_l] + 0.2[(40)(100 - q_h) + p_h q_h],$$

$$= 0.8[(20)(100 - q_l) + 30q_l] + 0.2[(40)(100 - q_h) + 50q_h]. \tag{10.17}$$

This is increasing in both q_l and q_h, so the seller would like to choose them to be as big as possible, subject to the constraints that $q_l = 3q_h$, $q_l \leq 100$, and $q_h \leq 100$. Thus, q_l will be the maximum possible, the first-best level $q_l = 100$, and q_h will be $q_h = q_l/3 = 33(1/3)$.

The equilibrium follows the general pattern for these games, though it has a twist because the informed player (the seller) has all the bargaining power, so it is the uninformed player (the buyer) whose participation constraint is binding. The incentive compatibility constraint is binding for the type with the most temptation to lie, and not for the other type. Using the two binding constraints, we can solve out for the values of some of the choice variables in terms of other choice variables, and then we can maximize the payoff of the player making the offer (the seller) to solve for values of those remaining variables. That is a useful general method, even though different games will have their own special features.

The mechanism will not work if further offers can be made after the end of the game. The mechanism is not first-best efficient; if the seller is high-quality, then he only sells 33(1/3) units to the buyer instead of all 100, even though both realize that the buyer's value is 50 and the seller's is only 40. If they could agree to sell the remaining 66(2/3) units, then the mechanism would not be incentive compatible in the first place, though, because then the low-quality seller would pretend to be high-quality, first selling 33(1/3) units and then selling the rest. The importance of commitment is a general feature of mechanisms.

A technical observation is that although we specified the contract in terms of (p, q), a price per unit p and a quantity q at that price, we could have set it up instead as (w, q), a total price amount w for the quantity q. That would be more in the style of mechanism design, with its emphasis on setting up the outcome of every outcome as the total transfers paid from one player to another and how an allocation or other decision is made.

10.3   An Example of Postcontractual Hidden Knowledge: The Salesman Game

Suppose the manager of a company has told his salesman to investigate a potential customer, who is either a *Pushover* or a *Bonanza*. If he is a *Pushover*, the efficient sales effort is low and sales should be moderate. If he is a *Bonanza*, the effort and sales should be higher. This is similar to Production Game VIII, but not the same. In the Salesman Game, the principal can perfectly deduce effort, even out of equilibrium. Also, there will be pooling as well as separating equilibria, and for the analysis we will make use of diagrams.

The Salesman Game

PLAYERS

A manager and a salesman.

THE ORDER OF PLAY

1   The manager offers the salesman a contract of the form $[w(m), q(m)]$, where w is the wage, q is sales, and m is a message.
2   The salesman decides whether or not to accept the contract.
3   Nature chooses whether the customer type t is a *Bonanza* or a *Pushover* with probabilities 0.2 and 0.8. The salesman observes the type, but the manager does not.
4   If the salesman has accepted the contract, he chooses his effort e. His sales level is $q = e$, so his sales perfectly reveal his effort.
5   The salesman's wage is $w(m)$ if he chooses $e = q(m)$ and zero otherwise.

PAYOFFS

The manager is risk-neutral and the salesman is risk-averse. If the salesman rejects the contract, his payoff is $\overline{U} = 8$ and the manager's is zero. If he accepts the contract, then

$$\pi_{manager} = q - w$$

$$\pi_{salesman} = U(e, w, \theta), \text{ where } \frac{\partial U}{\partial e} < 0, \ \frac{\partial^2 U}{\partial e^2} < 0, \ \frac{\partial U}{\partial w} > 0, \ \frac{\partial^2 U}{\partial w^2} < 0.$$

Figure 10.1 shows the indifference curves of manager and salesman, labelled with numerical values for exposition. The manager's indifference curves are straight lines with slope 1 because he is acting on behalf of a risk-neutral company. If the wage and the quantity both rise by a dollar, profits are unchanged, and the profits do not depend directly on whether s takes the value *Pushover* or *Bonanza*.

The salesman's indifference curves also slope upwards, because he must receive a higher wage to compensate for the extra effort that makes q greater. They are convex because the marginal utility of dollars is decreasing and the marginal disutility of effort is increasing. As figure 10.1 shows, the salesman has two sets of indifference curves, solid for *Pushovers* and dashed for *Bonanzas*, since the effort that secures a given level of sales depends on the state.

Because of the participation constraint, the manager must provide the salesman with a contract giving him at least his reservation utility of 8, which is the same in both states. If the true state is that the customer is a *Bonanza*, the manager would like to offer a contract that leaves the salesman on the dashed indifference curve $\widetilde{U}_S = 8$, and the efficient outcome is (q_2, w_2), the point at which the salesman's indifference curve is tangent to one of the manager's indifference curves. At that point, if the salesman sells an extra dollar he requires an extra dollar of compensation.

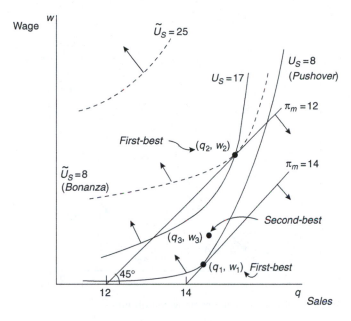

Figure 10.1   The Salesman Game with curves for pooling equilibria.

If it were common knowledge that the customer was a *Bonanza*, the principal could choose w_2 so that $U(q_2, w_2, Bonanza) = 8$ and offer the forcing contract

$$w = \begin{cases} 0 & \text{if } q < q_2, \\ w_2 & \text{if } q \geq q_2. \end{cases} \qquad (10.18)$$

The salesman would accept the contract and choose $e = q_2$. But if the customer were actually a *Pushover*, the salesman would still choose $e = q_2$, an inefficient outcome that does not maximize profits. High sales would be inefficient because the salesman would be willing to give up more than a dollar of wages to escape having to make his last dollar of sales. Profits would not be maximized, because the salesman achieves a utility of 17, and he would have been willing to work for less.

The revelation principle says that in searching for the optimal contract we need only look at contracts that induce the agent to truthfully reveal what kind of customer he faces. If it required more effort to sell any quantity to the *Bonanza*, as shown in figure 10.1, the salesman would always want the manager to believe that he faced a *Bonanza*, so he could extract the extra pay necessary to achieve a utility of 8 selling to *Bonanzas*. The optimal truth-telling contract is the pooling contract that pays the intermediate wage of w_3 for the intermediate quantity of q_3, and zero for any other quantity, regardless of the message. The pooling contract is a second-best contract, a compromise between the optimum for *Pushovers* and the optimum for *Bonanzas*. The point (q_3, w_3) is closer to (q_1, w_1) than to (q_2, w_2), because the probability of a *Pushover* is higher and the contract must satisfy the participation constraint,

$$0.8U(q_3, w_3, Pushover) + 0.2U(q_3, w_3, Bonanza) \geq 8. \qquad (10.19)$$

The nature of the equilibrium depends on the shapes of the indifference curves. If they are shaped as in figure 10.2, the equilibrium is separating, not pooling, and there does exist

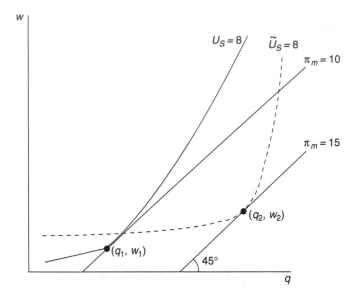

Figure 10.2   Indifference curves for a separating equilibrium.

a first-best, fully revealing contract.

$$
\text{Separating contract}\begin{cases} \text{Agent announces }\textit{Pushover:} \quad w = \begin{cases} 0 & \text{if } q < q_1, \\ w_1 & \text{if } q \geq q_1, \end{cases} \\[2ex] \text{Agent announces }\textit{Bonanza:} \quad w = \begin{cases} 0 & \text{if } q < q_2, \\ w_2 & \text{if } q \geq q_2. \end{cases} \end{cases} \tag{10.20}
$$

Again, we know from the revelation principle that we can narrow attention to contracts that induce the salesman to tell the truth. With figure 10.2's indifference curves, contract (10.20) induces the salesman to be truthful and the incentive compatibility constraint is satisfied. If the customer is a *Bonanza*, but the salesman claims to observe a *Pushover* and chooses q_1, his utility is less than 8 because the point (q_1, w_1) lies below the $\tilde{U}_S = 8$ indifference curve. If the customer is a *Pushover* and the salesman claims to observe a *Bonanza*, then although (q_2, w_2) does yield the salesman a higher wage than (q_1, w_1), the extra income is not worth the extra effort, because (q_2, w_2) is far below the indifference curve $U_S = 8$.

Another way to look at a separating equilibrium is to think of it as a choice of contracts rather than as one contract with different wages for different outputs. The salesman agrees to work for the manager, and after he discovers the customer's type he chooses either the contract (q_1, w_1) or the contract (q_2, w_2), where each is a forcing contract that pays him 0 if after choosing the contract (q_i, w_i) he produces output of $q \neq q_i$. In this interpretation, the manager offers a **menu of contracts** and the salesman selects one of them after learning his type.

Sales contracts in the real world are often complicated because it is easy to measure sales and hard to measure efforts when workers are out in the field away from direct supervision. The Salesman Game is a real problem. Gonik (1978) describes hidden knowledge contracts used by IBM's subsidiary in Brazil. Salesmen were first assigned quotas. They then announced their own sales forecasts as a percentage of quota and chose from among a set of contracts, one for each possible forecast. I'll invent some numbers for illustration. If

Smith were assigned a quota of 400 and he announced 100 percent, he would get $w = 70$ if he sold 400 and $w = 80$ if he sold 450. If he had announced 120 percent, he would have gotten $w = 60$ for 400 and $w = 90$ for 450. The contract encourages extra effort when the extra effort is worth the extra sales. The idea here, as in the Salesman Game, is to reward salesmen not just for high effort, but for appropriate effort.

The Salesman Game illustrates a number of ideas. It can have either a pooling or a separating equilibrium, depending on the utility function of the salesman. The revelation principle can be applied to avoid having to consider contracts in which the manager must interpret the salesman's lies. It also shows how to use diagrams when the algebraic functions are intractable or unspecified, a problem that does not arise in most of the two-valued numerical examples in this book.

*10.4   The Groves Mechanism

Hidden knowledge is particularly important in public economics, the study of government spending and taxation. In Mirrlees (1971), a classic article in the optimal taxation literature, citizens differ in their income-producing ability and the government wishes to demand higher taxes from the more able citizens. Since the government cannot observe ability directly, this is a problem of hidden knowledge. An even purer hidden knowledge problem is choosing the level of public goods based on private preferences. The government must decide whether it is worthwhile to buy a public good based on the combined preferences of all the citizens, but it needs to discover those preferences. Unlike so far in this chapter, a group of agents will now be involved, not just one agent. Moreover, here the principal is an altruistic government that cares directly about the utility of the agents rather than a car buyer or an insurance seller who cares about the agents' utility only in order to satisfy self-selection and participation constraints.

Our example is adapted from Varian (1992, p. 426). The mayor of a town is considering installing a streetlight costing $100. Each of the five houses near the light would be taxed exactly $20, but the mayor will only install it if he decides that the sum of the residents' valuations for it is greater than the cost.

The mayor's problem is to discover the valuations. If he could observe them directly, he would simply builds the streetlight if $\sum_{i=1}^{5} v_i > 100$. Otherwise, he has a problem. If he simply asks the householders and tells them that each must pay a tax of $20 if the streetlight is built, pro-light householder Smith might say that his valuation is $5,000, and anti-light householder Brown might say that he likes darkness and would pay $5,000 to *not* have a streetlight, but all the mayor could conclude would be that Smith's valuation exceeded $20 and Brown's did not. Talk is cheap, and the dominant strategy would be to overreport or underreport.

The flawed mechanism just described can be written as

$$M_1: \quad \left(w(m_i) = 20, \textit{Build iff} \sum_{i=1}^{5} m_i \geq 100 \right); \qquad (10.21)$$

that is, each resident pays $20, and the light is installed if the sum of the valuations exceeds 100.

The Streetlight Game

PLAYERS
The mayor and five householders.

THE ORDER OF PLAY
0 Nature chooses the value v_i that householder i places on having a streetlight installed, using distribution $f_i(v_i)$. Only Householder i observes v_i.
1 The mayor announces a mechanism, M, which requires a householder who reports m to pay $w(m)$ if the streetlight is installed and installs the streetlight if $g(m_1, m_2, m_3, m_4, m_5) \geq 0$.
2 Householder i reports value m_i simultaneously with all other householders.
3 If $g(m_1, m_2, m_3, m_4, m_5) \geq 0$, the streetlight is built and householder i pays $w(m_i)$.

PAYOFFS
The mayor tries to maximize social welfare, including the welfare of taxpayers besides the 5 householders. His payoff is zero if the streetlight is not built. Otherwise, it is

$$\pi_{mayor} = \left(\sum_{i=1}^{5} v_i \right) - 100, \qquad (10.22)$$

subject to the constraint that $\sum_{i=1}^{5} w(m_i) \geq 100$ so he can raise the taxes to pay for the light.
The payoff of householder i is zero if the streetlight is not built. Otherwise it is

$$\pi_i(m_1, m_2, m_3, m_4, m_5) = v_i - w(m_i). \qquad (10.23)$$

An alternative is to make resident i pay the amount of his message, or pay zero if it is negative. This mechanism is

$$M_2: \quad \left(w(m_i) = Max\{m_i, 0\}, \textit{Build iff } \sum_{j=1}^{5} m_j \geq 100 \right). \qquad (10.24)$$

Mechanism M_2 has no dominant strategy. Householder i would announce $m_i = 0$ if he thought the project would go through without his support, based on his estimates of other people's values, but he would announce up to his valuation if necessary.

If all the householders knew each others' values perfectly, then there would be a continuum of Nash equilibria that attained the efficient result, much as in the Holmstrom Teams Game of chapter 8. If, for example, the values were known to be (10, 30, 30, 30, 80), one equilibrium would be to report (0, 25, 25, 25, 25). Since typically equilibria would be asymmetric, though, it is problematic how the equilibrium to be played out would become common knowledge, as well as how the householders know the v's in the first place. M_2 is a simple mechanism, however, and it already teaches a lesson: people are more likely to report their true political preferences if they must bear part of the costs themselves.

It turns out, however, that not only can a mechanism be found which makes truth-telling a Nash equilibrium, one can be found which makes truth-telling the best strategy for a player regardless of what the other players do – a **dominant-strategy mechanism**. Consider the mechanism M_3.

$$M_3: \quad \left(w(m_i) = 100 - \sum_{j \neq i} m_j, \textit{Build iff} \sum_{j=1}^{5} m_j \geq 100 \right). \tag{10.25}$$

Under mechanism M_3, player i's message does not affect his tax bill except by its effect on whether or not the streetlight is installed. If player i's valuation is v_i, his full payoff is $v_i - 100 + \sum_{j \neq i} m_j$ if $m_i + \sum_{j \neq i} m_j \geq 100$, and zero otherwise. It is not hard to see that he will be truthful in a Nash equilibrium in which the other players are truthful, but we can go further: truthfulness is weakly dominant. Moreover, the players are strictly better off telling the truth whenever lying would alter the mayor's decision.

Consider a numerical example. Suppose Smith's valuation is 40 and the sum of the valuations is 110, so the project is indeed efficient. If the other players report their truthful sum of 70, Smith's payoff from truthful reporting is his valuation of 40 minus his tax of 30. Reporting more would not change his payoff, while reporting less than 30 would reduce it to 0.

If we are wondering whether Smith's strategy is dominant, we must also consider his best response when the other players lie. If they underreported, announcing 50 instead of the truthful 70, then Smith could make up the difference by overreporting 60, but his payoff would be $-10 (=40 + 50 - 100)$ so he would do better to report the truthful 40, killing the project and leaving himself with a payoff of 0. If the other players overreported, announcing 80 instead of the truthful 70, then Smith would benefit if the project went through, and he should report at least 20. Whether he reports 20, 21, 40, or 400, the streetlight is built and he pays a tax of 20 under mechanism M_3, leaving him with payoff of $20(=40 - 20)$. In particular, he is willing to report exactly 40, so it is a weakly best response to the other players' lies.

The problem with a dominant-strategy mechanisms like M_3 is that it is not budget balancing. This is not so bad if the budget had a surplus, as required in our game rules above, but it turns out to have a deficit except in special cases where it is perfectly balanced (e.g., $m_i = 20$ for all 5 householders). The first part of the tax $w(m)$ would collect 100 from each player, for 500, which leaves a surplus of 400 once we pay for the streetlight. The second part of $w(m)$, however, would subtract each player's value four times (1 for each other player), subtracting $4(\sum_{i=1}^{5} m_i)$. If the project goes through though, then $\sum_{i=1}^{5} m_i > 100$, so the budget would be left in deficit.

In fact, the total tax revenue could easily be negative too, because the "taxes" under M_3 are sometimes negative. If $v = 60$ for all five players, for example, then $m = 60$ and $w(m) = -140(=100 - 4(60))$.

Vickrey (1961) first suggested the non-budget-balancing mechanism for revelation of preferences, but that was in the context of auctions, not public economics. We will see in chapter 13 that the second-price auction has the same distinctive feature that a player's own report affects the allocative decision (whether the light is built, who wins the auction) but not the amount he pays conditional on the decision being made (the tax, the price the auction winner pays). The idea was rediscovered later and became known as the Groves Mechanism from Groves (1973).

10.5 Price Discrimination

Now let's go to algebra to do a more conventional mechanism design problem, where the agents not only select an action that reveals their information, but must choose to play the game in the first place.

When a firm has market power – most simply when it is a monopolist – it would like to charge different prices to different consumers. To the consumer who would pay up to $45,000 for a car, the firm would like to charge $45,000; to the consumer who would pay up to $36,000, the profit-maximizing price is $36,000. But how does the car dealer know how much each consumer is willing to pay?

He does not, and that is what makes this a problem of mechanism design under adverse selection. The consumer who would be willing to pay $45,000 can hide under the guise of being a less intense consumer, and despite facing a monopolist he can end up retaining consumer surplus – an **informational rent**, a return to the consumer's private information about his own type.[3]

Pigou was a contemporary of Keynes at Cambridge who usefully divided price discrimination into three types in 1920 but named them so obscurely that I relegate his names to the endnotes and use better ones here:

1 **Interbuyer price discrimination:** This is when the seller can charge different prices to different buyers. Smith's price for a hamburger is $4 per burger, but Jones's is $6.
2 **Interquantity price discrimination or nonlinear pricing:** This is when the seller can charge different unit prices for different quantities. A consumer can buy a first sausage for $9, a second sausage for $4, and a third sausage for $3. Rather than paying the "linear" total price of $9 for one sausage, $18 for two, and $27 for three, he thus pays the nonlinear price of $9 for one sausage, $13 for two, and $16 for three, the concave price path shown in figure 10.3.
3 **Perfect price discrimination:** This combines interbuyer and interquantity price discrimination. When the seller does have perfect information and can charge each buyer that buyer's reservation price for each unit bought, Smith might end up paying $50 for his first hot dog and $20 for his second, while next to him Jones pays $4 for his first and $3 for his second.

To illustrate price discrimination as mechanism design we will use a modified version of an example in chapter 14 of Hal Varian's third edition (Varian [1992]).

---

[3] A standard opening ploy of car salesman is to ask. "So, how much are you able to spend on a car today?" My recommendation: don't tell him. This may sound obvious, but remember it the next time your department chairman asks you how high a salary it would take to keep you from leaving for another university.

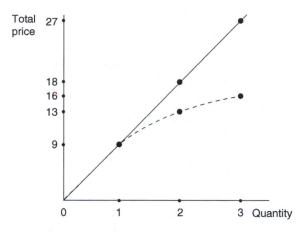

Figure 10.3   Linear and nonlinear pricing.

Varian's Nonlinear Pricing Game

PLAYERS
One seller and one buyer.

THE ORDER OF PLAY
0   Nature assigns the buyer a type, s. The buyer is "unenthusiastic" with utility function u or "valuing" with utility function v, with equal probability. The seller does not observe Nature's move, but the buyer does.
1   The seller offers mechanism $\{w_m, q_m\}$ under which the buyer can announce his type as m and buy amount q_m for lump sum w_m.
2   The buyer chooses a message m or rejects the mechanism entirely and does not buy at all.

PAYOFFS
The seller has a zero marginal cost, so his payoff is

$$w_u + w_v. \tag{10.26}$$

The buyers' payoffs are $\pi_u = u(q_u) - w_u$ and $\pi_v = v(q_v) - w_v$ if q is positive, and 0 if $q = 0$, with $u', v' > 0$ and $u'', v'' < 0$. The marginal willingness to pay is greater for the valuing buyer: for any q,

$$u'(q) < v'(q) \tag{10.27}$$

Condition (10.27) is an example of **the single-crossing property**, which we will discuss at the end of this section. Combined with the assumption that $v(0) = u(0) = 0$, it also implies that

$$u(q) < v(q) \tag{10.28}$$

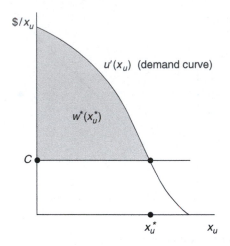

Figure 10.4   Perfect price discrimination.

for any value of q. Figure 10.7a, some pages below, shows an example of functions which satisfy it.

To ease into the difficult problem of solving for the equilibrium mechanism, let us start with two simpler versions of the game that limit it to (a) perfect price discrimination and (b) interbuyer discrimination.

Perfect Price Discrimination

The game would allow perfect price discrimination if the seller did know which buyer had which utility function. He can then just maximize profit subject to the participation constraints for the two buyers:

$$\underset{w_u, w_v, q_u, q_v}{\textit{Maximize}} \ w_u + w_v, \tag{10.29}$$

subject to

(a) $u(q_u) - w_u \geq 0$ and

(b) $v(q_v) - w_v \geq 0.$ \hfill (10.30)

The constraints will be satisfied as equalities, since the seller will charge all that the buyers will pay. Substituting for w_u and w_v into the maximand, the first order conditions become

(a) $u'(q_u^*) - c = 0$ and

(b) $v'(q_v^*) - c = 0.$ \hfill (10.31)

Thus, the seller will choose quantities so that each buyer's marginal utility equals the marginal cost of production, and will choose prices so that the entire consumer surpluses are eaten up: $w^*(q_u^*) = u(q_u^*)$ and $w^*(q_v^*) = v(q_v^*)$. Figure 10.4 shows this for the unenthusiastic buyer.

Interbuyer Price Discrimination

The interbuyer price discrimination problem arises when the seller knows which utility functions Smith and Jones have and can sell to them separately. If he can choose w_u and w_v as before and use forcing contracts, this is the same as the perfect price discrimination problem we just solved. If the seller must charge each buyer a single price per unit and let the buyer choose the quantity, however, the problem is quite different:

$$\text{Maximize}_{q_u, q_v, p_u, p_v} \ p_u q_u + p_v q_v, \tag{10.32}$$

subject to the participation constraints

$$u(q_u) - p_u q_u \geq 0 \quad \text{and} \quad v(q_v) - p_v q_v \geq 0 \tag{10.33}$$

and the incentive compatibility constraints

$$q_u = argmax[u(q_u) - p_u q_u] \quad \text{and} \quad q_v = argmax[v(q_v) - p_v q_v]. \tag{10.34}$$

This should remind you of moral hazard. It is very like the problem of a principal designing two incentive contracts for two agents to induce appropriate effort levels given their different disutilities of effort.

The agents will solve their quantity choice problems in (10.34), yielding

$$u'(q_u) - p_u = 0 \quad \text{and} \quad v'(q_v) - p_v = 0. \tag{10.35}$$

Thus, we can simplify the original problem in (10.32) to

$$\text{Maximize}_{q_u, q_v} \ u'(q_u)q_u + v'(q_v)q_v, \tag{10.36}$$

subject to the participation constraints

$$u(q_u) - u'(q_u)q_u \geq 0 \quad \text{and} \quad v(q_v) - v'(q_v)q_v \geq 0. \tag{10.37}$$

The participation constraints will not be binding. If they were, then $u(q)/q = u'(q)$, but since $u'' < 0$ there is diminishing utility of consumption and the average utility, $U(q)/q$, will be greater than the marginal utility, $u'(q)$. Thus we can solve problem (10.36) as if there were no constraints. The first-order conditions are

$$u''(q_u)q_u + u' = 0 \quad \text{and} \quad v''(q_v)q_v + v' = 0. \tag{10.38}$$

This is just the "marginal revenue equals marginal cost" condition that any monopolist uses, but one for each buyer instead of one for the entire market.

The assumption of constant marginal cost (equal to zero here) helps make this problem easier, because it makes it two independent problems, really. Choosing a contract for the valuing customer is completely separate from choosing one for the unenthusiastic customer. If the cost function were a more general convex $c(q_u + q_v)$, on the other hand, the two first-order conditions in (10.38) would have to be solved together, because each condition would depend on both q_u and q_v.

Back to Nonlinear Pricing

Neither the perfect price discrimination nor the interbuyer problems are mechanism design problems, since the seller is perfectly informed about the types of the buyers and has no need to worry about designing incentives to separate them. In the original game, however, separation is the seller's main concern. He must satisfy not just the participation constraints, but self-selection constraints. The seller's problem is

$$\text{Maximize}_{q_u, q_v, w_u, w_v} \ w_u + w_v, \tag{10.39}$$

subject to the participation constraints,

(a) $u(q_u) - w_u \geq 0$ and

(b) $v(q_v) - w_v \geq 0,$ $\tag{10.40}$

and the self-selection constraints,

(a) $u(q_u) - w_u \geq u(q_v) - w_v,$

(b) $v(q_v) - w_v \geq v(q_u) - w_u.$ $\tag{10.41}$

Not all of these constraints will be binding. If neither type had a binding participation constraint, however, the principal would be losing a chance to increase his profits. In a mechanism design problem like this, what always happens is that the contracts are designed so that one type of agent is pushed down to his reservation utility.

Suppose the optimal contract is in fact separating, and also that both types accept a contract. At least one type will have a binding participation constraint. Since the valuing consumer gets more consumer surplus from a given w and q than an unenthusiastic consumer, it must be the unenthusiastic consumer who is driven down to zero surplus for (w_u, q_u). The valuing consumer would get positive surplus from accepting that same contract, so his participation constraint is not binding. To persuade the valuing consumer to accept (w_v, q_v) instead, the seller must give him that same positive surplus from it. The seller will not be any more generous than he has to, though, so the valuing consumer's self-selection constraint will be binding.

Rearranging our two binding constraints and setting them out as equalities yields:

$$w_u = u(q_u) \tag{10.42}$$

and

$$w_v = w_u - v(q_u) + v(q_v). \tag{10.43}$$

This allows us to reformulate the seller's problem from (10.39) as

$$\text{Maximize}_{q_u, q_v} \ u(q_u) + u(q_u) - v(q_u) + v(q_v), \tag{10.44}$$

which has the first-order conditions

(a) $u'(q_u) + [u'(q_u) - v'(q_u)] = 0,$

(b) $v'(q_v) = 0.$ $\tag{10.45}$

The first-order conditions in (10.45) could be solved for exact values of q_u and q_v if we chose particular functional forms, but they are illuminating even if we do not. Equation (10.45b) tells us that the valuing type of buyer buys a quantity such that his last unit's marginal utility exactly equals the marginal cost of production; his consumption is at the efficient level. The unenthusiastic type, however, buys less than his first-best amount, something we can deduce using the single-crossing property, assumption (10.27b), that $u'(q) < v'(q)$, which implies from (10.45a) that $u'(q_u) > 0$ and the unenthusiastic type has not bought enough to drive his marginal utility down to marginal cost. The intuition is that the seller must sell less than first-best optimal to the unenthusiastic type so as not to make that contract too attractive to the valuing type. On the other hand, making the valuing type's contract more valuable to him actually helps separation, so q_v is chosen to maximize social surplus.

The single-crossing property has another important implication. Substituting from first-order condition (10.45b) into first-order condition (10.45a) yields

$$[u'(q_u) - v'(q_v)] + [u'(q_u) - v'(q_u)] = 0. \tag{10.46}$$

The second term in square brackets is negative by the single-crossing property. Thus, the first term must be positive. But since the single-crossing property tells us that $[u'(q_u) - v'(q_u)] < 0$, it must be true, since $v'' < 0$, that if $q_u \geq q_v$ then $[u'(q_u) - v'(q_v)] < 0$ – that is, that the first term is negative. We cannot have that without contradiction, so it must be that $q_u < q_v$. The unenthusiastic buyer buys strictly less than the valuing buyer. This accords with our intuition, and also lets us know that the equilibrium is separating, not pooling (though we still have not proven that the equilibrium involves both players buying a positive amount, something hard to prove elegantly since one player buying zero would be a corner solution to our maximization problem).

A Graphical Approach to the Same Problem

Under perfect price discrimination, the seller would charge $w_u = A + B$ and $w_v = A + B + J + K + L$ to the two buyers for quantities q_u^* and q_v^*, as shown in figure 10.5a. An attempt to charge $w_u^* = A + B$ and $w_v^* = A + B + J + K + L$, however, would simply lead to both buyers choosing to buy q_u^*, which would yield the valuing buyer a payoff of $J + K$ rather than the zero he would get as a payoff from buying q_v^*. The seller's payoff from this pooling equilibrium (which is the best pooling contract possible for him, since it drives the unenthusiastic type to a payoff of zero) is $2(A + B)$.

The seller could separate the two buyers by charging $w_u^* = A + B$ for q_u^* and $w_v^* = A + B + L$ for q_v^*, since the unenthusiastic buyer would have no reason to switch to the greater quantity, and that would increase his profits over pooling by amount L.

Figure 10.5b shows, however, that the seller would do better to slightly reduce the quantity sold to the unenthusiastic buyer, to below q_u^*, and reduce the price to him by the amount of the dark shading. He could then sell q_v^* to the valuing buyer and raise the price to him by the light shaded area. The valuing buyer will not be tempted to buy the smaller quantity at the lower price, and the seller will have gained profit by, loosely speaking, increasing the size of the L triangle.

Continuing this process until profit is maximized is what we did earlier using algebra. Our profit-maximizing mechanism is shown in figure 10.5a as $w_u' = A$ for q_u' and $w_v^* = A + B + K + L$ for q_v^*. The unenthusiastic buyer is left with a binding participation constraint and inefficiently low consumption, because $w_u' = A = u(q_u')$. The valuing

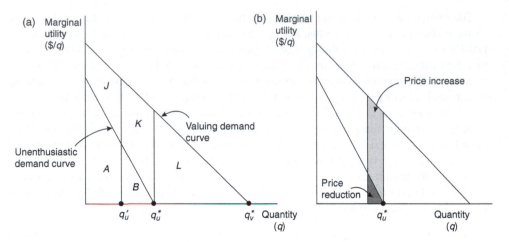

Figure 10.5   The Varian Nonlinear Pricing Game.

buyer has a nonbinding participation constraint, because $w_v^* = A + B + K + L < v(q_v^*) = A + B + J + K + L$; he is left with a surplus of J. Moreover, he consumes the efficient amount for him, which is q_v^*. He also has a binding self-selection constraint, because he is exactly indifferent between buying q_u' and q_v^*. His choice is between a payoff of $\pi_v(U) = (A+J) - A$ and $\pi_v(V) = (A + B + J + K + L) - (A + B + K + L)$. Thus, the diagram replicates the algebraic conclusions.

The Single-crossing Property

Condition (10.27) is an example of **the single-crossing property**, since it implies that the indifference curves of the two agents cross at most one time. Combined with the assumption that $v(0) = u(0) = 0$, it implies that $u(q) < v(q)$ for any value of q, as stated in inequality (10.28) earlier. Thus, in Varian's Nonlinear Pricing Game it is unambiguous that the valuing buyer has stronger demand than the unenthusiastic buyer.

When we say that Buyer V's demand is stronger than Buyer U's, however, there are two things we might mean:

1   Buyer V's *average demand* is stronger: $v(q)/q > u(q)/q$. Buyer V would pay more for quantity q than Buyer U would.
2   Buyer V's *marginal demand* is stronger: $v'(q) > u'(q)$. Buyer V would pay more for an additional unit than Buyer U would.

Definitions (1) and (2) are not equivalent. In figure 10.6a, Buyer U is willing to pay 5 per unit up to $q = 4$, but only 1 per unit thereafter. Buyer V is willing to pay only 2 per unit up to $q = 10$, and 1 per unit thereafter. As a result $u(q) > v(q)$, and U has the stronger demand by definition (1). But for $q \in [4, 10]$, Buyer V is willing to pay 2 per new unit while Buyer U is only willing to pay 1, so in that interval Buyber V has the stronger demand by definition (2).

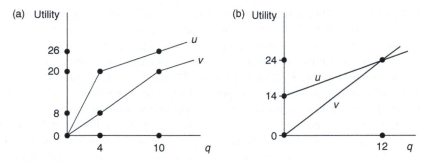

Figure 10.6   Marginal versus average demand.

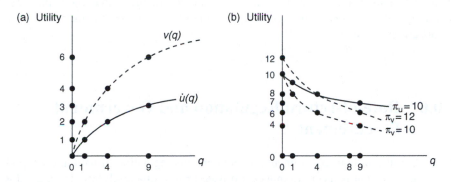

Figure 10.7   Two depictions of the single-crossing property.

It is the marginal demand that is more important to economic behavior and which forms the basis for the single-crossing property. The utility functions in figure 10.6b satisfy the single-crossing property, even though it is not true that $u(q) < v(q)$ (because they don't satisfy $u(0) = v(0) = 0$). Buyer V is always willing to pay 2 per unit, but Buyer U is only willing to pay 1 per unit. To be sure, $u(q) > v(q)$ for $u < 12$, but that is only because Buyer U starts with $u(0) = 14$, a "fixed benefit" which is irrelevant to his behavior. Buyer U may be the happier person at a consumption level of zero, but since that happiness is unaffected by his material circumstances, it is not going to affect any economic predictions we might want to make. Thus, definition (2) is best: when we say strong demand we should mean greater marginal demand. Indeed, that is what having a higher demand curve means in our usual diagrams, since the Marshallian demand curve is a marginal curve, showing not the total amount a consumer spends on quantity Q but the amount extra he willing to pay to buy a little more.

Figure 10.7a depicts functions which satisfy the assumptions of Varian's Nonlinear Pricing Game: $u = \sqrt{q}$ and $v = 2\sqrt{q}$. The two curves satisfy the single-crossing property, condition (10.27), because $v'(q) > u'(q)$ for all q and $u(0) = 0$ and $v(0) = 0$.

Another way to think about the single-crossing property, a way that makes the "single crossing" clearly visible, is using indifference curves. Since utility is a more theoretical concept than the idea of indifference between two consumption bundles, it is more reliable not to use graphs in utility space. The two goods in Varian's Nonlinear Pricing Game are (1) the commodity being, sold and (2) money, which enters linearly in the form of $-w$, the amount paid for the commodity. Another way to write the payoff functions would have been as $\pi_u(q, money) = money + u(q)$, where $money = wealth - w(q)$. Figure 10.7b shows how the buyers trade off money and the commodity. One comparison is between the curves for which $\pi = 10$, which both pass through the point $(0, 10)$ in $(q, money)$ space. The $\pi_u = 10$ indifference curve then descends more slowly than the $\pi_v = 10$ curve because the commodity is not so valued by Buyer U. Another comparison is between the two curves which contain the point $(4, 8)$, which are $\pi_u = 10$ and $\pi_v = 12$. These two curves also cross only once, at that point. In fact, if you pick any one indifference curve for Buyer U and any one for Buyer V, those curves will cross either not at all, or once.

It is often natural to assume that the single-crossing property holds, and it is a useful sufficient condition for separation to be possible, but it is not a necessary condition. If there are just two types of agents, as in many of our models, what matters is that the incentive compatibility constraints hold at the outputs that the principal specifies in the mechanism, not at all outputs. If the V player actually has a smaller marginal than the U player over a small range of consumption near zero, that will not hurt separation if the two contractual outputs are much larger.

*10.6   Rate-of-return Regulation and Government Procurement

The central idea in both government procurement and regulation of natural monopolies is that the government is trying to induce a private firm to efficiently provide a good to the public while covering the cost of production. If information is symmetric, this is an easy problem; the government simply pays the firm the cost of producing the good efficiently, whether the good be a missile or electricity. Usually, however, the firm has better information about costs and demand than the government does.

The variety of ways the firm might have better information and the government might extract it has given rise to a large literature in which moral hazard with hidden actions, moral hazard with hidden knowledge, adverse selection, and signalling all put in appearances. Suppose the government wants a firm to provide cable television service to a city. The firm knows more about its costs before agreeing to accept the franchise (adverse selection), discovers more after accepting it and beginning operations (moral hazard with hidden knowledge), and exerts greater or smaller effort to keep costs low (moral hazard with hidden actions). The government's problem is to acquire cable service at the lowest cost. It wants to be generous enough to induce the firm to accept the franchise in the first place but no more generous than necessary. It cannot simply agree to cover the firm's costs, because the firm would always claim high costs and exert low effort. Instead, the government might auction off the right to provide the service, might allow the firm a maximum price (a **price cap**), or might agree to compensate the firm to varying degrees for different levels of cost (**rate-of-return regulation**).

The problems of regulatory franchises and government procurement are the same in many ways. If the government wants to purchase a missile, it also has the problem of how much to offer the firm. Roughly speaking, the equivalent of a price cap is a flat price, and the equivalent of rate-of-return regulation is a cost-plus contract, although the details differ in interesting ways. (A price cap allows downwards flexibility in prices, and rate-of-return regulation allows an expected but not guaranteed profit, for example.)

Procurement I: Full Information[4]

PLAYERS
The government and the firm.

THE ORDER OF PLAY
0   Nature assigns the firm expensive problems with the project, which add costs of x, with probability θ. A firm is thus "normal," with type N and $s = 0$, or "expensive," with type X and $s = x$. The government and the firm both observe the type.
1   The government offers a contract $\{w(m) = c(m) + p(m), c(m)\}$ which pays the firm its observed cost c and a profit p if it announces its type to be m and incurs cost $c(m)$, and pays the firm zero otherwise.
2   The firm accepts or rejects the contract.
3   If the firm accepts, it chooses effort level e, unobserved by the government.
4   The firm finishes the missile at a cost of $c = \bar{c} + s - e$, which is observed by the government, plus an additional unobserved cost[5] of $f(e - \bar{c})$. The government reimburses $c(m)$ and pays $p(m)$.

PAYOFFS
Both firm and government are risk-neutral and both receive payoffs of zero if the firm rejects the contract. If the firm accepts, its payoff is

$$\pi_{firm} = p - f(e - \bar{c}) \tag{10.47}$$

where $f(e - \bar{c})$, the cost of effort, is increasing and convex, so $f' > 0$ and $f'' > 0$. Assume for technical convenience that f is increasingly convex, so $f''' > 0$.[6] The government's payoff is

$$\pi_{government} = B - (1 + t)c - tp - f, \tag{10.48}$$

where B is the benefit of the missile and t is the deadweight loss from the taxation needed for government spending. This is substantial. Hausman & Poterba (1987) estimate the loss to be around \$0.30 for each \$1 of tax revenue raised at the margin for the United States.

---

[4] I have changed the notation from the third edition of this book. The expensiveness variable x replaces the ability variable a; p replaces s; the type L firm becomes an expensive firm.

[5] The reader may ask why this disutility is specified as $f(e - \bar{c})$ rather than just $f(e)$. The reason is that we will later find an equilibrium cost level of $(\bar{c} - e^*)$, which would be negative if $c_0 = 0$.

[6] The argument of f is normalized to be $(\bar{c} - e)$ rather than just e to avoid clutter in the algebra later. The assumption that $f''' > 0$ allows the use of first-order conditions by making concave the maximand in (10.59), which is a difference of two concave functions. It will also make deterministic contracts superior to stochastic ones. See Laffont & Tirole (1993, p. 58).

Many of these situations are problems of moral hazard with hidden knowledge, because one player is trying to design a contract that the other will accept that will then induce him to use his private information properly.

Although the literature on mechanism design can be traced back to Mirrlees (1971) and in 1979 Loeb and Magat suggested using a Groves Mechanism to extract information from regulated firms, the extensive application to regulation began with Baron & Myerson's 1982 article, "Regulating a Monopolist with Unknown Costs." McAfee & McMillan (1988), and Laffont & Tirole (1993) provide 168-page, and 702-page treatments of the confusing array of possible models and policies in their books on government regulation. Here, we will look at a version of the model Laffont and Tirole use to introduce their book (pp. 55–62). This is a two-type model in which a special cost characteristic and the effort of a firm is its private information but its realized cost is public and nonstochastic. The model combines moral hazard and adverse selection, but it will behave more like an adverse selection model. The government will reimburse the firm's costs, but also fixes a price (which if negative becomes a tax) that depends on the level of the firm's costs. The questions the model hopes to answer are (1) whether effort will be too high or too low and (2) whether the price is positive and rises with costs.

The first version of the model will be one in which the government can observe the firm's type and so the first-best can be attained. It will be a benchmark for our later versions.

The model differs from most other principal–agent models in this book (though not from the Streetlight Game) because the principal cares about the welfare of the agent. If the government cared only about the value of the missile and the cost to taxpayers, its payoff would be $[B - (1+t)c - (1+t)p]$. Instead, the payoff function maximizes social welfare, the sum of the welfares of the taxpayers and the firm. The welfare of the firm is $(p - f)$, and summing the two welfares yields equation (10.48). Either kind of government payoff function may be realistic, depending on the political balance in the country being modelled, and the model will have similar properties whichever one is used. In the end, though, this model behaves in the same way as one with a selfish principal, because though the government does care about the welfare of the agent, the fact that taxation has deadweight loss means that the government will want to pay the firm as little as possible.

Assume for the moment that B is large enough that the government definitely wishes to build the missile (how large will become apparent later). Cost, not output, is the focus of this model. The optimal output is one missile regardless of agency problems, but the government wants to minimize the cost of producing the missile.

In Procurement I, whether the firm has expensive problems is observed by the government, which can therefore specify a contract conditioned on the type of the firm. The government pays p_N to a normal firm with the cost c_N, p_X to an expensive firm with the cost c_X, and $p = 0$ to a firm that does not achieve its appropriate cost level. The government thus maximizes its payoff, equation (10.48), by choice of p_X, p_N, c_X, and c_N, subject to participation and incentive compatibility constraints.

The expensive firm exerts effort $e = \bar{c} + x - c_X$, achieves $c = c_X$, generating unobserved effort disutility $f(e - \bar{c}) = f(x - c_X)$, so its participation constraint, that type X's payoff from reporting that it is type X, is

$$\pi_X(X) \geq 0,$$
$$p_X - f(x - c_X) \geq 0. \tag{10.49}$$

Similarly, in equilibrium the normal firm exerts effort $e = \bar{c} - c_N$, so its participation constraint is

$$\pi_N(N) \geq 0,$$
$$p_N - f(-c_N) \geq 0. \tag{10.50}$$

The incentive compatibility constraints are trivial here: the government can use a forcing contract that pays a firm zero if it generates the wrong cost for its type, since types are observable.

To make a firm's payoff zero and reduce the deadweight loss from taxation, the government will provide prices that do no more than equal the firm's disutility of effort. Since there is no uncertainty, we can invert the cost equation and write it as $e = \bar{c} + x - c$ or $e = \bar{c} - c$. The prices will be $p_X = f(e - \bar{c}) = f(x - c_X)$ and $p_N = f(e - \bar{c}) = f(-c_N)$.

Suppose the government knows the firm has expensive problems. Substituting the price p_X into the government's payoff function, equation (10.48), yields

$$\pi_{government} = B - (1 + t)c_X - tf(x - c_X) - f(x - c_X). \tag{10.51}$$

Since $f'' > 0$, the government's payoff function is concave, and standard optimization techniques can be used. The first-order condition for c_X is

$$\frac{\partial \pi_{government}}{\partial c_X} = -(1 + t) + (1 + t)f'(x - c_X) = 0, \tag{10.52}$$

so

$$f'(x - c_X) = 1. \tag{10.53}$$

Equation (10.53) is the crucial efficiency condition for effort. Since the argument of f is $(e - \bar{c})$, whenever $f' = 1$ the effort level is efficient. At the optimal effort level, the marginal disutility of effort equals the marginal reduction in cost because of effort. This is the first-best efficient effort level, which we will denote by $e^* \equiv e:\{f'(e - \bar{c}) = 1\}$.

If we derived the first-order condition for the normal firm we would find $f'(-c_N) = 1$ in the same way, so $c_N = c_X - x$. Also, if the equilibrium disutility of effort is the same for both firms, then both must choose the same effort, e^*, though the normal firm can reach a lower cost target with that effort. The cost targets assigned to each firm are $c_X = \bar{c} + x - e^*$ and $c_N = \bar{c} - e^*$. Since both types must exert the same effort, e^*, to achieve their different targets, $p_X = f(e^* - \bar{c}) = p_N$. The two firms exert the same efficient effort level and are paid the same price to compensate for the disutility of effort. Let us call this price level p^*.

The assumption that B is sufficiently large can now be made more specific: it is that $B - (1 + t)c_X - tf(e^* - \bar{c}) - f(e^* - \bar{c}) \geq 0$, which requires that $B - (1 + t)(\bar{c} + x - e^*) - (1 + t)p^* \geq 0$. If that were not true, then the government would not want to build the missile at all if the firm had an expensive cost function, as we will not treat of here.

Procurement II: Incomplete Information (Adverse Selection)

In the second variant of the game, the existence of expensive problems is not observed by the government, which must therefore provide incentives for the firm to volunteer its type if the normal firm is to produce at lower cost than the expensive firm.

If the government offered the two contracts of Procurement I, both types of firm would accept the expensive-cost contract, which has a price of p^* for a cost of $c = \bar{c} + x - e^*$, enough to compensate the expensive firm for its effort, and $p = 0$ for any other cost. That is the cheapest pooling contract, since any contract that paid less would violate the expensive-cost firm's participation constraint. It is inefficient, though, because the normal firm can reduce costs to $c = \bar{c} + x - e^*$ by exerting effort lower than e^*. The government would still be willing to build the missile, since the social cost of having the normal firm build the missile inefficiently is still lower than of having the expensive-cost firm build it efficiently. But it will turn out that separating contracts will yield higher welfare than the pooling contract.

First, let us establish that *some* pair of separating contracts is better than the pooling contract, and then we will find the *optimal separating contract*. A separating contract menu superior to the pooling contract would be a choice of (1) the old pooling contract $(p^*, c = \bar{c} + x - e^*)$, and (2) a new contract that offers a slightly higher price p but requires reimbursable costs c to be slightly lower. By definition of e^* in first-order condition (10.53), $f'(e^* - \bar{c}) = 1$, so $f'(e' - \bar{c}) < 1$ for the effort the normal firm exerts in the old pooling contract. If the normal firm increased its effort from e' by some small amount Δe, costs would fall by $(1)\Delta e$ but the firm would only have to be paid $f'(e' - \bar{c})\Delta e$ more to compensate for its extra disutility. Thus, there is a new contract that would draw the normal firm away from the old pooling contract and be preferred by the government.

We have shown that there is a pair of separating contracts that the government likes better than the pooling contract, but not whether that pair is optimal. We will therefore proceed to find the optimal pair of contracts (c_N, p_N) (c_X, p_X) for firms that announce *Normal* or *Expensive* (with $p = 0$ for other cost levels). Adapting the government's payoff in (10.48) to the probability θ of a expensive firm and probability $1 - \theta$ of a normal firm, the government's maximization problem under incomplete information is

$$\underset{c_N, c_X, p_N, p_X}{Maximize}\ \theta[B - (1 + t)c_X - tp_X - f(x - c_X)]$$

$$+ [1 - \theta][B - (1 + t)c_N - tp_N - f(-c_N)]. \tag{10.54}$$

A separating contract must satisfy participation constraints and incentive compatibility constraints for each type of firm. The participation constraints are the same as in Procurement I: inequalities (10.49) and (10.50):

$$\pi_X(X) = p_X - f(x - c_X) \geq 0 \tag{10.49}$$

and

$$\pi_N(N) = p_N - f(-c_N) \geq 0. \tag{10.50}$$

The incentive compatibility constraint for the expensive firm is

$$\pi_X(X) = p_X - f(x - c_X) \geq \pi_X(N) = p_N - f(x - c_N), \tag{10.55}$$

and the incentive compatibility constraint for the normal firm is

$$\pi_N(N) = p_N - f(-c_N) \geq \pi_N(X) = p_X - f(-c_X). \tag{10.56}$$

Since the normal firm can achieve the same cost level as the expensive firm with less effort, inequality (10.56) tells us that if we are to have $c_N < c_X$, as is necessary for us to have a separating equilibrium, we need $p_N > p_X$. The second half of inequality (10.56) must be positive. If the expensive firm's participation constraint, inequality (10.49), is satisfied, then $p_X - f(-c_X) > 0$. This, in turn implies that (10.50) is a strong inequality; the normal firm's participation constraint is nonbinding.

The expensive firm's participation constraint (10.49), will be binding (and therefore satisfied as an equality), because the government wishes to keep the price p low to reduce the deadweight loss of extra taxation, the $-tp_X$ term in problem (10.54). The normal firm's incentive compatibility constraint must also be binding, because if the pair (c_N, p_N) were strictly more attractive for the normal firm, the government could reduce the price p_N and save on the $-tp_N$ term in problem (10.54). Constraint (10.56) is therefore satisfied as an equality. Knowing that constraints (10.49) and (10.56) are binding, we can write, from constraint (10.49),

$$p_X = f(x - c_X) \tag{10.57}$$

and, making use of both (10.49) and (10.56),

$$p_N = f(-c_N) + f(x - c_X) - f(-c_X). \tag{10.58}$$

Substituting for p_X and p_N from (10.57) and (10.58) into the maximization problem (10.54), reduces the problem to

$$\text{Maximize}_{c_N, c_X} \theta[B - (1+t)c_X - tf(x - c_X) - f(x - c_X)]$$

$$+ [1 - \theta][B - (1+t)c_N - tf(-c_N) - tf(x - c_X) + tf(-c_X) - f(-c_N)]. \tag{10.59}$$

The first-order condition with respect to c_N is

$$(1 - \theta)[-(1+t) + tf'(-c_N) + f'(-c_N)] = 0, \tag{10.60}$$

which simplifies to

$$f'(-c_N) = 1. \tag{10.61}$$

Thus, as in Procurement I, $f'_N(e - \bar{c}) = 1$. The normal firm chooses the efficient effort level e^* in equilibrium, and c_N takes the same value as it did in Procurement I. Equation (10.58) can be rewritten as

$$p_N = p^* + f(x - c_X) - f(-c_X). \tag{10.62}$$

Because $f(x - c_X) > f(-c_X)$, equation (10.62) shows that $p_N > p^*$. Incomplete information increases the price for the normal firm, which earns more than its reservation utility in the game with incomplete information. Since the expensive firm will earn exactly zero, this means that the government is on average providing its supplier with an above-market rate of return, not because of corruption or political influence, but because that is the way to induce normal suppliers to reveal that they do not have expensive problems. This should be kept in mind as an alternative to chapter 5's product quality model and chapter 8's efficiency wage model for why above-average rates of return persist.

The first-order condition with respect to c_X is

$$\theta[-(1+t) + tf'(x - c_X) + f'(x - c_X)] + [1 - \theta][tf'(x - c_X) - tf'(-c_X)] = 0. \tag{10.63}$$

This can be rewritten as

$$f'(x - c_X) = 1 - \left(\frac{1 - \theta}{\theta(1 + t)}\right)[tf'(x - c_X) - tf'(-c_X)]. \tag{10.64}$$

Since the right hand side of equation (10.64) is less than one, the expensive firm has a lower level of f' than the normal firm, and if f' is lower and $f'' > 0$, effort must be less than the optimum, e^*. Perhaps this explains the expression "good enough for government work" – though our model can apply to any organization that is trying to buy goods instead of making them internally. Since, however, the expensive firm's participation constraint (10.49), is satisfied as an equality, it must also be true that $p_X < p^*$. The expensive firm's price is lower than under full information, although since its effort is lower its payoff stays the same.

I have not yet said whether the expensive firm's incentive compatibility constraint was binding. It is not: the expensive firm is not near being tempted to pick the normal firm's contract. This is a bit subtle. Setting the left-hand side of the incentive compatibility constraint (10.55) equal to zero because the participation constraint is binding for the expensive firm, substituting in for p_N from equation (10.58) and rearranging yields

$$f(x - c_N) - f(-c_N) \geq f(x - c_X) - f(-c_X). \tag{10.65}$$

As illustrated in figure 10.8, inequality (10.65) is true as a strict inequality, because f is convex ($f'' > 0$) and so the increment in f's value starting frome the lower base $-c_X$ is

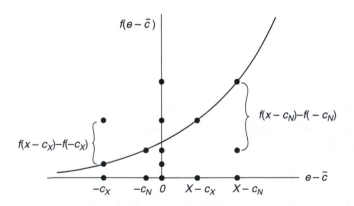

Figure 10.8   Why the expensive firm's incentive compatibility constraint is nonbinding.

smaller than starting from $-c_N$. Thus, the expensive firm's incentive compatibility constraint is nonbinding.

To summarize, the government's optimal contract will induce the normal firm to exert the first-best efficient effort level and achieve the first-best cost level, but will yield that firm a positive profit. The contract will induce the expensive firm to exert something less than the first-best effort level and result in a cost level higher than the first-best, but its profit will be zero.

There is a trade-off between the government's two objectives of inducing the correct amount of effort and minimizing the subsidy to the firm. Even under complete information, the government cannot provide a subsidy of zero, or the firms will refuse to build the missile. Under incomplete information, not only must the subsidies be positive but the normal firm earns **informational rents**; the government offers a contract that pays the normal firm more than under complete information to prevent it from mimicking an expensive firm and choosing an inefficiently low effort. The expensive firm, however, does choose an inefficiently low effort, because if it were assigned greater effort it would have to be paid a greater subsidy, which would tempt the normal firm to imitate it. In equilibrium, the government has compromised by having some probability of an inefficiently high subsidy ex post, and some probability of inefficiently low effort.

In the last version of the game, the firm's type is not known to either player until after the contract is agreed upon. The firm, however, learns its type before it must choose its effort level.

Procurement III: Moral Hazard with Hidden Information

THE ORDER OF PLAY

1 The government offers a contract $\{w(m) = c(m) + p(m), c(m)\}$ which pays the firm its observed cost c and a profit p if it announces its type to be m and incurs cost $c(m)$, and pays the firm zero otherwise.
2 The firm accepts or rejects the contract.
3 Nature assigns the firm expensive problems with the project, which add costs of x, with probability θ. A firm is thus "normal," with type N and $s = 0$, or "expensive," with type X and $s = x$. Only the firm observes its type.
4 If the firm accepted, it announces its type to be m and chooses effort level e, unobserved by the government.
5 If the firm accepted, it finishes the missile at a cost of $c = \bar{c} + x - e$ or $c = \bar{c} - e$ which is observed by the government, plus an additional cost $f(e - \bar{c})$ that the government does not observe. The government reimburses c and pays $p(c)$.

The firm's payoff $(p - f)$, as in Procurement I.

The government's payoff function is exactly the same as in Procurement II, equation (10.54)

$$\underset{c_N, c_X, p_N, p_X}{Maximize}\ \theta\left[B - (1+t)c_X - tp_X - f(x - c_X)\right]$$

$$+ [1 - \theta]\left[B - (1+t)c_N - tp_N - f(-c_N)\right]. \tag{10.54}$$

The incentive compatibility constraints are exactly the same as in Procurement II, equations (10.55) and (10.56). For the expensive firm the constraint is

$$\pi_X(X) \geq \pi_X(N),$$
$$p_X - f(x - c_X) \geq p_N - f(x - c_N), \tag{10.55}$$

and for the normal firm it is

$$\pi_N(N) \geq \pi_N(X),$$
$$p_N - f(-c_N) \geq p_X - f(-c_X) \tag{10.56}$$

The difference from Procurement II is that now there is just one participation constraint, not two, because the firm does not know its type at the time it agrees to the contract:

$$\theta[p_X - f(x - c_X)] + [1 - \theta][p_N - f(-c_N)] \geq 0. \tag{10.66}$$

Thus, the maximization problem is less constrained in Procurement III. The two participation constraints of Procurement II jointly imply constraint (10.66) is satisfied, but the reverse is not true. Now, the payoff of the expensive type can be negative, so long as the payoff of the normal type is positive enough to make the overall payoff non-negative.

The participation constraint, inequality (10.66), will be binding, because the government wants to keep the deadweight loss from taxation low, and it can now make the expensive firm's payoff negative enough to compensate for the normal firm's positive payoff. So long as the overall expected payoff is zero, the firm will still agree to the contract. There is no informational rent ex ante, unlike in Procurement II.

The normal firm's incentive compatibility constraint will still be binding. That firm does not want to admit that it can reduce costs easily, so it has a strong incentive to imitate the expensive firm, and must be bribed not to. The government will not want to pay a bigger bribe than necessary. If the pair (c_N, p_N) were strictly more attractive for the normal firm than (c_X, p_X), the government could reduce the price p_N. Constraint (10.56) is therefore satisfied as an equality.

Knowing that constraints (10.56) and (10.66) are binding, we can write from constraint (10.66),

$$p_X = f(x - c_X) - \frac{[1 - \theta][p_N - f(-c_N)]}{\theta}. \tag{10.67}$$

Substituting from (10.67) for p_X into (10.56), we get

$$p_N - f(-c_N) = f(x - c_X) - \frac{[1 - \theta][p_N - f(-c_N)]}{\theta} - f(-c_X). \tag{10.68}$$

This can be solved for p_N to yield

$$p_N = \theta[f(x - c_X) - f(-c_X)] + f(-c_N), \tag{10.69}$$

which when substituted into (10.67) yields

$$p_X = [1 - \theta][f(x - c_X) - f(-c_X)]. \tag{10.70}$$

Substituting for p_N and p_X from (10.69) and (10.70) into the maximization problem reduces the problem to

$$\underset{c_N, c_X}{Maximize}\ \theta\ \{B - (1+t)c_X - t[1-\theta][f(x-c_X) - f(-c_X)] - f(x-c_X)\}$$

$$+ [1-\theta]\ [B - (1+t)c_N - t\{\theta[f(x-c_X) - f(-c_X)] + f(-c_N)\} - f(-c_N)]. \tag{10.71}$$

The first-order condition with respect to c_N is

$$(1-\theta)[-(1+t) + tf'(-c_N) + f'(-c_N)] = 0, \tag{10.72}$$

just as under adverse selection, which simplifies to

$$f'(-c_N) = 1. \tag{10.73}$$

Thus, the crucial efficiency condition (10.53) is satisfied: $f'(e - c_0) = 1$. The normal firm chooses the efficient effort level e^* in equilibrium, and c_N takes the same value as it did in Procurement I and II.

Now that we know that the effort level is e^*, we can say something about the normal firm's payoff. Since $p^* = f(-c_N)$, the optimal price equation (10.69) can be rewritten as

$$p_N = \theta[f(x-c_X) - f(-c_X)] + p^*, \tag{10.74}$$

Because $f(x-c_X) > f(-c_X)$, equation (10.74) shows that $p_N > p^*$, even though $e_N = e^*$. The normal firm earns a positive payoff even though information was symmetric at the start of the game. It earns an informational rent because partway through the game it learns its type and the government does not, and the government needs to pay something to induce it to admit to its low-cost type. The expensive firm must earn less than its reservation utility so that the overall participation constraint will be satisfied as an equality.

The government could have made the expensive firm's payoff negative in either of two ways: (1) a lower p_X than in Procurement II, or (2) a lower c_X than in Procurement II (and thus higher e_X). Option (2) is what we just derived. It is beter than (1) because it raises the expensive firm's effort to closer to the efficient level. This increases the amount of surplus, and the government will get the entire surplus since there is now no informational rent. Hence, the expensive firm's effort is higher in Procurement III than in Procurement II.

Now that c_X is higher for the same p_X, the expensive cost-price pair is less attractive than in Procurement II. As a result, $\pi_N(X)$ is lower, and the government can make the normal firm's cost-price pair less attractive too. This is we found that though c_N is unchanged from Procurement II, p_N has fallen.

To summarize, the government's optimal contract in Procurement III will induce the normal firm to exert the first-best efficient effort level and achieve the first-best cost level, but will yield that firm a positive payoff, though smaller than in Procurement II. The contract will induce the expensive firm to exert less than the first-best effort level, though more than in Procurement II, and result in a cost level higher than the first-best and a negative payoff. Overall, the firm's expected payoff will be zero.

This is what one might expect of moral hazard with hidden information as compared to adverse selection. Starting with symmetric information results in less gaming at the time of contract formation, so the principal's maximization problem has three constraints to satisfy instead of four, and this results in effort choices closer to the first-best. Effort choices still do not always reach the first-best, however, because information about player types does become asymmetric midway through the game, and the contract has to be designed to induce the informed player, the firm, to disclose its information.

A practical implication is that the parties ought to agree on a contract as early as possible in the procurement process, before one of them acquires an informational advantage. Of course, this does not apply if one of them *starts* with an informational advantage; then, delay before agreement might actually help, by giving the uninformed party time to learn the facts it needs.

A little reflection will provide a host of additional ways to alter the Procurement Game. What if the firm discovers its costs only after accepting the contract? What if two firms bid against each other for the contract? What if the firm can bribe the government? What if the firm and the government bargain over the gains from the project instead of the government being able to make a take-it-or-leave-it contract offer? What if the game is repeated, so the government can use the information it acquires in the second period? If it is repeated, can the government commit to long-term contracts? Can it commit not to renegotiate? See Laffont & Tirole (1993) if these questions interest you. If they merely confuse you, an aphorism by Doug Larson that McAfee (2002, p. 202) quotes is an apt summary of the Procurement Game: "Accomplishing the impossible means only that the boss will add it to your regular duties."

Notes

N10.1 Production Game VIII, cross checking, unravelling, and the Revelation Principle

- The revelation principle was developed in Myerson (1979), though the idea can be traced back to Gibbard (1973). It was named in Myerson (1981). Myerson's game theory book is, as one might expect, a good place to look for further details (Myerson [1991, pp. 258–63, 294–99]). See also the books by Fudenberg & Tirole (1991a) and Laffont & Tirole (1993), Baron's chapter in the 1989 *Handbook of Industrial Organization*, the 2002 and 2005 books on the principal–agent problem by Laffont & Martimort and Bolton & Dewatripont, and Stole's 2001 manuscript.
- Levmore (1982) discusses hidden knowledge problems in tort damages, corporate freezeouts, and property taxes in a law review article. A legal application of the idea of the Sender–Receiver Game, pointing out the usefulness of a mediator as a mechanism is Brown & Ayres (1994).
- Postcontractual adverse selection is common in public policy. Should the doctors who prescribe drugs also be allowed to sell them? The question trades off the likelihood of overprescription against the potentially lower cost and greater convenience of doctor-dispensed drugs. See "Doctors as Druggists: Good Rx for Consumers?" *The Wall Street Journal*, June 25, 1987, p. 24.
- A hidden knowledge game requires that the state of the world matter to one of the players' payoffs, but not necessarily in the same way as in Production Game VII. The Salesman Game of section 10.2 effectively uses the utility function $U(e, w, \theta)$ for the agent and $V(q - w)$ for the principal. The state of the world matters because the agent's disutility of effort varies across states. In other problems, his utility of money might vary across states.
- Eric Maskin came up with the idea of cross-checking in a 1977 MIT working paper, "Nash Implementation and Welfare Optimality" The working paper became known as a classic, but was

not published until 22 years later, in a 1999 issue of the *Review of Economic Studies* with several other articles on mechanism design.

N10.3 An example of postcontractual private knowledge: the Salesman Game

- Sometimes students know more about their class rankings than the professor does. One professor of labor economics used a mechanism of the following kind for grading class discussion. Each student *i* reports a number evaluating other students in the class. Student *i*'s grade is an increasing function of the evaluations given *i* by other students and of the correlation between *i*'s evaluations and the other students'. There are many Nash equilibria, but telling the truth is a focal point.
- In dynamic games of moral hazard with hidden knowledge the **ratchet effect** is important: the agent takes into account that his information-revealing choice of contract this period will affect the principal's offerings next period. A principal might allow high prices to a public utility in the first period to discover that its costs are lower than expected, but in the next period the prices would be reduced. The contract is ratcheted irreversibly to be more severe. Hence, the company might not choose a contract which reveals its costs in the first period. This is modelled in Freixas, Guesnerie, & Tirole (1985).

  Baron (1989) notes that the principal might purposely design the equilibrium to be pooling in the first period so self selection does not occur. Having learned nothing, he can offer a more effective separating contract in the second period.

N10.5 Price discrimination

- The names for price discrimination in part 2, chapter 17, section 5 of Pigou (1920) are: (1) first-degree (perfect price discrimination), (2) second-degree (interquantity price discrimination), and (3) third-degree (interbuyer price discrimination). These arbitrary names have plagued generations of students of industrial organization, in parallel with the appalling Type I and Type II errors of statistics (better named as False Negatives and False Positives). I invented the terms **interbuyer price discrimination** and **interquantity price discrimination** for this edition, with the excuse that I think their meaning will be clear to anyone who already knows the concepts under their Pigouvian names.

  McAfee (2002, p. 261) has a new taxonomy that may catch on: direct versus indirect price discrimination. Direct price discrimination is based on observing characteristics of the customer and charging him a price for a given unit that depends on those characteristics, an offer not open to everyone. Indirect price discrimination makes offers open to everyone, but offers which will separate the customers, whether by quantity desired, quality desired, attention paid to newspaper coupons, or other unobservable characteristics.
- A narrower category of nonlinear pricing is the **quantity discount**, in which the price per unit declines with the quantity bought. Sellers are often constrained to this, since if the price per unit rises with the quantity bought, some means must be used to prevent a canny consumer from buying two batches of small quantities instead of one batch of a large quantity.
- Wilson's 1993 book, *Nonlinear Pricing*, is a good reference on price discrimination.
- In Varian's Nonlinear Pricing Game the probabilities of types for each player are not independent, unlike in most games. This does not make the game more complicated, though. If the assumption were "Nature assigns each buyer a utility function u or v with independent probabilities of 0.5 for each type," then there would be not just two possible states of the world in this game – uv and vu for Smith and Jones's types – but four – uv, vu, uu, and vv. How would the equilibrium change?
- The careful reader will think, "How can we say that Buyer V always gets higher utility than Buyer U for given x? Utility cannot be compared across individuals, and we could rescale Buyer V's utility function to make him always have lower utility without altering the essentials of the utility

function." My reply is that more generally we could set up the utility functions as $v(x) + y$ and $u(x) + y$, with y denoting spending on all other goods (as Varian does in his book). Then to say that V always gets higher utility for a given x means that he always has a higher relative value than U does for good x relative to money. Rescaling to give V the utility function $.001v(x) + .001y$ would not alter that.

- The notation I used in Varian's Nonlinear Pricing Game is optimized for reading. If you wish to write this on the board or do the derivations for practice, use abbreviations like u_1 for $u_1(x_1)$, a for $v(x_1)$, and b for $v(x_2)$ to save writing. The tradeoff between brevity and transparency in notation is common, and must be made in light of whether you are writing on a blackboard or on a computer, for just yourself or for the generations.

N10.6   Rate-of-return regulation and government procurement

- I changed the notation from Laffont and Tirole and from my own previous edition. Rather than assign each type of firm a cost parameter β for a cost of $c = \beta - e$, I now assign each type of firm an ability parameter a, for a cost of $c = c_0 - a - e$. This will allow the desirable type of firm to be the one with the *High* value of the type parameter, as in most models.
- In practice, whether procurement is by the government or by other large organizations it must balance a multitude of concerns, not just incentives for the supplier. Three of the most important concerns are giving performance incentives to the government's own agents (the ones who arrange the procurement), preventing corruption of those agents with kickbacks (a bribe awarded an agent in consideration of getting a contract), and transaction costs of various sorts. On this last, see Bajari & Tadelis (2001). Much insight can be had from auction theory as well, since auctions are frequently used for procurement. Paul Klemperer's 2004 *Auctions: Theory and Practice* (which is relatively nontechnical), and Paul Milgrom's 1999 *Auction Theory for Privatization* and 2004 *Putting Auction Theory to Work* are full of practical advice based on sound theory.

Problems

10.1:   Unravelling (hard)

An elderly prospector owns a gold mine worth an amount θ drawn from the uniform distribution $U[0, 100]$ which nobody knows, including himself. He will certainly sell the mine, since he is too old to work it and it has no value to him if he does not sell it. The several prospective buyers are all risk-neutral. The prospector can, if he desires, dig deeper into the hill and collect a sample of gold ore that will reveal the value of θ. If he shows the ore to the buyers, however, he must show genuine ore, since an unwritten Law of the West says that fraud is punished by hanging offenders from joshua trees as food for buzzards.

(a)   For how much can he sell the mine if he is clearly too feeble to have dug into the hill and examined the ore? What is the price in this situation if, in fact, the true value is $\theta = 70$?
(b)   For how much can he sell the mine if he can dig the test tunnel at zero cost? Will he show the ore? What is the price in this situation if, in fact, the true value is $\theta = 70$?
(c)   For how much can he sell the mine if, after digging the tunnel at zero cost and discovering θ, it costs him an additional 10 to verify the results for the buyers? What is his expected payoff?
(d)   Suppose that with probability 0.5 digging the test tunnel costs 5 for the prospector, but with probability 0.5 it costs him 120. Keep in mind that the 0–100 value of the mine is net of the buyer's digging cost. Denote the equilibrium price that buyers will pay for the mine after the

prospector approaches them without showing ore by P. What is the buyer's posterior belief about the probability it costs 120 to dig the tunnel, as a function of P? Denote this belief by $B(P)$. (Assume, as usual, that all these parameters are common knowledge, although only the prospector learns whether the cost is actually 0 or 120.)

(e)   What is the prospector's expected payoff in the conditions of part (d) if (i) the tunnel costs him 120, or (ii) the tunnel costs him 5?

(f)   What is the prospector's ex ante expected payoff in the conditions of part (d) – that is, what is his expected payoff viewed from before he knows the cost of digging a tunnel? How does that compare with his expected payoff when he can dig the tunnel at cost 5 with probability 1?

Table 10.1   The right to silence game payoffs

		Sally's Job		
		Job 1	*Job 2*	*Manager*
	Task 1 is efficient (0.5)	2, 5	1, −2	3, 3
Sally knows				
	Task 2 is efficient (0.5)	1, −2	2, 5	3, 3

Payoffs to: (Sally, Rayco).

10.2:   Task assignment (medium)

Table 10.1 shows the payoffs in the following game. Sally has been hired by Rayco to do either Job 1, to do Job 2, or to be a Manager. Rayco believes that Tasks 1 and 2 have equal probabilities of being the efficient ones for Sally to perform. Sally knows which task is efficient, but what she would like best is a job as Manager that gives her the freedom to choose rather than have the job designed for the task. The CEO of Rayco asks Sally which task is efficient. She can either reply "task 1," "task 2," or be silent. Her statement, if she makes one, is an example of "cheap talk," because it has no direct effect on anybody's payoff. See Farrell & Rabin (1996).

(a)   If Sally did not have the option of speaking, what would happen?

(b)   There exist perfect Bayesian equilibria in which it does not matter how Sally replies. Find one of these in which Sally speaks at least some of the time, and explain why it is an equilibrium. You may assume that Sally is not morally or otherwise bound to speak the truth.

(c)   There exists a perverse variety of equilibrium in which Sally always tells the truth and never is silent. Find an example of this equilibrium, and explain why neither player would have incentive to deviate to out-of-equilibrium behavior.

10.3:   Agency law (easy)

Mr. Smith is thinking of buying a custom-designed machine from either Mr. Jones or Mr. Brown. This machine costs $5,000 to build, and it is useless to anyone but Smith. It is common knowledge that with 90 percent probability the machine will be worth $10,000 to Smith at the time of delivery, one year from today, and with 10 percent probability it will only be worth $2,000. Smith owns assets of $1,000. At the time of contracting, Jones and Brown believe there is a 20 percent chance that Smith is actually acting as an "undisclosed agent" for Anderson, who has assets of $50,000.

Find the price be under the following two legal regimes: (1) An undisclosed principal is not responsible for the debts of his agent; and (2) even an undisclosed principal is responsible for the debts of his agent. Also, explain (as part [3]) which rule a moral hazard model like this would tend to support.

10.4: Incentive compatibility and price discrimination (medium)

Two consumers have utility functions $u_1(x_1, y_1) = a_1 log(1 + x_1) + y_1 - 15$ and $u_2(x_2, y_2) = a_2 log(1 + x_2) + y_2 - 15$ where $2 < a_1 < a_2 < 12$. The price of the y-good is 1 and each consumer has an initial wealth of 15. A monopolist supplies the x-good. He has a constant marginal cost of 1.2 up to his capacity constraint of 10. He will offer at most two price-quantity packages, (r_1, x_1) and (r_2, x_2), where r_i is the total cost of purchasing x_i units. He cannot identify which consumer is which, but he can prevent resale.

(a) Write down the monopolist's profit maximization problem. You should have four constraints plus a capacity constraint.
(b) Which constraints will be binding at the optimal solution?
(c) Substitute the binding constraints into the objective function. What is the resulting expression? What are the first-order conditions for profit maximization? What are the profit-maximizing values of x_1 and x_2?

10.5: The Groves Mechanism (easy)

A new computer costing 10 million dollars would benefit existing Divisions 1, 2, and 3 of a company with 100 divisions. Each divisional manager knows the benefit to his division (variables v_i, $i = 1, \ldots, 3$), but nobody else does, including the company CEO. Managers maximize the welfare of their own divisions. What dominant strategy mechanism might the CEO use to induce the managers to tell the truth when they report their valuations? Explain why this mechanism will induce truthful reporting, and denote the reports by x_i, $i = 1, \ldots, 3$. (You may assume that any budget transfers to and from the divisions in this mechanism are permanent – that the divisions will not get anything back later if the CEO collects more payments than he gives, for example.)

10.6: The two-part tariff (easy) (Varian 14.10, modified)

One way to price discriminate is to charge a lump sum fee L to have the right to purchase a good, and then charge a per-unit charge p for consumption of the good after that. The standard example is an amusement park where the firm charges an entry fee and a charge for the rides inside the park. Such a pricing policy is known as a **two-part tariff**. Suppose that all consumers have identical utility functions given by $u(x)$ and that the cost of production is cx. If the monopolist sets a two-part tariff, will it produce the socially efficient level of output, too little, or too much?

10.7: Selling cars (medium)

A car dealer must pay $10,000 to the manufacturer for each car he adds to his inventory. He faces three buyers. From the point of view of the dealer, Smith's valuation is uniformly distributed between $11,000 and $21,000, Jones's is between $9,000 and $11,000, and Brown's is between $4,000 and $12,000. The dealer's policy is to make a separate take-it-or-leave-it offer to each customer, and he is smart enough to avoid making different offers to customers who could resell to each other. Use the notation that the maximum valuation is $\overline{V}$ and the range of valuations is R.

(a) What will the offers be?
(b) Who is most likely to buy a car? How does this compare with the outcome with perfect price discrimination under full information? How does it compare with the outcome when the dealer charges $10,000 to each customer?

(c) What happens to the equilibrium prices if with probability 0.25 each buyer has a valuation of $0, but the probability distribution remains otherwise the same? What happens to the equilibrium expected profit?

(d) What happens to the equilibrium price the seller offers to seller Jones if with probability 0.25 Jones has a valuation of $30,000, but with probability 0.75 his valuation is uniformly distributed between $9,000 and $11,000 as before? Show the relation between price and profit on a rough graph.

Regulatory Ratcheting: A Classroom Game for Chapter 10

Electricity demand facing each of several firms is perfectly inelastic at 1 gigawatt per firm. A firm will supply either 0 or 1 gigawatt. The price is chosen by the regulator. The regulator cares about two things: (1) getting electrical service, and (2) getting it at the lowest price possible. The utilities like profit and dislike effort. Throughout the game, utility i has "cost reduction" parameter x_i, which it knows but the regulator does not. This parameter is big if the utility can reduce its costs with just a little effort. Each year, the following events happen.

1 The regulator offers price P_i to firm i.
2 Firm i accepts or rejects.
3 If Firm i accepts, it secretly chooses its effort level e_i,
4 Nature secretly and randomly chooses the economywide shock u (uniform from 1 to 6) and Firm i's shock u_i (uniform from 1 to 6) and announces Firm i's cost, c_i. That cost equals

$$c_i = 20 + u + u_i - x_i e_i. \tag{10.75}$$

5 Firm i earns a period payoff of 0 if it rejects the contract. If it accepts, its payoff is

$$\pi_i = p_i - c_i - e_i^2 \tag{10.76}$$

The regulator earns a period payoff of 0 from firm i if its contract is rejected. Otherwise, its payoff from that firm is

$$\pi_{regulator}(p_i) = 50 - p_i \tag{10.77}$$

All variables take integer values.
    The game repeats for as many years as the class has time for, with each firm keeping the same value of x throughout.

Chapter 11
signalling

11.1   The Informed Player Moves First: Signalling

Signalling is a way for an agent to communicate his type under adverse selection. The signalling contract specifies a wage that depends on an observable characteristic – the signal – which the agent chooses for himself after Nature chooses his type. Figures 7.1d and 7.1e showed the extensive forms of two kinds of models with signals. If the agent chooses his signal before the contract is offered, he is signalling to the principal. If he chooses the signal afterwards, the principal is screening him. Not only will it become apparent that this difference in the order of moves is important, it will also be seen that signalling costs must differ between agent types for signalling to be useful, and the outcome is often inefficient.

We begin with signalling models in which workers choose education levels to signal their abilities. Section 11.1 lays out the fundamental properties of a signalling model, and section 11.2 shows how the details of the model affect the equilibrium. Section 11.3 steps back from the technical detail to more practical considerations in applying the model to education. Section 11.4 turns the game into a screening model. Section 11.5 switches to diagrams and applies signalling to new stock issues to show how two signals need to be used when the agent has two unobservable characteristics. Section 11.6 addresses the rather different idea of signal jamming: strategic behavior a player uses to cover up information rather than to disclose it.

Spence (1973) introduced the idea of signalling in the context of education. We will construct a series of models which formalize the notion that education has no direct effect on a person's ability to be productive in the real world but useful for demonstrating his ability to employers. Let half of the workers have the type "high-ability" and half "low-ability," where ability is a number denoting the dollar value of his output. Output is assumed to be a noncontractible variable and there is no uncertainty. If output is contractible, it should be in the contract, as we have seen in chapter 7. Lack of uncertainty is a simplifying assumption, imposed so that the contracts are functions only of the signals rather than a combination of the signal and the output.

Employers do not observe the worker's ability, but they do know the distribution of abilities, and they observe the worker's education. To simplify, we will specify that the players are one worker and two employers. The employers compete profits down to zero and the worker receives the gains from trade. The worker's strategy is his education level

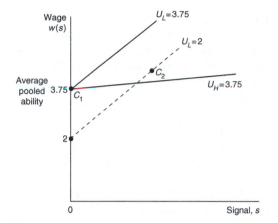

Figure 11.1   Education VI: no pooling equilibrium in a screening game.

and his choice of employer. The employers' strategies are the contracts they offer giving wages as functions of education level. The key to the model is that the signal, education, is less costly for workers with higher ability.

In the first four variants of the game, workers choose their education levels before employers decide how pay should vary with education.

Education I

PLAYERS
A worker and two employers.

THE ORDER OF PLAY
0   Nature chooses the worker's ability $a \in \{2, 5.5\}$, the *Low* and *High* ability each having probability 0.5. The variable a is observed by the worker, but not by the employers.
1   The worker chooses education level $s \in \{0, 1\}$.
2   The employers each offer a wage contract $w(s)$.
3   The worker accepts a contract, or rejects both of them.
4   Output equals a.

PAYOFFS
The worker's payoff is his wage minus his cost of education, and the employer's is his profit.

$$\pi_{worker} = \begin{cases} w - 8s/a & \text{if the worker accepts contract } w, \\ 0 & \text{if the worker rejects both contracts.} \end{cases}$$

$$\pi_{employer} = \begin{cases} a - w & \text{for the employer whose contract is accepted,} \\ 0 & \text{for the other employer.} \end{cases}$$

The payoffs assume that education is more costly for a worker if his ability takes a lower value, which is what permits separation to occur. As in any hidden knowledge game, we must think about both pooling and separating equilibria. Education I has both. In the pooling equilibrium, which we will call Pooling Equilibrium 1.1, both types of workers pick zero education and the employers pay the zero-profit wage of 3.75 regardless of the education level $(3.75 = [2 + 5.5]/2)$.

$$\text{Pooling Equilibrium 1.1} \begin{cases} s(Low) = s(High) = 0 \\ w(s = 0) = w(s = 1) = 3.75 \\ Prob(a = Low|s = 1) = 0.5 \end{cases}$$

Pooling Equilibrium 1.1 needs to be specified as a perfect Bayesian equilibrium rather than simply a Nash equilibrium because of the importance of the interpretation that the uninformed player puts on out-of-equilibrium behavior. The equilibrium needs to specify the employer's beliefs when he observes $s = 1$, since that is never observed in equilibrium. In Pooling Equilibrium 1.1, the beliefs are passive conjectures (see section 6.2): employers believe that a worker who chooses $s = 1$ is Low with the prior probability, which is 0.5. Given this belief, both types of workers realize that education is useless, and the model reaches the unsurprising outcome that workers do not bother to acquire unproductive education.

Under other beliefs, the pooling equilibrium breaks down. Under the belief $Prob(a = Low|s = 1) = 0$, for example, employers believe that any worker who acquired education is a $High$, so pooling is not Nash because the $High$ workers are tempted to deviate and acquire education. This leads to the separating equilibrium for which signalling is best known, in which the high-ability worker acquires education to prove to employers that he really has high ability.

$$\text{Separating Equilibrium 1.2} \begin{cases} s(Low) = 0, s(High) = 1, \\ w(s = 0) = 2, w(s = 1) = 5.5. \end{cases}$$

Following the method used in chapters 7–10, we will show that Separating Equilibrium 1.2 is a perfect Bayesian equilibrium by using the standard constraints which an equilibrium must satisfy. A pair of separating contracts must maximize the utility of the $High$s and the Lows subject to two constraints: (1) the participation constraints that the firms can offer the contracts without making losses; and (2) the self-selection constraints that the Lows are not attracted to the $High$ contract, and the $High$s are not attracted by the Low contract. The participation constraints for the employers require that

$$w(0) \leq a_L = 2 \quad \text{and} \quad w(1) \leq a_H = 5.5. \tag{11.1}$$

Competition between the employers makes the expressions in (11.1) hold as equalities. The self-selection constraint of the Lows is

$$U_L(s = 0) \geq U_L(s = 1), \tag{11.2}$$

which in Education I is

$$w(0) - 0 \geq w(1) - \frac{8(1)}{2}. \tag{11.3}$$

Since in Separating Equilibrium 1.2 the separating wage of the *Low*s is 2 and the separating wage of the *High*s is 5.5 from (11.1), the self-selection constraint (11.3) is satisfied.

The self-selection constraint of the *High*s is

$$U_H(s = 1) \geq U_H(s = 0), \tag{11.4}$$

which in Education I is

$$w(1) - \frac{8(1)}{5.5} \geq w(0) - 0. \tag{11.5}$$

Constraint (11.5) is satisfied by Separating Equilibrium 1.2.

There is another conceivable pooling equilibrium for Education I, in which $s(Low) = s(High) = 1$, but this turns out not to be an equilibrium, because the *Low*s would deviate to zero education. Even if such a deviation caused the employer to believe they were low-ability with probability 1 and reduce their wage to 2, the low-ability workers would still prefer to deviate, because

$$U_L(s = 0) = 2 \geq U_L(s = 1) = 3.75 - \frac{8(1)}{2}. \tag{11.6}$$

Thus, a pooling equilibrium with $s = 1$ would violate incentive compatibility for the *Low* workers.

Notice that we do not need to worry about a nonpooling constraint for this game, unlike in the case of the games of chapter 9. One might think that because employers compete for workers, competition between them might result in their offering a pooling contract that the high-ability workers would prefer to the separating contract. The reason this does not matter is that the employers do not compete by offering contracts, but by reacting to workers who have acquired education. That is why this is signalling and not screening: the employers cannot offer contracts in advance that change the workers' incentives to acquire education.

We can test the equilibrium by looking at the best responses. Given the worker's strategy and the other employer's strategy, an employer must pay the worker his full output or lose him to the other employer. Given the employers' contracts, the *Low* has a choice between the payoff 2 for ignorance (=2 − 0) and 1.5 for education (=5.5 − 8/2), so he picks ignorance. The *High* has a choice between the payoff 2 for ignorance (=2 − 0) and 4.05 for education (=5.5 − 8/5.5, rounded), so he picks education.

Unlike the pooling equilibrium, the separating equilibrium does not need to specify beliefs. Either of the two education levels might be observed in equilibrium, so Bayes' Rule always tells the employers how to interpret what they see. If they see that an agent has acquired education, they deduce that his ability is *High* and if they see that he has not, they deduce that it is *Low*. A worker is free to deviate from the education level appropriate to his type, but the employers' beliefs will continue to be based on equilibrium behavior. If a *High* worker deviates by choosing $s = 0$ and tells the employers he is a *High* who would rather pool than separate, the employers disbelieve him and offer him the *Low* wage of 2 that is appropriate to $s = 0$, not the pooling wage of 3.75 or the *High* wage of 5.5.

Separation is possible because education is more costly for workers if their ability is lower. If education were to cost the same for both types of worker, education would not work as a signal, because the low-ability workers would imitate the high-ability workers.

This requirement of different signalling costs is the **single-crossing property** that we have seen in chapter 10. When the costs are depicted graphically, as they will be in figure 11.1, the indifference curves of the two types intersect a single time.

A strong case can be made that the beliefs required for the pooling equilibria are not sensible. Harking back to the equilibrium refinements of section 6.2, recall that one suggestion (from Cho & Kreps [1987]) is to inquire into whether one type of player could not possibly benefit from deviating, no matter how the uninformed player changed his beliefs as a result. Here, the *Low* worker could never benefit from deviating from Pooling Equilibrium 1.1. Under the passive conjectures specified, the *Low* has a payoff of 3.75 in equilibrium versus -0.25 ($=3.75 - 8/2$) if he deviates and becomes educated. Under the belief that most encourages deviation – that a worker who deviates is *High* with probability one – the *Low* would get a wage of 5.5 if he deviated, but his payoff from deviating would only be 1.5 ($=5.5 - 8/2$), which is less than 2. The more reasonable belief seems to be that a worker who acquires education is a *High*, which does not support the pooling equilibrium.

The nature of the separating equilibrium lends support to the claim that education *per se* is useless or even pernicious, because it imposes social costs but does not increase total output. While we may be reassured by the fact that Professor Spence himself thought it worthwhile to become Dean of Harvard College, the implications are disturbing and suggest that we should think seriously about how well the model applies to the real world. We will do that later. For now, note that in the model, unlike most real-world situations, information about the agent's talent has no social value, because all agents would be hired and employed at the same task even under full information. Also, if side payments are not possible, Separating Equilibrium 1.2 is second-best efficient in the sense that a social planner could not make both types of workers better off. Separation helps the high-ability workers even though it hurts the low-ability workers.

Separation can also occur even if the signal of education has zero or negative cost for the high-ability workers, so long as it has positive cost for the low-ability workers. In such a case, however, the signalling is nonstrategic; it merely happens that the high-ability worker's efficient level of education is too high for low-ability workers to want to imitate them, and employers therefore deduce both natural and acquired ability from education.

11.2   Variants on the Signalling Model of Education

Although Education I is a curious and important model, it does not exhaust the implications of signalling. This section will start with Education II, which will show an alternative to the arbitrary assumption of beliefs in the perfect Bayesian equilibrium concept. Education III will be the same as Education I except for its different parameter values, and will have two pooling equilibrium rather than one separating and one pooling equilibrium. Education IV will allow a continuum of education levels, and will unify Education I and Education III by showing how all of their equilibria and more can be obtained in a model with a less restricted strategy space.

Education II: Modelling Trembles So Nothing Is Out of Equilibrium

The pooling equilibrium of Education I required the modeller to specify the employers' out-of-equilibrium beliefs. An equivalent model constructs the game tree to support the beliefs instead of introducing them via the equilibrium concept. This approach was briefly mentioned in connection with section 6.2's game of PhD Admissions. The advantage is that the assumptions on beliefs are put in the rules of the game along with the other assumptions. So let us replace Nature's move in Education I and modify the payoffs as follows.

Education II

THE ORDER OF PLAY

0   Nature chooses worker ability $a \in \{2, 5.5\}$, each ability having probability 0.5. (a is observed by the worker, but not by the employer.) With probability 0.001, Nature endows a worker with free education of $s = 1$.

1   The game continues in the same way as Education I.

PAYOFFS

$$\pi_{worker} = \begin{cases} w - 8s/a & \text{if the worker accepts contract } w \text{ (ordinarily)}, \\ w & \text{if the worker accepts contract } w \text{ (with free education)}, \\ 0 & \text{if the worker does not accept a contract.} \end{cases}$$

With probability 0.001 the worker receives free education regardless of his ability (this might model idiosyncratic reasons someone might be educated that are unrelated to job prospects). If the employer sees a worker with education, he knows that the worker might be one of this rare type, in which case the probability that the worker is *Low* is 0.5. Both $s = 0$ and $s = 1$ can be observed in any equilibrium and Education II has almost the same two equilibria as Education I, without the need to specify beliefs. The separating equilibrium did not depend on beliefs, and remains an equilibrium. What was Pooling Equilibrium 1.1 becomes "almost" a pooling equilibrium – almost all workers behave the same, but the small number with free education behave differently. The two types of greatest interest, the *High* and the *Low*, are not separated, but the ordinary workers are separated from the workers whose education is free. Even that small amount of separation allows the employers to use Bayes' Rule and eliminates the need for exogenous beliefs.

More formally, the pooling equilibrium would have both abilities of workers choosing $s = 0$ unless a worker was one of the few endowed with automatic $s = 1$. Out-of-equilibrium, if the employer observed $s = 1$, he could use Bayes' Rule:

$$Prob(a = Low|s = 1) = \frac{Prob(s = 1|a = L)Prob(L)}{Prob(s = 1|a = L)Prob(L) + Prob(s = 1|a = H)Prob(H)},$$

$$= \frac{(0.001)(0.5)}{(0.001)(0.5) + (0.001)(0.5)},$$

$$= 0.5. \tag{11.7}$$

Normal workers would not deviate from $s = 0$ because it would not increase the employer's estimate of their ability.

Education III: No Separating Equilibrium, Two Pooling Equilibria

Let us next modify Education I by changing the possible worker abilities from $\{2, 5.5\}$ to $\{2, 12\}$. The separating equilibrium vanishes, but a new pooling equilibrium emerges. In Pooling Equilibria 3.1 and 3.2, both pooling contracts pay the same zero-profit wage of 7 ($=[2 + 12]/2$), and both types of agents acquire the same amount of education, but the amount depends on the equilibrium.

Pooling Equilibrium 3.1 $\begin{cases} s(Low) = s(High) = 0, \\ w(0) = w(1) = 7, \\ Prob(a = Low|s = 1) = 0.5 \text{ (passive conjectures).} \end{cases}$

Pooling Equilibrium 3.2 $\begin{cases} s(Low) = s(High) = 1, \\ w(0) = 2, w(1) = 7, \\ Prob(a = Low|s = 0) = 1. \end{cases}$

Pooling Equilibrium 3.1 is similar to the pooling equilibrium in Education I and II, but Pooling Equilibrium 3.2 is inefficient. Both types of workers receive the same wage, but they incur the education costs anyway. Each type is frightened to do without education because the employer would pay him not as if his ability were average, but as if he were known to be *Low*.

Examination of Pooling Equilibrium 3.2 shows why a separating equilibrium no longer exists. Any separating equilibrium would require $w(0) = 2$ and $w(1) = 7$, but this is the contract that leads to Pooling Equilibrium 3.2. The self-selection and zero-profit constraints cannot be satisfied simultaneously, because the *Low* type is willing to acquire $s = 1$ to obtain the high wage.

It is not surprising that information problems create inefficiencies in the sense that first-best efficiency is lost. Indeed, the surprise is that in some games with asymmetric information, such as Broadway Game I in section 7.4, the first-best can still be achieved by tricks such as boiling-in-oil contracts. More often, we discover that the outcome is second-best efficient: given the informational constraints, a social planner could not alter the equilibrium without hurting some type of player. Pooling Equilibrium 3.2 is not even second-best efficient, because Pooling Equilibrium 3.1 and Pooling Equilibrium 3.2 result in the exact same wages and allocation of workers to tasks. The inefficiency is purely a problem of unfortunate expectations, like the inefficiency from choosing the dominated equilibrium in Ranked Coordination.

Pooling Equilibrium 3.2 also illustrates a fine point of the definition of pooling, because although the two types of workers adopt the same strategies, the equilibrium contract offers different wages for different education. The implied threat to pay a low wage to an uneducated worker never needs to be carried out, so the equilibrium is still called a pooling equilibrium. Notice that perfectness does not rule out threats based on beliefs. The model imposes these beliefs on the employer, and he would carry out his threats, because he believes they are best responses. The employer receives a higher payoff under some beliefs than under others, but he is not free to choose his beliefs.

Following the approach of Education II, we could eliminate Pooling Equilibrium 3.2 by adding an exogenous probability 0.001 that either type is completely unable to buy education. Then every possible actions might be observed in equilibrium and we end up with Pooling Equilibrium 3.1 because the only rational belief is that if $s = 0$ is observed, the worker has equal probability of being *High* or being *Low*. To eliminate Pooling Equilibrium 3.1 requires less reasonable beliefs; for example, a probability of 0.001 that a *Low* gets free education together with a probability of 0 that a *High* does.

These first three games illustrate the basics of signalling: (1) separating and pooling equilibria both may exist, (2) out-of-equilibrium beliefs matter, and (3) sometimes one perfect Bayesian equilibrium can Pareto-dominate others. These results are robust, but Education IV will illustrate some dangers of using simplified games with binary strategy spaces instead of continuous and unbounded strategies. So far education has been limited to $s = 0$ or $s = 1$; Education IV allows it to take greater or intermediate values.

Education IV: Continuous Signals and Continua of Equilibria

Let us now return to Education I, with one change: that education s can take any level on the continuum between 0 and infinity.

Education IV

PLAYERS
A worker and two employers.

THE ORDER OF PLAY
0   Nature chooses the worker's ability $a \in \{2, 5.5\}$, the *Low* and *High* ability each having probability 0.5. The variable a is observed by the worker, but not by the employers.
1   The worker chooses education level $s \in [0, \infty)$.
2   The employers each offer a wage contract $w(s)$.
3   The worker accepts a contract, or rejects both of them.
4   Output equals a.

PAYOFFS
The worker's payoff is his wage minus his cost of education, and the employer's is his profit.

$$\pi_{worker} = \begin{cases} w - 8s/a & \text{if the worker accepts contract } w, \\ 0 & \text{if the worker rejects both contracts.} \end{cases}$$

$$\pi_{employer} = \begin{cases} a - w & \text{for the employer whose contract is accepted,} \\ 0 & \text{for the other employer.} \end{cases}$$

The game now has continua of pooling and separating equilibria which differ according to the value of education chosen. In the pooling equilibria, the equilibrium education level is s^*, where each s^* in the interval $[0, \bar{s}]$ supports a different equilibrium. The out-of-equilibrium belief most likely to support a pooling equilibrium is $Prob(a = Low | s \neq s^*) = 1$, so let us use this to find the value of $\bar{s}$, the greatest amount of education that can be generated by a pooling equilibrium. The equilibrium is Pooling Equilibrium 4.1, where $s^* \in [0, \bar{s}]$.

Pooling Equilibrium 4.1 $\begin{cases} s(Low) = s(High) = s^*, \\ w(s^*) = 3.75, \\ w(s \neq s^*) = 2, \\ Prob(a = Low | s \neq s^*) = 1. \end{cases}$

The critical value $\bar{s}$ can be discovered from the incentive compatibility constraint of the *Low* type, which is binding if $s^* = \bar{s}$. The most tempting deviation is to zero education, so that is the deviation that appears in the constraint.

$$U_L(s = 0) = 2 \leq U_L(s = \bar{s}) = 3.75 - \frac{8\bar{s}}{2}. \tag{11.8}$$

Equation (11.8) yields $\bar{s} = 7/16$. Any value of s^* less than $7/16$ will also support a pooling equilibrium. Note that the incentive-compatibility constraint of the *High* type is not binding. If a *High* deviates to $s = 0$, he, too, will be thought to be a *Low*, so

$$U_H(s = 0) = 2 \leq U_H \left(s = \frac{7}{16} \right) = 3.75 - \frac{8\bar{s}}{5.5} \approx 3.1. \tag{11.9}$$

In the separating equilibria, the education levels chosen in equilibrium are 0 for the *Low*'s and s^* for the *High*'s, where each s^* in the interval $[\bar{s}, \bar{\bar{s}}]$ supports a different equilibrium. A difference from the case of separating equilibria in games with binary strategy spaces is that now there are possible out-of-equilibrium actions even in a separating equilibrium. The two types of workers will separate to two education levels, but that leaves an infinite number of out-of-equilibrium education levels. As before, let us use the most extreme belief for the employers' beliefs after observing an out-of-equilibrium education level: that $Prob(a = Low | s \neq s^*) = 1$. The equilibrium is Separating Equilibrium 4.2, where $s^* \in [\bar{s}, s]$.

Separating Equilibrium 4.2 $\begin{cases} s(Low) = 0, \quad s(High) = s^*, \\ w(s^*) = 5.5, \\ w(s \neq s^*) = 2, \\ Prob(a = Low | s \notin \{0, s^*\}) = 1. \end{cases}$

The critical value $\bar{s}$ can be discovered from the incentive-compatibility constraint of the *Low*, which is binding if $s^* = \bar{s}$.

$$U_L(s = 0) = 2 \geq U_L(s = \bar{s}) = 5.5 - \frac{8\bar{s}}{2}. \tag{11.10}$$

Equation (11.10) yields $\bar{s} = 7/8$. Any value of s^* greater than $7/8$ will also deter the *Low* workers from acquiring education. If the education needed for the wage of 5.5 is too great, the *High* workers will give up on education too. Their incentive compatibility constraint requires that

$$U_H(s = 0) = 2 \leq U_H(s = \bar{\bar{s}}) = 5.5 - \frac{8\bar{\bar{s}}}{5.5}. \tag{11.11}$$

Equation (11.11) yields $\bar{\bar{s}} = 77/32$. s^* can take any lower value than $77/32$ and the *High*'s will be willing to acquire education.

The big difference from Education I is that Education IV has Pareto-ranked equilibria. Pooling can occur not just at zero education but at positive levels, as in Education III, and the pooling equilibria with positive education levels are all Pareto inferior. Also, the separating equilibria can be Pareto ranked, since separation with $s^* = \bar{s}$ dominates separation with $s^* = \bar{\bar{s}}$. Using a binary strategy space instead of a continuum conceals this problem.

Education IV also shows how restricting the strategy space can alter the kinds of equilibria that are possible. Education III had no separating equilibrium because at the maximum possible signal, $s = 1$, the *Low*'s were still willing to imitate the *High*'s. Education IV would not have any separating equilibria either if the strategy space were restricted to allow only education levels less than $\frac{7}{8}$. Using a bounded strategy space eliminates possibly realistic equilibria.

This is not to say that models with binary strategy sets are always misleading. Education I is a fine model for showing how signalling can be used to separate agents of different types; it becomes misleading only when used to reach a conclusion such as "[i]f a separating equilibrium exists, it is unique." As with any assumption, one must be careful not to narrow the model so much as to render vacuous the question it is designed to answer.

11.3   General Comments on Signalling in Education

Signalling and Similar Phenomena

The distinguishing feature of signalling is that the agent's action, although not directly related to output, is useful because it is related to ability. For the signal to work, it must be less costly for an agent with higher ability. Separation can occur in Education I because when the principal pays a greater wage to educated workers, only the *High*s, whose utility costs of education are lower, are willing to acquire it. That is why a signal works where a simple message would not: actions speak louder than words.

Signalling is outwardly similar to other solutions to adverse selection. The high-ability agent finds it cheaper than the low-ability one to build a reputation, but the reputation-building actions are based directly on his high ability. In a typical reputation model he shows ability by producing high output period after period. Also, the nature of reputation is to require several periods of play, which signalling does not.

Another form of communication is possible when some observable variable not under the control of the worker is correlated with ability. Age, for example, is correlated with reliability, so an employer pays older workers more, but the correlation does not arise because it is easier for reliable workers to acquire the attribute of age. Because age is not an action chosen by the worker, we would not need game theory to model it.

Problems in Applying Signalling to Education

On the empirical level, the first question to ask of a signalling model of education is, "What is education?" For operational purposes this means, "In what units is education measured?"

330 Asymmetric Information

Two possible answers are "years of education" and "grade point average." If the sacrifice of a year of earnings is greater for a low-ability worker, years of education can serve as a signal. If less intelligent students must work harder to get straight As, then grade-point-average can also be a signal.

Layard & Psacharopoulos (1974) give three rationales for rejecting signalling as an important motive for education. First, dropouts get as high a rate of return on education as those who complete degrees, so the signal is not the diploma, although it might be the years of education. Second, wage differentials between different education levels rise with age, although one would expect the signal to be less important after the employer has acquired more observations on the worker's output. Third, testing is not widely used for hiring, despite its low cost relative to education. Tests are available, but unused: students commonly take tests like the American SAT whose results they could credibly communicate to employers, and their scores correlate highly with subsequent grade point average. One would also expect an employer to prefer to pay an 18-year-old low wages for four years to determine his ability, rather than waiting to see what grades he gets as a history major.

Productive Signalling

Even if education is largely signalling, we might not want to close the schools. Signalling might be wasteful in a pooling equilibrium like Pooling Equilibrium 3.2, but in a separating equilibrium it can be second-best efficient for at least three reasons. First, it allows the employer to match workers with jobs suited to their talents. If the only jobs available were "professor" and "typist," then in a pooling equilibrium, both *High* and *Low* workers would be employed, but they would be randomly allocated to the two jobs. Given the principle of comparative advantage, typing might improve, but I think, pridefully, that research would suffer.

Second, signalling keeps talented workers from moving to jobs where their productivity is lower but their talent is known. Without signalling, a talented worker might leave a corporation and start his own company, where he would be less productive but better paid. The naive observer would see that corporations hire only one type of worker (*Low*), and imagine there was no welfare loss.

Third, if ability is endogenous – moral hazard rather than adverse selection – signalling encourages workers to acquire ability. One of my teachers said that you always understand your next-to-last econometrics class. Suppose that solidly learning econometrics increases the student's ability, but a grade of A is not enough to show that he solidly learned the material. To signal his newly acquired ability, the student must also take "Time Series," which he cannot pass without a solid understanding of econometrics. "Time Series" might be useless in itself, but if it did not exist, the students would not be able to show he had learned basic econometrics.

11.4 The Informed Player Moves Second: Screening

In screening games, the informed player moves second, which means that he moves in response to contracts offered by the uninformed player. Having the uninformed player make the offers is important because his offer conveys no information about himself, unlike in a signalling model.

Education V: Screening with a Discrete Signal

PLAYERS
A worker and two employers.

THE ORDER OF PLAY
0   Nature chooses worker ability $a \in \{2, 5.5\}$, each ability having probability 0.5. Employers do not observe ability, but the worker does.
1   Each employer offers a wage contract $w(s)$.
2   The worker chooses education level $s \in \{0, 1\}$.
3   The worker accepts a contract, or rejects both of them.
4   Output equals a.

PAYOFFS

$$\pi_{worker} = \begin{cases} w - 8s/a & \text{if the worker accepts contract } w, \\ 0 & \text{if the worker rejects both contracts.} \end{cases}$$

$$\pi_{employer} = \begin{cases} a - w & \text{for the employer whose contract is accepted,} \\ 0 & \text{for the other employer.} \end{cases}$$

Education V has no pooling equilibrium, because if one employer tried to offer the zero profit pooling contract, $w(0) = 3.75$, the other employer would offer $w(1) = 5.5$ and draw away all the *High*s. The unique equilibrium is

Separating Equilibrium 5.1 $\begin{cases} s(Low) = 0, s(High) = 1, \\ w(0) = 2, w(1) = 5.5. \end{cases}$

Beliefs do not need to be specified in a screening model. The uninformed player moves first, so his beliefs after seeing the move of the informed player are irrelevant. The informed player is fully informed, so his beliefs are not affected by what he observes. This is much like simple adverse selection, in which the uninformed player moves first, offering a set of contracts, after which the informed player chooses one of them. The modeller does not need to refine perfectness in a screening model. The similarity between adverse selection and screening is strong enough that Education V would not have been out of place in chapter 9, but it is presented here because the context is so similar to the signalling models of education.

Education VI allows a continuum of education levels, in a game otherwise the same as Education V.

Education VI: Screening with a Continuous Signal

PLAYERS
A worker and two employers.

THE ORDER OF PLAY
0   Nature chooses worker ability $a \in \{2, 5.5\}$, each ability having probability 0.5. Employers do not observe ability, but the worker does.
1   Each employer offers a wage contract $w(s)$.
2   The worker choose education level $s \in [0, 1]$.
3   The worker chooses a contract, or rejects both of them.
4   Output equals a.

PAYOFFS

$$\pi_{worker} = \begin{cases} w - 8s/a & \text{if the worker accepts contract } w, \\ 0 & \text{if the worker rejects both contracts.} \end{cases}$$

$$\pi_{employer} = \begin{cases} a - w & \text{for the employer whose contract is accepted,} \\ 0 & \text{for the other employer.} \end{cases}$$

Pooling equilibria generally do not exist in screening games with continuous signals, and sometimes separating equilibria in pure strategies do not exist either – recall Insurance Game III from section 9.4. Education VI, however, does have a separating Nash equilibrium, with a unique equilibrium path.

Separating Equilibrium 6.1 $\begin{cases} s(Low) = 0, s(High) = 0.875, \\ w = \begin{cases} 2 & \text{if } s < 0.875, \\ 5.5 & \text{if } s \geq 0.875. \end{cases} \end{cases}$

In any separating contract, the *Low*s must be paid a wage of 2 for an education of 0, because this is the most attractive contract that breaks even. The separating contract for the *High*s must maximize their utility subject to the constraints discussed in Education I. When the signal is continuous, the constraints are especially useful to the modeller for calculating the equilibrium. The participation constraints for the employers require that

$$w(0) \leq a_L = 2 \quad \text{and} \quad w(s^*) \leq a_H = 5.5, \tag{11.12}$$

where s^* is the separating value of education that we are trying to find. Competition turns the inequalities in (11.12) into equalities. The self-selection constraint for the low-ability workers is

$$U_L(s = 0) \geq U_L(s = s^*), \tag{11.13}$$

which in Education VI is

$$w(0) - 0 \geq w(s^*) - \frac{8s^*}{2}. \qquad (11.14)$$

Since the separating wage is 2 for the *Low*s and 5.5 for the *High*s, constraint (11.14) is satisfied as an equality if $s^* = 0.875$, which is the crucial education level in Separating Equilibrium 6.1.

$$U_H(s = 0) = w(0) \leq U_H(s = s^*) = w(s^*) - \frac{8s^*}{5.5}. \qquad (11.15)$$

If $s^* = 0.875$, inequality (11.15) is true, and it would also be true for higher values of s^*. Unlike the case of the continuous-strategy signalling game, Education IV, however, the equilibrium contract in Education VI is unique, because the employers compete to offer the most attractive contract that satisfies the participation and incentive compatibility constraints. The most attractive is the separating contract that Pareto dominates the other separating contracts by requiring the relatively low separating signal of $s^* = 0.875$.

Similarly, competition in offering attractive contracts rules out pooling contracts. The nonpooling constraint, required by competition between employers, is

$$U_H(s = s^*) \geq U_H(pooling), \qquad (11.16)$$

which, for Education VI, is, using the most attractive possible pooling contract,

$$w(s^*) - \frac{8s^*}{5.5} \geq 3.75. \qquad (11.17)$$

Since the payoff of *High*s in the separating contract is 4.23 ($=5.5 - 8 \times 0.875/5.5$, rounded), the nonpooling constraint is satisfied.

No Pooling Equilibrium in Screening: Education VI

The screening game Education VI lacks a pooling equilibrium, which would require the outcome $\{s = 0, w(0) = 3.75\}$, shown as C_1 in figure 11.1. If one employer offered a pooling contract requiring more than zero education (such as the inefficient Pooling Equilibrium 3.2), the other employer could make the more attractive offer of the same wage for zero education. The wage is 3.75 to ensure zero profits. The rest of the wage function – the wages for positive education levels – can take a variety of shapes, so long as the wage does not rise so fast with education that the *High*s are tempted to become educated.

But no equilibrium has these characteristics. In a Nash equilibrium, no employer can offer a pooling contract, because the other employer could always profit by offering a separating contract paying more to the educated. One such separating contract is C_2 in figure 11.1, which pays 5 to workers with an education of $s = 0.5$ and yields a payoff of 4.89 to the *High*s ($=5 - [8 \times 0.5]/5.5$, rounded) and 3 to the *Low*s ($=5 - 8 \times 0.5/2$). Only *High*s prefer C_2 to the pooling contract C_1, which yields payoffs of 3.75 to both *High* and *Low*, and if only *High*s accept C_2, it yields positive profits to the employer.

Nonexistence of a pooling equilibrium in screening models without continuous strategy spaces is a general result. The linearity of the curves in Education VI is special, but in any screening model the *Low*s would have greater costs of education, which is equivalent to steeper indifference curves. This is the **single-crossing property** alluded to in Education I. Any pooling equilibrium must, like C_1, lie on the vertical axis where education is zero and the wage equals the average ability. A separating contract like C_2 can always be found to the northeast of the pooling contract, between the indifference curves of the two types, and it will yield positive profits by attracting only the *High*s.

Education VII: No Pure-strategy Equilibrium in a Screening Game

In Education VI we showed that screening models have no pooling equilibria. In Education VII the parameters are changed a little to eliminate even the separating equilibrium in pure strategies. Let the proportion of *High*s be 0.9 instead of 0.5, so the zero-profit pooling wage is 5.15 ($=0.9[5.5] + 0.1[2]$) instead of 3.75. Consider the separating contracts C_3 and C_4, shown in figure 11.2, calculated in the same way as Separating Equilibrium 5.1. The pair (C_3, C_4) is the most attractive pair of contracts that separates *High*s from *Low*s. *Low* workers accept contract C_3, obtain $s = 0$, and receive a wage of 2, their ability. *High*s accept contract C_4, obtain $s = 0.875$, and receive a wage of 5.5, their ability. Education is not attractive to *Low*s because the *Low* payoff from pretending to be *High* is 2 ($=5.5 - 8 \times 0.875/2$), no better than the *Low* payoff of 2 from C_3 ($=2 - 8 \times 0/2$).

The wage of the pooling contract C_5 is 5.15, so that even the *High*s strictly prefer C_5 to (C_3, C_4). But our reasoning that no pooling equilibrium exists is still valid; some contract C_6 would attract all the *High*s from C_5. No Nash equilibrium in pure strategies exists, either separating or pooling.

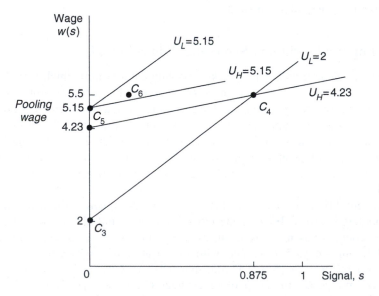

Figure 11.2 Education VII: neither separating nor pooling pure-strategy equilibria in a screening game.

Should the Modeller Worry about Multiple Equilibria, or Nonexistence of a Pure-strategy Equilibrium?

There is no reason why the modeller should be more worried about nonexistence of an equilibrium in pure strategies, per se, in a signalling model. As far back as chapter 3 we looked at games in which the only realistic equilibrium is in mixed strategies. In that chapter, and also in chapter 1 and in chapter 6 (on dynamic games with incomplete information) we discussed multiple equilibria, and why we should not be unduly worried about them either – the main reason being that under the logic of Nash equilibrium, which is self-fulfilling expectations, we should indeed expect different expectations to yield different outcomes.

It is in coordination models and signalling models that multiple equilibria have created the most anxiety among economists. For coordination models, there has been hope that cheap talk and focal points can often narrow down our predictions to a single outcome. For signalling models, the various refinements discussed in chapter 6 have been proposed, but with unenthusiastic reception. For both coordination games and signalling games, however, there is another way out: changing the order of moves. If moves are not simultaneous, and if, in the signalling game, it is not the informed player but the uninformed player who moves first, the outcome is much more likely to be both uniquely determined and efficient. Because the outcome is more likely to be efficient, it will also often be the case that the players would like the moves to be sequential, or that evolution will cause such a game to more often observed.

Consider what happens if the principal makes the offer of a particular reward for a particular signal level – a screening model instead of a signalling model. That simple change will eliminate Pareto-dominated contracts, because the uninformed player will not offer them.

As a specific example, suppose job candidates can heavily research the employer before an interview, and this works as a signal because less serious applicants are less willing to expend that effort.

One possibility is a pooling equilibrium in which both good and bad applicants signal by researching. The equilibrium is maintained by the fear that if an applicant does *not* he will be thought to be the bad type. This is inefficient, because the employer, in the end, gets no information.

An employer, therefore, would like to switch to a screening game. He would say to applicants that they should not research the company, because he knows that researching is not a good signal. In response, neither type of applicant would research. And the company would profit by reducing the salary it offers, acquiring some of the social savings from less researching. (A "no presents" rule at a birthday party is another example.)

Note, however, that just because you observe all applicants researching, an apparent pooling equilibrium, it might not be the case that the equilibrium really is pooling. It could be that the analyst's data has a self-selection problem: given that researching is necessary to have a chance at the job, only the good types apply – and they all research it. Be careful in concluding that a costly signal really is not separating out the types.

A second, related, inefficient equilibrium is when the equilibrium is separating but the signal is inefficiently high. In equilibrium, job applicants must be able to recite a list of the past four presidents of the company, but even requiring a list of two presidents would separate the good applicants from the bad. In response, the company could say before the interview that applicants need only know the history of the company for the past five years, and that it considers excess knowledge a sign of desperation on the part of the applicant.

A third, different kind of equilibrium is pooling where no signalling occurs: applicants believe that employers are unimpressed by their knowledge of company history and employers are unimpressed because only a blundering applicant would bother to research it. Such an equilibrium need not be inefficient. It might be that the cost of the signal is not worth the efficiency gains from separation. But it might be inefficient: the gains from hiring the most enthusiastic applicant, one who could stand to spend ten hours researching the history of an accounting firm merely to slightly increase his probability of getting a job there, might be worth the cost. If so, the employer could break out of the inefficient pooling equilibrium by announcing that applicants will be rated partly on their knowledge of company history. The pooling equilibrium would then be too delicate to survive.

A fourth kind of equilibrium is inefficient separation – an equilibrium where signalling occurs and separate good types of applicants from bad, but the cost to the applicants is not worth the social benefit. The good type of applicant may benefit, but the bad type loses even more, since the benefit is a pure transfer of who gets the job and this is achieved at a cost, the cost of the research.

Inefficient separation of this kind is more robust than the first three kinds of inefficient equilibria. The reason is that if one employer deviates and announces that it will no longer give applicants credit for their knowledge of company history, the result would simply be that they would attract even more low-quality applicants, while their high-quality applicants would desert them for employers who would respond to the research signal. If, however, there were only one employer, that employer could successfully pursue such a policy. It would change the signalling game to a screening game, and announce a reduction in the wage to the applicants' reservation level, but also ignore knowledge of company history in interviews. This is an interesting efficiency advantage of a monopsony.

Thus, very often, if not always, the timing of moves in a signalling game is flexible enough that in the metagame in which the players can choose the order of the moves, they will choose to convert it to a screening game. In the end, this will often eliminate all but one equilibrium outcome, and often the remaining outcome will be efficient, or at least Pareto-optimal.

A Summary of the Education Models

Because of signalling's complexity, most of this chapter has been devoted to elaboration of the education model. We began with Education I, which showed how with two types and two signal levels the perfect Bayesian equilibrium could be either separating or pooling. Education II took the same model and replaced the specification of out-of-equilibrium beliefs with an additional move by Nature, while Education III changed the parameters in Education I to increase the difference between types and to show how signalling could continue with pooling. Education IV changed Education I by allowing a continuum of education levels, which resulted in a continuum of inefficient equilibria, each with a different signal level. After a purely verbal discussion of how to apply signalling models, we looked at screening, in which the employer moves first. Education V was a screening reprise of Education I, while Education VI broadened the model to allow a continuous signal, which eliminates pooling equilibria. Education VII modified the parameters of Education VI to show that sometimes no pure-strategy Nash equilibrium exists at all.

Throughout it was implicitly assumed that all the players were risk-neutral. Risk-neutrality is unimportant, because there is no uncertainty in the model and the agents bear no risk. If the workers were risk-averse and they differed in their degrees of risk aversion, the contracts could try to use the difference to support a separating equilibrium because willingness to accept risk might act as a signal. If the principal were risk-averse he might offer a wage less than the average productivity in the pooling equilibrium, but he is under no risk at all in the separating equilibrium, because it is fully revealing. The models are also games of certainty, and this too is unimportant. If output were uncertain, agents would just make use of the expected payoffs rather than the raw payoffs and very little would change.

Ways to Communicate

We have by now seen a variety of ways one player can convey information to another. Following the Crawford–Sobel model of chapter 10, let us call these players the Sender and the Receiver. Why might the Receiver believe the Sender's message? The reason depends on the setting.

1 **Cheap talk games:** The Sender's message is costless and there is no penalty for lying.

In a cheap talk game, messages have no direct impact on payoff functions. If the Receiver ignores the message, the Sender's payoff is unaffected by the message. If the Receiver changes his action in response, though, that might affect the Sender. Usually, these are coordination games, where the Sender's preference for the action the Receiver will choose in response to the message is the same as the Receiver's, or at least correlated with it. Chapter 10's Crawford–Sobel model is an example of imperfect correlation, in which cheap talk results in some information being exchanged, even though the message is coarse and the Sender cannot convey precisely what he knows.

2 **Truthful announcement games:** The Sender may be silent instead of sending a message, but if he sends a message it must be truthful. The message might or might not be costly.

The Sender's type usually varies from bad to good in these models, and they are subject to the "unravelling" illustrated in chapter 10's example, since silence indicates bad news. As discussed there, unravelling might only be partial, for a variety of reasons such as some exogenous probability that the Sender actually is unable to send even a truthful message. One variant is when the Sender has committed to the truth, perhaps via a mechanism negotiated with the Receiver, converting a cheap talk game into a truthful announcement game.

3 **Auditing games:** The Receiver may audit the message at some cost and discover if the Sender was lying. The Sender's message might or might not be costly.

We saw examples of this in chapter 3, with commitment to auditing. A variant is when the Receiver cannot commit to auditing, in which case there will be an equilibrium in mixed strategies, with the Sender sometimes truthful, sometimes not, and the Receiver sometimes auditing, sometimes not. An example is Rasmusen (1993), in which the Sender is a lobbyist or protester who sends a costly message to the Receiver, a government official. That cost is wasted if the Receiver audits and finds the message is a lie, even if there is no additional punishment of the kind found in truthful announcement games.

4 **Mechanism games:** The Sender's message might or might not be costly. Before he sends it, he commits to a contract with the Receiver, with their decisions based on what they can observe and enforcement based on what can be verified by the courts.

Mechanisms were the topic of chapter 10. Commitment is the key. Mechanisms work out most simply if they are chosen before the Sender receives his private information, since otherwise the choice of mechanism may itself convey information.

5 **Signalling games:** The Sender's message is costly when he lies, and more costly when he lies than when he tells the truth. He sends it before the Receiver takes any action.

Signalling is the main topic of this chapter, chapter 11. The Sender's type usually varies from bad to good in these models. The single-crossing property is crucial – that if the Sender's type is better, it is cheaper for him to send a message that his type is good. It might well be costless for the Sender to send a truthful message (or even have negative costs), because what matters is the difference in costs between a truthful message and a false one. Usually in these models the message is an indirect one, conveyed by the choice of some action such as years of education seemingly unrelated to communication.

6 **Expensive-talk games:** The Sender's message is costly, but the cost is the same regardless of his type. There is no penalty for lying.

The difference between expensive talk and signalling is that in expensive talk the single-crossing property is not satisfied. Truthful communication might still work, for reasons akin to those in the Cheap-Talk Game, if the high-type Sender has a greater desire than the low type for the Receiver to adopt a high response. Chapter 6's PhD Admissions Game is an example. The student who hates economics has no incentive to pay the cost of applying for the PhD program. As with cheap talk and signalling, expectations are crucial because of multiple equilibria.

7 **Screening games:** The Sender's message is costly when he lies, and more costly when he lies than when he tells the truth. He sends it in response to an offer by the Receiver.

We have discussed screening games here in chapter 11. If the Receiver can commit to his response to a signal, this is a mechanism game. If he cannot, it is an expensive-talk game, where the Receiver's offer is made as part of an equilibrium in which the Sender's making the offer influences the Receiver's expectations of what the Sender will do.

In the rest of this chapter, we will look at more specialized models related to signalling.

*11.5   Two Signals: The Game of Underpricing New Stock Issues

One signal might not be enough when there is not one but two characteristics of an agent that he wishes to communicate to the principal. This has been generally analyzed in Engers (1987), and multiple signal models have been especially popular in financial economics, for example, the multiple signal model used to explain the role of investment bankers in new stock issues by Hughes (1986). We will use a model of initial public offerings of stock as the example in this section.

Empirically, it has been found that companies consistently issue stock at a price so low that it rises sharply in the days after the issue, an abnormal return estimated to average 11.4 percent (Copeland & Weston [1988], p. 377). The game of Underpricing New Stock Issues tries to explain this using the percentage of the stock retained by the original owner and the amount of underpricing as two signals. The two characteristics being signalled are the mean of the value of the new stock, which is of obvious concern to the potential buyers, and the variance, the importance of which will be explained later.

Underpricing New Stock Issues (Grinblatt & Hwang [1989])

PLAYERS
The entrepreneur and many investors.

THE ORDER OF PLAY
(See figure 2.3a for a time line.)

0 Nature chooses the expected value (μ) and variance (σ^2) of a share of the firm using some distribution F.
1 The entrepreneur retains fraction α of the stock and offers to sell the rest at a price per share of P_0.
2 The investors decide whether to accept or reject the offer.
3 The market price becomes P_1, the investors' estimate of μ.
4 Nature chooses the value V of a share using some distribution G such that μ is the mean of V and σ^2 is the variance. With probability θ, V is revealed to the investors and becomes the market price.
5 The entrepreneur sells his remaining shares at the market price.

PAYOFFS

$$\pi_{entrepreneur} = U([1-\alpha]P_0 + \alpha[\theta V + (1-\theta)P_1]), \quad \text{where } U' > 0 \text{ and } U'' < 0,$$

$$\pi_{investors} = (1-\alpha)(V - P_0) + \alpha(1-\theta)(V - P_1).$$

The entrepreneur's payoff is the utility of the value of the shares he issues at P_0 plus the value of those he sells later at the price P_1 or V. The investors' payoff is the true value of the shares they buy minus the price they pay.

Underpricing New Stock Issues subsumes the simpler model of Leland & Pyle (1977), in which σ^2 is common knowledge and if the entrepreneur chooses to retain a large fraction of the shares, the investors deduce that the stock value is high. The one signal in that model is fully revealing because holding a larger fraction exposes the undiversified entrepreneur to a larger amount of risk, which he is unwilling to accept unless the stock value is greater than investors would guess without the signal.

If the variance of the project is high, that also increases the risk to the undiversified entrepreneur, which is important even though the investors are risk-neutral and do not care directly about the value of σ^2. Since the risk is greater when variance is high, the signal α is more effective and retaining a smaller amount allows the entrepreneur to sell the remainder at the same price as a larger amount for a lower-variance firm. Even though the investors are diversified and do not care directly about firm-specific risk, they are interested in the variance because it tells them something about the effectiveness of entrepreneur-retained

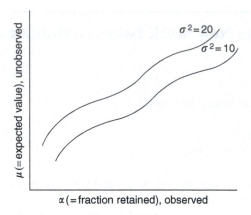

Figure 11.3   How the signal changes with the variance.

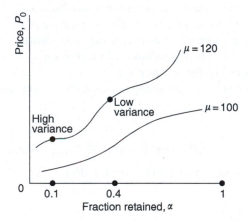

Figure 11.4   Different ways to signal a given company value.

shares as a signal of share value. Figure 11.3 shows the signalling schedules for two variance levels.

In the game of Underpricing New Stock Issues, σ^2 is not known to the investors, so the signal is no longer fully revealing. An α equal to 0.1 could mean either that the firm has a low value with low variance, or a high value with high variance. But the entrepreneur can use a second signal, the price at which the stock is issued, and by observing α and P_0, the investors can deduce μ and σ^2.

I will use specific numbers for concreteness. The entrepreneur could signal that the stock has the high mean value, $\mu = 120$, in two ways: (1) retaining a high percentage, $\alpha = 0.4$, and making the initial offering at a high price of $P_0 = 90$, or (2) retaining a low percentage, $\alpha = 0.1$, and making the initial offering at a low price, $P_0 = 80$. Figure 11.4 shows the different combinations of initial price and fraction retained that might be used. If the stock has a high variance, he will want to choose behavior (2), which reduces his risk. Investors deduce that the stock of anyone who retains a low percentage and offers a low price actually has $\mu = 120$ and a high variance, so stock offered at the price of 80 rises in price. If, on the other hand, the entrepreneur retained $\alpha = 0.1$ and offered the high price $P_0 = 90$, investors would conclude that μ was lower than 120 but that variance was low also, so the stock would not rise in price. The low price conveys the information that this stock has a high mean and high variance rather than a low mean and low variance.

This model explains why new stock is issued at a low price. The entrepreneur knows that the price will rise, but only if he issues it at a low initial price to show that the variance is high. The price discount shows that signalling by holding a large fraction of stock is unusually costly, but he is nonetheless willing to signal. The discount is costly because he is selling stock at less than its true value, and retaining stock is costly because he bears extra risk, but both are necessary to signal that the stock is valuable.

*11.6   Signal Jamming and Limit Pricing

This chapter has examined a number of models in which an informed player tries to convey information to an uninformed player by some means or other – by entering into an incentive contract, or by signalling. Sometimes, however, the informed party has the opposite problem: his natural behavior would convey his private information but he wants to keep it secret. This happens, for example, if one firm is informed about its poor ability to compete successfully, and it wants to conceal this information from a rival. The informed player may then engage in costly actions, just as in signalling, but now the costly action will be **signal jamming** (a term coined in Fudenberg & Tirole [1986c]): preventing information from appearing rather than generating information.

Limit pricing refers to the practice of keeping prices low to deter entry. Limit pricing can be explained in a variety of ways; notably, as a way for the incumbent to signal that he has low enough costs that rivals would regret entering, as in problem 6.2 and Milgrom & Roberts (1982a). Here, the explanation for limit pricing will be signal jamming: by keeping profits low, the incumbent keeps it unclear to the rival whether the market is big enough to accommodate two firms profitably. In previous editions I used a model from Rasmusen (1997) as an illustration, but in this edition I will use a simpler model that is still able to convey the idea of signal jamming. The market will be one with inelastic demand up to a reservation price. Entry would split that inelastic quantity evenly between the firms, and the price would fall. What is crucial is that before entry the entrant does not know the reservation price, and hence does not know how far the price would fall after entry. The incumbent may or may not find it worthwhile to keep his price low to prevent the entrant from learning something about the reservation price.

The incumbent needs to trade off a high price in the first period against the possibility of inducing entry. As always, work back from the end.

The incumbent's choice of p_{2m} is easy: choose $p_{2m} = v$, since there is no threat of future entry.

The rival's expected payoff from entry depends on his beliefs about v, which in turn depend upon which of the multiple equilibria of this game is being played out.

If the incumbent were nonstrategic, he would charge $p_1 = v$, maximizing his first-period profit. The rival would deduce the value v and would enter in the second-period

Limit Pricing as Signal Jamming

PLAYERS
The incumbent and the rival.

THE ORDER OF PLAY
0   Nature chooses the reservation price v using the continuous density $h(v)$ on the support $[c, d]$, observed only by the incumbent. (The parameter c is marginal cost.)
1   The incumbent chooses the first-period price p_1, generating sales of q if $p_1 \leq v$ and 0 otherwise. The variables p_1 and q are observed by both players.
2   The rival decides whether to enter at cost F or to stay out.
3   If the rival did not enter, the incumbent chooses the second period price, $p_{2,m}$, generating sales of q if $p_{2m} \leq v$ and 0 otherwise.
4   If the rival did enter, the duopoly price is $p_2(v)$, with $p_2 \geq c$ and $dp_2/dv > 0$.

Let us make more specific assumptions to avoid caveats later. Assume that the second-period duopoly price is halfway between marginal cost and the monopoly price, so

$$p_2(v) = \frac{c + v}{2}, \tag{11.18}$$

the distribution of reservation prices is uniform, so

$$h(v) = \frac{1}{d - c}, \tag{11.19}$$

that $c = 0$, and that $d > 6.4F/q$. We will defer using these special assumptions until midway through our exposition.

PAYOFFS
If the rival does not enter and p_1 and p_{2m} are no greater than v, the payoffs are

$$\pi_{incumbent} = (p_1 - c)q + (p_2 - c)q,$$
$$\pi_{rival} = 0 \tag{11.20}$$

If the rival does enter and p_1 are no greater than v, the payoffs are

$$\pi_{incumbent} = (p_1 - c)q + (p_2(v) - c)\left(\frac{q}{2}\right)$$
$$\pi_{rival} = -F + (p_2(v) - c)\left(\frac{q}{2}\right). \tag{11.21}$$

if p_1 exceeded the critical value $v^* = c + 2F/q$, a value which yields zero profits because

$$-F + \left[\left(c + \frac{2F}{q} - c \right) \left(\frac{q}{2} \right) \right] = 0. \tag{11.22}$$

If the incumbent is willing to charge a lower p_1, though, and accept lower first-period profits, he may be able to deter entry, and if he can, the higher second-period profits can more than make up for his sacrifice. Thus, nonstrategic behavior is not an equilibrium for this game. Instead, consider the strategy profile below.

A Limit Pricing Equilibrium

Incumbent: $p_2 = v$. For particular values a and b to be specified later,

$$p_1 = \begin{cases} v & \text{if } v < a, \\ a & \text{if } v \in [a, b], \\ v & \text{if } v > b. \end{cases}$$

Rival: Enter if $p_1 > a$. Otherwise, stay out. If the rival observes $p_1 \in (a, b]$, his out-of-equilibrium belief is that $v = h(v)/\int_{p_1}^{b} h(v) dv$, the expected value of v if it lies between p_1 and b.

The rival's equilibrium payoff if he enters is

$$\pi_{rival,enter} = -F + (Ep_2(v) - c) \left(\frac{q}{2} \right),$$

$$= -F + \left(\int_a^b p_2(v) \left(\frac{h(v)}{\int_a^b h(v) dv} \right) dv - c \right) \left(\frac{q}{2} \right), \tag{11.23}$$

where the density for the expectation $Ep_2(v)$ is $h(v)/\int_a^b h(v) dv$ instead of just $h(v)$ because it is conditional on v being between a and b, rather than v taking any of its possible values. The payoff in (11.23) equals zero in equilibrium for the entry-deterring values of a and b. If the incumbent deters entry, his payoff is

$$\pi_{incumbent}(no\ entry) = (p_1 - c)q + (v - c)q \tag{11.24}$$

and if he does not it is

$$\pi_{incumbent}(entry) = (v - c)q + (p_2(v) - c) \left(\frac{q}{2} \right). \tag{11.25}$$

The incumbent's advantage from limit pricing is the difference between these when $p_1 = a$, which is

$$[(a - c)q + (v - c)q] - \left[(v - c)q + (p_2(v) - c) \left(\frac{q}{2} \right) \right]. \tag{11.26}$$

This advantage is declining in v, and b is defined as the value at which it equals zero. Choosing $v = b$ in expression (11.26), equating to zero, and solving for a yields

$$a = \frac{c + p_2(b)}{2}. \tag{11.27}$$

We now have two equations (equation [11.27] and $\pi_{rival} = 0$ using expression [11.23]) for two unknowns (a and b). Now let us return to the special assumptions in equations (11.18) and (11.19). Given our specific assumptions on $h(v)$ and $p_2(v)$, $p_2(b) = b/2$ and $h(v) = 1/d$, so from (11.27),

$$a = \frac{b}{4}.$$ (11.28)

Since $\int_a^b h(v)dv = \int_a^b (1/d)dv = (b/d) - (a/d)$,

$$\pi_{rival} = -F + \left(\int_a^b \left(\frac{v}{2} \right) \left(\frac{1/d}{(b/d) - (a/d)} \right) dv \right) \left(\frac{q}{2} \right),$$

$$= -F + \left. \left(\frac{v^2}{4(b-a)} \right) \right|_{v=a}^{b} \left(\frac{q}{2} \right),$$

$$= -F + \left(\frac{b^2}{4(b-a)} - \frac{a^2}{4(b-a)} \right) \left(\frac{q}{2} \right),$$

$$= -F + \left(b^2 - \frac{b^2}{16} \right) \left(\frac{q}{8(b - (b/4))} \right),$$ (11.29)

so

$$b = \left(\frac{16}{5} \right) \left(\frac{2F}{q} \right).$$ (11.30)

where $b < d$ because of our special assumption that $d > 6.4F/q$. From equation (11.28),

$$a = \left(\frac{4}{5} \right) \left(\frac{2F}{q} \right).$$ (11.31)

It is useful to compare the limits a and b with v^*, the value of v for which entry yields a payoff of zero to the rival. That value, which we found above using equation (11.22), is

$$v^* = \frac{2F}{q}.$$ (11.32)

Thus, $a < v^* < b$. This makes sense. The values of a and b were chosen so that, in effect, v^* was the expected value of v on $[a, b]$, and the rival would be deterred even though he did not know the exact value of v. If $a \geq v^*$, then the expected value of v on $[a, b]$ would be greater than v^*, and the rival would feel safe in entering if the incumbent charged $p_1 = a$. Thus, to use limit pricing the incumbent must charge strictly less than the monopoly price appropriate if the duopoly market would yield zero profits to an rival. This kind of signal jamming reduces the information that reaches the rival compared to nonstrategic behavior, since the rival learns the precise value of v only if v is less than a or greater than b.

Note, however, that limit pricing would not work if this were a truthful announcement game, in which the incumbent could remain silent but could not lie to the rival.

The incumbent would then tell the rival the value of v whenever it was v^* or less – which means that limit pricing for values in the interval $[v^*, b]$ would no longer be effective.

*11.7   Countersignalling

Feltovich, Harbaugh, & To (2002) construct a model to explain a situation commonly observed: that although the worst types in a market do not signal, the best types do not signal either, and their very lack of signalling can be a sign of their confidence in their high quality (**countersignalling**). What is crucial in such situations is that the highest-quality types have an alternative way to convey their quality to the market besides costly signalling. We will illustrate that here with a model of banking.

Countersignalling

PLAYERS
Banks and depositors.

THE ORDER OF PLAY
0   There is a continuum of length 1 of banks. Nature chooses the solvency θ_i of each bank using cumulative distribution $F(\theta)$ on the support $[-10, 10]$ with $F(0) = 0.2$.
1   Bank i chooses to spend s_i on its building, where it must spend at least $\bar{s} = 9$ to operate at all, and otherwise must exit.
2   Depositors on a continuum of length $D = 1$ observe $\hat{\theta} = \theta_i + u_i$, where the u_i values are chosen independently and take values of -5, 0, and $+5$ with equal probability. The banks do not observe $\hat{\theta}$ in move (1).
3   Each depositor chooses a bank.

PAYOFFS
Bankers further from insolvency have cheaper access to capital, so if bank i attracts as many depositors as other active banks its payoff is

$$\pi_i = \frac{D}{B} - \left(\frac{s_i}{10 + \theta_i} \right), \tag{11.33}$$

where B is the interval of banks that attract depositors. If bank i attracts no depositors, its payoff is $-(s_i/(10 + \theta_i))$.
A depositor's payoff is 1 if he picks a bank with solvency θ at or above 0, and 0 if $\theta < 0$.

Equilibrium

Banks with solvency $\theta \in [-10, 0]$ choose $s = 0$. They do not signal, and attract no depositors.

Banks with solvency $\theta \in [0, 5)$ choose $s = s^* = 12.5$ and attract depositors.

Banks with solvency $\theta \in [5, 10]$ choose $s = 9$, and attract depositors.

Depositors choose banks with either $\hat{\theta} \geq 0$ or $s = 12.5$ or both. Out of equilibrium, they believe that no signal except 12.5 conveys information about a bank's solvency (passive conjectures).

Each bank has three reasonable choices: $s = 0$, $s = 9$, and $s = 12.5$. In equilibrium, $B = 1 - F(0) = 0.8$, because the solvent banks and only those banks enter.

A bank with $\theta \geq 5$ needn't worry about appearing insolvent, because its lowest possible observed solvency is $\hat{\theta} = \theta - 5 \geq 0$. Banks in the interval $[5, 10]$ will not spend more than the $s = 9$ necessary to enter because they attract all depositors anyway. They will enter with $s = 9$, though, because the least-profitable of those banks will then have a payoff of $D/B - (9/(10 + 5)) = 11/12 > 0$.

A bank with $\theta \in [0, 5)$ might be unlucky and have $u = -5$ and $\hat{\theta} < 0$, so signalling can be useful. The self-selection constraint requires that banks with $\theta < 0$ not signal. Thus, the crucial signal level, s^*, requires that the type of insolvent bank for which the signal is cheapest be unwilling to signal. We need $\pi_{\theta=0}(s = 0) = \pi_{\theta=0}(s = s^*)$, so

$$0 = \frac{D}{B} - \left(\frac{s^*}{10 + 0}\right). \tag{11.34}$$

Solving equation (11.34) for s^* and setting $B = 0.8$ and $D = 1$ yields

$$s^* = 12.5. \tag{11.35}$$

Alternatively, a bank with $\theta \in [0, 5)$ might enter with $s = 9$ and hope that $u = 0$ of $u = +5$ rather than $u = -5$. This has probability $2/3$, so in that case the payoff of the bank in that interval for which signalling is most costly is is negative:

$$\pi(s = K|\theta = 0) = \left(\frac{2}{3}\right)\left(\frac{D}{B}\right) - \left(\frac{9}{10 + 0}\right) = \frac{5}{6} - \left(\frac{9}{10}\right) < 0. \tag{11.36}$$

The insolvent banks with $\theta \in [-10, 0)$ choose $s = 0$ and a payoff of zero in equilibrium, but they also have the option to enter with $s = 12.5$, or with $s = 9$ in the hope that $u = +5$ and $\hat{\theta} \geq 0$. The expected payoffs from these strategies are

$$\pi(s = K|\theta < 0) < \left(\frac{1}{3}\right)\left(\frac{D}{B}\right) - \left(\frac{9}{10 + 0}\right) = \frac{5}{12} - \left(\frac{9}{10}\right) < 0 \tag{11.37}$$

and

$$\pi(s = s^*|\theta < 0) < \left(\frac{D}{B}\right) - \left(\frac{12.5}{10 + 0}\right) = \frac{5}{4} - \left(\frac{12.5}{10}\right) = 0. \tag{11.38}$$

As always, there also exists a nonsignalling perfect Bayesian equilibrium, in which depositors ignore any signal and only choose banks with $\hat{\theta} \geq 5$. And there exist other, inefficient, equilibria in which the crucial signal level is $s^* > 10D/(1 - F(0))$. You might also wish to investigate what happens if the number of consumers, D, takes values other than 1.

What is interesting in this model is that unlike in previous models, it is not the highest-quality players that signal, but the middle-quality ones. The highest-quality players have no need to signal, because their quality is so high that information about it reaches the market by a different means – here, the imperfect observation $\hat{\theta}$. The "countersignal" is the absence in the highest quality players of a normal signal. The crucial feature of countersignalling models that gives rise to this is that signalling not be the only way in which information reaches the market.

Another effect that can arise in countersignalling models (though it does not in the simple one here) is that the absence of a signal can have a positive, additional, effect on the uninformed player's estimate of the informed player's quality. In our banking game, that can't happen because if the noisy observation is $\hat{\theta} \geq 5$, depositors have the highest possible opinion of the bank's safety: that it is solvent with probability one. Thus, the high-quality banks abstain from signalling simply to save money, not because the countersignal actually helps them. Suppose, though, that we added new depositors to the model, an amount small enough to be measure zero so they would not affect the equilibrium, and these new depositors had the special features that: (1) they could not observe even $\hat{\theta}$, and (2) their payoffs were 0 not just for insolvent banks but for any bank with $\theta < 7$. These depositors would observe only that some banks have $s = 4$ and some have $s = s^*$. Since they would be looking for especially high-quality banks, they would actually prefer to choose a bank with the lower signal value of $s = 4$, because they could be sure that if $s = s^*$ then $\theta < 7$. Thus, having a smaller building acts as a countersignal, an indicator that this bank has such high quality that it does not need to be ostentatious.

This informational value of the countersignal is what prompted the title of Feltovich, Harbaugh, & To (2002): "Too Cool for School? Signalling and Countersignalling." Low-quality high-school students might do badly in their schoolwork because doing well is too costly a signal. Mid-quality students would do better, to separate themselves from the low-quality students. But high-quality students might also do badly in their schoolwork, as a form of countersignalling. An observable indicator of quality might already show them to be high-quality ("cool"), so they don't need the signal. But they might suppress their schoolwork even though they really would prefer to do well, because a student who does his schoolwork would be considered mid-quality, not high-quality. In such a case, the countersignal is actually costly – the student is refraining from schoolwork purely for strategic reasons. This is not quite signal jamming, because the high-quality students is trying to escape from pooling rather than hide in it, but it shares with signal jamming the idea of costly suppression of an observable variable.

The term "countersignalling" is new, but the idea that the more desirable type might signal less goes as far back as part III, article III of Adam Smith's *Wealth of Nations*, where he lays out a theory of morality and wealth, noting that the poor are often more rigorous than the rich in their morality. Most of his theory is based on the higher utility cost of vice to the poor rather than on information, but he also discusses the observable effects of vice. He suggests that for the urban poor, in the anonymity of the city, belonging to a strict church can signal their morality, while for rich people, the very indulgence in vice can signal wealth, since high expenditure would quickly ruin someone of moderate means. Countersignalling will be a fruitful area for empirical work to test whether it explains signalling by moderate types only in various situations. One fascinating study of quality and information provision is

Jin & Leslie (2003), a study of restaurant responses to government hygiene grade cards for restaurants in Los Angeles, cards whose posting in restaurant windows was optional and later was compulsory.

Notes

N11.1   The informed player moves first: signalling

- The term "signalling" was introduced by Spence (1973). The games in this book take advantage of hindsight to build simpler and more rational models of education than in his original article, which used a rather strange equilibrium concept: a strategy profile from which no worker has incentive to deviate and under which the employer's profits are zero. Under that concept, the firm's incentives to deviate are irrelevant.

    The distinction between signalling and screening has been attributed to Stiglitz & Weiss (1989). The literature has shown wide variation in the use of both terms, and "signal" is such a useful word that it is often used in models that have no signalling of the kind discussed in this chapter. Where confusion might arise, the word "indicator" might be better for an informative variable.

- The applications of signalling are too many to properly list. A few examples are the use of prices in Wilson (1980) and Stiglitz (1987), the payment of dividends in Ross (1977), and bargaining under asymmetric information (section 12.5). Banks (1991) has written a short book surveying signalling models in political science. Empirical papers include Layard & Psacharopoulos (1974) on education and Staten & Umbeck (1986) on occupational diseases. Riley (2001) surveys the signalling literature, and Rochet & Stole (2003) surveys multi-dimensional screening.

- Legal bargaining is one area of application for signalling. See Grossman & Katz (1983). Reinganum (1988) has a nice example of the value of precommitment in legal signalling. In her model, a prosecutor who wishes to punish the guilty and release the innocent wishes, if parameters are such that most defendants are guilty, to commit to a pooling strategy in which his plea bargaining offer is the same whatever the probability that a particular defendant would be found guilty.

- The peacock's tail may be a signal. Zahavi (1975) suggests that a large tail may benefit the peacock because, by hampering him, it demonstrates to potential mates that he is fit enough to survive even with a handicap. By now there is an entire literature on signalling in the natural world; see John Maynard-Smith & David Harper's 2004 book, *Animal Signals*.

- **Advertising:** Advertising is a natural application for signalling. The literature includes Nelson (1974), written before signalling was well known, Kihlstrom & Riordan (1984) and Milgrom & Roberts (1986). I will briefly describe a model based on Nelson's. Firms are one of two types, low quality or high quality. Consumers do not know that a firm exists until they receive an advertisement from it, and they do not know its quality until they buy its product. They are unwilling to pay more than zero for low quality, but any product is costly to produce. This is not a reputation model, because it is finite in length and quality is exogenous.

    If the cost of an advertisement is greater than the profit from one sale but less than the profit from repeat sales, high rates of advertising are associated with high product quality. Only firms with high quality would advertise.

    The model can work even if consumers do not understand the market and do not make rational deductions from the firm's incentives, so it does not have to be a signalling model. If consumers react passively and sample the product of any firm from whom they receive an advertisement, it is still true that the high-quality firm advertises more, because the customers it attracts become repeat customers. If consumers do understand the firms' incentives, signalling reinforces the result. Consumers know that firms which advertise must have high quality, so they are willing to try them. This understanding is important, because if consumers knew that 90 percent of firms were low quality but did not understand that only high-quality firms advertise, they would not respond to the advertisements which they received. This should bring to mind section 6.2's game of PhD Admissions.

- If there are just two workers in the population, the model is different depending on whether:

  1 Each is *High* ability with objective probability 0.5, so possibly both are *High* ability; or
  2 One of them is *High* and the other is *Low*, so only the subjective probability is 0.5.

The outcomes are different because in case (2) if one worker credibly signals he is *High* ability, the employer knows the other one must be *Low* ability.

Problems

11.1:   Is lower ability better? (medium)

Change Education I so that the two possible worker abilities are $a \in \{1,4\}$.

(a)   What are the equilibria of this game? What are the payoffs of the workers (and the payoffs averaged across workers) in each equilibrium?
(b)   Apply the Intuitive Criterion (see N6.2). Are the equilibria the same?
(c)   What happens to the equilibrium worker payoffs if the high ability is 5 instead of 4?
(d)   Apply the Intuitive Criterion to the new game. Are the equilibria the same?
(e)   Could it be that a rise in the maximum ability reduces the average worker's payoff? Can it hurt all the workers?

11.2:   Productive education and nonexistence of equilibrium (hard)

Change Education I so that the two equally likely abilities are $a_L = 2$ and $a_H = 5$ and education is productive: the payoff of the employer whose contract is accepted is $\pi_{employer} = a + 2s - w$. The worker's utility function remains $U = w - 8s/a$.

(a)   Under full information, what are the wages for educated and uneducated workers of each type, and who acquires education?
(b)   Show that with incomplete information the equilibrium is unique (except for beliefs and wages out of equilibrium) but unreasonable.

11.3:   Price and quality (medium)

Consumers have prior beliefs that Apex produces low-quality goods with probability 0.4 and high-quality with probability 0.6. A unit of output costs 1 to produce in either case, and it is worth 10 to the consumer if it is high quality and 0 if low quality. The consumer, who is risk-neutral, decides whether to buy in each of two periods, but he does not know the quality until he buys. There is no discounting.

(a)   What is Apex's price and profit if it must choose one price, p^*, for both periods?
(b)   What is Apex's price and profit if it can choose two prices, p_1 and p_2, for the two periods, but it cannot commit ahead to p_2?
(c)   What is the answer to part (b) if the discount rate is $r = 0.1$?

(d)   Returning to $r = 0$, what if Apex can commit to p_2?
(e)   How do the answers to (a) and (b) change if the probability of low quality is 0.95 instead of 0.4? (There is a twist to this question.)

11.4:   Signalling with a continuous signal (hard)

Suppose that with equal probability a worker's ability is $a_L = 1$ or $a_H = 5$, and the worker chooses any amount of education $y \in [0, \infty)$. Let $U_{worker} = w - 8y/a$ and $\pi_{employer} = a - w$.

(a)   There is a continuum of pooling equilibria, with different levels of y^*, the amount of education necessary to obtain the high wage. What education level, y^*, and wage, $w(y)$, are paid in the pooling equilibria, and what is a set of out-of-equilibrium beliefs that supports them? What are the incentive compatibility constraints?
(b)   There is a continuum of separating equilibria, with different levels of y^*. What are the education levels and wages in the separating equilibria? Why are out-of-equilibrium beliefs needed, and what beliefs support the suggested equilibria? What are the self-selection constraints for these equilibria?
(c)   If you were forced to predict one equilibrium to be the one played out, which would it be?

11.5:   Advertising (medium)

Brydox introduces a new shampoo which is actually very good, but is believed by consumers to be good with only a probability of 0.5. A consumer would pay 11 for high quality and 0 for low quality, and the shampoo costs 6 per unit to produce. The firm may spend as much as it likes on stupid TV commercials showing happy people washing their hair, but the potential market consists of 110 cold-blooded economists who are not taken in by psychological tricks. The market can be divided into two periods.

(a)   If advertising is banned, will Brydox go out of business?
(b)   If there are two periods of consumer purchase, and consumers discover the quality of the shampoo if they purchase in the first period, show that Brydox might spend substantial amounts on stupid commercials.
(c)   What is the minimum and maximum that Brydox might spend on advertising, if it spends a positive amount?

11.6:   Game theory books (easy)

In the preface, I explain why I listed competing game theory books by saying, "only an author quite confident that his book compares well with possible substitutes would do such a thing, and you will be even more certain that your decision to buy this book was a good one."

(a)   What is the effect of on the value of the signal if there is a possibility that I am an egotist who overvalues his own book?
(b)   Is there a possible nonstrategic reason why I would list competing game theory books?
(c)   If all readers were convinced by the signal of providing the list and so did not bother to even look at the substitute books, then the list would not be costly even to the author of a bad book, and the signal would fail. How is this paradox to be resolved? Give a verbal explanation.
(d)   Provide a formal model for part (c).

11.7:   Salesman clothing (medium)

Suppose a salesman's ability might be either $x = 1$ (with probability θ) or $x = 4$, and that if he dresses well, his output is greater, so that his total output is $(x + 2s)$ where s equals 1 if he dresses well and 0 if he dresses badly. The utility of the salesman is $U = w - (8s/x)$, where w is his wage. Employers compete for salesmen.

(a)   Under full information, what will the wage be for a salesman with low ability?
(b)   Show the self selection contraints that must be satisfied in a separating equilibrium under incomplete information.
(c)   Find all the equilibria for this game if information is incomplete.

11.8:   Signal jamming in politics (hard)

A congressional committee has already made up its mind that tobacco should be outlawed, but it holds televised hearings anyway in which experts on both sides present testimony. Explain why these hearings might be a form of signalling, where the audience to be persuaded is congress as a whole, which has not yet made up its mind. You can disregard any effect the hearings might have on public opinion.

11.9:   Crazy predators (hard) (adapted from Gintis [2000], problem 12.10)

Apex has a monopoly in the market for widgets, earning profits of m per period, but Brydox has just entered the market. There are two periods and no discounting. Apex can either *Prey* on Brydox with a low price or accept *Duopoly* with a high price, resulting in profits to Apex of $-p_a$ or d_a and to Brydox of $-p_b$ or d_b. Brydox must then decide whether to stay in the market for the second period, when Brydox will make the same choices. If, however, Professor Apex, who owns 60 percent of the company's stock, is crazy, he thinks he will earn an amount $p^* > d_a$ from preying on Brydox (and he does not learn from experience). Brydox initially assesses the probability that Apex is crazy at θ.

(a)   Show that under the following condition, the equilibrium will be separating, that is, Apex will behave differently in the first period depending on whether the Professor is crazy or not:

$$-p_a + m < 2d_a. \tag{11.39}$$

(b)   Show that under the following condition, the equilibrium can be pooling, that is, Apex will behave the same in the first period whether the Professor is crazy or not:

$$\theta \geq \frac{d_b}{p_b + d_b}. \tag{11.40}$$

(c)   If neither two condition (11.39) nor (11.40) apply, the equilibrium is hybrid, that is, Apex will use a mixed strategy and Brydox may or may not be able to tell whether the Professor is crazy at the end of the period. Let α be the probability that a sane Apex preys on Brydox in the first period, and let β be the probability that Brydox stays in the market in the second period after observing that Apex chose *Prey* in the first period. Show that the equilibrium values of α

and β are

$$\alpha = \frac{\theta p_b}{(1 - \theta)d_b}, \tag{11.41}$$

$$\beta = \frac{-p_a + m - 2d_a}{m - d_a}. \tag{11.42}$$

(d)   Is this behavior related to any of the following phenomenon? – Signalling, Signal Jamming, Reputation, Efficiency Wages.

11.11:   Monopoly quality (medium)

A consumer faces a monopoly. He initially believes that the probability that the monopoly has a high-quality product is H, and that a high-quality monopoly would be able to send him an advertisement at zero cost. With probability $(1 - H)$, though, the monopoly has low quality, and it would cost the firm A to send an ad. The firm does send an ad, offering the product at price P. The consumer's utility from a high-quality product is $X > P$, but from a low quality product it is 0. The production cost is C for the monopolist regardless of quality, where $C < P - A$. If the consumer does not buy the product, the seller does not incur the production cost.

You may assume that the high-quality firm always sends an ad, that the consumer will not buy unless he receives an ad, and that P is exogenous.

(a)   Draw the extensive form for this game.
(b)   What is the equilibrium if H is sufficiently high?
(c)   If H is low enough, the equilibrium is in mixed strategies. The high-quality firm always advertises, the low quality firm advertises with probability M, and the consumer buys with probability N. Show using Bayes' Rule how the consumer's posterior belief R that the firm is high-quality changes once he receives an ad.
(d)   Explain why the equilibrium is not in pure strategies if H is too low (but H is still positive).
(e)   Find the equilibrium probability of M. (You don't have to figure out N.)

Signalling Marriageability: A Classroom Game for Chapter 11

Each student is a Man or a Woman with a random and secret wealth level W distributed between 0 and 100. The wealth levels if there are ten people are 0, 10, 20, 30, 50, 60, 80, 90, 100, and 100 (100 appears twice). The instructor will choose from these values, repeating them if there are more than ten students, and omitting some values if the number of students is not divisible by ten.

A person's wealth level is secret, because the society has a taboo on telling your wealth level to someone else. Nonetheless, everybody is very interested in wealth because everyone's objective is to marry someone with high wealth.

Each year, each student first simultaneously writes down how much to spend on clothes that year. Then, in whatever order it happens, students pick someone else to pair up with temporarily. Both actions are publicly revealed – you may show people your scoresheet. In the fifth year, the pairings become permanent: marriage.

Your payoff is a concave function the original wealth minus clothing expenditures of you and your spouse (if you have one). Clothing has no value in itself. Thus, if i is married to j his payoff is, letting C_i and C_j denote the cumulative clothing purchases over the five periods,

$$U_i = log(W_i - C_i + W_j - C_j).$$

Table 11.1 shows some of the possible payoffs from this function.

Table 11.1 Marriage values

Remaining family wealth	0	1	2	5	10	25	50	100	150	200
Utility		$-\infty$	0	0.7	1.6	2.3	3.2	3.9	4.6	5.0	5.3

The first time you play the game, the only communication allowed is "Will you pair with me?" and "Yes" or "No." These pairing are not commitments, and can be changed even within the period.

If there is time, the game will be played over with new wealths and with unlimited communication.

Part 3
applications

Chapter 12
bargaining

12.1   The Basic Bargaining Problem: Splitting a Pie

Part 3 of this book is designed to stretch your muscles by providing more applications of the techniques from parts 1 and 2. The next three chapters may be read in any order. They concern three ways that prices might be determined. Chapter 12 is about bargaining – where both sides exercise market power. Chapter 13 is about auctions – where the seller has market power, but sells a limited amount of a good and wants buyers to compete against each other. Chapter 14 is about fixed-price models with a variety of different features such as differentiated or durable goods. One thing all these chapters have in common is that they use new theory to answer old questions.

Bargaining theory attacks a kind of price determination ill described by standard economic theory. In markets with many participants on one side or the other, standard theory does a good job of explaining prices. In competitive markets we find the intersection of the supply and demand curves, while in markets monopolized on one side we find the monopoly or monopsony output. Where theory is less satisfactory is when there are one or few players on both sides of the market. Early in one's study of economics, one learns that under bilateral monopoly (one buyer and one seller), standard economic theory is inapplicable because the traders must bargain. In the chapters on asymmetric information we would have come across this repeatedly except for our assumption that either the principal or the agent faced competition, which we could model as the other side's ability to make a take-it-or-leave-it offer.

Sections 12.1 and 12.2 introduce the archetypal bargaining problem, Splitting a Pie, ever more complicated versions of which make up the rest of the chapter. Section 12.2, where we take the original rules of the game and apply the Nash bargaining solution, is our one dip into cooperative game theory in this book. Section 12.3 looks at bargaining as a finitely repeated process of offers and counteroffers, and section 12.4 views it as an infinitely repeated process, leading up to the Rubinstein model. Section 12.5 returns to a finite number of repetitions (two, in fact), but with incomplete information. Finally, section 12.6 approaches bargaining from the different angle of the Myerson-Satterthwaite model: how people could try to construct a mechanism for bargaining, a prearranged set of rules that would maximize their expected surplus.

Splitting a Pie

PLAYERS
Smith and Jones.

THE ORDER OF PLAY
The players choose shares θ_s and θ_j of the pie simultaneously.

PAYOFFS
If $\theta_s + \theta_j \leq 1$, each player gets the fraction he chose:

$$\begin{cases} \pi_s = \theta_s, \\ \pi_j = \theta_j. \end{cases} \tag{12.1}$$

If $\theta_s + \theta_j > 1$, then $\pi_s = \pi_j = 0$.

Splitting a Pie resembles the game of Chicken except that it has a continuum of Nash equilibria: any strategy profile (θ_s, θ_j) such that $\theta_s + \theta_j = 1$ is Nash. The Nash concept is at its worst here, because the assumption that the equilibrium being played is common knowledge is very strong when there is a continuum of equilibria. The idea of the focal point (section 1.5) might help to choose a single Nash equilibrium. The strategy space of Chicken is discrete and it has no symmetric pure-strategy equilibrium, but the strategy space of Splitting a Pie is continuous, which permits a symmetric pure-strategy equilibrium to exist. That equilibrium is the even split, (0.5, 0.5), which is a focal point.

If the players moved in sequence, Splitting a Pie becomes what is known as the **Ultimatum Game**, which has a tremendous first-mover advantage. If Jones moves first, the unique Nash outcome would be (0, 1), although only weakly, because Smith would be indifferent as to his action. (This is the same open-set problem that was discussed in section 4.3.) In the unique equilibrium, Smith accepts Jones's offer by choosing $\theta_s = 0$ so that $\theta_s + \theta_j = 1$. Of course, if we add to the model even a small amount of ill will by Smith against Jones for making such a selfish offer, Smith would pick $\theta_s > 0$ and reject the offer. That is quite realistic, so depending on the amount of ill will, the equilibrium would have Jones making a more generous offer that depends on Smith's utility tradeoff between getting a share of the pie on the one hand and seeing Jones suffer on the other.

In many applications, this version of Splitting a Pie is unacceptably simple, because if the two players find their fractions add to more than 1 they have a chance to change their minds. In labor negotiations, for example, if manager Jones makes an offer which union Smith rejects, they do not immediately forfeit the gains from combining capital and labor. They lose a week's production and make new offers. We will model just such a sequence of offers, but before we do that let us see how cooperative game theory deals with the original game.

12.2   The Nash Bargaining Solution

A quite different approach to game theory than we have been using in this book is to describe the players and payoff functions for a game, decide upon some characteristics an equilibrium should have based on notions of fairness or efficiency, mathematicize the characteristics, and maybe add a few other axioms to make the equilibrium turn out neatly. This is a reduced-form approach, attractive if the modeller finds it difficult to come up with a convincing order of play but thinks he can say something about what outcome will appear. Nash (1950a) did this for the bargaining problem in what is the best-known application of cooperative game theory. Nash's objective was to pick axioms that would characterize the agreement the two players would anticipate making with each other. He used a game only a little more complicated than Splitting a Pie. In the Nash model, the two players can have different utilities if they do not come to an agreement, and the utility functions can be nonlinear in terms of shares of the pie. Figures 12.1a and b compare the two games.

In figure 12.1, the shaded region denoted by X is the set of feasible payoffs, which we will assume to be convex. The pair of disagreement payoffs or **threat point** is $\overline{U} = (\overline{U}_s, \overline{U}_j)$. The Nash bargaining solution, $U^* = (U_s^*, U_j^*)$, is a function of $\overline{U}$ and X that satisfies the following four axioms.

1   *Invariance*: For any strictly increasing linear function F,

$$U^*[F(\overline{U}), F(X)] = F[U^*(\overline{U}, X)]. \qquad (12.2)$$

This says that the solution is independent of the units in which utility is measured.

2   *Efficiency*: The solution is Pareto optimal, so the players cannot both be made better off by any change. In mathematical terms,

$$(U_s, U_j) > U^* \Rightarrow (U_s, U_j) \notin X. \qquad (12.3)$$

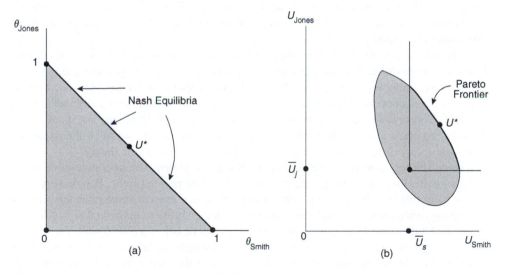

Figure 12.1   (a) Nash Bargaining Game (b) Splitting a Pie.

3   *Independence of irrelevant alternatives*: If we drop some possible utility profiles from X, leaving the smaller set Y, then if U^* was not one of the dropped points, U^* does not change.

$$U^*(\overline{U},X) \in Y \subseteq X \Rightarrow U^*(\overline{U},Y) = U^*(\overline{U},X). \tag{12.4}$$

4   *Anonymity (or symmetry)*: Switching the labels on players Smith and Jones does not affect the solution.

The axiom of Independence of Irrelevant Alternatives is the most debated of the four, but if I were to complain, it would be about the axiomatic approach itself, which depends heavily on the intuition behind the axioms. Everyday intuition says that the outcome should be efficient and symmetric, so that other outcomes can be ruled out a priori. But most of the games in the earlier chapters of this book turn out to have reasonable but inefficient outcomes, and games like Chicken have reasonable asymmetric outcomes.

Whatever their drawbacks, these axioms fully characterize the Nash solution. It can be proven that if U^* satisfies the four axioms above, then it is the unique strategy profile such that

$$U^* = \underset{U \in X, \, U \geq \overline{U}}{argmax} \, (U_s - \overline{U}_s)(U_j - \overline{U}_j). \tag{12.5}$$

Splitting a Pie is a simple enough game that not all the axioms are needed to generate a solution. If we put the game in this context, however, problem (12.5) becomes

$$\underset{\theta_s, \, \theta_j}{Maximize} \, (\theta_s - 0)(\theta_j - 0), \tag{12.6}$$

subject to $\theta_s + \theta_j \leq 1$, which generates the first-order conditions

$$\theta_s - \lambda = 0, \quad \text{and} \quad \theta_j - \lambda = 0, \tag{12.7}$$

where λ is the Lagrange multiplier on the constraint. From (12.6) and the constraint, we obtain $\theta_s = \theta_j = 1/2$, the even split that we found as a focal point of the noncooperative game.

Although Nash's objective was simply to characterize the anticipations of the players, I perceive a heavier note of morality in cooperative than in noncooperative game theory. Cooperative outcomes are neat, fair, beautiful, and efficient. In the next few sections we will look at noncooperative bargaining models that while plausible, lack every one of those features. Cooperative game theory may be useful for ethical decisions, but its attractive features are often inappropriate for economic situations, and the spirit of the axiomatic approach is very different from the utility maximization of economic theory.

It should be kept in mind, however, that the ethical component of cooperative game theory can also be realistic, because people are often ethical, or pretend to be. People very often follow rules that they believe represent virtuous behavior, even at some monetary cost. In bargaining experiments in which one player is given the ability to make a take-it-or-leave it offer (the Ultimatum Game) it is commonly found that he offers a 50–50 split. Presumably this is because either he wishes to be fair or he fears a spiteful response from the other player to a smaller offer. If the subjects are made to feel that they have "earned" the right to be the offering party, they behave much more like the players in noncooperative game theory

(Hoffman & Spitzer [1985]). Frank (1988) and Thaler (1992) describe numerous occasions where simple games fail to describe real-world or experimental results. People's payoffs include more than their monetary rewards, and sometimes knowing the cultural disutility of actions is more important than knowing the dollar rewards. This is one reason why it is helpful to a modeller to keep his games simple: when he actually applies them to the real world, the model must not be so unwieldy that it cannot be combined with details of the particular setting.

12.3 Alternating Offers over Finite Time

In the games of the next two sections, the actions are the same as in Splitting a Pie, but with many periods of offers and counteroffers. This means that strategies are no longer just actions, but rather are rules for choosing actions based on the actions chosen in earlier periods.

Alternating Offers

PLAYERS
Smith and Jones.

THE ORDER OF PLAY

1   Smith makes an offer θ_1.
1*   Jones accepts or rejects.
2   Jones makes an offer θ_2.
2*   Smith accepts or rejects.
. . .
T   Smith offers θ_T.
T*   Jones accepts or rejects.

PAYOFFS
The discount factor is $\delta \leq 1$.
If Smith's offer is accepted by Jones in round m,

$$\pi_s = \delta^m \theta_m,$$
$$\pi_j = \delta^m (1 - \theta_m).$$

If Jones's offer is accepted, reverse the subscripts.
If no offer is ever accepted, both payoffs equal zero.

When a game has many rounds we need to decide whether discounting is appropriate. If the discount rate is r then the discount factor is $\delta = 1/(1+r)$, so, without discounting, $r = 0$ and $\delta = 1$. Whether discounting is appropriate to the situation being modelled depends on whether delay should matter to the payoffs because the bargaining occurs over real time or the game might suddenly end (section 5.2). The game Alternating Offers can be interpreted

Table 12.1   Alternating offers over finite time

Round	Smith's share	Jones's share	Total value	Who offers?
$T-3$	0.819	0.181	0.9^{T-4}	Jones
$T-2$	0.91	0.09	0.9^{T-3}	Smith
$T-1$	0.9	0.1	0.9^{T-2}	Jones
T	1	0	0.9^{T-1}	Smith

in either of two ways, depending on whether it occurs over real time or not. If the players made all the offers and counteroffers between dawn and dusk of a single day, discounting would be inconsequential because, essentially, no time has passed. If each offer consumed a week of time, on the other hand, the delay before the pie was finally consumed would be important to the players and their payoffs should be discounted.

Consider first the game without discounting. There is a unique subgame-perfect outcome – Smith gets the entire pie – which is supported by a number of different equilibria. In each equilibrium, Smith offers $\theta_s = 1$ in each period, but each equilibrium is different in terms of when Jones accepts the offer. All of them are weak equilibria because Jones is indifferent between accepting and rejecting, and they differ only in the timing of Jones's final acceptance.

Smith owes his success to his ability to make the last offer. When Smith claims the entire pie in the last period, Jones gains nothing by refusing to accept. What we have here is not really a first-mover advantage, but a last-mover advantage, a difference not apparent in the one-period model.

In the game with discounting, the total value of the pie is 1 in the first period, δ in the second, and so forth. In period T, if it is reached, Smith would offer 0 to Jones, keeping 1 for himself, and Jones would accept under our assumption on indifferent players. In period $(T-1)$, Jones could offer Smith δ, keeping $(1-\delta)$ for himself, and Smith would accept, although he could receive a greater share by refusing, because that greater share would arrive later and be discounted.

By the same token, in period $(T-2)$, Smith would offer Jones $\delta(1-\delta)$, keeping $(1-\delta(1-\delta))$ for himself, and Jones would accept, since with a positive share Jones also prefers the game to end soon. In period $(T-3)$, Jones would offer Smith $\delta[1-\delta(1-\delta)]$, keeping $(1-\delta[1-\delta(1-\delta)])$ for himself, and Smith would accept, again to prevent delay. Table 12.1 shows the progression of Smith's shares when $\delta = 0.9$.

As we work back from the end, Smith always does a little better when he makes the offer than when Jones does, but if we consider just the class of periods in which Smith makes the offer, Smith's share falls. If we were to continue to work back for a large number of periods, Smith's offer in a period in which he makes the offer would approach $1/(1+\delta)$, which equals about 0.53 if $\delta = 0.9$. The reasoning behind that precise expression is given in the next section. In equilibrium, the very first offer would be accepted, since it is chosen precisely so that the other player can do no better by waiting.

12.4   Alternating Offers over Infinite Time

The Folk Theorem of section 5.2 says that when discounting is low and a game is repeated an infinite number of times, there are many equilibrium outcomes. That does not apply to the bargaining game, however, because it is not a repeated game. It ends when one player accepts an offer, and only the accepted offer is relevant to the payoffs, not the earlier proposals. In particular, there are no out-of-equilibrium punishments such as enforce the Folk Theorem's outcomes.

Let players Smith and Jones have discount factors of δ_s and δ_j which are not necessarily equal but are strictly positive and no greater than one. In the unique subgame-perfect outcome for the infinite-period bargaining game, Smith's share is

$$\theta_s = \frac{1 - \delta_j}{1 - \delta_s \delta_j}, \tag{12.8}$$

which, if $\delta_s = \delta_j = \delta$, is equivalent to

$$\theta_s = \frac{1}{1 + \delta}. \tag{12.9}$$

If the discount rate is high, Smith gets most of the pie: a 1,000 percent discount rate ($r = 10$) makes $\delta = 0.091$ and $\theta_s = 0.92$ (rounded), which makes sense, since under such extreme discounting the second period hardly matters and we are almost back to the simple game of section 12.1. At the other extreme, if r is small, the pie is split almost evenly: if $r = 0.01$, then $\delta \approx 0.99$ and $\theta_s \approx 0.503$.

It is crucial that the discount rate be strictly greater than 0, even if only by a little. Otherwise, the game has the same continuum of perfect equilibria as in section 12.1. Since nothing changes over time, there is no incentive to come to an early agreement. When discount rates are equal, the intuition behind the result is that since a player's cost of delay is proportional to his share of the pie, if Smith were to offer a grossly unequal split, such as (0.7, 0.3), Jones, with less to lose by delay, would reject the offer. Only if the split is close to even would Jones accept, as we will now prove.

Proposition 12.1 (Rubinstein [1982])[1]

In the discounted infinite game, the unique perfect equilibrium outcome is $\theta_s = (1 - \delta_j)/(1 - \delta_s \delta_j)$, where Smith is the first mover.

Proof. We found that in the T-period game Smith gets a larger share in a period in which he makes the offer. Denote by M the maximum nondiscounted share, taken over all the perfect equilibria that might exist, that Smith can obtain in a period in which he makes the offer. Consider the game starting at t. Smith is sure to get no more than M, as noted in table 12.2. (Jones would thus get $(1 - M)$, but that is not relevant to the proof.)

The trick is to find a way besides M to represent the maximum Smith can obtain. Consider the offer made by Jones at $(t - 1)$. Smith will accept any offer which gives him more than the discounted value of M received one period later, so Jones can make an offer

---

[1] The proof of proposition 12.1 is not from the original Rubinstein (1982), but is adapted from Shaked & Sutton (1984). The maximum rather than the supremum can be used because of the assumption that indifferent players always accept offers.

Table 12.2   Alternating offers over infinite time

Round	Smith's share	Jones's share	Who offers?
$t-2$	$1 - \delta_j(1 - \delta_s M)$		Smith
$t-1$		$1 - \delta_s M$	Jones
t	M		Smith

of $\delta_s M$ to Smith, retaining $(1 - \delta_s M)$ for himself. At $(t-2)$, Smith knows that Jones will turn down any offer less than the discounted value of the minimum Jones can look forward to receiving at $(t-1)$. Smith, therefore, cannot offer any less than $\delta_j(1 - \delta_s M)$ at $(t-2)$.

Now we have two expressions for "the maximum which Smith can receive," which we can set equal to each other:

$$M = 1 - \delta_j(1 - \delta_s M).   \tag{12.10}$$

Solving equation (12.10) for M, we obtain

$$M = \frac{1 - \delta_j}{1 - \delta_s \delta_j}.   \tag{12.11}$$

We can repeat the argument using m, the minimum of Smith's share. If Smith can expect at least m at t, Jones cannot receive more than $(1 - \delta_s m)$ at $(t-1)$. At $(t-2)$ Smith knows that if he offers Jones the discounted value of that amount, Jones will accept, so Smith can guarantee himself $(1 - \delta_j(1 - \delta_s m))$, which is the same as the expression we found for M. The smallest perfect equilibrium share that Smith can receive is the same as the largest, so the equilibrium outcome must be unique. QED.

This model from Rubinstein (1982) is widely used because of the way it explains why two players with the same discount rates tend to split the surplus equally (the limiting case in the model as the discount rate goes to zero and δ goes to one). Unfortunately, as with the Nash bargaining solution, there is no obvious best way to extend the model to three or more players – no best way to specify how they make and accept offers. Haller (1986) shows that for at least one specification, the outcome is not similar to the Rubinstein (1982) outcome, but rather is a return to the indeterminacy of the game without discounting.

No Discounting, but a Fixed Bargaining Cost

There are two ways to model bargaining costs per period: as proportional to the remaining value of the pie (the way used above), or as fixed costs each period, which we analyze next (again following Rubinstein [1982]). To understand the difference, think of labor negotiations during a construction project. If a strike slows down completion, there are two kinds of losses. One is the loss from delay in renting or selling the new building, a loss proportional to its value. The other is the loss from late-completion penalties in the contract, which often take the form of a fixed penalty each week. The two kinds of costs have very different effects on the bargaining process.

Here, let us assume that there is no discounting but whenever a period passes, Smith loses c_s and Jones loses c_j. In every subgame-perfect equilibrium, Smith makes an offer and Jones accepts, but there are three possible cases.

Delay costs are equal

$$c_s = c_j = c.$$

The Nash indeterminacy of section 12.1 remains almost as bad; any fraction such that each player gets at least c is supported by some perfect equilibrium.

Delay hurts Jones more

$$c_s < c_j.$$

Smith gets the entire pie. Jones has more to lose than Smith by delaying, and delay does not change the situation except by diminishing the wealth of the players. The game is stationary, because it looks the same to both players no matter how many periods have already elapsed. If in any period t Jones offered Smith x, in period $(t-1)$ Smith could offer Jones $(1-x-c_j)$, keeping $(x+c_j)$ for himself. In period $(t-2)$, Jones would offer Smith $(x+c_j-c_s)$, keeping $(1-x-c_j+c_s)$ for himself, and in periods $(t-4)$ and $(t-6)$ Jones would offer $(1-x-2c_j+2c_s)$ and $(1-x-3c_j+3c_s)$. As we work backwards, Smith's advantage rises to $\gamma(c_j-c_s)$ for an arbitrarily large integer γ. Looking ahead from the start of the game, Jones is willing to give up and accept zero.

Delay hurts Smith more

$$c_s > c_j.$$

Smith gets a share worth c_j and Jones gets $(1-c_j)$. The cost c_j is a lower bound on the share of Smith, the first mover, because if Smith knows Jones will offer $(0, 1)$ in the second period, Smith can offer $(c_j, 1-c_j)$ in the first period and Jones will accept.

12.5 Incomplete Information

Instant agreement has characterized even the multiperiod games of complete information discussed so far. Under incomplete information, knowledge can change over the course of the game and bargaining can last more than one period in equilibrium, a result that might be called inefficient but is certainly realistic. Models with complete information have difficulty explaining such things as strikes or wars, but if over time an uninformed player can learn the type of the informed player by observing what offers are made or rejected, such unfortunate outcomes can arise. The literature on bargaining under incomplete information is vast. For this section, I have chosen to use a model based on the first part of Fudenberg & Tirole (1983), but it is only a particular example of how one could construct such a model, and not a good indicator of what results are to be expected from bargaining.

Let us start with a one-period game. We will denote the price by p_1 because we will carry the notation over to a two-period version.

One-period Bargaining with Incomplete Information

PLAYERS
A seller, and a buyer called Buyer$_{100}$ or Buyer$_{150}$ depending on his type.

THE ORDER OF PLAY
0   Nature picks the buyer's type, his valuation of the object being sold, which is $b = 100$ with probability γ and $b = 150$ with probability $(1 - \gamma)$.
1   The seller offers price p_1.
2   The buyer accepts or rejects p_1.

PAYOFFS
The seller's payoff is p_1 if the buyer accepts the offer, and otherwise 0.
The buyer's payoff is $(b - p_1)$ if he accepts the offer, and otherwise 0.

Equilibrium:
Buyer$_{100}$: accept if $p_1 \leq 100$.
Buyer$_{150}$: accept if $p_1 \leq 150$.
Seller: offer $p_1 = 100$ if $\gamma \geq 1/3$ and $p_1 = 150$ otherwise.

Both types of buyers have a dominant strategy for the last move: accept any offer $p_1 < b$. Accepting any offer $p_1 \leq b$ is a weakly best response to the seller's equilibrium strategy. No equilibrium exists in which a buyer rejects an offer of $p_1 = b$, because we would fall into the open-set problem: there would be no greatest offer in $[0, b)$ that the buyer would accept, and so we could not find a best response for the seller.

The only two strategies that might be optimal for the seller are $p_1 = 100$ or $p_1 = 150$, since prices lower than 100 would lead to a sale with the same probability as $p_1 = 100$, prices in $(100, 150]$ would have the same probability as $p_1 = 150$, and prices greater than 150 would yield zero profits. The seller will choose $p_1 = 150$ if it yields a higher payoff than $p_1 = 100$; that is, if

$$\pi(p_1 = 100) = \gamma(100) + (1 - \gamma)(100) < \pi(p_1 = 150) = \gamma(0) + (1 - \gamma)(150),$$
(12.12)

which requires that

$$\gamma < 1/3. \tag{12.13}$$

Thus, if less than a third of buyers have a valuation of 100, the seller will charge 150, gambling that he is not facing such a buyer.

This means, of course, that if $\gamma < 1/3$, sometimes no sale will be made. This is the most interesting feature of the model. By introducing incomplete information into a bargaining model, we have explained why bargaining sometimes breaks down and efficient trades fail to be carried out. This suggests that when wars occur because nations cannot agree, or strikes occur because unions and employers cannot agree, we should look to information asymmetry for an explanation.

This has some similarity to a mechanism design problem. It is crucial that the seller commit to make only one offer. Once the offer $p_1 = 150$ is made and rejected, the seller realizes that $b = 100$. At that point, he would like to make a second offer, of $p_1 = 100$. But of course if he could do that, then rejection of the first offer would not convey the information that $b = 100$.

Now let us move to a two-period version of the same game. Let us restrict ourselves to the case of $\gamma = 1/6$. We will need to make an assumption on discounting – the loss that results from a delay in agreement. Let us assume that each player loses a fixed amount $D = 4$ if there is no agreement in the first period. (As a result, a player can end up with a negative payoff by playing this game, something experienced bargainers will find realistic.)

Two-period Bargaining with Incomplete Information

PLAYERS
A seller, and a buyer called Buyer$_{100}$ or Buyer$_{150}$ depending on his type.

THE ORDER OF PLAY
0   Nature picks the buyer's type, his valuation of the object being sold, which is $b = 100$ with probability $1/6$ and $b = 150$ with probability $5/6$.
1   The seller offers price p_1.
2   The buyer accepts or rejects p_1.
3   The seller offers price p_2.
4   The buyer accepts or rejects p_2.

PAYOFFS
The seller's payoff is p_1 if the buyer accepts the first offer, $(p_2 - 4)$ if he accepts the second offer, and -4 if he accepts no offer.
The buyer's payoff is $(b - p_1)$ if he accepts the first offer, $(b - p_2 - 4)$ if he accepts the second offer, and -4 if he accepts no offer.

Equilibrium Behavior (separating, in mixed strategies)

Buyer$_{100}$: Accept if $p_1 \leq 104$. Accept if $p_2 \leq 100$.
Buyer$_{150}$: Accept if $p_1 < 154$. Accept with probability $\theta \leq 0.6$ if $p_1 = 154$.
Accept if $p_2 \leq 150$.
Seller: Offer $p_1 = 154$ and $p_2 = 150$.

Buyer$_{100}$'s strategy
If Buyer$_{100}$ deviates and rejects an offer of p_1 less than 104, his payoff will be -4, which is worse than $(100 - p_1)$. Rejecting p_2 does not result in any extra transactions cost, so he rejects any $p_2 < 100$.

Buyer$_{150}$'s strategy

Buyer$_{150}$'s equilibrium payoff is either

$$\pi_{Buyer_{150}}(Accept\ p_1 = 154) = b - 154 = -4, \tag{12.14}$$

or

$$\pi_{Buyer_{150}}(Reject\ p_1 = 154) = -4 + (b - 150) = -4 \tag{12.15}$$

Thus, Buyer$_{150}$ is indifferent and is willing to mix in the first period. Or, out of equilibrium, if $p_1 < 154$ he can achieve a higher payoff by immediately accepting it. In the second period, the game is just like the one-period game, so he will accept any offer of $p_2 \leq 150$.

The seller's strategy

To check on whether the seller has any incentive to deviate, let us work back from the end. If the game has reached the second period, he knows that the fraction of Buyer$_{100}$'s has increased, since there was some probability that a Buyer$_{150}$ would have accepted $p_1 = 150$. The prior probability was $Prob(Buyer_{100}) = 1/6$, but the posterior is

$$
\begin{aligned}
&Prob(Buyer_{100}|Rejected\ p_1 = 154)\\
&= \frac{Prob(Rejected\ p_1 = 154|Buyer_{100})Prob(Buyer_{100})}{Prob(Rejected\ p_1 = 154)}\\
&= \frac{Prob(Rejected|100)Prob(Buyer_{100})}{Prob(Rej|100)Prob(100) + Prob(Rej|150)Prob(150)}\\
&= \frac{(1)(1/6)}{(1)(\theta) + (1 - \theta)(5/6)}\\
&\leq \frac{1}{3} \text{ if } \theta \leq 0.6.
\end{aligned}
\tag{12.16}
$$

In equilibrium the seller expects the $Prob(Buyer_{100})$ proportion in the second period to be no more than 1/3. If he chooses a price $p_2 > 150$ he will sell to nobody in the second period. If he chooses $p_2 \in (100, 150]$ he will sell only to high-valuing buyers. If he chooses $p_2 \leq 100$ he will sell to both types of buyers. This narrows down the possibly optimal prices to $p_2 = 150$ versus $p_2 = 100$. The payoffs from each, as viewed at the start of period 2, are

$$\pi_{Seller}(p_2 = 100) = 100 - 4 \tag{12.17}$$

and

$$\pi_{seller}(p_2 = 150) = Prob(Buyer_{150}/Rejected\ p_1 = 154) * 150 - 4 \tag{12.18}$$

$$= \left[1 - \left(\frac{(1)(1/6)}{(1)(\theta) + (1 - \theta)(5/6)}\right)\right] * 150 - 4. \tag{12.19}$$

If $\theta \leq 0.6$, then $p_2 = 150$ yields the higher payoff.

Thus, neither player has incentive to deviate from the proposed equilibrium.

The most important lesson of this model is that bargaining can lead to inefficiency. Some of the Buyer$_{150}$s delay their transactions until the second period, which is inefficient since the payoffs are discounted. Moreover, there is a positive probability that the Buyer$_{100}$s never buy at all, as in the one-period game, and the potential gains from trade are lost.

Note, too, that this is a model in which prices fall over time as bargaining proceeds. The first-period price is $p_1 = 154$, but the second-period price falls to $p_1 = 150$. This happens because high-valuation buyers know that though the price will fall if they waited, they would incur an extra delay cost. This result has close parallels to the durable-goods monopoly pricing problem that will be discussed in Chapter 14.

In both the one-period and the two-period models, the price the buyer pays depends heavily on the seller's equilibrium beliefs. If the seller thinks that the buyer has a high valuation with probability 0.5, the price is 100, but if he thinks the probability is 0.05, the price rises to 150. This implies that a buyer is unfortunate if he is part of a group which is believed to have high valuations more often. Even if his own valuation is low, what we might call his bargaining power is low when he is part of a high-valuing group. Ayres (1991) found that when he hired testers to pose as customers at car dealerships, their success depended on their race and gender even though they were given identical predetermined bargaining strategies to follow. Since the testers did as badly even when faced with salesmen of their own race and gender, it seems likely that they were hurt by being members of groups that usually can be induced to pay higher prices rather than out of animus to the group itself.

*12.6   Setting Up a Way to Bargain: The Myerson–Satterthwaite Model

Let us now think about a different way to approach bargaining under incomplete information. We will stay with noncooperative game theory, but now let us ask what would happen under different sets of formalized rules – different mechanisms.

We have seen in section 12.5 that under incomplete information, inefficiency can easily arise in bargaining. This inefficiency varies depending on the rules of the game. Thus, if feasible, the players might like to bind themselves in advance to follow whichever rules are best at avoiding inefficiency – at least as long as they can share the efficiency gains.

Suppose a group of players in a game are interacting in some way. They would like to set up some rules for their interaction in advance that would make the best use of the information they will later have, and this set of rules is what we call a mechanism, the topic of chapter 10. Usually, models analyze different mechanisms without asking how the players would agree upon them, taking that as exogenous to the model. This is reasonable – the mechanism may be assigned by history as an institution of the market. If it is not, then there is bargaining over which mechanism to use, an extra layer of complexity.

Let us consider the situation of two people trying to exchange a good under various mechanisms. The mechanism must do two things:

1   Tell under what circumstances the good should be transferred from seller to buyer; and

2   Tell the price at which the good should be transferred, if it is transferred at all.

Usually these two things are made to depend on **reports** of the two players – that is, on statements they make.
The first mechanisms we will look at are simple.

Bilateral Trading I: Complete Information

PLAYERS
A buyer and a seller.

THE ORDER OF PLAY
0   Nature independently chooses the seller to value the good at v_s and the buyer at v_b using the uniform distribution between 0 and 1. Both players observe these values.
1   The seller reports (v_s^s, v_b^s) and the buyer reports (v_s^b, v_b^b) as their observations of (v_b, v_s), simultaneously.
2   If $(v_s^s, v_b^s) = (v_s^b, v_b^b)$ then the seller keeps the good if $(v_s^s > v_b^s)$ and otherwise the buyer acquires it for a payment to the seller of

$$p = v_s^s + \frac{v_b^s - v_s^s}{2}.$$ (12.20)

If $(v_s^s, v_b^s) \neq (v_s^b, v_b^b)$, the good is destroyed and the buyer pays v_b^b to the court.

PAYOFFS
If the seller keeps the good, both players have payoffs of 0. If the buyer acquires the object, the seller's payoff is $(p - v_s)$ and the buyer's is $(v_b - p)$. If the reports disagree, the seller's payoff is $-v_s$ and the buyer's payoff is $-v_b^s$.

I have normalized the payoffs so that each player's payoff is zero if no trade occurs. I could instead have normalized to $\pi_s = v_s$ and to $\pi_b = 0$ if no trade occurred, a common alternative.

This is one of chapter 10's cross checking mechanisms. One equilibrium is for buyer and seller to both tell the truth. That is an equilibrium because if the buyer acquires the object, the payoffs are $\pi_s = (v_b^s - v_s^s)/2$ and $\pi_b = (v_b^s - v_s^s)/2$, both of which are positive if and only if $v_b > v_s$. This will result in the efficient allocation, in the sense that the good ends up with the player who values it most highly. This is, moreover an acceptable mechanism for both players if they expect this equilibrium to be played out, because they share any gains from trade that may exist.[2]

I include Bilateral Trading I to introduce the situation and provide a first-best benchmark, as well as to give another illustration of cross checking. Let us next look at a game of incomplete information and a mechanism which does depend on the players' actions.

Bilateral Trading II: Incomplete Information

PLAYERS
A buyer and a seller.

THE ORDER OF PLAY
0 Nature independently chooses the seller to value the good at v_s and the buyer at v_b using the uniform distribution between 0 and 1. Each player's value is his own private information.
1 The seller reports p_s and the buyer reports p_b.
2 The buyer accepts or rejects the seller's offer. The price at which the trade takes place, if it does, is p_s.

PAYOFFS
If there is no trade, the seller's payoff is 0 and the buyer's is 0.
If there is trade, the seller's payoff is $(p_s - v_s)$ and the buyer's is $(v_b - p_s)$.

This mechanism does not use the buyer's report at all, and so perhaps it is not surprising that the result is inefficient. It is easy to see, working back from the end of the game, that the buyer's equilibrium strategy is to accept the offer if $v_b \geq p_s$ and to reject it otherwise. If the buyer does that, the seller's expected payoff is

$$[p_s - v_s][Prob\{v_b \geq p_s\}] + 0[Prob\{v_b \leq p_s\}] = [p_s - v_s][1 - p_s]. \qquad (12.21)$$

Differentiating this with respect to p_s and setting equal to zero yields the seller's equilibrium strategy of

$$p_s = \frac{1 + v_s}{2}. \qquad (12.22)$$

This is inefficient because if v_b is just a little bigger than v_s, trade will not occur even though gains from trade do exist that is, even though $v_b > v_s$. In fact, trade will fail to occur whenever $v_b < (1 + v_s)/2$.

Let us try another simple mechanism, which at least uses the reports of both players, replacing move (2) with (2′).

---

[2] As usual, the efficient equilibrium is not unique. Another equilibrium would be for both players to always report $v_s = 0.5, v_b = 0.4$, which would yield zero payoffs and never result in trade. If either player unilaterally deviated, the punishment would kick in and payoffs would become negative.

(2′) The good is allocated to the seller if $p_s > p_b$ and to the buyer otherwise. The price at which the trade takes place, if it does, is p_s.

Suppose the buyer truthfully reports $p_b = v_b$. What will the seller's best response be? The seller's expected payoff for the p_s he chooses is now

$$[p_s - v_s][Prob\{p_b(v_b) \geq p_s\}] + 0[Prob\{p_b(v_b) \leq p_s\}] = [p_s - v_s][1 - p_s]. \qquad (12.23)$$

where the expectation has to be taken over all the possible values of v_b, since p_b will vary with v_b.

Maximizing this, the seller's strategy will solve the first-order condition $1 - 2p_s + v_s = 0$, and so will again be

$$p_s(v_s) = \frac{1 + v_s}{2} = \frac{1}{2} + \frac{v_s}{2}. \qquad (12.24)$$

Will the buyer's best response to this strategy be $p_b = v_b$? Yes, because whenever $v_b \geq 1/2 + v_s/2$ the buyer is willing for trade to occur, and the size of p_b does not affect the transactions price, only the occurrence or nonoccurrence of trade. The buyer needs to worry about causing trade to occur when $v_b < 1/2 + v_s/2$, but this can be avoided by using the truthtelling strategy. The buyer also needs to worry about preventing trade from occurring when $v_b > 1/2 + v_s/2$, but choosing $p_b = v_b$ prevents this from happening either.

Thus, it seems that either mechanism (2) or (2′) will fail to be efficient. Often, the seller will value the good less than the buyer, but trade will fail to occur and the seller will end up with the good anyway – whenever $v_b > (1 + v_s)/2$. Figure 12.2 shows when trades will be completed based on the parameter values.

As you might imagine, one reason this is an inefficient mechanism is that it fails to make effective use of the buyer's information. The next mechanism will do better. Its trading rule is called the **double auction mechanism**. The problem is like that of chapter 10's Groves Mechanism, because we are trying to come up with an action rule (allocate the object to the buyer or to the seller) based on the agents' reports (the prices they suggest), under the condition that each player has private information (his value).

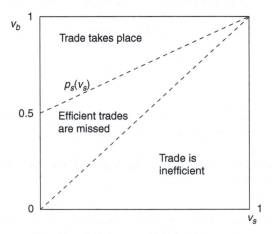

Figure 12.2   Trades in Bilateral Trading II.

Bilateral Trading III: The Double Auction Mechanism

PLAYERS
A buyer and a seller.

THE ORDER OF PLAY
0   Nature independently chooses the seller to value the good at v_s and the buyer at v_b using the uniform distribution between 0 and 1. Each player's value is his own private information.
1   The buyer and the seller simultaneously decide whether to try to trade or not.
2   If both agree to try, the seller reports p_s and the buyer reports p_b simultaneously.
3   The good is allocated to the seller if $p_s \geq p_b$ and to the buyer otherwise. The price at which the trade takes place, if it does, is $p = (p_b + p_s)/2$.

PAYOFFS
If there is no trade, the seller's payoff is 0 and the buyer's is zero. If there is trade, then the seller's payoff is $(p - v_s)$ and the buyer's is $(v_b - p)$.
The buyer's expected payoff for the p_b he chooses is

$$\left[v_b - \frac{p_b + E[p_s | p_b \geq p_s]}{2} \right] [Prob\{p_b \geq p_s\}], \tag{12.25}$$

where the expectation has to be taken over all the possible values of v_s, since p_s will vary with v_s.
The seller's expected payoff for the p_s he chooses is

$$\left[\frac{p_s + E(p_b | p_b \geq p_s)}{2} - v_s \right] [Prob\{p_b \geq p_s\}], \tag{12.26}$$

where the expectation has to be taken over all the possible values of v_b, since p_b will vary with v_b.

The game has lots of Nash equilibria. Let's focus on two of them, a **one-price equilibrium** and the unique **linear equilibrium**.

In the **one-price equilibrium**, the buyer's strategy is to offer $p_b = x$ if $v_b \geq x$ and $p_b = 0$ otherwise, for some value $x \in [0, 1]$. The seller's strategy is to ask $p_s = x$ if $v_s \leq x$ and $p_s = 1$ otherwise. Figure 12.3 illustrates the one-price equilibrium for a particular value of x. Efficient trade occurs in the shaded region, but is missed in regions A and B. Suppose $x = 0.7$. If the seller were to deviate and ask prices lower than 0.7, he would just reduce the price he receives. If the seller were to deviate and ask prices higher than 0.7, then $p_s > p_b$ and no trade occurs. So the seller will not deviate. Similar reasoning applies to the buyer, and to any value of x, including 0 and 1 (where trade never occurs).

The **linear equilibrium** can be derived very neatly. Suppose the seller uses a linear strategy, so $p_s(v_s) = \alpha_s + c_s v_s$. From the buyer's point of view, p_s will be uniformly distributed from $\alpha_s = 1/4$ to $(\alpha_s + c_s) = 1/12$ with density $1/c_s$, as v_s ranges from 0 to 1. Since $E_b[p_s | p_b \geq p_s] = E_b(p_s | p_s \in [a_s, p_b]) = (a_s + p_b)/2$, the buyer's expected payoff

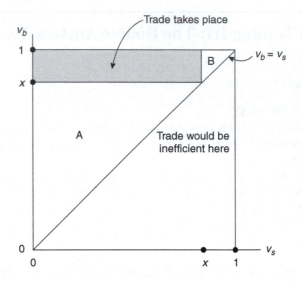

Figure 12.3 Trade in the one-price equilibrium.

(12.25) becomes

$$\left[v_b - \frac{p_b + \frac{\alpha_s + p_b}{2}}{2} \right] \left[\frac{p_b - \alpha_s}{c_s} \right]. \tag{12.27}$$

Maximizing with respect to p_b yields

$$p_b = \left(\frac{2}{3}\right) v_b + \left(\frac{1}{3}\right) \alpha_s. \tag{12.28}$$

Thus, if the seller uses a linear strategy, the buyer's best response is a linear strategy too! We are well on our way to a Nash equilibrium.

If the buyer uses a linear strategy $p_b(v_b) = \alpha_b + c_b v_b$, then from the seller's point of view p_b is uniformly distributed from α_b to $\alpha_b + c_b$ with density $1/c_b$ and the seller's payoff function, expression (12.26), becomes, since $E_s(p_b|p_b \geq p_s) = E_s(p_b|p_b \in [p_s, \alpha_b + c_b] = (p_s + \alpha_b + c_b)/2$,

$$\left[\frac{p_s + \frac{p_s + \alpha_b + c_b}{2}}{2} - v_s \right] \left[\frac{\alpha_b + c_b - p_s}{c_b} \right]. \tag{12.29}$$

Maximizing with respect to p_s yields

$$p_s = \left(\frac{2}{3}\right) v_s + \frac{1}{3}(\alpha_b + c_b). \tag{12.30}$$

Solving equations (12.28) and (12.30) together yields

$$p_b = \left(\frac{2}{3}\right) v_b + \frac{1}{12} \tag{12.31}$$

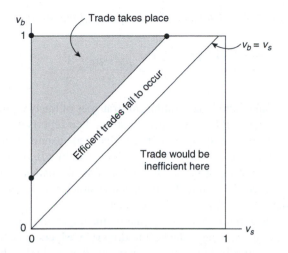

Figure 12.4   Trade in the linear equilibrium.

and

$$p_s = \left(\frac{2}{3}\right) v_s + \frac{1}{4}. \qquad (12.32)$$

So we have derived a linear equilibrium. Manipulation of the equilibrium strategies shows that trade occurs if and only if $v_b \geq v_s + (1/4)$, which is to say, trade occurs if the valuations differ enough. The linear equilibrium does not make all efficient trades, because sometimes $v_b > v_s$ and no trade occurs, but it does make all trades with joint surpluses of 1/4 or more. Figure 12.4 illustrates this.

One detail about equation (12.31) should bother you. The equation seems to say that if $v_b = 0$, the buyer chooses $p_b = 1/12$. If that happens, though, the buyer is bidding more than his value! The reason this can be part of the equilibrium is that it is only a weak Nash equilibrium. Since the seller never chooses lower than $p_s = 1/4$, the buyer is safe in choosing $p_b = 1/12$; trade never occurs anyway when he makes that choice. He could just as well bid 0 instead of 1/12, but then he wouldn't have a linear strategy.

The linear equilibrium is not a truth-telling equilibrium. The seller does not report his true value v_s, but rather reports $p_s = (2/3)v_s + 1/4$. But we could replicate the outcome in a truth-telling equilibrium. We could have the buyer and seller agree that they would make reports r_b and r_s to a neutral mediator, who would then choose the trading price p. He would agree in advance to choose the trading price p by (1) mapping r_s onto p_s just as in the equilibrium above, (2) mapping r_b onto p_b just as in the equilibrium above, and (3) using p_b and p_s to set the price just as in the double auction mechanism. Under this mechanism, both players would tell the truth to the mediator. Let us compare the original linear mechanism with a truth-telling mechanism.

The Chatterjee–Samuelson mechanism: *The good is allocated to the seller if $p_s \geq p_b$ and to the buyer otherwise. The price at which the trade takes place, if it does, is $p = (p_b + p_s)/2$.*

A direct incentive-compatible mechanism: *The good is allocated to the seller if $(2/3)p_s + 1/4 \geq (2/3)p_b + 1/12$, which is to say, if $p_s \geq p_b - 1/4$, and to the buyer* *otherwise. The price at which the trade takes place, if it does, is*

$$p = \frac{\left(\left(\frac{2}{3}\right)p_b + \frac{1}{12}\right) + \left(\left(\frac{2}{3}\right)p_s + \frac{1}{4}\right)}{2} = \frac{p_b + p_s}{3} + \frac{1}{6}. \tag{12.33}$$

What I have done is substituted the equilibrium strategies of the two players into the mechanism itself, so now they will have no incentive to set their reports different from the truth. The mechanism itself looks odd, because it says that trade cannot occur unless v_b is more than 1/4 greater than v_s, but we cannot use the rule of trading if $v_b > v_s$ because then the players would start misreporting again. The truth-telling mechanism only works because it does not penalize players for telling the truth, and in order not to penalize them, it cannot make full use of the information to achieve efficiency.

In this game we have imposed a trading rule on the buyer and seller, rather than letting them decide for themselves what is the best trading rule. Myerson & Satterthwaite (1983) prove that of all the equilibria and all the mechanisms that are budget balancing, the linear equilibrium of the double auction mechanism yields the highest expected payoff to the players, the expectation being taken ex ante, before Nature has chosen the types. The mechanism is not optimal when viewed after the players have been assigned their types, and a player might not be happy with the mechanism once he knew his type. He will, however, at least be willing to participate.

What mechanism would players choose, ex ante, if they knew they would be in this game? If they had to choose after they were informed of their type, then their proposals for mechanisms could reveal information about their types, and we would have a model of bargaining under incomplete information that would resemble signalling models. But what if they chose a mechanism before they were informed of their type, and did not have the option to refuse to trade if after learning their type they did not want to use the mechanism?

In general, mechanisms have the following parts.

1 Each agent i simultaneously makes a report p_i.
2 A rule $x(p)$ determines the action (such as who gets the good, whether a bridge is built, etc.) based on the p.
3 Each agent i receives an incentive transfer a_i that in some way depends on his own report.
4 Each agent receives a budget-balancing transfer b_i that does not depend on his own report.

We will denote the agent's total transfer by t_i, so $t_i = a_i + b_i$.

In Bilateral Trading III, the mechanism had the following parts.

1 Each agent i simultaneously made a report p_i.
2 If $p_s \geq p_b$, the good was allocated to the seller, but otherwise to the buyer.
3 If there was no trade, then $a_s = a_b = 0$. If there was trade, then $a_s = (p_b + p_s)/2$ and $a_b = -((p_b + p_s)/2)$.
4 No further transfer b_i was needed, because the incentive transfers balanced the budget by themselves.

It turns out that if the players in Bilateral Trading can settle their mechanism and agree to try to trade in advance of learning their types, an efficient budget-balancing mechanism exists that can be implemented as a Nash equilibrium. The catch will be that after discovering his type, a player will sometimes regret having entered into this mechanism.

This would actually be part of a subgame perfect Nash equilibrium of the game as a whole. The mechanism design literature tends not to look at the entire game, and asks "Is there a mechanism which is efficient when played out as the rules of a game?" rather than "Would the players choose a mechanism that is efficient?"

Bilateral Trading IV: The Expected Externality Mechanism

PLAYERS

A buyer and a seller.

THE ORDER OF PLAY

−1   Buyer and seller agree on a mechanism $(x(p), t(p))$ that makes decisions x based on reports p and pays t to the agents, where p and t are 2-vectors and x allocates the good either to the buyer or the seller.

0   Nature independently chooses the seller to value the good at v_s and the buyer at v_b using the uniform distribution between 0 and 1. Each player's value is his own private information.

1   The seller reports p_s and the buyer reports p_b simultaneously.

2   The mechanism uses $x(p)$ to decide who gets the good, and $t(p)$ to make payments.

PAYOFFS

Player i's payoff is $(v_i + t_i)$ if he is allocated the good, t_i otherwise.

Part (-1) of the order of play is vague on how the two parties agree on a mechanism. The mechanism design literature is also vague, and focuses on efficiency rather than payoff-maximization. To be more rigorous, we should have one player propose the mechanism and the other accept or reject. The proposing player would add an extra transfer to the mechanism to reduce the other player's expected payoff to his reservation utility.

Let me use the term **action surplus** to denote the utility an agent gets from the choice of action.

The **expected externality mechanism** has the following objectives for each of the parts of the mechanism.

1   Induce the agents to make truthful reports.
2   Choose the efficient action.
3   Choose the incentive transfers to make the agents choose truthful reports in equilibrium.
4   Choose the budget-balancing transfers so that the incentive transfers add up to zero.

First I will show you a mechanism that does this. Then I will show you how I came up with that mechanism. Consider the following three-part mechanism:

1   The seller announces p_s. The buyer announces p_b. The good is allocated to the seller if $p_s \geq p_b$, and to the buyer otherwise.
2   The seller gets transfer $t_s = (1 - p_s^2)/2 - (1 - p_b^2)/2$.
3   The buyer gets transfer $t_b = (1 - p_b^2)/2 - (1 - p_s^2)/2$.

This is budget-balancing:

$$\frac{(1 - p_s^2)}{2} - \frac{(1 - p_b^2)}{2} + \frac{(1 - p_b^2)}{2} - \frac{(1 - p_s^2)}{2} = 0. \tag{12.34}$$

The seller's expected payoff as a function of his report p_s is the sum of his expected action surplus and his expected transfer. We have already computed his transfer, which is not conditional on the action taken.

The seller's action surplus is 0 if the good is allocated to the buyer, which happens if $v_b > p_s$, where we use v_b instead of p_b because in equilibrium $p_b = v_b$. This has probability $(1 - p_s)$. The seller's action surplus is v_s if the good is allocated to the seller, which has probability p_s. Thus, the expected action surplus is $p_s v_s$.

The seller's expected payoff is therefore

$$p_s v_s + \frac{(1 - p_s^2)}{2} - \frac{(1 - p_b^2)}{2}. \tag{12.35}$$

Maximizing with respect to his report, p_s, the condition is

$$v_s - p_s = 0, \tag{12.36}$$

so the mechanism is incentive compatible – the seller tells the truth.

The buyer's expected action surplus is v_b if his report is higher, for example, if $p_b > v_s$, and zero otherwise, so his expected payoff is

$$p_b v_b + \frac{(1 - p_b^2)}{2} - \frac{(1 - p_s^2)}{2}. \tag{12.37}$$

Maximizing with respect to his report, p_s, the first-order condition is

$$v_b - p_b = 0, \tag{12.38}$$

so the mechanism is incentive compatible – the buyer tells the truth.

Now let us see how to come up with the transfers. The expected externality mechanism relies on two ideas.

The first idea is that to get the incentives right, each agent's incentive transfer is made equal to the sum of the expected action surpluses of the other agents, where the expectation is calculated conditionally on (1) the other agents reporting truthfully, and (2) our agent's report. This makes the agent internalize the effect of his externalities on the other agents. His expected payoff comes to equal the expected social surplus. Here, this means, for example, that the seller's incentive transfer will equal the buyer's expected action surplus. Thus, denoting the uniform distribution by F,

$$a_s = \int_0^{p_s} (0)\, dF(v_b) + \int_{p_s}^1 v_b\, dF(v_b),$$

$$= 0 + \left.\frac{v_b^2}{2}\right|_{p_s}^1,$$

$$= \frac{1}{2} - \frac{p_s^2}{2}. \tag{12.39}$$

The first integral is the expected buyer action surplus if no transfer is made because the buyer's value v_b is less than the seller's report p_s, so the seller keeps the good and the buyer's action surplus is zero. The second integral is the surplus if the buyer gets the good, which occurs whenever the buyer's value, v_b (and hence his report p_b), is greater than the seller's report, p_s.

We can do the same thing for the buyer's incentive, finding the seller's expected surplus.

$$a_b = \int_0^{p_b} 0\, dF(v_s) + \int_{p_b}^1 v_s\, dF(v_s),$$

$$= 0 + \left.\frac{v_s^2}{2}\right|_{p_b}^1,$$

$$= \frac{1}{2} - \frac{p_b^2}{2}. \tag{12.40}$$

If the seller's value v_s is low, then it is likely that the buyer's report of p_b is higher than v_s, and the seller's action surplus is zero because the trade will take place. If the seller's value v_s is high, then the seller will probably have a positive action surplus.

The second idea is that to get budget balancing, each agent's budget-balancing transfer is chosen to help pay for the other agents' incentive transfers. Here, we just have two agents, so the seller's budget-balancing transfer has to pay for the buyer's incentive transfer. That is very simple: just set the seller's budget-balancing transfer b_s equal to the buyer's incentive transfer a_b (and likewise set b_b equal to a_s).

The intuition and mechanism can be extended to N agents. There are now N reports $p_1, \ldots, p_N$. Let the action chosen be $x(p)$, where p is the N-vector of reports, and the action surplus of agent i is $W_i(x(p), v_i)$. To make each agent's incentive transfer equal to the sum of the expected action surpluses of the other agents, choose it so

$$a_i = E(\Sigma_{j\neq i} W_j(x(p), v_j)). \tag{12.41}$$

The budget balancing transfers can be chosen so that each agent's incentive transfer is paid for by dividing the cost equally among the other $(N-1)$ agents:

$$b_i = \left(\frac{1}{N-1}\right)(\Sigma_{j\neq i} E(\Sigma_{k\neq j} W_k(x(p), v_k))). \tag{12.42}$$

There are other ways to divide the costs that will still allow the mechanism to be incentive compatible, but equal division is the simplest.

The expected externality mechanism does have one problem: the participation constraint. If the seller knows that $v_s = 1$, he will not want to enter into this mechanism. His expected transfer would be $t_s = 0 - (1 - 0.5)^2/2 = -0.125$. Thus, his payoff from the mechanism is $1 - 0.125 = 0.875$, whereas he could get a payoff of 1 if he refused to participate. We say that this mechanism fails to be **interim incentive compatible**, because at the point when the agents discover their own types, but not those of the other agents, the agents might not want to participate in the mechanism or choose the actions we desire.

Ordinarily economists think of bargaining as being less structured than in the Bilateral Trading games, but it should be kept in mind that there are two styles of bargaining: bargaining with loose rules that are "made up as you go along," and bargaining with pre-determined rules to which the players can somehow commit. This second kind of bargaining is more common in markets where many bargains are going to be made and in situations where enough is at stake that the players first negotiate the rules under which the main bargaining will occur. Once bargaining becomes mechanism design, it becomes closer to the idea of simply holding an auction. Bulow & Klemperer (1996) compare the two means of selling an item, observing that a key feature of auctions is involving more traders, an important advantage.

Notes

N12.2   The Nash bargaining solution

- See Binmore, Rubinstein, & Wolinsky (1986) for a comparison of the cooperative and noncooperative approaches to bargaining. For overviews of cooperative game theory see Luce & Raiffa (1957) and Shubik (1982).
- While the Nash bargaining solution can be generalized to n players (see Harsanyi [1977], p. 196), the possibility of interaction between coalitions of players introduces new complexities. Solutions such as the Shapley value (Shapley [1953b]) try to account for these complexities.

   The **Shapley value** satisfies the properties of invariance, anonymity, efficiency, and linearity in the variables from which it is calculated. Let S_i denote a **coalition** containing player i; that is, a group of players including i that makes a sharing agreement. Let $v(S_i)$ denote the sum of the utilities of the players in coalition S_i, and $v(S_i - \{i\})$ denote the sum of the utilities in the coalition created by removing i from S_i. Finally, let $c(s)$ be the number of coalitions of size s containing player i. The Shapley value for player i is then

$$\phi_i = \frac{1}{n} \sum_{s=1}^{n} \frac{1}{c(s)} \sum_{S_i} [v(S_i) - v(S_i - \{i\})]. \tag{12.43}$$

where the S_i are of size s. The motivation for the Shapley value is that player i receives the average of his marginal contributions to different coalitions that might form. Gul (1989) has provided a noncooperative interpretation.

N12.5   Incomplete information

- Bargaining under asymmetric information has inspired a large literature. In early articles, Fudenberg & Tirole (1983) uses a two-period model with two types of buyers and two types of sellers. Sobel & Takahashi (1983) builds a model with either T or infinite periods, a continuum of types of buyers, and one type of seller. Cramton (1984) uses an infinite number of periods, a continuum of types of buyers, and a continuum of types of sellers. Rubinstein (1985a) uses an infinite number of periods, two types of buyers, and one type of seller, but the types of buyers differ not in their valuations, but in their discount rates. Samuelson (1984) looks at the case where one bargainer knows the size of the pie better than the other bargainer. Perry (1986) uses a model with fixed bargaining costs and asymmetric information in which each bargainer makes an offer in turn, rather than one offering and the other accepting or rejecting. For overviews, see the surveys of Sutton (1986) and Kennan & Wilson (1993).
- The asymmetric information model in section 12.5 has **one-sided** asymmetry in the information: only the buyer's type is private information. Fudenberg & Tirole (1983) and others have also built models with **two-sided** asymmetry, in which buyers' and sellers' types are both private information. In such models a multiplicity of perfect Bayesian equilibria can be supported for a given set of parameter values. Out-of-equilibrium beliefs become quite important, and provided much of the motivation for the exotic refinements mentioned in section 6.2.

N12.6   Setting up a way to bargain: the Myerson–Satterthwaite Model

- The Bilateral Trading model originated in Chatterjee & Samuelson (1983, p. 842), who also analyze the more general mechanism with $p = \theta p_s + (1 - \theta)p_b$. I have adapted this description from Gibbons (1992, p. 158).
- Discussions of the general case can be found in Fudenberg & Tirole (1991a, p. 273), and Mas-Colell, Whinston & Green (1994, p. 885). I have taken the term "expected externality mechanism" from MWG. Fudenberg and Tirole use "AGV mechanism" or "AGV-Arrow mechanism" for the same thing, because the idea was first published in and D'Aspremont & Gerard-Varet (1979) and Arrow (1979). It is also possible to add extra costs that depend on the action chosen (for example, a transactions tax if the good is sold from buyer to seller). See Fudenberg & Tirole (1991a, p. 274). Myerson (1991) is also worth looking into.

Problems

12.1:   A fixed cost of bargaining and grudges (medium)

Smith and Jones are trying to split 100 dollars. In bargaining round 1, Smith makes an offer at cost 0, proposing to keep S_1 for himself and Jones either accepts (ending the game) or rejects. In round 2, Jones makes an offer at cost 10 of S_2 for Smith and Smith either accepts or rejects. In round 3, Smith makes an offer of S_3 at cost c, and Jones either accepts or rejects. If no offer is ever accepted, the 100 dollars goes to a third player, Dobbs.

(a)   If $c = 0$, what is the equilibrium outcome?

(b)   If $c = 80$, what is the equilibrium outcome?

(c)   If $c = 10$, what is the equilibrium outcome?

(d)   What happens if $c = 0$, but Jones is very emotional and would spit in Smith's face and throw the 100 dollars to Dobbs if Smith proposes $S = 100$? Assume that Smith knows Jones's personality perfectly.

382   Applications

12.2:   Selling cars (medium)

A car dealer must pay $10,000 to the manufacturer for each car he adds to his inventory. He faces three buyers. From the point of view of the dealer, Smith's valuation is uniformly distributed between $12,000 and $21,000, Jones's is between $9,000 and $12,000, and Brown's is between $4,000 and $12,000. The dealer's policy is to make a single take-it-or-leave-it offer to each customer, and he knows these three buyers will not be able to resell to each other. Use the notation that the maximum valuation is $\overline{V}$ and the range of valuations is R.

(a)   What will the offers be?
(b)   Who is most likely to buy a car? How does this compare with the outcome with perfect price discrimination under full information? How does it compare with the outcome when the dealer charges $10,000 to each customer?
(c)   What happens to the equilibrium prices if, with probability 0.25, each buyer has a valuation of $0, but the probability distribution remains otherwise the same?

12.3:   The Nash bargaining solution (medium)

Smith and Jones, shipwrecked on a desert island, are trying to split 100 pounds of cornmeal and 100 pints of molasses, their only supplies. Smith's utility function is $U_s = C + 0.5M$ and Jones's is $U_j = 3.5C + 3.5M$. If they cannot agree, they fight to the death, with $U = 0$ for the loser. Jones wins with probability 0.8.

(a)   What is the threat point?
(b)   With a 50–50 split of the supplies, what are the utilities if the two players do not recontract? Is this efficient?
(c)   Draw the threat point and the Pareto frontier in utility space (put U_s on the horizontal axis).
(d)   According to the Nash bargaining solution, what are the utilities? How are the goods split?
(e)   Suppose Smith discovers a cookbook full of recipes for a variety of molasses candies and corn muffins, and his utility function becomes $U_s = 10C + 5M$. Show that the split of goods in part (d) remains the same despite his improved utility function.

12.4:   Price discrimination and bargaining (easy)

A seller with marginal cost constant at c faces a continuum of consumers represented by the linear demand curve $Q^d = a - bP$, where $a > c$. Demand is at a rate of one or zero units per consumer, so if all consumers between points 1 and 2.5 on the consumer continuum make purchases at a price of 13, we say that a total of 1.5 units are sold at a price of 13 each.

(a)   What is the seller's profit if he chooses one take-it-or-leave- it price?
(b)   What is the seller's profit if he chooses a continuum of take-it-or-leave-it prices at which to sell, one price for each consumer? (You should think here of a pricing function, since each consumer is infinitesimal.)
(c)   What is the seller's profit if he bargains separately with each consumer, resulting in a continuum of prices? You may assume that bargaining costs are zero and that buyer and seller have equal bargaining power.

12.5:   A fixed cost of bargaining and incomplete information (medium)

Up to part (c), this problem is identical with problem 12.1. Smith and Jones are trying to split 100 dollars. In bargaining round 1, Smith makes an offer at cost 0, proposing to keep S_1 for himself and Jones either accepts (ending the game) or rejects. In round 2, Jones makes an offer at cost 10 of S_2 for Smith and Smith either accepts or rejects. In round 3, Smith makes an offer of S_3 at cost c, and Jones either accepts or rejects. If no offer is ever accepted, the 100 dollars goes to a third player, Dobbs.

(a)   If $c = 0$, what is the equilibrium outcome?
(b)   If $c = 80$, what is the equilibrium outcome?
(c)   If Jones's priors are that $c = 0$ and $c = 80$ are equally likely, but only Smith knows the true value, what are the players' equilibrium strategies in rounds 2 and 3? (i.e., what are S_2 and S_3, and what acceptance rules will each player use?)
(d)   If Jones's priors are that $c = 0$ and $c = 80$ are equally likely, but only Smith knows the true value, what are the equilibrium strategies for round 1? (Hint: the equilibrium uses mixed strategies.)

12.6:   A fixed bargaining cost, again (easy)

Apex and Brydox are entering into a joint venture that will yield 500 million dollars, but they must negotiate the split first. In bargaining round 1, Apex makes an offer at cost 0, proposing to keep A_1 for itself. Brydox either accepts (ending the game) or rejects. In round 2, Brydox incurs a cost of 10 million to make an offer that gives A_2 to Apex, and Apex either accepts or rejects. In round 3, Apex incurs a cost of c to make an offer that gives itself A_3, and Brydox either accepts or rejects. If no offer is ever accepted, the joint venture is cancelled.

(a)   If $c = 0$, what is the equilibrium? What is the equilibrium outcome?
(b)   If $c = 10$, what is the equilibrium? What is the equilibrium outcome?
(c)   If $c = 300$, what is the equilibrium? What is the equilibrium outcome?

12.7:   Myerson–Satterthwaite (medium)

The owner of a tract of land values his land at v_s and a potential buyer values it at v_b. The buyer and seller do not know each other's valuations, but guess that they are uniformly distributed between 0 and 1. The seller and buyer suggest p_s and p_b simultaneously, and they have agreed that the land will be sold to the buyer at price $p = (p_b + p_s)/2$ if $p_s \leq p_b$.

The actual valuations are $v_s = 0.2$ and $v_b = 0.8$. What is one equilibrium outcome given these valuations and this bargaining procedure? Explain why this can happen.

12.8:   Negotiation (Rasmusen [2002]) (hard)

Two parties, the Offeror and the Acceptor, are trying to agree to the clauses in a contract. They have already agreed to a basic contract, splitting a surplus 50–50, for a surplus of Z for each player. The offeror can at cost C offer an additional clause which the acceptor can accept outright, inspect carefully (at cost M), or reject outright. The additional clause is either "genuine," yielding the Offeror X_g and the Acceptor Y_g if accepted, or "misleading," yielding the Offeror X_m (where $X_m > X_g > 0$) and the Acceptor $-Y_m < 0$.

What will happen in equilibrium?

Labor Bargaining: A Classroom Game for Chapter 12[3]

Currently, an employer is paying members of a labor union $46,000 per year, but the union has told its members it thinks $68,000 would be a fairer amount. Every $1,000 increase in salary costs the employer $30 million per year, and benefits the workers in aggregate by $25 million (the missing $5 million going to taxes, which are heavier for the workers).

If the workers go on strike, it will cost the players $25 million per week in foregone earnings, and it will cost the employer $60 million in lost profits. Interest rates are low enough that they can be ignored in this game.

The rules for bargaining are as follows. The union makes the first offer, on May 1 (time 0), and the employer accepts or rejects. If the employer accepts the offer, there is no strike. If the employer rejects it, there is a strike for the next week, but the employer then can make a counteroffer on May 8 (time 1). If it is accepted by the union, the strike has lasted one week. If it is rejected, the union has one week in which to put together its counteroffer for May 15 (time 2).

The workers' morale and bank accounts will run out after 7 weeks of a strike, at time 7. If no other agreement has been reached, the union must then accept an offer as low as $46,000. It will not accept an offer any lower, because the workers angrily refuse to ratify a lower offer.

Students will be put into groups of three that represent either the employer or the union. Employer groups and union groups will then pair up to simultaneously play the game. A group's objective is to maximize its payoff. The instructor will set up place on the blackboard for each group to record its weekly offers. If a group cannot agree on what offer to make and does not write it up on the board in time, then it forfeits its chance to make an offer that week. Each offer must be in thousands of dollars of annual salary – no offers of $52,932 are allowed.

---

[3] This game is adapted from a classroom game of Vijay Krishna.

Chapter 13
auctions

13.1 Values Private and Common, Continuous and Discrete

Bargaining and auctions are two extremes in the many ways to sell goods, as Bulow & Klemperer (1996) explain. In typical bargaining, one buyer faces one seller and they make offers and counteroffers free from the formal rules we impose in theoretical modelling (though as in Bulow & Klemperer, it is worth considering what happens if the bargaining does have rules to which the players commit). In typical auctions, many bidders face one seller and make offers according to formal rules as rigid as those of the theorist. Bargaining is slow but flexible; auctions are fast but rigid.

Bargaining models generate different results with different assumptions, but since it is usually hard to match the assumptions with particular real situations, the practical implications come from the simplest models – ideas such as the importance of avoiding misunderstanding, determining, and then concealing one's own reservation price, bluffing, and manipulating the timing of offers.

Auction models, on the other hand, may also generate different results with different assumptions but it is easier to match the assumptions with particular real situations, or even to create a real situation to match the model. That is because auctions vary not only in the underlying preferences of the players, as in bargaining, but in the specific rules used to play the game, and those rules are chosen by one of the players, usually with legal commitment to them. Thus, auction theory lends itself to what Alvin Roth (2002) calls "the economist as engineer": the use of technical economic theory to design institutions for specific situations. As with other engineering, the result may not be of general interest, but tailoring the model to the situation is both tricky and valuable, requiring the same kind of talent and care as developing the general theory.

Because auctions are stylized markets with well-defined rules, modelling them with game theory is particularly appropriate. Moreover, several of the motivations behind auctions are similar to the motivations behind the asymmetric information contracts of part 2 of this book. Besides the mundane reasons such as speed of sale that make auctions important, auctions are useful for a variety of informational purposes. Often bidders know more than the seller about the value of what is being sold, and the seller, not wanting to suggest a price first, uses an auction as a way to extract information. Art auctions are a good example, because the value of a painting depends on the bidder's tastes, which are known only to himself. Efficient allocation of resources is a goal different from profit maximization, but auctions are useful for that too. A good example is told in Boyes and Happel's 1989 article, "Auctions as an Allocation Mechanism in Academia: The Case of Faculty Offices." At their business school, the economics department used an auction to allocate new offices, whereas the management department used seniority, the statistics department used dice, and the finance department posted a first-come, first-serve sign-up sheet without warning. The auction has the best chance of coming up with an immediate efficient allocation. (Why do I say "immediate"? Why would the long-run probably stay the same?)

Auctions are also useful for agency reasons, because they hinder dishonest dealing. If the mayor were free to offer a price for building the new city hall and accept the first contractor who showed up, the lucky contractor would probably be the one who made the biggest political contribution. If the contract is put up for auction, cheating the public is more costly, and the difficulty of rigging the bids may outweigh the political gain.

We will spend most of this chapter on the effectiveness of different kinds of auction rules in extracting surplus from bidders, which will require finding the strategies with which bidders respond to the rules. Section 13.1 classifies auctions based on the relationships between different bidders' estimates of the value of what is being auctioned. Section 13.2, a necessarily very long section, explains the possible auction rules and the bidding strategies optimal for each rule. Section 13.3 compares the outcomes under the various rules, proving the Revenue Equivalence Theorem and showing how it becomes invalid if bidders are risk-averse. Section 13.4 shows how to choose an optimal reserve price using the similarity between optimal auctions and monopoly pricing. Section 13.5 analyzes common-value auctions, which can lead bidders into "the winner's curse" if they are not careful. Section 13.6 discusses asymmetric equilibria (the Wallet Game) and information affiliation.

Private-value and Common-value Auctions

Auctions differ enough for an intricate classification to be useful. One way to classify auctions is based on differences in the values bidders put on what is being auctioned. We will call the dollar value of the utility that bidder i receives from an object its **value** to him, v_i, and we will denote his estimate of the value by $\hat{v}_i$.

In a **private-value auction**, a bidder can learn nothing about his value from knowing the values of the other bidders. An example is the sale of antique chairs to people who will not resell them. Usually a bidder's value equals his value estimate in private-value auction models. If an auction is to be private value, it cannot be followed by costless resale of the object. If there were resale, a bidder's value would depend on the price at which he could resell, which would depend on the other bidders' values. What is special about a private-value auction is that a bidder cannot extract any information about his own value from the value estimates of the other bidders. Knowing all the other values in advance would not change his estimate. It might well change his bidding strategy, however, so we distinguish between the **independent private-value auction**, in which knowing his own value tells him nothing about other bidders' values, and other situations such as the **affiliated private-value auction** (affiliation being a concept which will be explained later) in which he might be able to use knowledge of his own value to deduce something about other players' values.

In a **pure common-value auction**, the bidders have identical values, but each bidder forms his own estimate on the basis of his own private information. An example is bidding for U.S. Treasury bills. A bidder's estimate would change if he could sneak a look at the other bidders' estimates, because they are all trying to estimate the same true value.

The values in most real-world auctions are a combination of private value and common value, because the value estimates of the different bidders are positively correlated but not identical. As always in modelling, we trade off descriptive accuracy against simplicity. It is common for economists to speak of mixed auctions as "common-value" auctions, since their properties are closer to those of common-value auctions. Krishna (2002) has used the term **interdependent value** for the mixed case.

The private value/common value dichotomy is about what a bidder knows about his own value, but a separate dimension of auctions is what a bidder knows about other bidders' values. One possibility is that the values are common knowledge.

This makes optimal bidding simple. In a private-value auction, the highest-valuing bidder can bid just above the second-highest value. In a common-value auction, the bidders will take into account each others' information and their value estimates will instantly converge to a single common estimate, the best one given all available information. In either case, bidders don't have to worry about cleverly deducing each others' information by observing how the bidding proceeds.

It would be odd, however, to observe an auction in the real world in which the seller knew the value estimates. In that case, the seller should not be using an auction. He should just charge a price equal to the highest value estimate, a price he knows will be accepted by one of the bidders.

More commonly, only the bidder himself knows his value, not other bidders or the seller. Most simply, the estimated values are statistically independent, the independent private value case that we will be analyzing for the first half of this chapter. If the estimates are independent, then a bidder's only source of information about his value is his private information and his only source of information about other bidders' value estimates is what he observes of their bidding. If the value estimates are not independent, a bidder can use his private information to help estimate other bidders' values (and thus how they will bid), and if he does not know his own value perfectly he can use observations of their value estimates to improve his estimate of his own value – which takes us to the common value case.

Lack of statistical independence can be present even in private-value auctions, however. Smith might know his own value perfectly, and so would not be able to learn anything about it by learning Jones's value. That is what makes the auction a private-value auction. But if the values are not independent – if, say, they are positively correlated – then if Smith knows that his own value is unusually high he could predict that Jones's value was also high. This would affect Smith's bidding strategy, even though it would not affect the maximum he would be willing to pay for the object being sold. I will not be analyzing private-value auctions with correlated values here, but as explained in Riley (1989) the difference can be important. Although bidding in the ascending and second-price auction rules that we will soon discuss is unchanged when values are correlated, bidding becomes lower in the descending and first-price auctions. In contrast, we will see that bidding in a common-value auction is generally more cautious than in a private-value auction even in ascending and second-price auctions.

To look at these various auction rules, we will use the following two games, which I have set up using the language of mechanism design since choosing auction rules fits well into that paradigm. The Ten-Sixteen Auction will be our running example for when values are discrete ($v = 10$ or $v = 16$), and the Continuous-Value Auction will be our example for when they are on a continuum ($v \sim f(v)$ on $[\underline{v}, \overline{v}]$).

The Ten-sixteen Auction

PLAYERS
One seller and two bidders.

ORDER OF PLAY
0   Nature chooses Bidder i's value for the object to be either $v_i = 10$ or $v_i = 16$, with equal probability. (The seller's value is zero.)

1   The seller chooses a mechanism $[G(\tilde{v}_i, \tilde{v}_{-i})v_i - t(\tilde{v}_i, \tilde{v}_{-i})]$ that takes payments t and gives the object with probability G to player i (including the seller) if he announces that his value is $\tilde{v}_i$ and the other players announce $\tilde{v}_{-i}$. He also chooses the procedure in which bidders select $\tilde{v}_i$ (sequentially, simultaneously, etc.).

2   Each bidder simultaneously chooses to participate in the auction or to stay out.

3   The bidders and the seller choose $\tilde{v}$ according to the mechanism procedure.

4   The object is allocated and transfers are paid according to the mechanism.

PAYOFFS
The seller's payoff is

$$\pi_s = \sum_{i=1}^{n} t(\tilde{v}_i, \tilde{v}_{-i}), \tag{13.1}$$

Bidder i's payoff is zero if he does not participate, and otherwise is

$$\pi_i(v_i) = G(\tilde{v}_i, \tilde{v}_{-i})v_i - t(\tilde{v}_i, \tilde{v}_{-i}). \tag{13.2}$$

To get around the open-set problem, we will assume for any auction rule that ties are broken in favor of whoever has the highest value, or randomly if the values are equal. Otherwise, if, for example, we said that ties simply split the probability of winning, then if $v_1 = 10$ and $v_2 = 16$ and this were known to both bidders, it would not be even a weak equilibrium to have them bid $p_1 = 10$ and $p_2 = 10$, because Bidder 2 would deviate to a slightly higher bid – but the smallest bid strictly greater than 10 does not exist if bid increments can be infinitesimal.

The second game will be our example for when values lie on a continuum.

The Continuous-value Auction

PLAYERS

One seller and two bidders.

ORDER OF PLAY

0 Nature chooses Bidder i's value for the object, v_i, using the strictly positive, atomless density $f(v)$ on the interval $[\underline{v}, \overline{v}]$.

1 The seller chooses a mechanism $[G(\tilde{v}_i, \tilde{v}_{-i})v_i - t(\tilde{v}_i, \tilde{v}_{-i})]$ that takes payments t and gives the object with probability G to player i (including the seller) if he announces that his value is $\tilde{v}_i$ and the other players announce $\tilde{v}_{-i}$. He also chooses the procedure in which bidders select $\tilde{v}_i$ (sequentially, simultaneously, etc.).

2 Each bidder simultaneously chooses to participate in the auction or to stay out.

3 The bidders and the seller choose $\tilde{v}$ according to the mechanism procedure.

4 The object is allocated and transfers are paid according to the mechanism, if it was accepted by all bidders.

PAYOFFS
The seller's payoff is

$$\pi_s = \sum_{i=1}^{n} t(\tilde{v}_i, \tilde{v}_{-i}). \tag{13.3}$$

Bidder i's payoff is zero if he does not participate, and otherwise is

$$\pi_i(v_i) = G(\tilde{v}_i, \tilde{v}_{-i})v_i - t(\tilde{v}_i, \tilde{v}_{-i}). \tag{13.4}$$

Many possible auction procedures fit the mechanism paradigm, even ones that are never used in practice. The mechanism could allocate the good with 70 percent probability to the highest bidder and with 30 percent probability to the lowest bidder, for example; or each bidder could be made to pay the amount he bids, even if he loses; or t could include an entry fee; or there could be a "reserve price," a minimum bid for which the seller will surrender the good. In this analysis, the seller will choose a direct mechanism that satisfies a participation constraint for each bidder type v_i (Bidder i will join the auction, so, for example, the entry fee is not too large), and an incentive compatibility constraint (the bidder will truthfully reveal his type; $\tilde{v}_i = v_i$).

13.2   Optimal Strategies under Different Rules in Private-value Auctions

Auctions have the same bewildering variety of rules as poker does. We will look at five different auction rules, using the private-value setting since it is simplest. In teaching this material, I ask each student to pick a value between 80 and 100, after which we conduct the various kinds of auctions. I advise the reader to try this. Pick two values and try out sample strategy profiles for the different auctions as they are described. Even though the values are private, it will immediately become clear that the best-response bids still depend on the strategies the bidder thinks other bidders have adopted.

The five auction rules we will consider (with common synonyms for them) are:

1   Ascending (English, open cry, open exit);
2   First price (first-price sealed bid);
3   Second price (second-price sealed bid, Vickrey);
4   Descending (Dutch)
5   All Pay

Ascending (English, open cry, open exit)

Rules
Each bidder is free to revise his bid upwards. When no bidder wishes to revise his bid further, the highest bidder wins the object and pays his bid.

Strategies
A bidder's strategy is his series of bids as a function of (1) his value, (2) his prior estimate of other bidders' values, and (3) the past bids of all the bidders. His bid can therefore be updated as his information set changes.

Payoffs
The winner's payoff is his value minus his highest bid ($t = p$ for him and $t = 0$ for everyone else). The losers' payoffs are zero.

Discussion
A bidder's dominant strategy in a private-value ascending auction is to stay in the bidding until bidding higher would require him to exceed his value and then to stop. This is optimal because he always wants to buy the object if the price is less than its value to him, but he wants to pay the lowest price possible. All bidding ends when the price reaches the second-highest value of any bidder present at the auction. The optimal strategy is independent of risk neutrality if bidders know their own values with certainty rather than having to estimate them, although risk-averse bidders who must estimate their values should be more conservative in bidding as we will see later.

The optimal private-value strategy is simple enough that details of the ascending auction usually do not make much difference, but there are a number of possibilities.

1   The **open-exit** auction, in which the price rises continuously and bidders show their willingness to pay the price by not dropping out, where a bidder's dropping out is publicly announced to the other bidders.
2   The **silent-exit** auction (my neologism), in which the price rises continuously and bidders show their willingness to pay the price by not dropping out, but a bidder's dropping out is not known to the other bidders.
3   The **eBay auction**, in which a bidder submits his "bid ceiling," the maximum price he is willing to pay. During the course of the auction the seller uses the bid ceilings to raise the current winning bid only as high as necessary, and the winner is the player whose bid is highest at a prespecified ending time.
4   The **Amazon auction**, in which a bidder submits his bid ceiling. During the course of the auction the seller uses the bid ceilings to raise the current winning bid only as high as necessary, and the winner is the player whose bid is highest at a prespecified ending time or ten minutes after the last increase in the current winning bid, whichever is later.

The precise method can be quite important in common-value auctions, where knowing what other players are doing alters a bidder's own value estimate. If the auction is open exit, for example, a bidder who observed that most of the other bidders dropped out at a low price would probably revise his own value estimate downwards, something he would not know to do in a silent-exit auction.

The ascending auction can be seen as a mechanism in which each bidder announces his value (which becomes his bid), the object is awarded to whoever announces the highest value (that is, bids highest), and he pays the second highest announced value (the second highest bid). In the Continuous-value Auction, denote the highest announced value by $\tilde{v}_{(1)}$, the second-highest by $\tilde{v}_{(2)}$, and so forth. The highest bidder gets the object with probability $G(\tilde{v}_{(1)}, \tilde{v}_{-1}) = 1$ at price $t(\tilde{v}_{(1)}, \tilde{v}_{-1}) = \tilde{v}_{(2)}$, and for $i \neq 1$, $G(\tilde{v}_{(i)}, \tilde{v}_{-i}) = 0$ and $t(\tilde{v}_{(1)}, \tilde{v}_{-1}) = 0$. This is incentive compatible, since a player's value announcement only matters if his value is highest, and he then wants to win if and only if the price is less than or equal to his value. It satisfies the participation constraint because his lowest possible payoff following that strategy is zero, and his payoff is higher if he wins and $\tilde{v}_{(1)} > \tilde{v}_{(2)}$.

Since each bidder's expected payoff is strictly positive, the *optimal* mechanism for the seller would be more complicated. As we will discuss later, it would include a **reserve price** p^* below which the object would remain unsold, changing the first part of the mechanism to $G(\tilde{v}_{(1)}, \tilde{v}_{-1}) = 1$ and $t(\tilde{v}_{(1)}, \tilde{v}_{-1}) = Max\{\tilde{v}_{(2)}, p^*\}$ if $\tilde{v}_{(1)} \geq p^*$ but $G(\tilde{v}_{(1)}, \tilde{v}_{-1}) = 0$ if $\tilde{v}_{(1)} < p^*$. We have seen in chapter 10 that optimal mechanisms are not always efficient, and that is so here, too: the object will go unsold if $\tilde{v}_{(1)} < p^*$.

In the Ten-Sixteen Auction, the seller's value is $v_s = 0$, and each of two bidders' private values v_1 and v_2 is either 10 or 16 with equal probability, known only to the bidder himself. A bidder's optimal strategy in the ascending auction would be to set his bid or bid ceiling to $p(v = 10) = 10$ and $p(v = 16) = 16$. His expected payoff would be

$$\pi(v = 10) = 0,$$
$$\pi(v = 16) = 0.5(16 - 10) + 0.5(16 - 16) = 3.$$

(13.5)

The expected price, the payoff to the seller, is

$$\pi_s = 0.5^2(10) + 0.5^2(16) + 2(0.5)^2(10) = 2.5 + 4 + 5 = 11.5. \qquad (13.6)$$

First Price (First-price Sealed Bid)

Rules
Each bidder submits one bid, in ignorance of the other bids. The highest bidder pays his bid and wins the object.

Strategies
A bidder's strategy is his bid as a function of his value.

Payoffs
The winner's payoff is his value minus his bid. The losers' payoffs are zero.

Discussion
In the first-price auction what the winning bidder wants to do is to have submitted a sealed bid just above the second-highest bid. If all the bidders' values are common knowledge and he can predict the second-highest bid perfectly, this is a simple problem. If the values are private information, then he has to guess at the second-highest bid, however, and take a gamble. His trade-off is between bidding high – thus winning more often – and bidding low – thus benefiting more if the bid wins. His optimal strategy depends on his degree of risk aversion and beliefs about the other bidders, so the equilibrium is less robust to mistakes in the assumptions of the model than the equilibria of ascending and second-price auctions. As we will see later, however, there are good reasons why sellers so often choose to use first-price auctions.

The First-price Auction with a Continuous Distribution of Values
Suppose Nature independently assigns values to n risk-neutral bidders using the continuous density $f(v) > 0$ (with cumulative probability $F(v)$) on the support $[0, \bar{v}]$.

A bidder's payoff as a function of his value v and his bid function $p(v)$ is, letting $G(p(v))$ denote the probability of winning with a particular $p(v)$:

$$\pi(v, p(v)) = G(p(v))[v - p(v)]. \qquad (13.7)$$

Let us first prove a lemma.

Lemma 13.1 *If player's equilibrium bid function is differentiable, it is strictly increasing in his value: $p'(v) > 0$.*

Proof.   The first-order condition from payoff (13.7) is

$$\frac{d\pi(v)}{dp} = G'(v - p) - G = 0. \qquad (13.8)$$

The optimum is an interior solution because at $p_i = 0$ the payoff is increasing and if p_i becomes large enough, π is negative. Thus, $d^2\pi(v_i)/dp_i^2 \leq 0$ at the optimum. Using the implicit function theorem and the fact that $d^2\pi(v_i)/dp_i dv_i = G' \geq 0$ because a higher bid does not yield a lower probability of winning, we can conclude that $dp_i/dv_i \geq 0$, at least if the bid function is differentiable. But it cannot be that $dp_i/dv_i = 0$, because then there would be values v_1 and v_2 such that $p_1 = p_2 = p$ and then

$$\frac{d\pi(v_1)}{dp_1} = G'(p)(v_1 - p) - G(p) = 0 = \frac{d\pi(v_2)}{dp_2} = G'(p)(v_2 - p) - G(p), \qquad (13.9)$$

which cannot be true. So the bidder bids more if his value is higher. QED.

Now let us try to find an equilibrium bid function. From equation (13.7), it is

$$p(v) = v - \frac{\pi(v, p(v))}{G(p(v))}. \qquad (13.10)$$

That is not very useful in itself, since it has $p(v)$ on both sides. We need to find ways to rewrite π and G in terms of just v.

First, tackle $G(p(v))$. Monotonicity of the bid function (from lemma 13.1) implies that the bidder with the greatest v will bid highest and win. Thus, the probability $G(p(v))$ that a bidder with price p_i will win is the probability that v_i is the highest value of all n bidders. The probability that a bidder's value v is the highest is $F(v)^{n-1}$, the probability that each of the other $(n-1)$ bidders has a value less than v. Thus,

$$G(p(v)) = F(v)^{n-1}. \qquad (13.11)$$

Next think about $\pi(v, p(v))$. The Envelope Theorem says that if $\pi(v, p(v))$ is the value of a function maximized by choice of $p(v)$ then its total derivative with respect to v equals its partial derivative, because $\partial\pi/\partial p = 0$:

$$\frac{d\pi(v, p(v))}{dv} = \frac{\partial\pi(v, p(v))}{\partial p}\frac{\partial p}{\partial v} + \frac{\partial\pi(v, p(v))}{\partial v} = \frac{\partial\pi(v, p(v))}{\partial v}. \qquad (13.12)$$

We can apply the Envelope Theorem to equation (13.7) to see how π changes with v assuming $p(v)$ is chosen optimally, which is appropriate because we are characterizing not just any bid function, but the optimal bid function. Thus,

$$\frac{d\pi(v, p(v))}{dv} = G(p(v)). \qquad (13.13)$$

Substituting from equation (13.11) gives us π's derivative, if not π, as a function of v:

$$\frac{d\pi(v, p(v))}{dv} = F(v)^{n-1}. \qquad (13.14)$$

To get $\pi(v, p(v))$ from its derivative, (13.14), integrate over all possible values from zero to v and include the a base value of $\pi(0)$ as the constant of integration:

$$\pi(v, p(v)) = \pi(0) + \int_0^v F(x)^{n-1}dx = \int_0^v F(x)^{n-1}dx. \qquad (13.15)$$

The last step is true because a bidder with $v = 0$ will never bid a positive amount and so will have a payoff of $\pi(0, p(0)) = 0$.

We can now return to the bid function in equation (13.10) and substitute for $G(p(v))$ and $\pi(v, p(v))$ from equations (13.11) and (13.15):

$$p(v) = v - \frac{\int_0^v F(x)^{n-1}dx}{F(v)^{n-1}}. \tag{13.16}$$

Suppose $F(v) = v/\bar{v}$, the uniform distribution. Then (13.16) becomes

$$p(v) = v - \frac{\int_0^v (x/\bar{v})^{n-1}dx}{(v/\bar{v})^{n-1}},$$

$$= v - \frac{\left|_{x=0}^v (1/\bar{v})^{n-1}(1/n)x^n\right.}{(v/\bar{v})^{n-1}},$$

$$= v - \frac{(1/\bar{v})^{n-1}(1/n)v^n - 0}{(v/\bar{v})^{n-1}},$$

$$= v - \frac{v}{n} = \left(\frac{n-1}{n}\right)v. \tag{13.17}$$

What a happy ending to a complicated derivation! If there are two bidders and values are uniform on [0, 1], a bidder should bid $p = v/2$, which since he has probability v of winning yields an expected payoff of $v^2/2$. If $n = 10$ he should bid $9/10v$, which since he has probability v^9 of winning yields him an expected payoff of $v^{10}/10$, quite close to zero if $v < 1$.

The First-price Auction: A Mixed-strategy Equilibrium in the Ten-sixteen Auction

The result in equation (13.17) depended crucially on the value distribution having a continuous support. When this is not true, the equilibrium in a first-price auction may not even be in pure strategies. Now let each of two bidders' private values v_1 and v_2 be either 10 or 16 with equal probability and known only to himself.

In a first-price auction, a bidder's optimal strategy is to bid $p(v = 10) = 10$, and if $v = 16$ to use a mixed strategy, mixing over the support $[\underline{p}, \bar{p}]$, where it will turn out that $\underline{p} = 10$ and $\bar{p} = 13$. The expected payoffs will be

$$\pi(v = 10) = 0,$$

$$\pi(v = 16) = 3, \tag{13.18}$$

$$\pi_s = 11.5.$$

These are the same payoffs as in the ascending auction, an equivalence we will come back to in a later section.

This will serve as an illustration of how to find an equilibrium mixed strategy when bidders mix over a continuum of pure strategies rather than just between two. The first step is to see why the equilibrium cannot be in pure strategies.

In any equilibrium, $p(v = 10) = 10$, because if either bidder used the bid $p < 10$, it would cause the other player to deviate to $(p + \epsilon)$, and a bid above 10 exceeds the object's value. If $v = 16$, however, a player will randomize his bid. Suppose the two bidders are using the pure strategies $p_1(v_1 = 16) = z_1$ and $p_2(v_2 = 16) = z_2$. The values of z_1 and z_2 would lie in $(10, 16]$ because a bid of exactly 10 would lose to the positive probability bid of $p(v = 10) = 10$ given our tie-breaking assumption and a bid over 16 would exceed the object's value, yielding a negative payoff. Either $z_1 = z_2$, or $z_1 \neq z_2$. If $z_1 = z_2$, then each bidder has incentive to deviate to $(z_1 - \epsilon)$ and win with probability one instead of tying. If $z_1 < z_2$, then Bidder 2 will deviate to bid $(z_1 + \epsilon)$. If he does that, however, Bidder 1 would deviate to bid $(z_1 + 2\epsilon)$, so he could win with probability one at trivially higher cost. The same holds true if $z_2 < z_1$. Thus, there is no equilibrium in pure strategies.

The second step is to figure out what pure strategies will be mixed between by a bidder with $v = 16$. It turns out that they form the interval $[10, 13]$. As just explained, the bid $p(v = 16)$ will be no less than 10 (so the bidder can win if his rival's value is 10) and no greater than 16 (which would always win, but unprofitably). The pure strategy of $(p = 10)|(v = 16)$ will win with probability of at least 0.50 (when the other bidder happens to have $v = 10$, given our tie-breaking rule), yielding a payoff of $0.50(16 - 10) = 3$. This rules out bids in $(13, 16]$, since even if they always win, their payoff is less than 3. Thus, the upper bound $\bar{p}$ must be no greater than 13.

The lower bound $\underline{p}$ must be exactly 10. If it were at $(10 + \epsilon)$ then a bid of $(10 - 2\epsilon)$ would have an equal certainty of winning the auction, but would have ϵ higher payoff. Thus, $\underline{p} = 10$.

The upper bound $\bar{p}$ must be exactly 13. If it were any less, then the other player would respond by using the pure strategy of $(\bar{p} + \epsilon)$, which would win with probability one and yield a payoff of greater than the payoff of 3 ($= 0.5(16 - 10)$) from $\underline{p} = 10$. In a mixed-strategy equilibrium, though, the payoff from any of the strategies mixed between must be equal. Thus, $\bar{p}$ cannot be less than 13.

We are not quite done looking at the strategies mixed between. When a player mixes over a continuum, the modeller must be careful to check for (1) atoms (some particular point which has positive probability, not just positive density), and (2) gaps (intervals within the mixing range with zero probability of bids). Are there any atoms or gaps within the interval $[10,13]$? No, it turns out.

1   Bidder 2's mixing density does not have an atom at any point a in $[10, 13]$ – no point a has positive probability, as opposed to positive density. An example of such an atom would be if the mixing distribution were the density $m(p) = 1/6$ over the interval $[10, 13]$ plus an atom of probability $1/2$ at $p = 13$, so the cumulative probability would be $M(p) = p/6$ over $[10, 13)$ and $M(13) = 1$. Using $M(p)$, a point such as 11 would have zero probability even though the interval, say, of $[10.5, 12.5]$ would have probability $2/6$.
    If there were an atom at a, Bidder 1 would respond by putting positive probability on $(a + \epsilon)$ and zero probability on a. But then Bidder 2 would respond by putting zero probability on a and shifting that probability to $(a + 2\epsilon)$.
2   Bidder 2's mixing density does not have a gap $[g, h]$ anywhere with $g > 10$ and $h < 13$. If it did, then Bidder 1's payoff from bidding g and h would be

$$\pi_1(g) = Prob(p_2 < g)v_1 - g \tag{13.19}$$

and

$$\pi_1(h) = Prob(p_2 < h)v_1 - h = Prob(p_2 < g)v_1 - h, \tag{13.20}$$

where the second equality in $\pi_1(h)$ is true because there is zero probability that p_2 is between g and h. Bidder 1 will put zero probability on $p_1 = h$, since its payoff is lower than the payoff from $p_1 = g$ and will put zero probability on slightly larger values of p_1 too, since by continuity their payoffs will also be less than the payoff from $p_1 = g$. This creates a gap $[h, h^*]$ in which $p_1 = 0$. But then Bidder 2 will want to put zero probability on $p_2 = h^*$ and slightly higher values, by the same reasoning, which means that our original hypothesis of only a gap $[g, h]$ is false.

Thus, we can conclude that the mixing density $m(p)$ is positive over the entire interval $[10, 13]$, with no atoms. What will it look like? Let us confine ourselves to looking for a symmetric equilibrium, in which both bidders use the same function $m(p)$. We know the expected payoff from any bid p in the support must equal the payoff from $p = 10$ or $p = 13$, which is 3. Therefore, since if our player has value $v = 16$ there is probability 0.5 of winning because the other player has $v = 10$ and probability $0.5M(p)$ of winning because the other player has $v = 16$ too but bid less than p, the payoff is

$$0.5(16 - p) + 0.5M(p)(16 - p) = 3. \tag{13.21}$$

This implies that $(16 - p) + M(p)(16 - p) = 6$, so

$$M(p) = \frac{6}{16 - p} - 1, \tag{13.22}$$

which has the density

$$m(p) = \frac{6}{(16 - p)^2} \tag{13.23}$$

on the support $[10, 13]$, rising from $m(10) = 1/6$ to $m(13) = 4/6$.

Since each bidder type has the same expected payoff in this first-price auction as in the ascending auction, and the object is sold with probability one, it must be that the seller's payoff is the same, too, equal to 11.5, as we found in equation (13.6).

You may find it odd that the general continuous-value auction has a pure-strategy equilibrium but our particular discrete-value auction does not. Usually if a game lacks a pure-strategy equilibrium in discrete type space, it also lacks one if we "smooth" the probability distribution by making it continuous but still putting almost all the weight on the old discrete types, as in figure 13.1.

This is related to a remarkable feature of private-value auctions with discrete values: the mixed-strategy equilibria do not necessarily block efficiency (and the revenue equivalence we study later). When players randomize, it would seem that sometimes by chance the highest-valuing player would be unlucky and lose the auction, which would be inefficient. Not so here. As explained in Riley (1989) and Wolfstetter (1999, p. 204), if the values of each player are distributed discretely over some set $\{0, v_a, v_b, \ldots, v_w\}$ then in the symmetric equilibrium mixed strategy, the supports of the mixing distributions are $v_a: [0, p_1], v_b: [p_1, p_2], v_w: [p_{w-1}, p_w]$, where $p_1 < p_2 < \cdots < p_w$. The supports do not

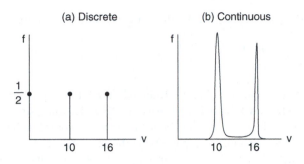

Figure 13.1   Smoothing a discrete distribution.

overlap. Each type of bidder acts as if he was in competition just with his own type (since he will surely win over the lower types and will surely lose to the higher types) and the object is allocated to a bidder who values it most. The mixing only determines who wins when two players happen to have the same type.

Second-price Auctions (Second-price Sealed Bid, Vickrey)

Rules
Each bidder submits one bid, in ignorance of the other bids. The bids are opened, and the highest bidder pays the amount of the second-highest bid and wins the object.

Strategies
A bidder's strategy is his bid as a function of his value.

Payoffs
The winning bidder's payoff is his value minus the second-highest bid. The losing bidders' payoffs are zero. The seller's payoff is the second-highest bid.

Discussion
Second-price auctions are similar to ascending auctions, but simpler, so although they are rarely used to actually sell products, they are useful for modelling. Bidding one's value is a weakly dominant strategy: a bidder who bids less is no more likely to win the auction (and probably less likely, depending on $f(v)$), but he pays the same price – the second-highest-valuing player's bid – if he does win. The structure of the payoffs is reminiscent of the Groves Mechanism of section 10.4, because in both games a bidder's strategy affects some major event (who wins the auction, or whether the project is undertaken), but his strategy affects his own payoff only via that event. In the auction's symmetric equilibrium, each bidder bids his value and the winner ends up paying the second-highest value. If bidders know their own values, the outcome does not depend on risk neutrality.

One difference between ascending and second-price auctions is that second-price auctions have peculiar asymmetric equilibria because the actions in them are simultaneous. Consider a variant of the Ten-Sixteen Auction, in which each of two bidders' values can be 10 or 16, but where the realized values are common knowledge. Bidding one's value is a **symmetric equilibrium**, meaning that the bid function $p(v)$ is the same for both bidders:

$\{p(v = 10) = 10, p(v = 16) = 16\}$. But there are asymmetric equilibria such as

$$p_1(v = 10) = 10, \quad p_1(v = 16) = 16,$$
$$p_2(v = 10) = 1, \quad p_2(v = 16) = 10. \tag{13.24}$$

Since Bidder 1 never bids less than 10, Bidder 2 knows that if $v_2 = 10$ he can never get a positive payoff, so he is willing to choose $p_2(v = 10) = 1$. Doing so results in a sale price of 1, for any $p_1 > 1$, which is better for Bidder 1 and worse for the seller than a price of 10, but Bidder 2 does not care about their payoffs. In the same way, if $v_2 = 16$, Bidder 2 knows that if he bids 10 he will win if $v_1 = 10$, but if $v_2 = 16$ he would have to pay 16 to win and would earn a payoff of zero. He might as well bid 10 and earn his zero by losing.[1]

Perhaps the seller's fear of asymmetric equilibria like this is why second-price auctions are so rare. They have actually been used, though, in a computer operating system. An operating system must assign a computer's resources to different tasks, and researchers at Xerox Corporation designed the Spawn system, under which users allocate "money" in a second-price auction for computer resources. See "Improving a Computer Network's Efficiency," *The New York Times*, p. 35 (March 29, 1989).

Descending Auctions (Dutch)

Rules
The seller announces a bid, which he continuously lowers until some bidder stops him and takes the object at that price.

Strategies
A bidder's strategy is when to stop the bidding as a function of his value.

Payoffs
The winner's payoff is his value minus his bid. The losers' payoffs are zero.

Discussion
The typical descending auction is **strategically equivalent** to the first-price auction, which means there is a one-to-one mapping between the strategy sets and the equilibria of the two games. The reason for the strategic equivalence is that no relevant information is disclosed in the course of the auction, only at the end, when it is too late to change anybody's behavior. In the first-price auction a bidder's bid is irrelevant unless it is the highest, and in the descending auction a bidder's stopping price is irrelevant unless it is the highest. The equilibrium price is calculated the same way for both auctions.

A descending auction does not have to be like a first-price auction as a matter of logic, though. Vickrey (1961) notes that a descending auction could be set up as a second-price auction. When the first bidder presses his button, he primes an auction-ending buzzer that

---

[1] Trembling-hand perfectness, however, would rule out this kind of equilibrium. If Bidder 1 might tremble and bid, for example, 4 by accident, Bidder 2 would not want to ever bid less than 4. Bidding less than one's value is weakly dominated by bidding exactly one's value – but Nash equilibrium strategies can be weakly dominated, as we saw with the Bertrand Game in chapter 3.

does not goes off until a second bidder presses his button. In that case, the descending auction would be strategically equivalent to a second-price auction. Economists almost always mean "first price descending auctions" when they use the term, however.

Descending – "Dutch" – auctions have been used in the Netherlands to sell flowers – see the Aalsmeer auction website at http://www.vba.nl for information and photos. They have also been used in Ontario to sell tobacco, using a clock four feet in diameter marked with quarter-cent gradations. Each of six or so bidders has a stop button. The clock hand drops a quarter-cent at a time, and the stop buttons are registered so that ties cannot occur (tobacco bidders need reflexes like race-car drivers). The farmer sellers watch from an adjoining room and can later reject the bids if they feel they are too low (a form of reserve price). The clock is fast enough to sell 2,500,000 lb. per day (Cassady [1967, p. 200]).

Descending auctions are common in less obvious forms. Filene's is one of the biggest stores in Boston, and Filene's Basement is its most famous department. In the basement are a variety of marked-down items formerly in the regular store, each with a price and date attached. The price customers pay at the register is the price on the tag minus a discount which depends on how long ago the item was dated. As time passes and the item remains unsold, the discount rises from 10 to 50 to 70 percent. The idea of pre-dictable time discounting has also been used by bookstores too ("Waldenbooks to Cut Some Book Prices in Stages in Test of New Selling Tactic," *The Wall Street Journal*, March 29, 1988, p. 34).

All-pay Auctions

Rules
Each bidder places a bid simultaneously. The bidder with the highest bid wins, and each bidder pays the amount he bid.

Strategies
A bidder's strategy is his bid as a function of his value.

Payoffs
The winner's payoff is his value minus his bid. The losers' payoffs are the negative of their bids.

Discussion
The winning bid will be lower in the all-pay auction than under the other rules, because bidders need a bigger payoff when they do win to make up for their negative payoffs when they lose. At the same time, since even the losing bidders pay something to the seller it is not obvious that the seller does badly (and in fact, it turns out to be just as good an auction rule as the others, in this simple risk-neutral context).

I do not know of the all-pay rule ever being used in a real auction, but it is a useful modelling tool because it models rent-seeking very well. When a number of companies lobby a politician for a privilege, they are in an all-pay auction because even the losers have paid by incurring the cost of lobbbying. When a number of companies pursue a patent, it is an all-pay auction because even the losers have incurred the cost of doing research.

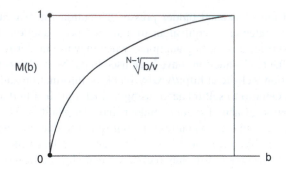

Figure 13.2   The bid function in an all-pay auction with identical bidders.

The Equal-value All-pay Auction

Suppose each of the n bidders has the same value, v. That is not a very interesting game for most of the auction rules, though it is true that for the second-price auction there exists the strange asymmetric equilibrium $\{v, 0, 0, \ldots, 0\}$. Under the all-pay auction rule, however, this game is quite interesting. The equilibrium is in mixed strategies. This is easy to see, because in any pure-strategy profile, either the maximum bid is less than v, in which case someone could deviate to $p = v$ and increase his payoff; or one bidder bids v and the rest bid at most $p' < v$, in which case the high bidder will deviate to bid just above p'.

Suppose we have a symmetric equilibrium, so all bidders use the same mixing cumulative distribution $M(p)$. Let us conjecture that $\pi(p) = 0$, which we will later verify.[2] The payoff function for each bidder is the probability of winning times the value of the prize minus the bid, which is paid with probability one, and if we equate that to zero we get

$$M(p)^{n-1}v = p,$$
(13.25)

so

$$M(p) = \sqrt[n-1]{\frac{p}{v}},$$
(13.26)

as shown in figure 13.2. At the extreme bids that a bidder with value v might offer, $M(0) = \sqrt[n-1]{0/v} = 0$ and $M(v) = \sqrt[n-1]{v/v} = 1$, so we have found a valid distribution function $M(p)$. Moreover, since the payoff from one of the strategies between which it mixes, $p = 0$, equals zero, we have verified our conjecture that $\pi(p) = 0$ in the equilibrium.

Consider now what happens with the all-pay rule in the Continuous-Value Auction Game, using an explanation adapted from Krishna (2002, chapter 3.2).

The Continuous-value All-pay Auction

Suppose each of the n bidders picks his value v from the same density $f(v)$. Conjecture that the equilibrium is symmetric, in pure strategies, and that the bid function, $p(v)$, is strictly

---

[2] It turns out there is a continuum of asymmetric equilibria in this game if $n > 2$, but a unique equilibrium if $n = 2$. See Kovenock, Baye, & de Vries (1996) for a full characterization of all-pay auctions with complete information.

increasing. The equilibrium payoff function for a bidder with value v who pretends he has value z is

$$\pi(v,z) = F(z)^{n-1}v - p(z), \tag{13.27}$$

since if our bidder bids $p(z)$, that is the highest bid only if all $(n-1)$ other bidders have $v < z$, a probability of $F(z)$ for each of them.

The function $\pi(v,z)$ is not necessarily concave in z, so satisfaction of the first-order condition will not be a sufficient condition for payoff maximization, but it is a necessary condition since the optimal z is not 0 (unless $v = 0$) or infinity and from (13.27) $\pi(v,z)$ is differentiable in z in our conjectured equilibrium. Thus, we need to find z such that

$$\frac{\partial \pi(v,z)}{\partial z} = (n-1)F(z)^{n-2}f(z)v - p'(z) = 0. \tag{13.28}$$

In the equilibrium, our bidder does follow the strategy $p(v)$, so $z = v$ and we can write

$$p'(v) = (n-1)F(v)^{n-2}f(v)v. \tag{13.29}$$

Integrating up, we get

$$p(v) = p(0) + \int_0^v (n-1)F(x)^{n-2}f(x)x\,dx,$$
$$= \int_0^v (n-1)F(x)^{n-2}F(x)x\,dx. \tag{13.30}$$

where we know that $p(0) = 0$ because if $p(0) > 0$ a bidder with $v = 0$ would have a negative expected payoff. The function $p(v)$ is thus deterministic, symmetric, and strictly increasing in v, so we have verified our conjectures. We can verify that truthtelling is a symmetric equilibrium strategy by substituting for $p(z)$ from (13.30) into payoff equation (13.27).

$$\pi(v,z) = F(z)^{n-1}v - p(z),$$
$$= F(z)^{n-1}v - \int_0^z (n-1)F(x)^{n-2}f(x)x\,dx,$$
$$= F(z)^{n-1}v - F(z)^{n-1}z + \int_0^z F(x)^{n-1}dx, \tag{13.31}$$

where the last step uses integration by parts ($\int gh' = gh - \int hg'$, where $g = x$ and $h' = (n-1)F(x)^{n-2}f(x)$). Maximizing (13.31) with respect to z yields

$$\frac{\partial \pi(v,z)}{\partial z} = (n-1)F(z)^{n-2}f(z)(v-z), \tag{13.32}$$

which is maximized by setting $z = v$. Thus, if $(n-1)$ of the bidders are using this $p(v)$ function, so will the remaining bidder, and we have a Nash equilibrium.

Let's see what happens with a particular value distribution. Suppose values are uniformly distributed over $[0, 1]$, so $F(v) = v$. Then equation (13.30) becomes

$$p(v) = \int_0^v (n-1)x^{n-2}(1)x\,dx,$$

$$= \Big|_{x=0}^v (n-1)\frac{x^n}{n},$$

$$= \left(\frac{n-1}{n}\right)v^n. \tag{13.33}$$

If there were $n = 2$ bidders, a bidder with value v would bid $v^2/2$, win with probability v, and have expected payoff $\pi = v(v) - v^2/2 = v^2/2$. If there were $n = 10$ bidders, a bidder with value v would bid $(9/10)v^{10}$, win with probability v^9, and have expected payoff $\pi = v(v^9) - (9/10)v^{10} = v^{10}/(10)$. As we will see when we discuss the Revenue Equivalence Theorem, it is no accident that this is the same payoff as for the first-price auction when values were uniformly distributed on $[0, 1]$.

The Dollar Auction

A famous example of an auction in which not just the winner pays is the dollar auction of Shubik (1971). This is an ascending auction to sell a dollar bill in which the players offer higher and higher bids, and the highest bidder wins – but both the first- and second-highest bidders pay their bids. If the players begin with infinite wealth, the game illustrates why equilibrium might not exist if strategy sets are unbounded. Once one bidder has started bidding against another, both of them do best by continuing to bid, so as to win the dollar as well as pay the bid. (If there are three or more players, all but the top two will be happy to stop bidding early in the game.) This auction may seem absurd, but as a variant on the all-pay auction it has considerable similarity to patent and arms races. See Baye & Hoppe (2003) for more on the equivalence between innovation games and auctions.

The all-pay auction and the dollar auction are just two examples of auctions in which a player must pay something even though he loses. Chapter 3's War of Attrition is another example, which is something like a second-price all-pay auction. Even odder is the **loser-pays auction**, a two-player auction in which only the loser pays. As we have seen with the all-pay auction and its revenue equivalence to other auction forms, however, the fact that an auction's rules are strange does not mean it is necessarily worse for bidders.

All-pay auctions are a standard way to model rentseeking: imagine that n players each exert e in effort simultaneously to get a prize worth V, the winner being whoever's effort is highest. Another common way to model rentseeking is as an auction in which the highest bidder has the best chance to win but lower bidders might win instead. Tullock (1980) started a literature on this in an article which was valuable despite a mistaken claim that the expected amount paid by the bidders might exceed the value of the prize. (See Baye, Kovenock, & de Vries [1999] for a more recent analysis of this **rent dissipation**.) There is no obvious way to model contests, and the functional form does matter to behavior, as Jack Hirshleifer (1989) tells us. In the most popular functional form, P_1 and P_2 are the probabilities of winning of the two players, e_1 and e_2 are their efforts, and R and θ are parameters which can be used to increase the probability that the high bidder wins or to give one player an advantage over the other. The victory function is then assumed to be

$$P_1 = \frac{\theta e_1^R}{\theta e_1^R + e_2^R} \quad \text{and} \quad P_2 = \frac{e_2^R}{\theta e_1^R + e_2^R}. \tag{13.34}$$

If $\theta = 1$ and R becomes large, this becomes close to the simple all-pay auction, because neither player has an advantage and the highest bidder wins with probability near one.

Once we depart from true auctions, however, the modeller must be careful about some seemingly obvious assumptions. Two bidders can simply refuse to enter the dollar auction, for example, but two countries have a harder time refusing to enter a situation in which an arms race is tempting, though they can try to collude in keeping the bids small. It is also often plausible that the size of the prize rises or falls with the bids – for example, when the contest is a mechanism used by a team to motivate its members to produce more (see Chung [1996]) or when the prize shrinks with effort because rent-seeking hurts the economy (see Alexeev & Leitzel [1996]).

13.3   Revenue Equivalence, Risk Aversion, and Uncertainty

We can now collect together the outcomes of these various auction rules and compare them. We have seen that the first-price and descending auctions are strategically equivalent, so the payoffs to the bidders and seller will be the same under each rule regardless of whether values are private or common and whether the players are risk-neutral or risk-averse.

When values are private and independent, the second-price and ascending auctions are the same in the sense that the bidder who values the object most highly wins and pays the second highest of the values of all the bidders present, but the strategies are different in the two auctions. In all five kinds of auctions, however, the seller's expected revenue is the same. This is the biggest result in auction theory: the **Revenue Equivalence Theorem** of Vickrey (1961). This has been variously generalized from Vickrey's original statement (e.g., Klemperer [2004, p. 40]), so there is no single Revenue Equivalence Theorem, but they all share the same idea of payoffs being the same under various auction rules. We will look at two versions, a general one for auctions with particular properties and a more specific one – a corollary, really – for the five auction rules just analyzed.

Theorem 13.1 (The Revenue Equivalence Theorem)

Let all players be risk-neutral with private values drawn independently from the same atomless, strictly increasing distribution $F(v)$ on $[\underline{v}, \bar{v}]$. If under either Auction Rule A_1 or Auction Rule A_2 it is true that:

(a)   the winner of the object is the player with the highest value; and
(b)   the lowest bidder type, $v = \underline{v}$, has an expected payment of zero;

then the symmetric equilibria of the two auction rules have the same expected payoffs for each type of bidder and for the seller.

Proof.   Let us represent the auction as the truthful equilibrium of a direct mechanism in which each bidder sends a message z of his type v and then pays an expected amount $p(z)$. (The Revelation Principle says that we can do this.) By assumption (a), the probability that a player wins the object given that he chooses message z equals $F(z)^{n-1}$, the probability that all $(n-1)$ other players have values $v < z$. Let us denote this winning probability by $G(z)$, with density $g(z)$. Note that $g(z)$ is well defined because we assumed that $F(v)$ is atomless and everywhere increasing.

The expected payoff of any player of type v is the same, since we are restricting ourselves to symmetric equilibria. It equals

$$\pi(z, v) = G(z)v - p(z). \tag{13.35}$$

The first-order condition with respect to the player's choice of type message z (which we can use because neither $z = 0$ nor $z = \bar{v}$ is the optimum if condition (a) is to be true) is

$$\frac{d\pi(z; v)}{dz} = g(z)v - \frac{dp(z)}{dz} = 0, \tag{13.36}$$

so

$$\frac{dp(z)}{dz} = g(z)v. \tag{13.37}$$

We are looking at a truthful equilibrium, so we can replace z with v:

$$\frac{dp(v)}{dv} = g(v)v. \tag{13.38}$$

Next, we integrate (13.38) over all values from zero to v, adding $p(\underline{v})$ as the constant of integration:

$$p(v) = p(\underline{v}) + \int_{\underline{v}}^{v} g(x)x dx. \tag{13.39}$$

We can use (13.39 to substitute for $p(v)$ in the payoff equation (13.35), which becomes, after replacing z with v and setting $p(\underline{v}) = 0$ because of assumption (b),

$$\pi(v, v) = G(v)v - \int_{\underline{v}}^{v} g(x)x dx. \tag{13.40}$$

Equation (13.40) says the expected payoff of a bidder of type v depends only on the $G(v)$ distribution, which in turn depends only on the $F(v)$ distribution, and not on the $p(z)$ function or other details of the particular auction rule. But if the bidders' payoffs do not depend on the auction rule, neither does the seller's. QED.

There are many versions of the revenue equivalence theorem, and the name of the theorem comes from a version that just says that the seller's revenue is the same across auction rules rather than including bidders too. The version proved above is adapted from proposition 3.1 of Krishna (2002, p. 30). Other versions, which use different proof approaches, can be found in Klemperer (1998, p. 40), and Milgrom (2004, p. 74). Two assumptions that are standard across versions are that the bidders are risk-neutral and that their values are drawn from the same distribution.

It is only when we apply the Revenue Equivalence Theorem to the diverse auction rules we laid out earlier that its remarkable nature can be appreciated. The symmetric equilibria of the ascending, first-price, second-price, descending, and all-pay auctions with continuous values all satisfy the two conditions of theorem 13.1: (1) the winner is the bidder with the highest value, and (2) the lowest type makes an expected payment of zero. Thus, the following corollary is true.

A Revenue Equivalence Corollary. *Let all players be risk-neutral with private values drawn from the same strictly increasing, atomless distribution $F(v)$. The symmetric equilibria of the ascending, first-price, second-price, descending, and all-pay auctions all have the same expected payoffs for each type of bidder and for the seller.*

Although the different auctions have the same expected payoff for the seller, they do not have the same realized payoff. In the first-price auction, for example, the winning bidder's payment depends entirely on his own value. In the second-price auction, the winning bidder's payment depends entirely on the second-highest value, which is sometimes close to his own value and sometimes much less. Thus, we will see that first-price auctions are better if players are risk-averse.

Remember, too, that the revenue equivalence theorem requires not just that the bidders have private values not common, but also that the private values be independent. To see why, consider what happens if there are two bidders, both with values drawn uniformly from [0,10], but interdependently, with $v_2 = 10 - v_1$. If we put aside equilibria with weakly dominated strategies (e.g., for a player to bid 0 if his value is less than 5), the second-price auction yields revenue equal to $p = v_{(2)}$, the second-highest value. The seller can extract more revenue, however, by using the auction rule that the winner is the highest bidder, and he pays 10 minus the second-highest bid. One equilibrium under that rule has both players bidding their values, and $p = 10 - v_{(2)} = v_{(1)} > v_{(2)}$.

Risk Aversion in Private-value Auctions[3]

When bidders are risk-averse, the Revenue Equivalence Theorem fails. Consider Bidder 1 in the Ten-Sixteen Auction when he knows his own value is $v_1 = 16$ but does not know v_2. In the second-price auction, he has an equal chance of a payoff of either 0 (if $v_2 = 16$) or 6 (if $v_2 = 10$), regardless of whether the bidders are risk-averse or not, because bidding one's value is a weakly dominant strategy.

Compare that with his payoff in the first-price auction, in which the equilibrium is in mixed strategies. If the bidders are risk-neutral, then as we found earlier, if the bidder has value 16 he wins using a bid in the mixing support [10, 13] and achieves a payoff in [3, 6] with probability 0.75, and he loses and earns payoff of zero with probability 0.25. The (0, 6) gamble of the second-price auction is riskier than the (0, 3 to 6) gamble of the first-price auction. The (0, 6) gamble is simpler, but it has more dispersion.

If the bidders are risk-averse, then the optimal strategies in the first-price auction change. It remains true that the bidders mix on an interval $[10, \bar{p}]$. We derived $\bar{p}$ and the optimal

[3] This explanation is adapted from chapter 8 of the English draft of the Chinese version of Wolfstetter (1999).

mixing distribution by equating expected payoffs, however, and a certain win at a price of 10 will now be worth more to a bidder than a 50 percent chance of winning at a price of 13. Let us denote the concave utility function of each bidder by $U(v - p)$ and normalize by defining $U(0) \equiv 0$. The expected payoff from $p = 10$, which wins with probability 0.5, must equal the expected payoff from the upper bound $\bar{p}$ of the mixing support, so

$$0.5U(6) = U(16 - \bar{p}). \tag{13.41}$$

Since $0.5U(6) < U(16 - 13)$ by concavity of U, it must be that $\bar{p} > 13$. We found the mixing distribution function $M(p)$ by equating $\pi(p)$ to the payoff from bidding 10, which is $0.5U(6)$, so

$$\pi(p) = 0.5U(16 - p) + 0.5M(p)U(16 - p) = 0.5U(6), \tag{13.42}$$

which can be solved to yield

$$M(p) = \frac{U(6)}{U(16 - p)} - 1, \tag{13.43}$$

which has the density

$$m(p) = \frac{U(6)U'(16 - p)}{U^2(16 - p)}, \tag{13.44}$$

compared with the risk-neutral density $m(p) = 6/(16 - p)^2$ from equation (13.23). Thus, risk aversion of the bidders actually spreads out their equilibrium bids (the support is broader than $[10, 13]$), but it remains true that the first-price auction is less risky than the second-price auction.

What happens in the Continuous-value Auction? In the second-price auction, the optimal strategies are unchanged, so seller revenue does not change if bidders are risk-averse. To solve for the equilibrium of the first-price auction, let us look at a given bidder's incentive to report his true type v as z in an auction in which the payment is $p(z)$ and the probability of winning the object is $G(z)$. The bidder maximizes by choice of z

$$\pi(v, z) = G(z)U[v - p(z)],$$
$$= F(z)^{n-1}U[v - p(z)], \tag{13.45}$$

where $\pi(v, 0) = 0$ because $F(0) = 0$. At the optimum,

$$\frac{\partial \pi(v, z)}{\partial z} = (n - 1)F(z)^{n-2}f(z)U[v - p(z)] + F(z)^{n-1}U'[v - p(z)][-p'(z)] = 0, \tag{13.46}$$

In equilibrium, $z = v$. Using that fact, for all $v > \underline{v}$ (since $F(\underline{v}) = 0$) we can solve equation (13.46) for $p(z)$ to get

$$p(v) = \left(\frac{(n-1)f(v)}{F(v)}\right)\left(\frac{U[v - p(v)]}{U'[v - p(v)]}\right) \tag{13.47}$$

Now let us look at the effect of risk aversion on $p(v)$. If U is linear, then

$$\frac{U[v - p(v)]}{U'[v - p(v)]} = v - p(v), \tag{13.48}$$

but if the bidder is risk-averse, so U is strictly concave,

$$\frac{U[v - p(v)]}{U'[v - p(v)]} > v - p(v). \tag{13.49}$$

Thus, for a given v, the bid function in (13.47) makes the bid higher if the bidder is risk-averse than if he is not. The bid for every value of v except $v = \underline{v}$ increases ($p(\underline{v}) = \underline{v}$, regardless of risk aversion). By increasing his bid from the level optimal for a risk-neutral bidder, the risk-averse bidder insures himself. If he wins, his surplus is slightly less because of the higher price, but he is more likely to win and avoid a surplus of zero.

As a result the seller's revenue is greater in the first-price than in the second-price auction if bidders are risk-averse. But since under risk neutrality the first-price and second-price auctions yield the same revenue, under risk aversion the first-price auction must yield greater revenue, both in expectation and conditional on the highest v present in the auction. The seller, whether risk-neutral or risk-averse, will prefer the first-price auction when bidders are risk-averse.

Uncertainty over One's Own Value

We have seen that when bidders are risk-averse, revenue equivalence fails because the second-price auction is riskier than the first-price auction. By the same reasoning, the ascending auction is riskier, and by strategic equivalence the descending auction is the same as the first price. Risk aversion matters for different reasons if the bidders do not know their values precisely. As we will see later, uncertainty over one's own value will generate conservative bidding behavior in common-value auctions for the strategic reason of the "Winner's Curse" – a reason which applies whether bidders are risk-averse or not – and because of the "Linkage Principle" of Milgrom & Weber (1982). Value uncertainty also has a simpler effect that is driven by risk aversion and applies even in independent private-value auctions: buying a good of uncertain value is instrinsically risky, whether buying it by auction or by a posted price.

Consider the following question:

If the seller can reduce bidder uncertainty over the value of the object being auctioned, should he do so?

Let us assume that the seller can precommit to reveal both favorable information and unfavorable information, since of course he would like best to reveal only information that raises bidder estimates of the object's value (though the unravelling effect of chapter 10 might undo such a strategy). It is often plausible that the seller can set up an auction system which reduces uncertainty – say, by a regular policy of allowing bidders to examine the goods before the auction begins. Let us build a model to show the effect of such a policy.

Suppose there are n bidders, each with a private value, in an ascending auction. Each measures his private value v with an independent error $\epsilon > 0$. This error is with equal probability $-x, +x$, or 0. The bidders have diffuse priors, so they take all values of v to be equally likely, ex ante. Let us denote a bidder's measured value by $\hat{v} = v + \epsilon$, which is an unbiased estimate of v. In the ascending auctions we have been studying so far, where $\epsilon = 0$, the optimal bid ceiling was v. Now, when $\epsilon > 0$, what bid ceiling should be used by a bidder with utility function $U(v - p)$?

If the bidder wins the auction and pays p for the object, his expected utility at that point is

$$\pi(p) = \frac{U([\hat{v} - x] - p)}{3} + \frac{U(\hat{v} - p)}{3} + \frac{U([\hat{v} + x] - p)}{3}. \tag{13.50}$$

If he is risk-neutral, this yields him a payoff of zero if $p = \hat{v}$, and winning at any lower price would yield a positive payoff. This is true because we can write $U(v - p) = v - p$ and

$$\pi(\textit{risk-neutral}, p = \hat{v}) = \frac{([\hat{v} - x] - \hat{v})}{3} + \frac{(\hat{v} - \hat{v})}{3} + \frac{(\hat{v} + x - \hat{v})}{3} = 0. \tag{13.51}$$

Thus, under risk-neutrality, uncertainty over one's own value does not affect the optimal strategy, except that the bidder's bid ceiling is his expected value for the object rather than his value. Adverse selection aside, there is no reason for the seller to try to improve bidder information.

If the bidder is risk-averse, however, then the utility function U is concave and

$$\frac{U([\hat{v} - x] - p)}{3} + \frac{U([\hat{v} + x] - p)}{3} < \left(\frac{2}{3}\right) U(\hat{v} - p), \tag{13.52}$$

so his expected payoff in equation (13.50) is less than $U(\hat{v} - p)$, and if $p = \hat{v}$ his payoff is less than $U(0)$. A risk-averse bidder will have a negative expected payoff from paying his bid ceiling unless it is strictly less than his estimated value.

Notice that the seller does not have control over all the elements of the model. The seller can often choose the auction rules unilaterally. This includes not just how bids are made, but such things as whether the bidders get to know how many potential bidders are in the auction, whether the seller himself is allowed to bid, and so forth. Also, the seller can decide how much information to release about the goods. The seller cannot, however, decide whether the bidders are risk-averse or not, or whether they have common or private values, no more than he can choose what their values are for the good he is selling. All of those assumptions concern the utility functions of the bidders. At best, the seller can do things such as choose to produce goods to sell at the auction which have common values instead of private values.

An error I have often observed is to think that the presence of uncertainty over one's value always causes the Winner's Curse that we will shortly examine. It does not, unless the auction is in common values. Uncertainty over one's value is a necessary but not sufficient condition for the Winner's Curse. It is true that risk-averse bidders should not bid as high as their value estimates if they are uncertain about them, even if the auction is in private values. That sounds a lot like a Winner's Curse, but the reason for the discounted bids is completely different, depending as it does on risk aversion. If bidders are uncertain about value estimates but they are risk-neutral, their dominant strategy is still to bid up to their value estimates. If the Winner's Curse is present, even if a bidder is risk-neutral he discounts his bid because if he wins, on average his estimate will be greater than the value.

13.4 Reserve Prices and the Marginal Revenue Approach

A **reserve price** p^* is a bid put in by the seller, secretly or openly, before the auction begins, which commits him not to sell the object if nobody bids more than p^*. The seller will often find that a reserve price can increase his payoff. If he does, it turns out that he will choose a reserve price strictly greater than his own value: $p^* > v_s$. To see this, we will use the **marginal revenue approach** to auctions, an approach developed in Bulow & Roberts (1989) for risk-neutral private values, and Bulow & Klemperer (1996) for common values and risk aversion. This approach compares the seller in an auction to an ordinary monopolist who sells using a posted price. We start with an auction to just one bidder, then extend the idea to an auction with multiple bidders, and finally return to the surprising similarity between an auction with one bidder and a monopoly selling to a continuum of bidders using a posted price.

1 One bidder. If there is just one bidder, the seller will do badly in any of the auction rules we have discussed so far. The single bidder would bid $p_1 = 0$ and win.

The situation is really better suited to bargaining or simple monopoly than to an auction. The seller could use an auction, but a standard auction yields him zero revenue, so posting a price offer to the bidder makes more sense. If the auction has a reserve price, however, it can be equivalent to posting a price, just as in bargaining the making of a single take-it-or-leave-it offer of p^* is equivalent to posting a price.

What should the offer p^* be? Let the bidder have value distribution $F(v)$ on $[\underline{v}, \bar{v}]$ which is differentiable and strictly increasing, so the density $f(v)$ is always positive. Let the seller value the object at $v_s \geq \underline{v}$. The seller's payoff is

$$\pi(p^*) = Pr(p^* < v)(p^* - v_s) + Pr(p^* > v)(0),$$
$$= [1 - F(p^*)](p^* - v_s). \tag{13.53}$$

This has first-order condition

$$\frac{d\pi(p^*)}{dp^*} = [1 - F(p^*)] - f(p^*)[p^* - v_s] = 0. \tag{13.54}$$

On solving (13.54) for p^* we get

$$p^* = v_s + \left(\frac{1 - F(p^*)}{f(p^*)}\right). \tag{13.55}$$

The optimal take-it-or-leave-it offer, the "reserve price" p^* satisfies equation (13.55). The reserve price is strictly greater than the seller's value for the object ($p^* > v_s$) unless the solution is such that $F(p^*) = 1$ because the optimal reserve price is the greatest possible bidder value, in which case the object has probability zero of being sold. One reason to use a reserve price is so the seller does not sell an object for a price worth less than its value to him, but that is not all that is going on.[4]

---

[4] The second-order condition for the problem is $d^2\pi(p^*)/dp*^2 = -2f(p^*) + f'(p^*)[p^* - v_s] \leq 0$. This might well be false, and in any case several values of p^* might satisfy equation (13.55) so it is only a necessary condition, not a sufficient one. Another way to see that $p^* > v_s$ is to observe that $d\pi(p^* = v_s)/dp^* = [1 - F(v_s) - f(v_s)][v_s - v_s] > 0$, so p^* should be increased beyond v_s.

2 Multiple bidders. Now let there be n bidders, all with values distributed independently by $F(v)$. Denote the bidders with the highest and second-highest values as bidders 1 and 2. The seller's payoff in a second-price auction is

$$\pi(p^*) = Pr(p^* > v_1)(0) + Pr(v_2 < p^* < v_1)(p^* - v_s) + Pr(p^* < Ev_2 < v_1)(v_2 - v_s),$$

$$= \int_{v_1=\underline{v}}^{p^*} f(v_1)(0)dv_1 + \int_{v_1=p^*}^{\bar{v}} \left(\int_{v_2=\underline{v}}^{p^*} (p^* - v_s)f(v_2)dv_2 \right.$$

$$\left. + \int_{v_2=p^*}^{v_1} (v_2 - v_s)f(v_2)dv_2 \right) f(v_1)dv_1. \qquad (13.56)$$

This expression integrates over two random variables. First, it matters whether v_1 is greater than or less than p^*, the outer integrals. Second, it matters whether v_2 is less than p^* or not, the inner integrals.

Now differentiate equation (13.56) to find the optimal reserve price p^* using Leibniz's integral rule (given in the mathematical appendix):

$$\frac{d\pi(p^*)}{dp^*} = 0 + -f(p^*)\left(\int_{v_2=\underline{v}}^{p^*} (p^* - v_s)f(v_2)dv_2 + \int_{v_2=p^*}^{p^*} (v_2 - v_s)f(v_2)dv_2 \right)$$

$$+ \int_{v_1=p^*}^{\bar{v}} \left((p^* - v_s)f(p^*) - (p^* - v_s)f(p^*) + \int_{v_2=\underline{v}}^{p^*} f(v_2)dv_2 \right) f(v_1)dv_1,$$

$$= -f(p^*)\left(\int_{v_2=\underline{v}}^{p^*} (p^* - v_s)f(v_2)dv_2 + 0 \right) + \int_{v_1=p^*}^{\bar{v}} \left(\int_{v_2=\underline{v}}^{p^*} f(v_2)dv_2 \right) f(v_1)dv_1,$$

$$= -f(p^*)F(p^*)(p^* - v_s) + (1 - F(p^*))F(p^*) = 0. \qquad (13.57)$$

Dividing by F, the last line of expression (13.57) implies that

$$p^* = v_s + \frac{1 - F(p^*)}{f(p^*)}, \qquad (13.58)$$

just what we found in equation (13.55) for the one-bidder case. Remarkably, the optimal reserve price is unchanged! Moreover, equation (13.58) applies to any number of bidders, not just $n = 2$. Only bidders 1 and 2 show up in the equations we used in the derivation, but that is because they are the only ones to affect the result in a second-price auction.

In fact, only the highest-valuing bidder matters to the optimal reserve price. The reserve price only affects the winning price if the second-highest-valuing bidder happens to have a rather low value. Conditioning on that, Bidder 1 would bid low if there were no reserve price – it is almost as if he faced no competition. But the seller, conditioning on that value being low, would want to set a reserve price so that Bidder 1 must pay more. Since the reserve price only matters if all but one of the bidders have low values, it does not matter whether "all but one" is 99 or 0. Conditioning on all but one bidder having low values, the seller is conditioning on the game having only one bidder who matters.

3 A continuum of bidders: the marginal revenue interpretation. Now think of a firm with a constant marginal cost of c facing a continuum of bidders along the same distribution

$F(v)$ that we have been using. The quantity of bidders with values above p will be $(1-F(p))$, so the demand equation is

$$q(p) = 1 - F(p) \tag{13.59}$$

and

$$Revenue \equiv pq = p(1 - F(p)). \tag{13.60}$$

The marginal revenue is then (keeping in mind that $dq/dp = -f(p)$)

$$\begin{aligned}
Marginal\ Revenue \equiv \frac{dR}{dq} &= p + \left(\frac{dp}{dq}\right)q, \\
&= p + \left(\frac{1}{dq/dp}\right)q, \\
&= p + \left(\frac{1}{-f(p)}\right)(1 - F(p)), \\
&= p - \frac{1 - F(p)}{f(p)}. \tag{13.61}
\end{aligned}$$

Setting marginal revenue to marginal cost, the profit-maximizing monopoly price is the one at which the marginal revenue in (13.61) equals c.

Does equation (13.61) look familiar?[5] Equating (13.61) to marginal cost, thinking of marginal cost as v_s, the seller's opportunity cost, and moving p to the left-hand side yields the optimal price equation we found for one bidder in equation (13.55). That is because the mathematics of the problem is identical whether the seller is facing a continuum of bidders on distribution $F(v)$ or one bidder drawn randomly from the continuum $F(v)$. The problem is just like that in a take-it-or-leave-it-offer bargaining model where the bidder's type is unknown to the seller. In all three situations – the continuum of bidders, the auction to one seller with a reserve price, and the single offer to a single bidder, the seller is in effect using the basic monopoly pricing rule of setting quantity so that marginal revenue equals marginal cost. The difference is in interpretation. In the auction and bargaining contexts, the marginal change in the number of units of quantity becomes the marginal change in the probability of selling one unit. The seller is still picking quantity, but he is picking it in the interval $[0, 1]$ instead of $[0, \infty]$ when he is selling just one unit to one bidder. To increase that probability, and thus the expected number of units sold, the seller must reduce his price, just as an ordinary monopolist must reduce his price to increase the number of units he sells.

Figure 13.3a shows this. In the auction context, c could represent the seller's production cost, or it could be any other kind of opportunity cost that creates the minimum price at which the seller would part with the good, v_{seller}. The auction seller should act like a monopolist with constant marginal cost of v_{seller} (constant because he is producing just one unit), facing the demand curve based on $f(v)$, which means he should set a reserve price for the quantity where marginal revenue equals marginal cost.

---

[5] As with monopoly in general, it might happen here that marginal revenue equals marginal cost at more than one quantity. The $MR = MC$ rule is only a necessary condition, not a sufficient one, for profit maximization.

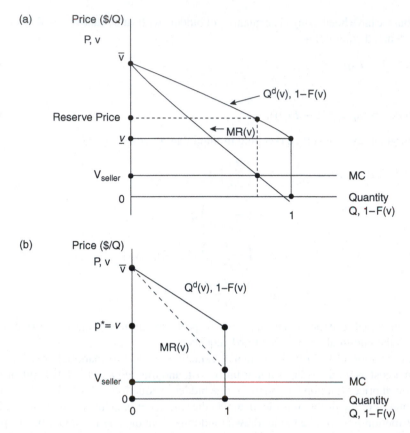

Figure 13.3 Auctions and marginal revenue: (a) reserve price needed and (b) no reserve price needed.

The optimal reserve price will always be positive. In figure 13.3a, even if v_s were zero instead of positive, the curves are such that the reserve price should be positive, even though the probability of making a sale would then equal one. This corresponds to the idea that a monopolist will always raise the price above marginal cost, even though in certain situations (such as the curves in figure 13.3b) he will not reduce output below the competitive level and a reserve price is redundant.

If output is reduced below the competitive level, the outcome is inefficient, something true both in conventional monopoly and here. Here, output is inefficiently low if no sale takes place of the one unit even though $v > v_s$ for some bidder. In that case, what the seller has done is to inefficiently reduce the expected output to below the one unit he has available, resulting in an expected welfare loss equal to the area of a triangle, just as in conventional monopoly.

Unlike in a conventional monopoly, there is a possibility of inefficient "overproduction" in an auction. That happens if the sale takes place even though no bidder values the good as much as the seller: $v < v_s$ for the winning bidder. A positive reserve price, therefore, can help efficiency rather than hurt it. All the five auction forms – first price, second price, descending, ascending, and all pay – can be efficient in a private-value setting, but only if the reserve price is set not at the profit-maximizing level but at $p^* = v_s$. We have also shown, however, that without a reserve price greater than v_s, none of the five auction rules is optimal for the seller. With the addition of an optimal reserve price, though, it can be shown (though we will not do so here) that in simple settings the seller need use no more complicated auction rules than one of the five we have studied.

In more complicated settings, of course, things do get more complicated, and there is the possibility of inefficiency not just because the object is not sold at all, but because it might be sold to the "wrong" bidder (i.e., not to the bidder who values it most). I have already mentioned that this can happen in asymmetric auctions, where the bidders have values drawn from different distributions instead of just one $F(v)$. It could happen that for two bidders, $(1 - F_1(v)/f_1(v)) > (1 - F_2(v)/f_2(v))$, in which case our rule for setting p^* becomes ambiguous. Which bidder's F function should we use? In such cases, the seller does best if he biases the auction rules in favor of bidder 2, who will then sometimes win even if $v_2 < v_1$. A similar problem can arise if F is an unusual distribution for which higher v does not imply that $(v - 1 - F(v)/f(v))$ is higher. For more on the intricacies of such situations, see Myerson (1981) or Bulow & Roberts (1989).

Hindering Bidder Collusion

The choice of auction rule can matter for another reason which comes to mind now that we have been discussing the seller as monopolist: the bidders may act as a monopsonist by colluding. If the bidders can cooperate as if they were one bidder, we are in the situation just described of an auction to one bidder, where use of a reserve price is critical and where the information-eliciting benefit of an auction to the seller evaporates. If the bidders try to collude but remain selfish, however, the choice of an auction rule can make the difference between successful collusion and failure for them. Some auction rules are more vulnerable to collusion than others.

Robinson (1985) has pointed out that whether the auction is private value or common value, the first-price auction is superior to the second-price or ascending auctions for deterring collusion among bidders. (See, too, Graham & Marshall [1987].) Consider a bidder's cartel in which bidder Smith has a private value of 20, the other bidders' values are each 18, and they agree that everybody will bid 5 except Smith, who will bid 6. (We will not consider the rationality of this choice of bids, which might be based on avoiding legal penalties.) In an ascending auction this is self-enforcing, because if somebody cheats and bids 7, Smith is willing to go all the way up to 20 and the cheater will end up with no gain from his deviation. Enforcement is also easy in a second-price auction, because the cartel agreement can be that Smith bids 20 and everyone else bids 6, and if anyone cheats and bids higher than 6 he still loses unless he bids 20 or more.

Unlike in an ascending or second-price auction, however, in a first-price auction the bidders have a strong temptation to cheat. The bid p' that the colluders would choose for Smith would be lower than $p' = 20$, since he would have to pay his bid, but if p' is anything less than the other bidders' value of 18 any one of them could gain by deviating to bid more than p' and win.

Thus, the seller should use a first-price auction if he fears collusion. Even then, cheating will be a problem if the game is repeated, and where collusive "bidding rings" are most often found is in markets where the same bidders meet over and over in auctions for similar objects. Thus, antique auctions are notorious for collusion among bidders who are professional antique dealers (and thus are "regulars" at the auctions and meet repeatedly). A similar problem arises when the same highway contractors repeatedly compete with each other in bidding for who will carry out a government job at the lowest cost. An example described in the book by Sultan (1974), is the Electric Conspiracy of the 1950's, in which antitrust authorities found and prosecuted collusion among executives in a few large companies bidding for electrical generating equipment contracts.

13.5   Common-value Auctions and the Winner's Curse

In section 13.1 we distinguished private-value auctions from common-value auctions, in which the bidders all have the same value for the object but their value estimates may differ. All five sets of rules discussed there can be used for common-value auctions, but the optimal strategies change. In common-value auctions, each bidder can extract useful information about the object's value to himself from the bids of the other bidders. Surprisingly enough, a bidder can use the information from other bidders' bids even in a sealed-bid auction, as will be explained below.

A common-value auction in which all the bidders knew the value would not be very interesting – or very different from a private-value auction – but more commonly the bidders must estimate the common value. The obvious strategy, especially following our discussion of private-value auctions, is for a risk-neutral bidder to bid up to his unbiased estimate of the value. But this strategy makes the winner's payoff negative, because the winner is the bidder who has made the largest positive error in his estimate. The bidders who underestimated the number of pennies lose the auction, but their payoff equals zero, which they would receive even if the true value were common knowledge. Only the winner suffers from his estimation error: he has stumbled into the **Winner's Curse**, a phenomenon first described in Rothkopf (1969) and Wilson (1969).

When some bidders are better informed than others, the Winner's Curse becomes even more severe. Naturally if a bidder knows that he is the worst informed, he should be cautious. Anyone, for example, who outbids 50 experts on the value of an object to win an auction should worry about why all the experts bid less. But the presence of the poorly informed bidder also increases the danger for the experts. Any experts who wins not just against 49 equally well-informed experts but also against a naive bidder who might well have made a large overestimation error and bid too high should worry too.

Once bidders recognize the possibility of the Winner's Curse and adjust their bidding strategies, the winner will no longer have to regret his victory. Having adjusted by scaling down their bids to be lower than their unbiased estimates, the winner may still be the bidder with the biggest overestimation error, but the winning bid can still be less than the true value. Thus, the problem is to decide how much less than one's value estimate to bid.

The mental process is a little like deciding how much to bid in a private-value, first-price auction. There, a bidder wants to bid less than his value, but he also wants to win if he can do so cheaply enough. He therefore tries to estimate the value of the second-highest bid conditional upon himself having the highest value and winning. In a common-value auction a bidder's first step is to use similar mathematics, but to estimate his own value conditional upon winning the auction, not the second-highest value.

One way to think about a bidder's conditional estimate is to think about it as a conditional bid. The bidder knows that if he wins using his unbiased estimate, he probably bid too high, so after winning with such a bid he would like to retract it. Instead, he would like to submit a bid of [X *if I lose, but* ($X - Y$) *if I win*], where X is his value estimate conditional on losing and ($X - Y$) is his estimate conditional on winning – a lower estimate, since winning implies his overestimation error was the biggest of anybody's. If he still won with a bid of ($X - Y$) he would be happy. If he lost, he would be relieved. But Smith can achieve the same effect by simply submitting the bid ($X - Y$) in the first place, since when he loses, the size of his bid is irrelevant.

Another way to look at the Winner's Curse is based on the Milgrom definition of "bad news" (Milgrom [1981b], appendix b). Suppose the government is auctioning off the mineral rights to a plot of land with common value v and that Bidder i has value estimate $\hat{v}_i$. Suppose also that the bidders are identical in everything but their value estimates, which are based on the various information sets Nature has assigned them, and that the equilibrium is symmetric, so the equilibrium bid function $p(\hat{v}_i)$ is the same for each bidder. If Bidder 1 wins with a bid $p(\hat{v}_1)$ that is based on his prior value estimate $\hat{v}_1$, his posterior value estimate $\tilde{v}_1$ is

$$\tilde{v}_1 = E(V|\hat{v}_1, p(\hat{v}_2) < p(\hat{v}_1), \ldots, p(\hat{v}_n) < p(\hat{v}_1)). \tag{13.62}$$

The news that $p(\hat{v}_2) < \infty$ would be neither good nor bad, since it conveys no information. The information that $p(\hat{v}_2) < p(\hat{v}_1)$, however, is bad news, since it rules out values of p more likely to be produced by large values of $\hat{v}_2$. In fact, the lower the winning value of $p(\hat{v}_1)$, the worse is the news of having won. Hence,

$$\tilde{v}_1 < E(V|\hat{v}_1) = \hat{v}_1, \tag{13.63}$$

and if Bidder 1 had bid $p(\hat{v}_1) = \hat{v}_1$ he would immediately regret having won. If his winning bid were enough below $\hat{v}_1$, however, he would be pleased to win.

Deciding how much to scale down the bid is a hard problem because the amount depends on how much all the other bidders scale down. In a second-price auction a bidder calculates the value of $\tilde{v}_1$ using equation (13.62), but that equation hides considerable complexity under the disguise of the term $p(\hat{v}_2)$, which is itself calculated as a function of $p(\hat{v}_1)$ using an equation like (13.62).

Oil Tracts and the Winner's Curse

The best known example of the Winner's Curse is from bidding for offshore oil tracts. Offshore drilling can be unprofitable even if oil is discovered, because something must be paid to the government for the mineral rights. Physicists Capen, Clapp, & Campbell suggested in a 1971 paper in the *Journal of Petroleum Engineering* that bidders' ignorance of what they termed "the Winner's Curse" caused overbidding in US government auctions of the 1960s. If the oil companies had bid close to what their engineers estimated the tracts were worth, rather than scaling down their bids, the winning companies would have lost on their investments. The hundredfold difference in the sizes of the bids in the sealed-bid auctions shown in table 13.1 lends some plausibility to the view that this is what happened.

Later studies such as Mead, Moseidjord, & Sorason (1984) that actually looked at profitability concluded that the rates of return from offshore drilling were not abnormally low,

Table 13.1   Bids by serious competitors in oil auctions

Offshore Louisiana 1967 Tract SS 207	Santa Barbara Channel 1968 Tract 375	Offshore Texas 1968 Tract 506	Alaska North Slope 1969 Tract 253
32.5	43.5	43.5	10.5
17.7	32.1	15.5	5.2
11.1	18.1	11.6	2.1
7.1	10.2	8.5	1.4
5.6	6.3	8.1	0.5
4.1		5.6	0.4
3.3		4.7	
		2.8	
		2.6	
		0.7	
		0.7	
		0.4	

so perhaps the oil companies did scale down their bids rationally. The spread in bids is surprisingly wide, but that does not mean that the bidders did not properly scale down their estimates. Although expected profits are zero under optimal bidding, realized profits could be either positive or negative. With some probability, one bidder makes a large overestimate which results in too high a bid even after rationally adjusting for the Winner's Curse. The knowledge of how to bid optimally does not eliminate bad luck; it only mitigates its effects.

Another consideration is the rationality of the other bidders. If bidder Apex has figured out the Winner's Curse, but bidders Brydox and Central have not, what should Apex do? Its rivals will overbid, which affects Apex's best response. Apex should scale down its bid even further than usual, because the Winner's Curse is intensified against overoptimistic rivals. If Apex wins against a rival who usually overbids, Apex has very likely overestimated the value.

Risk aversion affects bidding in a surprisingly similar way. If all the bidders are equally risk-averse, the bids would be lower, because the asset is a gamble, whose value is lower for the risk-averse. If Smith is more risk-averse than Brown, then Smith should be more cautious for two reasons. The direct reason is that the gamble is worth less to Smith – the reason analyzed above in the private-value setting. The indirect reason is that when Smith wins against a rival like Brown who regularly bids more, Smith probably overestimated the value. Parallel reasoning holds if the bidders are risk neutral, but the private value of the object differs among them.

In fact, Capen, Clapp, & Campbell all worked for the oil company Arco, and developed a bidding strategy for oil leases that took into account the Winner's Curse. Company executives realized that they were bidding too high, but were not clear about whether the solution was to reduce the geological estimates, raise the discount rate, or something else, before the three worked out their strategy. There was debate within the company as to whether to make the idea of the Winner's Curse public. The idea was a private advantage for Arco – but other oil company's ignorance of it meant that they were bidding too high, which may have hurt them most, but hurt Arco too. After some years, the company decided to let them reveal the secret. (See "The Tale of the 'Winner's Curse'" at http://www.aapg.org/explorer/2004/12dec/capen.cfm.)

The Winner's Curse crops up in situations seemingly far removed from auctions. An employer should beware of hiring a worker passed over by other employers. Someone renting an apartment should worry that he is the first potential renter who arrived when the neighboring trumpeter was asleep. A firm considering a new project should be concerned that the project has been considered and rejected by competitors. The Winner's Curse can even be applied to political theory; certain proposals for innovations keep reappearing in the political arena over time. Will the first electorate to adopt them fall prey to the Winner's Curse?

On the other hand, if information is revealed in the course of an auction, the fact that values are common can lead to higher bidding, not lower. "Getting carried away" may be a rational feature of a common-value auction. Suppose that the setting is not pure common value, but a mix of a common value and private values. If a bidder has a high private value and then learns in the course of the bidding that the common value is larger than he thought, he may well end up bidding more than he had planned and winning, but he would not regret it afterwards. Especially in these mixed situations, when bidders have different private values and when some but not all of each bidder's information is revealed by his bidding, common-value auctions can become very complicated indeed.

Strategies in Common-value Auctions

Milgrom & Weber (1982) found that when there is a common-value element in an auction and signals are "affiliated" then revenue equivalence fails. The first-price and descending auctions are still identical, but they raise less revenue than the ascending or second-price auctions. If there are more than two bidders, the ascending auction raises more revenue than the second-price auction. (In fact, if signals are affiliated then even in a private-value auction, in which each bidder knows his own value with certainty, the first-price and descending auctions will do worse.)

We will not prove the ranking of revenues by auction generally, but we will go through an example with estimation errors that are uniformly distributed. This example will be tractable because of some special properties of optimal estimates when errors are uniformly distributed, so let us start with discussion of those properties.

Suppose n signals are independently drawn from the uniform distribution on $[\underline{s}, \bar{s}]$. Denote the jth highest signal by $s_{(j)}$. The expectation of the kth highest value happens to be

$$Es_{(k)} = \underline{s} + \left(\frac{n+1-k}{n+1}\right)(\bar{s} - \underline{s}).\tag{13.64}$$

This means the expectation of the very highest value is

$$Es_{(1)} = \underline{s} + \left(\frac{n}{n+1}\right)(\bar{s} - \underline{s}).\tag{13.65}$$

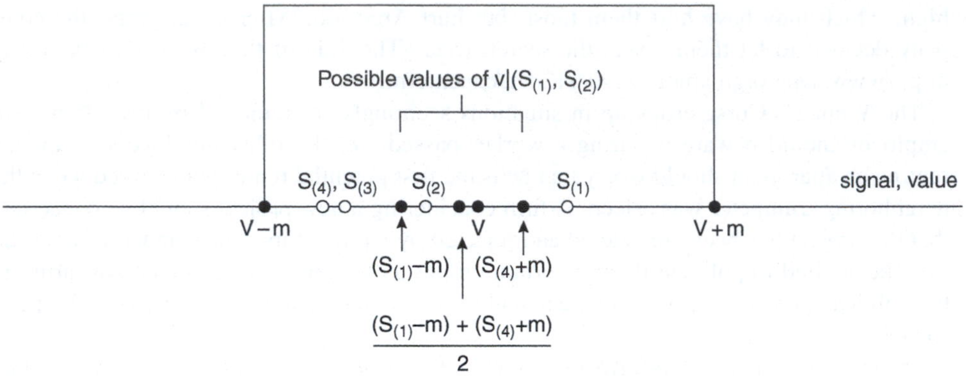

Figure 13.4   Extracting information from uniformly distributed signals.

The expectation of the second-highest value is

$$Es_{(2)} = \underline{s} + \left(\frac{n-1}{n+1}\right)(\bar{s} - \underline{s}). \tag{13.66}$$

The expectation of the lowest value, the n'th highest, is

$$Es_{(n)} = \underline{s} + \left(\frac{1}{n+1}\right)(\bar{s} - \underline{s}). \tag{13.67}$$

Let n risk-neutral bidders, $i = 1, 2, \ldots, n$ each receive a signal s_i independently drawn from the uniform distribution on $[v - m, v + m]$, where v is the true value of the object to each of them. Assume that they have "diffuse priors" on v, which means they think any values from $v = -\infty$ to $v = \infty$ are equally likely. The best estimate of the value given the set of n signals is

$$Ev|(s_1, s_2, \ldots, s_n) = \frac{s_{(n)} + s_{(1)}}{2}. \tag{13.68}$$

The estimate depends only on two out of the n signals – a remarkable property of the uniform distribution. If there were five signals $\{6, 7, 7, 16, 24\}$, the expected value of the object would be 15 ($=[6 + 24]/2$), well above the mean of 12 and the median of 7, because only the extremes of 6 and 24 are useful information. A density that had a peak, like the normal density, would yield a different result, but here all we can tell from the data is that all values of v between $(6 + m)$ and $(24 - m)$ are equally probable.

Figure 13.4 illustrates why this is true. Someone who saw just signals $s_{(4)}$ and $s_{(1)}$ could deduce that v could not be less than $(s_{(1)} - m)$ or greater than $(s_{(4)} + m)$. Learning the signals in between – would be unhelpful, because the only information that, for example, $s_{(2)}$ conveys is that $v \leq (s_{(2)} + m)$ and $v \geq (s_{(2)} - m)$, facts which our observer had already figured out from $s_{(4)}$ and $s_{(1)}$.

Now let us go to the game itself, which is based on the introductory chapter of Paul Klemperer's (2000) book.

The Uniform-signal Common-value Auction

PLAYERS
One seller and n bidders.

ORDER OF PLAY
0   Nature chooses the common value for the object v using the uniform density on $[-\infty, \infty]$ (the limit of $[-x, x]$ as x goes to infinity), and sends signal s_i to Bidder i using the uniform distribution on $[v - m, v + m]$.
1   The seller chooses a mechanism that allocated the object and payments based on each player's choice of p. He also chooses the procedure in which bidders select p (sequentially, simultaneously, etc.).
2   Each bidder simultaneously chooses to participate in the auction or to stay out.
3   The bidders and the seller choose value of p according to the mechanism procedure.
4   The object is allocated and transfers are paid according to the mechanism.

PAYOFFS
Payoff depends on the particular rules, but if the object is sold, the payoff to the seller is the sum of all the payments and the value to a bidder is the value of the object, if he wins, minus his payments.

What are the strategies in symmetric equilibria for the different auction rules? (We will ignore possible asymmetric equilibria.)

The Ascending Auction (Open Exit)

Equilibrium
If no bidder has quit yet, Bidder i should drop out when the price rises to s_i. Otherwise, he should drop out when the price rises to $p_i = p_{(n)} + s_i/2$, where $p_{(n)}$ is the price at which the first dropout occurred.

Explanation
If no other bidder has quit yet, Bidder i is safe in agreeing to pay his signal, s_i. Either (1) he has the lowest signal, or (2) everybody else has the same signal value s_i too, and they will all drop out at the same time. In case (1), having the lowest signal, he will lose anyway. In case (2), the best estimate of the value is s_i, and that is where he should drop out.

Once one bidder has dropped out at $p_{(n)}$, the other bidders can deduce that he had the lowest signal, so they know that signal $s_{(n)}$ must equal $p_{(n)}$. Suppose Bidder i has signal $s_i > s_{(n)}$. Either (1) someone else has a higher signal and Bidder i will lose the auction anyway and dropping out too early does not matter, or (2) everybody else who has not yet dropped out has signal s_i too, and they will all drop out at the same time, or (3) he would be the last to drop out, so he will win. In cases (2) and (3), his estimate of the value is $p_{(i)} = p_{(n)} + s_i/2$, since $p_{(n)}$ and s_i are the extreme signal values and the signals are uniformly distributed, and that is where he should drop out.

The price paid by the winner will be the price at which the second-highest bidder drops out, which is $s_{(n)} + s_{(2)}/2$. The expected values are, from equations (13.66) and (13.67),

$$Es_{(n)} = (v - m) + \left(\frac{n + 1 - n}{n + 1}\right)((v + m) - (v - m)),$$

$$= v + \left(\frac{1 - n}{n + 1}\right)m \tag{13.69}$$

and

$$Es_{(2)} = (v - m) + \left(\frac{n + 1 - 2}{n + 1}\right)((v + m) - (v - m)),$$

$$= v + \left(\frac{n - 3}{n + 1}\right)m. \tag{13.70}$$

Averaging them yields the expected winning price,

$$Ep_{(2)} = \frac{[v + (1 - n/n + 1)m] + [v + (n - 3/n + 1)m]}{2},$$

$$= v - \left(\frac{1}{2}\right)\left(\frac{1}{n + 1}\right)2m. \tag{13.71}$$

If $m = 50$ and $n = 4$, then

$$Ep_{(2)} = v - \left(\frac{1}{10}\right)(100) = v - 10. \tag{13.72}$$

Expected seller revenue increases in n, the number of bidders (and thus of independent signals) and falls in the uncertainty m (the inaccuracy of the signals). This will be true for all three auction rules we examine here.

It is not always true that the bidders can deduce the lowest signal in an ascending auction and use that to form their bid. Their ability to discover $s_{(n)}$ depended crucially on the open-exit feature of the auction – that the player with the lowest signal had to openly drop out, rather than lurk quietly in the background. A secret-exit ascending auction would behave like a second-price auction instead.

The Second-price Auction

Equilibrium
Bid $p_i = s_i - (n - 2/n)m$.

Explanation

In forming his strategy, Bidder i should think of himself as being tied for winner with one other bidder, and so having to pay exactly his bid. If he is tied (but not otherwise), his precise bid affects his payoff. Thus, he imagines himself as the highest of $(n-1)$ bidders drawn from $[v-m, v+m]$ and tied with one other. On average, if this happens,

$$s_i = (v-m) + \left(\frac{([n-1]+1-1)}{[n-1]+1} \right) ([v+m]-[v-m]),$$

$$= (v-m) + \left(\frac{n-1}{n} \right) (2m),$$

$$= v + \left(\frac{n-2}{n} \right) (m). \tag{13.73}$$

He will bid the value v which solves equation (13.73), yielding the optimal strategy, $p_i = s_i - (n-2/n)(m)$.

On average, the second-highest bidder actually has the signal $Es_{(2)} = v+(n-3/n+1)m$, from equation (13.70). So the expected price, and hence the expected revenue from the auction, is

$$Ep_{(2)} = \left[v + \left(\frac{n-3}{n+1} \right) m \right] - \left(\frac{n-2}{n} \right) (m),$$

$$= v + \left(\frac{n(n-3) - (n+1)(n-2)}{(n+1)n} \right) m,$$

$$= v - \left(\frac{n-1}{n} \right) \left(\frac{1}{n+1} \right) 2m. \tag{13.74}$$

If $m = 50$ and $n = 4$, then

$$Ep_{(2)} = v - \left(\frac{3}{4} \right) \left(\frac{1}{5} \right) (100) = v - 15. \tag{13.75}$$

If there are at least three bidders, expected revenue is lower in the second-price auction. (We found revenue of $(v-10)$ with $n=4$ in the ascending auction.) If $n=2$, however, the expected price is the same in the second-price and ascending auctions. Then, $v_{(n)} = v_{(2)}$, so the winning price is based on the same information in both auctions.

The First-price Auction

Equilibrium
Bid $(s_i - m)$.

Explanation

This is the simplest strategy of the three, but the hardest to derive. Bidder i bids $(s_i - z)$ for some amount z that does not depend on his signal, because given the assumption of diffuse priors, he does not know whether his signal is a high one or a low one. Define T_i to be how far the signal s_i is above its minimum possible value, $(v - m)$, so

$$T_i \equiv s_i - (v - m), \tag{13.76}$$

and $s_i \equiv v - m + T_i$. Bidder i has the highest signal and wins the auction if T_i is big enough, which has probability $(T_i/2m)^{n-1}$, which we will define as $G(T_i)$, because it is the probability that the $(n-1)$ other signals are all less than $s_i = v - m + T_i$. He earns v minus his bid of $(s_i - z)$ if he wins, which equals $(z + m - T_i)$.

If, instead, Bidder i deviated and bid a small amount ϵ higher, he would win with a higher probability, $G(T_i + \epsilon)$, but he would lose ϵ whenever he would have won with the lower bid. Using a Taylor expansion, $G(T_i + \epsilon) \approx G(T_i) + G'(T_i)\epsilon$, so

$$G(T_i + \epsilon) - G(T_i) \approx (n-1)T_i^{n-2} \left(\frac{1}{2m} \right)^{n-1} \epsilon. \tag{13.77}$$

The benefit from bidding higher is the higher probability, $[G(T_i + \epsilon) - G(T_i)]$ times the winning surplus $(z + m - T_i)$. The loss from bidding higher is that the bidder would pay an additional ϵ in the $(T_i/2m)^{n-1}$ cases in which he would have won anyway. In equilibrium, he is indifferent about this infinitesimal deviation, taking the expectation across all possible values of his "signal height" T_i, so

$$\int_{T_i=0}^{2m} \left[\left((n-1)T_i^{n-2} \left(\frac{1}{2m} \right)^{n-1} \epsilon \right)(z + m - T_i) - \epsilon \left(\frac{T_i}{2m} \right)^{n-1} \right] \left[\frac{1}{2m} \right] dT_i = 0. \tag{13.78}$$

This implies that

$$\epsilon \left(\frac{1}{2m} \right)^n \int_{T_i=0}^{2m} [((n-1)T_i^{n-2})(z + m) - (n-1)T_i^{n-1} - T_i^{n-1}] dT_i = 0, \tag{13.79}$$

which in turn implies that

$$\left|_{T_i=0}^{2m} (T_i^{n-1}(z + m) - T_i^n) = 0, \tag{13.80}$$

so $(2m)^{n-1}(z + m) - (2m)^n - 0 + 0 = 0$ and $z = m$. Bidder i's optimal strategy in the symmetric equilibrium is to bid $p_i = s_i - m$.

The winning bid is set by the bidder with the highest signal, and that highest signal's expected value is

$$Es_{(1)} = \underline{s} + \left(\frac{n+1-1}{n+1}\right)(\bar{s} - \underline{s}),$$

$$= v - m + \left(\frac{n}{n+1}\right)((v+m) - (v-m)),$$

$$= v - m + \left(\frac{n}{n+1}\right)(2m). \tag{13.81}$$

The expected revenue is therefore

$$Ep_{(1)} = v - (1)\left(\frac{1}{n+1}\right)2m. \tag{13.82}$$

If $m = 50$ and $n = 4$, then

$$Ep_{(1)} = v - \left(\frac{1}{5}\right)(100) = v - 20. \tag{13.83}$$

Here, the revenue is even lower than in the second-price auction, where it was $(v - 15)$ (and the revenue is lower even if $n = 2$).

The revenue ranking is thus that the ascending open-exit auction has the highest expected revenue for the seller, the second-price auction is in the middle, and the first-price auction is lowest. The revenue depends on how intensely bidders compete up the price under each auction rule, which in turn depends on how much of an informational advantage the highest-signal bidder has. In the ascending auction, all the bidders come to know $s_{(n)}$, and the winning price and who wins depends on $s_{(2)}$ and $s_{(1)}$, so the bidder with the highest signal has a relatively small advantage. In the second-price auction, the winning price and who wins depends on $s_{(2)}$ and $s_{(1)}$, and that information comes to be known only to those two bidders. In the first-price auction, the winning price and who wins depend only on $s_{(1)}$, so the bidder with the highest signal has the only relevant information. Thus, his informational rent is greatest under that auction rule. Paradoxically, the bidders prefer an auction rule which makes it harder for them to pool their information and accurately estimate v. Or perhaps this is not paradoxical. What the seller would like best would be for every bidder to truthfully announce his signal publicly, because then every bidder would have the same estimate, that would be the amount each would bid, and the informational rent would fall to zero.

13.6 Asymmetric Equilibria, Affiliation, and Linkage: The Wallet Game

Asymmetric Equilibria in Common-value Auctions

Besides the symmetric equilibria I have been discussing so far, asymmetric equilibria are typical, robust, and plausible in common-value auctions. That is because the severity of the winner's curse facing Bidder i depends on the bidding behavior of the other bidders. If other bidders bid aggressively, then if i wins anyway, he must have a big overestimate of the value of the object. So the more aggressive are the other bidders, the more conservative ought Bidder i to be – which in turn will make the other bidders more aggressive. The Wallet Game of Klemperer (1998) illustrates this.

The Wallet Game

PLAYERS

Smith and Jones.

ORDER OF PLAY

0   Nature chooses the amounts s_1 and s_2 of the money in each player's wallet using density functions $f_1(s_1)$ and $f_2(s_2)$. Each player observes only his own wallet's contents.

1   Each player chooses a bid ceiling p_1 or p_2. An auctioneer auctions off the two wallets by gradually raising the price until either p_1 or p_2 is reached.

PAYOFFS

The player who bids less has a payoff of zero. The winning player pays the bid ceiling of the loser and hence has a payoff of

$$s_1 + s_2 - Min(p_1, p_2) \qquad (13.84)$$

A symmmetric equilibrium is for Bidder i to choose bid ceiling $p_i = 2s_i$. This is an equilibrium because if he wins at exactly that price, Bidder j's signal must be $s_j = s_i$ and the value of the wallets is $2s_i$. If Bidder i bids any lower, he might pass up a chance to buy the wallet for less than its value. If he bids any higher, he would only win if $p > 2s_j$ too, which implies that $p > s_i + s_j$.

This equilibrium clearly illustrates how bidders should base their strategy on the strategy they expect the other bidders to use. Note that Bidder i's strategy is unrelated to his prior beliefs about Bidder j's value. It might be, for example, that using $f_2(s_2)$, the expected value of s_2 is 100, but if Bidder 1's wallet contains $s_1 = 8$, he should just bid 16. So doing, he will probably lose, but if he bids 108 and wins, it will only be because Bidder 2's wallet contains 54 or less. That is fine if it contains 8 or less, but if it contains, for example, $s_2 = 9$, then Bidder 2 will bid up to 18 and stop, Bidder 1 will win with his bid ceiling of 108, and his payoff will be $8 + 9 - 18 = -1$.

The Wallet Game has both independent values and pure common values, a curious combination. The value of the two wallets is the same for both bidders, but the signal each receives is independent. Knowing s_1 is useless in predicting s_2, though it is useful in predicting the common value.

The independence of the signals makes a bidder's optimal strategy particularly sensitive to what he thinks the other bidder's strategy is, since his own signal tells him nothing about the other player's signal and he must rely on the other player's bidding for any information about it. Thus, there are many asymmetric equilibria. One of them is $(p_1 = 10s_1, p_2 = (10/9)s_2)$. If the two players tie, having chosen $p = p_1 = p_2$, then $10s_1 = 10/9s_2$, which implies that $s_1 = 1/9s_2$, so $s_1 + s_2 = 10s_1 = p$, and $v = p$. This is a bad equilibrium for Bidder 2 because he hardly ever wins and when he does win it's because s_1 was very low – so there is hardly any money in Bidder 1's wallet. Being the aggressive bidder in an equilibrium is valuable. If there is a sequence of auctions, this means establishing a reputation for aggressiveness can be worthwhile, as shown in Bikhchandani (1988).

Asymmetric equilibria can even arise when the players are identical. Second-price, two-person, common-value auctions usually have many asymmetric equilibria besides the symmetric equilibrium we have been discussing (see Milgrom [1981c] and Bikhchandani [1988]). Suppose that Smith and Brown have identical payoff functions, but Smith thinks Brown is going to bid aggressively. The winner's curse is intensified for Smith, who would probably have overestimated if he won against an aggressive bidder like Brown, so Smith bids more cautiously. But if Smith bids cautiously, Brown is safe in bidding aggressively, and there is an asymmetric equilibrium. For this reason, acquiring a reputation for aggressiveness is valuable.

Oddly enough, if there are three or more bidders, the second-price, common-value auction has a unique equilibrium, which is also symmetric. The open-exit ascending auction is different: it has asymmetric equilibria, because after one bidder drops out, the two remaining bidders know that they are alone together in a subgame which is a two-bidder auction. Regardless of the number of bidders, first-price auctions do not have this kind of asymmetric equilibrium. Threats in a first-price auction are costly because the high bidder pays his bid even if his rival decides to bid less in response. Thus, a bidder's aggressiveness is not made safer by intimidation of another bidder.

Affiliation, the Monotone Likelihood Ratio Property, and the Linkage Principle[6]

Milgrom & Weber (1982) introduced the idea of **affiliation**: a formal definition of two variables tending to move upwards together that is useful in the auction context. Suppose Bidder 1 has a value v_1 which is a increasing function of a private signal x_1 that he receives, and which might also depend on the private signal of Bidder 2, x_2. What we need to know to analyze the auction is what happens to Bidder 1's estimate of his value as he observes or deduces more about Bidder 2's signal. A simple and plausible situation is that whenever he learns that x_2 takes a large value, his estimate of his value v_1 rises. Thus, if he observes Bidder 2 bid more and he deduces that x_2 is large, he should increase his estimate of v_1. Affiliation is defined so this will happen if the signals x_1 and x_2 are strongly affiliated, and if they are weakly affiliated, Bidder 1's estimate of v_1 at least will not fall as x_2 rises. For simplicity, I will define affiliation for the case of two signals.

---

[6] Much of this discussion is based on Cramton (undated), Klemperer (2004, p. 51), and Wolfstetter (1999).

Definition: The signals x_1 and x_2 are affiliated if for all possible realizations *Small* $<$ *Big* of x_1 and *Low* $<$ *High* of x_2, the joint probability $f(x_1, x_2)$ is such that

$$f(x_1 = Small, x_2 = Low)f(x_1 = Big, x_2 = High)$$
$$\geq f(x_1 = Small, x_2 = High)f(x_1 = Big, x_2 = Low). \tag{13.85}$$

Thus, affiliation says that the probability the values of x_1 and x_2 move in the same direction is greater than the probability they move oppositely. Notice that this allows a joint probability distribution such as the following, in which even if x_2 is *Low*, x_1 is probably *Big*.

$$Prob(x_1 = Big, x_2 = High) = 0.5$$
$$Prob(x_1 = Small, x_2 = Low) = 0.1$$
$$Prob(x_1 = Big, x_2 = Low) = 0.2$$
$$Prob(x_1 = Small, x_2 = High) = 0.2$$

Imagine that Bidder 3, who is ignorant of both x_1 and x_2, can deduce about x_1 if he learns that $x_2 = Low$. Bidder 3's prior is

$$Prob(x_1 = Big) = Prob(x_1 = Big, x_2 = High) + Prob(x_1 = Big, x_2 = Low),$$
$$= 0.5 + 0.2 = 0.7. \tag{13.86}$$

Suppose Bidder 3 finds out that x_2 is *Low*. We will use the same kind of manipulation as in Bayes' rule, though not Bayes' rule itself. Since

$$Prob(x_1 = Big, x_2 = Low) = Prob(x_1 = Bigh | x_2 = Low)Prob(x_2 = Low), \tag{13.87}$$

we can write Bidder 3's posterior as

$$Prob(x_1 = Big | x_2 = Low) = \frac{Prob(x_1 = Big, x_2 = Low)}{Prob(x_2 = Low)},$$
$$= \frac{0.2}{Prob(x_1 = Big, x_2 = Low) + Prob(x_1 = Small, x_2 = Low)},$$
$$= \frac{0.2}{0.2 + 0.1}. \tag{13.88}$$

Thus, observing $x_2 = Low$ leaves Bidder 3 still thinking that probably $x_1 = Big$, but the probability has fallen from 0.7 to 0.66. $x_2 = Low$ is bad news about the value of x_1.

The big implication of two signals being affiliated is that the expected value of the winning bid conditional on the signals is increasing in all the signals. When one signal rises, that has the positive direct effect of increasing the bid of the player who sees it, and nonnegative indirect effects once the other players see his bid increase and deduce that he had a high signal.

This is very much like the Monotone Likelihood Ratio Property, which is the same thing expressed in terms of the conditional densities, the posteriors.

Definition: The conditional probability $g(x_1|x_2)$ satisfies the Monotone Likelihood Ratio Property if the likelihood ratio is weakly decreasing in x_1, that is, for all possible realizations *Small* $<$ *Big* of x_1 and *Low* $<$ *High* of x_2,

$$\frac{g(Big|Low)}{g(Big|High)} \leq \frac{g(Small|Low)}{g(Small|High)}. \tag{13.89}$$

The Monotone Likelihood Ratio Property says that as x_2 goes from *Low* to *High*, the *Big* value of x_1 becomes relatively more likely. It can be shown that this implies that for any value z, the conditional cumulative distribution of x_1 up to $x_1 = z$ given x_2 weakly increases with x_2, which is to say that the distribution $G(x_1|x_2)$ conditional on a larger value of x_2 stochastically dominates the distribution conditional on a smaller value of x_2.

This no doubt leaves the reader's head spinning quite as much as it does the author's, despite my attempt at simplification. A final, equivalent definition of affiliation, applicable when the signals are distributed according to a joint density $f(x_1, x_2)$ that is continuous and twice differentiable is that x_1 and x_2 are affiliated if

$$\frac{\partial log(f)^2}{\partial x_1 \partial x_2} \geq 0. \tag{13.90}$$

One of the rewards of establishing that bidders' signals are affiliated is **the linkage principle**, which says that when the amount of affiliated information available to bidders increases, the equilibrium sales price becomes greater. Thus, the seller should have a policy of disclosing any affiliated information he possesses. Also, auction rules which reveal affiliated information in the course of the auction (e.g., open-exit auctions) or use it in determining the winner's payment (e.g., the second-price auction) will result in higher prices. We saw this in the Uniform-signal Common-value Auction examples. The result is not restricted to common-value auctions, however; seller revenue rises when affiliated information is released even in an affiliated private-value auction, in which the bidders each know their own private values but not those of other bidders. The intuition behind the linkage principle is hard to grasp, because it applies even when there is no winner's curse (as in the affiliated private-value auction), and it does not always apply in common value auctions (when there are just two bidders, the ascending auction is not superior to the second-price auction, as we saw above). The best intuition I have seen is on page 128 of Klemperer (2004): that bidder profits arise from their private information, and release of affiliated information reveals something about the private information of each bidder, including, especially, the one who will win, and thus heightens competition.

The linkage principle provides a reason why sellers may wish to extend auctions over time in multiple rounds, why they should encourage active bidding throughout rather than let bidders "lurk" and suddenly bid near the end, why they should lay out their own information as clearly and early as possible, and why they should let bidders know each others' identities. The idea is a slippery one, however, and Perry & Reny (1999) show that the linkage principle actually can fail if more than one unit of the good is being auctioned, so players submit bids for the possible purchase of multiple units. Multiple-unit auctions and "package auctions," in which not just multiple units but multiple objects are sold in a single auction, are active areas of research.

Notes

N13.1   Values private and common, continuous and discrete

- Milgrom & Weber (1982) is a classic article that covers many aspects of auctions. McAfee & McMillan (1987) is an excellent older survey of auction theory which takes some pains to relate it to models of asymmetric information. More recent is Maskin (2004). Klemperer (2000) collects many of the most important articles in an edited volume. Vijay Krishna's 2002 *Auction Theory*, Paul Klemperer's 2004 *Auctions: Theory and Practice* (which is relatively nontechnical), and Paul Milgrom's 2004 *Putting Auction Theory to Work* (which is very good on the mathematical assumptions) are good textbook treatments. I particularly like the auction chapters in Elmar Wolfstetter's 1999 *Topics in Microeconomics: Industrial Organization, Auctions, and Incentives*. Paul Milgrom's consulting firm, Agora Market Design, has a website with many good working papers that can be found via http://www.market-design.com.
- Cassady (1967) is an excellent source of pre-web institutional detail. The appendix to his book includes advertisements and sets of auction rules, and he cites numerous newspaper articles. The rise of the web, an ideal setting for auctions, fortuitously occurred at the same time as the rise of auction theory. See Bajari & Hortacsu's 2004 survey, "Economic Insights from Internet Auctions."

N13.2   Optimal strategies under different rules in private-value auctions

- Many (all?) leading auction theorists were involved in the seven-billion dollar spectrum auction by the United States government in 1994, either helping the government choose an auction rule to sell spectrum or helping bidders decide how to buy it. Paul Milgrom's 1999 book, *Auction Theory for Privatization*, tells the story. See also McAfee & McMillan (1996). Interesting institutional details have come in the spectrum auctions and stimulated new theoretical research. Ayres & Cramton (1996), for example, explore the possibility that affirmative action provisions designed to help certain groups of bidders may have actually increased the revenue raised by the seller by increasing the amount of competition in the auction.
- One might think that an ascending second-price, open-cry auction would come to the same results as an ascending first-price, open-cry auction, because if the price advances by ϵ at each bid, the first and second bids are practically the same. But the second-price auction can be manipulated. If somebody initially bids $10 for something worth $80, another bidder could safely bid $1,000. No one else would bid more, and he would pay only the second price: $10.
- Auctions are especially suitable for empirical study because they are so stylized and generate masses of data. Hendricks & Porter (1988) is a classic comparison of auction theory with data. See Bajari, Hong, & Ryan (2004) or the Athey & Haile (2005) and Hendricks & Porter (forthcoming) surveys of empirical work on auctions.
- After the last bid of an open-cry art auction in France, the representative of the Louvre has the right to raise his hand and shout "pre-emption de l'etat," after which he takes the painting at the highest price bid (*The Economist*, May 23, 1987, p. 98). How does that affect the equilibrium strategies? What would happen if the Louvre could resell?
- **Share auctions.** In a share auction each bidder submits a bid for both a quantity and a price. The bidder with the highest price receives the quantity for which he bid at that price. If any of the product being auctioned remains, the bidder with the second-highest price takes the quantity he bid for, and so forth. The rules of a share auction can allow each bidder to submit several bids,

often called a **schedule** of bids. The details of share auctions vary, and they can be either first price or second price. Modelling is complicated; see Wilson (1979).

N13.3 Revenue equivalence, risk aversion, and uncertainty

- Che & Gale (1998) point out that if bidders differ in their willingness to pay in a private-value auction because of budget constraints rather than tastes then the revenue equivalence theorem can fail. The following example from page 2 of their paper shows this. Suppose two budget-constrained bidders are bidding for one object. In Auction 1, each bidder has a budget of 2 and knows only his own value, which is drawn uniformly from [0, 1]. The budget constraints are never binding, and it turns out that the expected price is $1/3$ under either a first-price or a second-price auction. In Auction 2, however, each bidder knows only his own budget, which is drawn uniformly from [0, 1], and both have values for the object of 2. The budget constraint is always binding, and the equilibrium strategy is to bid one's entire budget under either set of auction rules. The expected price is still $1/3$ in the second-price auction, but now it is $2/3$ in the first-price auction. The seller therefore prefers to use a first-price auction.
- **A mechanism to extract all the surplus.** Myerson (1981) shows that if the bidders' private information is correlated, the seller can construct something akin to a cross checking mechanism of the kind discussed in Chapter 10 that extracts all the information and all the surplus. In the Uniform-signal Common-value Auction, where signals are uniform in $[v - m, v + m]$ ask Bidder i to bid s_i, allocate the good to the high bidder at the price $s_{(1)} + s_{(n)}/2$, which is an unbiased estimate of v, and ensure truthtelling by the boiling-in-oil punishment of a large negative payment if the reports are such that $s_{(n)} < s_{(1)} - m$, which cannot possibly occur if all bidders tell the truth.

N13.4 Common-value auctions and the Winner's Curse

- Rothkopf (1969) and Wilson (1969) seem to the be first published accounts of the Winner's Curse. An article on Edward Capen, "The Tale of the 'Winner's Curse' " at http://www.aapg.org/explorer/12dec/capen.cfm says that the term was first published in Capen, Clapp, & Campbell (1971). I recommend the article for its tale of the use of theory in business practice.
- The Winner's Curse and the idea of common values versus private values have broad application. The Winner's Curse is related to the idea of "regression to the mean" discussed in section 2.4 of this book. Kaplow & Shavell (1996) use the idea to discuss property versus liability rules, one of the standard rule choices in law-and-economics. If someone violates a property rule, the aggrieved party can undo the violation, as when a thief is required to surrender stolen property. If someone violates a liability rule, the aggrieved party can only get monetary compensation, as when someone who breaches a contract is required to pay damages to the aggrieved party. Kaplow and Shavell argue that if a good has independent values, a liability rule is best because it gives efficient incentives for rule violation; but if it has common value and courts make errors in measuring the common value, a property rule may be better (see especially page 761 of their article).

N13.6 Asymmetric equilibria, affiliation, and linkage: the Wallet Game

- Even if value estimates are correlated, the optimal bidding strategies can still be the same as in private-value auctions if the values are independent. If everyone overestimates their values by ten percent, a bidder can still extract no information about his value by seeing other bidders' value estimates.

Problems

13.1:   Rent seeking (medium)

Two risk-neutral neighbors in sixteenth century England, Smith and Jones, have gone to court and are considering bribing a judge. Each of them makes a gift, and the one whose gift is the largest is awarded property worth £2,000. If both bribe the same amount, the chances are 50 percent for each of them to win the lawsuit. Gifts must be either £0, £900, or £2,000.

(a)   What is the unique pure-strategy equilibrium for this game?
(b)   Suppose that it is also possible to give a £1,500 gift. Why does there no longer exist a pure-strategy equilibrium?
(c)   What is the symmetric mixed-strategy equilibrium for the expanded game? What is the judge's expected payoff?
(d)   In the expanded game, if the losing litigant gets back his gift, what are the two equilibria? Would the judge prefer this rule?

13.2:   The founding of Hong Kong (medium)

The Tai-Pan and Mr. Brock are bidding in an ascending auction for a parcel of land on a knoll in Hong Kong. They must bid integer values, and the Tai-Pan bids first. Tying bids cannot be made, and bids cannot be withdrawn once they are made. The direct value of the land is 1 to Brock and 2 to the Tai-Pan, but the Tai-Pan has said publicly that he wants it, so if Brock gets it, he receives 5 in "face" and the Tai Pan loses 10. Moreover, Brock hates the Tai-Pan and receives 1 in utility for each 1 that the Tai-Pan pays out to get the land.

Table 13.2   The Tai-Pan Game

Winning bid	1	2	3	4	5	6	7	8	9	10	11	12
If Brock wins:												
π_{Brock}												
$\pi_{Tai\text{-}Pan}$												
If Brock loses:												
π_{Brock}												
$\pi_{Tai\text{-}Pan}$												

(a)   First suppose there were no "face" or "hate" considerations, just the direct values. What are the equilibria if the Tai-pan bids first?
(b)   Continue supposing there were no "face" or "hate" considerations, just the direct values. What are the three possible equilibria if Mr. Brock bids first? (Hint: in one of them, Brock wins; in the other two, the Tai-pan wins.)
(c)   Fill in the entries in table 13.2, including the "face" and "hate" considerations.
(d)   In equilibrium, who wins, and at what bid?
(e)   What happens if the Tai-Pan can precommit to a strategy?

(f) What happens if the Tai-Pan cannot precommit, but he also hates Brock, and gets 1 in utility for each 1 that Brock pays out to get the land?

13.3: Government and monopoly (medium)

Incumbent Apex and potential entrant Brydox are bidding for government favors in the widget market. Apex wants to defeat a bill that would require it to share its widget patent rights with Brydox. Brydox wants the bill to pass. Whoever offers the chairman of the House Telecommunications Committee more campaign contributions wins, and the loser pays nothing. The market demand curve for widgets is $P = 25 - Q$, and marginal cost is constant at 1.

(a) Who will bid higher if duopolists follow Bertrand behavior? How much will the winner bid?
(b) Who will bid higher if duopolists follow Cournot behavior? How much will the winner bid?
(c) What happens under Cournot behavior if Apex can commit to giving away its patent freely to everyone in the world if the entry bill passes? How much will Apex bid?

13.4: An auction with stupid bidders (hard)

Smith's value for an object has a private component equal to 1 and another component Z that is common with Jones and Brown. Jones's and Brown's private components both equal zero. Each bidder estimates Z independently. Bidder i's estimate is either x_i above the true value or x_i below, with equal probability. Jones and Brown are naive and always bid their value estimates. The auction is ascending. Smith knows all three values of x_i, but not whether his estimate is too high or too low.

(a) If $x_{Smith} = 0$, what is Smith's dominant strategy if his estimate of Z is 20?
(b) If $x_i = 8$ for all bidders and Smith estimates that $Z = 20$, what are the probabilities that he puts on different possible values of Z?
(c) If $x_i = 8$ for Jones and Brown but $x_{Smith} = 0$, and Smith knows that $Z = 12$ with certainty, what are the probabilities he puts on the different combinations of bids by Jones and Brown?
(d) Why is 9 a better upper limit on bids for Smith than 21, if his estimate of Z is 20, and $x_i = 8$ for all three bidders?
(e) Suppose Smith could pay amount 0.001 to explain optimal bidding strategy to his rival bidders, Jones and Brown. Would he do so?

13.5: A teapot auction with incomplete information (easy)

Smith believes that Brown's value v_b for a teapot being sold at auction is 0 or 100 with equal probability. Smith's value of $v_s = 400$ is known by both bidders.

(a) What are the bidders' equilibrium strategies in an open-cry auction? You may assume that in case of ties, Smith wins the auction.
(b) What are the bidders' equilibrium strategies in a first-price sealed-bid auction? You may assume that in case of ties, Smith wins the auction.
(c) Now let $v_s = 102$ instead of 400. Will Smith use a pure strategy? Will Brown? You need not find the exact strategies used.

Auctions: A Classroom Game for Chapter 13

The instructor will bring to class a glass jar of pennies to be auctioned off. There are between 0 and 100 pennies in the jar, the number being drawn from a uniform distribution. Twenty percent of the students in the class must close their eyes while the jar is being displayed. The instructor will pass the jar around to the other students in the class to let them try to figure out how many pennies are inside. He will then auction off the jar five times, using five different sets of rules. (The instructor will decide for himself whether to play for real money or not.)

The first auction will be a first-price auction. Each student submits a bid, and also records his estimate of the number of pennies.

The second auction will be a second-price auction. Each student submits a bid, and also records his estimate of the number of pennies.

The third auction will be an all-pay auction. Each student submits a bid, and also records his estimate of the number of pennies.

The fourth auction will be a descending auction. After the auction, each student submits his estimate of the number of pennies.

The fifth auction will be an ascending auction. After the auction, each student submits his estimate of the number of pennies.

At this point, the instructor will announce the number of pennies in the jar, and the results of each auction.

Chapter 14
pricing

14.1 Quantities as Strategies: Cournot Equilibrium Revisited

Chapter 14 is about how firms with market power set prices. Section 14.1 extends the Cournot Game of section 3.5 in which two firms choose the quantities they sell, while section 14.2 extends the Bertrand model in which they choose prices to the case where capacity is limited. Section 14.3 goes back to the origins of product differentiation, and develops two Hotelling location models. Section 14.4 shows how to do comparative statics in games, using the differentiated Bertrand model as an example and supermodularity and the implicit function theorem as tools. Section 14.5 looks at another sort of differentiation: choice of "vertical" quality, from good to bad, by monopoly or duopoly. Section 14.6 concludes this book with the problem facing a firm selling a durable good because buyers foresee that it will be tempted to reduce the price over time to price-discriminate among them. At that point, perhaps you will wonder how much this book will cost next year!

Cournot Behavior with General Cost and Demand Functions

In the next few sections, sellers compete against each other while moving simultaneously. We will start by generalizing the Cournot Game of section 3.5 from linear demand and zero costs to a wider class of functions. The two players are firms Apex and Brydox, and their strategies are their choices of the quantities q_a and q_b. The payoffs are based on the total cost functions, $c(q_a)$ and $c(q_b)$, and the demand function, $p(q)$, where $q = q_a + q_b$. This specification says that only the sum of the outputs affects the price. The implication is that the firms produce an identical product, because whether it is Apex or Brydox that produces an extra unit, the effect on the price is the same.

Let us take the point of view of Apex. In the Cournot–Nash analysis, Apex chooses its output of q_a for a given level of q_b as if its choice did not affect q_b. From its point of view, q_a is a function of q_b, but q_b is exogenous. Apex sees the effect of its output on price as

$$\frac{\partial p}{\partial q_a} = \left(\frac{dp}{dq}\right)\left(\frac{\partial q}{\partial q_a}\right) = \frac{dp}{dq}. \tag{14.1}$$

Apex's payoff function is

$$\pi_a = p(q)q_a - c(q_a). \tag{14.2}$$

To find Apex's reaction function, we differentiate with respect to its strategy to obtain

$$\frac{d\pi_a}{dq_a} = p + \left(\frac{dp}{dq}\right)q_a - \frac{dc}{dq_a} = 0, \tag{14.3}$$

which implies

$$q_a = \frac{dc/dq_a - p}{dp/dq}, \tag{14.4}$$

or, simplifying the notation,

$$q_a = \frac{c' - p}{p'}. \tag{14.5}$$

If particular functional forms for $p(q)$ and $c(q_a)$ are available, equation (14.5) can be solved to find q_a as a function of q_b. More generally, to find the change in Apex's best response for an exogenous change in Brydox's output, differentiate (14.5) with respect to q_b, remembering that q_b exerts not only a direct effect on $p(q_a+q_b)$, but possibly an indirect effect via q_a.

$$\frac{dq_a}{dq_b} = \frac{(p - c')\left(p'' + p''\left(dq_a/dq_b\right)\right)}{p'^2} + \frac{c''\left(dq_a/dq_b\right) - p' - p'\left(dq_a/dq_b\right)}{p'}. \tag{14.6}$$

Equation (14.6) can be solved for $(dq_a)/(dq_b)$ to obtain the slope of the reaction function,

$$\frac{dq_a}{dq_b} = \frac{(p - c')p'' - p'^2}{2p'^2 - c''p' - (p - c')p''} \tag{14.7}$$

If both costs and demand are linear, as in section 3.5, then $c'' = 0$ and $p'' = 0$, so equation (14.7) becomes

$$\frac{dq_a}{dq_b} = -\frac{p'^2}{2p'^2} = -\frac{1}{2}. \tag{14.8}$$

The general model faces two problems that did not arise in the linear model: nonuniqueness and nonexistence. If demand is concave and costs are convex, which implies that $p'' < 0$ and $c'' > 0$, then all is well as far as existence goes. Since price is greater than marginal cost ($p > c'$), equation (14.7) tells us that the reaction functions are downward sloping, because $(2p'^2 - c''p' - (p - c')p'')$ is positive and both $(p - c')p''$ and $-p'^2$ are negative. If the reaction curves are downward sloping, they cross and an equilibrium exists, as is shown in figure 14.1a for the linear case represented by equation (14.8). We usually do assume that costs are at least weakly convex, since that is the result of diminishing or constant returns, but there is no reason to believe that demand is either concave, as in figure 14.1b, or convex, as in figure 14.1c. If the demand curves are not linear, the contorted reaction functions of equation (14.7) might give rise to multiple Cournot equilibria, as in figure 14.2.

If demand is convex or costs are concave, so $p'' > 0$ or $c'' < 0$, the reaction functions can be upward sloping, in which case they might never cross and no equilibrium would

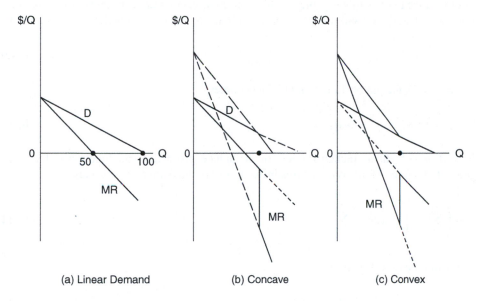

(a) Linear Demand   (b) Concave   (c) Convex

Figure 14.1   Different demand curves.

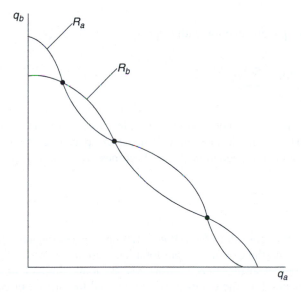

Figure 14.2   Multiple Cournot–Nash equilibria.

exist. The problem can also be seen from Apex's payoff function, equation (14.2). If $p(q)$ is convex, the payoff function might not be concave, in which case standard maximization techniques break down. The problems of the general Cournot model teach a lesson to modellers: sometimes simple assumptions such as linearity generate atypical results.

Many Oligopolists

Let us return to the simpler game in which production costs are zero and demand is linear. For concreteness, we will use the same specific inverse demand function as in chapter 3,

$$p(q) = 120 - q. \tag{14.9}$$

Using (14.9), the payoff function, (14.2), becomes

$$\pi_a = 120q_a - q_a^2 - q_b q_a. \tag{14.10}$$

In section 3.5, firms picked outputs of 40 apiece given demand function (14.9). This generated a price of 40. With n firms instead of two, the demand function is

$$p\left(\sum_{i=1}^{n} q_i\right) = 120 - \sum_{i=1}^{n} q_i, \tag{14.11}$$

and firm j's payoff function is

$$\pi_j = 120q_j - q_j^2 - q_j \sum_{i \neq j} q_i. \tag{14.12}$$

Differentiating j's payoff function with respect to q_j yields

$$\frac{d\pi_j}{dq_j} = 120 - 2q_j - \sum_{i \neq j} q_i = 0. \tag{14.13}$$

The first step in finding the equilibrium is to guess that it is symmetric, so that $q_j = q_i$ $(i = 1, \ldots, n)$. This is an educated guess, since every player faces a first-order condition like (14.13). By symmetry, equation (14.13) becomes $120 - (n+1)q_j = 0$, so that

$$q_j = \frac{120}{n+1}. \tag{14.14}$$

Consider several different values for n. If $n = 1$, then $q_j = 60$, the monopoly optimum; and if $n = 2$ then $q_j = 40$, the Cournot output found in section 3.5. If $n = 5$, $q_j = 20$; and as n rises, individual output shrinks to zero. Moreover, the total output of $nq_j = (n/(n+1))120$ gradually approaches 120, the competitive output, and the market price falls to zero, the marginal cost of production. As the number of firms increases, profits fall.

14.2   Capacity Constraints: The Edgeworth Paradox

In the last section we assumed constant marginal costs (of zero), and we assumed constant marginal costs of 12 in chapter 3 when we first discussed Cournot and Bertrand equilibrium. What if it were increasing, either gradually, or abruptly rising to infinity at a fixed capacity?

In the Cournot model, where firms compete in quantities, increasing marginal costs or a capacity constraint complicate the equations but do not change the model's features dramatically. Increasing marginal cost would reduce output as one might expect. If one firm had a capacity that was less than the ordinary Cournot output, that firm would produce only up to its capacity and the other firm would produce more than the ordinary Cournot output, since their outputs are strategic substitutes.

What happens in the Bertrand model, where firms compete in prices, is less straightforward. In chapter 3's game, the demand curve was $p(q) = 120 - q$, which we also used in the previous section of this chapter, and the constant marginal cost of firms Apex and Brydox was $c = 12$. In equilibrium, $p_a = p_b = 12$ and $q_a = q_b = 54$. If Apex deviated to a higher price such as $p_a = 20$, its quantity would fall to zero, since all customers would prefer Brydox's low price.

What happens if we constrain each firm to sell no more than its capacity of $K_a = K_b = 70$? The industry capacity of 140 continues to exceed the demand of 108 at $p_a = p_b = 12$. If, however, Apex deviates to the higher price of $p_a = 20$, it can still get customers. All 108 customers would prefer to buy from Brydox, but Brydox could only serve 70 of them, and the rest would have to go unhappily to Apex.

To discover what deviation is most profitable for Apex when $p_a = p_b = 12$, however, we need to know what Apex's exact payoff would be from deviation. That means we need to know not only that $38 (= 108 - 70)$ of the customers are turned away by Brydox, but which 38 customers. If they are the customers at the top of the demand curve, who are willing to pay prices near 100, Apex's optimal deviation will be much different than if they are ones towards the bottom, who are only willing to pay prices a little above 12.

Thus, in order to set up the payoff functions for the game, we need to specify a **rationing rule** to tell us which consumers are served at the low price and which must buy from the high-price firm. The rationing rule is unimportant to the payoff of the low-price firm, but crucial to the high-price firm.

One possible rule is

Intensity rationing (or efficient rationing, or high-to-low rationing). *The consumers able to buy from the firm with the lower price are those who value the product most.*

The inverse demand function from equation (14.9) is $p = 120 - q$, and under intensity rationing the K consumers with the strongest demand buy from the low-price firm. Suppose that Brydox is the low-price firm, charging (for illustration) a price of $p_b = 30$, so 90 consumers wish to buy from it though only K can do so, and Apex is charging some higher price p_a. The residual demand facing Apex is either 0 (if $p_a > 120 - K$) or

$$q_a = 120 - p_a - K. \tag{14.15}$$

That is the demand curve in figure 14.3(a).

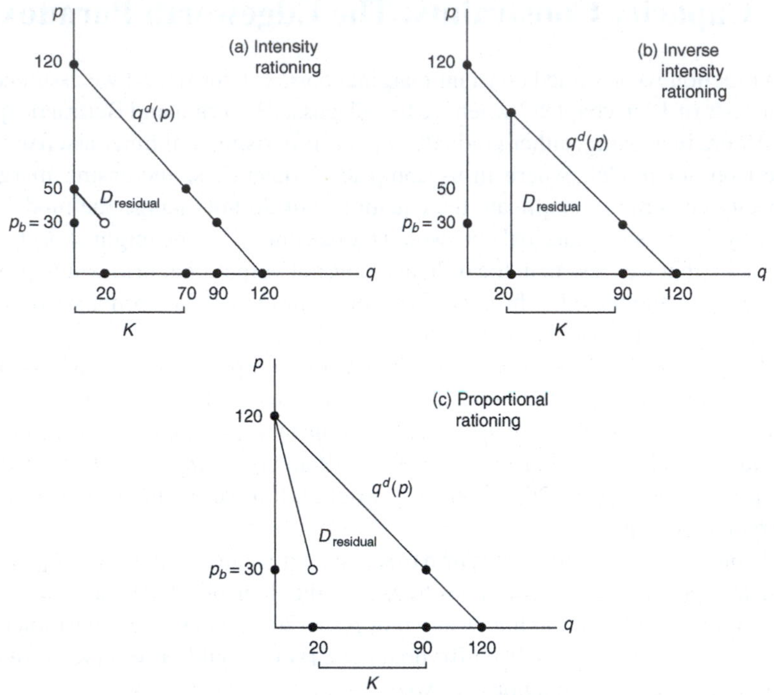

Figure 14.3 Rationing rules when $p_b = 30$, $p_a > 30$, and $K = 70$.

Under **intensity rationing**, if $K = 70$ the demand function for Apex (Brydox's is analogous) is

$$q_a = \begin{cases} Min\{120 - p_a, 70\} & \text{if } p_a < p_b & \text{(a)} \\ \dfrac{120 - p_a}{2} & \text{if } p_a = p_b & \text{(b)} \\ Max\{(120 - p_a - 70), 0\} & \text{if } p_a > p_b, p_b < 50 & \text{(c)} \\ 0 & \text{if } p_a > p_b, p_b \geq 50 & \text{(d)} \end{cases} \tag{14.16}$$

Equation (14.16a) is true because if Apex has the lower price, all consumers will want to buy from Apex if they buy at all. All of the $(120 - p_a)$ customers who want to buy at that price will be satisfied if there are 70 or less; otherwise only 70. Equation (14.16b) simply says the two firms split the market equally if prices are equal. Equation (14.16c) is true because if Brydox's price is the lowest and is less than 50, Brydox will sell 70 units, and the residual demand curve facing Apex will be as in equation (14.15). If Brydox's price is the lowest but exceeds 50, then less than 70 customers will want to buy at all, so Brydox will satisfy all of them and zero will be left for Apex – which is equation (14.16d).

The appropriate rationing rule depends on what is being modelled. Intensity rationing is appropriate if buyers with more intense demand make greater efforts to obtain low prices. If the intense buyers are wealthy people who are unwilling to wait in line, the least intense buyers might end up at the low-price firm which is the case of the **inverse-intensity rationing** (or **low-to-high rationing**) in figure 14.3b. An intermediate rule is proportional rationing, under which every type of consumer is equally likely to be able to buy at the low price.

Proportional rationing: *Each consumer has the same probability of being able to buy from the low-price firm.*

Under proportional rationing, if $K = 70$ and 90 consumers wanted to buy from Brydox, 2/9 ($=(q(p_b) - K)/(q(p_b))$) of each type of consumer will be forced to buy from Apex (e.g., 2/9 of the type willing to pay 120). The residual demand curve facing Apex, shown in figure 14.3c and equation (14.17), intercepts the price axis at 120, but slopes down at a rate three times as fast as market demand because there are only 2/9 as many remaining consumers of each type.

$$q_a = (120 - p_a)\left(\frac{120 - p_b - K}{120 - p_b}\right). \tag{14.17}$$

We thus have three choices for rationing rules, with no clear way to know which to use. Let us use intensity rationing. That is the rule which makes deviation to high prices least attractive, since the low-price firm keeps the best customers for itself, so if we find that the normal Bertrand equilibrium breaks down there, we will know it would break down under the other rationing rules too.

The Bertrand Game with Capacity Constraints

PLAYERS
Firms Apex and Brydox.

THE ORDER OF PLAY
Apex and Brydox simultaneously choose prices p_a and p_b from the set $[0, \infty)$.

PAYOFFS
Marginal cost is constant at $c = 12$. Demand is a function of the total quantity sold, $Q(p) = 120 - p$. The payoff function for Apex (Brydox's would be analogous) is, using equation (14.16) for q_a,

$$\pi_a = \begin{cases} (p_a-c)\cdot Min\{120-p_a,70\} & \text{if } p_a < p_b & \text{(a)} \\ (p_a-c)\left(\frac{120-p_a}{2}\right) & \text{if } p_a = p_b & \text{(b)} \\ (p_a-c)\cdot Max\{(120-p_a-70),0\} & \text{if } p_a > p_b, p_b < 50 & \text{(c)} \\ 0 & \text{if } p_a > p_b, p_b \geq 50 & \text{(d)} \end{cases} \tag{14.18}$$

The capacity constraint has a very important effect: ($p_a = 12, p_b = 12$) is no longer a Nash equilibrium in prices, even though the industry capacity of 140 is well over the market demand of 108 when price equals marginal cost. Apex's profit would be zero in that strategy profile. If Apex increased its price to $p_a = 20$, Brydox would immediately sell $q_b = 70$, and to the most intense 70 of buyers. Apex would be left with all the buyers between $p_a = 20$ and $p_a = 12$ on the demand curve for sales of $q_a = 30$ and a payoff of 240 from equation (14.18c). So deviation by Apex is profitable. (Of course, $p_a = 20$ is not necessarily the most profitable deviation – but we do not need to check that; any profitable deviation is enough to refute the proposed equilibrium.)

Equilibrium prices must be lower than 120, because that price yields a zero payoff under any circumstance. There are three remaining possibilities (now that we have ruled out $p_a = p_b = 12$) for prices chosen in the open interval [12, 120).

1   Equal prices with $p_a = p_b > 12$ are not an equilibrium. Even if the price is close to 12, Apex would sell at most 54 units as its half of the market, which is less than its capacity of 70. Apex could profitably deviate to just below p_b and have a discontinuous jump in sales for an increase in profit, just as in the basic Bertrand game.
2   Unequal prices with one equal to 12 are not an equilibrium. Without loss of generality, suppose $p_a > p_b = 12$. Apex could not profitably deviate, but Brydox could deviate to $p_b = p_a - \epsilon$ and make positive instead of zero profit.
3   Unequal prices of (p_a, p_b) with both greater than 12 are not an equilibrium. Without loss of generality, suppose $p_a > p_b > 12$. Apex's profits are shown in equation (14.18c). If $\pi_a = 0$, it can gain by deviating to $p_a = p_b - \epsilon$. If $\pi_a = (p_a - c)(50 - p_a)$, it can gain by deviating to $p_a = p_b - \epsilon$, because equation (14.18c) tells us that Apex's payoff will rise to either $\pi_a = (p_a - c)(70)$ (if $p_b \geq 50$) or $\pi_a = (p_a - c)(120 - p_a)$ (if $p_b < 50$).

Thus, no equilibrium exists in pure strategies under intensity rationing, and similar arguments rule out pure-strategy equilibria under other forms of rationing. This is known as the **Edgeworth paradox** after Edgeworth (1897, 1922).

Nowadays we know that the resolution to many a paradox is mixed strategies, and that is the case here too. A mixed-strategy equilibrium does exist, calculated using intensity rationing and linear demand by Levitan & Shubik (1972). Expected profits are positive, because the firms charge prices above marginal cost. In the symmetric equilibrium, the firms mix using distribution $F(p)$ with a support $[\underline{p}, \bar{p}]$, where $\underline{p} > c$ and $\bar{p}$ is the monopoly price for the residual demand curve (14.15), which happens to be $\bar{p} = 36$ in our example. The upper bound $\bar{p}$ is that monopoly price because $F(\bar{p}) = 1$ and the firm choosing that price certainly is the one with the highest price and so should maximize its profit using the residual demand curve. The payoff from playing the lower bound, $\underline{p}$, is $(\underline{p} - c)(70)$ from equation (14.18c), so since that payoff must equal the payoff of 336 $(=(p-\bar{c})q = (36-12)(50-36))$ from $\bar{p}$, we can conclude that $\underline{p} = 16.8$. The mixing distribution $F(p)$ could then be found by setting $\pi(p) = 336 = F(p)(p - c)(50 - p) + (1 - F(p))(p - c)(70)$ and solving for $F(p)$.

If capacities are large enough – above the capacity of $K = Q(c) = 108$ in this example – the Edgeworth paradox disappears. The argument made above for why equal prices of c is not an equilibrium fails, because if Apex were to deviate to a positive price, Brydox would be fully capable of serving the entire market, leaving Apex with no consumers.

If capacities are small enough – less than $K = 36$ in our example – the Edgeworth paradox also disappears, but so does the Bertrand paradox. The equilibrium is in pure strategies, with each firm using its entire capacity, so $q_a = q_b = K$ and charging the same price. There is no point in a firm reducing its price, since it cannot sell any greater quantity. How about a deviation to increasing its price and reducing its quantity? Its best deviation is to the price which maximizes profit using the residual demand curve $(120 - K - p)$. This turns out to be $p^* = (120 - K + c)/2$, in which case

$$q^* = \frac{120 - K - c}{2}. \tag{14.19}$$

But if

$$K < \frac{120 - c}{3}, \tag{14.20}$$

then $q^* > K$ in equation (14.19) and is infeasible – the profit-maximizing price is from using all the capacity. The critical level from inequality (14.20) is $K = 36$ in our example. For any lower capacities, firms simply dump their entire capacity onto the market and the price, $p_a = p_b = 120 - 2K$, exceeds marginal cost.

14.3   Location Models

In chapter 3 we analyzed the Bertrand model with differentiated products using demand functions whose arguments were the prices of both firms. Such a model is suspect because it is not based on primitive assumptions. In particular, the demand functions might not be generated by maximizing any possible utility function. A demand curve with a constant elasticity less than one, for example, is impossible because as the price goes to zero, the amount spent on the commodity goes to infinity. Also, the demand curves were restricted to prices below a certain level, and it would be good to be able to justify that restriction.

Location models construct demand functions like those in chapter 3 from primitive assumptions. In location models, a differentiated product's characteristics are points in a space. If cars differ only in their mileage, the space is a one-dimensional line. If acceleration is also important, the space is a two-dimensional plane. An easy way to think about this approach is to consider the location where a product is sold. The product "gasoline sold at the corner of Wilshire and Westwood Streets," is different from "gasoline sold at the corner of Wilshire and Fourth." Depending on where consumers live, they have different preferences over the two, but, if prices diverge enough, they will be willing to switch from one gas station to the other.

Location models form a literature in themselves. We will look at the first two models analyzed in the classic article of Hotelling (1929), a model of price choice and a model of location choice. Figure 14.4 shows what is common to both. Two firms are located at points x_a and x_b along a line running from zero to one, with a constant density of consumers throughout. In the Hotelling Pricing Game, firms choose prices for given locations. In the Hotelling Location Game, prices are fixed and the firms choose the locations.

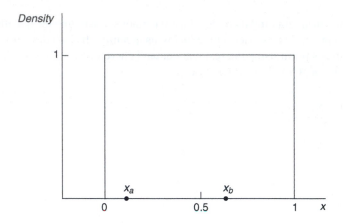

Figure 14.4   Location models.

The Hotelling Pricing Game (Hotelling [1929])

PLAYERS
Sellers Apex and Brydox, located at x_a and x_b, where $x_a < x_b$, and a continuum of buyers indexed by location $x \in [0, 1]$.

THE ORDER OF PLAY
1   The sellers simultaneously choose prices p_a and p_b.
2   Each buyer chooses a seller.

PAYOFFS
Demand is uniformly distributed on the interval [0, 1] with a density equal to one (think of each consumer as buying one unit). Production costs are zero. Each consumer always buys, so his problem is to minimize the sum of the price plus the linear transport cost, which is θ per unit distance travelled.

$$\pi_{buyer\,at\,x} = V - Min\{\theta|x_a - x| + p_a, \theta|x_b - x| + p_b\}. \tag{14.21}$$

$$\pi_a = \begin{cases} p_a(0) = 0 & \text{if } p_a - p_b > \theta(x_b - x_a) \quad \text{(a)} \\ & \text{(Brydox captures entire market)} \\[4pt] p_a(1) = p_a & \text{if } p_b - p_a > \theta(x_b - x_a) \quad \text{(b)} \\ & \text{(Apex captures entire market)} \\[4pt] p_a\left(\dfrac{1}{2\theta}[(p_b - p_a) + \theta(x_a + x_b)]\right) & \text{otherwise (the market is divided) \quad (c)} \end{cases}$$

$$\tag{14.22}$$

Brydox has analogous payoffs.

The payoffs result from buyer behavior. A buyer's utility depends on the price he pays and the distance he travels. Price aside, Apex is most attractive of the two sellers to the consumer at $x = 0$ ("Consumer 0") and least attractive to the consumer at $x = 1$ ("Consumer 1"). Consumer 0 will buy from Apex so long as

$$V - (\theta x_a + p_a) > V - (\theta x_b + p_b), \tag{14.23}$$

which implies that

$$p_a - p_b < \theta(x_b - x_a), \tag{14.24}$$

which yields payoff (14.22a) for Apex. Consumer 1 will buy from Brydox if

$$V - [\theta(1 - x_a) + p_a] < V - [\theta(1 - x_b) + p_b], \tag{14.25}$$

which implies that

$$p_b - p_a < \theta(x_b - x_a), \tag{14.26}$$

which yields payoff (14.22b) for Apex.

Very likely, inequalities (14.24) and (14.26) are both satisfied, in which case Consumer 0 goes to Apex and Consumer 1 goes to Brydox. This is the case represented by payoff (14.22c), and the next task is to find the location of Consumer x^*, defined as the consumer who is at the boundary between the two markets, indifferent between Apex and Brydox. First, notice that if Apex attracts Consumer x_b, he also attracts all $x > x_b$, because beyond x_b the consumers' distances from both sellers increase at the same rate. So we know that if there is an indifferent consumer he is between x_a and x_b. Knowing this, the consumer's payoff equation, (14.21), tells us that

$$V - [\theta(x^* - x_a) + p_a] = V - [\theta(x_b - x^*) + p_b], \tag{14.27}$$

so that

$$p_b - p_a = \theta(2x^* - x_a - x_b), \tag{14.28}$$

and

$$q_a = x^* = \frac{1}{2\theta}[(p_b - p_a) + \theta(x_a + x_b)], \tag{14.29}$$

which generates demand curve (14.22c).

Remember, however, that equation (14.29) is valid only if there really does exist a consumer who is indifferent. If such a consumer does not exist, equation (14.29) will generates a number for x^*, but that number is meaningless.

Since Apex keeps all the consumers between 0 and x^*, equation (14.29) is the demand function facing Apex so long as he does not set his price so far above Brydox's that he loses even consumer 0. The demand facing Brydox equals $(1 - x^*)$. Note that if $p_b = p_a$, then from (14.29), $x^* = (x_a + x_b)/2$, independent of the travel cost, θ, which is just what we would expect. Demand is linear in the prices of both firms, and looks similar to the demand curves used in section 3.6 for the Bertrand game with differentiated products.

Now that we have found the demand functions, the Nash equilibrium can be calculated in the same way as in section 14.2, by setting up the profit functions for each firm, differentiating with respect to the price of each, and solving the two first-order conditions for the two prices. If there exists an equilibrium in which the firms are willing to pick prices to satisfy inequalities (14.24) and (14.26), then it is

$$p_a = \frac{(2 + x_a + x_b)\theta}{3}, \quad p_b = \frac{(4 - x_a - x_b)\theta}{3}. \tag{14.30}$$

From (14.30) one can see that Apex charges a higher price if a large x_a gives it more safe consumers or a large x_b makes the number of contestable consumers greater. The simplest case is when $x_a = 0$ and $x_b = 1$, when (14.30) tells us that both firms charge a price equal to θ. Profits are positive and increasing in the transportation cost.

We cannot rest satisfied with the neat equilibrium of equation (14.30), because the assumption that there exists an equilibrium in which the firms choose prices so as to split the market on each side of some boundary consumer x^* is often violated. Hotelling did not notice this, and fell into a common mathematical trap. Economists are used to models in which the calculus approach gives an answer that is both the local optimum and the global optimum. In games like this one, however, the local optimum is not always global, because of the discontinuity in the objective function. Vickrey (1964) and D'Aspremont, Gabszewicz, & Thisse (1979) have shown that if x_a and x_b are close together, no pure-strategy equilibrium exists, for reasons similar to why none exists in the Bertrand model with capacity constraints. If both firms charge nonrandom prices, neither would deviate to a slightly different price, but one might deviate to a much lower price that would capture every single consumer. But if both firms charged that low price, each would deviate by raising his price slightly. It turns out that if, for example, Apex and Brydox are located symmetrically around the center of the interval, $x_a \geq 0.25$, and $x_b \leq 0.75$, no pure-strategy equilibrium exists (although a mixed-strategy equilibrium does, as Dasgupta & Maskin [1986b] show).

Hotelling should have done some numerical examples. And he should have thought about the comparative statics carefully. Equation (14.30) implies that Apex should choose a higher price if both x_a and x_b increase, but it is odd that if the firms are locating closer together, say at 0.90 and 0.91, that Apex should be able to charge a higher price, rather than suffering from more intense competition. This kind of odd result is a typical clue that the result has a logical flaw somewhere. Until the modeller can figure out an intuitive reason for his odd result, he should suspect an error. For practice, let us try a few numerical examples, illustrated in figure 14.5.

Example 14.1: Everything works out simply

Try $x_a = 0$, $x_b = 0.7$ and $\theta = 0.5$. Then equation (14.30) says $p_a = (2+0+0.7)0.5/3 = 0.45$ and $p_b = (4 - 0 - 0.7)0.5/3 = 0.55$. Equation (14.29) says that $x^* = 1/(2 * 0.5)[(0.55 - 0.45) + 0.5(0.0 + 0.7)] = 0.45$.

In example 14.1, there is a pure-strategy equilibrium and the equations generated sensible numbers given the parameters we chose. But it is not enough to calculate just one numerical example.

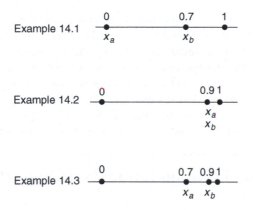

Figure 14.5   Numerical examples for Hotelling pricing.

Example 14.2: Same location – but different prices?

Try $x_a = 0.9$, $x_b = 0.9$ and $\theta = 0.5$. Then equation (14.30) says $p_a = (2.0 + 0.9 + 0.9)0.5/3 \approx 0.63$ and $p_b = (4.0 - 0.9 - 0.9)0.5/3 \approx 0.37$.

Example 14.2 shows something odd happening. The equations generate numbers that seem innocuous until one realizes that if both firms are located at 0.9, but $p_a = 0.63$ and $p_b = 0.37$, then Brydox will capture the entire market! The result is nonsense, because equation (14.30)'s derivation relied on the assumption that $x_a < x_b$, which is false in this example.

Example 14.3: Locations too near each other

$x^* < x_a < x_b$. Try $x_a = 0.7$, $x_b = 0.9$, and $\theta = 0.5$. Then equation (14.30) says that $p_a = (2.0 + 0.7 + 0.9)0.5/3 = 0.6$ and $p_b = (4 - 0.7 - 0.9)0.5/3 = 0.4$. As for the split of the market, equation (14.29) says that $x^* = 1/(2*0.5)[(0.4-0.6)+0.5(0.7+0.9)] = 0.6$.

Example 14.3 shows a serious problem. If the market splits at $x^* = 0.6$ but $x_a = 0.7$ and $x_b = 0.9$, the result violates our implicit assumption that the players split the market. Equation (14.29) is based on the premise that there does exist some indifferent consumer, and when that is a false premise, as under the parameters of example 14.3, equation (14.29) will still spit out a value of x^*, but the value will not mean anything. In fact the consumer at $x = 0.6$ is not really indifferent between Apex and Brydox. He could buy from Apex at a total cost of $0.6 + 0.1(0.5) = 0.65$ or from Brydox, at a total cost of $0.4 + 0.3(0.5) = 0.55$. There exists no consumer who strictly prefers Apex. Even Apex's "home" consumer at $x = 0.7$ would have a total cost of buying from Brydox of $0.4 + 0.5(0.9 - 0.7) = 0.5$ and would prefer Brydox. Similarly, the consumer at $x = 0$ would have a total cost of buying from Brydox of $0.4 + 0.5(0.9 - 0.0) = 0.85$, compared to a cost from Apex of $0.6 + 0.5(0.7 - 0.0) = 0.95$, and he, too, would prefer Brydox.

The problem in examples 14.2 and 14.3 is that the firm with the higher price would do better to deviate with a discontinuous price cut, to just below the other firm's price. Equation (14.30) was derived by calculus, with the implicit assumption that a local profit maximum was also a global profit maximum, or, put differently, that if no small change could raise a firm's payoff, then it had found the optimal strategy. Sometimes a big change will increase a player's payoff even though a small change would not. Perhaps this is what they mean in business by the importance of "nonlinear thinking" or "thinking out of the envelope." The everyday manager or scientist as described by Schumpeter (1934) and Kuhn (1970) concentrates on analyzing incremental changes and only the entrepreneur or genius breaks through with a discontinuously new idea, the profit source or paradigm shift.

Let us now turn to the choice of location. We will simplify the model by pushing consumers into the background and imposing a single exogenous price on all firms.

The Hotelling Location Game (Hotelling [1929])

PLAYERS
n Sellers.

THE ORDER OF PLAY
The sellers simultaneously choose locations $x_i \in [0, 1]$.

PAYOFFS
Consumers are distributed along the interval $[0, 1]$ with a uniform density equal to one. The price equals one, and production costs are zero. The sellers are ordered by their location so $x_1 \leq x_2 \leq \cdots \leq x_n$, $x_0 \equiv 0$ and $x_{n+1} \equiv 1$. Seller i attracts half the consumers from the gaps on each side of him, as shown in figure 14.6, so that his payoff is

$$\pi_1 = x_1 + \frac{x_2 - x_1}{2}, \tag{14.31}$$

$$\pi_n = \frac{x_n - x_{n-1}}{2} + 1 - x_n, \tag{14.32}$$

or, for $i = 2, \ldots, n - 1$,

$$\pi_i = \frac{x_i - x_{i-1}}{2} + \frac{x_{i+1} - x_i}{2}. \tag{14.33}$$

With **one seller**, the location does not matter in this model, since the consumers are captive. If price were a choice variable and demand were elastic, we would expect the monopolist to locate at $x = 0.5$.

With **two sellers**, both firms locate at $x = 0.5$, regardless of whether or not demand is elastic. This is a stable Nash equilibrium, as can be seen by inspecting figure 14.4 and imagining best responses to each other's location. The best response is always to locate ε

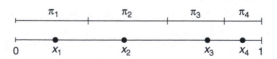

Figure 14.6   Payoffs in the Hotelling Location Game.

closer to the center of the interval than one's rival. When both firms do this, they end up splitting the market since both of them end up exactly at the center.

With **three sellers** the model does not have a Nash equilibrium in pure strategies. Consider any strategy profile in which each player locates at a separate point. Such a strategy profile is not an equilibrium, because the two players nearest the ends would edge in to squeeze the middle player's market share. But if a strategy profile has any two players at the same point a, as in figure 14.7, the third player would be able to acquire a share of at least $(0.5 - \epsilon)$ by moving next to them at b; and if the third player's share is that large, one of the doubled-up players would deviate by jumping to his other side and capturing his entire market share. The only equilibrium is in mixed strategies.

Suppose all three players use the same mixing density, with $m(x)$ the probability density for location x, and positive density on the support $[g, h]$, as depicted in figure 14.8. We will need the density for the distribution of the minimum of the locations of players 2 and 3. Player 2 has location x with density $m(x)$, and Player 3's location is greater than that with probability $(1 - M(x))$, letting M denote the cumulative distribution, so the density for Player 2 having location x and it being smaller is $m(x)[1 - M(x)]$. The density for either Player 2 or Player 3 choosing x and it being smaller than the other firm's location is then $2m(x)[1 - M(x)]$.

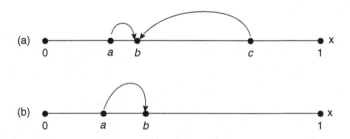

Figure 14.7   Nonexistence of pure strategies with three players.

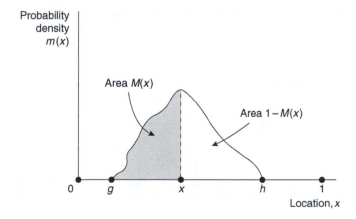

Figure 14.8   An equilibrium mixed-strategy density in the three-player location game.

If Player 1 chooses $x = g$ then his expected payoff is

$$\pi_1(x_1 = g) = g + \int_g^h 2m(x)[1 - M(x)] \left(\frac{x - g}{2}\right) dx, \tag{14.34}$$

where g is the safe set of consumers to his left, $2m(x)[1 - M(x)]$ is the density for x being the next biggest location of a firm, and $(x - g)/2$ is Player 1's share of the consumers between his own location of g and the next biggest location.

If Player 1 chooses $x = h$ then his expected payoff is, similarly,

$$\pi_1(x_1 = h) = (1 - h) + \int_g^h 2m(x)M(x) \left(\frac{h - x}{2}\right) dx, \tag{14.35}$$

where $(1 - h)$ is the set of safe consumers to his right.

In a mixed strategy equilibrium, Player 1's payoffs from these two pure strategies must be equal, and they are also equal to his payoff from a location of 0.5, which we can plausibly guess is in the support of his mixing distribution. Going on from this point, the algebra and calculus start to become fierce. Shaked (1982) has computed the symmetric mixing probability density $m(x)$ to be as shown in figure 14.9,

$$m(x) = \begin{cases} 2 & \text{if } \frac{1}{4} \leq x \leq \frac{3}{4} \\ 0 & \text{otherwise} \end{cases} \tag{14.36}$$

You can check this equilibrium by seeing that with the mixing density (14.36) (depicted in figure 14.9) the payoffs in equations (14.34) and (14.35) do equal each other. This method has only shown what the symmetric equilibrium is like, however; it turns out that asymmetric equilibria also exist (Osborne & Pitchik [1986]).

Strangely enough, three is a special number. With **more than three sellers**, an equilibrium in pure strategies does exist if the consumers are uniformly distributed, but this is a delicate result (Eaton & Lipsey [1975]). Dasgupta & Maskin (1986b), as amended by Simon (1987), have also shown that an equilibrium, possibly in mixed strategies, exists for any number of players n in a space of any dimension m.

Since prices are inflexible, the competitive market does not achieve efficiency. A benevolent social planner or a monopolist who could charge higher prices if he located his outlets

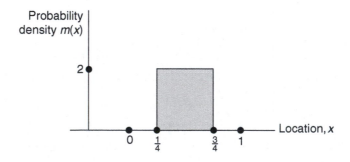

Figure 14.9   The equilibrium mixing density for location.

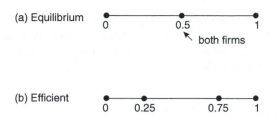

Figure 14.10   Equilibrium versus efficiency in location.

closer to more consumers would choose different locations than competing firms. In particular, when two competing firms both locate in the center of the line, consumers are no better off than if there were just one firm. As shown in figure 14.10, the average distance of a consumer from a seller would be minimized by setting $x_1 = 0.25$ and $x_2 = 0.75$, the locations that would be chosen either by the social planner or the monopolist.

The Hotelling Location Model, however, is very well suited to politics. Often there is just one dimension of importance in political races, and voters will vote for the candidate closest to their own position, so there is no analog to price. The Hotelling Location Model predicts that the two candidates will both choose the same position, right on top of the median voter. This seems descriptively realistic; it accords with the common complaint that all politicians are pretty much the same.

14.4   Comparative Statics and Supermodular Games

Comparative statics is the analysis of what happens to endogenous variables in a model when the exogenous variables change. This is a central part of economics. When wages rise, for example, we wish to know how the price of steel will change in response. Game theory presents special problems for comparative statics, because when a parameter changes, not only does Smith's equilibrium strategy change in response, but Jones's strategy changes as a result of Smith's change as well. A small change in the parameter might produce a large change in the equilibrium because of feedback between the different players' strategies.

Let us use a differentiated Bertrand game as an example. Suppose there are N firms, and for firm j the demand curve is

$$Q_j = Max \left\{ \alpha - \beta_j p_j + \sum_{i \neq j} \gamma_i p_i, 0 \right\},$$

(14.37)

with $\alpha \in (0, \infty)$, $\beta_i \in (0, \infty)$, and $\gamma_i \in (0, \infty)$ for $i = 1, \ldots, N$. Assume that the effect of p_j on firm j's sales is larger than the effect of the other firms' prices, so that

$$\beta_j > \sum_{i \neq j} \gamma_i.$$

(14.38)

Let firm i have constant marginal cost κc_i, where $\kappa \in \{1, 2\}$ and $c_i \in (0, \infty)$, and let us assume that each firm's costs are low enough that it does operate in equilibrium. (The shift variable κ could represent the effect of the political regime on costs.)
The payoff function for firm j is

$$\pi_j = (p_j - \kappa c_j) \left(\alpha - \beta_j p_j + \sum_{i \neq j} \gamma_i p_i \right). \tag{14.39}$$

Firms choose prices simultaneously.

Does this game have an equilibrium? Does it have several equilibria? What happens to the equilibrium price if a parameter such as c_j or κ changes? These are difficult questions because if c_j increases, the immediate effect is to change firm j's price, but the other firms will react to the price change, which in turn will affect j's price. Moreover, this is not a symmetric game – the costs and demand curves differ from firm to firm, which could make algebraic solutions of the Nash equilibrium quite messy. It is not even clear whether the equilibrium is unique.

Two approaches to comparative statics can be used here: the implicit function theorem and supermodularity. We will look at each in turn.

The Implicit Function Theorem

The implicit function theorem says that if $f(y, z) = 0$, where y is endogenous and z is exogenous, then

$$\frac{dy}{dz} = - \left(\frac{\partial f / \partial z}{\partial f / \partial y} \right). \tag{14.40}$$

It is worth knowing how to derive this. We start with $f(y, z) = 0$, which can be rewritten as $f(y(z), z) = 0$, since y is endogenous. Using the calculus chain rule,

$$\frac{df}{dz} = \frac{\partial f}{\partial z} + \left(\frac{\partial f}{\partial y} \right) \left(\frac{dy}{dz} \right) = 0. \tag{14.41}$$

where the expression equals zero because after a small change in z, f will still equal zero after y adjusts. Solving for dy/dz yields equation (14.40).

The implicit function theorem is especially useful if y is a choice variable and z a parameter, because then we can use the first-order condition to set $f(y, z) \equiv \partial \pi / \partial y = 0$ and the second-order condition tells us that $\partial f / \partial y = \partial^2 \pi / \partial y^2 \leq 0$. One only has to make certain that the solution is an interior solution, so the first- and second-order conditions are valid, and keep in mind that if the solution is only a local maximum, not a global one, the maximizing choice might "jump" up or down when an exogenous variable changes.

We do have a complication if the model is strategic: there will be more than one endogenous variable, because more than one player is choosing variable values. Suppose that instead of simply $f(y, z) = 0$, our implicit equation has two endogenous and two exogenous variables, so $f(y_1, y_2, z_1, z_2) = 0$. The extra z_2 is no problem; in comparative statics we are holding all but one exogenous variable constant. But the y_2

does add some complexity to the mix. Now, using the calculus chain rule yields not equation (14.41) but

$$\frac{df}{dz_1} = \frac{\partial f}{\partial z_1} + \left(\frac{\partial f}{\partial y_1}\right)\left(\frac{dy_1}{dz_1}\right) + \left(\frac{\partial f}{\partial y_2}\right)\left(\frac{dy_2}{dz_1}\right) = 0. \tag{14.42}$$

Solving for dy_1/dz_1 yields

$$\frac{dy_1}{dz_1} = -\left(\frac{\partial f/\partial z_1 + (\partial f/\partial y_2)\,(dy_2/dz_1)}{\partial f/\partial y_1}\right). \tag{14.43}$$

It is often unsatisfactory to solve out for dy_1/dz_1 as a function of both the exogenous variables z_1 and z_2 and the endogenous variable y_2 (though it is okay if all you want is to discover whether the change is positive or negative), but ordinarily the modeller will also have available an optimality condition for Player 2 also: $g(y_1, y_2, z_1, z_2) = 0$. This second condition yields an equation similar to (14.43), so that two equations can be solved for the two unknowns.

We can use the differentiated Bertrand game to see how this works out. Equilibrium prices will lie inside the interval $(c_j, \bar{p})$ for some large number $\bar{p}$, because a price of c_j would yield zero profits, rather than the positive profits of a slightly higher price, and $\bar{p}$ can be chosen to yield zero quantity demanded and hence zero profits. The equilibrium or equilibria are, therefore, interior solutions, in which case they satisfy the first-order condition

$$\frac{\partial \pi_j}{\partial p_j} = \alpha - 2\beta_j p_j + \sum_{i \neq j} \gamma_i p_i + \kappa c_j \beta_j = 0, \tag{14.44}$$

and the second-order condition,

$$\frac{\partial^2 \pi_j}{\partial p_j^2} = -2\beta_j < 0. \tag{14.45}$$

Next, apply the implicit function theorem by using p_i and c_i, $i = 1, \ldots, N$, instead of y_i and z_i, $i = 1, 2$, and by letting $\partial \pi_j/\partial p_j = 0$ from equation (14.44) be our $f(y_1, y_2, z_1, z_2) = 0$. The chain rule yields

$$\frac{df}{dc_j} = -2\beta_j\left(\frac{dp_j}{dc_j}\right) + \sum_{i \neq j} \gamma_i\left(\frac{dp_i}{dc_j}\right) + \kappa\beta_j = 0, \tag{14.46}$$

so

$$\frac{dp_j}{dc_j} = \frac{\sum_{i \neq j} \gamma_i(dp_i/dc_j) + \kappa\beta_j}{2\beta_j}. \tag{14.47}$$

Just what is dp_i/dc_j? For each i, we need to find the first-order condition for firm i and then use the chain rule again. The first-order condition for Player i is that the derivative of π_i with respect to p_i (not p_j) equals zero, so

$$g^i \equiv \frac{\partial \pi_i}{\partial p_i} = \alpha - 2\beta_i p_i + \sum_{k \neq i} \gamma_k p_k + \kappa c_i \beta_i = 0. \tag{14.48}$$

The chain rule yields (keeping in mind that it is a change in c_j that interests us, *not* a change in c_i),

$$\frac{dg^i}{dc_j} = -2\beta_i \left(\frac{dp_i}{dc_j}\right) + \sum_{k \neq i} \gamma_k \left(\frac{dp_k}{dc_j}\right) = 0. \tag{14.49}$$

With equation (14.47), the $(N-1)$ equations (14.49) give us N equations for the N unknowns dp_i/dc_j, $i = 1, \ldots, N$.

It is easier to see what is going on if there are just two firms, j and i. Equations (14.47) and (14.49) are then

$$\frac{dp_j}{dc_j} = \frac{\gamma_i(dp_i/dc_j) + \kappa\beta_j}{2\beta_j}. \tag{14.50}$$

and

$$-2\beta_i \left(\frac{dp_i}{dc_j}\right) + \gamma_j \left(\frac{dp_j}{dc_j}\right) = 0. \tag{14.51}$$

Solving these two equations for dp_j/dc_j and dp_i/dc_j yields

$$\frac{dp_j}{dc_j} = \frac{2\beta_i\beta_j\kappa}{4\beta_i\beta_j - \gamma_i\gamma_j} \tag{14.52}$$

and

$$\frac{dp_i}{dc_j} = \frac{\gamma_j\beta_j\kappa}{4\beta_i\beta_j - \gamma_i\gamma_j}. \tag{14.53}$$

Keep in mind that the implicit function theorem only tells about infinitesimal changes, not finite changes. If c_n increases enough, then the nature of the equilibrium changes drastically, because firm n goes out of business. Even if c_n increases a finite amount, the implicit function theorem is not applicable, because then the change in p_n will cause changes in the prices of other firms, which will in turn change p_n again.

We cannot go on to discover the effect of changing κ on p_n, because κ is a discrete variable, and the implicit function theorem only applies to continuous variables. The implicit function theorem is none the less very useful when it does apply. This is a simple example, but the approach can be used even when the functions involved are very complicated. In complicated cases, knowing that the second-order condition holds allows the modeller to avoid having to determine the sign of the denominator if all that interests him is the sign of the relationship between the two variables.

Supermodularity

The second approach uses the idea of the supermodular game, an idea related to that of strategic complements (section 3.6). Suppose that there are N players in a game, subscripted by i and j, and that player i has a strategy consisting of $\bar{s}^i$ elements, subscripted by s and

t, so his strategy is the vector $y^i = (y^i_1, \ldots, y^i_{\bar{s}^i})$. Let his strategy set be S^i and his payoff function be $\pi^i(y^i, y^{-i}; z)$, where z represents a fixed parameter. We say that the game is a **smooth supermodular game** if the following four conditions are satisfied for every player $i = 1, \ldots, N$:

A1′ The strategy set is an interval in $R^{\bar{s}^i}$:

$$S^i = [\underline{y^i}, \overline{y^i}]. \tag{14.54}$$

A2′ π^i is twice continuously differentiable on S^i.

A3′ (Supermodularity) Increasing one component of player i's strategy does not decrease the net marginal benefit of any other component: for all i, and all s and t such that $1 \leq s < t \leq \bar{s}^i$,

$$\frac{\partial^2 \pi^i}{\partial y^i_s \partial y^i_t} \geq 0. \tag{14.55}$$

A4′ (Increasing differences in strategies) Increasing one component of j's strategy does not decrease the net marginal benefit of increasing any component of player i's strategy: for all $j \neq i$, and all s and t such that $1 \leq s \leq \bar{s}^i$ and $1 \leq t \leq \bar{s}^j$,

$$\frac{\partial^2 \pi^i}{\partial y^i_s \partial y^j_t} \geq 0. \tag{14.56}$$

In addition, we will be able to talk about the comparative statics of smooth supermodular games if a fifth condition is satisfied, increasing differences in parameters.

A5′ (Increasing differences in parameters) Increasing parameter z does not decrease the net marginal benefit to player i of any component of his own strategy: for all i, and all s such that $1 \leq s \leq \bar{s}^i$,

$$\frac{\partial^2 \pi^i}{\partial y^i_s \partial z} \geq 0. \tag{14.57}$$

The heart of supermodularity is in assumptions $A3'$ and $A4'$. Assumption $A3'$ says that the components of player i's strategies are all **complementary inputs**; when one component increases, it is worth increasing the other components too. This means that even if a strategy is a complicated one, one can still arrive at qualitative results about the strategy, because all the components of the optimal strategy will move in the same direction together. Assumption $A4'$ says that the strategies of players i and j are **strategic complements**; when player i increases a component of his strategy, player j will want to do so also. When the strategies of the players reinforce each other in this way, the feedback between them is less tangled than if they undermined each other.

I have put primes on the assumptions because they are the special cases, for smooth games, of the general definition of supermodular games in the Mathematical Appendix. Smooth games use differentiable functions, but the supermodularity theorems apply more generally. One condition that is relevant here is condition A5:

A5 (Increasing differences in parameters) π^i has increasing differences in y^i and z for fixed y^{-i}; for all $y^i \geq y^{i'}$, the difference $\pi^i(y^i, y^{-i}, z) - \pi^i(y^{i'}, y^{-i}, z)$ is nondecreasing with respect to z.

Is the differentiated Bertrand game supermodular? The strategy set can be restricted to $[c_i, \overline{p}]$ for player i, so A1′ is satisfied. π_i is twice continuously differentiable on the interval $[c_i, \overline{p}]$, so A2′ is satisfied. A player's strategy has just one component, p_i, so A3′ is immediately satisfied. The following inequality is true,

$$\frac{\partial^2 \pi_i}{\partial p_i \partial p_j} = \gamma_j > 0, \tag{14.58}$$

so A4′ is satisfied. And it is also true that

$$\frac{\partial^2 \pi_i}{\partial p_i \partial c_i} = \kappa \beta_i > 0, \tag{14.59}$$

so A5′ is satisfied for c_i.

From equation (14.44), $\partial \pi_i / \partial p_i$ is increasing in κ, so $\pi_i(p_i, p_{-i}, \kappa) - \pi_i(p'_i, p_{-i}, \kappa)$ is nondecreasing in κ for $p_i > p'_i$, and A5 is satisfied for κ.

Thus, all the assumptions are satisfied. This being the case, a number of theorems can be applied, including the following two.

Theorem 14.1 *If the game is supermodular, there exists a largest and a smallest Nash equilibrium in pure strategies.*

Theorem 14.2 *If the game is supermodular and assumption (A5) or (A5′) is satisfied, then the largest and smallest equilibrium are nondecreasing functions of the parameter z.*

Applying theorems 14.1 and 14.2 yields the following results for the differentiated Bertrand game:

1   There exists a largest and a smallest Nash equilibrium in pure strategies (theorem 14.2).
2   The largest and smallest equilibrium prices for firm i are nondecreasing functions of the cost parameters c_i and κ (theorem 14.2).

Supermodularity, unlike the implicit function theorem, has yielded comparative statics on κ, the discrete exogenous variable. It yields weaker comparative statics on c_i, however, because it just finds the effect of c_i on p_i^* to be nondecreasing, rather than telling us its value or whether it is actually increasing.

For more on supermodularity, see Milgrom & Roberts (1990), Fudenberg & Tirole (1991, pp. 489–97), or Vives's 2005 survey.

*14.5   Vertical Differentiation

In previous sections of this chapter we have been looking at product differentiaton, but differentiation in dimensions that cannot be called "good" versus "bad." Rather, location along a line is a matter of taste and "de gustibus non est disputandum." Another form of product differentiation is from better to worse, as analyzed in Shaked & Sutton (1983) and around pp. 150 and 296 of Tirole (1988). Here, we will look at that in a simpler game in which there are just two types of buyers and two levels of quality, but we will compare a monopoly to a duopoly under various circumstances.

Vertical Differentiation I: The One-product Monopoly

PLAYERS
A seller and a continuum of buyers.

THE ORDER OF PLAY
0   Nature assigns quality values to a continuum of buyers of length 1. Half of them are "weak" buyers ($\theta = 0$) who value high quality at 20 and low quality at 10. Half of them are "strong" buyers ($\theta = 1$) who value high quality at 50 and low quality at 15.
1   The seller picks quality s to be either 0 (low) or 1 (high).
2   The seller picks price p from the interval $[0, \infty)$.
3   Each buyer chooses one unit of a good, or refrains from buying. The seller produces at constant marginal cost $c = 1$, which does not vary with quality.

PAYOFFS
The seller's payoff is

$$\pi_{seller} = (p - 1)q. \tag{14.60}$$

The buyer's payoff is zero if he does not buy. If he does buy, it is

$$\pi_{buyer} = (10 + 5\theta) + (10 + 25\theta)s - p. \tag{14.61}$$

Payoff (14.61) represents a base value of $(10+5\theta)$ plus $(10+25\theta)$ per unit of quality beyond that.

The seller should clearly set the quality to be high since then he can charge more to the buyer (though note that this runs contrary to a common misimpression that a monopoly will result in lower quality than a competitive market). The price should be either 50, which is the most the strong buyers would pay, or 20, the most the weak buyers would pay. Since $\pi(50) = 0.5(50 - 1) = 24.5$ and $\pi(20) = 0.5(20 - 1) + 0.5(20 - 1) = 19$, the seller should choose $p = 50$. Separation (by inducing only the strong buyers to buy) is better for the seller than pooling. Note that the payoffs satisfy the single-crossing property.

Next we will allow the seller to use two quality levels. A social planner would just use one – the maximal one of $s = High$ – since it is no cheaper to produce lower quality. The monopoly seller might use two, however, because it helps him to price-discriminate.

Vertical Differentiation II: The Two-product Monopoly

PLAYERS

A seller and a continuum of buyers.

THE ORDER OF PLAY

0   Nature assigns quality values to a continuum of buyers of length 1. Half of them are "weak" buyers ($\theta = 0$) who value high quality at 20 and low quality at 10. Half of them are "strong" buyers ($\theta = 1$) who value high quality at 50 and low quality at 15.

1   The seller decides to sell both qualities $s = 0$ (low) and $s = 1$ (high) or just one of them.

2   The seller picks prices p_L and p_H from the interval $[0, \infty)$.

3   Each buyer chooses one unit of a good, or refrains from buying. The seller produces at constant marginal cost $c = 1$, which does not vary with quality.

PAYOFFS

$$\pi_{seller} = (p_L - 1)q_L + (p_H - 1)q_H \tag{14.62}$$

and

$$\pi_{buyer} = (10 + 5\theta) + (10 + 25\theta)s - p. \tag{14.63}$$

This is a problem of mechanism design. The seller needs to pick p_1 and p_2 to satisfy incentive compatibility and participation constraints if he wants to offer two qualities with positive sales of both, and he also needs to decide if that is more profitable than offering just one quality.

We already solved the one-quality problem in Vertical Differentiation I, yielding profit of 24.5. The monopolist cannot simply add a second, low-quality, low-price good for the weak buyers, because the strong buyers, who derive zero payoff from the high-quality good, would switch to the low-quality good, which would give them a positive payoff. In equilibrium, the monopolist will have to give the strong buyers a positive payoff. Their participation constraint will be non-binding, as we have found so many times before for the "good" type.

Following the usual pattern, the participation constraint for the weak buyers will be binding, so $p_L = 10$. The self-selection constraint for the strong buyers will also be binding, so

$$\pi_{strong}(L) = 15 - p_L = 50 - p_H. \tag{14.64}$$

Since $p_L = 10$, this results in $p_H = 45$. The price for high quality must be at least 35 higher than the price for low quality to induce separation of the buyer types. Profits will now be:

$$\pi_{seller} = (10 - 1)(0.5) + (45 - 1)(0.5) = 26.5. \tag{14.65}$$

This exceeds the one-quality profit of 24.5, so it is optimal for the seller to sell two qualities.

This result, is, of course, dependent on the parameters chosen, but it is nonetheless a fascinating special case, and one which is perhaps no more special than the other special case, in which the seller finds that profits are maximized with just one quality. The outcome of allowing price discrimination is a Pareto improvement. The seller is better off, because profit has risen from 24.5 to 26.5. The strong buyers are better off, because the price they pay has fallen from 50 to 45. And the weak buyers are no worse off. In Vertical Differentiation I their payoff was zero because they chose not to buy; in Vertical Differentiation II their payoffs are zero because they buy at a price exactly equal to their value for the good.

Indeed, we can go further. Suppose the cost for the low-quality good is actually *higher* than for the high-quality good, for example, $c_L = 3$ and $c_H = 1$, because the good is normally produced as high quality and needs to be purposely damaged before it becomes low quality. The price-discrimination profit in (14.65) would then be $\pi_{seller} = (10 - 3)$ $(0.5) + (45 - 1)(0.5) = 25.5$. Since that is still higher than 24.5, the seller would still price-discriminate. The buyers' payoffs would be unaffected. Thus, allowing the seller to damage some of the good at a cost in real resources of 2 per unit, converting it from high to low quality, can result in a Pareto improvement!

This is the point made in Deneckere & McAfee (1996), which illustrates the theory with real-world examples of computer chips and printers purposely damaged to allow price discrimination. See too McAfee (2002, p. 265), which tells us, for example, that Sony made two sizes of minidisc in 2002, a 60-minute and a 74-minute version. Production of both starts with a capacity of 74 minutes, but Sony added code to the 60-minute disc to make 14 minutes of it unusable. That code is an extra fixed cost, but IBM's 1990 Laserprinter E is an example of a damaged product with extra marginal cost. The Laserprinter E was a version of the original Laserprinter that was only half as fast. The reason? IBM added five extra chips to the Laserprinter E to slow it down.

We will analyze one more version of the product differentiation game: with two sellers instead of one. This will show how the product differentiation which increases profits in the way we have seen in the Hotelling games can occur vertically as well as horizontally.

Vertical Differentiation III: Duopoly Quality Choice

PLAYERS
Two sellers and a continuum of buyers.

THE ORDER OF PLAY

0   Nature assigns quality values to a continuum of buyers of length 1. Half of them are "weak" buyers ($\theta = 0$) who value high quality at 20 and low quality at 10. Half of them are "strong" buyers ($\theta = 1$) who value high quality at 50 and low quality at 15.

1   Sellers 1 and 2 simultaneously choose values for s_1 and s_2 from the set $\{0, 1\}$. They may both choose the same value.

2   Sellers 1 and 2 simultaneously choose prices p_1 and p_2 from the interval $[0, \infty)$.

3   Each buyer chooses one unit of a good, or refrains from buying. The sellers produce at constant marginal cost $c = 1$, which does not vary with quality.

PAYOFFS

$$\pi_{seller} = (p - 1)q, \tag{14.66}$$

and

$$\pi_{buyer} = (10 + 5\theta) + (10 + 25\theta)s - p. \tag{14.67}$$

If both sellers both choose the same quality level, their profits will be zero, but if they choose different quality levels, profits will be positive. Thus, there are three possible equilibria in the quality stage of the game: (Low, High), (High, Low), and a symmetric mixed-strategy equilibrium. Let us consider the pure-strategy equilibria first, and without loss of generality suppose that Seller 1 is the low-quality seller and Seller 2 is the high-quality seller.

1   The equilibrium prices of Vertical Differentiation II, ($p_L = 10, p_H = 45$), will no longer be equilibrium prices. The problem is that the low-quality seller would deviate to $p_L = 9$, doubling his sales for a small reduction in price.
2   Indeed, there is no pure-strategy equilibrium in prices. We have seen that ($p_L = 10, p_H = 45$) is not an equilibrium, even though $p_H = 45$ is the high-quality seller's best response to $p_L = 10$. $P_L > 10$ will attract no buyers, so that cannot be part of an equilibrium. Suppose $P_L \in (1, 10)$. The response of the high-quality seller will be to set $p_H = p_L + 35$, in which case the low-quality seller can increase his profits by slightly reducing p_L and doubling his sales. The only price left for the low-quality seller that does not generate negative profits is $p_L = 1$, but that yields zero profits, and so is worse than $p_L = 10$. Thus, no choice of p_L is part of a pure-strategy equilibrium.
3   As always, an equilibrium does exist, so it must be in mixed strategies, as shown below.

The Asymmetric Equilibrium: Pure Strategies for Quality, Mixed for Price

The low-quality seller picks p_L on the support [5.5, 10] using the cumulative distribution

$$F(p_L) = 1 - \left(\frac{39.5}{p_L + 34} \right) \tag{14.68}$$

with an atom of probability 39.5/44 at $p_L = 10$.
The high-quality seller picks p_H on the support [40.5, 45] using the cumulative distribution

$$G(p_H) = 2 - \left(\frac{9}{p_H - 36} \right). \tag{14.69}$$

Weak buyers buy from the low-quality seller if $10 - p_L \geq 20 - p_H$, which is always true in equilibrium. Strong buyers buy from the low-quality seller if $15 - p_L > 50 - p_H$, which has positive probability, and otherwise from the high-quality seller.

This equilibrium is noteworthy because it includes a probability atom in the mixed-strategy distribution, something not uncommon in pricing games. The low-quality seller usually chooses $p_L = 10$, but with some probability he mixes between 5.5 and 10. The intuition for why this happens is that for the low-quality seller the weak buyers are "safe" customers, for whom the monopoly price is 10, but unless the low-quality seller chooses to shade the price with some probability to try to attract the strong customers, the high-quality seller will maintain such a high price ($p_H = 45$) as to make such shading irresistible.

To start deriving this equilibrium, let us conjecture that the low-quality seller will not include any prices above 10 in his mixing support but will include $p_L = 10$ itself. That is plausible because he would lose all the low-quality buyers at prices above 10, but $p_L = 10$ yields maximal profits whenever p_H is low enough that only weak consumers buy low quality.

The low-quality seller's profit from $p_L = 10$ is $\pi_L(p = 10) = 0.5(10 - 1) = 4.5$. Thus, the lower bound of the support of his mixing distribution (denote it by a_L) must also yield a profit of 4.5. There is no point in charging a price less than the price which would capture even the strong consumers with probability one, in which case

$$\pi_L(a_L) = 0.5(a_L - 1) + 0.5(a_L - 1) = 4.5 \tag{14.70}$$

and $a_L = 5.5$. Thus, the low-quality seller mixes on $[5.5, 10]$.

On that mixing support, the low-quality seller's profit must equal 4.5 for any price. Thus,

$$\pi_L(p_L) = 4.5 = 0.5(p_L - 1) + 0.5(p_L - 1)Prob(15 - p_L > 50 - p_H),$$
$$= 0.5(p_L - 1) + 0.5(p_L - 1)Prob(p_H > 35 + p_L),$$
$$= 0.5(p_L - 1) + 0.5(p_L - 1)[1 - G(35 + p_L)]. \tag{14.71}$$

Therefore, the $G(p_H)$ function is such that

$$1 - G(35 + p_L) = \frac{4.5}{0.5(p_L - 1)} - 1, \tag{14.72}$$

and

$$G(35 + p_L) = 2 - \left(\frac{4.5}{0.5(p_L - 1)}\right). \tag{14.73}$$

We want a G function with the argument p_H, not $(35 + p_L)$, so

$$G(p_H) = 2 - \left(\frac{4.5}{0.5([p_H - 35] - 1)}\right) = 2 - \left(\frac{9}{p_H - 36}\right). \tag{14.74}$$

As explained in chapter 3, what we have just done is to find the strategy for the high-quality seller that makes the low-quality seller indifferent among all the values of p_L in his mixing support.

We can find the support of the high-quality seller's mixing distribution by finding values a_H and b_H such that $G(a_H) = 0$ and $G(b_H) = 1$, so

$$G(a_H) = 2 - \left(\frac{9}{a_H - 36}\right) = 0, \tag{14.75}$$

which yields $a_H = 40.5$, and

$$G(b_H) = 2 - \left(\frac{9}{(0) \cdot b_H - 36}\right) = 1, \tag{14.76}$$

which yields $b_H = 45$. Thus the support of the high-quality seller's mixing distribution is $[40.5, 45]$.

Now let us find the low-quality seller's mixing distribution, $F(p_L)$. At $p_H = 40.5$, the high-quality seller has zero probability of losing the strong buyers to the low-quality seller, so his profit is $0.5(40.5 - 1) = 19.75$. Now comes the tricky step. At $p_h = 45$, if the high-quality seller had probability one of losing the strong buyers to the low-quality seller, his profit would be zero, and he would strictly prefer $p_H = 40.5$. Thus, it must be that at $p_h = 45$ there is strictly positive probability that $p_L = 10$ – not just a positive density. So let us continue, using our finding that the profit of the high-quality seller must be 19.75 from any price in the mixing support. Then,

$$\pi_H(p_H) = 19.75 = 0.5(p_H - 1)Prob(15 - p_L < 50 - p_H),$$

$$= 0.5(p_H - 1)Prob(p_H - 35 < p_L),$$

$$= 0.5(p_H - 1)[1 - F(p_H - 35)], \tag{14.77}$$

so

$$F(p_H - 35) = 1 - \left(\frac{19.75}{0.5(p_H - 1)}\right). \tag{14.78}$$

Using the same substitution trick as in equation (14.74), putting p_L instead of $(p_H - 35)$ as the argument for F, we get

$$F(p_L) = 1 - \left(\frac{19.75}{0.5(p_L + 35 - 1)}\right) = 1 - \left(\frac{39.5}{p_L + 34}\right) \tag{14.79}$$

In particular, note that

$$F(5.5) = 1 - \left(\frac{39.5}{5.5 + 34}\right) = 0, \tag{14.80}$$

confirming our earlier finding that the minimum p_L used is 5.5, and

$$F(10) = 1 - \left(\frac{39.5}{10 + 34}\right) = 1 - \frac{39.5}{44} < 1. \tag{14.81}$$

Equation (14.81) shows that at the upper bound of the low-quality seller's mixing support the cumulative mixing distribution does not equal 1, an oddity we usually do not see in mixing distributions. What it implies is that there is an atom of probability at $p_L = 10$, soaking up all the remaining probability beyond what equation (14.81) yields for the prices below 10. The atom must equal $39.5/44 \approx 0.9$.

Happily, this solves our paradox of zero high-quality seller profit at $p_H = 45$. If $p_L = 10$ has probability $39.5/44$, the profit from $p_H = 45$ is $0.5(39.5/44)(45 - 1) = 19.75$. Thus, the profit from $p_H = 45$ is the same as from $p_H = 40.5$, and the seller is willing to mix between them.

One of the technical lessons of chapter 3 is that if your attempt to calculate mixing probability results in probabilities of less than zero or more than one, then probably the equilibrium is not in mixed strategies (algebra mistakes being another possibility). The lesson here is that if your attempt to calculate the support of a mixing distribution results in impossible bounds, then you should consider the possibility that the distribution has atoms of probability.

The duopoly sellers' profits are 4.5 (for low quality) and 19.75 (for high quality) in the asymmetric equilibrium of Vertical Differentiation III, a total of 24.25 for the industry. This is less than either the 24.5 earned by the nondiscriminating monopolist of Vertical Differentiation I or the 26 earned by the discriminating monopolist of Vertical Differentiation II. But what about the mixed-strategy equilibrium for Vertical Differentiation III?

The Symmetric Equilibrium: Mixed Strategies for both Quality and Price

Each player chooses low quality with probability $\alpha = 4.5/24.25$ and high quality otherwise. If they choose the same quality, they next both choose a price equal to 1, marginal cost. If they choose different qualities, they choose prices according to the mixing distributions in the asymmetric equilibrium.

This equilibrium is easier to explain. Working back from the end, if they choose the same qualities, the two firms are in undifferentiated price competition and will choose prices equal to marginal cost, with payoffs of zero. If they choose different qualities, they are in the same situation as they would be in the asymmetric equilibrium, with expected payoffs of 4.5 for the low-quality firm and 19.75 for the high-quality firm. As for choice of product quality, the expected payoffs from each quality must be equal in equilibrium, so there must be a higher probability of both choosing high quality:

$$\pi(Low) = \alpha(0) + (1-\alpha)4.5 = \pi(High) = \alpha(19.75) + (1-\alpha)(0). \tag{14.82}$$

Solving equation (14.82) yields $\alpha = 4.5/24.25 \approx 0.17$, in which case each player's payoff is about 3.75. Thus, even if a player is stuck in the role of low-quality seller in the pure-strategy equilibrium, with an expected payoff of 4.5, that is better than the expected payoff he would get in the "fairer" symmetric equilibrium.

We can conclude that if the players could somehow arrange what equilibrium would be played out, they would arrange for a pure-strategy equilibrium, perhaps by use of cheap talk and some random focal point variable.

Or, perhaps they could change the rules of the game so that they would choose qualities sequentially. Suppose one seller gets to choose quality first. He would of course choose high quality, for a payoff of 19.75. The second-mover, however, choosing low-quality, would have a payoff of 4.5, better than the expected payoff in the symmetric mixed-strategy equilibrium of the simultaneous quality-choice game. This is the same phenomenon as the Pareto superiority of a sequential version of the Battle of the Sexes over the symmetric mixed-strategy equilibrium of the simultaneous-move game.

What if Seller 1 chooses both quality and price first, and Seller 2 responds with quality and price? If Seller 1 chooses low quality, then his optimal price is $p_L = 10$, since the second player will choose high quality and a price low enough to attract the strong buyers – $p_H = 45$, in equilibrium – so Seller 1's payoff would be $0.5(10 - 1) = 4.5$. If Seller 1 chooses high quality, then his optimal price is $p_H = 40.5$, since the second player will choose low quality and would choose a price high enough to lure away the strong buyers if $p_H < 40.5$. If, however, $p_H = 40.5$, Seller 2 would give up on attracting the strong buyers and pick $p_L = 10$. Thus, if Seller 1 chooses both quality and price first, he will choose high quality and $p_H = 40.5$ while Seller 2 will choose low quality and $p_L = 10$, resulting in the same payoffs as in the asymmetric equilibrium of the simultaneous-move game, though no longer in mixed strategies.

What Product Differentiation III shows us is that product differentiation can take place in oligopoly vertically as well as horizontally. Head-to-head competition reduces profits, so firms will try to differentiate in any way that they can. This increases their profits, but it can also benefit consumers – though more obviously in the case of horizontal differentiation than in vertical. Keep in mind, though, that in our games here we have assumed that high quality costs no more than low quality. Usually high quality is more expensive, which means that having more than one quality level can be efficient. Often poor people prefer lower quality, given the cost of higher quality, and even a social planner would provide a variety of quality levels. Here, we see that even when only high quality would be provided in the first best, it is better that a monopolist provide two qualities rather than one, and a duopoly is even better for consumers.

*14.6   Durable Monopoly

Introductory economics courses are vague on the issue of the time period over which transactions take place. When a diagram shows the supply and demand for widgets, the x-axis is labelled "widgets," not "widgets per week" or "widgets per year." Also, the diagram splits off one time period from future time periods, using the implicit assumption that supply and demand in one period is unaffected by events of future periods. One problem with this on the demand side is that the purchase of a good which lasts for more than one use is an investment; although the price is paid now, the utility from the good continues into the future. If Smith buys a house, he is buying not just the right to live in the house tomorrow, but the right to live in it for many years to come, or even to live in it for a few years and then sell the remaining years to someone else. The continuing utility he receives from this durable good is called its **service flow**. Even though he may not intend to rent out the house, it is an investment decision for him because it trades off present expenditure for future utility. Since even a shirt produces a service flow over more than an instant of time, the durability of goods presents difficult definitional problems for national income accounts. Houses are counted as part of national investment (and an estimate of their service flow as part of services consumption), automobiles as durable goods consumption, and shirts as nondurable goods consumption, but all are to some extent durable investments.

In microeconomic theory, "durable monopoly" refers not to monopolies that last a long time, but to monopolies that sell durable goods. These present a curious problem. When a monopolist sells something like a refrigerator to a consumer, that consumer drops out of the market until the refrigerator wears out. The demand curve is, therefore, changing over time as a result of the monopolist's choice of price, which means that the modeller should not make his decisions in one period and ignore future periods. Demand is not **time separable**, because a rise in price at time t_1 affects the quantity demanded at time t_2.

The durable monopolist has a special problem because in a sense he does have a competitor – himself in the later periods. If he were to set a high price in the first period, thereby removing high-demand buyers from the market, he would be tempted to set a lower price in the next period to take advantage of the remaining consumers. But if it were expected that he would lower the price, the high-demand buyers would not buy at a high price in the first period. The threat of the future low price forces the monopolist to keep his current price low.

This presents another aspect of product differentiation: the durability of a good. Will a monopolist produce a shoddier, less durable product? Durability is different from the vertical differentiation we have already analyzed because durability has temporal implications. The buyer of a less durable product will return to the market sooner than the buyer of a more durable one, regardless of other aspects of product quality.

To formalize this situation, let the seller have a monopoly on a durable good which lasts two periods. He must set a price for each period, and the buyer must decide what quantity to buy in each period. Because this one buyer is meant to represent the entire market demand, the moves are ordered so that he has no market power, as in the principal–agent models in chapter 7 and onwards. Alternatively, the buyer can be viewed as representing a continuum of consumers (see Coase [1972] and Bulow [1982]). In this interpretation, instead of "the buyer" buying q_1 in the first period, q_1 of the buyers each buy one unit in the first period.

Durable Monopoly

PLAYERS
A buyer and a seller.

THE ORDER OF PLAY

1 The seller picks the first-period price, p_1.
2 The buyer buys quantity q_1 and consumes service flow q_1.
3 The seller picks the second-period price, p_2.
4 The buyer buys additional quantity q_2 and consumes service flow $(q_1 + q_2)$.

PAYOFFS
Production cost is zero and there is no discounting. The seller's payoff is his revenue, and the buyer's payoff is the sum across periods of his benefits from consumption minus his expenditure. The buyer's benefits arise from his being willing to pay as much as

$$B(q_t) = 60 - \frac{q_t}{2} \tag{14.83}$$

for the marginal unit service flow consumed in period t, as shown in figure 14.10. The payoffs are therefore

$$\pi_{seller} = q_1 p_1 + q_2 p_2 \tag{14.84}$$

and, since a consumer's total benefit is the sum of a triangle plus a rectangle of benefit, as shown in figure 14.10,

$$\pi_{buyer} = [consumer\ surplus_1] + [consumer\ surplus_2],$$
$$= [total\ benefit_1 - expenditure_1] + [total\ benefit_2 - expenditure_2],$$
$$= \left[\left(\frac{(60 - B(q_1))q_1}{2} + B(q_1)q_1 \right) - p_1 q_1 \right]$$
$$+ \left[\left(\frac{60 - B(q_1 + q_2)}{2}(q_1 + q_2) + B(q_1 + q_2)(q_1 + q_2) \right) - p_2 q_2 \right]. \tag{14.85}$$

Thinking about durable monopoly is hard because we are used to one-period models in which the demand curve, which relates the price to the quantity demanded, is identical to

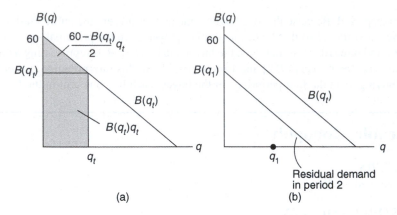

Figure 14.11   The buyer's marginal benefit per period in durable monopoly.

the marginal-benefit curve, which relates the marginal benefit to the quantity consumed. Here, the two curves are different. The marginal benefit curve is the same each period, since it is part of the rules of the game, relating consumption to utility. The demand curve will change over time and depends on the equilibrium strategies, depending as it does on the number of periods left in which to consume the good's services, expected future prices, and the quantity already owned. Marginal benefit is a given for the buyer; quantity demanded is his strategy.

The buyer's total benefit in period 1 is the dollar value of his utility from his purchase of q_1, which equals the amount he would have been willing to pay to rent q_1. This is composed of the two areas shown in figure 14.11a, the upper triangle of area $(1/2)(q_1 + q_2)(60 - B(q_1+q_2))$ and the lower rectangle of area $(q_1+q_2)B(q_1+q_2)$. From this must be subtracted his expenditure in period 1, $p_1 q_1$, to obtain what we might call his consumer surplus in the first period. Note that $p_1 q_1$ will not be the lower rectangle, unless by some strange accident, and the "consumer surplus" might easily be negative, since the expenditure in period 1 will also yield utility in period 2 because the good is durable.

To find the equilibrium price path one cannot simply differentiate the seller's utility with respect to p_1 and p_2, because that would violate the sequential rationality of the seller and the rational response of the buyer. Instead, one must look for a subgame perfect equilibrium, which means starting in the second period and discovering how much the buyer would purchase given his first-period purchase of q_1, and what second-period price the seller would charge given the buyer's second-period demand function.

In the first period, the marginal unit consumed was the q_1th. In the second period, it will be the $(q_1 + q_2)$th. The residual demand curve after the first period's purchases is shown in figure 14.11b. It is a demand curve very much like the demand curve resulting from intensity rationing in the capacity-constrained Bertrand game of section 14.2, as shown in figure 14.11a. The most intense portion of the buyer's demand, up to q_1 units, has already been satisfied, and what is left begins with a marginal benefit of $B(q_1)$, and falls at the same slope as the original marginal benefit curve. The equation for the residual demand is therefore, using equation (14.83),

$$p_2 = B(q_1) - \frac{q_2}{2} = 60 - \left(\frac{1}{2}\right)q_1 - \left(\frac{1}{2}\right)q_2. \tag{14.86}$$

Solving for the monopoly quantity, q_2^*, the seller maximizes $q_2 p_2$, solving the problem

$$\underset{q_2}{\text{Maximize}}\ q_2 \left(60 - \left(\frac{1}{2} \right) (q_1 + q_2) \right), \tag{14.87}$$

which generates the first-order condition

$$60 - q_2 - \left(\frac{1}{2} \right) q_1 = 0, \tag{14.88}$$

so that

$$q_2^* = 60 - \left(\frac{1}{2} \right) q_1. \tag{14.89}$$

From equations (14.86) and (14.89), it can be seen that $p_2^* = 30 - q_1/4$.

We must now find q_1^*. In period one, the buyer looks ahead to the possibility of buying in period two at a lower price. Buying in the first period has two benefits: consumption of the service flow in the first period and consumption of the service flow in the second period. The price he would pay for a unit in period one cannot exceed the marginal benefit from the first-period service flow in period one plus the foreseen value of p_2, which from (14.89) is $30 - q_1/4$. If the seller chooses to sell q_1 in the first period, therefore, he can do so at the price

$$p_1(q_1) = B(q_1) + p_2,$$

$$= \left(60 - \left(\frac{1}{2} \right) q_1 \right) + \left(30 - \left(\frac{1}{4} \right) q_1 \right),$$

$$= 90 - \left(\frac{3}{4} \right) q_1. \tag{14.90}$$

Knowing that in the second period he will choose q_2 according to (14.89), the seller combines (14.89) with (14.90) to give the maximand in the problem of choosing q_1 to maximize profit over the two periods, which is

$$\pi_{seller} = (p_1 q_1 + p_2 q_2) = \left(90 - \frac{3q_1}{4} \right) q_1 + \left(30 - \frac{q_1}{4} \right)(60 - \frac{q_1}{2}),$$

$$= 1800 + 60 q_1 - \frac{5 q_1^2}{8}, \tag{14.91}$$

which has the first-order condition

$$60 - \frac{5 q_1}{4} = 0, \tag{14.92}$$

so that

$$q_1^* = 48 \tag{14.93}$$

and, making use of (14.90), $p_1^* = 54$.

It follows from (14.89) that $q_2^* = 36$ and $p_2 = 18$. The seller's profits over the two periods are $\pi_s = 3{,}240\ (= 54(48) + 18(36))$.

The purpose of these calculations is to compare the situation with three other market structures: a competitive market, a monopolist who rents instead of selling, and a monopolist who commits to selling only in the first period.

A *competitive market* bids down the price to the marginal cost of zero. Then, $p_1 = 0$ and $q_1 = 120$ from (14.83) because buyers buy till their marginal benefit is zero, and profits equal zero also.

If the monopolist *rents* instead of selling, then equation (14.83) is like an ordinary demand equation, because the monopolist is effectively selling the good's services separately each period. He could rent a quantity of 60 each period at a rental fee of 30 and his profits would sum to $\pi_s = 3,600$. That is higher than 3,240, so profits are higher from renting than from selling outright. The problem with selling outright is that the first-period price cannot be very high or the buyer knows that the seller will be tempted to lower the price once the buyer has bought in the first period. Renting avoids this problem.

If the monopolist can *commit to not producing in the second period*, he will do just as well as the monopolist who rents, since he can sell a quantity of 60 at a price of 60, the sum of the rents for the two periods. An example is the artist who breaks the plates for his engravings after a production run of announced size. We must also assume that the artist can convince the market that he has broken the plates. People joke that the best way an artist can increase the value of his work is by dying, and that, too, fits the model.

If the modeller ignored sequential rationality and simply looked for the Nash equilibrium that maximized the payoff of the seller by his choice of p_1 and p_2, he would come to the commitment result. An example of such an equilibrium is $(p_1 = 60, p_2 = 200, Buyer$ *purchases according to* $q_1 = 120 - p_1$, *and* $q_2 = 0)$. This is Nash because neither player has incentive to deviate given the other's strategy, but it fails to be subgame perfect, because the seller should realize that if he deviates and chooses a lower price once the second period is reached, the buyer will respond by deviating from $q_2 = 0$ and will buy more units.

With more than two periods, the difficulties of the durable-goods monopolist become even more striking. In an infinite-period model without discounting, if the marginal cost of production is zero, the equilibrium price for outright sale instead of renting is constant – at zero! Think about this in the context of a model with many buyers. Early consumers foresee that the monopolist has an incentive to cut the price after they buy, in order to sell to the remaining consumers who value the product less. In fact, the monopolist would continue to cut the price and sell more and more units to consumers with weaker and weaker demand until the price fell to marginal cost. Without discounting, even the high-valuation consumers refuse to buy at a high price, because they know they could wait until the price falls to zero. And this is not a trick of infinity: a large number of periods generates a price close to zero.

We can also use the durable monopoly model to think about the durability of the product. If the seller can develop a product so flimsy that it only lasts one period, that is equivalent to renting. A consumer is willing to pay the same price to own a one-hoss shay that he knows will break down in one year as he would pay to rent it for a year. Low durability leads to the same output and profits as renting, which explains why a firm with market power might produce goods that wear out quickly. The explanation is not that the monopolist can use his market power to inflict lower quality on consumers – after all, the price he receives is lower too – but that the lower durability makes it credible to high-valuation buyers that the seller expects their business in the future and will not reduce his price.

With durable-goods monopoly, this book is concluded. Is this book itself a durable good? As I am now writing its fourth edition, I cannot say that it is perfectly durable, because it has improved with each edition, and I can honestly say that a rational consumer who liked the first edition should have bought each successive edition. If you can benefit from this book, your time is valuable enough that you should substitute book reading for solitary thinking even at the expensive prices my publisher and I charge.

Yet although I have added new material, and improved my presentation of the old material, the basic ideas remain the same. The central idea is that in modern economic modelling the modeller starts by thinking about players, actions, information, and payoffs, stripping a situation down to its essentials. Having done that, he sees what payoff-maximizing equilibrium behavior arises from the assumptions. This book teaches a variety of common ways that assumptions link to conclusions just as a book on chess strategy teaches how variety of common configurations of a chessboard lead to winning or losing. Just as with a book on chess, however, the important thing is not just to know common tricks and simplifications, but to be able to recognize the general features of a situation and know what tricks to apply.

Notes

N14.1   Quantities as strategies: the Cournot equilibrium revisited

- Articles on the existence and uniqueness of a pure-strategy equilibrium in the Cournot model include Roberts & Sonnenschein (1976), Novshek (1985), and Gaudet & Salant (1991).
- **Merger in a Cournot model.** A problem with the Cournot model is that a firm's best policy is often to split up into separate firms. Apex gets half the industry profits in a duopoly game. If Apex split into firms $Apex_1$ and $Apex_2$, it would get two thirds of the profit in the Cournot triopoly game, even though industry profit falls.

    This point was made by Salant, Switzer, & Reynolds (1983) and is the subject of problem 14.2. It is interesting that nobody noted this earlier, given the intense interest in Cournot models. The insight comes from approaching the problem from asking whether a player could improve his lot if his strategy space were expanded in reasonable ways.

- An ingenious look at how the number of firms in a market affects the price is Bresnahan & Reiss (1991a), which looks empirically at a number of very small markets with one, two, three or more competing firms. They find a big decline in the price from one to two firms, a smaller decline from two to three, and not much change thereafter.

    Exemplifying theory, as discussed in the Introduction to this book, lends itself to explaining particular cases, but it is much less useful for making generalizations across industries. Empirical work associated with exemplifying theory tends to consist of historical anecdote rather than the linear regressions to which economics has become accustomed. Generalization and econometrics are still often useful in industrial organization, however, as Bresnahan & Reiss shows. The most ambitious attempt to connect general data with the modern theory of industrial organization is Sutton's 1991 book, *Sunk Costs and Market Structure*, which is an extraordinarily well-balanced mix of theory, history, and numerical data.

N14.2   Prices as strategies: the Bertrand equilibrium

- As Morrison (1998) points out, Cournot actually does (in chapter 7) analyze the case of price competition with imperfect substitutes, as well as the quantity competition that bears his name. It is convenient to continue to contrast "Bertrand" and "Cournot" competition, however, though a case can be made for simplifying terminology to "price" and "quantity" competition instead. For the history of how the Bertrand name came to be attached to price competition, see Dimand & Dore (1999).

- Intensity rationing has also been called **efficient rationing**. Sometimes, however, this rationing rule is inefficient. Some low-intensity consumers left facing the high price decide not to buy the product even though their benefit is greater than its marginal cost. The reason intensity rationing has been thought to be efficient is that it is efficient if the rationed-out consumers are unable to buy at any price.

- OPEC has tried both price and quantity controls ("OPEC, Seeking Flexibility, May Choose Not to Set Oil Prices, but to Fix Output," *Wall Street Journal*, October 8, 1987, p. 2; "Saudi King Fahd Is Urged by Aides to Link Oil Prices to Spot Markets," *Wall Street Journal*, October 7, 1987, p. 2). Weitzman (1974) is the classic reference on price versus quantity control by regulators, although he does not use the context of oligopoly. The decision rests partly on enforceability, and OPEC has also hired accounting firms to monitor prices ("Dutch Accountants Take On a Formidable Task: Ferreting Out 'Cheaters' in the Ranks of OPEC," *Wall Street Journal*, February 26, 1985, p. 39).

- Kreps & Scheinkman (1983) show how capacity choice and Bertrand pricing can lead to a Cournot outcome. Two firms face downward-sloping market demand. In the first stage of the game, they simultaneously choose capacities, and in the second stage they simultaneously choose prices (possibly by mixed strategies). If a firm cannot satisfy the demand facing it in the second stage (because of the capacity limit), it uses intensity rationing (the results depend on this). The unique subgame perfect equilibrium is for each firm to choose the Cournot capacity and price.

- Haltiwanger & Waldman (1991) have suggested a dichotomy applicable to many different games between players who are **responders**, choosing their actions flexibly, and those who are **nonresponders**, who are inflexible. A player might be a nonresponder because he is irrational, because he moves first, or simply because his strategy set is small. The categories are used in a second dichotomy, between games exhibiting **synergism**, in which responders choose to do whatever the majority do (upward sloping reaction curves), and games exhibiting **congestion**, in which responders want to join the minority (downward sloping reaction curves). Under synergism, the equilibrium is more like what it would be if all the players were nonresponders; under congestion, the responders have more influence. Haltiwanger and Waldman apply the dichotomies to network externalities, efficiency wages, and reputation.

- There are many ways to specify product differentation. This chapter looks at horizontal differentiation where all consumers agree that products A and B are more alike than A and C, but they disagree as to which is best. Another way horizontal differentiation might work is for each consumer to like a particular product best, but to consider all others as equivalent. See Dixit & Stiglitz (1977) for a model along those lines. Or, differentiation might be vertical: all consumers agree that A is better than B and B is better than C but they disagree as to how *much* better A is than B. Firms therefore offer different qualities at different prices. Shaked & Sutton (1983) have explored this kind of vertical differentation.

N14.3 Location models

- For a booklength treatment of location models, see Greenhut & Ohta (1975).
- Vickrey notes the possible absence of a pure-strategy equilibrium in Hotelling's model in pp. 323–4 of his 1964 book *Microstatics*. D'Aspremont, Gabszewicz, & Thisse (1979) work out the mixed-strategy equilibrium for the case of quadratic transportation costs, and Osborne & Pitchik (1987) do the same for Hotelling's original model.
- Location models and switching cost models are attempts to go beyond the notion of a market price. Antitrust cases are good sources for descriptions of the complexities of pricing in particular

markets. See, for example, Sultan's 1974 book on electrical equipment in the 1950s, or antitrust opinions such as *US v. Addyston Pipe & Steel Co.*, 85 F. 271 (1898).

- It is important in location models whether the positions of the players on the line are moveable (see, e.g., Lane [1980]).

- The location games in this chapter model use a one-dimensional space with end points, that is, a line segment. Another kind of one-dimensional space is a circle (not to be confused with a disk). The difference is that no point on a circle is distinctive, so no consumer preference can be called extreme. It is, if you like, Peoria versus Berkeley. The circle might be used for modelling convenience or because it fits a situation: for example, airline flights spread over the 24 hours of the day. With two players, the Hotelling location game on a circle has a continuum of pure-strategy equilibria that are one of two types: both players locating at the same spot, versus players separated from each other by 180°. The three-player model also has a continuum of pure-strategy equilibria, each player separated from another by 120°, in contrast to the nonexistence of a pure-strategy equilibrium when the game is played on a line segment.

- Characteristics such as the color of cars could be modelled as location, but only on a player-by-player basis, because they have no natural ordering. While Smith's ranking of (red=1, yellow=2, blue=10) could be depicted on a line, if Brown's ranking is (red=1, blue=5, yellow=6) we cannot use the same line for him. In the text, the characteristic was something like physical location, about which people may have different preferences but agree on what positions are close to what other positions.

N14.6   Durable monopoly

- The proposition that price falls to marginal cost in a durable monopoly with no discounting and infinite time is called the "Coase Conjecture," after Coase (1972). It is really a proposition and not a conjecture, but alliteration was too strong to resist.

- Gaskins (1974) has written a well-known article on the problem of the durable monopolist who foresees that he will be creating his own future competition in the future because his product can be recycled, using the context of the aluminum market.

- Leasing by a durable monopoly was the main issue in the antitrust case *US v. United Shoe Machinery Corporation*, 110 F. Supp. 295 (1953), but not because it increased monopoly profits. The complaint was rather that long-term leasing impeded entry by new sellers of shoe machinery, a curious idea when the proposed alternative was outright sale. More likely, leasing was used as a form of financing for the machinery consumers; by leasing, they did not need to borrow as they would have to do if it was a matter of financing a purchase. See Wiley, Ramseyer, & Rasmusen (1990a).

- Another way out of the durable monopolist's problem is to give best-price guarantees to consumers, promising to refund part of the purchase price if any future consumer gets a lower price. Perversely, this hurts consumers, because it stops the seller from being tempted to lower his price. The "most-favored-consumer" contract, which is the analogous contract in markets with several sellers, is analyzed by Holt & Scheffman (1987), for example, who demonstrate how it can maintain high prices, and Png & Hirshleifer (1987), who show how it can be used to price discriminate between different types of buyers.

- The durable monopoly model should remind you of bargaining under incomplete information. Both situations can be modelled using two periods, and in both situations the problem for the seller is that he is tempted to offer a low price in the second period after having offered a high price in the first period. In the durable monopoly model this would happen if the high-valuation buyers bought in the first period and thus were absent from consideration by the second period. In the bargaining model this would happen if the buyer rejected the first-period offer and the seller could conclude that he must have a low valuation and act accordingly in the second period. With a rational buyer, neither of these things can happen, and the models' complications arise from the attempt of the seller to get around the problem. For further discussion, see the survey by Kennan & Wilson (1993).

Problems

14.1:   Differentiated Bertrand with advertising (medium)

Two firms that produce substitutes are competing with demand curves

$$q_1 = 10 - \alpha p_1 + \beta p_2 \tag{14.94}$$

and

$$q_2 = 10 - \alpha p_2 + \beta p_1. \tag{14.95}$$

Marginal cost is constant at $c = 3$. A player's strategy is his price. Assume that $\alpha > \beta/2$.

(a)   What is the reaction function for firm 1? Draw the reaction curves for both firms.
(b)   What is the equilibrium? What is the equilibrium quantity for firm 1?
(c)   Show how firm 2's reaction function changes when β increases. What happens to the reaction curves in the diagram?
(d)   Suppose that an advertising campaign could increase the value of β by one, and that this would increase the profits of each firm by more than the cost of the campaign. What does this mean? If either firm could pay for this campaign, what game would result between them?

14.2:   Cournot mergers (easy) (See Salant, Switzer, & Reynolds [1983])

There are three identical firms in an industry with demand given by $P = 1 - Q$, where $Q = q_1 + q_2 + q_3$. The marginal cost is zero.

(a)   Compute the Cournot equilibrium price and quantities.
(b)   How do you know that there are no asymmetric Cournot equilibria, in which one firm produces a different amount than the others?
(c)   Show that if two of the firms merge, their shareholders are worse off.

14.3:   Differentiated Bertrand (medium)

Two firms that produce substitutes have the demand curves

$$q_1 = 1 - \alpha p_1 + \beta(p_2 - p_1) \tag{14.96}$$

and

$$q_2 = 1 - \alpha p_2 + \beta(p_1 - p_2), \tag{14.97}$$

where $\alpha > \beta$. Marginal cost is constant at c, where $c < 1/\alpha$. A player's strategy is his price.

(a)   What are the equations for the reaction curves $p_1(p_2)$ and $p_2(p_1)$? Draw them.
(b)   What is the pure-strategy equilibrium for this game?
(c)   What happens to prices if α, β, or c increase?
(d)   What happens to each firm's price if α increases, but only firm 2 realizes it (and firm 2 knows that firm 1 is uninformed)? Would firm 2 reveal the change to firm 1?

14.4:   Asymmetric Cournot duopoly (easy)

Apex has variable costs of q_a^2 and a fixed cost of 1,000, while Brydox has variables costs of $2q_b^2$ and no fixed cost. Demand is $p = 115 - q_a - q_b$.

(a) What is the equation for Apex's Cournot reaction function?
(b) What is the equation for Brydox' Cournot reaction function?
(c) What are the outputs and profits in the Cournot equilibrium?

14.5:   Price discrimination (medium)

A seller faces a large number of buyers whose market demand is given by $P = \alpha - \beta Q$. Production marginal cost is constant at c.

(a) What is the monopoly price and profit?
(b) What are the prices under perfect price discrimination if the seller can make take-it-or-leave-it offers? What is the profit?
(c) What are the prices under perfect price discrimination if the buyer and sellers bargain over the price and split the surplus evenly? What is the profit?

The Kleit Oligopoly Game: A Classroom Game for Chapter 14

The widget industry in Smallsville has N firms. Each firm produces 150 widgets per month. All costs are fixed, because labor is contracted for on a yearly basis, so we can ignore production cost for the purposes of this case. Widgets are perishable; if they are not sold within the month, they explode in flames.

There are two markets for widgets, the national market, and the local market. The price in the national market is $20 per widget, with the customers paying for delivery, but the price in the local market depends on how many are for sale there in a given month. The price is given by the following market demand curve:

$$P = 100 - \frac{Q}{N},$$

where Q is the total output of widgets sold in the local market. If, however, this equation would yield a negative price, the price is just zero, since the excess widgets can be easily destroyed.

$20 is the opportunity cost of selling a widget locally – it is what the firm loses by making that decision. The benefit from the decision depends on what other firms do. All firms make their decisions at the same time on whether to ship widgets out of town to the national market. The train only comes to Smallsville once a month, so firms cannot retract their decisions. If a firm delays making its decision till too late, then it misses the train, and all its output will have to be sold in Smallsville.

General procedures
For the first seven months, each of you will be a separate firm. You will write down two things on an index card: (1) the number of the month, and (2) your LOCAL-market sales for that month. Also record your local and national market sales

The Kleit Oligopoly Game: A Classroom Game for Chapter 14 (Continued)

on your scoresheet. The instructor will collect the index cards and then announce the price for that month. You should then calculate your profit for the month and add it to your cumulative total, recording both numbers on your scoresheet.

For the last five months, you will be organized into five different firms. Each firm has a capacity of 150, and submits a single index card. The card should have the number of the firm on it, as well as the month and the local output. The instructor will then calculate the market price, rounding it to the nearest dollar to make computations easier. Your own computations will be easier if you pick round numbers for your output.

If you do not turn in an index card by the deadline, you have missed the train and all 150 of your units must be sold locally. You can change your decision up until the deadline by handing in a new card noting both your old and your new output, for example, "I want to change from 40 to 90."

Procedures each month
1   Each student is one firm. No talking.
2   Each student is one firm. No talking.
3   Each student is one firm. No talking.
4   Each student is one firm. No talking.
5   Each student is one firm. No talking.
6   Each student is one firm. You can talk with each other, but then you write down your own output and hand all outputs in separately.
7   Each student is one firm. You can talk with each other, but then you write down your own output and hand all outputs in separately.
8   You are organized into firms, 1 through 5, so $N = 5$. People can talk within the firms, but firms cannot talk to each other. The outputs of the firms are secret.
9   You are organized into firms, 1 through 5, so $N = 5$. People can talk within the firms, but firms cannot talk to each other. The outputs of the firms are secret.
10 You are organized into firms, 1 through 5, so $N = 5$. You can talk to anyone you like, but when the talking is done, each firm writes down its output secretly and hands it in.
11 You are organized into firms, 1 through 5, so $N = 5$. You can talk to anyone you like, but when the talking is done, each firm writes down its output secretly and hands it in. Write the number of your firm with your output. This number will be made public once all the outputs have been received.

You may be wondering about the "Kleit". Andrew Kleit is an economics professor in at Pennsylvania State University who originated the ancestor of this oligopoly game for classroom use.

mathematical appendix

This appendix has three purposes: to remind some readers of the definitions of terms they have seen before, to give other readers an idea of what the terms mean, and to list a few theorems for reference. In accordance with these limited purposes, some terms such as "boundary point" are left undefined. For fuller exposition, see Rudin (1964) on real analysis, Debreu's *Theory of Value* (1959), and Chiang (1984) and Takayama (1985) on mathematics for economists. Intriligator (1971) and Varian (1992) both have good mathematical appendices and are strong in discussing optimization, and Kamien & Schwartz (1991) covers maximizing by choice of functions. Border's 1985 book is entirely about fixed point theorems. Stokey & Lucas (1989) is about dynamic programming. Fudenberg & Tirole (1991a) is the best source of mathematical theorems for use in game theory.

The web is very useful for mathematical definitions. See http://en.wikipedia.org, http://mathworld.wolfram.com, and http://planetmath.org.

*A.1 Notation

$\sum$ **Summation.** $\sum_{i=1}^{3} x_i = x_1 + x_2 + x_3$.

Π **Product.** $\Pi_{i=1}^{3} x_i = x_1 x_2 x_3$.

$|x|$ **Absolute value** of x. If $x \geq 0$ then $|x| = x$ and if $x < 0$ then $|x| = -x$.

$|$ **"Such that,"** "given that," or "conditional upon." $\{x|x < 3\}$ denotes the set of real numbers less than three. $Prob(x|y < 5)$ denotes the probability of x given that y is less than 5.

:   **"Such that."** $\{x: x < 3\}$ denotes the set of real numbers less than three. The colon is a synonym for $|$.

$\mathbf{R}^n$ The set of n-dimensional vectors of **real numbers** (integers, fractions, and the least upper bounds of any subsets thereof).

$\{x, y, z\}$ **A set of elements** x, y, and z. The set $\{3, 5\}$ consists of two elements, 3 and 5.

$\in$ **"Is an element of."** $a \in \{2, 5\}$ means that a takes either the value 2 or 5.

$\subset$ **Set inclusion.** If $X = \{2, 3, 4\}$ and $Y = \{2, 4\}$, then $Y \subset X$ because Y is a subset of X.

$[x, y]$ The **closed interval** with endpoints x and y. The interval $[0, 1{,}000]$ is the set $\{x | 0 \leq x \leq 1{,}000\}$. Square brackets are also used as delimiters.

(x, y) The **open interval** with endpoints x and y. The interval $(0, 1{,}000)$ is the set $\{x | 0 < x < 1{,}000\}$. $(0, 1{,}000]$ would be a half-open interval, the set $\{x | 0 < x \leq 1{,}000\}$. Parentheses are also used as delimiters.

$x!$ **x-factorial.** $x! = x(x - 1)(x - 2) \ldots (2)(1)$. $4! = 4(3)(2)(1) = 24$.

$\binom{a}{b}$ The number of unordered combinations of b elements from a set with a elements. $\binom{a}{b} = a!/b!(a - b)!$, so $\binom{4}{3} = 4!/3!(4 - 3)! = 24/6 = 4$. (See *combination* and *permutation* below.)

$\times$ The **Cartesian product.** $X \times Y$ is the set of points $\{x, y\}$, where $x \in X$ and $y \in Y$.

ϵ An **arbitrarily small positive number.** If my payoff from both *Left* and *Right* equals 10, I am indifferent between them; if my payoff from *Left* is changed to $(10 + \epsilon)$, I prefer *Left*.

$\sim$ We say that $X \sim F$ if the random variable X is **distributed according to** distribution F.

$\exists$ **"There exists. . ."** $\exists x > 0 : 9 - x^2 = 0$.

$\forall$ **"For all. . ."** $\forall x \in [0, 3]$, $x^2 < 10$.

$\equiv$ **"Equals by definition"** "For clarity, let us define the average income $x \equiv \theta^{w-1}/(a - 1)^2 + b^2 + c$ for use in the expressions below."

$\rightarrow$ If f **maps** space X into space Y then $f : X \rightarrow Y$.

$\dfrac{df}{dx}, \dfrac{d^2f}{dx^2}$ The **first and second derivatives** of a function. If $f(x) = x^2$ then $df/dx = 2x$ and $d^2f/dx^2 = 2$.

f', f'' The **first and second derivatives** of a function. If $f(x) = x^2$ then $f' = 2x$ and $f'' = 2$. Primes are also used on variables (not functions) for other purposes: x' and x'' might denote two particular values of x.

$\dfrac{\partial f}{\partial x}, \dfrac{\partial^2 f}{\partial x \partial y}$ **Partial derivatives** of a function. If $f(x, y) = x^2 y$ then $\partial f/\partial x = 2xy$ and $\partial^2 f/\partial x \partial y = 2x$.

y_{-i} The set y minus element i. If $y = \{y_1, y_2, y_3\}$, then $y_{-2} = \{y_1, y_3\}$.

$Max(x, y)$ The **maximum** of two numbers x and y. $Max(8, 24) = 24$.

$Min(x, y)$ The **minimum** of two numbers x and y. $Min(5, 3) = 3$.

$\lceil x \rceil$ **Ceiling**(x). A number rounded up to the nearest integer. $\lceil 4.2 \rceil = 5$. This notation is not well known in economics.

$\lfloor x \rfloor$ **Floor**(x). A number rounded down to the nearest integer. $\lfloor 6.9 \rfloor = 6$. This notation is not well known in economics.

Sup X   The **supremum (least upper bound)** of set X. If $X = \{x|0 \leq x < 1,000\}$, then *sup* $X = 1,000$. The supremum is useful because sometimes, as here, no maximum exists.

Inf X   The **infimum (greatest lower bound)** of set X. If $X = \{x|0 \leq x < 1,000\}$, then *inf* $X = 0$.

Argmax   The **argument that maximizes** a function. If $e^* = argmax\ EU(e)$, then e^* is the value of e that maximizes the function $EU(e)$. The argmax of $f(x) = x - x^2$ is $1/2$.

Maximum   The **greatest value** that a function can take. $Maximum(x - x^2) = 1/4$ for $x \geq 0$ (at $x = 0$).

Minimum   The **least value** that a function can take. $Minimum(-5 + x^2) = -5$ (at $x = 0$).

*A.2 The Greek Alphabet

A	α	alpha	N	ν	nu
B	β	beta	Ξ	ξ	xi
Γ	γ	gamma	O	o	omicron
Δ	δ	delta	Π	π	pi
E	ϵ or ε	epsilon	P	ρ	rho
Z	ζ	zeta	Σ	σ	sigma
H	η	eta	T	τ	tau
Θ	θ	theta	Υ	υ	upsilon
I	ι	iota	Φ	ϕ	phi
K	κ	kappa	X	χ	chi
Λ	λ	lambda	Ψ	ψ	psi
M	μ	mu	Ω	ω	omega

*A.3 Glossary

almost always See "generically."

annuity A riskless security paying a constant amount each year for a given period of years, with the amount conventionally paid at the end of each year.

closed A closed set in $\mathbf{R}^n$ includes its boundary points. The set $\{x: 0 \leq x \leq 1,000\}$ is closed.

combination The number of unordered sets of b elements from a set with a elements, denoted $\binom{a}{b} = a!/b!(a - b)!$. If we form sets of 2 elements from the set $A = \{w, x, y, z\}$, the possibilities are $\{w, x\}, \{w, y\}, \{w, z\}, \{x, y\}, \{x, z\}, \{y, z\}$. Thus, $\binom{4}{2} = 4!/2!(4 - 2)! = 24/6 = 6$. (See *permutation* for the ordered version.)

compact If set X in $\mathbf{R}^n$ is closed and bounded, then X is compact. Outside of Euclidean space, however, a set being closed and bounded does not guarantee compactness.

complete metric space A metric space that includes the limits of all possible Cauchy sequences. All compact metric spaces and all Euclidean spaces are complete.

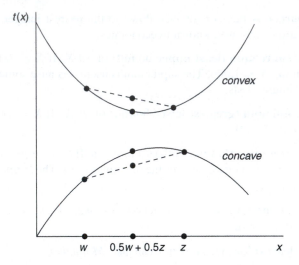

Figure A.1   Concavity and convexity.

concave function The continuous function $f(x)$ defined on interval X is concave if for all elements w and z of X, $f(0.5w + 0.5z) \geq 0.5f(w) + 0.5f(z)$. If f maps $\mathbf{R}$ into $\mathbf{R}$ and f is concave, then $f'' \leq 0$. See figure A.1.

continuous function Let $d(x, y)$ represent the distance between points x and y. The function f is continuous if for every $\epsilon > 0$ there exists a $\delta(\epsilon) > 0$ such that $d(x, y) < \delta(\epsilon)$ implies $d(f(x), f(y)) < \epsilon$.

continuum A continuum is a closed interval of the real line, or a set that can be mapped one-to-one onto such an interval.

contraction The mapping $f(x)$ is said to be a contraction if there exists a number $c < 1$ such that for the metric d of the space X,

$$d(f(x), f(y)) \leq c * d(x, y), \quad \text{for all } x, y \in X. \tag{A.1}$$

convex function The continuous function $f(x)$ is convex if for all elements w and z of X, $f(0.5w + 0.5z) \leq 0.5f(w) + 0.5f(z)$. See figure A.1. Convex functions are only loosely related to convex sets.

convex set If set X is convex, then if you take any two of its elements w and z and a real number $t: 0 \leq t \leq 1$, then $tw + (1 - t)z$ is also in X.

correspondence A correspondence is a mapping that maps each point to one or more other points, as opposed to a function, which only maps to one.

domain The domain of a mapping is the set of elements it maps from – something like the land that it can alter as it pleases. (The mapping maps from the domain onto the range.)

function If f maps each point in X to exactly one point in Y, f is called a function. The two mappings in figure A.1 are functions, but the mapping in figure A.2 is not.

generically If a fact is true on set X generically, "except on a set of measure zero," or "almost always," then it is false only on a subset of points Z that have the property that if a point is randomly chosen using a density function with support X, a point in Z is chosen with probability zero. This implies that if the fact is false on $z \in \mathbf{R}^n$ and z is perturbed by adding a random amount ϵ, the fact is true on $(z + \epsilon)$ with probability one.

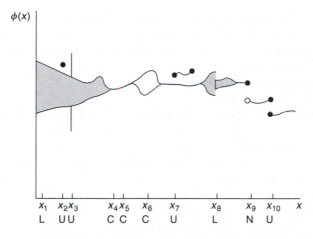

Note: Points at which the correspondence is just upper semi continuous are labelled U; just lower semicontinuous, L; both, C; and neither, N.

Figure A.2   Upper semicontinuity.

integration by parts This is a technique to rearrange integrals so they can be solved more easily. It uses the formula

$$\int_{z=a}^{b} g(z)h'(z)dz = g(z)h(z)\Big|_{z=a}^{b} - \int_{z=a}^{b} h(z)g'(z)dz. \tag{A.2}$$

To derive this, differentiate $g(z)h(z)$ using the chain rule, integrate each side of the equation, and rearrange.

Lagrange multiplier The Lagrange multiplier λ is the marginal value of relaxing a constraint in an optimization problem. If the problem is

$$\left\{ \underset{x}{Maximize} \; x^2 \; \text{subject to} \; x \; \leq 5 \right\} \; \text{then} \; \lambda = 2x^* = 10.$$

lattice A lattice is a partially ordered set (the $\geq$ ordering is defined) where for any two elements a and b, the values $inf(a, b)$ and $sup(a, b)$ are also in the set. A lattice is **complete** if the infimum and supremum of each of its subsets are in the lattice.

Leibniz's integral rule This is the rule for differentiation under the integral sign.

$$\frac{\partial}{\partial z} \int_{a(z)}^{b(z)} f(x, z)dx = f(b(z), z)\frac{\partial b(z)}{\partial z} - f(a(z), z)\frac{\partial a(z)}{\partial z} + \int_{a(z)}^{b(z)} \frac{\partial f(x, z)}{\partial z}dx. \tag{A.3}$$

list (or *n*-Tuple) A set of n elements in which the element positions are ordered. $(Up, Down, Up)$ is a list, but $(Down, Up, Up)$ and $(Up, Down)$ are different lists. See *set* and *multiset*.

lower semicontinuous correspondence The correspondence ϕ is lower semicontinuous at the point x_0 if

$$x_n \to x_0, \; y_0 \in \phi(x_0), \quad \text{implies} \; \exists y_n \in \phi(x_n) \; \text{such that} \; y_n \to y_0, \tag{A.4}$$

which means that associated with every x sequence leading to x_0 is a y sequence leading to its image. See figure A.2. This idea is not as important as upper semicontinuity.

maximand A maximand is what is being maximized. In the problem "Maximize $f(x, \theta)$ by choice of x," the maximand is f.

mean-preserving spread See the **Risk** section below.

measure zero See "generically."

metric The function $d(w, z)$ defined over elements of set X is a metric if (1) $d(w, z) > 0$ if $w \neq z$ and $d(w, z) = 0$ if and only if $w = z$; (2) $d(w, z) = d(z, w)$; and (3) $d(w, z) \leq d(w, y) + d(y, z)$ for points $w, y, z \in X$.

metric space Set X is a metric space if it is associated with a metric that defines the distance between any two of its elements.

multiset A set of n elements in which position in the listing is does not matter but multiplicity does. $(Up, Down, Up)$ is a multiset, and $(Down, Up, Up)$ is the same multiset, but $(Up, Down)$ is a different multiset. See *list* and *set*.

n-Tuple (or Tuple). See *list*.

one-to-one The mapping $f: X \to Y$ is one-to-one if every point in set X maps to a different point in Y, so $x_1 \neq x_2$ implies $f(x_1) \neq f(x_2)$. An example is $f(x) = x/2$ with $X = [0, 1]$ and $Y = [0, 2]$.

onto The mapping $f: X \to Y$ is onto Y if every point in Y is mapped onto by some point in X. An example is $f(x) = x^2$ with $X = [-1, 1]$ and $Y = [0, 1]$.

open In the space $\mathbf{R}^n$, an open set is one that does not include all its boundary points. The set $\{x: 0 \leq x < 1,000\}$ is open (even though it does include *one* of its boundary points). In more general spaces, an open set is a member of a topology.

permutation The number of lists (sets with an order) of b elements from a set with a elements, which equals $a!/(a - b)!$ If we form sets of 2 elements from the set $A = \{w, x, y, z\}$, the possibilities are

$$\{w, x\}, \{x, w\}, \{w, y\}, \{y, w\}, \{w, z\}, \{z, w\}, \{x, y\}, \{y, x\}, \{x, z\}, \{z, x\}, \{y, z\}, \{z, y\}.$$

The number of these is $4!/(4 - 2)! = 24/2 = 12$. (See *combination* for the unordered version.)

perpetuity A riskless security paying a constant amount each year in perpetuity, with the amount conventionally paid at the end of each year.

quasi-concave The continuous function f is quasi-concave if for $w \neq z, f(0.5w + 0.5z) > min[f(w), f(z)]$, or, equivalently, if the set $\{x \in X | f(x) > b\}$ is convex for any number b. Every concave function is quasi-concave, but not every quasi-concave function is concave.

quasilinear utility A utility function is quasilinear in variable w if a monotonic transformation can make it linear in w and w is separable from all other variables in the utility function. $u(w, x) = w + \sqrt{x}$ and $u(w, x) = log(w + \sqrt{x})$ are quasilinear; $u(w, x) = wx$ and $u(w, x) = log(w) + \sqrt{x}$ are not.

range The range of a mapping is the set of elements to which it maps – the property over which it can spew its output. (The mapping maps from the domain onto the range.)

risk See the **Risk** section below.

set A set is a collection of objects in which position of listing and multiplicity do not matter. $\{Up, Down\}$, $\{Down, Up\}$, and $\{Up, Down, Down\}$ are all the same set of 2 elements. See *list* and *multiset*.

stochastic dominance See the **Risk** section below.

strict The word "strict" is used in a variety of contexts to mean that a relationship does not hold with equality or is not arbitrarily close to being violated. If function f is concave and $f' > 0$, then $f'' \leq 0$, but if f is strictly concave, then $f'' < 0$. The opposite of "strictly" is "weakly." The word "strong" is used as a synonym for "strict."

supermodular See the **Supermodularity** section below.

support The support of a probability distribution $F(x)$ is the closure of the set of values of x such that the density is positive. If each output between 0 and 20 has a positive probability density, and no other output does, then the support of the output distribution is [0, 20].

topology Besides denoting a field of mathematics, a topology is a collection of subsets of a space called "open sets" that includes (1) the entire space and the empty set, (2) the intersection of any finite number of open sets, and (3) the union of any number of open sets. In a metric space, the metric "induces" a topology by defining an open set. Imposing a topology on a space is something like defining which elements are close to each other, which is easy to do for $\mathbf{R}^n$, but not for every space (e.g., spaces consisting of functions or of game trees).

upper semicontinuous correspondence The correspondence $\phi: X \to Y$ is upper semicontinuous at point x_0 if

$$x_n \to x_0, \ y_n \in \phi(x_n), \ y_n \to y_0, \quad \text{implies} \ y_0 \in \phi(x_0), \qquad (A.5)$$

which means that every sequence of points in $\phi(x)$ leads to a point also in $\phi(x)$. See figure A.2. An alternative definition, appropriate only if Y is compact, is that ϕ is upper semicontinuous if the set of points $\{x, \phi(x)\}$ is closed.

vector A vector is a list (a set with order) that has a certain structure I will not describe here, but which, for example, a list of real numbers, a point in $\mathbf{R}^n$, will satisfy. The point $(2.5, 3, -4)$ is a vector in $\mathbf{R}^3$.

weak The word "weak" is used in a variety of contexts to mean that a relationship might hold with equality or be on a borderline. If f is concave and $f' > 0$, then $f'' \leq 0$, but to say that f is weakly concave, while technically adding nothing to the meaning, emphasizes that $f'' = 0$ under some or all parameters. The opposite of "weak" is "strict" or "strong."

*A.4   Formulas and Functions

$log(xy) = log(x) + log(y)$.

$log(x^2) = 2log(x)$.

$a^x = (e^{log(a)})^x$.

$e^{rt} = (e^r)^t$.

$e^{a+b} = e^a e^b$.

$a > b \Rightarrow ka < kb, \quad \text{if } k < 0$.

The Quadratic Formula: Let $ax^2 + bx + c = 0$. Then $x = -b \pm \sqrt{b^2 - 4ac}/2a$.

Derivatives

$f(x)$	$f'(x)$
x^a	ax^{a-1}
$1/x$	$-\dfrac{1}{x^2}$
$\dfrac{1}{x^2}$	$-\dfrac{2}{x^3}$
e^x	e^x
e^{rx}	re^{rx}
$log(x)$	$\dfrac{1}{x}$
$log(ax)$	$\dfrac{1}{ax}a = \dfrac{1}{x}$
a^x	$a^x log(a)$
$f(g(x))$	$f'(g(x))g'(x)$

See also Lawrence Spector's 2006 "An Approach to Calculus," http://www.themath-page.com/aCalc/exponential.htm

Table A.1   Some useful functional forms

$f(x)$	$f'(x)$	$f''(x)$	*Slope for $x > 0$*	*Curvature*
$log(x)$	$\dfrac{1}{x}$	$-\dfrac{1}{x^2}$	Increasing	Concave
$\sqrt{x}$	$\dfrac{1}{2\sqrt{x}}$	$-\dfrac{1}{4x^{(3/2)}}$	Increasing	Concave
x^2	$2x$	2	Increasing	Convex
$\dfrac{1}{x}$	$-\dfrac{1}{x^2}$	$\dfrac{2}{x^3}$	Decreasing	Convex
$7 - x^2$	$-2x$	-2	Decreasing	Concave
$7x - x^2$	$7 - 2x$	-2	Increasing/Decreasing	Concave

The signs of derivatives can be confusing. The function $f(x) = x^2$ is increasing at an *increasing* rate, but the function $f(x) = 1/x$ is decreasing at a *decreasing* rate, even though $f'' > 0$ in each case.

Determinants

$$\begin{vmatrix} a_{11} & a_{12} \\ a_{21} & a_{22} \end{vmatrix} = a_{11}a_{22} - a_{21}a_{12}.$$

$$\begin{vmatrix} a_{11} & a_{12} & a_{13} \\ a_{21} & a_{22} & a_{23} \\ a_{31} & a_{32} & a_{33} \end{vmatrix} = a_{11}a_{22}a_{33} - a_{11}a_{23}a_{32} + a_{12}a_{23}a_{31}$$
$$- a_{12}a_{21}a_{33} + a_{13}a_{21}a_{32} - a_{13}a_{22}a_{31}.$$

*A.5   Probability Distributions

The definitive listing of probability distributions and their characteristics is the three-volume series of Johnson & Kotz (1970). A few major distributions are listed here. A **probability distribution** is the same as a **cumulative density function** for a continuous distribution. Any single value has infinitesimal probability if the distribution is continuous (unless there is a probability atom there), so rather than speaking of the probability of a value, we speak of the probability of the value being in an interval, or of the **density** at a single value.

The Exponential Distribution

The exponential distribution, which has the set of nonnegative real numbers as its support, has the density function for mean λ of

$$f(x) = \frac{e^{-x/\lambda}}{\lambda}. \tag{A.6}$$

The cumulative density function is

$$F(x) = 1 - e^{-x/\lambda}. \tag{A.7}$$

The Uniform Distribution

A variable is uniformly distributed over support X if each point in X has equal probability. If the support is $[\alpha, \beta]$, the mean is $(\alpha + \beta)/2$, the density is

$$f(x) = \begin{cases} 0 & x < \alpha, \\ \dfrac{1}{\beta - \alpha} & \alpha \le x \le \beta, \\ 0 & x > \beta, \end{cases} \tag{A.8}$$

and the cumulative density function is

$$F(x) = \begin{cases} 0 & x < \alpha, \\ \dfrac{x - \alpha}{\beta - \alpha} & \alpha \le x \le \beta, \\ 1 & x > \beta. \end{cases} \tag{A.9}$$

The Normal Distribution

The normal distribution is a two-parameter single-peaked distribution which has as its support the entire real line. The density function for mean μ and variance σ^2 is

$$f(x) = \frac{1}{\sqrt{2\pi\sigma^2}} e^{-(x-\mu)^2/2\sigma^2} \tag{A.10}$$

The cumulative density function is the the the integral of this, often denoted $\Phi(x)$, which cannot be simplified analytically. You can find values on web sites such as http://www.math2.org/math/stat/distributions/z-dist.htm or from a spreadsheet program.

The Lognormal Distribution

If $log(x)$ has a normal distribution, x has a lognormal distribution. This is a skewed distribution which has the set of positive real numbers as its support since the logarithm of a negative number is not defined. The mean is $e^{\sigma^2/2}$.

A.6   Supermodularity

Suppose that there are N players in a game, subscripted by i and j, and that player i has a strategy consisting of $\bar{s}^i$ elements, subscripted by s and t, so his strategy is the vector $y^i = (y^i_1, \ldots, y^i_{\bar{s}^i})$. Let his strategy set be S^i and his payoff function be $\pi^i(y^i, y^{-i}; z)$, where z represents a fixed parameter. We say that the game is a **supermodular game** if the following four conditions are satisfied for every player $i = 1, \ldots, N$:

(A1) S^i is a complete lattice.

(A2) $\pi^i : S \to R \cup \{-\infty\}$ is order semicontinuous in y^i for fixed y^{-i}, and order continuous in y^{-i} for fixed y^i, and has a finite upper bound.

(A3) π^i is supermodular in y^i, for fixed y^{-i}. For all strategy profiles y and y' in S,

$$\pi^i(y) + \pi^i(y') \le \pi^i(supremum\{y, y'\}) + \pi^i(infimum\{y, y'\}). \tag{A.11}$$

(A4) π^i has increasing differences in y^i and y^{-i}. For all $y^i \ge y^{i'}$, the difference $\pi^i(y^i, y^{-i}) - \pi^i(y^{i'}, y^{-i})$ is nondecreasing in y^{-i}.

In addition, it is sometimes useful to use a fifth assumption:

(A5) π^i has increasing differences in y^i and z for fixed y^{-i}; for all $y^i \ge y^{i'}$, the difference $\pi^i(y^i, y^{-i}, z) - \pi^i(y^{i'}, y^{-i}, z)$ is nondecreasing with respect to z.

The conditions for **smooth supermodularity** are

A1′   The strategy set is an interval in $R^{\bar{s}^i}$:

$$S^i = [\underline{y^i}, \overline{y^i}]. \tag{A.12}$$

A2′ π^i is twice continuously differentiable on S^i.

A3′ (Supermodularity) Increasing one component of player i's strategy does not decrease the net marginal benefit of any other component: for all i, and all s and t such that $1 \leq s < t \leq \bar{s}^i$,

$$\frac{\partial^2 \pi^i}{\partial y_s^i \partial y_t^i} \geq 0. \tag{A.13}$$

A4′ (Increasing differences in one's own and other strategies) Increasing one component of i's strategy does not decrease the net marginal benefit of increasing any component of player j's strategy: for all $i \neq j$, and all s and t such that $1 \leq s \leq \bar{s}^i$ and $1 \leq t \leq \bar{s}^j$,

$$\frac{\partial^2 \pi^i}{\partial y_s^i \partial y_t^j} \geq 0. \tag{A.14}$$

The fifth assumption becomes

A5′ (Increasing differences in parameters) Increasing parameter z does not decrease the net marginal benefit to player i of any component of his own strategy: for all i, and all s such that $1 \leq s \leq \bar{s}^i$,

$$\frac{\partial^2 \pi^i}{\partial y_s^i \partial z} \geq 0. \tag{A.15}$$

Theorem A.1 *If the game is supermodular, there exists a largest and smallest Nash equilibrium in pure strategies.*

Theorem A.1 is useful because it shows (1) existence of an equilibrium in pure strategies, and (2) if there are at least two equilibria (note that the largest and smallest equilibria might be the same strategy profile), then two of them can be ranked in the magnitudes of the components of each player's equilibrium strategy.

Theorem A.2 *If the game is supermodular and assumption (A5′) is satisfied, then the largest and smallest equilibria are nondecreasing functions of the parameter z.*

Theorem A.3 *If a game is supermodular, then for each player there is a largest and smallest serially undominated strategy, where both of these strategies are pure.*

Theorem A.4 *Let $\underline{y}^i$ denote the smallest element of player i's strategy set S^i in a supermodular game. Let y^* and $y^{*'}$ denote two equilibria, with $y^* \geq y^{*'}$, so y is the "big" equilibrium. Then,*

1 *If $\pi^i(\underline{y}^i, y^{-i})$ is increasing in y^{-i}, then $\pi^i(y^*) \geq \pi^i(y^{*'})$.*
2 *If $\pi^i(\underline{y}^i, y^{-i})$ is decreasing in y^{-i}, then $\pi^i(y^*) \leq \pi^i(y^{*'})$.*
3 *If the condition in (1) holds for a subset N_1 of players, and the condition in (2) holds for the remainder of the players, then the big equilibrium y^* is the best equilibrium for players in N_1 and the worst for the remaining player, and the small equilibrium $y^{*'}$ is the worst equilibrium for players in N_1 and the best for the remaining players.*

The theorems here are taken from Milgrom & Roberts (1990). Theorem A.1 is their corollary to theorem 5. Theorem A.2 is their theorem 6 and corollary. Theorem A.3 is their

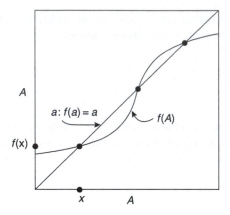

Figure A.3   A mapping with three fixed points.

theorem 5, and Theorem A.4 is their theorem 7. For more on supermodularity, see Milgrom & Roberts (1990), Fudenberg & Tirole (1991, pp. 489–97), or Vives's 2005 survey article. For a mathematician's view, see Topkis's 1998 *Supermodularity and Complementarity*.

A.7   Fixed Point Theorems

Fixed points theorems say that various kinds of mappings from one set to another result in at least one point being mapped back onto itself. The most famous fixed point theorem is Brouwer's Theorem, illustrated in figure A.3. I will use a formulation from page 952 of Mas-Colell, Whinston, & Green (1994).

The Brouwer Fixed Point Theorem

Suppose that set A in R^N is nonempty, compact, and convex; and that $f: A \to A$ is a continuous function from A into itself. ("Compact" means closed and bounded, in Euclidean space.) Then f has a fixed point; that is, there is an x in A such that $x = f(x)$.

The usefulness of fixed point theorems is that an equilibrium is a fixed point. Consider equilibrium prices. Let p be a point in N-space consisting of one price for each good. Let P be the set of all possible price points. P will be convex and compact if we limit it to finite prices. Agents in the economy look at p and make decisions about consumption and output. These decisions change p into $f(p)$. An equilibrium is a point p^* such that $f(p^*) = p^*$. If you can show that f is continuous, you can show that p^* exists.

This is also true for Nash equilibria. Let s be a point in N-*space* consisting of one strategy for each player – a strategy profile. Let S be the set of all possible strategy profiles. This will be compact and convex if we allow mixed strategies (for convexity) and if strategy sets are closed and bounded. Each strategy profile s will cause each player to react by choosing his best response $f(s)$. A Nash equilibrium is s^* such that $f(s^*) = s^*$. If you can show that f is continuous – which you can do if payoff functions are continuous – you can show that s^* exists.

The Brouwer theorem is useful in itself, and conveys the intuition of fixed point theorems, but to prove existence of prices in general equilibrium and existence of Nash equilibrium in game theory requires the Kakutani fixed point theorem. That is because the mappings involved are not one-to-one functions, but one-to-many-point correspondences. In general equilibrium, one firm might be indifferent between producing various amounts of output. In game theory, one player might have two best responses to another player's strategy.

The Kakutani Fixed Point Theorem (Kakutani [1941])

Suppose that set A in R^N is a nonempty, compact, convex set and that $f: A \to A$ is an upper hemicontinuous correspondence from A into itself, with the property that the set $f(x)$ is nonempty and convex for every x. Then f has a fixed point; that is, there is an x in A such that x is one element of $f(x)$.

Other fixed point theorems exist for other kinds of mappings – for example, for a mapping from a set of functions back into itself. In deciding which theorem to use, care must be taken to identify the mathematical nature of the set of strategy profiles and the smoothness of the best response functions.

*A.8   Genericity

Suppose we have a space X consisting of the interval between 0 and 100 on the real line, $[0, 100]$, and a function f such that $f(x) = 3$ except that $f(15) = 5$. We can then say any of the following:

1 $f(x) = 3$ except on a set of measure zero.
2 $f(x) = 3$ except on a null set.
3 Generically, $f(x) = 3$.
4 $f(x) = 3$ almost always.
5 The set of x such that $f(x) = 3$ is dense in X.
6 The set of x such that $f(x) = 3$ has full measure.

These all convey the idea that if parameters are picked using a continuous random density, $f(x)$ will be 3 with probability one, and any other value of $f(x)$ is very special in that sense. If you start with point x, and add a small random perturbation ϵ, then with probability one, $f(x + \epsilon) = 3$. So unless there is some special reason for x to take the particular value of 15, you can count on observation $f(x) = 3$.

Statements like these always depend on the definition of the space X. If, instead, we took a space Y consisting of the integers between 0 and 100, which is $0, 1, 2, \ldots, 100$, then it is not true that "$f(x) = 3$ except on a set of measure zero." Instead, if x is chosen randomly, there is a $1/101$ probability that $x = 15$ and $f(x) = 5$.

The concept of "a set of measure zero" becomes more difficult to implement if the space X is not just a finite interval. I have not defined the concept in these notes; I have just pointed to usage. This, however, is enough to be useful to you. A course in real analysis would teach you the definitions. As with the concepts of "closed" and "bounded," complications can arise even in economic applications because of infinite spaces and in dealing with spaces of functions, game tree branchings, or other such objects.

Now, let us apply the idea to games. Here is an example of a theorem that uses genericity.

Theorem A.5 *"Generically, all finite games of perfect information have a unique subgame perfect equilibrium."*

Proof.   A game of perfect information has no simultaneous moves, and consists of a tree in which each player moves in sequence. Since the game is finite, each path through the tree leads to an end node. For each end node, consider the decision node just before it. The player making the decision there has a finite number N of choices, since this is a finite game. Denote the payoffs from these choices as $(P_1, P_2, \ldots, P_N)$. This set of payoffs has a unique maximum, because generically no two payoffs will be equal. (If they were, and you perturbed the payoffs a little, with probability one they would no longer be equal, so games with equal payoffs have measure zero.) The player will pick the action with the biggest payoff. Every subgame perfect equilibrium must specify that the players choose those actions, since they are the unique Nash strategies in the subgames at the end of the game.

Next, consider the next-to-last decision nodes. The player making the decision at such a node has a finite number of choices, and using the payoffs determined from the optimal choice of final moves, he will find that some move has the maximum payoff. The subgame perfect equilibrium must specify that move. Continue this procedure until you reach the very first move of the game. The player there will find that some one of his finite moves has the largest payoff, and he will pick that one move. Each player will have one best action choice at each node, and so the equilibrium will be unique. QED.

Genericity entered this as the condition that we are ignoring special games in the theorem's statement – games that have tied payoffs. Whether those are really special or not depends on the context.

*A.9   Discounting

A model in which the action takes place in real time must specify whether payments and receipts are valued less if they are made later, that is, whether they are **discounted**. Discounting is measured by the discount rate or the discount factor.

> *The* **discount rate***, r, is the extra fraction of a unit of value needed to compensate for delaying receipt by one period.*

> *The* **discount factor***, δ, is the equivalent in present units of value of one unit to be received one period from the present.*

The discount rate is analogous to the interest rate, and in some models the interest rate determines the discount rate. The discount factor represents exactly the same idea as the discount rate, and $\delta = 1/1 + r$. Models use r or δ depending on notational convenience. Not discounting is equivalent to $r = 0$ and $\delta = 1$, so the notation includes zero discounting as a special case.

Whether to put discounting into a model involves two questions. The first is whether the added complexity will be accompanied by a change in the results or by a surprising demonstration of no change in the results. A second, more specific question is whether the events of the model occur in real time, so that discounting is appropriate. The bargaining game of Alternating Offers from section 12.3 can be interpreted in two ways. One way is that the players make all their offers and counteroffers between dawn and dusk of a single day, so essentially no real time has passed. The other way is that each offer consumes a week of time, so that the delay before the bargain is reached is important to the players. Discounting is appropriate only in the second interpretation.

Discounting has two important sources: time preference and a probability that the game might end, represented by the rate of time preference, ρ, and the probability each period that the game ends, θ. It is usually assumed that ρ and θ are constant. If they both take the value zero, the player does not care whether his payments are scheduled now or ten years from now. Otherwise, a player is indifferent between $x/1 + \rho$ now and x guaranteed to be paid one period later. With probability $(1 - \theta)$ the game continues and the later payment is actually made, so the player is indifferent between $(1 - \theta)x/(1 + \rho)$ now and the promise of x to be paid one period later contingent upon the game still continuing. The discount factor is therefore

$$\delta = \frac{1}{1 + r} = \frac{(1 - \theta)}{(1 + \rho)}. \tag{A.16}$$

Table A.2 summarizes the implications of discounting for the value of payment streams of various kinds. We will not go into how these are derived, but they all stem from the basic fact that a dollar paid in the future is worth δ dollars now. Continuous time models usually refer to rates of payment rather than lump sums, so the discount factor is not so useful a concept, but discounting works the same way as in discrete time except that payments are continuously compounded. For a full explanation, see a finance text (e.g., Appendix A of Copeland & Weston [1988]).

The way to remember the formula for an annuity over a period of time is to use the formulas for a payment at a certain time in the future and for a perpetuity. A stream of x paid at the end of each year is worth x/r. A payment of Y at the end of period T has a present value of $-Y/(1 + r)^T$. Thus, if at the start of period T you must pay out a perpetuity of x at the end of each year, the present value of that payment is $(x/r)(1/1 + r)^T$. One may also view a stream of payments each year from the present until period T as the same thing as owning a perpetuity but having to give away a perpetuity in period T. This leaves a present value of $(x/r)(1 - (1/1 + r)^T)$, which is the second formula for an annuity given in table A.2. Figure A.4 illustrates this approach to annuities and shows how it can also be used to value a stream of income that starts at period S and ends at period T.

Discounting will be left out of most dynamic games in this book, but it is an especially important issue in infinitely repeated games, and is discussed further in section 5.2.

*A.10   Risk

We say that a player is **risk-averse** if his utility function is strictly concave in money, which means that he has diminishing marginal utility of money. He is **risk-neutral** if his utility

Table A.2 Discounting

Payoff Stream	Discounted Value	
	r-notation (discount rate)	*δ-notation* (discount factor)
x at the end of one period	$\dfrac{x}{1+r}$	δx
x at the end of each period in perpetuity	$\dfrac{x}{r}$	$\dfrac{\delta x}{1-\delta}$
x at the start of each period in perpetuity	$x+\dfrac{x}{r}$	$\dfrac{x}{1-\delta}$
x at the end of each period up through T (first formula)	$\displaystyle\sum_{t=1}^{T}\dfrac{x}{(1+r)^t}$	$\displaystyle\sum_{t=1}^{T}\delta^t x$
x at the end of each period up through T (second formula)	$\dfrac{x}{r}\left(1-\dfrac{1}{(1+r)^T}\right)$	$\dfrac{\delta x}{1-\delta}(1-\delta^T)$
x at time t in continuous time	xe^{-rt}	—
Flow of x per period up to time T in continuous time	$\displaystyle\int_{0}^{T}xe^{-rt}\,dt$	—
Flow of x per period in perpetuity, in continuous time	$\dfrac{x}{r}$	—

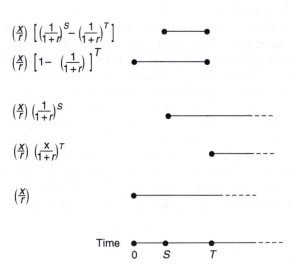

$$\left(\tfrac{x}{r}\right)\left[\left(\tfrac{1}{1+r}\right)^S-\left(\tfrac{1}{1+r}\right)^T\right]$$

$$\left(\tfrac{x}{r}\right)\left[1-\left(\tfrac{1}{1+r}\right)\right]^T$$

$$\left(\tfrac{x}{r}\right)\left(\tfrac{1}{1+r}\right)^S$$

$$\left(\tfrac{x}{r}\right)\left(\tfrac{x}{1+r}\right)^T$$

$$\left(\tfrac{x}{r}\right)$$

Time   0   S   T

Figure A.4 Discounting.

function is linear in money. The qualifier "in money" is used because utility may be a function of other variables too, such as effort.

We say that probability distribution F **dominates** distribution G in the sense of **first-order stochastic dominance** if the cumulative probability that the variable will take a value less than x is greater for G than for F, that is, if

$$\text{for any } x, \quad F(x) \le G(x), \tag{A.17}$$

and (A.17) is a strong inequality for at least one value of x. The distribution F dominates G in the sense of **second-order stochastic dominance** if the area under the cumulative distribution G up to $G(x)$ is greater than the area under F, that is, if

$$\text{for any } x, \quad \int_{-\infty}^{x} F(y)dy \le \int_{-\infty}^{x} G(y)dy, \tag{A.18}$$

and (A.18) is a strong inequality for some value of x. Equivalently, F dominates G if, limiting U to increasing functions for first-order dominance and increasing concave functions for second-order dominance,

$$\text{for all functions } U, \quad \int_{-\infty}^{+\infty} U(x)dF(x) > \int_{-\infty}^{+\infty} U(x)dG(x). \tag{A.19}$$

If F is a first-order dominant gamble, it is preferred by all players; if F is a second-order dominant gamble, it is preferred by all risk-averse players. If F is first-order dominant it is second-order dominant, but not vice versa.

Milgrom (1981b) has used stochastic dominance to carefully define what we mean by **good news**. Let θ be a parameter about which the news is received in the form of message x or y, and let utility be increasing in θ. The message x is more favorable than y (is "good news") if for every possible nondegenerate prior for $F(\theta)$, the posterior $F(\theta|x)$ first-order dominates $F(\theta|y)$.

Rothschild & Stiglitz (1970) shows how two gambles can be related in other ways equivalent to second-order dominance, the most important of which is the **mean-preserving spread**. Informally, a mean-preserving spread is a density function which transfers probability mass from the middle of a distribution to its tails. More formally, for discrete distributions placing sufficient probability on the four points a_1, a_2, a_3, and a_4,

A **mean-preserving spread** is a set of four locations $a_1 < a_2 < a_3 < a_4$ and four probabilities $\gamma_1 \ge 0, \gamma_2 \le 0, \gamma_3 \le 0, \gamma_4 \ge 0$ such that $-\gamma_1 = \gamma_2$, $\gamma_3 = -\gamma_4$, and $\sum_i \gamma_i a_i = 0$.

Figure A.5 shows how this works. Panel (a) shows the original distribution with solid bars. The mean is $0.1(2) + 0.3(3) + 0.3(4) + 0.2(5) + 0.1(6)$, which is 3.9. The spread has mean $0.1(1) - 0.3(.3) - 0.1(4) + 0.2(6)$, which is 0, so it is mean-preserving. Panel (b) shows the resulting spread-out distribution.

The definition can be extended to continuous distributions, and can be alternatively defined by taking probability mass from one point in the middle and moving it to the sides; panel (c) of figure A.5 shows an example. See Rasmusen & Petrakis (1992), which also, with Leshno, Levy, & Spector (1997), fixes an error in the original Rothschild & Stiglitz proof.

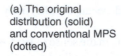

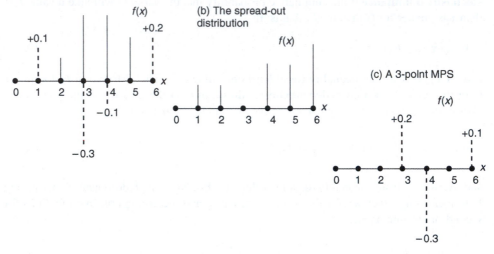

Figure A.5   Mean-preserving spreads.

Hazard Rates

The hazard rate has been important in the analysis above. Suppose we have a density $f(v)$ for a buyer's value for an object being sold, with cumulative distribution $F(v)$ on support $[\underline{v}, \overline{v}]$. The hazard rate $h(v)$ is defined as

$$h(v) = \frac{f(v)}{1 - F(v)} \tag{A.20}$$

What this means is that $h(v)$ is the probability density of v for the distribution which is like $F(v)$ except cutting off the lower values, so its support is limited to $[v, \overline{v}]$. In economic terms, $h(v)$ is the probability density for the valuing equalling v given that we know that value equals at least v.

For most distributions we use, the hazard rate is increasing, including the uniform, normal, logistic, and exponential distributions, and any distribution with increasing density over its support (see Bagnoli & Bergstrom [1994]). Figure A.6 shows three of them.

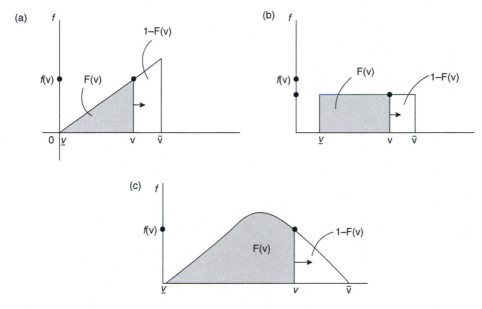

Figure A.6   Three densities to illustrate increasing hazard rates $f(v)/(1 - F(v))$.

references and name index

The page numbers where a reference is mentioned in the text are listed after the reference. The date of first publication, which may differ from the date of the printing cited, follows the author's name. Some publications (e.g., *The Wall Street Journal*) are cited in footnotes in the main text but are not in the bibliography. In the case of newspapers, I provide page numbers, but the exact page may differ among regional and time-of-day editions.

Abreu, Dilip, David Pearce, & Ennio Stacchetti (1986) "Optimal Cartel Equilibria with Imperfect Monitoring," *The Journal of Economic Theory*, 39(1): 251–269 (June 1986). **120**

Abreu, Dilip, David Pearce, & Ennio Stacchetti (1990) "Toward a Theory of Discounted Repeated Games with Imperfect Monitoring," *Econometrica*, 58(5): 1041–1064 (September 1990). **149**

Akerlof, George (1970) "The Market for Lemons: Quality Uncertainty and the Market Mechanism," *The Quarterly Journal of Economics*, 84(3): 488–500 (August 1970). Reprinted in Rasmusen (2001). **249, 269, 270**

Akerlof, George (1980) "A Theory of Social Custom, of Which Unemployment May Be One Consequence," *The Quarterly Journal of Economics*, 94(4): 749–775 (June 1980). **266**

Akerlof, George (1983) "Loyalty Filters," *The American Economic Review*, 73(1): 54–63 (March 1983). **216, 266**

Akerlof, George & Janet Yellen, eds., (1986) *Efficiency Wage Models of the Labor Market*, Cambridge: Cambridge University Press (1986). **236**

Alchian, Armen. See Klein et al. (1978).

Alchian, Armen & Harold Demsetz (1972) "Production, Information Costs and Economic Organization," *The American Economic Review*, 62(5): 777–795 (December 1972). **201**

Alexeev, Michael & James Leitzel (1996) "Rent-Shrinking," *The Southern Economic Journal*, 62(3): 620–626. **403**

Aliprantis, Charalambos & Subir Chakrabarti (1999) *Games and Decisionmaking*, Oxford: Oxford University Press (1999). **xxvi**

Anderson Lisa R. See Holt & Anderson (1996).

Antle, Rick & Abbie Smith (1986) "An Empirical Investigation of the Relative Performance Evaluation of Corporate Executives," *The Journal of Accounting Research*, 24(1):1–39 (Spring 1986). **236**

Arrow, Kenneth (1979) "The Property Rights Doctrine and Demand Revelation under Incomplete Information," in *Economics and Human Welfare*, ed. Michael Boskin, New York: Academic Press (1979). **381**

Arrow, Kenneth (1985) "The Economics of Agency," in *Principals and Agents: The Structure of Business*, pp. 37–51, John Pratt & Richard Zeckhauser, eds., Boston: Harvard Business School Press (1985). **183**

Athey, Susan & Philip A. Haile (2005) "Nonparametric Approaches to Auctions," *The Handbook of Econometrics, Vol. 6*, http://athens.src.uchicago.edu/jenni/handbookv6/athey-haile-handbook.pdf. Elsevier (2005). **428**

Aumann, Robert (1964a) "Markets with a Continuum of Traders," *Econometrica*, 32: 39–50 (January/April 1964). **99**

Aumann, Robert (1964b) "Mixed and Behavior Strategies in Infinite Extensive Games," in *Annals of Mathematics Studies, No. 52*, M. Dresher, L. S. Shapley, and A. W. Tucker, eds., pp. 627–650, Princeton: Princeton University Press (1964). **99**

Aumann, Robert (1974) "Subjectivity and Correlation in Randomized Strategies," *The Journal of Mathematical Economics*, 1(1): 67–96 (March 1974). **80**

Aumann, Robert (1976) "Agreeing to Disagree," *Annals of Statistics*, 4(6): 1236–1239 (November 1976). **64**

Aumann, Robert (1981) "Survey of Repeated Games," in *Essays in Game Theory and Mathematical Economics in Honor of Oscar Morgenstern*, ed. Robert Aumann, Mannheim: Bibliographisches Institut (1981). **149**

Aumann, Robert (1987) "Correlated Equilibrium As an Expression of Bayesian Rationality," *Econometrica*, 55(1): 1–18 (January 1987). **80**

Aumann, Robert (1997) "On the State of the Art in Game Theory," in *Understanding Strategic Interaction*, Wulf Albers, Werner Guth, Peter Hammerstein, Benny Moldovanu, & Eric van Damme, eds., Berlin: Springer-Verlag (1997). **22**

Aumann, Robert. See Hart (2005).

Aumann, Robert & Sergiu Hart (1992) *Handbook of Game Theory with Economic Applications*, New York: North-Holland (1992). **xxv, xxv, xxvii**

Axelrod, Robert (1984) *The Evolution of Cooperation*, New York: Basic Books (1984). **169, 175**

Axelrod, Robert & William Hamilton (1981) "The Evolution of Cooperation," *Science*, 211(4489): 96 (March 1981). Reprinted in Rasmusen (2001a). **151**

Ayres, Ian (1990) "Playing Games with the Law," *Stanford Law Review*, 42(5): 1291–1317 (May 1990). **113**

Ayres, Ian (1991) "Fair Driving: Gender and Race Discrimination in Retail Car Negotiations," *Harvard Law Review*, 104(4): 817–872 (February 1991). **369**

Ayres, Ian & Peter Cramton (1996) "Deficit Reduction through Diversity: How Affirmative Action at the FCC Increased Auction Competition," *Stanford Law Review*, 48: 761–814 (April 1996). **428**

Ayres, Ian. See Brown & Ayres (1994).

Bagchi, Arunabha (1984) *Stackelberg Differential Games in Economic Models*, Berlin: Springer-Verlag (1984). **99**

Bagehot, Walter (1971) "The Only Game in Town," *Financial Analysts Journal*, 27(2): 12–22 (March/April 1971). Reprinted in Rasmusen (2001). **259**

Bagnoli, Mark & Theodore Bergstrom (1994) "Log-Concave Probability and Its Applications," working paper, http://ideas.repec.org/p/wpa/wuwpmi/9410002.html (1994). **490**

Baird, Douglas, Gertner Robert, & Randal Picker (1994) *Strategic Behavior and the Law: The Role of Game Theory and Information Economics in Legal Analysis*, Cambridge, MA: Harvard University Press (1994). **xxv**

Bajari, Patrick & Ali Hortacsu (2004) "Economic Insights from Internet Auctions," *The Journal of Economic Literature*, 42(2): 457–486 (2004). **428**

Bajari, Patrick, Han Hong, & Stephen Ryan (2004) "Identification and Estimation of Discrete Games of Complete Information," NBER Working Paper No. T0301, http://ssrn.com/abstract = 601103 (October 2004). **99**

Bajari, Patrick & Stephen Tadelis (2001) "Incentives versus Transaction Costs: A Theory of Procurement Contracts," *The RAND Journal of Economics*, 32(3): 387–407 (Autumn 2001). **316**

Baker, George, Michael Jensen, & Kevin J. Murphy (1988) "Compensation and Incentives: Practice vs. Theory," *The Journal of Finance*, 43(3): 593–616 (July 1988). **216**

Baldwin, B. & G. Meese (1979) "Social Behavior in Pigs Studied by Means of Operant Conditioning," *Animal Behavior*, 27: 947–957 (August 1979). **26, 35**

Baliga, Sandeep (2002) "Research Summary," http://www.kellogg.northwestern.edu/faculty/baliga/htm/resumm.pdf (undated: 2002?). **281**

Banks, Jeffrey (1991) *Signalling Games in Political Science*, Chur, Switzerland: Harwood Publishers (1991). **348**

Bannerjee, A. V. (1992) "A Simple Model of Herd Behavior," *The Quarterly Journal of Economics*, 107(3): 797–817 (August 1992). **61**

Baron, David (1989) "Design of Regulatory Mechanisms and Institutions," in Schmalensee & Willig (1989). **314, 315**

Baron, David & David Besanko (1984) "Regulation, Asymmetric Information, and Auditing," *The RAND Journal of Economics*, 15(4): 447–470 (Winter 1984). **100**

Baron, David & Robert Myerson (1982) "Regulating a Monopolist with Unknown Costs," *Econometrica*, 50(4): 911–930 (July 1982). **306**

Basar, Tamar & Geert Olsder (1999) *Dynamic Noncooperative Game Theory*, 2nd edition, revised, Philadelphia: Society for Industrial and Applied Mathematics (1st edition 1982, 2nd edition 1995). **xxvi**

Basu, Kaushik (1993) *Lectures in Industrial Organization Theory*, Oxford: Blackwell Publishers (1993). **xxv**

Baumol, William & Stephen Goldfeld (1968) *Precursors in Mathematical Economics: An Anthology*, London: London School of Economics and Political Science (1968). **6**

Baye, Michael R. & Heidrun H. Hoppe (2003) "The Strategic Equivalence of Rent-Seeking, Innovation, and Patent-Race Games," *Games and Economic Behavior*, 44(2): 217–226. **402**

Baye, Michael. See Kovenock, Baye & de Vries (1996).

Becker, Gary (1968) "Crime and Punishment: An Economic Approach," *The Journal of Political Economy*, 76(2): 169–217 (March/April 1968). **198**

Becker, Gary & George Stigler (1974) "Law Enforcement, Malfeasance and Compensation of Enforcers," *The Journal of Legal Studies*, 3(1): 1–18 (January 1974). **213**

Benoit, Jean-Pierre & Vijay Krishna (1985) "Finitely Repeated Games," *Econometrica*, 17(4): 317–320 (July 1985). **147, 152**

Benoit, Jean-Pierre & Vijay Krishna (2000) "The Folk Theorems for Repeated Games: A Synthesis," Pennsylvania State University working paper, http://econ.la.psu.edu/~vkrishna/papers/synth34.pdf (March 10, 2000).

Bernanke, Benjamin (1983) "Nonmonetary Effects of the Financial Crisis in the Propagation of the Great Depression," *The American Economic Review*, 73(3): 257–276 (June 1983). **265**

Bernheim, B. Douglas (1984a) "Rationalizable Strategic Behavior," *Econometrica*, 52(4): 1007–1028 (July 1984). **35**

Bernheim, B. Douglas (1984b) "Strategic Deterrence of Sequential Entry into an Industry," *The RAND Journal of Economics*, 15(1): 1–11 (Spring 1984). **230**

Bernheim, B. Douglas, Bezalel Peleg, & Michael Whinston (1987) "Coalition-Proof Nash Equilibria I: Concepts," *The Journal of Economic Theory*, 42(1): 1–12 (June 1987). **120**

Bernheim, B. Douglas & Michael Whinston (1987) "Coalition-Proof Nash Equilibria II: Applications," *The Journal of Economic Theory*, 42(1): 13–29 (June 1987). **120**

Bertrand, Joseph (1883) "Rechercher sur la theorie mathematique de la richesse," *Journal des Savants*, 48: 499–508 (September 1883). **90**

Besanko, David, David Dranove, & Mark Shanley (1996) *Economics of Strategy*, New York: John Wiley and Sons (1996). **xxvi**

Besanko, David. See Baron & Besanko (1984).

Bierman, H. Scott & Fernandez, Luis (1998) *Game Theory with Economic Applications*, 2nd edition, Reading, MA: Addison-Wesley (1st edition 1993). **xxvi**

Bikhchandani, Sushil (1988) "Reputations in Repeated Second Price Auctions," *The Journal of Economic Theory*, 46(1): 97–119 (October 1988). **425**

Bikhchandani, Sushil, David Hirshleifer, & Ivo Welch (1992) "A Theory of Fads, Fashion, Custom, and Cultural Change As Informational Cascades," *The Journal of Political Economy*, 100(5): 992–1026 (October 1992). **61**

Binmore, Ken (1990) *Essays on the Foundations of Game Theory*, Oxford: Basil Blackwell (1990). **173**

Binmore, Ken (1992) *Fun and Games: A Text on Game Theory*, Lexington: D. C. Heath (1992). **xxv**

Binmore, Ken & Partha Dasgupta, eds., (1986) *Economic Organizations as Games*, Oxford: Basil Blackwell (1986). **6**

Binmore, Ken, Ariel Rubinstein, & Asher Wolinsky (1986) "The Nash Bargaining Solution in Economic Modelling," *The RAND Journal of Economics*, 17(2): 176–188 (Summer 1986). **380**

Blanchard, Olivier (1979) "Speculative Bubbles, Crashes, and Rational Expectations," *Economics Letters*, 3(4): 387–389 (1979). **149**

Bognanno, Michael L. See Ehrenberg & Bognanno (1990).

Bolton, Patrick & Mathias Dewatripont (2005) *Contract Theory*, Cambridge, MA: MIT Press (2005). **xxviii, 201**

Bond, Eric (1982) "A Direct Test of the 'Lemons' Model: The Market for Used Pickup Trucks," *The American Economic Review*, 72(4): 836–840 (September 1982).

Border, Kim (1985) *Fixed Point Theorems with Applications to Economics and Game Theory*, Cambridge: Cambridge University Press (1985). **473**

Border, Kim & Joel Sobel (1987) "Samurai Accountant: A Theory of Auditing and Plunder," *The Review of Economic Studies*, 54(4): 525–540 (October 1987). **100**

Bowersock, G. (1985) "The Art of the Footnote," *The American Scholar*, 52: 54–62 (Winter 1983/84). **7**

Boyd, Robert & Jeffrey Lorberbaum (1987) "No Pure Strategy Is Evolutionarily Stable in the Repeated Prisoner's Dilemma Game," *Nature*, 327(6117): 58–59 (May 1987). **149**

Boyd, Robert & Peter Richerson (1985) *Culture and the Evolutionary Process*, Chicago: University of Chicago Press (1985). **151**

Boyes, William J. & Stephen K. Happel, "Auctions As an Allocation Mechanism in Academia: The Case of Faculty Offices," *The Journal of Economic Perspectives*, 3(3): 37–40 (Summer 1989). **385**

Brams, Steven (1980) *Biblical Games: A Strategic Analysis of Stories in the Old Testament*, Cambridge, MA: MIT Press (1980). **34**

Brams, Steven (1983) *Superior Beings: If They Exist, How Would We Know?* New York: Springer-Verlag (1983). **34**

Brams, Steven & D. Marc Kilgour (1988) *Game Theory and National Security*, Oxford: Basil Blackwell (1988). **35**

Brandenburger, Adam (1992) "Knowledge and Equilibrium in Games," *The Journal of Economic Perspectives*, 6(4): 83–102 (Fall 1992). **49, 64**

Bresnahan, Timothy & Peter Reiss (1990) "Entry in Monopoly Markets," *The Review of Economic Studies*, 57(4): 531–553. **99**

Bresnahan, Timothy & Peter Reiss (1991a) "Empirical Models of Discrete Games," *The Journal of Econometrics*, 48(1–2): 57–81. **99, 467**

Bresnahan, Timothy & Peter Reiss (1991b) "Entry and Competition in Concentrated Markets," *The Journal of Political Economy*, 99(5): 977–1009 (October 1991). **467**

Brown, Jennifer & Ian Ayres (1994) "Economic Rationales for Mediation," *Virginia Law Review*, 80(2): 323–401 (March 1994). **314**

Bulow, Jeremy (1982) "Durable-Goods Monopolists," *The Journal of Political Economy*, 90(2): 314–332 (April 1982). **463**

Bulow, Jeremy, John Geanakoplos, & Paul Klemperer (1985) "Multimarket Oligopoly: Strategic Substitutes and Complements," *The Journal of Political Economy*, 93(3): 488–511 (June 1985). **94, 102**

Bulow, Jeremy & Paul Klemperer (1996) "Auctions versus Negotiations," *The American Economic Review*, 86(1): 180–194 (March 1996). **380, 385, 409**

Bulow, Jeremy & John Roberts (1989) "The Simple Economics of Optimal Auctions," *The Journal of Political Economy*, 97(5): 1060–1090 (October 1989). **409, 413**

Calfee, John. See Craswell & Calfee (1986).

Calomiris, Charles & Joseph Mason (1997) "Contagion and Bank Failures During the Great Depression: The June 1932 Chicago Banking Panic," *The American Economic Review*, 87(5): 863–883 (December 1997).

Campbell, Richmond & Lanning Sowden (1985) *Paradoxes of Rationality and Cooperation: Prisoner's Dilemma and Newcomb's Problem*, Vancouver: University of British Columbia Press (1985). **34**

Campbell, W. See Capen et al. (1971).

Canzoneri, Matthew & Dale Henderson (1991) *Monetary Policy in Interdependent Economies*, Cambridge, MA: MIT Press (1991). **35**

Capen, E., R. Clapp, & W. Campbell (1971) "Competitive Bidding in High-Risk Situations," *The Journal of Petroleum Technology*, 23(1): 641–653 (June 1971). **415, 416, 429**

Cass, David & Karl Shell (1983) "Do Sunspots Matter?" *The Journal of Political Economy*, 91(2): 193–227 (April 1983). **80**

Cassady, Ralph (1967) *Auctions and Auctioneering*, Berkeley: California University Press (1967). **399, 428**

Chakrabarti, Subir. See Aliprantis & Chakrabarti (1999).

Chammah, Albert. See Rapoport & Chammah (1965).

Chatterjee, Kalyan and William Samuelson (1983) "Bargaining Under Incomplete Information," *Operations Research*, 31(5): 835–851 (September/October 1983). **381**

Che Yeon-Koo & Ian Gale (1998) "Standard Auctions with Financially Constrained Bidders," *The Review of Economic Studies*, 65(1): 1–21 (January 1998). **429**

Che Yeon-Koo. See Polinsky & Che (1991).

Chiang, Alpha (1984) *Fundamental Methods of Mathematical Economics*, 3rd edition, New York: McGraw-Hill (1984, 1st edition 1967). **473**

Chiappori, P. A., Steven Levitt, & T. Groseclose (2002) "Testing Mixed Strategy Equilibria when Players Are Heterogeneous: The Case of Penalty Kicks in Soccer," *The American Economic Review*, 92(4): 1138–1151 (September 2002). **98**

Chiappori, P. A. & B. Salanie (2003) "Testing Contract Theory: A Survey of Some Recent Work," in *Advances in Economics and Econometrics – Theory and Applications, Eighth World Congress*, pp. 115–149, M. Dewatripont, L. Hansen, & P. Turnovsky, eds., Econometric Society Monographs, Cambridge: Cambridge University Press (2003). **201**

Cho, In-Koo & David Kreps (1987) "Signaling Games and Stable Equilibria," *The Quarterly Journal of Economics*, 102(2): 179–221 (May 1987). **324, 173**

Chung, Tai-Yeong (1996) "Rent-Seeking Contest when the Prize Increases with Aggregate Efforts," *Public Choice*, 87(1–2): 55–65 (1996). **403**

Clapp, R. See Capen et al. (1971).

Coase, Ronald (1960) "The Problem of Social Cost," *The Journal of Law and Economics*, 3: 1–44 (October 1960). **192, 217**

Coase, Ronald (1972) "Durability and Monopoly," *The Journal of Law and Economics*, 15(1): 143–149 (April 1972). **463, 469**

Cooper, Russell (1999) *Coordination Games: Complementarities and Macroeconomics*, Cambridge: Cambridge University Press (1999). **35**

Cooter, Robert & Peter Rappoport (1984) "Were the Ordinalists Wrong about Welfare Economics?" *The Journal of Economic Literature*, 22(2): 507–530 (June 1984). **33**

Cooter, Robert & Daniel Rubinfeld (1989) "Economic Analysis of Legal Disputes and Their Resolution," *The Journal of Economic Literature*, 27(3): 1067–1097 (September 1989). **115**

Copeland, Thomas & J. Fred Weston (1988) *Financial Theory and Corporate Policy*, 3rd edition, Reading, MA: Addison-Wesley (1st edition, 1983). **338, 487**

Cosmides, Leda & John Tooby (1993) "Cognitive Adaptions for Social Change," in *The Adapted Mind: Evolutionary Psychology and the Generation of Culture*, pp. 162–228, J. H. Barkow, Leda Cosmides, & John Tooby, eds., Oxford: Oxford University Press (1993). **68**

Cournot, Augustin (1838) *Recherches sur les Principes Mathematiques de la Theorie des Richesses*, Paris: M. Riviere & C. (1838). Translated in *Researches into the Mathematical Principles of Wealth*, New York: A. M. Kelly (1960). **88**

Cox, David & David Hinkley (1974) *Theoretical Statistics*, London: Chapman and Hall (1974). **203**

Cramton, Peter (1984) "Bargaining with Incomplete Information: An Infinite Horizon Model with Two-Sided Uncertainty," *The Review of Economic Studies*, 51(4): 579–593 (October 1984). **381**

Cramton, Peter (undated) "Economics 703: Lecture Note 6: Auctions, Reputations, and Bargaining," http://www.cramton.umd.edu/econ703/note6-auctions-reputations-and-bargaining.pdf. **425**

Cramton, Peter. See Ayres & Cramton (1996).

Crawford, Robert. See Klein et al. (1978).

Crawford, Vincent & Hans Haller (1990) "Learning How to Cooperate: Optimal Play in Repeated Coordination Games," *Econometrica*, 58(3): 571–597 (May 1990). **36**

Crawford, Vincent & Joel Sobel (1982) "Strategic Information Transmission," *Econometrica*, 50(6): 1431–1452 (November 1982). **80**

Dalkey, Norman (1953) "Equivalence of Information Patterns and Essentially Determinate Games," pp. 217–243 of Kuhn & Tucker (1953).

Dasgupta, Partha. See Binmore & Dasgupta (1986).

Dasgupta, Partha & Eric Maskin (1986b) "The Existence of Equilibrium in Discontinuous Economic Games, II: Applications," *The Review of Economic Studies*, 53(1): 27–41 (January 1986). **258, 444, 448**

D'Aspremont, Claude, J. Gabszewicz, & Jacques Thisse (1979) "On Hotelling's 'Stability of Competition'," *Econometrica*, 47(5): 1145–1150 (September 1979). Reprinted in Rasmusen (2001). **381, 444, 468**

D'Aspremont, Claude & L. Gerard-Varet (1979) "Incentives and Incomplete Information," *The Journal of Public Economics*, 11(1): 25–45 (February 1979). **444**

David, Paul (1985) "CLIO and the Economics of QWERTY," *AEA Papers and Proceedings*, 75(2): 332–337 (May 1985). **30**

Davis, Philip, Reuben Hersh, & Elena Marchisotto (1981) *The Mathematical Experience*, Boston: Birkhauser (1981). **6**

Dawes, Robyn (1988) *Rational Choice in an Uncertain World*, Fort Worth, Texas: Harcourt Brace (1988). **65, 236**

Dawkins, Richard (1989) *The Selfish Gene*, 2nd edition, Oxford: Oxford University Press (1st edition 1976). **151**

Debreu, Gerard (1959) *Theory of Value: An Axiomatic Analysis of Economic Equilibrium*, New Haven: Yale University Press (1959). **473**

Debreu, Gerard. See Arrow & Debreu (1954).

Debreu, Gerard & Herbert Scarf (1963) "A Limit Theorem on the Core of an Economy," *The International Economic Review*, 4(3): 235–246 (September 1963). **2**

Demsetz, Harold. See Alchian & Demsetz (1972).

Deneckere, Raymond J. & R. Preston McAfee (1996) "Damaged Goods," *The Journal of Economics and Management Strategy*, 5(2): 149–174 (Summer 1996). **457**

de Vries, Casper G. See Kovenock, Baye & de Vries (1996).

Dewatripont, Mathias (1989) "Renegotiation and Information Revelation over Time in Optimal Labor Contracts," *The Quarterly Journal of Economics*, 104(3): 589–620 (August 1989). **219**

Dewatripont, Mathias. See Bolton & Dewatripont (2005).

Diamond, Douglas W. (1984) "Financial Intermediation and Delegated Monitoring," *The Review of Economic Studies*, 51(3): 393–414 (July 1984). **100**

Diamond, Douglas W. (1989) "Reputation Acquisition in Debt Markets," *The Journal of Political Economy*, 97(4): 828–862 (August 1989). **170, 265**

Diamond, Douglas W. & P. Dybvig (1983) "Bank Runs, Deposit Insurance, and Liquidity," *The Journal of Political Economy*, 91(3): 401–419 (June 1983). **102**

Diamond, Peter (1982) "Aggregate Demand Management in Search Equilibrium," *The Journal of Political Economy*, 90(5): 881–894 (October 1982). **102**

Diamond, Peter & Michael Rothschild, eds., (1978) *Uncertainty in Economics: Readings and Exercises*, New York: Academic Press (1978). **6**

Dimand, Mary Ann & Robert Dimand (1996) *A History of Game Theory*, London: Routledge (1996). **6, 35**

Dimand, Mary Ann & Robert Dimand (1997) *The Foundations of Game Theory*, 3 Vol., Cheltenham, England: Edward Elgar Publishing (1997). **6**

Dimand, Robert & Mohammed Dore (1999) "Cournot, Bertrand, and Game Theory: A Further Note," *Atlantic Economic Journal*, 27: 325–333 (September 1999). **468**

Dixit, Avinash & Barry Nalebuff (1991) *Thinking Strategically: The Competitive Edge in Business, Politics, and Everyday Life*, New York: Norton (1991). **xxiv, 115**

Dixit, Avinash & Susan Skeath (1998) *Games of Strategy*, New York: Norton (1998). **xxvi**

Dixit, Avinash & Joseph Stiglitz (1977) "Monopolistic Competition and Optimum Product Diversity," *The American Economic Review*, 67(3): 297–308 (June 1977). **468**

Dore, Mohammed. See Dimand & Dore (1999).

Dranove, David. See Besanko, Dranove, & Shanley (1996).

Dubey, Pradeep, Ori Haimanko & Andriy Zapechelnyuk (2006) "Strategic Substitutes and Potential Games," forthcoming, *Games and Economic Behavior*, http://ideas.repec.org/p/nys/sunysb/02-02.html (2005). **102**

Duggan, Mark & Steven D. Levitt (2002) "Winning Isn't Everything: Corruption in Sumo Wrestling," *The American Economic Review*, 92(5): 1594–1605 (December 2002). **237**

Dugatkin, Lee & Hudson Reeve, eds., (1998) *Game Theory & Animal Behavior*, Oxford: Oxford University Press (1998). **xxvi, 151**

Dunbar, Robin (1995) *The Trouble with Science*, Cambridge, MA: Harvard University Press (1995). **68**

Dutta, Prajit (1999) *Strategies and Games: Theory and Practice*, Cambridge, MA: MIT Press (1999). **xxvi**

Dybvig, P. See Diamond & Dybvig (1983).

Eaton, C. & Richard Lipsey (1975) "The Principle of Minimum Differentiation Reconsidered: Some New Developments in the Theory of Spatial Competition," *The Review of Economic Studies*, 42(1): 27–49 (January 1975). **448**

Eatwell, John, Murray Milgate, & Peter Newman (1989) *The New Palgrave: Game Theory*, New York: W.W. Norton & Co. (1989). **xxiv**

Edgeworth, Francis (1897) "La Teoria Pura del Monopolio," *Giornale Degli Economisti*, 40: 13–31 (1925). Translated in pp. 111–142 of Edgeworth, Francis, *Papers Relating to Political Economy*, Vol. I, London: Macmillan (1925). **440**

Edgeworth, Francis (1922) "The Mathematical Economics of Professor Amoroso," *Economic Journal*, 32(127): 400–407 (September 1922). Reprinted in Rasmusen (2001). **440**

Ehrenberg, Ronald G. & Michael L. Bognanno (1990) "Do Tournaments Have Incentive Effects?" *The Journal of Political Economy*, 98(6): 1307–1324 (December 1990). **237**

Eichberger, Jurgen (1993) *Game Theory for Economists*, San Diego: Academic Press (1993). **xxv**

Engers, Maxim (1987) "Signalling with Many Signals," *Econometrica*, 55(3): 663–674 (May 1987). **338**

Fama, Eugene (1980) "Banking in the Theory of Finance," *The Journal of Monetary Economics*, 6(1): 39–57 (January 1980). **201**

Farrell, Joseph (2001) "Monopoly Slack and Competitive Rigor: A Simple Model," MIT mimeo (February 1983). Published in Rasmusen (2001). **214**

Farrell, Joseph (1987) "Cheap Talk, Coordination, and Entry," *The RAND Journal of Economics*, 18(1): 34–39 (Spring 1987). Reprinted in Rasmusen (2001). **80**

Farrell, Joseph & Matthew Rabin (1996) "Cheap Talk," *The Journal of Economic Perspectives*, 10(3): 103–118 (Summer 1996). **317**

Farrell, Joseph & Garth Saloner (1985) "Standardization, Compatibility, and Innovation," *The RAND Journal of Economics*, 16(1): 70–83 (Spring 1985). **30**

Farrell, Joseph & Carl Shapiro (1988) "Dynamic Competition with Switching Costs," *The RAND Journal of Economics*, 19(1): 123–137 (Spring 1988). **141**

Feltovich, Nick, Richmond Harbaugh, & Ted To (2002) "Too Cool for School? Signalling and Countersignalling," *The RAND Journal of Economics*, 33(4): 630–649 (Winter 2002). **xxi**, **345**, **347**

Fisher, D. C. & J. Ryan (1992) "Optimal Strategies for a Generalized 'Scissors, Paper, and Stone' Game," *The American Mathematical Monthly*, 99(10): 935–942 (1992). **98**

Fisher, Franklin (1989) "Games Economists Play: A Noncooperative View," *The RAND Journal of Economics*, 20(1): 113–124 (Spring 1989). **2**

Flanagan, Thomas (1998) *Game Theory and Canadian Politics*, Toronto: University of Toronto Press (1998). **35**

Fowler, Henry (1926) *A Dictionary of Modern English Usage*, Herefordshire: Wordsworth Editions reprint, (1997). **7**

Fowler, Henry & Frank Fowler (1931) *The King's English*, 3rd edition, Oxford: Clarendon Press (1949). **7**

Frank, Robert (1988) *Passions within Reason: The Strategic Role of the Emotions*, New York: Norton (1988). **361**

Freixas, Xavier, Roger Guesnerie, & Jean Tirole (1985) "Planning under Incomplete Information and the Ratchet Effect," *The Review of Economic Studies*, 52(2): 173–191 (April 1985). **315**

Friedman, James (1990) *Game Theory with Applications to Economics*, New York: Oxford University Press (2nd edition, 1986). **xxiv**

Friedman, Milton (1953) *Essays in Positive Economics*, Chicago: University of Chicago Press (1953). **6**

Fudenberg, Drew & David Levine (1986) "Limit Games and Limit Equilibria," *The Journal of Economic Theory*, 38(2): 261–279 (April 1986). **100**, **148**, **148**

Fudenberg, Drew & David K. Levine (1989) "Reputation and Equilibrium Selection in Games with a Patient Player," *Econometrica*, 57(4): 759–778 (July 1989).

Fudenberg, Drew & Eric Maskin (1986) "The Folk Theorem in Repeated Games with Discounting or with Incomplete Information," *Econometrica*, 54(3): 533–554 (May 1986). **149**, **169**

Fudenberg, Drew & Jean Tirole (1983) "Sequential Bargaining with Incomplete Information," *The Review of Economic Studies*, 50(2): 221–247 (April 1983). **365**

Fudenberg, Drew & Jean Tirole (1986b) "A Theory of Exit in Duopoly," *Econometrica*, 54(4): 943–960 (July 1986). **148**

Fudenberg, Drew & Jean Tirole (1986c) "A Signal-Jamming Theory of Predation," *The RAND Journal of Economics*, 17(3): 366–376 (Autumn 1986). **341**

Fudenberg, Drew & Jean Tirole (1991a) *Game Theory*, Cambridge, MA: MIT Press (1991). **xix, xxiv, 65, 77, 120, 149, 195, 306, 381, 454, 473, 484**

Fudenberg, Drew & Jean Tirole (1991b) "Perfect Bayesian Equilibrium and Sequential Equilibrium," *The Journal of Economic Theory*, 53(2): 236–260 (April 1991). **173**

Gabszewicz, J. See d'Aspremont et al. (1979).

Galbraith, John Kenneth (1954) *The Great Crash*, Boston: Houghton Mifflin (1954). **238**

Gale, Ian. See Che & Gale (1998).

Gal-Or, Esther (1985) "First Mover and Second Mover Advantages," *International Economic Review*, 26(3): 649–653 (October 1985). **94**

Gardner, Roy, *Games for Business and Economics*, New York: John Wiley and Sons (2nd edition 2003). **xxv**

Gaskins, Darius (1974) "Alcoa Revisited: The Welfare Implications of a Second-Hand Market," *The Journal of Economic Theory*, 7(3): 254–271 (March 1974). **469**

Gates, Scott & Brian Humes (1997) *Games, Information, and Politics: Applying Game Theoretic Models to Political Science*, Ann Arbor: University of Michigan Press (1997). **xxvi**

Gaudet, Gerard & Stephen Salant (1991) "Uniqueness of Cournot Equilibrium: New Results from Old Methods," *The Review of Economic Studies*, 58: 399–404 (April 1991). **467**

Gaver, Kenneth & Jerold Zimmerman (1977) "An Analysis of Competitive Bidding on BART Contracts," *The Journal of Business*, 50(3): 279–295 (July 1977). **213**

Geanakoplos, John (1992) "Common Knowledge," *The Journal of Economic Perspectives*, 6(4): 53–82 (Fall 1992). **64**

Geanakoplos, John. See Bulow et al. (1985).

Geanakoplos, John & Heraklis Polemarchakis (1982) "We Can't Disagree Forever," *The Journal of Economic Theory*, 28(1): 192–200 (October 1982). **65**

Gerard-Varet, L. See D'Aspremont & Gerard-Varet (1979).

Gertner, Robert. See Baird, Gertner, & Picker (1994).

Ghemawat, Pankaj (1997) *Games Businesses Play: Cases and Models*, Cambridge, MA: MIT Press (1997). **xxvi**

Ghemawat, Pankaj & Barry Nalebuff (1985) "Exit," *The RAND Journal of Economics*, 16(2): 184–194 (Summer 1985). **76**

Gibbard, Allan (1973) "Manipulation of Voting Schemes: A General Result," *Econometrica*, 41(4): 587–601 (July 1973). **314**

Gibbons, Robert (1992) *Game Theory for Applied Economists*, Princeton: Princeton University Press (1992). **xxv, 284, 381**

Gillies, Donald (1953) "Locations of Solutions," in *Report of an Informal Conference on the Theory of n-Person Games*, pp. 11–12, Princeton Mathematics mimeo (1953). **1**

Gintis, Herbert (2000) *Game Theory Evolving*, Princeton: Princeton University Press (2000). **xxvii, 144, 351**

Gjesdal, Froystein (1982) "Information and Incentives: The Agency Information Problem," *The Review of Economic Studies*, 49(3): 373–390 (July 1982). **203**

Glazer, Jacob & Albert Ma (1989) "Efficient Allocation of a 'Prize': King Solomon's Dilemma," *Games and Economic Behavior*, 1(3): 222–233 (1989). **281**

Glosten, Lawrence & Paul Milgrom (1985) "Bid, Ask, and Transaction Prices in a Specialist Model with Heterogeneously Informed Traders," *The Journal of Financial Economics*, 14(1): 71–100 (March 1985). **259**

Goldfeld, Stephen. See Baumol & Goldfeld (1968).

Gonik, Jacob (1978) "Tie Salesmen's Bonuses to Their Forecasts," *Harvard Business Review*, 56: 116–123 (May/June 1978). Reprinted in Rasmusen (2001). **292**

Gordon, David. See Rapaport, Guyer, & Gordon (1976).

Graham, Daniel & Robert Marshall (1987) "Collusive Bidding Behavior at Single-Object Second-Price and English Auctions," *The Journal of Political Economy*, 95(6): 1217–1239. **413**

Green, Jerry. See Mas-Colell, Whinston, & Green (1994).

Greenhut, Melvin & Hiroshi Ohta (1975) *Theory of Spatial Pricing and Market Areas*, Durham, N. C.: Duke University Press (1975). **468**

Grinblatt, Mark & Chuan-Yang Hwang (1989) "Signalling and the Pricing of New Issues," *The Journal of Finance*, 44(2): 393–420 (June 1989). **339**

Groseclose, T. See Chiappori, Levitt, & Groseclose (2002).

Grossman, Gene & Michael Katz (1983) "Plea Bargaining and Social Welfare," *The American Economic Review*, 73(4): 749–757 (September 1983). **348**

Grossman, Sanford & Oliver Hart (1980) "Takeover Bids, the Free-Rider Problem, and the Theory of the Corporation," *The Bell Journal of Economics*, 11(1): 42–64 (Spring 1980). **230**

Grossman, Sanford & Oliver Hart (1983) "An Analysis of the Principal Agent Problem," *Econometrica*, 51(1): 7–45 (January 1983). **195**

Groves, Theodore (1973) "Incentives in Teams," *Econometrica*, 41(4): 617–631 (July 1973). **296**

Guasch, J. Luis & Andrew Weiss (1980) "Wages as Sorting Mechanisms in Competitive Markets with Asymmetric Information: A Theory of Testing," *The Review of Economic Studies*, 47(4): 653–664 (July 1980). **272**

Guesnerie, Roger. See Freixas et al. (1985).

Guth, Werner, Rold Schmittberger, & Bernd Schwarze (1982) "An Experimental Analysis of Ultimatum Bargaining," *The Journal of Economic Behavior and Organization*, 3(4): 367–388 (December 1982). **118**

Guyer, Melvin. See Rapaport, Guyer & Gordon (1976).

Haile, Philip A. See Athey & Haile (2005).

Haimanko, Ori. See Dubey, Haimanko, & Zapechelnyuk (2002).

Haller, Hans (1986) "Noncooperative Bargaining of $N \geq 3$ Players," *Economics Letters*, 22: 11–13 (1986). **364**

Haller, Hans. See Crawford & Haller(1990).

Halmos, Paul (1970) "How to Write Mathematics," *L'Enseignement Mathematique*, 16(2): 123–152 (May/June 1970). **7**

Haltiwanger, John & Michael Waldman (1991) "Responders versus Nonresponders: A New Perspective of Heterogeneity," *Economic Journal*, 101(408): 1085–1102 (September 1991). **468**

Hamilton, William. See Axelrod & Hamilton (1981).

Han Fei Tzu (c. 250 B.C.) *Basic Writings*, translated by Burton Watson, New York: Columbia University Press (1964). **216, 217**

Happel, Stephen K. See Boyes & Happel (1989).

Harbaugh, Richmond. See Feltovich, Harbaugh, & To (2002).

Harper, David. See Maynard-Smith & Harper (2004).

Harrington, Joseph (1987) "Collusion in Multiproduct Oligopoly Games under a Finite Horizon," *The International Economic Review*, 28(1): 1–14 (February 1987). **147**

Harris, Milton & Bengt Holmstrom (1982) "A Theory of Wage Dynamics," *The Review of Economic Studies*, 49(3): 315–334 (July 1982). **52**

Harris, Milton & Arthur Raviv (1992) "Financial Contracting Theory," in *Advances in Economic Theory: Sixth World Congress*, ed. Jean-Jacques Laffont, Cambridge: Cambridge University Press (1992).

Harris, Milton & Arthur Raviv (1995) "The Role of Games in Security Design," *The Review of Financial Studies*, 8(2): 327–367 (Summer 1995). **263**

Harris, Robert. See Franks et al. (1988).

Harsanyi, John (1967) "Games with Incomplete Information Played by 'Bayesian' Players, I: The Basic Model," *Management Science*, 14(3): 159–182 (November 1967). **2, 53**

Harsanyi, John (1968a) "Games with Incomplete Information Played by 'Bayesian' Players, II: Bayesian Equilibrium Points," *Management Science*, 14(5): 320–334 (January 1968).

Harsanyi, John (1968b) "Games with Incomplete Information Played by 'Bayesian' Players, III: The Basic Probability Distribution of the Game," *Management Science*, 14(7): 486–502 (March 1968).

Harsanyi, John (1973) "Games with Randomly Disturbed Payoffs: A New Rationale for Mixed Strategy Equilibrium Points," *The International Journal of Game Theory*, 2(1): 1–23 (1973). **73**

Harsanyi, John (1977) *Rational Behavior and Bargaining Equilibrium in Games and Social Situations*, New York: Cambridge University Press (1977). **380**

Harsanyi, John & Reinhard Selten (1988) *A General Theory of Equilibrium Selection in Games*, Cambridge, MA: MIT Press (1988). **31**

Hart, Oliver & Bengt Holmstrom (1987) "The Theory of Contracts," in *Advances in Economic Theory*, ed. T. F. Bewley, pp. 71–155, Cambridge: Cambridge University Press (1987). **183**

Hart, Oliver & John Moore (1990), "Property Rights and the Nature of the Firm," *The Journal of Political Economy*, 98(6): 1119–1158 (December 1990). **218, 219**

Hart, Oliver. See Grossman & Hart (1980, 1983).

Hart, Sergiu (2005) "An Interview with Robert Aumann," http://www.ma.huji.ac.il/~hart/abs/aumann.html (January 2005; updated April 2005). **35**

Hart, Sergiu. See Aumann & Hart (1992).

Hausman, Jerry & James Poterba (1987) "Household Behavior and the Tax Reform Act of 1986," *The Journal of Economic Perspectives*, 1(1): 101–119 (Summer 1987). **305**

Haywood, O. (1954) "Military Decisions and Game Theory," *Journal of the Operations Research Society of America*, 2(4): 365–385 (November 1954). **22**

Henderson, Dale. See Canzoneri & Henderson (1991).

Hendricks, Ken, Andrew Weiss, & Charles A. Wilson (1988) "The War of Attrition in Continuous Time with Complete Information," *International Economic Review*, 29(4): 663–680 (November 1988).

Hendricks, Ken & Robert Porter (1988) "An Empirical Study of an Auction with Asymmetric Information," *The American Economic Review*, 78(5): 865–883 (December 1988). **428**

Hendricks, Ken & Robert Porter (forthcoming), "Lectures on Auctions: An Empirical Perspective," in *The Handbook of Industrial Organization, Vol. III*, M. Armstrong and R. Porter, eds., Elsevier, forthcoming. **428**

Herodotus (c. 429 B.C.) *The Persian Wars*, George Rawlinson, translator, New York: Modern Library (1947). **34**

Hersh, Reuben. See Davis & Hersh (1981).

Hines, W. (1987) "Evolutionary Stable Strategies: A Review of Basic Theory," *Theoretical Population Biology*, 31(2): 195–272 (April 1987). **151**

Hinkley, David. See Cox & Hinkley (1974).

Hirshleifer, David (1995) "The Blind Leading the Blind: Social Influence, Fads, and Informational Cascades," in *The New Economics of Human Behavior*, Mariano Tommasi and Kathryn Ierulli, eds., pp. 188–215 (chapter 12), Cambridge: Cambridge University Press (1995). **61**

Hirshleifer, David & Eric Rasmusen (1989) "Cooperation in a Repeated Prisoner's Dilemma with Ostracism," *The Journal of Economic Behavior and Organization*, 12(1): 87–106 (August 1989). **147**

Hirshleifer, David. See Png & Hirshleifer (1987), Bikhchandani, Hirshleifer, & Welch (1992).

Hirshleifer, Jack (1982) "Evolutionary Models in Economics and Law: Cooperation versus Conflict Strategies," *Research in Law and Economics*, 4: 1–60 (1982). **35, 151**

Hirshleifer, Jack (1987) "On the Emotions as Guarantors of Threats and Promises," in *The Latest on the Best: Essays on Evolution and Optimality*, ed. John Dupre, Cambridge, MA: MIT Press (1987). **150**

Hirshleifer, Jack (1989) "Conflict and Rent-Seeking Success Functions: Ratio and Difference Models of Relative Success," *Public Choice*, 63(2): 101–112. **402**

Hirshleifer, Jack & Juan Martinez-Coll (1988) "What Strategies Can Support the Evolutionary Emergence of Cooperation?" *The Journal of Conflict Resolution*, 32(2): 367–398 (June 1988). **149**

Hirshleifer, Jack & Eric Rasmusen (1992) "Are Equilibrium Strategies Unaffected by Incentives?" *The Journal of Theoretical Politics*, 4: 343–357 (July 1992). **100**

Hirshleifer, Jack & John Riley (1979) "The Analytics of Uncertainty and Information: An Expository Survey," *The Journal of Economic Literature*, 17(4): 1375–1421 (December 1979).

Hirshleifer, Jack & John Riley (1992) *The Analytics of Uncertainty and Information*, Cambridge: Cambridge University Press (1992). **xxv, 49**

Hoffman, Elizabeth & Matthew Spitzer (1985) "Entitlements, Rights and Fairness: An Experimental Examination of Subjects' Concepts of Distributive Justice," *The Journal of Legal Studies*, 14(2): 269–297 (June 1985). **360**

Hofstadter, Douglas (1983) "Computer Tournaments of the Prisoner's Dilemma Suggest How Cooperation Evolves," *Scientific American*, 248(5): 16–26 (May 1983). **175**

Holmes, Oliver (1881) *The Common Law*, Boston: Little, Brown and Co. (1923). **217, 217**

Holmstrom, Bengt (1979) "Moral Hazard and Observability," *The Bell Journal of Economics*, 10(1): 74–91 (Spring 1979). **197, 202**

Holmstrom, Bengt (1982) "Moral Hazard in Teams," *The Bell Journal of Economics*, 13(2): 324–340 (Autumn 1982). **227, 230, 238**

Holmstrom, Bengt & Paul Milgrom (1987) "Aggregation and Linearity in the Provision of Intertemporal Incentives," *Econometrica*, 55(2): 303–328 (March 1987). **xx**

Holmstrom, Bengt & Paul Milgrom (1991) "Multitask Principal-Agent Analyses: Incentive Contracts, Asset Ownership, and Job Design," *The Journal of Law, Economics and Organization*, 7: 24–52 (Special Issue, 1991). **xx, xx, 230**

Holmstrom, Bengt & Roger Myerson (1983) "Efficient and Durable Decision Rules with Incomplete Information," *Econometrica*, 51(6): 1799–1819 (November 1983).

Holmstrom, Bengt. See Harris & Holmstrom (1982), Hart & Holmstrom (1987).

Holt Charles A. & Lisa R. Anderson (1996) "Classroom Games: Understanding Bayes Rule," *The Journal of Economic Perspectives*, 10(2): 179–187 (Spring 1996). **68**

Holt, Charles & David Scheffman (1987) "Facilitating Practices: The Effects of Advance Notice and Best-Price Policies," *The RAND Journal of Economics*, 18(2): 187–197 (Summer 1987). **469**

Hong, Han. See Bajari, Hong, & Ryan (2004).

Hoppe, Heidrun H. See Baye & Hoppe (2003).

Hortacsu, Ali. See Bajari & Hortacsu (2004).

Hotelling, Harold (1929) "Stability in Competition," *Economic Journal*, 39: 41–57 (March 1929). Reprinted in Rasmusen (2001). **441, 446**

Hughes, Patricia (1986) "Signalling by Direct Disclosure under Asymmetric Information," *The Journal of Accounting and Economics*, 8(2): 119–142 (June 1986). **338**

Humes, Brian. See Gates & Humes (1996).

Hwang, Chuan-Yang. See Grinblatt & Hwang (1989).

Intriligator, Michael (1971) *Mathematical Optimization and Economic Theory*, Englewood Cliffs, NJ: Prentice-Hall (1971). **473**

Isoda, Kazuo. See Nikaido & Isoda (1955).

Jarrell, Gregg & Sam Peltzman (1985) "The Impact of Product Recalls on the Wealth of Sellers," *The Journal of Political Economy*, 93(3): 512–536 (June 1985). **150**

Jensen, Michael C. (2003) "Paying People to Lie: The Truth about the Budgeting Process," *European Financial Management*, 9(3): 379–406 (September 2003). **201**

Jensen, Michael C. See Baker et al. (1988).

Jin, Ginger & Philip Leslie (2003) "The Effect of Information on Product Quality: Evidence from Restaurant Hygiene Grade Cards," *The Quarterly Journal of Economics*, 118(2): 409–451 (2003). **348**

Johnson, Norman & Samuel Kotz (1970) *Distributions in Statistics*, 3 vol., New York: John Wiley and Sons (1970). **481**

Kahneman, Daniel, Paul Slovic, & Amos Tversky, eds., (1982) *Judgement Under Uncertainty: Heuristics and Biases*, Cambridge: Cambridge University Press (1982). **65, 236**

Kakutani, Shizuo (1941) "A Generalization of Brouwer's Fixed Point Theorem," *Duke Mathematical Journal*, 8(3): 457–459 (September 1941). **485**

Kalai, Ehud, Dov Samet, & William Stanford (1988) "Note on Reactive Equilibria in the Discounted Prisoner's Dilemma and Associated Games," *The International Journal of Game Theory*, 17: 177–186 (1988). **131**

Kamien, Morton & Nancy Schwartz (1982) *Market Structure and Innovation*, Cambridge: Cambridge University Press (1982).

Kamien, Morton & Nancy Schwartz (1991) *Dynamic Optimization: The Calculus of Variations and Optimal Control in Economics and Management*, 2nd edition, New York: North Holland (1991, 1st edition 1981). **473**

Kandori, Michihiro (2002) "Introduction to Repeated Games with Private Monitoring," *The Journal of Economic Theory*, 102(1): 1–15 (January 2002). **149**

Kandori, Michihiro & H. Matsushima (1998) "Private Observation, Communication, and Collusion," *Econometrica*, 66(3): 627–652. **87**

Kaplow, Louis & Steven Shavell (1996) "Property Rules versus Liability Rules: An Economic Analysis," *Harvard Law Review*, 109(4): 713–789 (February 1996). **429**

Karlin, Samuel (1959) *Mathematical Methods and Theory in Games, Programming and Economics*, Reading, MA: Addison-Wesley (1959). **77**

Katz, Lawrence (1986) "Efficiency Wage Theory: A Partial Evaluation," in *NBER Macroeconomics Annual 1986*, ed. Stanley Fischer, Cambridge, MA: MIT Press (1986). **236**

Katz, Michael & Carl Shapiro (1985) "Network Externalities, Competition, and Compatibility," *The American Economic Review*, 75(3): 424–440 (June 1985). **30**

Katz, Michael. See Grossman & Katz (1983).

Katz, Michael. See Moskowitz et al. (1980).

Kennan, John & Robert Wilson (1993) "Bargaining with Private Information," *The Journal of Economic Literature*, 31(1): 45–104 (March 1993). **115, 381, 469**

Kennedy, Peter (1979) *A Guide to Econometrics*, 1st edition, Cambridge, MA: MIT Press (1979, 5th edition 2003).

Keynes, John Maynard (1933) *Essays in Biography*, New York: Harcourt, Brace and Company (1933). **6**

Keynes, John Maynard (1936) *The General Theory of Employment, Interest and Money*, London: Macmillan (1947). **35**

Kierkegaard, Soren (1938) *The Journals of Soren Kierkegaard*, translated by Alexander-Dru, Oxford: Oxford University Press (1938). **129**

Kihlstrom, Richard & Michael Riordan (1984) "Advertising as a Signal," *The Journal of Political Economy*, 92(3): 427–450 (June 1984). **348**

Kilgour, D. Marc. See Brams & Kilgour (1988).

Kindleberger, Charles (1983) "Standards as Public, Collective and Private Goods," *Kyklos*, 36: 377–396 (1983). **30**

Klein, Benjamin, Robert Crawford, & Armen Alchian (1978) "Vertical Integration, Appropriable Rents, and the Competitive Contracting Process," *The Journal of Law and Economics*, 21(2): 297–326 (October 1978). **201, 218**

Klein, Benjamin & Keith Leffler (1981) "The Role of Market Forces in Assuring Contractual Performance," *The Journal of Political Economy*, 89(4): 615–641 (August 1981). **138, 140, 150, 236**

Klein, Benjamin & Lester Saft (1985) "The Law and Economics of Franchise Tying Contracts," *The Journal of Law and Economics*, 28(2): 345–361 (May 1985). **203**

Klemperer, Paul (1987) "The Competitiveness of Markets with Switching Costs," *The RAND Journal of Economics*, 18(1): 138–150 (Spring 1987). **141**

Klemperer, Paul (1998) "Auctions with Almost Common Values: The 'Wallet Game' and Its Applications," *European Economic Review*, 42(3–5): 757–769 (May 1998). **424**

Klemperer, Paul, ed. (2000) *The Economic Theory of Auctions*. Cheltenham, England: Edward Elgar (2000). http://www.paulklemperer.org. **6, 419, 428**

Klemperer, Paul (2004) *Auctions: Theory and Practice*, Princeton: Princeton University Press (2004). http://www.paulklemperer.org. **403, 425, 427, 428**

Klemperer, Paul. See Bulow, Geanakoplos, & Klemperer (1985), Bulow & Klemperer (1996).

Kohlberg, Elon & Jean-Francois Mertens (1986) "On the Strategic Stability of Equilibria," *Econometrica*, 54(5): 1003–1007 (September 1986). **101**

Kotz, Samuel. See Johnson & Kotz (1970).

Kovenock, Dan, Michael R. Baye, & Casper G. de Vries (1996) "The All-Pay Auction with Complete Information," *Economic Theory*, 8(2): 291–305. **400**

Kreps, David (1990a) *A Course in Microeconomic Theory*, Princeton: Princeton University Press (1990). **xxiv, 65**

Kreps, David (1990b) *Game Theory and Economic Modeling*, Oxford: Oxford University Press (1990). **xxiv, 173**

Kreps, David, Paul Milgrom, John Roberts, & Robert Wilson (1982) "Rational Cooperation in the Finitely Repeated Prisoners' Dilemma," *The Journal of Economic Theory*, 27: 245–252 (August 1982). Reprinted in Rasmusen (2001). **2, 167**

Kreps, David & Jose Scheinkman (1983) "Quantity Precommitment and Bertrand Competition Yield Cournot Outcomes," *The Bell Journal of Economics*, 14(2): 326–337 (Autumn 1983). **468**

Kreps, David & A. Michael Spence (1985) "Modelling the Role of History in Industrial Organization and Competition," in *Issues in Contemporary Microeconomics and Welfare*, ed. George Feiwel, London: Macmillan (1985). **3**

Kreps, David & Robert Wilson (1982a) "Reputation and Imperfect Information," *Journal of Economic Theory*, 27(2): 253–279 (August 1982).

Kreps, David & Robert Wilson (1982b) "Sequential Equilibria," *Econometrica*, 50(4): 863–894 (July 1982). **2**

Krishna, Vijay (2002) *Auction Theory*, San Diego: Academic Press (2002). **xxvii, 387, 400, 404, 428**

Krishna, Vijay. See Benoit & Krishna (1985, 2000).

Krouse, Clement (1990) *Theory of Industrial Economics*, Oxford: Blackwell (1990). **xxiv**

Kuhn, Harold (1953) "Extensive Games and the Problem of Information," in Kuhn & Tucker (1953). **98**

Kuhn, Harold, ed. (1997) *Classics in Game Theory*, Princeton: Princeton University Press (1997). **6**

Kuhn, Harold & Albert Tucker, eds., (1953) *Contributions to the Theory of Games, Volume II, Annals of Mathematics Studies, No. 28*, Princeton: Princeton University Press (1953).

Kuhn, Thomas (1970) *The Structure of Scientific Revolutions*, Chicago: University of Chicago Press (1970). **446**

Kydland, Finn & Edward Prescott (1977) "Rules rather than Discretion: The Inconsistency of Optimal Plans," *The Journal of Political Economy*, 85(3): 473–491 (June 1977). **122**

Kyle, Albert (1985) "Continuous Auctions and Insider Trading," *Econometrica*, 53(6): 1315–1336 (November 1985). **261**

Laffont, Jean-Jacques & David Martimort (2001) *The Theory of Incentives: The Principal-Agent Model*, Princeton: Princeton University Press (2001). **xxv**

Laffont, Jean-Jacques & Jean Tirole (1986) "Using Cost Observation to Regulate Firms," *Journal of Political Economy*, 94(3): 614–641 (June 1986).

Laffont, Jean-Jacques & Jean Tirole (1993) *A Theory of Incentives in Procurement and Regulation*, Cambridge, MA: MIT Press (1993). **120, 305, 314**

Lakatos, Imre (1976) *Proofs and Refutations: The Logic of Mathematical Discovery*, Cambridge: Cambridge University Press (1976). **3**

Lane, W. (1980) "Product Differentiation in a Market with Endogenous Sequential Entry," *The Bell Journal of Economics*, 11(1): 237–260 (Spring 1980). **469**

Layard, Richard & George Psacharopoulos (1974) "The Screening Hypothesis and the Returns to Education," *The Journal of Political Economy*, 82(5): 985–998 (September/October 1974). **330, 348**

Lazear, Edward & Sherwin Rosen (1981) "Rank-Order Tournaments As Optimum Labor Contracts," *The Journal of Political Economy*, 89(5): 841–864 (October 1981). **236**

Leffler, Keith. See Klein & Leffler (1981).

Leibenstein, Harvey (1950) "Bandwagon, Snob and Veblen Effects in the Theory of Consumers' Demand," *The Quarterly Journal of Economics*, 64(2): 183–207 (May 1950). **270**

Leitzel, James. See Alexeev & Leitzel (1996).

Leland, Hayne & David Pyle (1977) "Informational Asymmetries, Financial Structure, and Financial Intermediation," *The Journal of Finance*, 32(2): 371–387 (May 1977). **339**

Leonard, Robert J. (1995) "From Parlor Games to Social Science: Von Neumann, Morgenstern, and the Creation of Game Theory 1928–1944," *The Journal of Economic Literature*, 33(2): 730–761 (June 1995). **35**

Leshno, Moshe, Haim Levy, & Yishay Spector (1997) "A Comment on Rothschild and Stiglitz's 'Increasing Risk I: A Definition'," *The Journal of Economic Theory*, 77(1): 223–228 (November 1997). **489**

Leslie, Philip. See Jin & Leslie (2003).

Levering, Robert. See Moskowitz et al. (1980).

Levine, David. See Fudenberg & Levine (1986, 1989).

Levitan, Richard & Martin Shubik (1972) "Price Duopoly and Capacity Constraints," *The International Economic Review*, 13(1): 111–122 (February 1972). **440**

Levitt, Steven. See Chiappori, Levitt, & Groseclose (2002), Duggan & Levitt (2002).

Levmore, Saul (1982) "Self-Assessed Valuation for Tort and Other Law," *Virginia Law Review*, 68(4): 771–861 (April 1982). **314**

Levy, Haim. See Leshno, Levy, & Spector (1997).

Lewis, David (1969) *Convention: A Philosophical Study*, Cambridge: Harvard University Press (1969). **64**

Liebowitz, S. & Stephen Margolis (1990) "The Fable of the Keys," *The Journal of Political Economy*, 33(1): 1–25 (April 1990). Reprinted in *Famous Fables of Economics: Myths of Market Failures*, ed. Daniel F. Spulber, Oxford: Blackwell Publishers (2001). **30**

Lipsey, Richard. See Eaton & Lipsey (1975).

Lively, C. M. See Sinervo & Lively (1996).

Loeb, Martin & Wesley A. Magat (1979) "A Decentralized Method for Utility Regulation," *The Journal of Law and Economics*, 22(2): 399–404 (October 1979). **306**

Lorberbaum, Jeffrey. See Boyd & Lorberbaum (1987).

Lucas, Robert. See Stokey & Lucas (1989).

Luce, R. Duncan & Howard Raiffa (1957) *Games and Decisions: Introduction and Critical Survey*, New York: Wiley (1957). **xxiii, xxiii, 35, 134, 148, 380**

Ma, Albert. See Glazer & Ma (1989).

Macaulay, Stewart (1963) "Non-Contractual Relations in Business," *The American Sociological Review*, 28(1): 55–70 (February 1963). **150**

Macho-Stadler, Ines & J. David Perez-Castillo (1997) *An Introduction to the Economics of Information: Incentives and Contracts*, Oxford: Oxford University Press (1997). **xxvi, 201**

Macrae, Norman (1992) *John von Neumann*, New York: Random House (1992). **18, 35**

Magat, Wesley A. See Loeb & Magat (1979).

Margolis, Stephen. See Liebowitz & Margolis (1990).

Mason, Joseph. See Calomiris & Mason (1997).

Maynard-Smith, John & David Harper (2004) *Animal Signals*, Oxford: Oxford University Press (2004). **348**

Marschak, Jacob & Roy Radner (1972) *Economic Theory of Teams*, New Haven: Yale University Press (1972). **238**

Martin, Stephen (1993) *Advanced Industrial Economics*, Oxford: Blackwell Publishers (1993). **xxv**

Martinez-Coll. See J. Hirshleifer & Martinez-Coll (1988).

Mas-Colell, Andreu, Michael Whinston, & Jerry Green (1995) *Microeconomic Theory*, Oxford: Oxford University Press (1995). **xxvi, 381, 484**

Maskin, Eric (1977) "Nash Implementation and Welfare Optimality," mimeo, MIT. Published in 1999 in the *The Review of Economic Studies*, 66(1): 23–38 (January 1999). **280**

Maskin, Eric (2004) "The Unity of Auction Theory: Milgrom's Masterclass," *The Journal of Economic Literature*, 42(4): 1102–1115 (December 2004). **428**

Maskin, Eric. See Dasgupta & Maskin (1986a, 1986b), Fudenberg & Maskin (1986).

Maskin, Eric & John Riley (1985) "Input vs. Output Incentive Schemes," *Journal of Public Economics*, 28: 1–23 (October 1985).

Maskin, Eric & Jean Tirole (1987) "Correlated Equilibria and Sunspots," *The Journal of Economic Theory*, 43(2): 364–373 (December 1987). **80**

Mathewson, G. Frank & Ralph Winter (1985) "The Economics of Franchise Contracts," *The Journal of Law and Economics*, 28(3): 503–526 (October 1985). **203**

Matsushima, H. See Kandori & Matsushima (1998).

Mayer, Colin. See Franks et al. (1988).

Maynard Smith, John (1974) "The Theory of Games and the Evolution of Animal Conflicts," *The Journal of Theoretical Biology*, 47(1): 209–221 (September 1974). **76**

Maynard Smith, John (1982) *Evolution and the Theory of Games*, Cambridge: Cambridge University Press (1982). **151**

Maynard Smith, John & G. A. Parker (1976) "The Logic of Asymmetric Contests," *Animal Behavior*, 24: 159–175.

McAfee, R. Preston (2002) *Competitive Solutions: The Strategist's Toolkit*, Princeton: Princeton University Press (2002). **xxvii, 77, 226, 315, 457**

McAfee, R. Preston & John McMillan (1986) "Bidding for Contracts: A Principal-Agent Analysis," *The RAND Journal of Economics*, 17(3): 326–338 (Autumn 1986).

McAfee, R. Preston & John McMillan (1987) "Auctions and Bidding," *The Journal of Economic Literature*, 25(2): 699–754 (June 1987). **428**

McAfee, R. Preston & John McMillan (1988) *Incentives in Government Contracts*, Toronto: University of Toronto Press (1988). **314**

McAfee, R. Preston & John McMillan (1996) "Analyzing the Airwaves Auction," *The Journal of Economic Perspectives*, 10(1): 159–175 (Winter 1996). Reprinted in Rasmusen (2001). **428**

McAfee, R. Preston. See Deneckere & McAfee (1996).

McCloskey, Donald (1985) "Economical Writing," *Economic Inquiry*, 24(2): 187–222 (April 1985). **7**

McCloskey, Donald (1987) *The Writing of Economics*, New York: Macmillan (1987). **7**

McDonald, John & John Tukey (1949) "Colonel Blotto: A Problem of Military Strategy," *Fortune*, 40: 102 (June 1949). Reprinted in Rasmusen (2001). **101**

McGee, John (1958) "Predatory Price Cutting: The Standard Oil (N.J.) Case," *The Journal of Law and Economics*, 1: 137–169 (October 1958). **111**

McMillan, John (1992) *Games, Strategies, and Managers: How Managers Can Use Game Theory to Make Better Business Decisions*, Oxford: Oxford University Press (1992). **xxv, 66**

McMillan, John. See McAfee & McMillan (1986, 1987, 1988, 1996).

Mead, Walter, Asbjorn Moseidjord, & Philip Sorenson (1984) "Competitive Bidding under Asymmetrical Information: Behavior and Performance in Gulf of Mexico Drainage Lease Sales 1959–1969," *The Review of Economics and Statistics*, 66(3): 505–508 (August 1984). **415**

Meckling, William. See Jensen & Meckling (1976).

Meese, G. See Baldwin & Meese (1979).

Mertens, Jean-Francois. See Kohlberg & Mertens (1986).

Mertens, Jean-Francois & S. Zamir (1985) "Formulation of Bayesian Analysis for Games with Incomplete Information," *The International Journal of Game Theory*, 14(1): 1–29 (1985). **65**

Milgate, Murray. See Eatwell et al. (1989).

Milgrom, Paul (1981a) "An Axiomatic Characterization of Common Knowledge" *Econometrica*, 49(1): 219–222 (January 1981). **64**

Milgrom, Paul (1981b) "Good News and Bad News: Representation Theorems and Applications," *The Bell Journal of Economics*, 12(2): 380–391 (Autumn 1981). **203**

Milgrom, Paul (1981c) "Rational Expectations, Information Acquisition, and Competitive Bidding," *Econometrica*, 49(4): 921–943 (July 1981). **425**

Milgrom, Paul (1999) *Auction Theory for Privatization*, Cambridge: Cambridge University Press (1999). **316, 428**

Milgrom, Paul (2004) *Putting Auction Theory to Work*, Cambridge: Cambridge University Press (2004). **xxvii, 404, 316**

Milgrom, Paul & John Roberts (1982) "Limit Pricing and Entry under Incomplete Information: An Equilibrium Analysis," *Econometrica*, 50(2): 443–459 (March 1982). **175, 341**

Milgrom, Paul & John Roberts (1986) "Price and Advertising Signals of Product Quality," *The Journal of Political Economy*, 94(4): 796–821 (August 1986). **348**

Milgrom, Paul & John Roberts (1990) "Rationalizability, Learning, and Equilibrium in Games with Strategic Complementarities," *Econometrica*, 58(61): 1255-1279 (November 1990). **102, 454, 483, 484**

Milgrom, Paul & John Roberts (1992) *Economics, Organizations, and Management*, Englewood Cliffs, NJ: Prentice-Hall (1992). **xxiv, 201**

Milgrom, Paul & Robert Weber (1982) "A Theory of Auctions and Competitive Bidding," *Econometrica*, 50(5): 1089–1122 (September 1982). **407, 417, 425, 428**

Milgrom, Paul. See Kreps et al. (1982), Glosten & Milgrom (1985), and Holmstrom & Milgrom (1987, 1991).

Milinski, M. (1987) "TIT FOR TAT in Sticklebacks and the Evolution of Cooperation," *Nature*, 325: 433–435 (January 29, 1987). **149**

Miller, Geoffrey (1986) "An Economic Analysis of Rule 68," *The Journal of Legal Studies*, 15: 93–125 (January 1986). **113**

Mirrlees, James (1971) "An Exploration in the Theory of Optimum Income Taxation," *The Review of Economic Studies*, 38(114): 175–208 (April 1971). **269, 293, 306**

Mirrlees, James (1974) "Notes on Welfare Economics, Information and Uncertainty," in *Essays on Economic Behavior under Uncertainty*, M. Balch, Daniel McFadden, and S. Wu, eds., Amsterdam: North Holland (1974). **203, 272**

Mookherjee, Dilip & Ivan Png (1989) "Optimal Auditing, Insurance, and Redistribution," *The Quarterly Journal of Economics*, 104(2): 399–415 (May 1989). **100**

Moore, John. See Hart & Moore (1990).

Moreaux, Michel (1985) "Perfect Nash Equilibria in Finite Repeated Game and Uniqueness of Nash Equilibrium in the Constituent Game," *Economics Letters*, 17(4): 317–320 (1985). **147**

Morgenstern, Oskar. See von Neumann & Morgenstern (1944).

Morris, Peter (1994) *Introduction to Game Theory*, Berlin: Springer-Verlag (1994). **xxv**

Morrison, Clarence (1998) "Cournot, Bertrand, and Modern Game Theory," *Atlantic Economic Review*, 26: 172–174 (June 1998). **467**

Morrow, James (1994) *Game Theory for Political Scientists*, Princeton: Princeton University Press (1994). **xxv**

Moseidjord, Asbjorn. See Mead et al. (1984).

Moulin, Herve (1986) *Eighty-Nine Exercises with Solutions from Game Theory for the Social Sciences*, 2nd and revised edition, New York: NYU Press (1986). **xxiii**

Murphy, Kevin J. See Baker et al. (1988).

Muthoo, Abhinay (1999) *Bargaining Theory With Applications*, Cambridge: Cambridge University Press (1999). **xxvii**

Muzzio, Douglas (1982) *Watergate Games*, New York: New York University Press (1982). **35**

Myerson, Roger (1979) "Incentive Compatibility and the Bargaining Problem," *Econometrica*, 47(1): 61–73 (January 1979). **314**

Myerson, Roger (1981) "Optimal Auction Design," *Mathematics of Operations Research*, 6(1): 58–73 (February 1981). **314, 413, 429**

Myerson, Roger (1991) *Game Theory: Analysis of Conflict*, Cambridge: Harvard University Press (1991). **xxiv, 413**

Myerson, Roger (1999) "Nash Equilibrium and the History of Economic Theory," *The Journal of Economic Literature*, 37(3): 1067–1082 (September 1999). **6, 34**

Myerson, Roger. See Holmstrom & Myerson (1983).

Myerson, Roger & Mark Satterthwaite (1983) "Efficient Mechanisms for Bilateral Trading," *The Journal of Economic Theory*, 29(2): 1–21 (April 1983). **376**

Nalebuff, Barry. See Ghemawat & Nalebuff (1985), Dixit & Nalebuff (1991).

Nalebuff, Barry & John Riley (1985) "Asymmetric Equilibria in the War of Attrition," *The Journal of Theoretical Biology*, 113(3): 517–527 (April 1985). **76**

Nalebuff, Barry & David Scharfstein (1987) "Testing in Models of Asymmetric Information," *The Review of Economic Studies*, 54(2): 265–278 (April 1987). **272**

Nalebuff, Barry & Joseph Stiglitz (1983) "Prizes and Incentives: Towards a General Theory of Compensation and Competition,"*The Bell Journal of Economics*, 14(1): 21-43 (Spring 1983). **237**

Nasar, Sylvia (1998) *A Beautiful Mind*, New York: Simon and Schuster (1998). **6, 35**

Nash, John (1950a) "The Bargaining Problem," *Econometrica*, 18(2): 155–162 (January 1950). Reprinted in Rasmusen (2000). **1**

Nash, John (1950b) "Equilibrium Points in n-Person Games," *Proceedings of the National Academy of Sciences, USA*, 36(1): 48–49 (January 1950). Reprinted in Rasmusen (2001). **1**

Nash, John (1951) "Non-Cooperative Games," *Annals of Mathematics*, 54(2): 286–295 (September 1951). Reprinted in Rasmusen (2001). **1**

Nelson, Philip (1974) "Advertising as Information," *The Journal of Political Economy*, 84(4): 729–754 (July/August 1974). **348**

Newman, John. See Eatwell et al. (1989).

Novshek, William (1985) "On the Existence of Cournot Equilibrium," *The Review of Economic Studies*, 52(1): 85–98 (January 1985). **467**

Ohta, Hiroshi. See Greenhut & Ohta (1975).

Olsder, Geert. See Basar & Olsder (1999).

Ordeshook, Peter (1986) *Game Theory and Political Theory: An Introduction*, Cambridge: Cambridge University Press (1986). **xxiii**

Osborne, Martin (2003) *An Introduction to Game Theory*, Oxford: Oxford University Press (2003). **xxvii**

Osborne, Martin & Carolyn Pitchik (1986) "The Nature of Equilibrium in a Location Model" *International Economic Review*, 27(1): 223–237 (February 1986). **448**

Osborne, Martin & Carolyn Pitchik (1987) "Equilibrium in Hotelling's Model of Spatial Competition," *Econometrica*, 55(4): 911–922 (July 1987). **468**

Osborne, Martin & Ariel Rubinstein (1994) *A Course in Game Theory*, Cambridge, MA: MIT Press (1994). **xxv**

Owen, Guillermo (1995) *Game Theory*, 3rd edition, New York: Academic Press (1st edition 1968) (1995). **xxvi**

Parker, G. A. See Maynard Smith & Parker (1976).

Pearce, David (1984) "Rationalizable Strategic Behavior and the Problem of Perfection," *Econometrica*, 52(4): 1029–1050 (July 1984). **35**

Pearce, David. See Abreu et al. (1986, 1990).

Peleg, Bezalel. See Bernheim et al. (1987).

Peltzman, Sam (1991) "The Handbook of Industrial Organization: A Review Article," *The Journal of Political Economy*, 99(1): 201–217 (February 1991). **98**

Peltzman, Sam. See Jarrell & Peltzman (1985).

Perez-Castillo. See Macho-Stadler & Perez-Castillo (1997).

Perri, Timothy (2001). See Rasmusen & Perri (2001).

Perry, Motty (1986) "An Example of Price Formation in Bilateral Situations: A Bargaining Model with Incomplete Information," *Econometrica*, 54(2): 313–321 (March 1986). **381, 401**

Perry, Motty & Philip J. Reny (1999) "On the Failure of the Linkage Principle," *Econometrica*, 67(4): 895–890. **427**

Petrakis, Emmanuel. See Rasmusen & Petrakis (1992).

Picker, Randal. See Baird, Gertner & Picker(1994).

Pigou, A. (1920), *The Economics of Welfare*, 4th edition (1932), London: Macmillan and Company (1952, 1st edition 1920). **201**

Pitchik, Carolyn. See Osborne & Pitchik (1986, 1987).

Png, Ivan (1983) "Strategic Behaviour in Suit, Settlement, and Trial," *The Bell Journal of Economics*, 14(2): 539–550 (Autumn 1983). **61**

Png, Ivan. See Mookherjee & Png (1989).

Png, Ivan & David Hirshleifer (1987) "Price Discrimination through Offers to Match Price," *The Journal of Business*, 60(3): 365–383 (July 1987). **469**

Polemarchakis, Heraklis. See Geanakoplos & Polemarchakis (1982).

Polinsky, A. Mitchell & Yeon-Koo Che (1991) "Decoupling Liability: Optimal Incentives for Care and Litigation," *The RAND Journal of Economics*, 22(4): 562–570 (Winter 1991). **198**

Popkin, Samuel (1979) *The Rational Peasant: The Political Economy of Rural Society in Vietnam*, Berkeley: University of California Press (1979). **218**

Porter, Robert (1983a) "Optimal Cartel Trigger Price Strategies," *The Journal of Economic Theory*, 29(2): 313–338 (April 1983). **149, 230**

Porter, Robert (1983b) "A Study of Cartel Stability: The Joint Executive Committee, 1880–1886," *The Bell Journal of Economics*, 14(2): 301–314 (Autumn 1983). **149**

Porter, Robert. See Hendricks & Porter (1988, forthcoming).

Posner, Richard (1975) "The Social Costs of Monopoly and Regulation," *The Journal of Political Economy*, 83(4): 807–827 (August 1975). **76**

Poterba, James. See Hausman & Poterba (1987).

Prescott, Edward. See Kydland & Prescott (1977).

Poundstone, William (1992) *Prisoner's Dilemma: John von Neumann, Game Theory, and the Puzzle of the Bomb*, New York: Doubleday (1992). **33**

Psacharopoulos, George. See Layard & Psacharopoulos (1974).

Pyle, David. See Leland & Pyle (1977).

Quine, William (1953) "On a So-Called Paradox," *Mind*, 62: 65–67 (January 1953). **123**

Rabin, Matthew. See Farrell & Rabin (1996).

Radner, Roy (1980) "Collusive Behavior in Oligopolies with Long but Finite Lives," *The Journal of Economic Theory*, 22(2): 136–156 (April 1980). **148**

Radner, Roy (1985) "Repeated Principal-Agent Games with Discounting," *Econometrica*, 53(5): 1173–1198 (September 1985). **216**

Radner, Roy. See Marschak & Radner (1972).

Raff, Daniel & Lawrence Summers (1987) "Did Henry Ford Pay Efficiency Wages?" *The Journal of Labor Economics*, 5(4): 57–86 (October 1987). **265**

Raiffa, Howard (1992) "Game Theory at the University of Michigan, 1948–52," in *Toward a History of Game Theory*, ed. E. Roy Weintraub, pp. 165–176, Durham: Duke University Press (1992). **33**

Raiffa, Howard. See Luce & Raiffa (1957).

Ramseyer, J. Mark. See Wiley, Rasmusen, & Ramseyer (1990).

Rapoport, Anatol (1960) *Fights, Games and Debates*, Ann Arbor: University of Michigan Press (1960). **xxiii**

Rapoport, Anatol (1970) *N-Person Game Theory: Concepts and Applications*, Ann Arbor: University of Michigan Press (1970). **xxiii**

Rapoport, Anatol & Albert Chammah (1965) *Prisoner's Dilemma: A Study in Conflict and Cooperation*, Ann Arbor: University of Michigan Press (1965). **169**

Rapoport, Anatol, Melvin Guyer, & David Gordon (1976) *The 2×2 Game*, Ann Arbor: University of Michigan Press (1976). **33**, **34**

Rappoport, Peter. See Cooter & Rappoport (1984).

Rasmusen, Eric (1987) "Moral Hazard in Risk-Averse Teams," *The RAND Journal of Economics*, 18(3): 428–435 (Fall 1987). **230**, **237**, **238**

Rasmusen, Eric (1988a) "Entry for Buyout," *The Journal of Industrial Economics*, 36(3): 281–300 (March 1988). **3**

Rasmusen, Eric (1988b) "Mutual Banks and Stock Banks," *The Journal of Law and Economics*, 31(2): 395–422 (October 1988). **216**, **206**

Rasmusen, Eric (1989a) *Games and Information*, Oxford: Basil Blackwell (1989) (second edition, 1994, third edition 2001) Japanese translation by Moriki Hosoe, Shozo Murata, and Yoshinobu Arisada, Kyushu University Press, vol. I (1990), vol. 2 (1991). Italian translation (*Teoria dei Giochi e Informazore*) by Alberto Bernardo, Milan: Ulrico Hoepli Editore (1993). Spanish translation (*Juegos e Informacion*) by Roberto Mazzoni, Mexico City: Fondo de Cultura Economica (1997). Chinese Complex Characters translation, Wu-Nan Book Company, Taipei (2003). Chinese Simplified Characters translation, Yang Yao, Liangjing Publishing. French translation, *Jeux et information*, Brussels: Editions de Boeck & Larcier (2004). **xxiv**, **xxvi**, **xxvii**

Rasmusen, Eric (1989b) "A Simple Model of Product Quality with Elastic Demand,"*Economics Letters*, 29(4): 281–283 (1989). **138**

Rasmusen, Eric (1992a) "Folk Theorems for the Observable Implications of Repeated Games," *Theory and Decision*, 32: 147–164 (March 1992). **133, 149**

Rasmusen, Eric (1992b) "Managerial Conservatism and Rational Information Acquisition," *The Journal of Economics and Management Strategy*, 1(1): 175–202 (Spring 1992). **60**

Rasmusen, Eric (1992c) "An Income-Satiation Model of Efficiency Wages," *Economic Inquiry*, 30(3): 467–478 (July 1992). **241**

Rasmusen, Eric (1993) "Lobbying when the Decisionmaker Can Acquire Independent Information," *Public Choice*, 77: 899–913 (1993). **337**

Rasmusen, Eric (2000) "Writing, Speaking, and Listening," in Rasmusen (2001). **7**

Rasmusen, Eric, ed. (2001) *Readings in Games and Information*, Oxford: Blackwell Publishing (2001). **140**

Rasmusen, Eric & Timothy Perri (2001) "Can High Prices Ensure Product Quality when Buyers Do Not Know the Sellers' Cost?" *Economic Inquiry*, 39(4): 561–567 (October 2001). **6, 140**

Rasmusen, Eric & Emmanuel Petrakis (1992) "Defining the Mean-Preserving Spread: 3-pt versus 4-pt," *Decision Making Under Risk and Uncertainty: New Models and Empirical Findings*, ed. John Geweke, Amsterdam: Kluwer (1992). **489**

Rasmusen, Eric & Todd Zenger (1990) "Diseconomies of Scale in Employment Contracts," *The Journal of Law, Economics and Organization*, 6(1): 65–92 (June 1990). **238**

Rasmusen Eric. See D. Hirshleifer & Rasmusen (1989), J. Hirshleifer & Rasmusen (1992), and Wiley, Rasmusen, & Ramseyer (1990).

Ratliff, Jim (1997a) "Nonequilibrium Solution Concepts: Iterated Dominance and Rationalizability," lecture notes, http://www.virtualperfection.com/gametheory/2.2.IteratedDominanceRationality.1.0.pdf (1997). **24, 33, 35**

Ratliff, Jim (1997b). "Strategic Dominance," lecture notes, http://www.virtualperfection.com/gametheory/2.1.StrategicDominance.1.0.pdf, (1997). **33**

Raviv, Arthur. See M. Harris & Raviv (1992, 1995).

Ray, D. See Mookherjee & Ray (1992).

Reeve, Hudson. See Dugatkin & Reeve (1998).

Reinganum, Jennifer (1988) "Plea Bargaining and Prosecutorial Discretion," *The American Economic Review*, 78(4): 713–728 (September 1988). **348**

Reinganum, Jennifer & Nancy Stokey (1985) "Oligopoly Extraction of a Common Property Natural Resource: The Importance of the Period of Commitment in Dynamic Games," *The International Economic Review*, 26(1): 161–174 (February 1985). **123**

Reiss, Peter. See Bresnahan & Reiss (1991).

Reny, Philip J. See Perry & Reny (1999).

Reynolds, Robert. See Salant et al. (1983).

Richerson, Peter. See Boyd & Richerson (1985).

Riker, William (1986) *The Art of Political Manipulation*, New Haven: Yale University Press (1986). **35, 124**

Riley, John G. (1980) "Strong Evolutionary Equilibrium and the War of Attrition," *The Journal of Theoretical Biology*, 82(3): 383–400 (February 1980). **76**

Riley, John G. (1989) "Expected Revenues from Open and Sealed Bid Auctions," *The Journal of Economic Perspectives*, 3(3): 41–50 (Summer 1989). **76, 406, 396**

Riley, John G. (2001) "Silver Signals: Twenty-Five Years of Screening and Signaling," *The Journal of Economic Literature*, 39(2): 432–478 (June 2001). **348**

Riley, John G. See Hirshleifer & Riley (1979, 1992), Maskin & Riley (1984, 1985), and Nalebuff & Riley (1985).

Riordan, Michael. See Kihlstrom & Riordan (1984).

Roberts, John. See Kreps et al. (1982) and Milgrom & Roberts (1982a, 1982b, 1986, 1990, 1992).

Roberts, John & Hugo Sonnenschein (1976) "On the Existence of Cournot Equilibrium without Concave Profit Functions," *The Journal of Economic Theory*, 13(1): 112–117 (August 1976). **467**

Robinson, Marc (1985) "Collusion and the Choice of Auction," *The RAND Journal of Economics*, 16(1): 1–5 (Spring 1985). **413**

Rochet, Jean-Charles, & Lars Stole (2003) "The Economics of Multidimensional Screening," in *Advances in Economics and Econometrics: Theory and Applications, Eighth World Congress*, M. Dewatripont, L. Hansen and S. Turnovsky, eds., Cambridge: Cambridge University Press (2003). http://gsblas.uchicago.edu/papers/worldcongress.pdf (2003). **348**

Rogerson, William (1982) "The Social Costs of Monopoly and Regulation: A Game–Theoretic Analysis,"*The Bell Journal of Economics*, 13(2): 391–401 (Autumn 1982). **80**

Romp, Graham (1997) *Game Theory: Introduction and Applications*, Oxford: Oxford University Press (1997). **xxvi**

Rosen, Sherwin (1986) "Prizes and Incentives in Elimination Tournaments," *The American Economic Review*, 76(4): 701–715 (September 1986). **236**

Rosen, Sherwin. See Lazear & Rosen (1981).

Rosenberg, David & Steven Shavell (1985) "A Model in Which Suits Are Brought for Their Nuisance Value," *The International Review of Law and Economics*, 5: 3–13 (June 1985). **115**

Ross, Steven (1977) "The Determination of Financial Structure: The Incentive-Signalling Approach," *The Bell Journal of Economics*, 8(1): 23–40 (Spring 1977). **348**

Roth, Alvin (1984) "The Evolution of the Labor Market for Medical Interns and Residents: A Case Study in Game Theory," *The Journal of Political Economy*, 92(6): 991–1016 (December 1984).

Roth, Alvin (2002) "The Economist as Engineer: Game Theory, Experimental Economics and Computation As Tools of Design Economics," Fisher Schultz lecture, *Econometrica*, 70(4): 1341–1378 (July 2002). **385**

Rothkopf, Michael H. (1969) "Competitive Bidding with Asymmetric Information," *Management Science*, 15(7): 362–373 (March 1969). **429**

Rothkopf, Michael H. (1980) "TREES: A Decision-Maker's Lament," *Operations Research*, 28(1): 3 (January/February 1980). Reprinted in Rasmusen (2001).

Rothschild, Michael (1974) "A Two-Armed Bandit Theory of Market Pricing," *The Journal of Economic Theory*, 9(2): 185–202 (October 1974). **60**

Rothschild, Michael & Joseph Stiglitz (1970) "Increasing Risk I. A Definition" *The Journal of Economic Theory*, 2(2): 225–243 (September 1970). Reprinted in Diamond & Rothschild (1978). **489**

Rothschild, Michael & Joseph Stiglitz (1976) "Equilibrium in Competitive Insurance Markets: An Essay on the Economics of Imperfect Information," *Quarterly Journal of Economics*, 90(4): 629–649 (November 1976). **255**

Rothschild, Michael. See Diamond & Rothschild (1978).

Rubin, Paul (1978) "The Theory of the Firm and the Structure of the Franchise Contract," *The Journal of Law and Economics*, 21(1): 223–233 (April 1978). **203**

Rubinfeld, Daniel. See Cooter & Rubinfeld (1989).

Rubinstein, Ariel (1979) "An Optimal Conviction Policy for Offenses That May Have Been Committed by Accident," in *Applied Game Theory*, Steven Brams, A. Schotter, Gerhard Schrodiauer, eds., pp. 406–413, Physica-Verlag (1979). Reprinted in Rasmusen (2001). **239**

Rubinstein, Ariel (1982) "Perfect Equilibrium in a Bargaining Model," *Econometrica*, 50(1): 97–109 (January 1982). Reprinted in Rasmusen (2001). **363, 364**

Rubinstein, Ariel (1985) "A Bargaining Model with Incomplete Information about Time Preferences," *Econometrica*, 53(5): 1151–1172 (September 1985). **381**

Rubinstein, Ariel. See Binmore et al. (1986), Osborne & Rubinstein (1994).

Rudin, Walter (1964) *Principles of Mathematical Analysis*, New York: McGraw-Hill (1964). **473**

Ryan, Stephen. See Bajari, Hong, & Ryan (2004).

Saft, Lester. See Klein & Saft (1985).

Salanie, Bernard (1997) *The Economics of Contracts: A Primer*, Cambridge, MA: MIT Press (1997). **xxvi**

Salanie, Bernard. See Chiappori & Salanie (2003).

Salant, Stephen, Sheldon Switzer, & Robert Reynolds (1983) "Losses from Horizontal Merger: The Effects of an Exogenous Change in Industry Structure on Cournot–Nash Equilibrium," *The Quarterly Journal of Economics*, 98(1): 185–199 (May 1983). **467**

Salant, Stephen. See Gaudet & Salant (1991).

Saloner, Garth. See Farrell & Saloner (1985).

Salop, Steven & Joseph Stiglitz (1977) "Bargains and Ripoffs; A Model of Monopolistically Competitive Price Dispersion," *The Review of Economic Studies*, 44(3): 493–510 (October 1977). **263**

Samet, Dov. See Kalai, Samet, & Stanford (1988).

Samuelson, Paul (1958) "An Exact Consumption-Loan Model of Interest with or without the Social Contrivance of Money," *The Journal of Political Economy*, 66(6): 467–482 (December 1958). **141, 151**

Samuelson, William (1984) "Bargaining under Asymmetric Information," *Econometrica*, 52(4): 995–1005 (July 1984). **381**

Samuelson, William. See Chatterjee & Samuelson (1983).

Satterthwaite, Mark. See Myerson & Satterthwaite (1983).

Savage, Leonard (1954) *The Foundations of Statistics*, New York: Wiley (1954). **65**

Scarf, Herbert. See Debreu & Scarf (1963).

Scharfstein, David. See Nalebuff & Scharfstein (1987).

Scheffman, David. See Holt & Scheffman (1987).

Scheinkman, Jose. See Kreps & Scheinkman (1983).

Schelling, Thomas (1960) *The Strategy of Conflict*, Cambridge: Harvard University Press (1960). **2, 32**

Schelling, Thomas (1978) *Micromotives and Macrobehavior*, New York: W. W. Norton (1978). **35**

Schick, Frederic (2003) *Ambiguity and Logic*, Cambridge: Cambridge University Press (2003). Chapter 5: http://www.lucs.lu.se/spinning/categories/decision/Schick/Schick.pdf. **123**

Schmalensee, Richard (1982) "Product Differentiation Advantages of Pioneering Brands,"*The American Economic Review*, 72(3): 349–365 (June 1982). **140**

Schmalensee, Richard & Robert Willig, eds., (1989) *The Handbook of Industrial Organization*, New York: North-Holland (1989). **xxiv**

Schmittberger, Rold. See Guth et al. (1982).

Schumpeter, Joseph (1911/1934) *Theory of Economic Development*, translated from the German 3rd edition by Redvers Opie, Cambridge: Harvard University Press (1st edition 1911). **446**

Schwartz, Nancy. See Kamien & Schwartz (1981, 1991).

Schwarze, Bernd. See Guth et al. (1982).

Seligman, Daniel (1992) *A Question of Intelligence: The IQ Debate in America*, New York: Carol Publishing (1992). **269**

Selten, Reinhard (1965) "Spieltheoretische Behandlung eines Oligopolmodells mit Nachfragetragheit," *Zeitschrift f'ur die gesamte Staatswissenschaft*, 121: 301–324, 667–689 (October 1965). **2, 122**

Selten, Reinhard (1975) "Reexamination of the Perfectness Concept for Equilibrium Points in Extensive Games," *The International Journal of Game Theory*, 4(1): 25–55 (1975). **2, 122**

Selten, Reinhard (1978) "The Chain-Store Paradox," *Theory and Decision*, 9(2): 127–159 (April 1978). **129, 148**

Selten, Reinhard. See Harsanyi & Selten (1988).

Shaked, Avner (1982) "Existence and Computation of Mixed Strategy Nash Equilibrium for 3-Firms Location Problem," *The Journal of Industrial Economics*, 31(1/2): 93–96 (September/December 1982). Reprinted in Rasmusen (2001). **448**

Shaked, Avner & John Sutton (1983) "Natural Oligopolies," *Econometrica*, 51(5): 1469–1483 (September 1983). **455, 468**

Shaked, Avner & John Sutton (1984) "Involuntary Unemployment as a Perfect Equilibrium in a Bargaining Model," *Econometrica*, 52(6): 1351–1364 (November 1984). **363**

Shanley, Mark. See Besanko, Dranove, & Shanley (1996).

Shapiro, Carl (1982) "Consumer Information, Product Quality and Seller Reputation," *Bell Journal of Economics*, 13(1): 20–35 (Spring 1982).

Shapiro, Carl (1983) "Premiums for High Quality Products as Returns to Reputation," *The Quarterly Journal of Economics*, 98(4): 659–679 (November 1983). **150**

Shapiro, Carl (1989) "The Theory of Business Strategy," *The RAND Journal of Economics*, 20(1): 125–137 (Spring 1989).

Shapiro, Carl. See Farrell & Shapiro (1988), Katz & Shapiro (1985).

Shapiro, Carl & Joseph Stiglitz (1984) "Equilibrium Unemployment As a Worker Discipline Device," *The American Economic Review*, 74(3): 433–444 (June 1984). **150, 213**

Shapley, Lloyd (1953a) "Open Questions," in *Report of an Informal Conference on the Theory of n-Person Games*, p. 15, Princeton Mathematics mimeo (1953). **1**

Shapley, Lloyd (1953b) "A Value for n-Person Games," pp. 307–317 of Kuhn & Tucker (1953). **1, 380**

Shavell, Steven (1979) "Risk Sharing and Incentives in the Principal and Agent Relationship," *The Bell Journal of Economics*, 10(1): 55–73 (Spring 1979). **202**

Shavell, Steven. See Rosenberg & Shavell (1985), Kaplow & Shavell (1996).

Shell, Karl. See Cass & Shell (1983).

Shubik, Martin (1954) "Does the Fittest Necessarily Survive?" in *Readings in Game Theory and Political Behavior*, ed. Martin Shubik, pp. 43–46, Garden City, New York: Doubleday (1954). Reprinted in Rasmusen (2001). **77, 124**

Shubik, Martin (1971) "The Dollar Auction Game: A Paradox in Noncooperative Behavior and Escalation," *The Journal of Conflict Resolution*, 15: 109–111 (March 1971). Reprinted in Rasmusen (2001). **402**

Shubik, Martin (1982) *Game Theory in the Social Sciences: Concepts and Solutions*, Cambridge, MA: MIT Press (1982). **xxiii, 64, 380**

Shubik, Martin (1992) "Game Theory at Princeton, 1949–1955: A Personal Reminiscence," in *Toward a History of Game Theory*, ed. E. Roy Weintraub, pp. 151–164, Durham: Duke University Press (1992). **6**

Shubik, Martin. See Levitan & Shubik (1972).

Shy, Oz (1996) *Industrial Organization, Theory and Applications*, Cambridge, MA: MIT Press (1996). **xxvi**

Simon, Leo (1987) "Games with Discontinuous Payoffs," *The Review of Economic Studies*, 54(4): 569–598 (October 1987). **448**

Sinervo, B. & C. M. Lively (1996) "The Rock-Paper-Scissors Game and the Evolution of Alternative Male Strategies," *Nature*, 380: 240–243 (March 21, 1996). **98**

Skeath, Susan. See Dixit & Skeath (1999).

Slade, Margaret (1987) "Interfirm Rivalry in a Repeated Game: An Empirical Test of Tacit Collusion," *The Journal of Industrial Economics*, 35(4): 499–516 (June 1987). **149**

Slatkin, Montgomery (1980) "Altruism in Theory," review of Scott Boorman & Paul Levitt, *The Genetics of Altruism. Science*, 210: 633–647 (November 1980). **3**

Slovic, Paul. See Kahneman, Slovic, & Tversky (1982).

Smith, Abbie. See Antle & Smith (1986).

Smith, Adam (1776) *An Inquiry into the Nature and Causes of the Wealth of Nations*, Chicago: University of Chicago Press (1977). **213, 347**

Smith, J. See DeBrock & Smith (1983).

Sobel, Joel. See Border & Sobel (1987), Crawford & Sobel (1982).

Sobel, Joel & Ichiro Takahashi (1983) "A Multi-Stage Model of Bargaining," *The Review of Economic Studies*, 50(3): 411–426 (July 1983). **381**

Sonnenschein, Hugo. See Roberts & Sonnenschein (1976).

Sorenson, Philip. See Mead et al. (1984).

Sowden, Lanning. See Campbell & Sowden (1985).

Spector, Yishay. See Leshno, Levy & Spector (1997).

Spence, A. Michael (1973) "Job Market Signalling," *The Quarterly Journal of Economics*, 87(3): 355–374 (August 1973). **320**

Spence, A. Michael. See Kreps & Spence (1984).

Spitzer, Matthew. See Hoffman & Spitzer (1985).

Stacchetti, Ennio. See Abreu et al. (1986, 1990).

Stackelberg, Heinrich von (1934) *Marktform und Gleichgewicht*, Berlin: J. Springer. Translated by Alan Peacock as *The Theory of the Market Economy*, London: William Hodge (1952). **101, 101**

Stahl, Saul (1998) *A Gentle Introduction to Game Theory*, Providence, RI: American Mathematical Society (1998). **xxvii**

Stanford, William. See Kalai, Samet, & Stanford (1988).

Starmer, Chris (2000) "Developments in Non-Expected Utility Theory, " *The Journal of Economic Literature*, 38(2): 332–382 (June 2000). **33, 65**

Staten, Michael & John Umbeck (1986) "A Study of Signaling Behavior in Occupational Disease Claims," *The Journal of Law and Economics*, 29(2): 263–286 (October 1986). **348**

Stigler, George (1964) "A Theory of Oligopoly," *The Journal of Political Economy*, 72(1): 44–61 (February 1964). **149**

Stigler, George. See Becker & Stigler (1974).

Stiglitz, Joseph (1987) "The Causes and Consequences of the Dependence of Quality on Price," *The Journal of Economic Literature*, 25(1): 1–48 (March 1987). **140, 150, 270, 348**

Stiglitz, Joseph & Andrew Weiss (1981) "Credit Rationing in Markets with Imperfect Information," *The American Economic Review*, 71(3): 393–410 (June 1981). **265**

Stiglitz, Joseph. See Dixit & Stiglitz (1977), Nalebuff & Stiglitz (1983), Rothschild & Stiglitz (1970, 1976), Salop & Stiglitz (1977), and Shapiro & Stiglitz (1984).

Stokey, Nancy & Robert Lucas (1989) *Recursive Methods in Economic Dynamics*, Cambridge: Harvard University Press (1989). **473**

Stokey, Nancy. See Reinganum & Stokey (1985).

Stole, Lars (2001) "Lecture Notes on the Theory of Contracts and Organizations," 17 February 2001 draft, http://gsblas.uchicago.edu/papers/lectures.pdf. **314**

Stole, Lars. See Rochet & Stole (2003).

Straffin, Philip (1980) "The Prisoner's Dilemma," *UMAP Journal*, 1: 101–103 (1980). Reprinted in Rasmusen (2001). **33**

Strunk, William & E. B. White (1959) *The Elements of Style*, New York: Macmillan (1959). **7**

Sugden, Robert (1986) *The Economics of Rights, Co-operation and Welfare*, Oxford: Blackwell (1986). **129**

Sultan, Ralph (1974) *Pricing in the Electrical Oligopoly, Vol I: Competition or Collusion*, Cambridge: Harvard University Press (1974). **413, 469**

Summers, Larry. See Raff & Summers (1987).

Sutton, John (1986) "Non-Cooperative Bargaining Theory: An Introduction," *The Review of Economic Studies*, 53(5): 709–724 (October 1986). **381**

Sutton, John (1991) *Sunk Costs and Market Structure: Price Competition, Advertising, and the Evolution of Concentration*, Cambridge, MA: MIT Press (1991). **467**

Sutton, John. See Shaked & Sutton (1983, 1984).

Switzer, Sheldon. See Salant et al. (1983).

Szenberg, Michael, ed. (1992) *Eminent Economists: Their Life Philosophies*, Cambridge: Cambridge University Press (1992). **35**

Szenberg, Michael, ed. (1998) *Passion and Craft: Economists at Work*, Ann Arbor: University of Michigan Press (1998). **6**

Tadelis, Stephen. See Bajari & Tadelis (2001).

Takahashi, Ichiro. See Sobel & Takahashi (1983).

Takayama, Akira (1985) *Mathematical Economics*, 2nd edition, Cambridge: Cambridge University Press (1985). **473**

Telser, Lester (1966) "Cutthroat Competition and the Long Purse," *The Journal of Law and Economics*, 9: 259–277 (October 1966). **170**

Telser, Lester (1980) "A Theory of Self-Enforcing Agreements," *The Journal of Business*, 53(1): 27–44 (January 1980). **140**

Thaler, Richard (1992) *The Winner's Curse: Paradoxes and Anomalies of Economic Life*, New York: The Free Press (1992). **65, 361**

Thisse, Jacques. See d'Aspremont et al. (1979).

Tirole, Jean (1986) "Hierarchies and Bureaucracies: On the Role of Collusion in Organizations," *The Journal of Law, Economics, and Organization*, 2(2): 181–214 (Fall 1986). **218**

Tirole, Jean (1988) *The Theory of Industrial Organization*, Cambridge, MA: MIT Press (1988). **xxiv, xxiv, 65, 455**

Tirole, Jean. See Freixas et al. (1985), Fudenberg & Tirole (1983, 1986a, 1986b, 1988, 1991a, 1991b), Laffont & Tirole (1986, 1993), and Maskin & Tirole (1987).

To, Ted. See Feltovich, Harbaugh, & To (2002).

Tooby, John. See Cosmides & Tooby (1993).

Topkis, Donald (1998) *Supermodularity and Complementarity*, Princeton: Princeton University Press (1998). **484**

Tsebelis, George (1989) "The Abuse of Probability in Political Analysis: The Robinson Crusoe Fallacy," *The American Political Science Review*, 83(1): 77–91 (March 1989). **100**

Tucker, Albert (1950) "A Two-Person Dilemma," Stanford University mimeo. May 1950. Reprinted in Straffin (1980). Reprinted in Rasmusen (2001). **1, 33**

Tucker, Albert. See Kuhn & Tucker (1953).

Tukey, John (1949) "A Problem in Strategy," *Econometrica*, (supplement), 17: 73 (abstract) (July 1949). **101**

Tukey, John. See McDonald & Tukey (1949).

Tullock, Gordon (1967) "The Welfare Costs of Tariffs, Monopolies, and Theft," *The Western Economic Journal*, 5(3): 224–232 (June 1967). **76**

Tullock, Gordon (1980) "Efficient Rent-Seeking," in *Toward a Theory of the Rent-Seeking Society*, James Buchanan, G. Tollison & Gordon Tullock, eds., pp. 97–112. College Station, TX: Texas A&M University Press (1980). **402**

Tversky, Amon. See Kahneman, Slovic, & Tversky (1982).

Umbeck, John. See Staten & Umbeck (1986).

Van Damme, Eric (1989) "Stable Equilibria and Forward Induction," *The Journal of Economic Theory*, 48(2): 476–496 (August 1989). **173, 176**

Van Damme, Eric (2002) "Strategic Equilibrium," in the *Handbook of Game Theory with Economic Applications, vol. 3*, Chapter 41, pp. 1521–1596, Elsevier (2002). Also: http://greywww.kub.nl:2080/greyfiles/center/2000/doc/115.pdf.

Varian, Hal (1992) *Microeconomic Analysis*, 3rd edition. New York: W. W. Norton, 1992 (2nd edition 1984) (1992). **xxv, 65, 293, 473**

Vickrey, William (1961) "Counterspeculation, Auctions, and Competitive Sealed Tenders," *The Journal of Finance*, 16(1): 8–37 (March 1961). **295, 398, 403**

Vickrey, William (1964) *Microstatics*, New York: Harcourt, Brace and World (1964). **444**

Vives, Xavier (1990), "Nash Equilibrium with Strategic Complementarities," *The Journal of Mathematical Economics*, 19: 305–321. **102**

Vives, Xavier (2000) *Oligopoly Pricing*, Cambridge, MA: MIT Press (2000). **xxvii**

Vives, Xavier (2005) "Complementarities and Games: New Developments," *The Journal of Economic Literature*, 63(2): 437–479 (June 2005). **95, 454, 484**

Von Neumann, John (1928) "Zur Theorie der Gesellschaftspiele," *Mathematische Annalen*, 100: 295–320 (1928). Translated by Sonya Bargmann as "On the Theory of Games of Strategy," pp. 13–42 of Luce & Tucker (1959). **135**

Von Neumann, John & Oskar Morgenstern (1944) *The Theory of Games in Economic Behavior*, New York: Wiley (1944). **1, 6, 51, 101**

Waldegrave, James (1713) "Excerpt from a Letter," (with a preface by Harold Kuhn), in Baumol & Goldfeld (1968). **98**

Waldman, Michael (1987) "Noncooperative Entry Deterrence, Uncertainty, and the Free Rider Problem," *The Review of Economic Studies*, 54(2): 301–310 (April 1987). **230**

Waldman, Michael. See Haltiwanger & Waldman (1991).

Watson, Joel (2002) *Strategy: An Introduction to Game Theory*, W. W. Norton & Co. (2002). **xxvii**

Weber, Robert. See Milgrom & Weber (1982).

Weiner, E. (1984) *The Oxford Guide to the English Language*, Oxford: Oxford University Press (1984). **7**

Weintraub, E. Roy, ed. (1992) *Toward a History of Game Theory*, Durham: Duke University Press (1992). **6, 34**

Weiss, Andrew (1990) *Efficiency Wages*, Princeton: Princeton University Press (1990). **236**

Weiss, Andrew. See Guasch & Weiss (1980), Stiglitz & Weiss (1981, 1989).

Weitzman, Martin (1974) "Prices vs. Quantities," *The Review of Economic Studies*, 41(1): 477–491 (October 1974). **468**

Welch, Ivo. See Bikhchandani, David Hirshleifer, & Welch (1992).

Weston, J. Fred. See Copeland & Weston (1988).

Whinston, Michael. See Bernheim et al. (1987), Bernheim & Whinston (1987), and Mas-Colell, Whinston, & Green (1994).

White, E. B. See Strunk & White (1959).

Wicksteed, Philip (1885) *The Common Sense of Political Economy*, New York: Kelley (1950). **4**

Wiley, John, Eric Rasmusen, & Mark Ramseyer (1990) "The Leasing Monopolist," *UCLA Law Review*, 37: 693–732 (April 1990). **469**

Williamson, Oliver (1975) *Markets and Hierarchies: Analysis and Antitrust Implications: A Study in the Economics of Internal Organization*, New York: Free Press (1975). **218**

Willig, Robert. See Schmalensee & Willig (1989).

Wilson, Charles (1980) "The Nature of Equilibrium in Markets with Adverse Selection," *The Bell Journal of Economics*, 11(1): 108–130 (Spring 1980). **254, 234**

Wilson, Robert (1969) "Competitive Bidding with Disparate Information," *Management Science*, 15(7): 446–448 (March 1969). **429**

Wilson, Robert (1979) "Auctions of Shares," *The Quarterly Journal of Economics*, 93(4): 675–689 (November 1979). **429**

Wilson, Robert (1993) *Nonlinear Pricing*, Oxford: Oxford University Press (1993). **315**

Wilson, Robert (unpublished) Stanford University 311b Course notes. **168**

Wilson, Robert. See Kennan & Wilson (1993), Kreps & Wilson (1982a, 1982b), and Kreps et al. (1982).

Winter, Ralph. See Mathewson & Winter (1985).

Wolfstetter, Elmar (1999) *Topics in Microeconomics: Industrial Organization, Auctions, and Incentives*, Cambridge: Cambridge University Press (1999). See also http://www.wiwi.hu-berlin.de/~wolf/chap-08-new.pdf. **xxvii, 396, 405, 428, 428**

Wolinsky, Asher. See Binmore et al. (1986).

Wydick, Richard (1978) "Plain English for Lawyers," *California Law Review*, 66: 727–764 (1978). **7**

Yellen Janet. See Akerlof & Yellen (1986).

Zahavi, Amotz (1975) "Mate Selection: A Selection for a Handicap," *The Journal of Theoretical Biology*, 53(1): 205–214 (September 1975). **348**

Zamir, S. See Mertens & Zamir (1985).

Zapechelnyuk, Andriy. See Dubey, Haimanko, & Zapechelnyuk (2002).

Zenger, Todd. See Rasmusen & Zenger (1990).

Von Zermelo, E. (1913) "Uber eine Anwendung der Mengenlehre auf die Theorie des Schachspiels," *Proceedings, Fifth International Congress of Mathematicians*, 2: 501–504 (1913). Reprinted in Rasmusen (2001) in the translation by Ulrich Schwalbe and Paul Walker, "On an Application of Set Theory to the Game of Chess."

Zimmerman, Jerold. See Gaver & Zimmerman (1977).

subject index

Lightning Source UK Ltd.
Milton Keynes UK
UKOW07n0618251117
313290UK00002B/4/P

9 781405 136662